Madam Secretary
Frances Perkins

Books by George Martin

The Opera Companion:
A Guide for the Casual Operagoer (*1961*)

The Battle of the Frogs and the Mice:
An Homeric Fable (*1962*)

Verdi: His Music, Life and Times (*1963*)

The Red Shirt and the Cross of Savoy:
The Story of Italy's Risorgimento, 1748–1871 (*1969*)

Causes and Conflicts: The Centennial History
of the Association of the Bar of the
City of New York, 1870–1970 (*1970*)

Madam Secretary: Frances Perkins (*1976*)

Madam Secretary

Frances Perkins

by

George Martin

Houghton Mifflin Company Boston

1976

A portion of this book has
appeared in *American Heritage*.

Library of Congress Cataloging in Publication Data
Martin, George Whitney.
Madam Secretary, Frances Perkins.
Bibliography: p.   Includes index.
1. Perkins, Frances, 1882–1965. 2. Women in
politics — United States — Biography. 3. Labor policy
— United States — History. I. Title.
HD8073.P38M37   973.917'092'4 [B]   75-38637
ISBN 0-395-24293-2

Printed in the United States of America

v 10 9 8 7 6 5 4 3 2 1

. . . be ye stedfast . . .

1 COR. 15:58

Preface

A WORD about the book: It is the first biography of Perkins because until recently her papers and oral history at Columbia University have not been open to the public. Though several other important collections of her papers exist, they lack the depth and range to support a biography.

But for other reasons, too, I have attempted a biography rather than a history. Perkins's personality informed all her work. The Social Security Act and the Fair Labor Standards Act, her greatest glories, might seem too technical to allow personality to enter, but what Perkins chose to do was determined by her religion. Many Democrats supported the Social Security Act because it attracted votes; others, for humanitarian reasons; Perkins, "for Jesus' sake," because it brought the City of God closer to the cities of toil and industry.

She seldom used such terms because she knew that they made many people nervous. But her religion was the source of her strength. For years she and others recommended programs of unemployment and old age insurance for industrial workers, but not until the Social Security Act of 1935 did Congress pass laws to implement them. The moment of that success made the programs part of the New Deal, but for her and her fellows their origins went back at least as far as 1907 and the great survey of industrial conditions in Pittsburgh. The best way to trace those origins as well as the development of her religious life, it seemed to me, was through biography rather than history.

The decision, however, raises a well-known danger: biographers tend to favor their subject. But through the portraits of Florence Kelley, Robert F. Wagner, Paul U. Kellogg, Alfred E. Smith, Franklin D. Roosevelt and others less well known, I hope that the sense of a movement for reform will always be present. For though Perkins's hard work, stamina and luck carried her further than most, she was only one among many.

The luck was extraordinary. To have found one man, who, as governor of New York, would put her, a woman, in his cabinet, was remarkable. But, following his defeat, to have found in his successor a second man, who, as governor of New York, would put her, a woman, in the cabinet, was incredible. And then, where the first had failed, to have the second succeed in becoming President of the United States and appoint her United States Secretary of Labor was against all odds.

Such luck, however, has its burdens: to some extent she lost control of her life. For the sake of all women she had little choice but to accept the post regardless of the cost to her and her family. Though she was eager for it, she was not so ambitious that she was unaware of its costs, which is part of her interest as a person.

In telling her story I have used a great deal of dialogue, most of it taken from her oral history (102 tape-recorded interviews) and her biography of Roosevelt, also based on oral history (she talked into a recording machine). Though she was not much of a writer, she was a brilliant talker, and her colleagues have confirmed the accuracy of her memory. It is unlikely that she has recalled perfectly every word for every sentence, but for many scenes others who were present report that the tone and relationship between the people is exactly right: this is the way the conversation went; most of the words, at least, are right. Except to straighten out the grammatical tangles or delete the repetitions that occur in anyone's speech I have not changed her language, nor have I entered her mind unless in a letter or document she has stated her thoughts.

But my reliance on her accounts of various events has a consequence. Inevitably it has meant that to some extent reality is perceived through her eyes. If on any point I discovered her memory had played her false, I did not follow her. But in something like the firing of Johnson as director of the NRA I have, in effect, given her version. He published his in 1935, and she, characteristically, kept silent.

A different case is the San Francisco strike of 1934. It was not a typical strike of the period, and in a history it would deserve less space. But it was crucial in her career because it led ultimately to a resolution of impeachment against her. In her biography, I believe, it should be emphasized.

I think Perkins needs a biography. Not only was she one of the most important women of her generation, but even today, because of her work on minimum wage and on accident, unemployment and old age insurance, she has a hand in our daily lives. Of few cabinet officers can so much be said a quarter of a century after they have left office. For several reasons I think her achievements have been too little appreciated. She disliked personal publicity and often would do nothing to counter criticism even when it was patently unfair. Then, just as the legislation for which she was chiefly responsible began to bear fruit, World War II intervened, and after it few people bothered to recall the source of legislation already a decade old. And in particular, I think, because historians and biographers of Al Smith have reported only the first half of her career, and those of Roosevelt only the second, its continuity has been lost. Consider: for roughly twenty years, from 1925 to 1945, on social legislation hers was the knowledgeable, dominant voice at the ear of the leader of the Democratic party, and among the party's most lasting achievements in that period are several for which she was the prime mover.

Many persons have helped me in my research, particularly several librarians, directors of oral history collections and friends of Perkins. Her friends, despite her well-known aversion to publicity, believed her story should be told, that she was too extraordinary a person with too large a part in the country's history to be left in the shadows of privacy. Four who were especially helpful were Agnes Leach, Vira Peters Towle, Isador Lubin and Perkins's daughter, Susanna Coggeshall. But even old friends could not reveal Perkins's thoughts on events that she apparently discussed with no one, such as the death of her first child or her father, and there are gaps in her life that probably will never be closed.

Among the librarians, I want to mention Anne C. Edmonds and her staff at Mount Holyoke and Kenneth A. Lohf and his in the Rare Book and Manuscript Library (Special Collections) at Columbia. Because of lack of space Lohf had me at a table in his office for almost a year while I searched through the Perkins collection. Similarly, at the Oral History Research Office Elizabeth Mason, Assistant Director, was faced with my presence day after day; as in Washington was Dr. Jonathan P. Grossman, the historian of the Department of Labor. It cannot have been easy for any of them, and for their courtesies I am grateful.

I also wish to thank Susanna Coggeshall, who allowed me to use her copy of her mother's oral history; Charles E. Wyzanski, Jr., and Ewan Clague for permission to cite and quote from theirs; and Dr. Louis M. Starr, Director of the Columbia Oral History Collection for permission to cite and quote from the other Columbia reminiscences listed in the bibliography. Dr. Starr, like Anne Edmonds, Elizabeth Mason and Kenneth Lohf, also made a number of decisions and suggestions that greatly helped me. For permission to quote from Roger Lapham's "An Interview on Shipping, Labor, City Government and American Foreign Aide," the transcript of a tape-recorded interview conducted by Corrine L. Gilb, 515 pages, Regional Cultural History Project, General Library, University of California, Berkeley, 1957, pp. 85 and 95, I am grateful to Professor James D. Hart, Director of the Bancroft Library. And to all those others listed in the bibliography who responded to my questions or were in charge of collections, I am grateful. For the use of certain pictures I thank Mount Holyoke, the Rare Book and Manuscript Library (Special Collections) at Columbia and Susanna Coggeshall.

I should like to express my gratitude to Professor William E. Leuchtenburg, who read the book in typescript and saved me from many factual errors. He also questioned some of my portrayals — had I not made Al Smith appear more liberal than he was? — and for such probing of substance I am especially grateful. But I should add, to save him from any criticism: What mistakes remain, in fact or opinion, are mine.

With regard to the notes and bibliography: Because this is the first book on Perkins to make use of most of the Perkins collections, I have emphasized them and the oral history in the citations. Conversely I have left much of what might be called general history unannotated. I hope the result proves useful to others.

GEORGE MARTIN

New York City
May 1975

Contents

PART III

Quasi-Public Office: The Factory Investigating Commission.
Marriage and Mayor Mitchel

PART IV

Public Office: The New York State Labor Department

PART V

The United States Department of Labor

PART VI

After Sixty-Five

Illustrations

PART I

Appointment as United States Secretary of Labor

Chapter 1

>>)<<<

*Her appointment announced. The AFL objects. Roosevelt's inaugu-
ration. The cabinet sworn in.*

THOUGH THE POSSIBILITY of her appointment as Secretary of Labor had
been discussed publicly for months, she was one of the last named by
Franklin D. Roosevelt to his cabinet. On Tuesday, February 28, 1933,
only four days before his inauguration, he called newsmen into his
study at Hyde Park and without comment announced that to complete
it he had selected "Dan" Roper and Miss Perkins.

Roper's appointment as Secretary of Commerce caused little excitement, but on the naming of Frances Perkins a storm broke. Many
women's organizations, professional groups, state labor officials and
individuals in the labor movement rejoiced.[1] But in the headquarters
of the country's largest and most powerful labor organization, the
American Federation of Labor, there was fury.

"Labor," announced William Green, the president, "can never become reconciled to the selection." He listed in general terms the
qualifications he sought in a Secretary, but his specific grievance was
plain: Perkins — besides the shock, the insult of her being a woman —
was not a union official or even a union member; Roosevelt had
ignored the AFL, when he should have chosen one of its leaders.

Two years earlier Green had objected almost as rigorously to Herbert Hoover's appointment of William N. Doak as Secretary, because
Doak's union, the Brotherhood of Railway Trainmen, was not in the
AFL. For the federation to be passed over again was public evidence of
its weakness after four years of depression.

Perkins moved quickly to placate Green and the leaders of his 108
unions. As Industrial Commissioner of New York she had an office in
New York City, and the day after Green's blast she asked reporters to

meet her there. Twenty came, many more than she was used to dealing with, and the small room was crowded.

"Mr. Green and the American Federation of Labor are entirely within their rights," she replied to the first question. "I am glad they expressed themselves openly and frankly. It creates a more wholesome situation, and I do not in any way regard it as an expression of ill-will against me."

She could not be coaxed into acknowledging offense. Green, she insisted, was "a man of great integrity, vision and patriotism." She predicted that she would have much to discuss with him, as well as with other representatives of organized labor, and "if they cannot find the time to come and see me, I will hasten to see them."

To the question "How do you feel to be the first woman in the cabinet?" after hesitating she answered, "Well, I feel just a little odd."

As the questions grew more personal, touching on her husband, Paul Wilson, and their sixteen-year-old daughter, Susanna, she began to flush, played first with a pen and then a pencil and soon was visibly irritated. After evading several questions about her husband, she expressed the hope that the newspapers would not "exploit" the members of her family who were not in public life.

Though some reporters may have known that her husband was ill, what they did not realize, because she could not bring herself to tell them, was that he was in a mental institution, suffering from alternating moods of elation and depression and terrified of publicity. But instead of speaking out — off the record, perhaps — she began to fend unwelcome questions with the remark, "Is this quite necessary?"

By the time she was asked, "Will you sign Frances Perkins to your pay checks?" instead of a simple, "Yes. I always have," she orated. "I will do what the President instructs me to do. I have been confirmed in office by the Senate in this State six times. On each occasion I signed Frances Perkins."

The next morning in the papers the tone of her remarks on labor subjects, such as Green, unemployment insurance and the scandal-ridden immigration bureau, was splendidly right. On personal matters she sounded schoolmarmish and stuffy. But her friends and her colleagues in the state Labor Department would have testified that, though she was often prosy in speech and didactic in manner, she was never stuffy.[2]

On Friday, March 3, 1933, she and Susanna took the train to Washington for the inauguration. Their New York apartment at

Madison Avenue and Eighty-ninth Street was filled with flowers, telegrams and tissue paper. Her friend Margaret Poole, insisting that
Perkins must have new clothes for a new job, had telephoned several
shops to send dresses on approval. She even had persuaded the shops
to send along seamstresses, saying it would be a disgrace to the trade if
the first woman cabinet member were improperly fitted.[3]

Out of all that was sent Perkins had bought a new suit, a black
velvet evening dress with iridescent sequins and a plain black dress
appropriate, as her grandmother used to say, "for mill and for meeting." She balked at a new hat, however, and wore her usual tricorn,
which in its current model had a touch of white on the side.

As a girl of twelve she had been taken by her mother one day in
Boston to shop for a hat. After visiting several stores and finding
nothing they went to Lamston & Hubbard, the leading milliner.
There her mother seized a tricorn of Milan straw, placed it on her
daughter's head and said: "My dear, that is your hat. You should
always wear a hat something like it. You have a very broad face. Your
head is actually narrower above the temples than it is at the cheekbones. Also, it slopes off very suddenly into your chin. The result is
you always need to have as much width in your hat as you have in
your cheekbones. Never let yourself get a hat that is narrower than
your cheekbones, because it makes you look ridiculous."

Thereafter she always kept at least one tricorn in the closet, though
she sometimes bought broad-brimmed summer hats as well. As she
became a national figure, reporters made a symbol of the tricorns and
sometimes teased her about them, saying that she must have had them
designed at the Bureau of Standards. But she never wavered in her
allegiance. "My mother was an artist," she would say, "aware of
proportions and anatomy. She saw I needed that balance."[4]

At Union Station in Washington, while waiting with Susanna for a
cab, Perkins saw a number of familiar faces. After noting four or five,
she realized that the people arriving in the city were all Democrats,
and those departing, Republicans. Suddenly the change of administration and her opportunity to succeed or fail with the Department of
Labor seemed very close.

She had half-expected Doak, the retiring Secretary, to call or write,
offering, perhaps, to introduce her to the Department or to send an
assistant to meet her at the station. But except for personal notes from
Grace Abbott and Mary Anderson, the heads of the Children's and
Women's bureaus, she had not heard from anyone in the Department.

There was an inauguration committee, she knew, for it had sent her two tickets to the inauguration, the parade and the afternoon reception at the White House; beyond that it seemed not to function. Earlier in the week she had feared that she might not get into a hotel at all, but a friend who had business dealings with the Willard House managed to reserve a room for her.

In 1933, the Willard, at Pennsylvania Avenue and Fourteenth Street, was already an old-fashioned hotel and in financial difficulties. The rooms were large, with high ceilings, heavy flowered carpets and wardrobes of carved wood with mirrored doors. When Susanna saw the bed ends of voluptuously curled brass she burst out laughing.

Family pride had stirred a first cousin by marriage, Jack Johnston, to come from Boston with his two boys "to see Frances inaugurated," and they all had dinner together. Afterward the young people went off on adventures of their own, and Perkins asked her cousin if he would take her to a reception at the Pan American Union.

"Certainly," he replied. "I came down to be useful to you."

She showed him the tickets, which had arrived with a large, beautifully inscribed invitation. She knew nothing about the reception but supposed it was something official; in any event, they agreed, it might be fun. Changing into evening clothes, they met again in the hotel lobby and started off in a cab.

By now the city was filled with visitors, and they had hardly pulled away from the Willard's door when their cab became one in a long line, inching forward. Minutes passed, quarter- and half-hours, then over an hour. Johnston, a practical man, began to wonder aloud how they would get home.

The driver assured them that he would not wait. No cabs would wait — only the limousines hired for important people.

After more than an hour and a half they reached the Pan American Union building. From its door emerged Mrs. Woodrow Wilson, the President's widow, who advised them on no account to enter. People had been standing for three hours to reach the receiving line. It was jammed. Unbearable. "Take my advice and leave now," she said.

"I think that's good advice," said Johnston.

So they hurried back to the cab, which was still in line, and by a roundabout way returned to the Willard.

On her door was a message to call Stephen Early at once. He was Roosevelt's press secretary, and she felt comforted to have an official contact.

He was aghast to hear that she had tried to go to the reception at the Union. "Nobody goes to that," he said. "It's just to entertain the riffraff."

The remark startled her. His purpose, however, was to ask her to be at St. John's Episcopal Church at ten the next morning. Roosevelt, as President-elect, wanted his official family to join him in a service of prayer at the start of their adminisration. She could bring her daughter but no one else.

"Where is St. John's?" she asked.

Now he was startled. "Why, you know. On Lafayette Square."

"All right," she said, thinking a cab driver would know.

But the next morning at twenty minutes of ten there were no cabs. After consulting the doorman she and Susanna began to hurry toward the church on foot, frequently stopping passersby to confirm the directions. Lafayette Square, which faces the White House, was not far, and they arrived in time.

St. John's, called the Church of Presidents because every President since Jefferson has attended a service there, is not large, but even so the official family did not fill the nave. To the front and right near a side door, pew 54 was reserved for Roosevelt and his family. Others came in through the main doors, which opened on the nave at the rear, and sat where they chose.

It was her first sight of many of her future colleagues. From news pictures she recognized Cordell Hull, who was to be Secretary of State, Claude Swanson, Secretary of the Navy and Homer Cummings, Attorney General (in place of Senator Thomas J. Walsh of Montana, who had died Thursday on his way to Washington). She knew William Woodin, who was to be the Secretary of the Treasury, for in the early 1920s they had worked together in New York on a Council of Immigrant Education; and she knew James A. Farley, Roosevelt's campaign manager, who was to be Postmaster General. She liked them both, particularly Farley, who looked elegant in a top hat and Chesterfield with immaculate velvet collar. He was tall and impressive, and there was something in his features and complexion that always made him look wonderfully clean. Like her, he had worked in Albany with Roosevelt during his four years as governor of New York.

Soon Roosevelt and his family entered and filled the front pews. Then came the clergy: Robert Johnson, the rector of St. John's, and Endicott Peabody, the headmaster and rector of Groton School, whom Roosevelt had invited to officiate.

Peabody had arranged a service based on the Order for Morning Prayer but modified to include special collects and prayers and two of Roosevelt's favorite hymns, "Oh God Our Help in Ages Past" and "Faith of Our Fathers." Perkins was a devout Episcopalian, and the familiar words had meaning for her. In the years to come the fact that she and Roosevelt were of the same church was a bond. It did not increase her influence with him, but it eased communication. If she talked to him about social justice or urged him to do something simply because it was right, the words tended to have the same resonance in both minds. As she listened now to Peabody — "May Thy son Franklin, chosen to be our President, and all of his advisers, be enlightened and strengthened for Thy service" — she was moved.

After the service, while the others waited, Roosevelt continued for a moment in prayer. Then he rose, turned to smile briefly at his friends and colleagues and, with a cane and leaning on a son's arm, went out the side door to his car. The others, smiling and nodding, slowly filed down the aisles to the front doors.

Outside the church Hull and Swanson, who had been senators and were experienced in the perils and perquisites of a Washington occasion, drove off with their wives in government limousines. Those who had rented cars and chauffeurs for the day disappeared around the corner, and a few of the rest were fortunate enough to find cabs promptly. Soon four of the least experienced and aggressive found themselves alone on the curb.

"I suppose we are all going to the same place," she remarked to the only man among them.

"You're Miss Perkins, aren't you?" he replied.

"And you're the Wallaces, I'm sure," she said to him and his companion. She then introduced Susanna, and Henry Wallace presented his wife, Ilo.

They agreed to share a cab, but none appeared. Finally, by posting themselves on different corners and waving frantically at any that came in sight, they succeeded in attracting one and started for the Capitol.

Their tickets stated they were to enter the building through Statuary Hall, but since neither she nor Wallace was familiar enough with Washington to give the driver directions, he simply aimed straight for the Capitol. Eventually he reached the western edge of the grounds, where they were stopped by a wooden barrier and a policeman who, despite Wallace's pleas, refused to let them drive further. "You should have gone some other way or come earlier. Look at the crowd!" Beyond the barrier the road was jammed with people.

They got out and started pushing through the crush. Wallace tried to clear their way: "Will you let us through. Please. Kindly make way." But their progress was slow, and as time passed both she and Wallace became increasingly agitated. Neither wished to go down in history as the cabinet officer, designated by Roosevelt, who had failed to appear at his inauguration.

The day was overcast, misting heavily, and finally Wallace said, "I hope you have your rubbers on." She did not, but she agreed that, to reach the platform before the ceremony began, they would have to abandon the crowded roadway and run to the Capitol across the open lawn. She hesitated to leave Susanna, whose ticket was for the distinguished visitors' section, not for the platform. But so was Ilo's, and the two agreed to look out for each other. Among the four, in that moment of agitation, an enduring friendship was formed, and as Ilo and Susanna watched, the two future cabinet members ducked under the barrier at the road's edge and started running awkwardly uphill on the wet grass to the back of the Capitol.[5]

They were in time, but their seats on the platform were taken and, rather than make a fuss, they took others at the edge of the stand. Inside the Capitol, while waiting, Roosevelt went over his speech once again and added an opening sentence: "This is a day of consecration."

The ceremony began. In taking his oath of office as governor of New York in 1929 and 1931, Roosevelt had used his family's old Dutch Bible, and now again he made his profession on it, repeating each word after the Chief Justice in a clear voice. Then he turned to the people, perhaps a hundred thousand in the crowd before him and millions more across the country at their radios.

"This is a day of *national* consecration," he began, adding another word to his opening sentence. "I am certain that my fellow Americans expect that on my induction into the Presidency I will address them with a candor and a decision which the present situation of our Nation impels. This is pre-eminently the time to speak the truth, the whole truth, frankly and boldly. Nor need we shrink from honestly facing conditions in our country today. This great Nation will endure as it has endured, will revive and will prosper."

The crowd waited. Perhaps not since Lincoln, had a President been inaugurated under more ominous portents. In the past three years over 5000 banks had failed. By March 2, only two days before the inauguration, governors in twenty-one states had either closed the banks or put severe limits on withdrawals. Shortly before dawn on inauguration day the governors of New York and Illinois announced that the banks in their states were closed. Chicago had stopped paying its schoolteachers, Boston its police; in Detroit municipal workers, unable to cash their paychecks, were collapsing from hunger. Unemployment, larger than Hoover's administration had ever been willing to admit, was increasing and was thought to be at fifteen million, or almost a third of the working population. Bands of unemployed men had begun to drift from state to state in search of jobs that did not exist. In the cities the breadlines grew longer. To many people, even those with food and money, the future seemed terrifying.

"So, first of all," Roosevelt said, "let me assert my firm belief that the only thing we have to fear is fear itself [a phrase he had added at his hotel only that morning], nameless, unreasoning, unjustified terror which paralyzes needed efforts to convert retreat into advance." The country's difficulties, he said, sprang from false spiritual values.

> Our distress comes from no failure of substance. . . . Plenty is at our doorstep, but a generous use of it languishes in the very sight of the supply. Primarily this is because rulers of the exchange of mankind's goods have failed through their own stubbornness and their own incompetence, have admitted their failure, and have abdicated . . . True they have tried, but their efforts have been cast in the pattern of an outworn tradition . . . They know only the rules of a generation of self-seekers. They have no vision, and when there is no vision the people perish.
>
> The money changers have fled from their high seats in the temple of our civilization. We may now restore that temple to the ancient truths. The measure of the restoration lies in the extent to which we apply social values more noble than mere monetary profit . . . Restoration calls, however, not for changes in ethics alone. This Nation asks for action, and action now.

The outgoing President, Hoover, might have delivered the first part of the speech. He had tried again and again to persuade the bankers to act voluntarily and loosen credit in order to stimulate the economy, and always they had insisted they must first receive aid from the federal government. Even his own Secretary of the Treasury, Andrew Mellon, had refused to act personally or through his Pittsburgh bank without some tax or credit benefit from the government. As a result Hoover's first step in active relief, the Reconstruction Finance Corporation, was primarily designed to aid the banks, insurance companies and railroads. The fact disgusted many, including Hoover, who felt that the bankers had abdicated their responsibilities and forced the government to act in places and ways it should not in a capitalistic economy.

It was Roosevelt's insistence on the government's right and duty to act that distinguished him from Hoover.

We must act and act quickly . . . With this pledge taken, I assume unhesitatingly the leadership of this great army of our people dedicated to a disciplined attack upon our common problems.

It is to be hoped that the normal balance of Executive and legislative authority may be wholly adequate to meet the unprecedented task before us. But it may be that an unprecedented demand and need for un-delayed action may call for temporary departure from that normal balance of public procedure.

I am prepared under my constitutional duty to recommend the measures that a stricken Nation in the midst of a stricken world may re-quire. These measures, or such other measures as the Congress may build out of its experience and wisdom, I shall seek, within my constitutional authority, to bring to speedy adoption.

But in the event that the Congress shall fail to take one of these two courses, and in the event that the national emergency is still critical, I shall not evade the clear course of duty that will then confront me. I shall ask the Congress for the one remaining instrument to meet the crisis — broad Executive power to wage a war against the emergency, as great as the power that would be given to me if we were in fact invaded by a foreign foe . . .

In this dedication of a Nation, we humbly ask the blessing of God. May He protect each and every one of us. May He guide me in the days to come.

Roosevelt had written the speech himself in longhand on yellow legal cap paper as he sat by the fire at Hyde Park, and he had worked on it steadily until the moment of delivery. Listening to it, Perkins realized that he had made great changes in the draft she had seen. Sitting beside her was Raymond Moley, at that time one of Roose-velt's closest advisers, a stocky, soft-spoken man with sparkling eyes. He listened with elbows on his knees and his hat dangling between his legs, and at the end he turned to her with a great sigh and said: "Well, he's taken the ship of state and he's turned it right around. We're going in the opposite direction."

All across the country others said the same. Though Roosevelt actually had said very little, his manner of saying it had radiated purpose and courage. Addressing a people beginning to sink into despair, he had revived their faith in themselves and restored their will to work at their problems. In later years Perkins came to feel that he had had a kind of religious revelation when preparing the speech, perhaps after he had arrived in Washington and sensed the despera-tion of people of all conditions and parties. She noticed that he never referred to the address when he spoke to her, though he was always ready to gloat over his others: "Now I said . . . Wasn't that good?" But his first inaugural was something else. If she mentioned it to him, he would talk of it in a quiet, hesitant manner "that made you realize you were on quite sacred ground so far as he was concerned. He would never claim credit for that. It was something not of his own making. I'm sure he thought of it as direct divine guidance."[6]

That day she seemed to be forever taking cabs, abandoning them because of the crowds, rushing on foot to the next event, fearing to be late and meeting others who shared or rescued her from her predicament. Once Harold Ickes, who was to be Secretary of the Interior, seeing her and Susanna in a crowd, invited them to share his limousine. Another time, when her cab was at a standstill in the traffic, Grace Abbott, the chief of the Children's Bureau, and her assistant, Katharine Lenroot, Republicans both, came over to exclaim on the excellence of Roosevelt's speech and to welcome her to the Department of Labor. It was a pleasant interlude. In the midst of the confusion and agitation of the day she resolved that if she lived to see her successor into office she would do better by him than Secretary Doak and the inauguration committee had done by her.

The Wallaces came independently to the same decision. "We were very green," Mrs. Wallace remarked years later, "and knew nothing about the sort of arrangements that could be made, not even that we could ask for a limousine from the Department of Agriculture — and Henry's father had been Secretary of Agriculture under Harding. But life was simpler then, and no one told us."

Following the inaugural parade there was a reception at the White House. Perkins's tickets for herself and Susanna were marked "East Gate," a side entrance opposite the Treasury, most often used by tourists. The line there was long and moved slowly, but it was a relief for once to be on time and in the right place. Besides, she enjoyed talking to the people. They were the Democratic rank and file who had come to Washington to celebrate the first Democratic administration in twelve years — the first since Woodrow Wilson. Though they were worried about the country and about how they would pay their hotel bills in the morning, they were a happy lot, pleased with Roosevelt's speech and sure that he would be able to do something. She did not ask their names or volunteer her own; that was not her way. To demand a person's name seemed to her an invasion of privacy quite unnecessary in a conversation.

Gradually the line moved up into the main hall. There Marguerite

"Missy" LeHand, Roosevelt's secretary, passed through. Seeing Perkins and her daughter, she rushed over.

"Miss Perkins! What are you doing here?"

"I'm just waiting on the line to be received."

"Why didn't you come in the front door?"

Her card, she said, had read East Gate.

LeHand laughed. "Don't you know cabinet officers are supposed to come in the front door?"

She did not.

"I'm just as new at it," LeHand exclaimed. "But most of the others are here, and we've been wondering where you were. Now come with me." She led Perkins and Susanna through the main reception area to a room in which the President and Mrs. Roosevelt were greeting cabinet members and their families.

Later, while the reception continued on the main floor, Perkins and the others were led to the Oval Room upstairs, where to her surprise they were told that the Senate had already met and confirmed their appointments: they would be sworn in immediately. Perkins was eager for Susanna to be present, but she had disappeared and Perkins dared not leave the room to search for her. Ilo Wallace, seeing the situation, hurried downstairs, found Susanna and returned with her in time for the ceremony.

The President sat at his desk with Supreme Court Justice Benjamin Cardozo, in judicial robes, standing before him. Around the Justice in a large semicircle the usher placed the designated cabinet officers in order of precedence determined by the date when the department of each was founded. The arrangement put Perkins, whose Department of Labor was the most recent, on Cardozo's left and across from Hull, whose Department of State was the oldest. After Hull came the Secretaries of the Department of the Treasury and of War, the Attorney General, the Postmaster General, the Secretaries of the Navy and the Departments of the Interior, of Agriculture, Commerce and, finally, Labor. Behind each man stood his wife or relatives; behind Perkins, Susanna.

When all were in order, Roosevelt explained that because of the emergency he wanted them sworn in that evening and had asked Cardozo, an old friend from New York, to administer the oaths. "I hope you don't mind being sworn in on my old Dutch Bible. You won't be able to read a word of it," he said, smiling broadly, "but it's the Holy Scriptures all right."

Starting with Hull, he called the name of the officer to be sworn.

Each stepped forward and repeated the oath of office after Cardozo, closing with "So help me God!"

The President welcomed them all to the administration and said he hoped they would work for the common good and best interests of the nation. "No cabinet," he concluded, "has ever been sworn in before in this way. I am happy to do it because it gives the families of the new cabinet an opportunity to see the ceremony. It is my intention to inaugurate precedents like this from time to time."

It was absolutely without precedent. Quite aside from the Dutch Bible, no cabinet in the country's history had been sworn in at the White House, sworn in as a single group or had included among its members a woman. It was the last that caught the country's interest.[7]

Chapter 2

➤➤➤❮❮❮

Speaker Rainey on how she should be addressed. Her entrance into office and her predecessor's exit.

TRANSFERS OF POWER are usually difficult: those relinquishing it are often reluctant and sullen; those taking it overeager and triumphant. It proved easier, however, for Roosevelt at the White House than for Perkins at the Department of Labor.

At the White House the usher recorded:

> Saturday, March 4, 1933 . . .
> 10:50 Pres. Elect & Mrs. Roosevelt arrived but remained in cars under North Portico where the Pres. & Mrs. Hoover greeted them.
> 10:55 Party left for Capitol.
> 1:30 The President, Mrs. Roosevelt and Family arrived from Capitol.[1]

So it was done: one administration, Democratic, succeeded another, Republican. Hoover left for New York directly from the Capitol, and Roosevelt returned to the White House, moving from the Mayflower Hotel into a home with a large staff and an office ready to function.

For Perkins the succession was more complicated. She had heard nothing from the Department of Labor; her predecessor, William N. Doak, apparently did not plan any ceremonial welcome. Also, she could not combine home and office and could not stay much longer at the Willard. Except for an occasional fee from an article or speech, she had only her salary as a cabinet officer, $13,000 a year, to support herself, her child and husband. Susanna was doing well at the Brearley School in New York, and Wilson was in a sanatorium in White Plains, able on occasion to come home. In order not to disturb their routines she had decided to keep the apartment in New York and return to it on weekends. During the week Susanna would stay with friends whose daughter was in her class. In Washington Perkins felt she needed, perhaps could afford, only a small apartment or a single room.[2]

She had intended to come down for the inauguration and, while the Senate debated her appointment, return to New York to wind up affairs as the state's Industrial Commissioner. She would settle Susanna with their friends and then come back to Washington to establish herself. But the banking crisis upset her plans. The Senate had met following Roosevelt's inaugural address and approved all his appointments without debate, so by Saturday evening, as she dressed to go to the inaugural ball, not Doak but Frances Perkins was Secretary of Labor with duties to perform.

On Sunday she sent Susanna back to New York with Jack Johnston and asked her New York secretary, Frances Jurkowitz, who had come down for the inauguration, to stay over and work for several days. Already at the Willard there were letters to be answered, phone calls to be taken and memoranda to be prepared, and Sunday afternoon at the White House there was a cabinet meeting on the banking crisis. Several congressional leaders attended as well as Roosevelt's Director of the Budget, Lewis W. Douglas. Perkins, knowing little about the technicalities of banking, merely listened.

As she came out of the cabinet room in the west, or office, wing of the White House, she found herself beside the Speaker-elect of the House of Representatives, Henry T. Rainey. Reporters quickly surrounded them, eager to know about the meeting. While she was passing the questions to Rainey, who neatly evaded them, one reporter asked her directly, "What do we call you?"

"My name is Perkins."

"Yes, but what do we call you? How do we address you?"

"*Miss* Perkins," she suggested.

"But we say 'Mr. Secretary' to the Secretary of State and 'Mr. Secretary' to the Secretary of the Interior. What do we say to you?"

She deferred to Rainey. "The Speaker of the House, who is an expert on parliamentary procedure, will know better than I."

Rainey, a tall, picturesque man from Illinois, with curly white hair almost to his shoulders, drew himself up. "When the Secretary of Labor is a lady, she should be addressed with the same general formalities as the Secretary of Labor who is a gentleman. You call him 'Mr. Secretary.' You will call her 'Madam Secretary.' You gentlemen know that when a lady is presiding over a meeting, she is referred to as

'Madam Chairman' when you rise to address the chair. If she is president of the Women's Temperance League, she is addressed as 'Madam President' when in her official capacity she is presiding over a meeting or taking some official action as president of that organization. This is all in the *Robert's Rules of Order* revisions. She will be addressed as 'Madam Secretary.' "

The next day the newspapers carried Rainey's answer, though some attributed it directly to Perkins. Not everyone in the press corps, however, seemed able to grasp its logic. Frequently reporters in their stories or editors in their headlines would refer to her as Madam Perkins or the Madam Secretary or even the Madam, instead of simply Miss Perkins or the Secretary of Labor. Her sex seemed to confuse them. Some addressed her not as Miss Perkins or Madam Secretary, but as Madam Perkins. That mistake "is one of the things that gets me down," she confessed years later, after the newspapers had spread the confusion. Most persons, she knew, blundered in ignorance, but she came to feel that a few did it deliberately as a crude form of insult — like continually mispronouncing a person's name.[3]

Monday morning Roosevelt and the cabinet attended a memorial service at the Capitol for Senator Thomas J. Walsh, who was to have been the Attorney General. Immediately afterward Perkins, Roper, George Dern and Harold Ickes, the Secretaries of Labor, Commerce, War and the Interior, went to the East Room of the White House for a governors' conference on unemployment.

With the roving bands of unemployed in mind, Perkins had prepared a memorandum on interstate agreements with regard to labor legislation, using as a model the Port of New York Authority, created by an interstate compact between New York and New Jersey in 1921. It was a solution she and Roosevelt had discussed in Albany while planning the conference. Now, however, he suggested that it might be wiser to let the governors do the talking, and as the hours passed, one after another rose to tell of conditions in his state: how industry had broken down, how charities could no longer cope with the mass misery, how the state had reached the limit of its power to borrow and in a month or a week would no longer be able to provide bread for the breadlines.

She did not stay to the end. She could see that nothing specific would emerge; the gain would be in good will between the President and the governors. Everyone would understand that the problem of unemployment was nationwide and not limited to the industrial centers. Also, she still had not set foot in the Department of Labor. She must go and take command.[4]

She went first to the Willard to check with Miss Jurkowitz, usually called Miss Jay. There was still no message from anyone at the Department of Labor. As Doak evidently did not intend to open its door for her, she would have to push it open herself. "I am the Secretary," she said to Jay, "and I have not only a right but a duty to take possession of the premises." Looking up the number in the phone book, she called.

She reached a male secretary, who said, "We were expecting to hear from you." After a long wait, Doak came on the phone. "Good morning."

"You know I've been sworn in," she began.

"I read in the paper that the whole cabinet was sworn in," he said. "I didn't know whether you were going to stay in Washington now or not."

"We were all sworn in, asked to stay, and take over our duties at once."

"Oh, yes," he said.

"I'm here, and I thought I would like to come over to the department while you are still there." She stressed the "still." "Perhaps you will introduce me to the principal members of the staff and show me the general works of the place."

He agreed, though her suggestion that she be in his office in half an hour plainly took him by surprise.

Doak, a short, stout Virginian with deep-set brown eyes made larger by thick glasses, had been a controversial figure in Hoover's cabinet. Compared with the more patrician members, Henry L. Stimson or Charles F. Adams, he seemed uncouth. He dressed sloppily, spoke profanely and strove constantly to appear a backslapping friend of labor leaders. Compared in ability with others in Hoover's cabinet he seemed incompetent. He developed few services or programs for working people and devoted most of his time to deporting aliens. And even in this matter he was ineffective. A commission appointed by Hoover to study problems of law enforcement, with such men as George W. Wickersham, Newton Baker and Roscoe Pound among its members, reported in May 1931 that the administration of the deportation laws was poor, that many aliens were being harassed unnecessarily and that the constitutional rights of many citizens were being violated.

In other areas Doak had done little better. His reorganization of the U.S. Employment Service, started largely in response to pressure from Senator Robert F. Wagner, had failed to satisfy the critics of the service. His refusal to reappoint the chief of the Bureau of Labor Statistics, after the man had publicly questioned some of the administration's optimistic reports on employment, had lowered the bureau's standing and morale. To many persons interested in the federal government, the Department of Labor, more than any other, needed overhauling.[5]

Perkins, with Jay at her side, went directly to 1712 G Street, where the department had a nine-story, boxlike building, put up during the First World War. She had hoped that Doak might have a secretary waiting at the entrance, but none was on hand. Inside, the elevator man refused to take them up until he had confirmed their appointment.

"I've already telephoned," she assured him, "but I am Miss Perkins, the new Secretary of Labor."

He said he had seen in the paper that the new Secretary was to be a lady.

Their names cleared, she and Jay were taken up to the seventh floor, where they stepped off into a large and gloomy outer office filled with hard, straightbacked chairs interspersed with ashtrays, most of them unemptied. A Negro, whose name she later learned was Callus, came toward them. He was a big man, stooped, with many teeth missing, his jacket spotted with food, his cuffs frayed and his shirt dirty. "All of this may spell a poor man," she observed later, "but that is also a peculiar man to have as a receptionist." When he discovered who she was, he put his hand on his heart, bowed very low and welcomed her to the department.

He led her into a dingy office where three men were working, two of them on immigration matters and the third as Doak's private secretary. She identified herself and explained that she had come to see Mr. Doak. The secretary rose and said, "I'll see if he's free." In a few minutes she and Jay were shown into Doak's office and greeted by the man himself.

His room was cleaner than the others, though even here the chairs were battered and unwaxed, the windows grimy, the desk top pitted and stained. But what struck her most forcefully was that nothing had been packed. There was no sign that Doak or his staff had any thought of leaving.

He greeted them pleasantly and offered them chairs; she introduced Jay as her assistant. Because Doak seemed uncertain what to say, she took the lead and asked general questions about the department. She quickly concluded that he had little information. To a question about his channels of communication with union leaders he replied, "Oh, they're around here all the time." But he could not describe any ideas they had discussed for combating the Depression. When she mentioned a program of public works as a method of providing employment and increasing purchasing power, he seemed to have no ideas beyond his feeling that "it'll cost a lot of money and wreck the Treasury."

Time was passing and the amenities, she felt, had been observed sufficiently. Perhaps before lunch, she suggested, he could introduce her to the staff. "I would prefer to be introduced by you," she explained.[6]

While the secretary was assembling the higher officials in the outer office, she questioned Doak about the department's chief problems. "Well, the immigration business is always serious," he said. "We have lots of trouble with those people who come in illegally. That's a never-ending problem." For a few minutes he was eloquent on the pressures exerted on the department, the constant phone calls from immigrants' friends, families, congressmen; the requests for favors, for review or for action.

She sympathized in part, for the pressure, particularly from Congress, doubtless was great. On the other hand, Hoover's Commission on Law Observance and Enforcement had condemned several of the procedures Doak's men used, such as illegal search and seizure of persons as well as property, and had questioned the continued use of others.

Moreover, she had reason to fear that the situation was worse than the commission, and perhaps Doak, knew. The previous week a New York police lieutenant[7] whom she trusted had come to her office to describe how a group within the Bureau of Immigration was extorting money from aliens. Members of the group were known as Section 24 men, from the section of the statute authorizing their appointment. They would "raid" a place where aliens gathered — a Finnish Community Dance Hall, for example, or a Slovakian beer parlor — round up the aliens, scare some of them into believing that their papers were incorrect and for a price agree to drop the charges. It was a difficult crime to prevent; the aliens, who often spoke little or no English, would not go to the police, and the shakedowns were small amounts of cash. Specifically, the lieutenant warned her to watch for Murray Garsson and his brother Henry, the leaders of the Section 24 group.

Doak had created the special section and appointed both men. Presumably he did not know what was going on. It was not the sort of labor problem Perkins had discussed with Roosevelt, but here it was in her department.

Finally the staff was assembled. The secretary ushered them in, more or less in order of precedence, and Doak introduced them. At the head of the line was Robe Carl White, the First Assistant Secretary. She did not know him, but he looked intelligent and trustworthy. She thought he would know something about the department's operations, and she shook his hand warmly, saying she wanted to see him very soon.

William W. Husband, the Second Assistant Secretary, was an acquaintance; they had served together on several committees in New York. He came from Vermont, she remembered, and had worked both in and out of the government on immigration matters. She liked him and was confident that he had had no part in any crookedness in the Bureau of Immigration.

She also knew Grace Abbott, chief of the Children's Bureau, and Mary Anderson, chief of the Women's Bureau. Both were prominent in their fields — popular, strong leaders who ran their bureaus as independent of the department as possible. Abbott was a national figure, and there had been a movement to urge Hoover to appoint her instead of Doak as his Secretary of Labor. Though the effort had failed, it encouraged women's groups to hope for a representative in the cabinet and prepared the way for Perkins's appointment.[8]

As the line continued to move past them, Doak soon proved unable to match names, faces and jobs, and the people began to introduce themselves. To her surprise four or five men described themselves as "in charge of immigration."[9] She had heard that the bureau suffered from divided command but had never imagined that its authority was so fragmented. Soon another man introduced himself as in charge of immigration: "My name is Murray Garsson." He was trimly built, with dark hair, well-cut clothes — too well-cut for her taste — and a shrewd expression. Then someone else took his place and was speaking to her.

After the last man had shaken her hand and murmured his name, and while the others, still nodding and chatting, were drifting out of the room, she went over to Robe Carl White with a question about the department's operations.

"I don't want to be in your way," he said quickly. "I have prepared my resignation." But she asked him to wait for a few days.

With White still at her side, she turned to Doak, determined now to get him out of the office. "I presume you have a luncheon engagement," she said, "but if not, I should like you to come to my hotel and lunch with me."

His surprise was evident. He murmured that — well, yes, as a matter of fact — he was engaged for lunch.

She expressed regret, adding, "I hope you will come in to see me often. I presume that you have a few articles here in the office that you would like to take with you. Is this Negro man in the outer office the person you would call on to pack those?"

He hesitated. "I suppose so."

"Perhaps it would be a good idea," she said, "to have him pack them now while you're at lunch. I don't lunch, you see, so I'll stay here. If it's all right with you, I'll tell the man to pack your things now."

He looked at her in astonishment. "Are you going to stay on in Washington?" he asked.

"Yes. I'm going to stay."

"I thought perhaps you'd go back to New York."

"No. I shan't go back to New York. I'll send for my trunks and stay right here. I'll spend the afternoon in the office. I'll come in tomorrow morning early. It's been most kind of you to introduce the people. By the way, is there a car or any other conveyance at the disposal of the Secretary?"

There were several small cars, a limousine and a truck.

"That's quite a fleet," she remarked. "That must be very convenient for you. Since you're going to lunch, won't you take the car and the chauffeur as you've been accustomed?" In order to leave no doubt in his mind, she added, "Would you be kind enough to tell the chauffeur, once he has left you at your home after lunch, to come back here? If he'll come directly to the office, I'll give him his further orders."

White, who had been standing beside them, moved to the window and then left the room.

"I'll have to telephone," Doak said.

To give him privacy she went to the outer office and told the secretary that, as soon as Mr. Doak had gone to lunch, she would have some letters to dictate. When he came out, she shook his hand and invited him back for a visit. Once he was gone she sat down at her desk and dictated the letters.

Chapter 3

→»)«←

Cleaning the office. The problem of Section 24. The department ball.

THE AFTERNOON of her first day at the department was a succession of interruptions as people came and went with routine matters. Callus, packing Doak's belongings, hovered about. "I'll take good care of you," he kept saying. "I was a butler once. I know just how to take care of ladies."

When he showed Perkins and Jay the washroom, a large one containing a couch, he said, "This is where the Secretary used to take his nap every afternoon. You'll do the same, I hope."

Perkins protested, saying that she never napped.

"You'll find you get tired," he said. "You'll find that you need to lie down. I'll tell you what — I'll wash your gloves every morning. Bring your white gloves in and I'll wash and dry them in here."

She and Jay stifled their laughter. What did he expect; what did others expect of the first woman Secretary? He was so obviously well intentioned that it was impossible not to like him. The washroom was dirty, however, and she asked him to clean the basin with scouring powder and to put out fresh towels.

Then she asked the secretary to empty Doak's desk, for the drawers might hold personal papers. She had Callus pack the books and knickknacks. When he came in to say that he had run out of cardboard boxes, she sent him to a grocery for more. She was determined to have Doak out of the office by the end of the day, with all his belongings delivered to his home by the department's truck.

When the last carton had disappeared to the outer office, she sat at the desk. As she pulled open the lowest drawer, a small black animal leapt at her face. She shrieked. It fell back and she slammed the drawer. "Quick!" she called to Callus. "There's a mouse here. Get rid of it."

Investigating, Callus reported, "That's no mouse. That's a cock-roach." After studying the animal herself, she agreed, though it was larger than any cockroach she had ever seen.

There were more in the middle drawer. Disturbed by the clean-up, they had abandoned their lairs. So Callus again departed for the grocery, this time to buy ammonia to wash the drawers. After he'd gone, Perkins said to Jay, "See if there's any roach paste in Washington. We'll have to do the job ourselves. It's too deep-seated to respond to an old colored man flopping around with a rag. There's got to be drastic treatment."

In the coming weeks an army of cockroaches was to die by poison. Callus's desk in particular was infested. As a Negro he had few places nearby where he could eat, and every day he had brought his lunch in a paper bag and stored it in his desk. Perkins couldn't change the city's law, but she bought him a lunch pail and saw that he used it.

Eighteen months later when the department moved to a new build-ing on Constitution Avenue she opened the cafeteria with a ruling that all employees, regardless of color, could use it. Though she had made the ruling on larger grounds, to one white man who complained she explained it not in terms of racial justice, but of cockroaches: it was merely sensible housekeeping.[1]

In the midst of the packing and the cockroaches the First Assistant Secretary, Robe Carl White, returned. "I want to congratulate you," he said. "I didn't think our former Secretary would be able to leave so quickly."

"I hope I wasn't rude."

"You were all right. He simply wasn't counting on your coming to stay."

Doak's behavior puzzled her. "What did he think I was going to do?"

"He just thought you wouldn't come down for a while and things would go on as usual. I'm glad you made the break, because it is going to be difficult. There are some serious situations here."

Instinctively she trusted him. He was elderly, tall, thin, with white hair and glasses. His expression was a bit sour — his mouth was tight and severe — but also intelligent. "Mr. White," she said, "will you stay on with me a while?"

"I'll stay as long as you need me," he replied, "but, of course, you know I am a Republican and a Republican appointee."

"But you know the ropes here. Perhaps you'll give me guidance."

"I will. I'm a Republican and I don't like Democrats" — he evidently wanted to make that plain — "but I like my country, and I want it well governed."[2]

He told her his background. He was a lawyer from Muncie, Indiana. He had been the city attorney in Muncie, then the city postmaster and the Delaware County Republican chairman. In 1922, when he was fifty-three, he had taken his first post in the federal government as chairman of the board of review of the Bureau of Immigration. Later that same year he became Second Assistant Secretary of the Department of Labor. The position had recently been created to handle administrative problems arising from the immigration law of 1921, which set up the first quota system for the admission of immigrants. In 1925 he was promoted to First Assistant Secretary, a post he had held now for eight years, all but two under Doak's predecessor, James J. Davis. White's background therefore was largely in law and immigration work, and most of what he had to tell her concerned the Bureau of Immigration.

To a greater extent than she had realized it dominated the department. Its various activities absorbed 3659 of the 5113 employees and nearly $10 million of the $13.5 million budget, even though the number of immigrants and aliens in the country, partly because of the new quota law, was fast declining.[3]

Much of the bureau's work was routine, but under Doak one aspect, the deportation of aliens, had become highly visible and controversial.[4] He wrote and spoke often of the "radical element" among laborers; he stressed constantly the threat to the country from "alien agitators"; and in order to find and deport aliens illegally in the country he had formed a special corps of investigators, the Section 24 men led by Murray Garsson. This force of about ninety men and women was constantly in the news. One of its most sensational "raids," conducted even after Hoover's Commission on Law Observance and Enforcement had criticized its work, was carried out in Detroit in 1932. Assisted by the local police, a group of Section 24 investigators surrounded a block of buildings late at night, and without warrants of any kind, either for entry or arrest, forced their way into the people's rooms and apartments and took away 606 suspects. These were lodged in the local jails, where the investigators began to examine them. Of the 606, two were found to be subject to deportation; the rest were citizens or aliens legally in the country.[5]

White quickly made it plain that he and many others in the bureau considered Garsson's group a disgrace to the department and to the country. They could do little about it, however, because it had been set up by Doak and its members were not required to report to anyone but him. No one else in the department could find out what they did or were about to do until it was reported in the newspaper.

Didn't Husband, the Second Assistant Secretary, work on immigration matters? asked Perkins. "Husband does nothing but immigration!" White said. But the Secretary "has put so many 'buttinskeys' in that Husband can hardly function. Doak has divided it all up."

Seven men that morning, she remarked, had introduced themselves as "in charge of immigration." "That's just it!" exclaimed White. "Doak puts them in charge of special branches and Husband can't follow them. They don't report to him. God knows who they report to. They supposedly report to the Secretary."

"The whole thing is in a bad way," he said. "It's all very irregular. I don't even like to think what's going on there."

While they were talking, the chief clerk came in to invite her to the department's annual reception and ball being held that evening at the Mayflower Hotel. To anyone familiar with the American labor movement, the first meeting with the chief clerk was a startling experience. His name was Samuel Gompers and he was the son of *the* Samuel Gompers, founder and first president of the American Federation of Labor. Not only did the chief clerk have his father's name, but he looked exactly like him — short, thick-set, with a prominent jaw and a strong forehead. Inside the head, however, most people agreed, all resemblance stopped; his name alone won him the job and kept him in it.

Though Perkins had not known of the reception, she decided instantly to attend; it would provide an opportunity to meet more of the department's employees. Turning to White, she said, "You will go, of course."

"I hadn't thought of it."

"Well, I think it would be nice," she said. "I'm sure Mr. Doak won't come, so you can represent the outgoing administration." The idea of making visible the continuity of the department appealed to her. "It would be a pleasure for me," she added. He agreed to go.

"We'll stand in a receiving line," she said to Gompers. "Mr. White will be next to me, and you can stand between me and the door. You know the people, and you can introduce them to me."

After Gompers had left, White began to explain the background of Section 24.[6] It had been possible for Doak to create a force of special investigators only because of unusual language in the statute under which he appointed them. Section 24 of the Immigration Act of 1917 permitted a Secretary of Labor, without regard to civil service requirements, to appoint to the bureau any persons he thought specially qualified to enforce the contract labor provisions of the immigration laws.

These provisions made it illegal for an employer to bring in foreign laborers under a contract to work — five hundred men, for example, from Dublin or Naples to work in New York or Chicago. Usually such contracts had undercut the local wage scale and depressed local wages; hence the ban.

For many years, however, there had been very little contract labor entering the country. Doak's Section 24 men worked almost entirely on the deportation of aliens under a clause in the statute providing that the special investigators might be assigned to other duties when not engaged in contract labor problems. Many people assumed this meant *temporarily* assigned to other duties and were astonished to see a new, permanent force for work with aliens created by Doak outside the regular body of immigration inspectors. To these critics the perversion of the statute's intent had reached a climax in January, when Garsson announced an investigation of Hollywood in search of foreign actors or scriptwriters who had overstayed their allotted time. It seemed likely that there would be lots of publicity for the investigators and high living at government expense, while the real problems of immigration, such as migrant labor from Mexico, were ignored.

In White's opinion most of the men Doak had appointed, which, protected by the statute, he had done "without reference" to the civil service act, were dishonest. They had been recruited, White said, "out of the gutter."

"If you plan to get rid of these men, you had better do it quickly," he advised, "because they'll plant something on you."

"Is it that bad?" she asked. "Did they plant something on Mr. Doak?"

"I wouldn't like to say, but they have something on him, and that's why he never could disturb them no matter what they did. Nothing I ever said could make him touch this crowd."

She found herself inclined to believe him. Still, though she was prepared to doubt Doak's honesty, she was not prepared to doubt Hoover's. "You knew all about this Section Twenty-four squad," she said. "Didn't you ever tell the President?"

"I never had the opportunity." In the last years of Hoover's administration, he explained, the President saw his cabinet officers one by one. If Doak was out of town, no substitute was requested or sent. White had hinted to some members of Congress that all was not well with the Section 24 group, but no one seemed to want to challenge Doak's policy of deporting aliens. Doak was apt to characterize any critic as un-American, and Congress was always ready to support his program with another appropriation.

Gompers reappeared at the door. He was troubled that he might not know the names of all the people coming to the ball.

"But you probably would know more than anybody else," Perkins said.

He wasn't sure. He thought the payroll clerk would know even more, and he went off to find the payroll clerk.

Except in the force of special investigators, White continued, morale within the bureau was poor. The Section 24 men roamed the country on large travel allowances, and their projects often wasted the time and hurt the pride of the local inspectors. The special investigators would arrive, give orders to the local force, perhaps set up a separate office, reap publicity for themselves and then depart, often leaving a mess for the local men to clean up. Moreover, Doak's brother and nephew were on the special force, and that was resented, too.

Perkins had assumed that since the group had been appointed without regard to civil service requirements they could be discharged without regard to them. She was dumbfounded when White told her that Hoover, on Doak's recommendation, in the last week of his administration, had given them all civil service status. This meant that not one could be retired unless charges were brought against him for some delinquency in his work, an impossible undertaking with a force of eighty-seven.

Gompers appeared at the door with the payroll clerk, to whom he had explained the plan for a receiving line at the ball. The clerk's appearance amused her; he seemed "a funny kind of flibbertigibbet sort of man." She said to him, "You know everyone's name, I suppose."

"Well, I ought to. I go over their checks every two weeks." Then, suddenly cautious, he added, "But I don't know whether I know the faces." He agreed, however, to join Perkins and White in the receiving line.

The two clerks left. Turning back to White, she said, "How am I going to get rid of these investigators now they're in civil service?"

White had a memorandum, a single sheet, which he handed her. It contained a statement of the financial underpinning of the Section 24 group.

"There's a special appropriation to support this operation," he explained. "Two hundred thousand dollars was appropriated. That will lapse on the fifteenth of March. They've spent it all. There's just twelve thousand dollars left in the fund and that isn't enough to pay their wages, and we owe traveling expenses besides. You haven't got any more money."

"You mean the function can be eliminated because there's no money?"

"That's right. Now I think I should tell you that if you will make an application and go before Congress and ask for one hundred thousand dollars on the ground that the money has all been spent, they will give it to you without a minute's thought or questioning."

"I think I won't do that," she replied. "The Roosevelt administration is for economy. I couldn't possibly ask for more money for this function which I don't think necessary. Of course I couldn't pledge any more money to these men. They'll have to go because there's no money to pay them."

It was not a final decision. She felt she should talk to Garsson first and also to the President, for the firing of an entire section of the department, particularly its best known, might cause political problems. But she indicated to White that she took his advice seriously and was inclined to act on it.

That night at the ball the payroll clerk proved to know almost no one by sight and was soon released from duty in the receiving line. White knew many employees but not all, and often Perkins simply grasped a stranger's hand, sometimes to his astonishment, and said, "I'm glad to see you. Do tell me your name and where you work." She was eager to impress them that they were "not just driven cattle so far as I was concerned, but coworkers."

When the band began to play, she said to White, "I suppose you and I will have to start the dancing." He looked so surprised that she added, "We'll dance just a minute or two and that will start the others." But evidently it was a formality that neither Davis nor Doak had made familiar, for, as she admitted later, the sight of herself and White gliding around the floor "created great astonishment." As they started around a second time she called to the people at the tables, "Take a partner! Begin to dance."

They did, and soon the floor was full. Then she and White retired to a box at the side of the room. After a time he went home, but she stayed almost to the end, circulating from box to box, stopping at tables, introducing herself to everyone and asking each to tell her who he was and where he worked. She met, she said later, a lot of "awfully nice people."[7]

According to the *New York Times* the next morning, Frances Perkins on her first day in office had

> . . . arrived at the department between one and two o'clock to find her desk covered with flowers, including a basket from bureau chiefs, who came in to greet her and to assure her of their readiness to be of every assistance.
>
> Former Secretary Doak spent much of the day at the department, having come with similar offers of aid and cooperation.[8]

Chapter 4

-»»×««-

Her first words at a cabinet meeting. Vice-President Garner. Section 24 abolished. The Garsson brothers return.

SHORTLY BEFORE 2:00 P.M. on Tuesday, March 7, Perkins reported to the office wing of the White House for the first scheduled meeting of the President and his cabinet.

The office wing lies 165 feet to the west of the central, residential part of the White House, to which it is attached by a gallery. On its long north side are several entrances, reached from a side street, which are generally used by visitors, staff and cabinet officers. Although it and a similar wing on the east are both three-story buildings, each is so well nestled into the sloping ground that it is almost completely concealed by planting. Persons looking at the White House from Lafayette Square, the traditional view from the north, are often unaware of either structure. They see only the green park and, at its center, in apparent isolation, the beautiful building with the columned porch that for generations has symbolized the American presidency.

The cabinet room is in the northeast corner of the office wing. Four large french windows look out on the rose garden, the south side of the White House with its curved balcony and down the south lawn through elms and oaks to the Washington Monument. During Roosevelt's presidency the windows were draped in red, and the white walls held portraits of Jefferson, Jackson and Wilson. Dominating the room was a large, eight-sided mahogany table four or five times as long as it was wide. The President sat at one end and the Vice-President at the other, with the cabinet officers alternating along either side in order of precedence. Thus Hull, the Secretary of State, was on the President's right, and Perkins, the Secretary of Labor, was on Vice-President

Garner's right. Opposite her on Garner's left was the Secretary of Commerce, Roper; on her right was the Secretary of Agriculture, Wallace.

This meeting, like the unscheduled two before it, was devoted to the banking crisis. On inauguration day Roosevelt had directed his Secretary of the Treasury, William Woodin, to draft an emergency banking bill, and the next day, to provide Woodin time to prepare it, he had issued two proclamations: one calling Congress into special session on Thursday, March 9, to vote on the bill that Woodin would have ready, and the other halting transactions in gold and closing all the country's banks for four days. During the bank holiday the people lived on credit, spent what cash they had or, in some cases, went hungry. Meanwhile Woodin sent his Treasury agents around the country to see what could be done for banks in trouble.

After a hopeful report from Woodin — people were redepositing money in the banks and the emergency bill would be ready by Thursday noon when Congress reconvened — Roosevelt turned to the rest of the cabinet, saying that he would ask each Secretary in turn to report on whatever seemed important in his department. The atmosphere, already formal, stiffened. Roosevelt knew well only Farley and Perkins; the others represented political decisions and compromises. Garner had been an opponent for the nomination. Hull and Swanson, the Secretary of the Navy, had been congressional leaders. Wallace and Ickes were former Republicans from the Midwest, and George Dern, Secretary of the Army, had been governor of Utah. Each was eager to take the measure of the others, and all were curious about the woman at the table.

As Hull described the situation in the Far East and Dern discussed the economy in general terms, she became aware that the other cabinet members were covertly studying her face, her clothes and her manner, even as she was studying theirs. Garner, immediately on her left, fascinated her. Short, plump, with a round face and a little beak of a nose, he had white hair, reddish pink complexion and eyes so blue that they blazed. "Red, white and blue," people used to say of him, summarizing his frontier style and appearance. On meeting Perkins, he had slapped his hand into hers, given her whole arm a shake and burst out heartily in a Texas accent, "Glad to see you, sister." The effect was homespun, genuine yet honed to perfection; he was aware of the source and power of his charm.

She also liked what she knew of his politics. In the House of Representatives, of which he had been a member since 1903 and

Speaker for the last two years, he had supported Wilson's program for a Federal Reserve System and a graduated income tax, and had fought Andrew Mellon's regressive tax policies of the twenties. He had few ideas of his own, however, for combating the Depression and in the recent Congress had proved a somewhat ineffectual leader of the Democratic majority in the House. Nevertheless, he was one of the party's recognized leaders, and at the national convention in Chicago the previous summer, when the nomination for President had threatened to become deadlocked among him, Roosevelt, Newton Baker and Al Smith, he had thrown his votes to Roosevelt in order to assure a quick decision and preserve party unity. It was the sort of action, the placing of principle before personal glory, that appealed to her.

As she listened to her colleagues, one after another, she tried to keep her face expressionless. Even when several discussed problems that bore on her department, she did not lean forward or make a note on the pad before her. The others occasionally asked questions; she did not. She wanted to impress them as a quiet, orderly woman who, as she later said, "did not buzz-buzz all the time or butt in where she was not wanted but who could be trusted not to be an embarrassment."

When Roper finished, Roosevelt turned to her with a private, brotherly smile. She knew that he understood why she had been silent and that he too wanted her to succeed with these men. "Well, Miss Perkins," he said, "have you anything to say, anything to contribute?" And, still smiling, "What have you been thinking about?"

She had decided against discussing any of the department's particular problems, such as the Bureau of Immigration. Instead she spoke in general terms of the need for some sort of immediate temporary relief for the unemployed and then for legislation, using all practical means, such as public works, to ensure the country against any further depression. To that end, she said, she and her staff were drafting plans for free public employment offices and for some kind of regulation of workers' hours.

She tried to say it all in one minute, in a flat, unemotional voice. She was aware, as she spoke, that every man in the room was looking at her. Garner, who was a bit deaf, took the cigar from his mouth and swung around in his chair to face her. When she stopped speaking, he swung back and resumed smoking.

Later that month she met Mrs. Garner, who for years had acted as her husband's secretary. Mrs. Garner said that he had come home from the White House and remarked, "Well, we had our first cabinet meeting."

"Was Miss Perkins there?" she had asked.

"Oh, yes."

"What kind of woman is she?"

"I guess she's all right," he had said. "She didn't interrupt. She didn't butt in. She didn't ask any questions. She kept still until the President asked her what she had to say. Then she said it. She said it loud enough so I could hear. She said it plain and distinct. She said it short. When she was through, she stopped. I guess she's all right."[1]

Although she had not mentioned the problem in the Immigration Bureau at the cabinet meeting, she knew she must do something about it immediately. She was inclined to be sceptical of White's suggestion that Garsson might plant something on her. But if she once went to Congress for money to continue the force, she would appear to have acquiesced in its operations. Cutting it back or abolishing it later would be far more difficult.

She talked with Murray Garsson and learned much about other inspectors in the bureau but little about him. Some of what he said, however, aggravated her suspicions of him. No one on the force had ever made a study of contract labor problems; in fact, Garsson had never heard of the provisions under which his section had been created. He spoke of it exclusively as a detective agency working on all immigration affairs and reporting only to the Secretary. Where were his written reports to Doak? On file, he thought, but he was not sure where; from his description of them, they were not extensive. The force, he complained, was "dogged by White."[2]

By Wednesday, the day after the cabinet meeting, she had decided to abolish the group in the manner suggested by White. But first she went to talk to the President. She saw him privately in his office in the west wing, told him briefly about the force, quoted the report of Hoover's commission and described what she had found in the department.

He was astonished and at the same time amused. "It's a great joke," he said, "that it should be you who runs into crooks. Go ahead and clean them out. You are lucky to have that way of doing it, darn lucky. I suppose," he added, "there are some Democrats among these people."

"I guess we'll learn in a day or two that there are. We'll begin hearing from Congress. We'll find that Doak appointed two or three just to keep the kitty sweet. What'll I do?"

"Don't do a thing. Just let them go. Tell the same story to the Democratic congressmen that you tell to the others. Tell them the money was gone; you couldn't keep them because there wasn't any money. You can be as polite as you want about how far you'll go to help a man to get another job. But I suppose there's not going to be much money available for new jobs."[3]

She set about eliminating the group as quickly and quietly as possible. She did not call in the newspapers; her purpose was not to blacken the Hoover administration or to lay charges against Garsson or his men, but to reorganize the largest bureau in her department. Garsson was asked to submit his resignation as Special Assistant Secretary of Labor, effective March 15. Sixteen members of the force, among them Doak's brother and nephew, who had been transferred by Hoover's executive order to the department's regular payroll, were put on furlough for the balance of the fiscal year; and the other seventy-one members were informed that, for lack of funds under Section 24 of the statute, their jobs as of March 15 were abolished.[4]

A day or two later she returned to the office after dinner to work, not expecting to find anyone in the building except the night watchman. As the elevator took them past the fourth floor, however, she heard a murmur of voices. Curious, she asked who was there.

"Mr. Garsson and all them fellows came back," the watchman replied. "They said they was working late."

"Don't stop at my floor," she said. "Take me back down there."

The elevator door opened directly on Garsson, his brother and several other men. They were rifling the files. She had no doubt of it. They had their sleeves rolled, and were pulling out the folders, going through them, taking papers out and piling them on the floor.

"Hold the elevator," she told the watchman. Though he was fat, slow and old enough to be a Spanish-American War veteran, she wanted some kind of backing.

"What are you doing, Mr. Garsson?"

He answered calmly. "You know we're all out. Well, the notice was so sudden we had no time to get our personal belongings and correspondence."

"These files can't be personal," she said. "They look like official files, immigration files, files of investigations."

"Well, we're just trying to get ours."

"Surely anything personal must be in your desks and not in the files."

"We just wanted to get a few little belongings."

She looked at the stacks of papers on the floor. "Where are your belongings?"

"Well . . . they're scattered."

"I shall have to decide quickly," she said, "and say that you are not to take anything out of the files and that you are to leave the building at once." Her eye swept over the group to include them all. "If you have anything personal here, I suggest that you come back tomorrow after the department is open, and that you tell Mr. White what you want. He will assist you in getting your personal belongings. Meanwhile I ask you to leave the building now."

The "now" resounded. On the faces of several of the more thuglike men she could see a determination not to leave. Garsson's face was a mask. She could only guess what was going through his mind: the consequences of staying — what would they do with her? — and the consequences of not staying.

He decided to go. Following his lead, the men put on their coats. She insisted they leave the papers where they were, on the floor; file clerks would clear up the room in the morning. She demanded the key to the files from Garsson, and he gave it to her. After they left, she telephoned for an additional guard and waited until he came. The next day she had the locks changed on the cabinets. Once she had some programs for unemployment started, she would see what could be done about prosecution.[5]

The reaction within the bureau to the breakup of the Section 24 group was immediate and joyful. One employee had written an account of the squad's corruption and through a friend in New York had sent it to her anonymously. Now that her position was clear, others told her in person what they knew.[6]

Her letter to the inspectors in the field announcing the squad's abolition stated without apology: "It will be necessary for each district to take over all the activities of the nature performed by these employees." More work for fewer people; yet the president of the Association of Immigration Inspectors sent a telegram of approval, and from others in the bureau and outside it she received letters of praise. One district director wrote: "I also wish . . . to congratulate you for the prompt action taken to correct certain conditions which, to my mind at least, have been detrimental to the personnel and the efficient and economical administration of the Immigration Law." The unstated reasons for her action were understood.[7]

As she declared later of the bureau's employees: "None of them were miracles of liberalism. Their hearts didn't bleed for the immigrants, but they liked things to be done right and not crooked. They were horrified at the shakedowns."

As she learned more, she came to believe that most if not all of the special force had been corrupt. Ultimately she accused even Doak of complicity: "He was not an honest man, I'm quite convinced. He died rich. I don't hold that against anybody. I'd like to die rich myself. But there was something sinister in his relationship to these people and in their relationship to the gangster world."[8]

Nevertheless she said nothing about corruption when she announced the abolition of the force at her first press conference, on March 21. She put the cause entirely on the lack of money, which the reporters and public accepted as the reason. By this time, too, her news was relatively stale, and most editors put the "clean sweep" at the Department of Labor on the back pages. Roosevelt's economy act, which slashed millions from the payments to veterans and federal employees, the regulation of the stock exchange and the legalization of 3.2 beer were all more topical and exciting stories. Undoubtedly this was the treatment she wanted and a reason for delaying her first meeting with the press until she had been in office almost three weeks. What with the power of patriotic groups in the country and the hostility, especially in bad times, toward immigrants — aliens — the less excitement stirred by the bureau's reorganization the better.

She intended, though she did not announce it, to lessen the bureau's importance in the department, chiefly by increasing the strength of the other five bureaus: Labor Statistics, Women, Children, and the Employment and Conciliation services. Though Immigration was the largest, in her view it had little to do with the country's problems. When she and Roosevelt had first discussed the possibility of her appointment, she had given him a list of policies that as Secretary of Labor she would like to pursue. Most dealt directly with unemployment: public works, minimum wages, maximum hours, unemployment insurance, old age or retirement insurance, abolition of child labor, creation of a federal employment service, federal aid to the states for direct relief and the promotion within the states of state labor laws. Immigration was peripheral.

She did not have these policies set in a grand design with position and priority established. She expected simply to take up each as soon as she could and carry it as far as she was able. She was aware from her experience with the legislature in New York that labor legislation, like oysters, could be swallowed only in certain seasons, and she was prepared to work on whatever at the moment seemed most likely to succeed.

Her pragmatism would conceal from almost everyone, perhaps even from herself, the extent to which she and her assistants eventually reorganized the department, for they not only transformed its point of view on labor problems, but also revived the quality of its daily work. The same pragmatism tended to conceal the importance of her role in some of the greatest accomplishments of the Roosevelt administration. She more than anyone else in the administration, for example, was responsible for the preparation and passage of the Social Security Act. If she had wanted, she might have become known as "the mother of social security." But after arranging for the appointment to the first Social Security Board of John Winant and Arthur Altmeyer, two men she greatly respected, she left the program to them and went back to some of her others.

Few of her ideas were new; she never claimed they were. Several had already been tried in various states and most had their origins in the progressive era of Theodore Roosevelt, the fifteen years leading up to World War I. At that time she was a young college graduate determined to make herself independent and useful to society. After the war had come years under New York's liberal governor, Alfred E. Smith, when she had a hand in putting some of the progressive ideas of her youth into practice. Though neither she nor anyone else at the time realized it, her experience was to make her uniquely qualified for her position in the cabinet. But her qualifications interested many persons less than the fact of her sex. Though almost no one approved of Green's declaration that "Labor can never become reconciled to the selection," many thought they understood what had caused it. Who was this woman who called herself Miss Perkins and yet had a teen-age daughter? How had she been able to get within sight of such a job as Secretary of Labor?

PART II

Youth, Settlement Work
and the Consumers' League

Chapter 5

>>><<<

*Birth, grandmother and the Brick House in Maine. Family life in
Worcester. Four years at Mount Holyoke.*

SHE WAS BORN in Boston on April 10, 1880. Seven years later, when
both her parents were active in the Congregational church, she was
baptized under the name given her at birth, Fannie Coralie Perkins.
Fannie, or Fanny as her family usually spelled it, was not an uncommon name in New England, but when she was about twenty-five she
began to call herself Frances, though continuing happily as Fanny
among friends and family.[1]

At the same time she also left her parents' church and still later,
apparently in genuine confusion and not from vanity, she subtracted
two years from her age. The mistake was costly, for it encouraged
some of her political enemies to whisper that she was not the person
she claimed to be, that the Boston Registrar reported no record of a
Frances Perkins born in 1882 and that she was in fact an immigrant
Russian Jewess with communist sympathies. Her mistake followed her
beyond the grave, for a memorial service and many of her obituary
notices gave the incorrect date, and some reference works still do.

Despite her birth in Boston, her tie with the city was slight, for her
parents soon moved to Worcester. Both originally came from Maine,
where for generations their families had been farmers, local businessmen or people of the sea. But with the rise of industry after the Civil
War, the larger manufacturing cities of Maine began to prosper at the
expense of the smaller towns and countryside. Since Colonial times
the Perkins family had farmed a holding at Newcastle, a small town
on the Damariscotta River about sixty miles east of Portland, and
from the clay in the river bank they had also made bricks, which they
shipped by barge to Boston. By 1875 the brick business was beginning

to fail. Fanny's father, Fred Perkins, was the second of three brothers, and after graduating in 1865 from a local academy he had gone up to Boston for a course in accounting. There prospects had seemed brighter, and he stayed on, first as a clerk in Jordan Marsh Company, and then in business for himself as a stationer, with a circulating library and periodicals for sale. But every summer on vacation he returned to the family farm at Newcastle.

In 1877, at thirty-three, he married Susie E. Bean of Bethel, Maine, who was five years younger than he. In 1882, two years after Fanny was born, he moved the family to Worcester and with a single assistant, George S. Butler, started a retail and wholesale stationery business. His only other child, Ethel, was born in Worcester in December 1884. The family, though never rich, soon was living comfortably. By 1900, when Perkins and Butler formed a partnership, their business was well known throughout western Massachusetts.

Despite his success in Worcester, Fred Perkins nurtured the family ties with Maine. His children heard constant talk of the Natives of Maine Association, of which he was a leader, and most of every summer they spent with their grandmother at Newcastle. Their father and mother would come down for vacation, and their uncle, Fred Perkins's younger brother, Augustus, a lawyer in Boston, also would return with his daughter Nan. Over the summers Fanny and this cousin, who in time married Jack Johnston, formed a friendship that lasted their lives.[2]

Though Fanny had been named after her mother's elder sister and though the Bean side of the family was more numerous than the Perkins, the latter, with its place at Newcastle, dominated the family life. Her father's elder brother, Charles, who never married and was perhaps, as they say in Maine, a "little touched in the head," managed the farm; but its spiritual center was her grandmother, Cynthia Otis Perkins, by then a widow in her seventies. She was small and wiry, with white hair, spectacles, extraordinary blue eyes and a fund of pithy sayings. Years later Fanny described her to a friend as "an extremely wise woman — worldly-wise as well as spiritually wise" and concluded, "I am extraordinarily the product of my grandmother . . . Scarcely a week goes by that I don't find myself saying, 'As my grandmother used to say,' and then repeating something that apparently has been a guiding principle all of my life." The influence, however, was unconscious on both sides. Among the three grandchildren, all girls, Fanny was not favored in any way.[3]

By the time she began to visit the farm in summers "the Brick

House" in which her grandmother and uncle lived was already fifty years old and filled with memories. Her great-grandmother, Thankful Otis, who had been born before the Revolution and talked with veterans of the French and Indian wars, had spent her last years in it, and stories of prerevolutionary days came down to the three grandchildren as vivid family history.[4]

The house was small, its only distinction that it was made of brick. The door and windows facing the road were balanced, but to the rear the symmetry collapsed into Maine farm architecture: a short kitchen wing pushed out and connected with a wooden carriage house and barn, both painted red. Beyond, standing separately, were the privy, the ice house and chicken coop. On the road to the front were maples; beside the house, clumps of lilacs and barberries; and on all sides in the distance, a forest of oaks and pines waiting to recapture the cleared fields.

Behind the house a lane descended for half a mile through woods and a great meadow to the edge of the Damariscotta, which at Newcastle is as much an inlet of the sea as a freshwater river. In summer the family kept a canoe, a rowboat and a sailboat beached on the shore. In the river were fish and clams, and for those who could take the cold water there was swimming.

Up-river and down were friends. Some, whose fathers worked in Damariscotta or Bath, lived there the year round; others, like the Perkins grandchildren, came only for the summer. The people of the area were relatively homogeneous. Few were very rich, few were very poor, and the general level of education was high. Doubtless there were tensions in the community, but they did not snap into violence for a child to see as they sometimes did in the big cities. One of Fanny's earliest unhappy memories was of a street fight in Boston.

She was six or seven and on a visit to her uncle's family in Boston. She and her nurse had been sent downtown to buy a pair of shoes. Suddenly the street filled with noise, and some large boys shouting, "Paddys! Paddys!" began to throw rocks and debris at a group of Irish boys, who retaliated in kind with cries of "Yankees!" She could remember her sense of alarm as the nurse hurried her into a recessed doorway and stood with skirts spread to protect her from the street.[5]

In Worcester, Fred Perkins moved his family every year or two as his fortunes rose. They lived first in a boardinghouse and then in various private houses, all close to the Plymouth Congregational Church. With the help of a maid and a cook, who were generally Irish immigrants, Mrs. Perkins ran an efficient, hospitable household — quiet, decorous, filled with family. Sometimes in the winter Uncle Charles would come down from the farm for five or six weeks, bringing his miniature violin to play for the children. Whenever an aunt or cousin fell sick, Mrs. Perkins would take in her children. Through the church Fanny's parents also befriended one of the poorer families in the neighborhood. Her father sometimes helped with their rent, and her mother was always hustling to find them some clothing, a barrel of flour or part-time jobs for the children.

Mrs. Perkins was a large, heavy woman, rather emotional and often unconventional. Persons of all ages found her good fun. She was skillful with her hands, sewed well, sketched and modeled in clay. When thieves one time broke into the house in Maine, most of what they stole was her hand-painted china. Yet with this artistic flair she combined a vigorous, practical temperament. One cousin described her as "not bashful about expressing her ideas" and, with underlinings, as having "a square face with a *good square jaw.*"

Mr. Perkins was of slighter build and more elegant appearance. At an early age his hair had turned white, and the color suited him, for he had his mother's startling blue eyes. His hands were remarkably beautiful and unusually small, attributes inherited by Fanny, and he wore a full beard, always neatly trimmed. He was more reserved than his wife, and most persons, particularly the young, found him harder to know.

He was bookish and enjoyed discussing problems of law and government. As a legacy from his days at school he still read Greek poetry in the original. Sometimes with two friends, one a Catholic priest, he would read Greek plays aloud over coffee. Each would take a role, and all would declaim the choruses together. When Fanny was seven or eight, going to a small private school, he began to teach her Greek grammar. Within the shadings of affection in a happy family it was evident that Fanny, as she matured, was becoming more compatible with her father than with her mother or sister.[6]

Worcester in 1895 had three public high schools, of which Worcester Classical High prepared students for college. Though there were relatively few girls in the school, Fanny's father enrolled her. She was never consulted about whether she would go to college; it was always assumed.[7]

The most violent events in the family's life were her sister's tantrums. Ethel's personality, like her mother's, was vigorous and transparently honest. But when she was crossed, she was likely to erupt in a fit, kicking chairs, banging tables and breaking dishes.

Ethel struggled to match what was tirelessly presented to her as good behavior, but she often failed. Once when Uncle Charles was paying a long visit, Ethel exploded during breakfast. As she beat the table, swept knives and forks to the floor and overturned her chair, her mother pleaded, "Darling, you mustn't. It's terrible. We have company — Uncle Charles!"

Ethel, with another blow at the table, cried: "I don't care! He's been here two months. He isn't company anymore."

Fanny watched her sister learn to control her temper in time, and she admired her for it. Years later in Washington when she saw grown men, with red faces, pound the table, she was unimpressed. If a girl could learn to control her temper, why not a man?[8]

Her own temperament was quite different; she was a natural actress and had little trouble masking her feelings. Bored by a conversation, she could extract some enjoyment from the art of feigning interest. If the situation proved more than she could handle, she did not explode like Ethel but slipped away to read a book.

A friend of her parents described her at this time as "pretty and articulate," but to one of her own generation she was "plump and plain." Friends of all ages, however, agreed that she was articulate. She liked to talk and developed a habit of arguing positions she did not hold, just to shock or anger the other person. Her father and uncles were fervent Republicans, and so were the parents of her friends. Sometimes at school for amusement, or perhaps out of irritation at the parroting of parental ideas, she would insist, "I'm a Democrat." When she tried it at home her father laughed and looked patient.

Despite her ease with words, she was shy and somewhat solitary. In later years she would demonstrate an extraordinary gift for friendship, but with the exception of her cousin Nan and a schoolmate, William Piper, all her lasting friendships developed after her twentieth year. By then she was in South Hadley, Massachusetts, at Mount Holyoke, a college for women.[9]

In Worcester Classical High School Fanny had been only a fair student, not truly involved in her work. She had taken the traditional humanities course based on Latin and Greek and, backed at home by her father's interest, had found it easy to make a little learning pass for more. But in her freshman Latin course at Mount Holyoke she came up against a teacher, Esther Van Dieman, who at once recognized a student with a good mind sliding by on bluff and a glib tongue.

Suddenly it was not enough to rattle off an approximate translation of the Latin sentence: it had to be exact. Not only for the grammar — why the verb was in the subjunctive rather than the indicative; but also for style — why the author had used one construction rather than another and how that choice was to be reflected in an English sentence. It was hard work, and at least once Fanny was pressed until she burst into tears. Yet looking back she acknowledged that Miss Van Dieman had taught her something about work and a person's handling of it: "For the first time I became conscious of character."

She had a similar experience in the sophomore chemistry course given by Nellie Esther Goldthwaite. She had taken very little science at Worcester Classical High School and, perhaps because of her extensive reading, vaguely hoped to be a writer or an actress. History and literature were what she felt drawn to, and she might not have taken chemistry at all if it had not been required. Once in it, she floundered badly. The terminology and methods bewildered her. She wondered if she would be able to pass the course.

Dr. Goldthwaite "hounded" her, as Fanny said later, until her pride was at stake, and she became determined to prove she could do it. In the end she not only passed but, with Dr. Goldthwaite as her faculty adviser, elected chemistry as her major subject with supporting work in physics and biology. This decision, which she never regretted, was possibly the first twinkle of her own personality as opposed to her childlike reflection of her parents' interests.

Her years at Mount Holyoke, from 1898 to 1902, were extremely happy. The situation of the college in South Hadley was beautiful, and she responded to it. Most of the buildings, built of brick or stone in Gothic or Romanesque style, were set on the east side of College Street in two large quadrangles. The land sloped gently to a stream with a pond and an old stone mill. Dams above and below had formed upper and lower lakes whose further shores were embedded in woods.

The west side of College Street was lined with white clapboard houses of which the most distinctive, standing clear of trees, was the college observatory, thimble-shaped and with a domed roof opening to the stars. At the village green the street divided: to the left, "the Smith ferry road," leading down to Hadley and the Connecticut River; to the right, slowly rising to cross over "the Notch," the road to Amherst. The area's industry was on the river five miles to the south in the town of Holyoke. At South Hadley the air was clear, the birds plentiful and the snow clean all winter.

At the turn of the century the college was relatively isolated. Clothes then were bulky, travel with trunks difficult, and girls once settled at the college seldom left until the end of term. In their free time they made their own fun, and the sense of community was strong.

Fanny Perkins, entering with a class of 150, found her way slowly. Basketball, played in bloomers, was the great excitement, and girls who scored the winning baskets were much admired. Fanny, though an outdoor girl in Maine, was not much of an indoor athlete.

When she entered, the college had five Greek letter societies, each of which elected six or seven freshmen during the year. Neither she nor any of the girls who were to be her closest friends were elected. The fact was not important. The societies were small and, without houses of their own, not visibly exclusive.

Her marks, though they improved in her last year, were poor; but she took the hardest courses and passed them, and this gave her confidence. With it gradually came social leadership. In her third year she was elected vice-president of the class and became absorbed in its activities. She also cut her hair, transforming herself from a round-faced girl with a brown pigtail into a young woman with her hair in a bun. In her final year she was elected class president. In order to have more time for class activities and "walks," she enrolled in a course reputed to be "comparatively restful." Dr. Goldthwaite, however, would have none of it. She expressed pained surprise, then indignation at the waste of time and talent and, finally, downright anger. In the end a chastened Fanny took a course in advanced physics.

She had the energy to do it all and more. Despite the demands of that "wretched physics laboratory," her social life was full; sometimes too full for her roommate, Amy Peters of Portland. Amy, as chairman of Mead House, was responsible for enforcing the student rules, one of which was that socializing should end at 9:40 P.M. with lights out at 10:00. Frequently Fanny, ignoring Amy's protests and her own responsibilities as class president, invited a classmate, Alice Cook, to stay after "lights out" and talk. On such nights Amy would leave to sleep in Alice Cook's bed, protesting the false position in which she had been put. The friendship survived because Fanny was not usually thoughtless and because Amy, like Fanny's other close friends, saw that she had a streak of bravado that could not always be denied. From time to time she had to kick over the traces and prove that she was superior to constraining rules. Not all her professors or classmates found this streak endearing. Yet by her senior year she was a genuinely popular leader. Her classmates in their Class Book proclaimed her "the girl who has done the most for her class" and elected her their permanent class president.[10]

Fifteen years later a sizable number questioned their judgment. Many were shocked by her "modern notions," and at reunions some openly disapproved of her retaining her maiden name after marriage and the birth of a child. On occasion she felt forced to justify her actions. As time passed, and as many of the ideas she supported became the law of the land, the friction disappeared. But that was less important to her and to her classmates than the fact that their friendships had survived the strain. Some friends were closer than others, but within the class there was a general affection that supported all and excluded none.[11]

"Perk," as she was known, felt the bond deeply, perhaps because she had sensed the loss implicit in exclusion. After the fiftieth reunion, held at the college in the spring of 1952, she wrote in a report of it to her classmates that the class had a "living personality," which was more than loyalty to a place or an experience, or to a group accidentally brought together for four years. She recalled that during the three-day reunion:

> I didn't hear one biting remark, I didn't see one unkind look or excluding act, I didn't hear one complaint or one reference to trouble or disappointment or disillusionment, although every one of us has known these human experiences. Quite a feat, I think, for sixty women, no longer young, with widely varied habits, living together dormitory style, with unaccustomed rules, "early rising" and late noise, semi-public toilet arrangements, a triumph of adaptability and good will. I was proud of *us*. I think that this was a demonstration of the exercise of Christian love.[12]

The religious cast to her thinking came naturally to her and her classmates, for Mount Holyoke, started in 1837 as a nondenominational female seminary, had always had a strong religious emphasis. Its founder and first principal, Mary Lyon, had been determined that women should have available to them the same kind of higher education that Harvard and Yale offered men. Education, however, implied a responsibility, and she insisted that the purpose of the college was "to cultivate the missionary spirit among its pupils: that they should live for God and do something."

It was a robust form of Christianity — "Do what nobody else wants to do; go where nobody else wants to go" — and did not appeal to everyone. Emily Dickinson, who enrolled in 1847 with eager anticipation, soon inquired of her brother: "Do you know of any nation about to besiege South Hadley? If so, do inform me of it, for I would be glad of a chance to escape, if we are to be stormed. I suppose Miss Lyon would furnish us all with daggers and order us to fight for our lives." Though Dickinson did well in her work, she found much in the college life and rules ridiculous and the constant stress on sin and duty intolerable. At the end of the year she withdrew.

Most of the girls, however, caught from Mary Lyon and her successors a strong sense of mission. By the thousands they went out to teach, to found schools, to serve as missionaries and to marry schoolteachers and missionaries.[13]

In 1902 the tradition was still strong. Every Saturday night each class would hold a prayer meeting, and as graduation approached these became more solemn, filled with a sense of parting. For the final meeting of her class Perkins, as president, was the speaker. Her text was St. Paul's passage on the immortality of the soul, 1 Cor. 15:58, which includes "O death where is thy sting?" and ends with the verse:

> Therefore my beloved brethren, be ye stedfast, unmoveable, always abounding in the work of the Lord, forasmuch as ye know that your labour is not in vain in the Lord.

The class had chosen "Be ye stedfast" as its motto, a more serious choice than the class color, crimson, or flower, Jacqueminot Rose, which determined that on special occasions, like the birth of a child, one classmate would send another red roses. The motto, constantly quoted at reunions and in class letters published in the years between, was a shorthand statement of what the class felt it had learned at Mount Holyoke: in Mary Lyon's words, "Education was to fit one to do good." If the class was "a living personality," then emblazoned on its standard to aid the faltering, encourage the despondent and remind the strong of their duty was "Be ye stedfast."[14]

Unlike Emily Dickinson, Fanny Perkins found the religious tone of Mount Holyoke easy to accept. It corresponded not only to a strain in her own nature, but also to the traditions of her home. Once in a conversation with Agnes Leach, a friend with a Philadelphia, Quaker background, she described trying on a new party dress that she had very much wanted and that her parents had bought for her. She had gone downstairs to show it off and her father had remarked that, although it did not make her look pretty, it was ladylike. "But then," she commented to Leach, "even if I had ever succeeded in making myself look pretty — which, mind you, I'm not saying I ever succeeded in doing — my father would never have told me. That would have been a sin."

To Leach, whose family was more openly affectionate and whose background perhaps allowed a little more easy living and frivolity, the incident seemed a touch hard. Yet she recognized that few grown children had greater affection for their parents than Perkins, or more respect. Evidently, as a child, the pattern of her parents' life and thinking had not been galling.[15]

As she went through Mount Holyoke, however, she came into contact with ideas that, taken home, her parents must have found upsetting or incomprehensible. Amy Peter's mother, for example, on being presented with the theory of evolution taught in Mount Holyoke's zoology course, cut off discussion by murmuring, "It does not seem according to Scripture." Almost certainly the response of Fanny's parents would have been the same.[16]

Even if they had been able to entertain the theory, in their daily lives they would not have accepted its implications about man and his position in the universe. Their daughter Fanny, however, almost forty years younger than they and majoring in science, pursued the implications. Often she reached conclusions that struck her parents as extraordinary, or even wrong, and one about which they disagreed was the idea that poverty might have little connection with moral worth.

The idea was beginning to be much debated, particularly in England, but Fanny discovered it at Mount Holyoke in a course in American history. The professor, Annah May Soule, had what was then the novel idea of taking her students into the factories of Holyoke and asking them to make a survey of working conditions. Years later this form of study was called social or economic history. But to most men of Mr. Perkins's generation it was not history at all. History was wars, men or great ideas. American history was the Declaration of Independence, the Bill of Rights, Abolition, the Civil War: What had any of these to do with a canning factory?

In Professor Soule's course Fanny had an opportunity to use her scientific training to test and build conclusions in a humanistic field. She discovered that one serious accident — say, the loss of a man's hand — could drive a steady, sober working family into penury. Factory work, she learned, was so irregular that savings were continually exhausted. Avoiding poverty therefore was not a question simply of liquor or laziness but also of safety devices on machines and of regularity of employment.

These ideas were difficult for her parents' generation to absorb. In 1900 two thirds of all Americans still lived on farms. Even of those in the cities many knew little or nothing about factories. They were still close enough to their agricultural backgrounds to know that hard work on a farm would produce enough food for a family and much of its clothing. Hard work was the clue; they were not aware of the enormous differences in conditions between farm and factory.

Similarly, many of the urban problems emerging in the United States were hard for the older generation to grasp. One summer during college Fanny had read Jacob Riis's study of the tenements in New York City, *How the Other Half Lives.* Her young, fresh imagination was seared by his statistics, descriptions and photographs. So long as she lived, the impact of that first reading remained.

To most of her father's generation the book was less vivid. Their imaginations were already filled with images of other great events: the Civil War, the linking of East and West, the technological changes following the discovery of oil. Parents living in Worcester and vacationing in Maine, however well intentioned, were unlikely to grasp the problems of life in New York, Chicago or St. Louis, or even to think much about them — unless they had an articulate daughter who talked of little else. And their response then was more likely to be puzzled or irritated than understanding.[17]

Fifteen-year-old Vira Peters, at the college with her parents to see Amy graduate — such a happy, exciting day — was astonished to hear Mrs. Perkins remark to Mrs. Peters, in a voice tinged with dismay, "I don't recognize my daughter Fanny anymore. I can't understand it. She's a stranger to me."[18]

Chapter 6

-»>«<-

Florence Kelley speaks at Mount Holyoke. Perkins teaches for five years. She changes her name and religion. Settlement work.

HER PARENTS hoped Fanny on graduation would return to Worcester and, after a round of visiting friends in the summer, either teach school or work for the church and, sooner or later, marry. This was the pattern of life most of her classmates began to follow.[1] She had a different idea.

During her senior year at college a group of Professor Soule's students had organized a Mount Holyoke chapter of the National Consumers' League, which, through the improvement of state laws and education of the public, was striving to abolish child labor and tenement sweatshops. The term sweatshop then was peculiar to the clothing industry; manufacturers often sent out sewing to be done in an employee's home or in a subcontractor's loft or basement. The wages were low, the hours long and the conditions of work frightful: a small, dark, dirty room crowded with women and children, all trying desperately to earn enough to survive.

Fanny was not a leader in the college chapter of the league, but she went to its meetings and on February 20, 1902, heard a talk by Mrs. Florence Kelley, the national secretary. Years later she wrote a friend that Kelley's speech "first opened my mind to the necessity for and the possibility of the work which became my vocation."[2]

At forty-three, Kelley was beginning a career that would help to shape the country's social history. She had served four years as Chief Inspector of Factories for Governor Altgeld of Illinois, had worked for two with Jane Addams at Hull House in Chicago and in 1899 had gone to New York to enlarge the league, which had started locally, into a national movement. She was a large woman, her head crowned with heavy braids of dark hair, her face quick to reflect her emotions.

About her appearance she was careless — "always in black, no stays" — but about social justice she was a "raging furnace," an "impatient crusader." Her great gift as a speaker was her ability to infuse the facts of industrial conditions with the humanity they represented. As she described the poorhouse boys employed by the Illinois Glass Company, an audience would begin to see the small, dark silhouettes running back and forth before the red-hot ovens. And after she told how each boy crouched at a glassblower's foot, ready at a nudge or kick to fetch and carry, even the least imaginative in the audience would stir uneasily to hear that the boys were called "dogs."

Aside from her cause, in herself she was an exciting, controversial person. Kelley was her own name; she had divorced her husband, an immigrant doctor, for nonsupport and alone had raised their three children. Her father for almost thirty years had been a congressman from Philadelphia, and after she had graduated from Cornell and been refused because of her sex by the law school of the University of Pennsylvania, he had taken her on a walking tour through the English industrial counties. What she had seen of human exploitation and misery had fixed her life's work. She went on for graduate study to the University of Zurich and while there translated from the German a small book by Engels, *Die Lage der Arbeiten Klassen in England* (*The Condition of the Working Classes in England in 1844*). She also married a socialist, Dr. Lazare Wishniewski, and was converted to socialism. In such a life there was plenty to twist into something sinister or disreputable — she once was described in Congress as "the only communist leader trained by Engels"— and plenty to admire and defend.[3]

Kelley's dynamic personality, her practical experience, her demand for drastic improvements and the "sense of crusade" surrounding her all appealed to Fanny. In the tradition of Mount Holyoke, she determined to put her education to social use; like Kelley, she would devote herself to urban and industrial problems. Over her father's protests she went to New York immediately after graduation to apply for a job with the New York Charity Organization Society. This group, older and larger than the Consumers' League, acted as a coordinating agency. It did not give alms or direct relief but referred the person in need to the proper charity. It also conducted surveys and research programs of its own. Like the league, its larger purpose was to determine and remove the causes of poverty. But unlike the league, which concentrated on manufacturers, retailers and state legislators, it worked more directly with the individual poor.

From Professor Soule Fanny had learned the name of the society's

director, Edward T. Devine, and on arriving at the Charities Building
in New York, at Twenty-second Street and Fourth Avenue, she asked
for him. As she had no appointment, his secretary for a time tried to
deflect her to someone else. But she was determined, and Devine
perhaps was amused by his secretary's description of the young, wide-
eyed New England girl who was so insistent. Certainly he was kind to
her.

Once in his office she came right to the point. She wanted a job, she
said, in the Charity Organization Society.

He asked her what she would like to do.

"You have visitors," she explained, "who go out to see families
applying for help. They make investigations, distribute food and help
the families unravel their problems."

Devine smiled thoughtfully. "Suppose you were sent out to a family
and found the dishes in the sink, no food in the house, the children
sick with sore throats, the mother disheveled, with a black eye and
bruises, and the father drunk on the bed. What would you do?"

"I'd send for the police at once," she replied, "and have the man
arrested."

The smile on Devine's face broadened. "That isn't exactly what *we*
would recommend." Their aim, he explained, was to get the father
back to work, in a position to discharge his responsibilities, not into
jail. Then he added gently that he had no place for anyone so young;
that she needed more experience of life before she could have sound
judgment on how to help the unemployed and poor.

A girl more sophisticated than she, or less, might have left. But she
was modest enough to accept his judgment without rancor, and yet
eager enough for instruction to be oblivious of how much she was
imposing on his time. How, she asked, should she prepare for such
work?

He questioned her on her education and then suggested that she
find a job teaching. "There's always opportunity. Just the passing of
years, what you observe and read, will give you experience. You
obviously," he pointed out, "have never even read in this field."
When she left, she had in her bag a list of books he had recommended
and under her arm several issues of *Charities,* the society's bulletin.[4]

Optimistic by nature, Fanny did not see the trip to New York as a
defeat. She had met and talked with a leader in the field, and she
started at once to follow his advice. She applied to the New York City
school system for a job but was told that the next trial examination

would not be given until midwinter. She went on a round of visits to classmates, asking always about teaching positions, but none was open. Finally she went to her grandmother's farm at Newcastle and invited her roommate, Amy, for a visit. Though young ladies then were supposed to protect their complexions from the sun, Amy returned to Portland "brown as a berry," explaining to her family that she and Fanny had spent all their time on the Damariscotta in a rowboat.[5]

By early September nothing had turned up for Fanny, and she went back to Worcester to keep house for her father while her mother and sister stayed on at Newcastle. Three days later, when Mr. Perkins was on a business trip, she was asked by Bacon Academy in Colchester, Connecticut, to substitute for a teacher who was ill. Abandoning her father, she went to Colchester for two and a half weeks. With her earnings she returned to Mount Holyoke for a visit. She was lonely, as she confessed in her contribution to the first class letter, published that winter, and missed the college life.

Bacon Academy soon called again, and this time she stayed until Thanksgiving. Thereafter there were no more sudden departures from home, and for the spring term she accepted a job teaching at Leicester Academy in Worcester, meanwhile settling into the life of good works that her parents expected of her. She taught a class in the church Sunday school and another in sewing at the Union Gospel Mission, a local settlement house. Using the mission's facilities, she organized a club for about twenty-five teen-age girls working in stores and a candy factory. One night a week was devoted to exercises and games in the gymnasium, and the other to something educational. But as she reported in the Class Letter: "The girls are very much afraid of being improved. They want fun. They like to sing, and so I keep them at that a good deal. We are going to give an entertainment about New Year's time to get some money to buy a basket-ball, so I'm going to keep them rehearsing for that. The whole thing," she concluded, "is just as entertaining as it can be."

Then a girl, Mary Hogan, had her hand cut off in a candy dipper. Fanny visited her in her home, arranged for a doctor (the factory had simply sent her home) and tried to collect some money for her from the employer. But she discovered the girl had no legal right to an award. In the end a clergyman intervened and persuaded the manufacturer to give her $100.

Meanwhile word of Fanny's "readiness to work" and "enthusiasm," which had impressed the administration of Bacon Academy, was circulating in the academic world, and for the following year Monson

Academy in Monson, Massachusetts, offered her a job teaching general science and history.[6] It meant living away from home, but she accepted, apparently with her parents' approval. They would have felt that until she married she ought to do something; idleness was sin.

Her year at home had not been unhappy, but there were signs that she was restless, uncertain of what she was doing and why. Either before or during her year at Monson Academy, she told her parents she was considering conversion to Catholicism. Almost nothing could have upset them more. To a Congregational family in New England at the turn of the century it was just conceivable that in Baltimore or New Orleans an educated person might be Catholic; in New England, with only the rarest exceptions, it was not. Her parents must have gasped at the idea. Her friends took it less seriously, putting it down to her quick tongue and occasional desire to shock people.

This trait, that same year, almost lost her a friend. She was visiting Amy Peters in Portland, and another Portland classmate, Janet Stevenson, had joined them for the evening. Janet was perhaps the least sophisticated of the three and also the most devout. She was teaching Sunday school for the Congregational church and working in its program for young people, Christian Endeavor, which had been founded in Portland and was spreading through a great interdenominational organization all over the world.

Fanny began by questioning the value of the church and its program but continued to a point where questioning turned mockery. After a time Janet stood up: "Perk, you are making fun of things for which I care very deeply, and I can't take it." Saying good night, she went home, and what had been a close friendship was never so close again.

In later years Fanny was more careful of the damage a quick tongue can do. All her life she enjoyed making and sustaining what she called "sallies of wit," but she had learned there were many persons in the world who carried away from such encounters real injuries, and she restricted her "sallies" to those who enjoyed them.[7]

After a year at Monson Academy she took a post at Ferry Hall in Lake Forest, Illinois. Whether she sought the school, so far from home, is not clear, but she had no hesitation in going. Founded in 1869 by a Presbyterian minister, Ferry Hall was possibly the largest and most famous girls' school west of the Appalachians. She was to teach physics and biology and to manage a dormitory. Presumably she got the job through Mount Holyoke, which served as a sort of clearinghouse for teachers and had close ties with Ferry Hall.

She stayed three years, did her work well, was popular with the students and administration, but left, in June 1907, because she wanted to do something else even more. Except for an occasional class, until she became a college lecturer fifty years later, Ferry Hall was the end of her teaching career. While there, what interest she had in it was overwhelmed by two preoccupations outside the school: the church and the settlement house.

Lake Forest was predominantly a Presbyterian community, and as the chief difference in the Presbyterian and Congregational churches relates to organization rather than doctrine, she might have been expected to join the Presbyterian congregation. Instead she joined the Episcopalian — "half-way to the Catholics," she remarked later.

The Episcopal church in Lake Forest, when she arrived in the autumn of 1904, was at an exciting moment in its history. The cornerstone of its first building, the Church of the Holy Spirit, had been laid in 1902, and although services had been held in it while it was under construction, the church was not consecrated until June 11, 1905. At that service, which doubtless was particularly moving and joyful, the rector presented several members of his congregation to the bishop for confirmation, and among them was Fanny Perkins — except that at her request she was confirmed and enrolled in the church as Frances C. Perkins.[8]

At Ferry Hall she continued to be Fanny, but after the spring of 1905 she presented herself to new friends or projects as Frances. Soon she dropped the middle initial, and in December 1905 she signed the register of Chicago Commons, a settlement house, simply as Frances Perkins.

It seems unlikely that a woman of twenty-five would change her name and religion without a sense of making a fresh start. With Frances Perkins, however, there was no sharp break with the past. In the register at Chicago Commons, though the information was not requested, she added, "Home address, 50 Queen Street, Worcester, Mass.," her parents' home.[9] Her affection for her family, for Maine, for Mount Holyoke and her classmates continued just as strong. Her conversion and change of name apparently were orderly steps in self-identification, which did not require a rupture with the past.

She was drawn to the Episcopal church chiefly by its ritual and by the sense of discipline and authority implicit in ritual. She would remark often in the future that American political life sorely needed more ritual, that transfers of power would be accomplished more surely and with less bitterness if each party knew in advance where to stand, what words to say and which gestures to make.

Moreover she saw ritual not in black and white but in color. She liked political and even personal events to be well staged, in every theatrical sense, for thus the public or family was best induced to share the occasion. She herself had a strong sense of event and never failed to write a friend or even an acquaintance on the birth of a child, a marriage or a death in the family. As a friend observed, she had a rare gift for noting "the milestones in life." Far more than the Congregational or Presbyterian, the Episcopal church, with its liturgy and vestments, especially if high-church (to which she was increasingly drawn), points up the milestones of its services and the changing seasons of the church year.

Evidently there was no thought of social advantage in her conversion. The Episcopal church was not strong in Maine and no more socially acceptable in Massachusetts than the Congregational and Unitarian churches. As for Lake Forest, the swells were Presbyterians; the local story is that the Presbyterians helped to build the Episcopal church in order to provide their Church of England butlers with a place to worship.

Possibly there was a touch of filial rebellion in her action. In Portland her friends said that Perk must do things her own way, not as her parents or others do them. Her conversion, however, was for life. After a time her interest in religion waned; still later it revived, stronger than before; but she always remained within the Episcopal church.[10]

Her other interest during her years at Ferry Hall was the work of the settlement houses in Chicago. Two of the country's oldest and most famous were there: Hull House, founded in 1889 by Ellen Gates Starr and Jane Addams, and Chicago Commons, founded in 1894 by the Reverend Graham Taylor. The settlement house movement, which was spreading rapidly in the United States, was originally inspired by an English model, Toynbee Hall in London. The idea was that men and women who had recently graduated from the universities would make a "settlement" in a slum, share the problems of the poor and work with them to reform neighborhood conditions.

The English movement was precipitated by the poverty the industrial revolution had spawned in all the larger cities. Its impulse was both artistic and religious. John Ruskin, critic and professor of fine arts at Oxford, argued that beauty and a meaningful life could be brought back to the cities only by such programs as a social security system and public works projects and by minimum wage laws and improved housing. Church of England clergymen, who often worked directly with the poor, were even more aware of the horrors of the London slums. Also, they wanted to do something about the spiritual poverty not only of the poor but of the rich, and they urged the children of the rich — university students — to make a meaningful life out of service to the poor.

The emphasis of Toynbee Hall, founded in 1884 by Oxford University students, was on education, culture and projects of social reform, like parks, playgrounds, better housing, sanitation. Through these means the gulf that industrialism had widened between rich and poor was to be narrowed, and the mutual suspicion and ignorance of each class lessened. One of the clerical founders described it as a program of "practicable socialism."

In the United States there were 6 settlement houses by 1891, more than 100 by 1900 and more than 200 by 1905. By 1910 the number would exceed 400. Though most of them were the direct result of what their founders saw or read of Toynbee Hall, others sprang up independently. The conditions of work and living created by the industrial revolution in many cities were sufficiently shocking to arouse an identical response in people living far apart. The American settlements, however, developed differently from the English. Their emphasis shifted from education and culture toward social reform, and their leaders often entered politics to demand that sanitation laws be enforced, new parks opened and new laws passed.

A reason for the difference was that the American settlements were usually in immigrant neighborhoods, where a language barrier complicated efforts to spread education and culture. Another was the close connection between religion and culture: the American settlements, which were predominantly Protestant with strong Jewish backing, had to avoid any appearance of religious proselytizing. It was hard enough to make headway against the local politician without also taking on the local rabbi or priest.[11]

The few Catholic settlements were essentially "missions"; they concentrated almost entirely on saving the individual's soul and left his surroundings and working conditions to the care of others. They tended to remain small and, aside from their spiritual value, were of little significance.

Few Americans at first knew what to make of this movement. The older generation, exemplified by Fanny's parents, thought of charity in terms of giving money or food to the poor. Settlement workers tended to scoff at that; they said that industrialism had created whole armies of the poor and that the traditional methods of aiding them, through church and county poorhouse, were inadequate. They also argued that aiding the people of a city ward to obtain facilities, such as sanitation, to which they were entitled by law was not charity but the enforcement of rights. And they talked much about the superiority of fraternal as opposed to paternal aid.

There was a difference between the kinds of aid but less perhaps than the settlement workers liked to think. Both the settlement house and the church's poor fund depended on gifts, and as far as the donor was concerned both were charities. Nevertheless the difference was important in that it determined the kind of activity the traditional charity or the new settlement house was likely to undertake. The charity tended to work with individuals who were unemployed and destitute; the settlement with groups of the working class, tenants or clothing workers, who were just above the poverty line.

Chicago Commons, to which Frances Perkins first turned, was housed in a five-story building at the corner of Morgan Street and Grand Avenue in Chicago's seventeenth ward. Its neighborhood included large blocs of Polish, Irish, German and Scandinavian immigrants. Its founder and leader, Graham Taylor, was a Dutch Reform and Congregational clergyman, a professor at the Chicago Theological Seminary, an adroit city politician and the publisher of *The Commons*, which from 1896 until 1905 was the outstanding magazine of the settlement movement. Its merger in November 1905 with *Charities*, the New York Charity Organization Society's bulletin, and the new journal's absorption the following year of *Jewish Charity*, the journal of the United Hebrew Charities of New York, symbolized the growing acceptance of settlement work as a worthy ally by the older, established charity organizations.

Undoubtedly Perkins had been reading *The Commons*, and perhaps its lively articles on every sort of neighborhood and industrial problem attracted her to the settlement. Possibly during her first year at Ferry Hall she went there for an occasional lecture or meeting. In any event in December 1905 for her Christmas vacation she joined its staff in a capacity known as "temporary resident."

Since part of the settlement idea was to expose people who were well educated and endowed to conditions in a poor neighborhood, most settlement houses kept a few small rooms for visitors. Sometimes a lecturer or settlement worker from out of town would stay overnight, but more often a "temporary resident" would take a room for several weeks or months. In return for a small fee to cover bed and board he or she would have the opportunity to work on the tasks at hand. These might include helping the nurse with a sick family, working in a political campaign, joining a picket line, compiling statistics on infant mortality, proofreading the magazine, browbeating employers into paying wages unfairly withheld or raising money to keep the settlement going. Often in the evenings there was a lecture or a meeting to attend, but if not, the staff and visitors would linger over dinner, served boardinghouse style. The head resident would preside and everyone would discuss the day's events. The talk at these sessions was said to be the best in town.

The whirlwind of new experiences left Perkins alternately dazed and belligerent. In Chicago about forty-five thousand persons worked in the clothing industry, three quarters of them immigrants. Half were women and girls, most of whom received $2.50 to $3.00 a week when a living wage was estimated at $8.00.[12] She was stunned by the number of hours they worked, the wages and conditions and their terror of losing a job, however bad. Among the unemployed, the sickness, despair, degradation and deaths were worse than anything she had imagined.

One Sunday afternoon, after she and Dr. Taylor's son, Graham R. Taylor, had been hosts for a neighborhood party, she burst out: "What *is* the trouble? How *can* we cure this? Is it to go on forever, these people being so poor that we have to give out free milk, we have to have free nursing services, the babies die, there's nothing to do on a Sunday afternoon but get drunk? What *can* be done? What *should* be done?"

They were standing by the elevator shaft in the entrance hall of the Commons. Around the open cage the heavy staircase curled to the upper floors. The hallway was busy as people gathered in the "neighborhood parlor," went into the settlement office or hurried up the stairs.

For young Graham Taylor, who was just her age, the "only answer" was the organization of trade unions. "If every working man and woman would join a union," he insisted, "then their wages would be sufficient to support them and the families would be able to look after themselves. There would be no need for the charity societies and settlements."

She was less sure. In Worcester and Maine there were few trade unions, and those existing were often held in ill repute. He tried to convince her. Since graduating from Harvard in 1903 he had been helping to edit *The Commons,* and he had seen more of trade unions than she. The carpenters, plumbers and bricklayers, he pointed out, were organized, got good pay and were no bother to anyone. The worst abuses were in the unorganized industries, like clothing. Wasn't it true? Hadn't she seen it for herself?

For more than an hour they talked and argued, as people stepped around them, in and out of the elevator, up and down the stairs. Forty years later he was still clear in her memory: slim, fair-haired, leaning against the iron grill and so intense about the need for trade unions.[13]

Soon after returning to Ferry Hall she wrote a letter to her classmates — signed Frances Perkins — that was published that spring in their Second Class Letter. "I have been spending my recent Christmas vacation at Chicago Commons — the settlement of which Dr. Graham Taylor is head resident. I never got so many ideas in my life as I did in those three weeks. I'm more interested than ever in settlement work; and I do hope to be able to do it for at least a year very soon."[14]

Chapter 7

-»>»«««-

More settlement work. Saving girls in Philadelphia. The Pittsburgh Survey. Simon Patten. New York and a master's degree at Columbia.

NOW SHE SPENT her vacations, as well as any weekends that she could be away from Ferry Hall, helping with the work at Chicago Commons or Hull House. Like the Commons, Hull House on South Halsted Street was at the center of an immigrant neighborhood — Chicago's nineteenth ward, composed mostly of Italians, Greeks, Slavs and, after 1905, Jews who had fled the pogroms in Russia. Possibly Hull House had more cultural and educational programs than the Commons, which concentrated on industrial problems and the development of unions. But the differences were slight; the needs of the poor determined the services of both.

At Hull House she made the rounds with the district nurse, visiting desperate and disintegrating families, such as that which Devine had put to her in his example. In one tenement, after she had gone down to the street again and again for water from the hydrant to wash the dishes and then the children, the nurse, who was tending the mother of the family, told her to wash the father. He was drunk and vomiting.

In a spasm of anger and disgust Perkins said, "Why don't you let him rot?"

The nurse passed no judgment on her outburst but answered quietly, "We have to straighten the family out. This woman is very sick."

Another job she undertook was collecting wages. Sometimes when pieceworkers in a sweatshop returned the garments with bastings removed, scams sewn and buttons in place, the employer would accept the work and then refuse to pay. It was an easy cheat, for how could an Italian woman with little or no English go to court? She lacked not only the language, but the time and money. Often the women came to the settlement with their complaints, and if the sweatshop was still in the neighborhood, someone like Perkins would try to collect the wages.

Once when an employer refused to pay up, she threatened to tell his landlord that he was running a dishonest shop. No one had told her to say that. It just came to her. But it worked, and after that she used it often. Meanwhile everywhere she went she saw that workers who were organized — the plumbers and carpenters, for example, in their trade unions — got paid for their work.

It was probably while she was at the Commons that she went as an observer to her first organizational meeting. A middle-aged woman, a fiery speaker named Gertrude Barnum, was urging the women of the neighborhood to join a clothing union. Her argument was very raw: Bosses, all bosses, were cruel swindlers. The only hope for the poor, their only defense, lay in the union. Join the union.

Perkins was repelled by the emotion and prejudice, yet she realized that without such a highly charged delivery little or none of the appeal would have reached its audience. The women were too exhausted by long hours of work, too run down in health and spirit to respond to any speech that did not stir them to hatred.

Later she went to a meeting of the bookbinders' union and was deeply impressed. This union had always admitted women, and one was a vice-president. The men treated her almost as an equal. Perkins also attended meetings of the printers' union, which did not allow women to join though many worked in the shops. Still, they were better off simply because the union existed.[1]

This wasn't true in all cases. Jane Addams had a policy at Hull House of hiring only union members. Once when she took on a Negro cook no Chicago union would admit him, and she arranged for him to join a Negro union in St. Louis. But at Hull House everyone knew that he had a good job in Chicago despite the unions, not because of them.[2]

Her work in the Chicago settlements convinced Perkins that her vocation lay not in teaching but in settlement work. "I had to do something," she explained later, "about unnecessary hazards to life, unnecessary poverty. It was sort of up to me. This feeling . . . sprang out of a period of great philosophical confusion which overtakes all young people. One thing seemed perfectly clear. Our Lord had directed all those who thought they were following in His path to visit the widows, the orphans, the fatherless, the prisoners and so forth. Definitely the circumstances of the life of the people of my generation was my business, and I ought to do something about it."[3]

At Hull House she and two other young residents, Allen Burns and Robert Hunter, started out on a project one winter morning. There had been snow, and while they waited for a streetcar they watched a man across the street who was shivering in ragged clothes. His toes stuck through the uppers of his shoes, and one of the young people asked the others, "Is there any way to get that man a new pair of shoes?"

As they debated, the question turned to why they should want to give him new shoes. Burns, describing himself as a humanitarian, said, "Because his feet are cold." Hunter, calling himself a Christian sociologist, said, "For Jesus' sake." She was not sure where she stood or what the difference was or even whether it was important. Clearly the end result would be the same. For her purpose, she thought, the argument could be left unresolved; what mattered was taking action.[4]

She had a financial problem, however, for unless she lived at home she had to earn a living, and the paid jobs in settlement work were limited mostly to administrators and professionals — nurses or experts on some special project. Nevertheless she kept trying, doggedly writing to persons in charity and settlement work. Through a friend in Boston she heard of a group in Philadelphia just organizing and calling itself the Philadelphia Research and Protective Association. She wrote and soon was hired as its general secretary, starting in September 1907 at a salary of fifty dollars a month. Without the clothes her parents had already given her and their letters of introduction, which would lead to invitations to dinner, she could not have taken the job. Though her salary at Ferry Hall is not known, it probably was $250 a year plus room and board. Financially the job in Philadelphia was a step backward.[5]

That summer she went on a tour of Italy with two Chicago friends and their aunt. Though she had a lifelong interest in art and on this trip filled a sketchbook with drawings of architectural detail, her pleasure and excitement in what she saw did not cause her to question her aim in life. Her deepest emotions were already committed.[6]

The Philadelphia Research and Protective Association was concerned with immigrant girls, including Negroes from the South, who were preyed on as soon as they reached the city. Waiting on the dock or railway platform there often happened to be a man of their background who was glad to give them advice about lodgings. Sometimes for a price, generally the greater part of a girl's money, he would conduct her to the boardinghouse he recommended. All too often it was a brothel. The less evil of these shills would take the girls to decent lodgings but then recommend an employment agency that effectively enslaved them by charging enormous fees to hire them out to conspiring employers.

A group in Philadelphia, including several prominent Quakers, had become aware of what was happening and started the association: "research" because no one as yet knew the facts of the problem — where the girls came from or went, or how they were treated — and "protective" because, after the facts were established, a program would have to be devised to protect the girls. Clearly the program would involve the city government, starting with the police.

Although there was nothing industrial about the problem — it doubtless predated discovery of the wheel — the association's method of attacking it was typical of the new settlement approach: First make a survey, then devise and start a program and, finally, persuade the government, municipal or state, to take on its financing and administration. The traditional charitable approach would have been less broad, confined to rescuing individual girls. But because of their large number, a result of the industrial revolution, the traditional approach seemed inadequate.

Perkins was to do everything. The association kept a small office, with a stenographer, in the business section of the city. Some of the association's officers worked part-time and helped to raise money, and she was allowed to hire an occasional assistant. But there was nothing she didn't do some of, and most of what was done she did. Years later when social workers asked her how she got to the top, she would shake her head and say, "I don't know. I began at the top."

It was true, because the idea of social work was then so new that the top was also the bottom. Her job had no formal requirements. She had no degree in what came to be called social work. The first course in it, loosely defined, was not offered until 1898; the first school not opened until 1903; and in the next thirteen years only six more were started. After World War I came a period of expansion, and by 1930 there were more than forty schools of social work.[7] When Perkins started in 1907, however, she had not studied how to make a survey, create a program or press a city government into action. She began simply by doing what she had done in Chicago: she went into the poor and bawdy districts and asked questions.

Some persons were nice to her; others not. But after a time she had a survey of the city showing which districts were inhabited by which ethnic group. She had lists of decent and indecent lodgings and boardinghouses, and of honest and dishonest employment agencies.

She had part-time assistants, including two educated Negro women, who met the boats and trains, and she had obtained for them a measure of police protection — for not everyone was pleased with what she was doing.

One rainy night about eleven, as she was returning home, she realized that two Negro men were following her. One of them she recognized as a pimp in charge of a crooked employment agency. The faster she walked, the faster they followed. She recalled her father's advice for such an occasion. Rounding a corner, she stopped, turned, lowered her umbrella so they collided with it and began to scream the name of the man she knew: "Sam Smith! Sam Smith!" Along the street windows went up, heads came out and the men fled.

She was shaken, and her employers at the association were distressed. Presumably she did not mention the incident to her parents, for beyond gossipy tales of the prominent persons she sometimes met, she told them very little about her work. Some good came from the experience, however; when she reported it to the police and they saw that she was truly frightened, they agreed to close Smith's agency — provided that the socially respectable members of the association backed them when Smith "squawked" to city hall. In the end several of the worst agencies were closed and a city ordinance, with specifications drawn by the association, was passed, requiring all lodgings to be licensed.

Though her hours were long and the responsibility great, she found the work profoundly satisfying because it engaged every side of her personality. Underlying all else was her religious desire to serve the poor or, as she put her conviction in a letter to her classmates, "weaker people than I needed the aid I could give."

She was never more herself than in her reply to the Irish police officer's question: "So you want Sam Smith put out of business, do you?" "Well," she said, "we think it's the right thing to do . . ." And having put the moral conclusion first, she then listed the reasons, based on religious conviction and statistical data, that had led her to it. She was not unique; most settlement workers would have answered the same way.

She also enjoyed the sociability of the work: hobnobbing with politicians at city hall, with the officers in the police courts and with the socially prominent members of her association. She believed that there was good and bad in all groups, and that the trick in routing the bad was to get the good everywhere working together. She was not indignant that the police refused to close down Sam Smith's agency

unless they were promised support by "respectable people." Bringing
the police and these people together was her job, and she found it
more varied and exciting than teaching school.

Finally she was stimulated by the theoretical, intellectual side of the
work. Why did the capitalist system produce so many poor? Was it
necessary? Could it be avoided? Where was the justice in it? Could
some other system do better? In search of answers she joined the
Socialist party, which in the 1912 presidential election would win
almost 6 percent of the vote. But of much greater importance in her
life was that in the fall of 1908 she enrolled in several evening and
Saturday courses in economics and sociology at the University of
Pennsylvania's Graduate School of Arts and Sciences.[8]

That year in particular the questions that preoccupied her were
much debated, for in the winter came the first magazine reports of
what was later combined into six volumes and called *The Pittsburgh
Survey*. This presented for the first time the entire life of an industrial
community, not only the conditions of work but the structure and
quality of family and civic life. Its massive accumulation of details
revealed a dark side indeed of the country's industrial development.[9]

The survey apparently originated in June 1906 with a letter from
the chief probation officer of Pittsburgh's juvenile court to Paul U.
Kellogg, managing editor of *Charities and the Commons*. The officer,
Alice B. Montgomery, had been impressed by the special March issue
of the magazine, "Neglected Neighborhoods in the Alleys, Shacks and
Tenements of the National Capital." Washington was not an industrial city; Pittsburgh was. She thought that a similar study was needed
there, especially since many of the city's leaders seemed unconcerned
about the conditions of life around them.

The idea appealed to Edward T. Devine and the New York Charity
Organization Society. They made a preliminary study, which confirmed the need for such a survey and indicated that the job was larger
than local settlement workers and probation officers could handle.
The society persuaded the newly formed Russell Sage Foundation to
underwrite the project, and over the next four years the foundation
contributed about $45,000 as its first extensive investment in social
research. The Pittsburgh Civic Association contributed $350, which
suggests that Montgomery's appraisal of local civic leaders was accurate.

Kellogg, who was twenty-eight, was put in charge, and in September
1907, with the help of a staff drawn mostly from New York but also
using hundreds of local workers, he began the field surveys. By the

summer of 1908 these had been completed, and the following winter articles based on their data began to appear in national magazines — not only in *Charities and the Commons,* read by Perkins and other settlement workers, but in such popular journals as *Collier's Weekly, American Magazine* and *Review of Reviews.* The Pittsburgh Survey made good copy.

It covered hours, wages, conditions of work, housing, health, taxation, education, fire and police protection, recreation, land values and more. It revealed that the dominant fact of life for Pittsburgh's largest group of workers, the steelworkers, was the twelve-hour day. Many of the men worked seven days a week, but even those who worked only six were too exhausted to share in any sort of community life. Once they reached home most of them had a smoke and then dropped into bed. Workers on some shifts did not see their children for days at a time. The burden on the mothers was correspondingly greater, and for both men and women fatigue increased the likelihood and persistence of sickness.

As for accidents in the mills, the report showed that about one-third were the result of workers' negligence and another third were caused by the employers' failure to provide safety devices. Yet the burden of any accident, no matter whose fault, fell on the worker and his family. And accidents were common: aside from injuries, 526 men were killed on the job in Allegheny County from June 1906 to June 1907.

Few of those who died had been able to afford adequate insurance for their families. In the country's bituminous coal mines, where there was a union, the miners received $2.36 for an eight-hour day (the survey estimated that $2.25 was needed to support an average family). In Pittsburgh's steel mills, where there was no union, the majority of unskilled workers averaged $1.42 for a twelve-hour day in a seven-day week. This enabled a man with a wife and three children to pay for "a two-room tenement in a crowded court, with no sanitary conveniences, a supply of food below the minimum sufficient for mere physical well-being" and very little else.

Though wages may have been higher in Pittsburgh than in Poland or southern Europe, the immigrants who had come with hope for a better life had merely exchanged one form of bondage for another. It was the policy of the steel companies to discourage any effort at self-determination or improvement. Fear pervaded the mills — fear of losing the job, fear of being blacklisted. "If you want to talk in Homestead," Kellogg's researchers were told, "you must talk to yourself."

Though men's wages were low, those of working women, often

widows or spinsters, were lower still. The data collected showed that "where skill and occupation are comparable, alike in skilled trade and is unskilled occupation, the man's wage is double the woman's." On this point the survey concluded that "in Pittsburgh there is scarcely a minimum to which women's wages may not be depressed."

A study of ninety households showed that the long hours and low wages destroyed all initiative. "Somehow it is easier to pay a neighbor 50 cents a month for the privilege of bringing drinking water three times a day from his well, than to insist that the borough provide a wholesome supply." Men and women alike felt they were without power to change their lives or jobs or conditions of work. The decisions affecting them seemed always to be made by others "in New York," who were unapproachable and uninterested.

> The workers not only have no representatives who can confer with the local management on disputed points, but they have a sense of being utterly outside the great moving center of the industry. The thing that is clear to them is that, for many, rates have been cut and earnings lowered, while the men whose names are linked with steel finance are making fortunes. Nor is this feeling lessened by the part which these same men have actually played in Homestead. Mr. Carnegie has given a library, Mr. Schwab a manual training school, and Mr. Frick a charming little park in the centre of the hill section. These generous gifts beautify Homestead . . . Yet . . . many a man said to me, "We'd rather they hadn't cut our wages and'd let us spend the money for ourselves. What use has a man who works twelve hours a day for a library?"

Nothing seemed to function to their advantage. The school system was financed by a general property tax whose proceeds were administered by wards. In the rich wards, where lawyers and bankers kept an eye on the political boss, the schools were good; in the poor neighborhoods the money was often stolen or wasted.

Much the same was true of hospital and medical services. Yet as one report emphasized, "For health's sake, the community cannot afford to permit its girl members to receive a wage too low for nutrition." An epidemic of typhoid fever once started would not stop at ward boundaries. In the year of the survey the city had 622 deaths by typhoid, a rate of 102.5 per 100,000. New York City's rate that same year was 18.2.

Yet Pittsburgh as a whole was prosperous. In summarizing the survey, Devine concluded that no community had ever applied its wealth "so meagerly to the rational purposes of human life." The fantastic industrial profits, he suggested, should be returned to the community — not in libraries or parks but in shorter hours, higher wages and increased safety in order to raise "the standards of domestic life."

One immediate result of the survey was that *Charities and the Commons* changed its name. For several years the staff and trustees had felt that the title did not adequately reflect the size and complexity of the problems they wished to attack: "Charities" seemed too limited and "the Commons" too local. With the April 1909 issue they renamed it *Survey,* aiming it at community leaders across the country. In the next forty years, with Paul Kellogg as its editor, though its subscriptions did not pass forty thousand, it became extremely influential. For all those, including Perkins, who were interested in social justice, in curbing the anarchy of industrial life, it was one of the chief forums where ideas were tested.

The impact of the Pittsburgh Survey was soon felt in economic theories and political platforms. Its revelations may have influenced Theodore Roosevelt in his Osawatomie, Kansas, speech on August 31, 1910: "I stand for the square deal . . . I mean not merely that I stand for fair play under the present rules of the game, but I stand for having these rules changed so as to work for a more substantial equality of opportunity and of reward for equally good service." Unquestionably the survey, together with advice from such social welfare leaders as Kellogg, Julia Lathrop, Florence Kelley and John A. Ryan, influenced the platform of Roosevelt's Progressive party in 1912. And in the campaign Roosevelt and his supporters put the issues of social justice directly before the country.[10]

Perkins, because she was a woman, had no vote in 1912, but if she had, she would have cast it for Roosevelt. Years later in Washington she told his daughter, Alice Roosevelt Longworth, how much she admired her father: he had had such a great influence on American life.

"Yes, didn't he!" said Longworth. "He built the Panama Canal and was the only man to see we needed a big navy." When Perkins looked surprised, she added, "That was his *great* contribution."

"I'm sorry, Alice," Perkins said, "but you know I never thought of that. I meant to tell you he had been the first to reach the peak of political life who pointed out a social obligation: the sufferings of the poor, of the oppressed, of the immigrants, and the right and duty of those with advantages to do something about it."

"Oh," said Longworth.[11]

On economic theories, as opposed to political platforms, Perkins was always less committed. She was a pragmatist and saw no virtue in theories. For her the test of any economic system was "whether or not it serves the people who depend upon it for the goods which they need; and whether it contributes to the moral and spiritual development of men to know, love and serve God."[12]

At the Pennsylvania Graduate School of Arts and Sciences the reigning professor in economics was Simon N. Patten, whose ideas, collectively known as "the theory of abundance," profoundly influenced many charity and social workers. Foremost among these, perhaps, was Edward T. Devine, who had earned a doctor's degree under Patten and later provided him with the chance to test several of his ideas in practice. From 1896, when Devine was appointed general secretary of the New York Charity Organization Society, until Patten's death in 1917 the two consulted regularly about the society's policies and programs. According to Devine, Patten had "far more to do with the developments in social work" for which Devine received the "main credit" than was generally realized.

Roughly, Patten's theory was that the industrial revolution, by greatly increasing per capita production, had made it possible for every man to have enough food, clothing and shelter to live in health. This made unnecessary the traditional battle between rich and poor for the basic goods of life. With the proper adjustments in the economic system, poverty would disappear and with it many of the aggressive attitudes usual among men of different classes.

In practice the theory led to such ideas as there being no need for men to work twelve hours a day. Hours could be shorter and wages higher because the money to support the workers was available within the industries, as was evident in the fantastic fortunes made simply in three of them: steel, oil and railroads. With a "surplus civilization" a better life for the many as well as the few was possible.[13]

Although Perkins admired Patten as a man and a teacher, she was too pragmatic by nature to become a disciple. She was impressed by his ideas, however, and eventually helped to enact some of their applications into law (see Appendix A). He considered her an exceptional student, and it was at his suggestion and with his help that she left Philadelphia for New York in the summer of 1909 with a $500 fellowship from the Russell Sage Foundation.

This was one of a group of fellowships established at the New York School of Philanthropy to train advanced students in methods of making surveys. In conjunction with it she planned to take courses at Columbia that would lead to a master's degree in economics and sociology. The project set by the foundation for her and the ten other fellows was to make under supervision a survey of Hell's Kitchen, a district on New York's West Side extending from Thirty-fourth to Fifty-third streets and from Eighth Avenue west to the river. Her subject was undernourished children, who were referred to her from the lower grades of the public school by the board of health doctor.

On most days she worked on the survey in the morning and attended classes in the afternoon or evening. She lived first at Hartley House, a settlement in the district, and then at Greenwich House in the Village. She wrote excitedly to her classmates, "I am in the very heart of both the theoretical and practical efforts to socialize the life of the modern city."[14]

She also enjoyed the city's artistic and social life. She went to art exhibits, tea dances and quaint restaurants in the Village. Sometimes on Sundays she would sketch or paint, though without pretending to talent. She haunted the Macbeth Gallery, which specialized in painters of realistic, everyday subjects. Their opponents labeled them the Ashcan School, but for just that reason she liked them; "they too had been touched by a feeling for social justice, a concern with how the other half lives." Her favorite picture was *Portrait of a Little Girl* by George Bellows, "a child of the poor — no question about it. You knew from the look on her face." Yet her likes were not restricted to realism. When the Armory Show opened in 1913, she was tremendously stimulated by the new fauve and cubist styles. But in her own painting she tended to follow Ralph A. Blakelock, a romantic landscape painter. "I was interested in dark, misty backgrounds and how he got them. The figures moved vaguely."

She was almost as interested in the literary world. While in Chicago she had written several "true love" stories and offered them under assumed names to magazines published by Street and Smith. Two pseudonyms she used were Bertha Warren, the name of a childhood friend, and Josie Sherman, though she couldn't remember her reason for choosing the latter. She always believed she had sold several but she was never able to trace them. Her stories were often about some innocent girl who worked in a station restaurant of the Atchison, Topeka and the Santa Fe and had terrible adventures that ended happily. "The happy ending was absolutely essential."

In New York she attempted stories and articles based on her work and almost sold one to *Delineator,* a women's magazine. But Theodore Dreiser, who was then the editor, thought it too sophisticated for his audience. She left his office discouraged but still full of admiration for him. She thought *Sister Carrie* "the most important book written in America for a generation." She could never forget Carrie's husband, sitting by the radiator and making believe that he was looking at the advertisements for help wanted.

Her energy and enthusiasm must have been attractive, for she made an astonishing number of acquaintances. She was always ready on Sundays for an outing to Staten Island, and on a picnic up the Hudson she met Paul Kellogg and formed a friendship that continued until his death in 1958. She went dancing often with Will Irwin, a journalist and writer, and one warm summer evening when all windows in her apartment house were open Sinclair Lewis proposed marriage to her "at the top of his lungs." Neither seem to have taken it seriously; both were more interested in their work. Perhaps because so many of her friends had come to the city to establish careers, the pressure on her to pair off was less than if she had remained in Portland or Worcester.[15]

In the spring she submitted her essay to Columbia, "A Study of Malnutrition in 107 Children from Public School 51," and on June 10, 1910, the university awarded her a master's degree in political science.[16] Her courses, however, had been almost entirely in economics and sociology. Several were concerned with historical types of social organization and social evolution. Others treated American social legislation, fiscal and industrial history, railroad problems, efficiency and relief, housing, and the theory and practice of charity organizations. One, given by Devine, was entitled "Misery and Its Causes." In her four years at Mount Holyoke she had never received an A; in her year at Columbia, with her whole personality engaged, she had several.[17]

Her essay, cut to the bone and without tables or footnotes, appeared in *Survey* in October 1910 — her first published article in her field. It presented a number of ideas that would be characteristic of her over the years. The statistics on malnutrition, she wrote, were "a mass of human documents full of human misery," and she insisted that human as well as economic values should be considered in any proposal for reform. Relief, she said, although an immediate necessity, was only an expedient until "society adjusts itself and provides adequate incomes and adequate education to all its workers." Because she was one of Patten's pupils, she was sure the adjustment was possible.

Her work in Philadelphia had made her a small reputation, which her record in New York enlarged. In April, before receiving her degree, she was offered a job as secretary of the New York City Consumers' League, the first of the leagues and perhaps the most important in the national federation. It meant she would be working closely with Florence Kelley, whose speech at Mount Holyoke had determined the direction of her life. She would have an office in the Charities Building and be in frequent contact with Devine, Kellogg and others like them. She would be close to a center of the national movement for social justice.

The salary offered for the first year was $1000, about half what a skilled worker in an organized trade might make and about double the estimated minimum wage on which a single worker could survive. She requested $1200, twice her starting salary three years earlier in Philadelphia. She also asked that a full-time stenographer be attached to the office. Promised the stenographer, she agreed to the lower salary.[18] Though she had not charted her course to this end, she had reached it by doing what Devine had advised eight years earlier when he refused her a job: she had gained the practical and theoretical experience that brought her at the age of thirty the position she wanted.

In retrospect she felt she had been slow to mature and discover her interests. "I was a late bloomer," she once remarked.[19] Probably most people would say that despite obstacles and confusion she had done a remarkable job of discovering and fostering her true nature and arranging her life around it.

Chapter 8

→>><<<-

Florence Kelley and the Consumers' League: bakeries, fire prevention, lobbying and Alfred E. Smith. The Triangle fire and origin of the Factory Investigating Commission.

WORKING WITH Florence Kelley, Perkins discovered, with an extraordinary experience: "She was no gentle saint." She was warm, violent and sometimes unjust. She was keen, sparkling and exciting. Defeated in a cause, she had patience and good humor.

She could grasp the essentials of a problem with incredible rapidity. She could amass and marshal the facts behind it and throw off a stream of ideas for its solution. But she was not an effective administrator, and her failure to develop a consistent pattern of purpose and organization for the affiliated leagues sometimes lost her the full benefit of their work. Her greatest quality as a leader was a flair for enlisting in her cause people of ability and character. In almost every state there was a group, inspired by her moral fervor, seeking to abolish child labor and to erect some defense against the industrial exploitation of unorganized workers, particularly women.

Her approach to any problem was factual and pragmatic. Whenever Perkins proposed a program to improve some aspect of working conditions, Kelley would begin with questions: "How many people are involved? How much damage, distributed or special? How can you correct it? Will the program work? How will you get it started? How will you enforce it?" It was a pattern she had developed from her days in Illinois as Chief Inspector of Factories, and perhaps because of her governmental experience she thought in terms of legislative reform. Most of the league's programs aimed at revising laws or, because at the time there was so little labor legislation, extending law into new areas.[1]

In defending one law — during the year Perkins was in Philadelphia — Kelley helped to validate a new approach to labor legislation.
In Portland, Oregon, a laundryman, Curt Muller, had been arrested
for violating a state law prohibiting women in laundries from working
more than ten hours a day. The Oregon Supreme Court upheld the
statute, but Muller appealed to the U.S. Supreme Court.

Though the state's attorney would argue the case for Oregon, Kelley
asked Louis Brandeis to present the league's arguments to the Court.
He agreed, and they planned to submit a new sort of brief. For three
weeks she and her assistants, particularly Josephine and Pauline Goldmark, dug out all the facts they could find on the effect of fatigue on
women and on the regeneration of their lives following a decent
limitation of hours. Brandeis organized the material and on January
15, 1908, presented it to the Court. At the time such social and
economic facts were generally considered irrelevant to the issue, which
would turn on Muller's and his employees' freedom to make their own
contracts. The Supreme Court, however, in upholding the validity of
the statute, explicitly noted the economic and social reasons for it,
opening a new line of defense for labor legislation. The league
promptly reprinted "the Brandeis Brief" along with the Court's opinion and distributed the two across the country to law schools, libraries
and labor unions.[2]

In the following year when Perkins succeeded Pauline Goldmark as
secretary of the New York City Consumers' League, she worked primarily on local problems, and on three so intensively that people in
the city and state began to associate her name with them. These were
sanitary regulations for cellar bakeries, fire prevention techniques in
factories and the league's "54-hour bill" to prohibit women of any age
and boys under eighteen from working in factories more than fifty-four
hours a week. By the end of two years Perkins had emerged as a
recognized expert on bakeries and fire prevention and was known in
Albany as an effective lobbyist for labor legislation. Yet, like Kelley,
she always had energy to do more. The first year in her spare time she
took additional courses in sociology at Columbia and the following
year taught a course in it at Adelphi.[3] She also took an active part in
the women's suffrage movement, speaking whenever asked and in the
process becoming an accomplished soapbox orator.

She began her survey of bakeries in October 1910. The large bread
companies had not yet developed; each community of a few blocks
had, besides its own saloon and laundry, its own bakery. There were

an estimated 2500 in the city, and she and her staff, mostly volunteers, visited about 250; she personally went to more than 100. Most bakeries, she discovered, were below street level, often in cellars, without adequate light and ventilation. The floors were dirty; some were made of dirt. Rats multiplied, and the bakery cats jumped up and down, slept and gave birth on the breadboards. In summer with the ovens going the heat was stifling, and the workers' sweat poured from their arms into the dough. In many cellars there were no closets or hooks, and clothing was thrown onto the breadboards. Some bakeries had no wash basins or toilets; in others these were located in the working area. Families sometimes lived in the workroom. In one Perkins found a child with a tubercular cough.[4]

These were the bakeries in the poorer districts. Conditions were considerably better on much of Manhattan's East Side, where a union of German bakers observed a code of sanitary regulations and empowered a doctor to prohibit a sick member from working. Yet the Germans' vision of their union struck her as extremely limited. Though women formed a large part of the work force, they could not be members. And because the union functioned partly as a fraternal order, the men had no interest in recruiting non-Germans. So the union did not spread, and the majority of bakers remained unorganized.[5]

Even before she completed the bakery report and presented it, with recommendations, to the city's Board of Health, a fire in a loft in Newark, New Jersey, had started her on another major survey. On November 26, 1910, some gasoline exploded in the Anchor Lamp Company factory on the third floor of a four-story building. A fire station was just across the street, yet in ten minutes there were twenty-five dead and forty injured, all of them from the fourth floor. Of the dead, nineteen had jumped from windows because there was no way to pass through the fire below.[6]

Manhattan Fire Chief Edward Croker warned New Yorkers that their safety measures were no better than Newark's. "A fire in the daytime," he said, "would be accompanied by a terrible loss of life." According to the 1910 census, Greater New York had about twenty-six thousand factories with six hundred and fifty thousand employees. This was roughly three out of four factory workers in the state, and fifty-thousand more than in all of Massachusetts. About half the factories were in lofts above the seventh floor, beyond which even the best-equipped firemen were not effective. Most hook-and-ladder engines reached only to the sixth floor; sprinkler systems, although they existed, were not yet required by law. It was still legal for buildings up to a height of 150 feet (roughly ten stories) to have window frames, trim and floors of wood.

With the aim of marshaling consumer pressure to force improvements, the Consumers' League undertook a survey of fire problems in industry. Perkins began to study sprinkler systems, horizontal exits, fireless ovens, the width and placement of fire stairways and the number of safety devices needed relative to the number of persons employed on each floor.

Meanwhile, women's suffrage was a cause to which she was increasingly drawn as she saw women working longer hours than men, earning less and often being excluded from the unions that might have helped them. Influenced perhaps by Kelley, who believed that "the enfranchisement of women is indispensable to the solution of the child labor problem," Perkins hoped that "women, when they once got the vote, would take a great interest in the social projects to which I was already committed." Until the vote was won (in 1917 in New York State, but not until 1920 in the nation as a whole), she marched in parades and made speeches wherever the Suffrage Office sent her. At first she was asked to address small groups in churches, union halls and immigrant societies; later, as the movement gained momentum, she was sent out to speak on street corners. She would set down her wooden grocery box, step upon it and, as a partner raised a banner proclaiming "Women's Suffrage," begin to speak.

She learned to project her voice over the noise of traffic and the passing crowd. To deal with hecklers she collected funny stories that were short, pointed and good-natured, for she found that if she could make the audience laugh with her, it would discipline itself. After a time she realized that she had nothing to fear from street corner crowds. Campaigning for the vote, she said later, "did more to make me truly at ease with everybody and fully democratic in my feeling about the roughest kind of people than anything else I ever did."

Suffrage was a movement she could share with her college classmates, most of whom worked for it, and with her parents, who sympathized. Several years earlier her father, while on a business trip, had heard a speech by Dr. Anna Howard Shaw and become a convert. He had returned home and announced to his startled family that the short, stocky Dr. Shaw was the greatest orator since William Lloyd Garrison. Later he asked an elderly hired hand in Newcastle, "Joe, what do you think about this idea of women voting?" Joe replied, "Fred, if Jake

Francis, the town fool, can vote, I don't know why your daughter Frances can't. She's a smart girl." In Yankee New England, where for years women had owned property, gone to school and played a role in public life, the denial of their right to vote seemed an anomaly.[7]

In January 1911 she began to learn a new set of skills when she went to Albany to lobby for legislation that the Consumers' League wanted. Its chief interest that year was the 54-hour bill. There had been such a law for a brief time, but in 1909 the Court of Appeals, New York's highest court, had declared it unconstitutional on technical grounds. Kelley had had the law redrafted to meet the court's objections and hoped to persuade the legislature to pass it in the 1911 session.

The New York legislature always convened on the first Wednesday of January and sat through March or April; a longer session was unusual. The two chambers, the Senate with 51 members and the Assembly with 150, met in opposite wings of the Capitol, a large Victorian Gothic pile perched almost at the top of a steep hill and facing down a broad avenue to the railroad station on the bank of the Hudson.

Despite its pretentions to grandeur, the building impressed Perkins as dilapidated. As she learned later, it was clean only for the opening day of the session. Thereafter the red carpeting quickly became gray with cigar ash, and there was a great deal of spitting, not always into spittoons. In the Assembly the red curtains hung in limp, uneven folds, and the huge chandelier was dull with dust.

Both chambers were shaped in a half-moon. The presiding officer sat on a dais overlooking clerks in a slight well and facing legislators sitting in curved and rising rows of desks. At the top and back of each room was a brass rail marking off an area ten or fifteen feet wide that was known as the lobby. Here the "lobbyists" would stand, recording votes and sending messages by the attendants to legislators on the floor.

In the corridor connecting the two chambers was a small, partitioned area, not very clean, called the Assembly Lunchroom. It had a few tables and a short counter without stools, and sold sandwiches, pie and coffee. For months, although often hungry, Perkins would not enter it for fear she would seem "too bold" and offend the legislators whose votes she was seeking. They, as often as not, carried the food back to their desks and ate without forks or spoons. The Assembly, she wrote later, frequently presented "an interesting and sometimes revolting spectacle."

On her first day in Albany a fellow lobbyist, Joseph Hammitt of the

Citizens Union, showed her around the Capitol. That morning the Assembly was not sitting; most of its members were in committee meetings, though a few stood talking in the aisles. One, a fairly young man, was reading at his desk, and she remarked on his studious appearance. Hammitt identified him as Alfred E. Smith, an assemblyman from New York. "That's what he does," Hammitt said. "He's reading the bills introduced last night. When he first came to the Assembly, he used to read every bill introduced and send out to the library for the law it amended. He seemed to think he had to know the business of the Chamber, and the only way to know it was to read the material as it turned up. Now he's one of the best-informed men on the floor."

She was eager to meet Smith, and just then another lobbyist, Robert S. Binkerd of the City Club of New York, joined them. He knew Smith well and, leaning across the rail, he loudly exhaled, "Al!"

Smith looked round, smiled and came up the aisle. Binkerd introduced her and she and Smith chatted for a few minutes. As he turned to go, he told her pleasantly, "Jackson's got your bill. It's still in committee and not moving very fast. Better ask for a hearing."

Later she learned that Assemblyman Edward D. Jackson, a heavy-set railroad man from Buffalo, was not pushing the bill, and that if no one requested a hearing, there would be none. She was grateful to Smith for his casual remark. As the winter wore on, she discovered that what he told her was invariably true. He was a politician and an orator, but he never used words to evade a question. He might say little, withholding something she wanted to know, but what he said was reliable.[8]

Smith's integrity and position were to be important to her. That winter, for the first time in a generation, Democrats controlled both chambers and the governorship, and Charles F. Murphy, the leader of the party in the state and the head of Tammany Hall in New York City, ordered a revolution in the party's legislative organization. Instead of promoting two elderly orators to be majority leaders in the Senate and Assembly, Murphy reached down into his "kindergarten class" and named Robert F. Wagner and Al Smith. Later Wagner would represent New York in the U.S. Senate from 1927 to 1949, and Smith would serve four terms as the state's governor. The two men, both under forty, were friends, and though they were Tammany men and took orders from Murphy, they also influenced him. More than any others, these three brought the Democratic party of New York into the twentieth century.[9]

Perkins quickly came to respect Smith's power and to admire the way he used it. When she seemed to be getting nowhere with her demand for a hearing, she went to him and complained: "It isn't moving at all. They've killed the bill for the last two years."

Smith, a member of Jackson's committee, said, "The canners want an amendment to let employees in canneries out."

She agreed that was the case but insisted that the Consumers' League and the other organizations supporting the bill could not accept an amendment exempting a large group of women workers.

"I'll talk to Jackson," Smith promised. "I think you might get it through."

At the hearings she made a "presentation": she described the bill, the people to whom it would apply, the means of enforcement and the reasons for it. She quoted authorities on the effects of ten- eleven- or twelve-hour days on the health of women and children. She gave specific examples of long hours in New York factories and supported them with photographs showing the conditions of work and the obvious exhaustion on the women's faces and in their bodies at the end of the day.

The most searching questions generally were asked by Smith. He seemed genuinely interested and constantly forced her to be specific: Where is that factory? When was the photograph taken? What is that woman's name? Has she a family? Perkins prepared carefully and usually could answer. She soon realized, however, that he asked many questions less for his own information than to arouse interest in the other committee members.

In the Senate the questioning was less close. The chairman of its Committee on Labor and Industry was Thomas J. MacManus, "The MacManus," boss of Hell's Kitchen. An old-style Irish ward boss, he was a large man but a careful dresser, with a neatly trimmed beard. In the eyes of most reformers he was irredeemably corrupt. She did not doubt the fact, but while working on her survey for the Russell Sage Foundation, she had had a happy experience with him.

A boy from the district had committed a crime and been caught. He was put in the Tombs to await trial, and his mother and two sisters, whom he supported, began to starve. The head resident at Hartley House, which was in MacManus's district, sent Perkins to the local office of the Charity Organization Society for help. The office made its investigation and then refused to make a referral for direct relief because the mother drank and one of the children was illegitimate.

Angered by such a pharisaical ruling, Perkins went from the society's office directly to the Tammany clubhouse. Inside, men were milling about, talking, smoking and spitting. She asked if she could see MacManus. "Sure, lady, sure. He'll be glad to see you," someone said.

The MacManus's office was as full of men, talk and smoke as the outer room, but he gave her his entire attention. "Go ahead; what's troubling you?"

She said she knew a boy in trouble.

"Well, I'm always glad to help anybody in trouble. Does he live in this district?"

"Yes."

"Do you live in the district?"

"Yes." She gave her address without identifying it as Hartley House for fear that might throw him off.

"What's the boy's name?"

She told him and described the circumstances. Thirty-six hours later the boy was out of prison and back at work.

She did not ask how it was done. She was not sure she approved of it, but thereafter she had some sympathy for MacManus. Nevertheless, despite a good presentation and every indication that she had enough votes among the senators to pass the bill, she could not persuade the committee to report it out.[10]

Meanwhile, partly because of a fire in the Capitol but even more because of a fight within the Democratic party over the nomination of the U.S. senator, the session continued into May and seemed likely to go on for another month. In June she had planned to go to Europe with friends, but she wanted to see the bill passed first.

She went again to Smith, pointing out that she had sufficient votes pledged in both the Senate and Assembly to pass the bill if only the committee would report it out. "You're in favor of this bill," she said. "Can't you give me some assurance it will be voted on?"

He was silent, and she realized that he was in some way taking her measure. Finally he said, "Now, I'm going to tell you something. You'll have to be very careful. You mustn't repeat this. You can go along to Europe with perfect ease of mind. The bill isn't going to be passed or reported this year."

"Mr. Smith!" she exclaimed. "How do you know? How can you possibly know that?"

"I had a talk with Murphy. You can never get it out of committee. That's the truth, and you go do as you please. You won't do any good staying around here because it's not going to be taken up."

"But why?"

"There's lots of good Democrats who don't believe in this kind of thing."

"Tell me who," she insisted. "The Democratic party had a kind of resolution in favor of it at the last convention."

"Yeah, but that don't mean anything. That was for the front. That sounded good because the Republicans didn't have any such thing. Your people agitated enough. Some of them got it introduced. The Democrats couldn't vote against it, and so they voted for it. Do you know who one of the big contributors to the Democratic fund is?"

She shook her head.

"It's the Huyler Candy Factory. They're great friends of Mr. Murphy's, and they live right down there near him. It's not going to go through yet. You can take that as a tip, but don't you tell anybody."

Recognizing that he had been extraordinarily frank, she was careful not to betray him. But she could not bring herself to follow his advice. Her friends sailed without her, and she continued to appear in Albany several days each week, talking, urging, asking why and why not. As long as the legislature was in session, there was a chance. But when it finally adjourned on October 6, Smith proved right.[11]

On the afternoon of Saturday, March 25, at about 4:40, the fire predicted by Chief Croker broke out in a factory building near Washington Square. Perkins, who lived on Waverly Place close by, was having tea that afternoon with a neighbor, Mrs. Gordon Norrie, on the Square's north side. Hearing the fire engines, they went out to investigate and, abandoning tea, ran across the small park to the street entering from the east. Fifty yards along it, on the northwest corner of Washington Place and Greene Street, the top of the Asch Building was ablaze. Fire enveloped the eighth, ninth and tenth floors, occupied by the Triangle Shirtwaist Company. Flames flashed from the windows, and workers who had crawled onto the sills and cornices were beginning to jump.

As far as investigators later could determine, the fire started on the eighth floor, probably from a cigarette falling into a bin of cotton scraps. The Triangle company made ladies' shirtwaists in the fashionable "Gibson girl" style. The cutters, forty of them, using a paper pattern, would cut a bodice front or right sleeve, hang the pattern on a wire over the table, put the part aside, cut to another pattern, hang and put aside, and from time to time sweep the scraps into a bin under the table. These were collected six times a year, most recently on

January 15, when the scraps had weighed 2252 pounds. By March 25, the day of the fire, there probably was a ton of cotton scraps on the eighth floor, all flammable as paper.

Because of the cotton on the tables and in the bins, the hanging paper patterns and oil in the sewing machines, the fire in minutes was everywhere. No fire drills had ever been held, and on the three floors were about 500 persons. Of the 70 on the top floor all but one escaped, most of them over the roof. But on the eighth and ninth floors the majority panicked. For all 430 there were only two passenger elevators (two freight elevators had shut down for the day), two narrow stairways and a fire escape. Several of the stairway exits, however, were either locked — it was never proved — or jammed, and the fire escape killed more than it saved. The iron shutters opening onto it jammed in a position to block the workers trying to come down. Meanwhile, through the windows came the fire, feeding on the wooden trim and frames and threatening the trapped workers.

Even the first few who had been lucky enough to reach the lowest level had then been forced to drop through a glass skylight into an enclosed court, where they would have suffocated if firemen had not managed to break down the locked cellar doors. Moments later the entire fire escape, under the weight of the people, collapsed, dumping them onto the skylight and into the court, eight floors below. The best means of escape proved to be the two passenger elevators, which the operators, by pulling the cables running through the open cage cars, moved up and down until heat bent the tracks of one and the other was broken by bodies falling on its roof.

The collapse of the fire escape was seen across the interior court by only one person, but from the two streets beside the Asch Building hundreds saw workers leap from the windows. In fifteen minutes — about as long as the firemen required to stop the fire from spreading — forty-seven persons jumped from the eighth and ninth floors. The fire horses, trained to stand quietly in noise and confusion, began to lunge, terrified by the rain of bodies, the concussion and the splattering blood. Some bodies, hitting the sidewalks where vaults were underneath, went through the pavement. Firemen held nets and blankets to break the fall, but the bodies hit with such force the firemen frequently were somersaulted. Not one of those who jumped was saved.

In all, 146 died in the Triangle fire. Of the injured there was never an exact count. Many, staggering home in a state of shock, disappeared into the city's multitude.

In the months after the fire, as investigations turned into trials, it became clear that the proprietors of the Triangle company, Max Blanck and Isaac Harris, were morally responsible for much of the disaster. Despite eight fires in nine years they had refused to hold fire drills. But it also became clear that they were not responsible legally. In the end, by jury verdict, they went free and collected $64,925 from their insurance company for property damage — roughly $445 for each Triangle worker who died.

The owner of the building, Joseph J. Asch, was able to show that his architects had met all the existing fire regulations when the building was completed in 1901. He had never been asked by the city to make any changes. Almost three years to the day after the fire, he settled twenty-three individual suits for lives lost in his building at a rate of $75 a life.

From the start there was a strong sense in the city that society itself was partially at fault. The religiously minded talked of the increasing substitution of business for spiritual values, property put ahead of life. The politically oriented pointed to the failure in government organization, as one city bureau chief after another demonstrated that he did not have the funds, personnel or power to enforce even the existing regulations. Many economic theorists — particularly the socialists, who were strong among the immigrant clothing workers — denounced capitalism's inherent inhumanity. However expressed, at all levels of society there was a feeling that the community in recent years had failed its members who worked in factories.

Eighteen months earlier a small union of shirtwaist workers had struck for shorter hours, safer working conditions and recognition of their union. They had set up picket lines and despite mass arrests had stayed out for almost three months. There had been violence, much of it by the police, and several extraordinarily one-sided judgments against individual strikers by the city magistrates. The union gained some favorable publicity when the police by mistake arrested Mary E. Dreier, president of the Women's Trade Union League, for she was not an unknown immigrant worker but a well-known figure in the city; many society women raised money for the strikers and tried to rally the public behind them. But the public had been uninterested and the first great strike by women in American labor history had failed.

Now, at a mass meeting in the Metropolitan Opera House on Sunday evening, April 2, the public and its leaders had its former attitude put before it. The groups sponsoring the meeting, among them the Consumers' League, had asked a leader of the Shirtwaist

Makers Union, Rose Schneiderman, to speak, and as every newspaper reader by then was aware, one of the companies that had defeated the union in its strike and had fired all union members was Triangle.

Perkins, as the league's representative, was seated on the stage not far from Schneiderman, who looked almost like a child and who early in the meeting had begun to tremble. Watching with sympathy, Perkins wondered whether the trembling was from nerves or anger. The meeting was not going easily. The sponsoring organizations had a plan for the creation of a new bureau of fire prevention and a system of workmen's compensation, but several of the speeches had drawn shouts of disapproval as well as applause. Evidently there were groups in the audience of 3500 who felt the plan was mere words, another resolution leading to nothing.

When Schneiderman rose to talk, the audience fell silent. A small woman, she appeared even smaller as she moved alone to the front of the stage. She began softly. Probably very few heard her first sentence. But then the slow, even intensity with which she spoke began to carry her words to the back rows.

> I would be a traitor to those poor burned bodies, if I were to come here to talk good fellowship. We have tried you good people of the public — and we have found you wanting.
>
> The old Inquisition had its rack and its thumbscrews and its instruments of torture with iron teeth. We know what these things are today: the iron teeth are our necessities, the thumbscrews are the high-powered and swift machinery close to which we must work, and the rack is here in the firetrap structures that will destroy us the minute they catch fire.
>
> This is not the first time girls have been burned alive in this city. Every week I must learn of the untimely death of one of my sister workers. Every year thousands of us are maimed. The life of men and women is so cheap and property is so sacred! There are so many of us for one job, it matters little if 140-odd are burned to death.
>
> We have tried you, citizens! We are trying you now and you have a couple of dollars for the sorrowing mothers and brothers and sisters by way of a charity gift. But every time the workers come out in the only way they know to protest against conditions which are unbearable, the strong hand of the law is allowed to press down heavily upon us.
>
> Public officials have only words of warning for us — warning that we must be intensely orderly and must be intensely peaceable, and they have the workhouse just back of all their warnings. The strong hand of the law beats us back when we rise — back into the conditions that make life unbearable.
>
> I can't talk fellowship to you who are gathered here. Too much blood

has been spilled. I know from experience it is up to the working people
to save themselves. And the only way is through a strong working-class
movement.

Three days later, the Women's Trade Union League held a funeral
procession for the fire's seven unidentified victims. About one hundred thousand workers and representatives of all professions marched.
In the rain, another four hundred thousand lined the streets. There
were no banners and no music; only the sound of marching feet.[12]

Out of the various protest meetings there emerged a single Committee on Safety, with Henry L. Stimson, soon to become Taft's Secretary
of War, as its president. The executive committee included R. Fulton
Cutting, Mary E. Dreier, Henry Morgenthau, Sr., Daniel Harris, Dr.
Henry Moskowitz, Anne Morgan and other civic leaders. Among the
groups to which it turned for help was the Consumers' League, and
Perkins was put on a committee to petition Governor Dix for action
by the state.

In Albany the governor listened politely to the committee's spokesmen and then referred them to Smith and Wagner, the majority
leaders in the Assembly and Senate. Perkins took this to mean that
the governor, whom she considered "not a very forceful man," wanted
the legislative leaders to share the responsibility for any action.

The committee saw Smith first. Perkins had met him by chance in
Grand Central Station just after he had called on several families who
had lost relatives in the fire, and she knew that he had been talking to
other legislators about what could be done. Now she watched with
admiration and amusement as he gently led the committee in the
direction he wanted it to go.

The committee, fearing "the hand of politics," wished to avoid a
close connection with the legislature. It hoped to persuade the governor to appoint an executive commission of "the finest people in the
state" and to fund its work with money from the executive budget or
from public contributions. Smith, to the contrary, wanted to make use
of politics in what he considered the right way. He suggested a
legislative commission, composed mostly of senators and assemblymen
and funded directly by legislative appropriations. He pointed out
that no one yet knew the size of the problem — how many other
factories in the state were firetraps. The legislature, he reminded
the petitioners, had great powers: its commission would have the right
of entry into buildings anywhere in the state as well as the right to
subpoena witnesses and records.

"These fellows in the Assembly," he said, "are good men at heart. They don't want to burn up people in factories. They just don't know anything about how to prevent it, and they don't really believe that there is any hazard until you show them. And they'll be more impressed if it is shown them by their own commission and own members."

Perkins already was convinced, but some members of the committee kept returning to the idea of recruiting the finest and ablest people for the governmental commission.

"Have you ever noticed," Smith asked, "how much these finest people in the State of New York have to do besides the thing you want them to do? They're always very busy, and you can't get their attention for long. Besides, you know, it isn't the finest people in the state who have the most influence in the legislature. The members there are just like everybody else — they think their own work is the best. If you want to get anything done, ladies and gentlemen, I advise you to ask for a legislative commission."

In the end, after conferring with Wagner, the committee followed Smith's plan, and in May the legislature approved the Wagner-Smith Resolution creating a New York State Factory Investigating Commission, effective June 30, 1911. The members were Senators Wagner (chairman) and Charles M. Hamilton; Assemblymen Smith (vice-chairman), Edward D. Jackson and Cyrus W. Phillips; and four public members, "finest people," appointed by the governor: Simon Brentano, a publisher and bookseller; Robert E. Dowling, a realtor; Mary E. Dreier, president of the Women's Trade Union League; and Samuel Gompers, president of the American Federation of Labor.

The commission's scope and powers were extremely broad, largely because of Smith's influence, and went beyond fire prevention and safety to sanitation, industrial disease, machinery, hours, workmen's compensation and, later, wages. In the three and a half years of its existence it conducted the most intensive study of industry undertaken in the United States until that time. It was the Pittsburgh Survey extended to an entire state, the major industrial state in the country.[13]

In October the commission held its first public hearing in New York, and on November 14 Perkins was called to testify on cellar bakeries. After she had given her name and address, her competence as an expert was questioned by a representative of some real estate interests, Stewart Browne, who was often considered a crank. Wagner at the moment was absent and Smith presiding. He allowed Browne to question her.

"Have you ever been a baker?" "No, sir." "Have you ever made a loaf of bread in your home?" "No, sir." "Have you ever marketed bread?" "No, sir." "Have you a degree and a license to practice medicine?" "No, sir." "Have you a degree and a license to practice engineering?" "No, sir." "Then by what right do you propose to testify here?"

Smith answered. "Because we've asked her to."

But Browne would not be stopped. He declared she had no education or training to qualify her as a witness on bakeries, and concluded triumphantly, "She's a totally ignorant and incompetent person and a *girl,* and I protest her being allowed to testify."

Whereupon Smith shifted his cigar to the other side of his face and said, "Let *me* ask her a few questions now." He took her through a series of questions to which she could answer yes. "Have you ever been in a cellar bakery? "Yes, sir." — and announced firmly at the end that she was a qualified expert.

While the audience tittered and members of the commission exchanged surreptitious smiles, Smith winked at her and said, "Give 'em the best you've got." In response to an occasional question by counsel she presented her report, backed up by notes and photographs. At subsequent hearings she testified on work done in tenements and twice on fire hazards and prevention.[14]

Throughout the commission's life she was associated with it as an expert witness, an investigator and a guide who arranged trips to factories so that the commissioners could see for themselves what conditions were. Just as the commission's work proved a seminal experience for Wagner and Smith, setting the course of their careers, so it was for her. And just as they took their experience on the state level and eventually transferred it to a larger, national plane, so did she.

Thirty years after the Triangle fire, Wagner won a bet by recalling the exact date and hour it began. Fifty years after, in 1961, Perkins, Schneiderman and fourteen survivors attended a meeting conducted by the New York City Fire Department to remember the dead. For those present the horrors of the Triangle fire never faded into history.[15]

Chapter 9

>>><<<

The Consumers' League: the 54-hour bill.

WHEN THE NEW YORK legislature convened in January 1912, Perkins began again her weekly trips to Albany to lobby for the 54-hour bill. As she remarked later with amusement, to others she must have appeared to think the session's only purpose was to pass that bill. But her intensity contributed to her effectiveness as a lobbyist. She cared that women and children should not work more than fifty-four hours in a week, and her knowledge of the ills caused by longer hours was formidable. With eyes burning, she often could transfix an assembly-man or senator until he, too, was ready to cry out that the hours must be limited by law.[1]

She started again with Smith. Although the Democrats had retained control of the Senate and the governorship, the Republicans controlled the Assembly and he was only the minority leader. Because of their work together on the Factory Investigating Commission she knew him better than before, yet they continued, as they would for life, to address each other as "Miss Perkins" and "Mr. Smith," or by title, "Madam Chairman" and "Governor." Yet their friendship already was intimate and subtle. She never asked him directly whether he would vote for the 54-hour bill. She knew that he personally was for it, but she also knew that Murphy, the head of Tammany, was against it and might demand Smith to vote against it. He on his side never volunteered how he would vote on the bill, though he was always willing to advise her on ways to advance it. At times, as in the case of the Huylers' opposition, he would even reveal what Murphy would have kept secret. But he never promised anything he could not deliver, and for that she liked him very much.

She made use of everything he told her. In the autumn, for help with the Huyler brothers, she had turned to some of the socially prominent members of her league's board of directors. Mr. and Mrs. R. Fulton Cutting and Mrs. Benjamin Nicoll began to include the Huylers and their wives in social gatherings at which the bemused guests discovered that their hosts favored the 54-hour bill. To influence the Bloomingdale brothers, who owned a large department store, she talked to their rabbi, Stephen Wise. It was all part of lobbying.

At her first meeting with Smith that winter she said, "I've done a lot. I took your hint. I don't think all the opposition that was going round about this bill will be present now."

"Perhaps," he said, adding, "I noticed you stuck around all summer even though I told you to go on to Europe."

"Well, I thought there might just be a chance."

"There wasn't any chance; I told you the truth. But you didn't lose anything by staying around. You made friends up here because they all knew that you were staying when it was hopeless; that you weren't going to give up. They know you mean business, so they'll listen to you more than they used to."

Her conversations with Wagner, who was still the majority leader in the Senate, were never as frank. She admired Wagner, an immigrant who had supported himself through college and law school, and she liked the way he relied on fact rather than exaggeration in his speeches. But he lacked Smith's charm. He was better looking — Smith had a scrawny neck and a beak of a nose — but his language was less vivid, his appearance and expression more austere. For her at least he had none of "that quality which makes you feel that, even if he might be wrong, you will go along with him."[2]

After she had been lobbying for almost three months, the bill's first progress came in the Senate on March 27, two days before the legislature was scheduled to adjourn. MacManus, the chairman of the Committee on Labor and Industry, presented it for debate and final passage. The bill's opponents, led by Senator Victor M. Allen of Troy, offered three amendments, but its supporters held ranks and voted them down. In the debate Senator Allen insisted that the factories of Troy were bright and airy and that the women preferred working in them to staying at home.

He was answered by "Big Tim" Sullivan, who was, like MacManus, a ward boss in New York. Where MacManus was famous for paying the funeral bills of supporters, Sullivan gave away shoes. He was a man of sentiment, and every year on his mother's birthday he gave each of the children in his ward — there were about 2000 of them — a pair of shoes. Not just any old shoes. The child, by going to the

Democratic clubhouse, received a ticket to exchange at a local store for shoes that fit.

Sullivan was also a bit of a poet and much of an actor, and chose to reply to Allen in an ironic vein:

> Mr. President, I wish to endorse everything my honored friend, the Senator from Troy, has just said. I've seen the shirt factories of Troy, and I want to tell you that it's a fine sight, too, to see them women and girls working in those bright, airy places the Senator has so eloquently described. But I also want to tell you that it's a far finer sight at noon-time to see the fine, big, up-standing men fetching around the women's dinner pails.

Amid the laughter the vote was called, and the bill passed, 32–15. To her delight Perkins saw that both Wagner and James A. Foley, who was Murphy's son-in-law and unofficial representative in the legislature, voted for it. The fact seemed to substantiate rumors that Murphy had given the bill his approval.

But in the Assembly, where the upstate canning and candy industries had concentrated their efforts, the bill had a rougher passage. An amendment to exempt the candy manufacturers for the three months before Christmas had been defeated; but another, exempting canners altogether, had passed, on the ground that canning was a seasonal industry that required long hours for a short period to avoid spoilage.

The Assembly's Rules Committee, therefore, had two bills: its own amended bill exempting the canners, known as the Jackson bill, and the unamended MacManus bill sent from the Senate. All day on Thursday, March 28, she tried to persuade the chairman and members of the Rules Committee to report out the MacManus bill. But in the half-hour while she was at dinner, the committee reported out the Jackson bill.

When she complained to Smith, he said, "I'm afraid that was intended."

"What do you mean?"

"I can't tell you any more about it," he said, "but I am sure that was intended."

The next day, when the amended bill was put to a vote, it passed the Assembly, 104–26, and was sent to the Senate.

She was left with a problem: the Senate and Assembly bills were not identical, and with the session in its last hours there was no chance to reconcile them. Either the Assembly must accept the Senate's bill, which it plainly would not do since it had just voted to exempt the canneries, or the Senate must accept the Assembly's bill, which it might do since the amended bill with the cannery exemption was less stringent than the one the Senate already had passed.

For three years the Consumers' League had proclaimed the length and breadth of the state that it would never accept a bill that exempted the canneries. She called New York but could not reach Kelley. The league's lawyers and several of its directors insisted that she stand firm: she must try to persuade the Assembly to pass the Senate's bill. Pauline Goldmark, the chairman of the league's Committee on Legislation, was on her way to Albany to lend a hand.

The session had been scheduled to end at noon, but the leaders had stopped the clocks, declaring the session would continue until the work was done. A band from the Catholic Protectory in New York, which had come up to enliven the closing hours with music, instead played in the Assembly's gallery during a short recess while some of the rowdier assemblymen bombarded each other with copies of unpassed bills. Yet the stopped clocks notwithstanding, time ran on. Hurrying back to the Senate from the Assembly, Perkins met one of her senatorial stalwarts by the elevator. He had his coat and was leaving to catch an evening train.

She talked to MacManus, but he could not help her in the Assembly. She appealed to Tim Sullivan, who said:

> Me girl, I seen you around here and I know you worked hard on this and I know you done your duty and I know it's very hard for a young lady like you to work away from home. I'll tell you; it's the truth. Murphy told them to go ahead and put out the bill, but the idea is that the Assembly will pass a different bill. They say, of course, you can't accept it — you're under instructions not to accept it. They don't mean to put it through. They don't mean to let you get that law this year because they know you won't accept the bill that's over in the Assembly with the canners' amendment on it. That's the idea.

It drove her nearly crazy. It was an election year, and the Republicans who controlled the Assembly would claim that they had done something for labor; the Democrats in the Senate, with an unamended bill, would claim that they had done even more; and everyone would deplore that time had run out before the bills could be reconciled. "That'll be fine publicity," she exclaimed frantically to Pauline Goldmark, "but no law this year."

As Goldmark hurried off to see what she could do, Joseph Hammitt, the lobbyist for the Citizens Union, asked Perkins quietly, "Do you really want that bill?"

"Yes!"

"How many women work in canneries?"

"About ten thousand."

"How many work in factories throughout the state?"

"About four hundred thousand."

"If I were you," he suggested, "I'd do what I could for the four hundred thousand."

She went out to the corridor to grapple with her conscience. Where did the worse betrayal lie? Her orders were explicit and recently confirmed. All over the state, league members had worked for a law without exemptions. Suppose, in the league's name, she abandoned the women in the canneries and then failed to achieve any law at all? What would be left of the league's program for another year?

Alone in the corridor, she decided to accept the amendment, to work for the majority of women this year and those in the canneries next. Without daring to confess her decision to Goldmark, she went directly to Wagner and MacManus. They protested that the league was against the canners' amendment. No more, she insisted. She wanted the bill even if amended. Wagner, expressing his surprise, agreed to report it out.

But before he had done so, he was called to preside over the meeting while the lieutenant governor went out to confer with the governor. Minutes slipped by and to her horror she discovered, on a tally of heads, that four of her votes had gone home. At best she had thirty-two; by constitutional requirement, in order to pass the bill she needed at least twenty-six, a majority of the fifty-one Senators. Then she saw Big Tim and his cousin Christy Sullivan, also a senator, with coats in hand leaving to catch the eight o'clock boat.

She was dismayed. She begged them to stay. Wagner had promised to have the Assembly bill reported out of the Rules Committee.

Big Tim, whom a reporter once described as "no lily" but "human," looked at her, considered and then explained: "Wagner's the chairman of the Rules Committee, and you'll have to have a rule. He's now the temporary president of the Senate so he can't call the Rules Committee together to pass a rule." He smiled at her. "That's the plan."

"Oh, Mr. Sullivan!" she gasped. The guile of it left her speechless.

Her disappointment must have touched him, for after a moment he said: "Me sister was a poor girl, and she went out to work when she was young. I feel kinda sorry for them poor girls that work the way you say they work. I'd like to do them a good turn. I'd like to do you a good turn. You don't know much about this parliamentary stuff, do you?"

She shook her head.

"Well, I'm the ranking Senate member of the Rules Committee. Wagner is presiding officer, and his orders are not to recognize anybody to move for reconsideration. If you don't believe me, you just try it. You get Newcomb to ask for a rule."

When she realized the extent of his offer to help her and the theatricality of the role he was preparing to play, she began to enjoy the intrigue. Hastily she collected for him the signatures of a majority of the committee. Then she sent Josiah Newcomb and Mayhew Wainright, two of the committee's lesser members, down the aisle asking to be recognized. Standing almost directly in front of Wagner, they raised their hands, waved their arms and called, "Mr. President! Mr. President!" But he wouldn't look at them. Ignored, as everyone saw, they came back to her in defeat.

Then Big Tim, his point proved, his role created, went down the aisle in splendid fashion. "A report from the Rules Committee," he called. "A report from the Rules Committee." Wagner turned white. Even from the back of the chamber she could see it. Lawyerlike he began to splutter, "I can't receive any additional rules. No rules to be given."

"I am the acting chairman of the Rules Committee," Sullivan proclaimed, "and I *de-mand* a vote on whether I can make a report or not!"

He stood at the foot of the aisle absolutely confident, beaming. Wagner called in a parliamentarian, who ruled in Sullivan's favor. The Assembly's bill exempting the canneries was called up for a vote.

The two Sullivans, with overcoats on, voted first and then left to catch the boat. Meanwhile pandemonium had broken out, for many of the senators, knowing nothing of her switch, shouted to colleagues to vote against the bill while others shouted back that they were now to vote for it. In the confusion many hurried up to her, behind the brass rail, asking, "Is this right? Are you for it? Is it a trick?"

"Yes, yes," she said excitedly. "I'm for it. I've authorized it. We want it. We want it." But to increase the confusion, at her side Pauline Goldmark was saying, "No. We don't want it. You mustn't say that."

"Pauline, this is *my* responsibility," she insisted. "I'll do it and hang for it if necessary."

But at the end of the roll call, the bill had failed of its required majority by two votes, 24–14. After Big Tim's departure two waverers had switched to vote against it. Wagner, at the end of the roll call, perhaps because he could see the bill already had been lost, voted for it. More significantly Murphy's lieutenant, Foley, who came early in the call, had not voted.

Having made her decision to compromise on the original bill, she refused to abandon the fight for the amended substitute. She told MacManus that she would call the Sullivans back from the boat and urged him to demand immediate reconsideration of the Assembly's bill. Under the Senate rules he could do this as one who had voted for the bill, and his motion, as a matter of internal Senate action, would need a majority only of senators present and voting in order to pass: 24–14 would be more than enough. Now the rising excitement in the chamber aided her. As she hurried to phone the Sullivans on the boat, she heard MacManus taunt one of the waverers: "We'll make you eat crow."

Her opponents, however, were not yet defeated. Recognizing that MacManus's motion to reconsider would pass easily, they concentrated on the vote on the bill itself, which would follow. They demanded a "closed call of the house," which meant that during the roll call the doors of the chamber would be locked. The Sullivans would have to arrive before the call began or they would be locked out. Wagner ruled in favor of a "closed call."

Under the rules, on a motion to reconsider each senator was allowed five minutes to explain his vote. When the call reached MacManus he rose and for five minutes talked what later was described as "drivel." Several other senators also used their full time, and one allegedly gave a lecture on birds. Just before the end of the call the Sullivans burst in: Big Tim red-faced and puffing; Christy, white-faced and gasping. They had missed the taxi she had sent for them and had run up the hill. "Record me in the affirmative," roared Big Tim as he came through the door.

"It's all right, me girl," he said to her while order was being restored. "We is with you. The bosses thought they was going to kill your bill, but they forgot about Tim Sullivan."

With Big Tim in charge the final vote on the bill was 27–16: passed. The Senate and galleries broke into loud applause. Wagner and Foley, though they had voted in favor, looked sulky, but Big Tim grinned and beamed and accepted congratulations all around.[3]

Later still, in the Capitol, she met a smiling Smith, who said to her, "You pulled a smart one. That was very smart. I didn't think you had the courage to do it."

There was still the Consumers' League to be faced, and Florence Kelley was an emotional woman who said exactly what she thought. As it turned out, Kelley fell on her neck with praise and joy because for the first time in years there would be some limitation on the hours women could be required to work. Pauline Goldmark was reconciled then.[4]

The next year the law, without much opposition, was broadened to include the canneries.

There are experiences that seem to be decisive in a person's life. This was one for Perkins. Ever after in personal life or politics she was, as her friend Agnes Leach described her, "a half-loaf girl: take what you can get now and try for more later."[5]

On April 19 Governor Dix signed the bill. There was a small ceremony in his office with representatives of the Consumers' League and other organizations that had supported it. Though Perkins made a short speech about what the bill would mean to women, Governor Dix signed it with misgivings. "I don't think this is a good idea," he said. "I think it will put women out of work. I think they'll hire men instead. I think women will lose their jobs. Anyhow, it's not good for them not to be fully occupied." He evidently subscribed to the argument, put forward in the legislative debates, that women who worked only fifty-four hours a week would use their free time for immoral practices.[6]

Perkins received considerable publicity for her part in the bill's passage. In July the popular *Metropolitan Magazine* carried an article about her entitled "Behind the Rail: Being the Story of a Woman Lobbyist." The author, Leroy Scott, was an acquaintance and must have obtained much of his information from her, but she was careful not to aggravate anyone's wounds. Sullivan is the hero of the story; neither Foley nor Murphy is mentioned; the two senators who wavered are not named; and Wagner, because most of his role is omitted, appears as well intentioned but, in his position as presiding officer, powerless to help.[7]

According to some later historians the senator who supposedly filibustered for her with a lecture on birds — an incident she never could recall — was Franklin D. Roosevelt. She knew him slightly at the time, socially and in politics, and did not like him in either setting. She describes him in her book *The Roosevelt I Knew* as having at this time "an unfortunate habit — so natural that he was unaware of it — of throwing his head up. This, combined with his pince-nez and great height, gave him the appearance of looking down his nose at most people."

It was not until 1933, when Roosevelt was about to become President, that accounts of his record on labor issues began to refer to a speech on birds. That winter an article in the *Saturday Evening Post* by Louis Howe, Roosevelt's assistant, gave him entire credit for the bill's passage and included an extended account of the bird speech. Howe would have known that the Senate's official record reports only how senators voted, not who spoke for and against, so his claim for Roosevelt could not be disproved. No contemporary report yet found, however, mentions that Roosevelt spoke, and it would seem that the speech as well as the alleged distinction of his record on labor issues was fabricated (see Appendix B). Certainly Perkins thought so, for so unfavorably did she recall his labor record as a state senator that for years she claimed he had voted against the bill. Even after discovering, in the official report, his vote for it, she wrote bluntly: "Franklin Roosevelt did not associate himself actively with this bill, which was a measure of the progressive politicians of 1910. I remember it clearly because I took it hard that a young man of so much spirit did not do so well in this, which I thought a test, as did Tim Sullivan and The MacManus, undoubtedly corrupt politicians."[8]

Several years after the 54-hour bill became law, Perkins went to Tammany Hall on Fourteenth Street to ask Murphy to support some legislation on factory buildings. By that time Smith and Wagner were making statewide reputations from their work on the Factory Investigating Commission, and the Democratic party, largely by supporting the commission's recommendations, was becoming the dominant party in the state.

Murphy, dignified and reserved, was extremely courteous. He listened to her argument for the factory bill, and then, leaning forward in his chair, said quietly, "You are the young lady, aren't you, who managed to get the fifty-four–hour bill passed?"

She admitted she was.

"Well, young lady, I opposed that bill."

"Yes, I so gathered, Mr. Murphy."

"It is my observation," he said, "that the bill made us many votes. I will tell the boys to give all the help they can to this new bill. Goodbye."

As she left, murmuring her thanks, he asked, "Are you one of these women suffragists?"

"Yes, I am," she stammered.

"Well, I am not," he replied, "but if anyone ever gives them the vote, I hope you will remember that you would make a good Democrat."[9]

PART III

Quasi-Public Office

The Factory Investigating Commission.

Marriage and Mayor Mitchel

Chapter 10

->>|<<-

The Committee on Safety. The Factory Investigating Commission: fire hazards, labor department reorganized, the canneries and minimum wage. The moral basis for action, and legislation the best means of improvement.

IN MAY 1912 she resigned as executive secretary of the Consumers' League to accept a similar position with the Committee on Safety of the City of New York. The change, which focused her attention for the next three years on the work of the Factory Investigating Commission, was made with the league's blessing; she continued to serve on its committees and was elected to its board of directors. Though she worked with many different organizations in her first decade in New York, 1909 to 1919, her tie with the league was never broken.

The Committee on Safety was the citizens' group that had emerged from the protest meetings following the Triangle fire. Together with the Fifth Avenue Association, it had led the demand for action by the state and had succeeded in having the Factory Investigating Commission appointed. Thereafter it had all but died, and Perkins was hired to revive it. "Under your leadership" was how the committee's spokesman, John A. Kingsbury, put it: she was to lead; the committee would follow.[1]

As the committee's purpose was to keep alive the public's interest in the Factory Investigating Commission and to ensure support for its recommendations, she worked closely with its leaders: Robert Wagner (chairman), Al Smith, Mary Dreier, Abram I. Elkus (counsel) and Bernard L. Shientag (assistant counsel). It was a historic association. Through these investigations, she wrote later, Wagner and Smith "got a firsthand look at industrial and labor conditions, and from that look they never recovered." Among the other members the most exotic and attentive was Mary Dreier — young and rich, with china blue eyes — not the kind of woman, Perkins once remarked, whom "one expected to find in social work." Yet as president of the Women's Trade Union League she was an able, dedicated leader.

Besides Wagner and Smith, the commission's legislative members were Assemblymen Edward Jackson and Cyrus Phillips, both of whom attended most of the factory inspections throughout the state, and Senator Charles M. Hamilton, less active in the field but a loyal advocate in Albany of the commission's recommendations. Of the nonlegislative members, Simon Brentano and Robert Dowling were interested almost exclusively in New York City, and AFL president Samuel Gompers proved indifferent to any problem not directly related to his unions. He cared nothing about working women, in sweatshops or not, and even among union men he drew harsh distinctions: "What swine in that outfit!" Perkins was disappointed. She had expected a staunch ally with a broad, generous outlook.[2]

For the commissioners she arranged factory inspections throughout the state, testified on surveys she and her associates had made and brought in experts to advise on such subjects as building construction, fire prevention and insurance. Her responsibilities also included raising money by public subscription to send civic groups to Albany to demonstrate for the commission's bills. The public and sometimes the press incorrectly assumed that she had some official tie to the commission, but as she explained once to a reporter, "The Committee on Safety lent me to the Commission, to organize and supervise its investigations."[3]

Others — witnesses, specialists and civic groups — also lent services or personnel. Without their help the commission could not have accomplished half of what it did, for its appropriations from the legislature were always small. In one six-month period, for example, it received only $10,000, yet held twenty-two public hearings, examined 222 witnesses, published 1986 pages of testimony and met in fifteen executive sessions to formulate recommendations. Its achievements were possible because Wagner and Smith, developing an interest in the problems, provided extraordinary leadership, and because experts in all fields, seeing a chance to make an impact on industrial conditions, provided extraordinary support.[4]

An early inspection tour Perkins arranged for the commissioners was to factories in Buffalo. They started with a candy factory, chosen because its main floor exhibited almost every type of fire hazard. The manager had no idea of the true reason for the visit. Perkins had represented it as something of an honor: Senator Wagner and Assemblyman Smith were coming.

They entered the building from the street, mounting several steps that had no railing, and were greeted in a small front hall. Ahead, an open stairway led to the candy works on the second and third floors. The stairs were wooden, unusually wide, steeply pitched and with a handrail on only one side. In a fire with 300 workers descending in a hurry, some would almost certainly fall and be trampled. A second handrail would be an improvement, but most of the hazards would remain. A fire stair ideally should accommodate only two abreast and not encourage a third to run down the middle without a handrail.

On the landing at the second floor and even on the steps leading to the third was a jumble of mops, pails and brooms. The manager explained that the cleaners often left them there. "Ah," murmured Wagner in the new terminology he was learning, "an obstructed exit."

The second and main floor was a single great room filled with large copper kettles of boiling candy. About 200 employees, mostly young women, were at work. Gas flame was used, and the room was extremely hot. Occasionally, when a kettle boiled over, flames sputtered up the sides. There were no sprinklers. On the floor above there were about 100 more employees at the same sort of work, under similar conditions.

The commissioners began to ask questions. Was there anything to prevent a girl's hair catching fire? Nothing special. How did they keep their hair clean? The manager was not sure, and a glance at the girls' uncovered heads revealed that they did not: globs of chocolate hung in their hair. They had no aprons or uniforms but wore their own clothes, mostly cotton dresses, which were covered with chocolate and sugar filling. Their hands, too, were coated with candy. Was there a washroom? Yes.

They were shown a room containing a sink with cold running water. There were no towels. Of the two toilets, one was plugged, leaving one toilet for all 300 employees, because there was no toilet on the third floor. "It's the best we can do," the manager said.

Were there ever accidents? The girls sometimes got burns, he said, usually on their hands and fingers. One day a girl's dress had caught fire, but others near her had smothered it. He spoke of the accidents as unforeseeable acts of God. To Perkins he seemed a decent man, but without any sense of responsibility.

Hours were long, he admitted: eleven or twelve a day, and seven days a week in the rush season. No, he did not hire children.

But an advantage of visiting a factory in a group was that while one commissioner talked with the manager others could question the workers. In this way Smith learned from two young girls and a boy that children without working papers were regularly employed.

The windows were dirty. "It doesn't pay to have them washed," said the manager. "They just get all steamed up and the syrup evaporates and sticks to the glass. You can't keep them clean in a candy factory."

Did the girls complain of the heat? Yes, they were always complaining. "But you can't boil sugar without heating up the place." The kettles had no hoods or ventilators.

The commissioners went to the rear of the building to look at the fire escape. Three steps led up to a window. Across the window there were three steam pipes through which a person would have to climb in order to reach the fire escape. Smith did it and, looking down, called that he didn't see a ladder at the bottom. The manager explained that it had been removed because boys used to climb up it at night to break in and steal the candy.

As they started back to the front of the factory, they noticed that the aisles were not straight; anyone heading for the exit would have to detour around the tables, kettles and machinery. Some employees would have to move away from the exit in order to reach it.

Downstairs they thanked the manager and left for the next factory, a two-story building. Some experts were arguing that no regulation of two-story buildings was necessary because escape from a window was always possible. In this case, however, the building was almost a block deep, with the windows and the single stairway all to the front. On the ground floor was a novelty shop; upstairs were three small businesses with only a few employees. The novelty shop sold everything that was cheap or gaudy: the counters were covered with displays, the walls and aisles were piled with cardboard boxes, and large baskets were filled with excelsior and wrapping paper. The counters and aisles formed a maze, and at the front of the store the owner was selling, quite legally, all kinds of fireworks. An explosion, a flash fire, and possibly no one would escape, even from the first floor.

By way of contrast Perkins took the commissioners to a pearl button factory that was a model of its kind. The industry had a special problem in that dust produced by grinding the shells was both a health and fire hazard. It damaged the lungs, and particles hanging in the air could cause an explosion. The management had installed a ventilating system with hoods directly over the benches where the buttons were cut and polished. The floor was kept moist so that the dust would stick when it settled. All employees wore uniforms and caps. There were good washrooms, clear aisles to fireproof doors opening outward and three fireproof enclosed stairways leading directly to the street. In New York City, on the other hand, some of the pearl button factories were horrors. But if one company in an industry could make a profit with a fireproof factory, why not another?[5]

Having looked at the fire hazards in factories, studied the best technical advice and held public hearings on its proposals, the commission sent its bills to amend the fire laws to the legislature. The civic groups supporting the bills sent lobbyists and delegations to Albany and in general courted publicity and exploited their channels of influence. Opposition was strong, particularly among conservative businessmen and real estate owners. In a public hearing in December 1912 Perkins, speaking for the Committee on Safety, told the commissioners:

> A great deal of testimony is being given to you to try to influence you to the belief that this legislation is too drastic. I want to say for the Committee that our investigation into the fire hazard in New York City leads us to believe your legislation is not by any means drastic; in our opinion it is not sufficiently drastic.[6]

Later she analyzed the commission's proposals in an article for *Survey*, emphasizing that in addition to such measures as fire drills, sprinkler systems, guards for gas jets and enclosed fire stairways, the commission was advocating a new principle of building construction: the number of exits should not depend upon the structure's area or height but upon the number of persons who must use them. This was a lesson learned from the Triangle fire. Too many workers had been concentrated on the top three stories for the number of exits available. The fire occurred on a Saturday afternoon when only the Triangle workers were in the building. Even if every exit had been open and functioning, it is unlikely that the three floors could have been cleared of 500 workers within three minutes. Certainly it would have been impossible if the six floors below had been disgorging workers into the elevators and stairways at the same time.[7]

In Robert Dowling, the realtor, the conservative business opposition had a spokesman within the commission. During executive sessions when the members were formulating their recommendations he continually emphasized cost, especially the expense of installing improvements like sprinkler systems and enclosed stairways in existing buildings. His role, the accountant of dollars and cents, was unattractive but quite necessary, and he had the respect of the other commissioners. But sometimes his choice of words brought underlying tensions to the surface.

Protesting a proposal one day, he quoted some Fire Department figures on the percentage of people who had lost their lives in factory fires and concluded, "It is an infinitesimal proportion of the population."

Mary Dreier, ordinarily calm, flared up, blue eyes flashing. "But Mr. Dowling, they were men and women! They were human souls! It was a hundred per cent for them!"

Dowling blushed, and Smith made everyone laugh by remarking, "Good Catholic doctrine, Robert!"[8]

In the end Dowling almost always supported the recommendations, a fact that impressed the legislature. In 1913, when the Democrats controlled both the Senate and the Assembly, eight of the commission's fifteen bills were passed, including two of the most important: mandatory fire drills for factories with more than twenty-five employees, and an automatic sprinkler system for buildings of seven or more stories.[9] The following year twenty-six out of twenty-eight bills passed, including a limitation on the number of workers per floor, depending on the number and kind of exits provided, and a construction code requiring more enclosed stairways and fire escapes on new buildings.

The next year, when the Democrats no longer controlled the Assembly, it seemed possible that the new laws might be weakened by amendment. In the closing hours of the session, conservative legislators almost managed to slip through a bill exempting certain types of factory buildings from the new regulations. Amendments, however, can be amended. From the office of the Committee on Safety, Perkins issued a reassuring statement: "Those who think the real estate interests gained these concessions no doubt read copies of their bill *before* it was passed, and not *after* we had amended it . . . The result is that the status remains unchanged."[10]

From that time on, though some of the real estate and business interests continued to lament, the laws were secure. "To own a factory building in New York is now a calamity," said the lawyer for the Real Estate Board of New York, and a spokesman for the Associated Industries of New York insisted that the Wagner-Smith acts would mean "the wiping out of industry in this state." But in a four-story clothing factory in Binghamton on July 22, 1913, a fire killed thirty-five, and another at the Diamond Candy factory in Brooklyn on November 6, 1915, killed twelve. To most persons the new regulations seemed even yet "not sufficiently drastic."[11]

The Factory Investigating Commission also reorganized the state's Department of Labor. Even the legislative members of the commission had been startled to hear the Commissioner of Labor testify that he could not provide them with a list of all the factories in the state. A manufacturer was not required by law to register his building or his product or report the start of his operations or the number of persons he employed. In amazement Smith had asked, "How do your inspectors make their inspections?"

"We have to guess at it or learn by experience," the commissioner replied. "The inspectors get around about once in two years, and if they find a new factory in some building, they write up a report on it."

But with only eighty-five inspectors and 30,699 factories already on the list, there was little time to search out more. In this area, therefore, the commission's first recommendation, passed in 1912, was that all factories be required to register with the Department of Labor within thirty days after beginning operations.[12]

Another problem, especially troublesome in New York City, was the conflict of jurisdiction among the various state and municipal departments. In its *Preliminary Report* to the legislature of 1912 the commission pointed out: "If a man had an obstruction on the fire escape, the Police Department alone could compel him to remove it. He could then move it into the passageway leading to the fire escape and it would come under the jurisdiction of the labor department. It was possible in one factory to have a condition of affairs which called for the intervention of all six [city] Departments in one day" — the Police and Fire departments, the Board of Health, and the Departments of Buildings, Water Supply and Tenement Houses.

The commission recommended that the Department of Labor be given broader powers, many of them to be lodged in a new industrial board of five members. The board would have the authority to amplify existing laws by special rulings "against fire hazards, personal injuries, and disease" in particular industries. For example, the requirement that a manufacturer must provide two exits in his plant could be waived in the case of a salt mine in a tunnel under Elmira Lake, and the mine owner could be asked to furnish some other form of protection. Codes for the various industries would be drawn up by subcommittees of the board composed of architects, engineers, businessmen and realtors.

The commission presented its recommendations in a single omnibus bill, passsed in 1913. In succeeding years the subcommittees were appointed, codes were promulgated and a new kind of department of labor emerged. The change was more than a reorganization; it was a recognition by the state's lawmakers that the industrial revolution had created enormous new problems in labor and industry, which required new solutions.[13]

For similar reasons, at this time the United States Department of Labor was founded, though its role in labor legislation, until Perkins became the Secretary in 1933, was less significant. Established in 1913, when President Taft reluctantly signed the bill on his last day in office, it had few powers, small funds and four ill-matched bureaus to administer: the Children's Bureau and the Bureaus of Labor Statistics, Immigration and Naturalization. Immigration and Naturalization employed about 1800 of the total staff of 2000. Many people then thought that, under the Constitution, labor legislation was not within the federal government's jurisdiction. And indeed, on that ground in 1918 the Supreme Court struck down a federal statute aimed at abolishing the employment of children under fourteen.

During World War I, the U.S. Department of Labor blossomed into the central agency for the government's war labor policies, but after the war Congress again restricted its scope. In the years 1921 to 1929 the Republicans were in power nationally, the country appeared prosperous and the Secretary of Labor was a millionaire who had no feeling of urgency about labor problems. The department, he announced, should be "run for the general benefit and not for the particular interest of organized or unorganized labor." Critics, citing the department's organic act, argued that the purpose for which it had been founded was to help the worker, but they did not prevail. Of this period, Perkins said, "I had some contact with the Labor Department, but not too much because the Labor Department really didn't do too much."[14] The New York Department of Labor in these years was saved from stagnation partly by its broad powers but chiefly by Smith's four terms as governor and by his regular appointment of Perkins to departmental posts. Between them they continued to develop the programs started by the Factory Investigation Commission.

Because of the broad purposes written at Smith's suggestion into the commission's enabling act, it was empowered to investigate working conditions in general, not simply those related to fire. As the commissioners examined labor conditions, they became extremely concerned over child labor and the long hours in some industries. Here the canners, the only ones to win exemption from the 54-hour law covering women and children, were the notorious offenders.

Canneries, which in 1912 employed about 7000 women and 2000 children, were usually located near the crops. A factory would be a one-story summer shed with relatively simple machinery and, as fire escapes, doors and windows opening directly into the fields. The canners, in arguing for their exemption, had made much of their rural surroundings — the sun and air — and of the industry's seasonal nature and problems of spoilage.[15]

The commission's local inspectors, who often worked part-time in factories, kept Perkins advised of the harvests in the farming counties. Once when she had Wagner, Smith, Dreier and Phillips at Auburn to see the rope factories, she also took them to a pea cannery. The inspectors suggested that the visit be unannounced, because it was easy for the canners to send the children into the fields, or even to close down for half a day. They also suggested that any inspection be early in the morning, about five, and that the group on arrival should divide, part going to the back sheds where the peas were shelled and part to the front where the peas were sorted and canned.

One morning, shortly after four, she and the commissioners left Auburn in two dingy Model T Fords and headed into the farming country south of the city. A short distance from the cannery they dropped their guides, who might be recognized, and turned down a lane leading into the fields. Soon they reached a low building with the sun already on it. Getting out quickly, Wagner and Phillips hurried into the front; Smith, Dreier and Perkins went around to the back.

They found a group of women and about a dozen children, all seated on little stools or piles of hay, shelling peas. The older children seemed eleven or twelve, the younger five or six. The women were working extremely fast. A man materialized almost immediately and asked their purpose. Introducing themselves, they said they had come to inspect a cannery.

The man began at once to explain the children: The cannery did not hire them; it was simply that most mothers were unable to leave them at home. And because children are a nuisance unless occupied, their mothers gave them peas to shell. No, the children's names did not appear on the books; a mother submitted a child's work as her own. Pay was by the basket of shelled peas. A fast worker with perhaps a child or two to help her could earn as much as two dollars a day.

He implied it was a good wage, and for an eight-hour day it would have been. But the commissioners discovered that the women worked from four or five in the morning until midnight, and the children until seven or eight in the evening or until they fell asleep. The traditional argument for such long hours, heard often in the debates in Albany, was that the growing and ripening of crops was an act of God and could not be regulated. Though apples could be kept uncanned for long periods and tomatoes for short, peas and beans were perishable and had to be canned at once. Some canners were already using freezing techniques to preserve the vegetables and spread the canning time, and others were planting and harvesting only so much as a regular work crew could handle.[16]

At a public hearing in Auburn the local inspectors brought in a number of women to testify. Several, asked why they worked so long for so little, replied that it was the only "cash work," open to country women. Yes, they were tired. Yes, it was too long to work on one day. Yes, the children got "short shrift" during the summer and fall. Yes, they neglected their families during this period. But they needed the money.

What did they need it for? To pay for a child's education, for a mother's operation, for a new roof, for a cow so they and their neighbors could have milk for the children. None of the reasons could be called foolish.[17]

In this particular pea cannery the front shed, which housed the machinery, was clean and airy. Even so, picking out foreign particles from the peas as they swept by on a belt caused eyestrain, especially at night when the only lighting was a few bare bulbs hanging from the ceiling. And the steady stream of peas on the moving belt often produced a nausea akin to seasickness, in some cases so severe that the women had to quit work. One told an inspector that when she finally got home and sat down with the newspaper, "the print kept flying by just like the peas."[18]

Conditions in other canneries were often worse. Gears and choppers were unguarded, the machines noisy, the floors slippery with mashed vegetables and the lighting poor even in daytime. And there were children everywhere. Once Wagner, arriving at a cannery at seven in the morning, two hours after it had opened, saw a six-year-old leaving. "Where are you going?" he asked. "They say they don't need me today," the boy replied. "I'll have to come back at five tomorrow."[19]

Some canners stoutly denied the bad conditions, the long hours and the children. At a hearing in the Assembly Parlor in the Capitol, one was vehemently contesting the allegations of the witnesses when the commission's lawyer confronted him with a recent Vassar College graduate, Mary L. Chamberlin, who, at the commission's request, had worked in his cannery. The man recognized her at once, broke down and admitted the truth of the charges.[20]

In its *Second Report* to the legislature the commission used its strongest language on the canners: "No words of ours can express too strongly our condemnation of the inhuman greed and avarice that permit women to be thus exploited." It recommended a limit of a ten-hour day and a six-day week, and an absolute prohibition on the employment of children under fourteen.[21]

The canners opposed the bills, and Smith in the debate, while supporting the requirement for one day's rest in seven, gave his shortest and perhaps most quoted speech:

> I have read carefully the commandment "Remember the Sabbath Day, to keep it holy"; but I am unable to find in it any language that says, "except in the canneries."[22]

The bills passed as recommended, with the single amendment that women might be employed for sixty-six hours a week during the pea season, on permission of the Industrial Board. Contrary to the predictions of the canners, the next year there was no shortage of canned vegetables or fruits.

Though a recommendation about wages was not among the commission's original purposes, it was added by the legislature in March 1913, since by then almost everyone could see that the underlying cause of long hours was low wages.[23] No worker, once he had achieved food and shelter, would choose to work twelve or fourteen hours a day.

Investigations of several industries had revealed an astonishingly low wage scale and a sense of desperation among the workers. At a time when $8.00 a week was considered a minimum living wage, workers in the paper box industry averaged $6.50, in the candy industry $6.00 and in department stores $6.00.

The lowest wages and most depressed conditions were in New York City, among the tenement workers. Most of them sewed, made artificial flowers or did some work related to clothing. Typically they were immigrants, women and children, despite the new law forbidding

the employment of children under fourteen. The commissioners, led
by settlement workers and investigators from the Consumers' League,
saw tenement after tenement in which women, sometimes alone, sometimes with their entire families, were doing piecework contracted out
to them by a factory or middleman. Depending on the rate and
number of pieces finished, wages ranged from $.50 to $8.00 a week; the
majority fell between $2.00 and $3.00.[24]

The wages were lower than they seemed, for the work was seasonal
and ceased almost entirely in the late spring and early summer. The
women were old at forty. The children were anemic, and fell asleep in
school from exhaustion. There was also a health hazard to the consumer: in some instances clothing or flowers had been made by people
with contagious diseases.

On an afternoon in December 1912, in the New York County Hall
of Records, an impressive group of women testified before the commission about tenement home work: Dr. F. Josephine Baker, director of
Child Hygiene in the Department of Health; Lillian D. Wald, director of Nurses' Settlement (Henry Street); Rose Schneiderman for
the Women's Trade Union League; Pauline Goldmark for the New
York City Consumers' League; Florence Kelley for the National Consumers' League; and Frances Perkins for the Committee on Safety. In
the course of her testimony Perkins described the life of a woman who
attempted to exist by crocheting slippers.

The wool comes to her from the factory, in the skein, and they also
send from the factory the lamb's wool soles. They are the ordinary
crocheted bedroom slippers. This wool she has to wind into balls,
crochet the slippers, put the fluffy stuff around top, sew the slippers together, with the soles, and complete a pair . . .

She gets up as soon as it is light in the morning and begins to work at
once. She has dependent upon her a little grandchild, who is still a
baby. She works all day without stopping even to prepare her own
meals, only stopping occasionally to give a little food to the child. She
works on steadily until eight o'clock at night, when she is so exhausted
she cannot work longer. She takes a nap — takes literally a nap — for an
hour and a half or two hours. By ten o'clock she is up and at her work
crocheting again, and she works at this crocheting until about two or
half past two in the morning, when she again drops from sheer exhaustion, and goes to bed until half past four or five o'clock and gets
up and begins the day all over again.

The reason she works these hours is because the pay is so low that in
order to make a little money, to make any money at all, she must work
unspeakably long. She gets paid at the rate of 40 cents per dozen pairs

of slippers — 40 cents for 24 slippers. Women who do this work for mere recreation know how long it takes to make a pair. She can make a dozen pairs in two days.

By Mr. Elkus, Commission's counsel:

Q. And these are the kind of slippers here on the table? A. Exactly that kind of slipper.

Q. Well, a manufacturer was here this morning and he said the ladies did that for pin money. A. This woman does it for the bare necessities of life.

By Commissioner Hamilton:

Q. How much does she average a day? A. She makes a dozen pairs in two days, that is 40 cents for two days' work.

Q. Twenty cents a day? A. Yes, sir . . .

By Assemblyman Phillips:

Q. Why doesn't she do something else? A. That is the question again. Because, you see, she has this child whom she must take care of. She is an average talented woman who can do this work, and feels that any work she can do she must do with her hands.

Q. She must be strong if she can work those hours. A. She hasn't any muscular strength to do washing and scrubbing and so on. As a matter of fact, the sum she earns does not support her; she is dependent upon charity for rent, which is paid by a charitable society in this city. It is one dark little room.

By Mr. Elkus:

Q. Suppose work of this character were prohibited now, would she be able to get any other? What would become of her? A. She would be entirely dependent upon charity, possibly, or possibly she would find work in a factory and would have her grandchild cared for by charity. In my opinion it would be infinitely better to have her adequately supported, adequately taken care of, and the child adequately brought up, by a charitable organization. That child is being deprived of the necessities of life altogether, because the money this grandmother earns is not sufficient to provide proper food or a proper place to live for them all.

By Assemblyman Phillips:

Q. As a matter of fact, the charitable organizations are now paying for making those slippers, aren't they A. You mean that they are paying her while she makes them?

Q. They pay the difference? A. Yes.

By Mr. Elkus:

Q. Then it comes out of the consumer in another form, doesn't it?
A. Exactly.

Q. If the price of labor was raised, she would not have to be an applicant for charity? A. Not at all. She might even go to work in the factory and find some suitable place for the child, to have the child cared for. So long as this work continues, I believe you will find just such inhumane hours for the women who do it, for I want to point out that the low wage paid is a lash which is more potent in driving the women on to exhausting hours of work and to exhausting forms of work than any lash of the overseer. The wage of all these industries is so low that in order to make something which will buy even a loaf of bread, the worker must sit up another hour and another hour, and the temptation to do it is almost unbelievable . . .

And I want to point out that there is another attack being made upon an institution which we believe to be of existing value to our social life. I refer to the home; and I mean that as I have seen this system of home-work, I have seen the factory invading and breaking down the home. You cannot have a factory and a home existing inside the same four walls without the home suffering. And it is always the home that suffers, for the mother cannot do for her children what she would ordinarily do. She can't stop making coats at four and five cents apiece and in the middle of the day prepare the nice warm lunch which the children ought to have when they get home from school. And she can't do all the other things that should be done around the home. Yet the poor people have a right to their homes the same as the rich, and simply because they are poor and in need, we should not be allowed to enslave them to a form of industry which refuses them not only all their liberty, but the wage which they ought to have in return for the labor they perform.[25]

For these reasons Perkins wanted the commission to recommend a law absolutely forbidding home work. But the commissioners were not willing to go so far: no one was quite sure what the effect would be on the workers if all sweatshop jobs were abolished. Its recommendation, which the 1913 legislature passed, prohibited home work only in the manufacture of infants' apparel, children's toys and food products. In the same session, however, it put through a bill giving the state Department of Labor power to regulate and inspect all home industries. Though the department might never have enough inspectors, their number was increased, and it seemed likely that in the tenements child labor at least would be reduced. On the whole, reformers were encouraged.

The following year the commission recommended the creation of a wage board with power to suggest minimum wages in accordance with location, industry and general cost of living in a particular section of the state. This was an idea Florence Kelley had brought back in 1908 from an international meeting of Consumers' Leagues held at Geneva. She had heard a report on British legislation, to become effective in 1910, that would create minimum wage boards for certain industries. Similar boards already existed in Australia.

In 1910 the national league adopted it as part of a ten-year program, and in 1912 the Massachusetts legislature passed a weak version of the plan. That year Theodore Roosevelt adopted a minimum wage law as part of the Progressive party platform. Though he was defeated, the idea was discussed, and in 1913 eight more states passed minimum wage laws.[26]

In this area therefore the Factory Investigating Commission followed rather than led what seemed to be a national trend. But the New York legislature refused to pass the bill establishing a wage board. The movement for minimum wage laws slowed, and throughout the 1920s, when there was a reaction against labor legislation, the idea was dormant. In the 1930s it revived with the Depression, and in 1938 Congress passed the Fair Labor Standards Act, which established a nationwide floor for wages. In New York in 1915, however, reformers succeeded in attacking the problem only indirectly: by publicity, by laws prohibiting child labor under fourteen, by laws restricting the goods that could be made at home and by increasing the power and personnel of the state's Department of Labor.

On February 14, 1915, while the commissioners were circulating their final report, which included the recommendation for a minimum wage board, Simon Brentano died. Though he had not signed the report — he was reading it when he died — he had already agreed by letter to its contents, so the others submitted it to the legislature "as having the approval of our lamented colleague."[27]

Samuel Gompers at first refused to sign it, because of the minimum wage recommendation. He and many others in the union movement were against minimum wage laws for fear that in many communities they would be intentionally misconstrued as also setting the maximum wage for the jobs covered. Besides, in trade union theory it was better for workers to win improvements by strike or threat of strike than by legislation. Then they had a reason to belong to a union, and unions would remain strong. Unions did not betray the workers; governments frequently did. "Look to the union" was the first and great commandment — but it offered no protection to women, children or Negroes, whom the unions often excluded.

Smith, who considered himself a friend of organized labor (though Perkins felt that he "knew very little about it"), was astonished by Gompers's refusal. He grabbed his derby and rushed to Gompers's office, where he set out to be charming. Fourteen years later, writing of this meeting, he said of Gompers, "He likes to sit and talk, smoking a cigar and drinking his glass of beer" — all activities in which Smith himself excelled. Sitting, smoking, drinking, describing the women's plight and interlarding his stories with affection and good cheer, he melted Gompers's opposition and left with his signature.[28]

One commissioner, however, not only refused to sign the report but wrote a dissent. Laurence M. D. McGuire, president of the Real Estate Board of New York City, had been appointed in July 1914 in place of Dowling, who had resigned to become the first chairman of the State Workmen's Compensation Board. Dowling's departure, the only break in the commission's continuity of personnel, was a real loss, for he had attended some of the early investigations and hearings of which McGuire had no direct knowledge.

His dissent was more philosophical than factual: he disliked the trend toward regulation of business. No one, he suggested, could show that the new fire laws had saved a single life, yet they were the cause of the decline in building construction in the city. "Thousands of workmen," he wrote, "are without employment and it would be difficult to estimate accurately the privation and hardship which has resulted therefrom." Even so, he said, the "professional agitator" was still driving for more regulation. As evidence he appended a form letter, signed by Perkins, that asked for contributions to the Committee on Safety to support the legislative campaign for better fire laws.

Labor, McGuire concluded, needed no special protection.

> To my mind this is all wrong. We live in a representative democracy and all are laborers. The employer of today is the laborer of yesterday . . . The experience of the past proves conclusively that the best government is the least possible government, that the unfettered initiative of the individual is the force that makes a country great and that this initiative should never be bound except where it becomes a menace to the liberty and initiative of others.
>
> Those laws that are said to be progressive are really reactionary and belong rather to the days of so-called beneficent despotism than to the era of representative government.[29]

The commission's majority issued an answer, in the course of it regretting his attack on Perkins, but there was little ground on which the points of view could meet. Wagner, for example, was an immigrant, brought over by his parents in 1886 when he was nine. At the time he spoke no English, and as the youngest of six children he alone went to school; the others worked. In the end his parents returned to Germany, defeated. Once when a reporter spoke of immigrants "making their way," Wagner burst out, "I came through it, yes. But that was luck, luck, luck! Think of the others!"[30]

Smith was not an immigrant, nor was either of his parents, but he was only twelve when his father died in 1886, and thereafter he had worked to help his mother support the family. They had lived on New York's Lower East Side, and he had seen poverty. Even so he had been shaken by some of the factory investigations.

In Auburn one dawn Perkins had taken him and several other commissioners to the rope works. They watched the women, thin, pale and stooped, coming off their twelve-hour shift as the men for the day shift went in. Some couples stopped for a second to exchange a word or kiss. "It's uncivilized," Smith murmured, and indeed while Perkins watched the two groups, men and women, waiting for the gate to open, meeting briefly and parting as the gate closed, she felt she was watching captives of some unthinking force.

"Let's go with them," she said to Smith and Dreier, and they followed one woman home, while a local inspector with Wagner and Phillips followed another. Though the woman was exhausted, she invited them into her house for coffee, and, after preparing breakfast for her three children and starting them to school, she described her life to them.

With her husband working the day shift and she herself the night, it was the loss in family living that she regretted most. "It's almost impossible for the whole family to do things together," she told them. "When I was a child, we used to go places with my father and mother. My mother never worked. She stayed in a nice farmhouse, and when we came home from school, we knew that she would be there and we'd have a nice time, and when my father came in from the field it was fun. We did things together. He was a working man too, but things were different in those days."

Almost all the women on her street worked at night; it was the only work they could get. But even with double wages in most homes, she felt they were all losing ground. Houses and people alike were deteriorating. She and her husband didn't drink because her family was "strictly temperance," but "down the street there's a crowd that drink as soon as they get home. They say they're so tired they have to have a drink before they can get to their housework."

From that time on Smith would argue with anyone about night

work. "You can't tell me," he'd say. "I've seen these women. I've seen their faces. I've seen them."

Reading the newspaper that evening on the train to Albany, he came across some views that were similar to those in McGuire's dissenting report. Looking up, he said to Perkins: "I can't see what all this talk is about. How is it wrong for the State to intervene with regard to the working conditions of people who work in the factories and mills. I don't see what they mean. What did we set up the government for?" He believed that the purpose of government was to help all the people achieve the "decencies of life":

> The industries of this state can surely afford to put their premises into condition that won't burn people or poison them or give them industrial diseases or cut off their hands or put out their eyes. And it can afford, too, to make their hours of work civilized so that they can stay home nights. And if that means raising the wages then I think they've got to do that. I don't think it's right to let this kind of thing go on unchecked.[31]

She didn't think it right either, and for both of them the moral issue preceded any political or economic program.

Later, in the midst of the Republican "return to normalcy" after World War I, Smith was almost the only governor of the forty-eight to press constantly for more social legislation. An old Tammany politician accounted for Smith's interest in it by saying, "He read a book" — an astonishing judgment, for Smith learned almost nothing by reading books and almost everything by talking to others and observing for himself. Asked to explain, the Tammany man said, "He knew Frances Perkins and she was a book." An exaggeration, certainly; yet with a grain of truth.[32]

The Factory Investigating Commission's term of office was not renewed in 1915, probably as much because the legislature felt that it had completed its work as because the Republicans now controlled both the Senate and the Assembly. In the three and a half years, from 1911 to 1915, it had conducted a revolution in the field of labor and industry. Perkins later spoke of its achievements as "a turning point" in American attitudes and policies toward social responsibility. Its effect on the persons who worked for it was likewise profound. Not only did it give Smith and Wagner an indelible impression of labor problems, but it caused her to develop a lifelong conviction that the best way to improve conditions for workers was through legislation, not unions.[33]

She believed that a union was "a natural and good institution," important to workers for "the raising of their self-respect, of their personal standards, education and capacity to participate in every aspect of American life." Unions were a necessary complement to legislation, yet, as she said in 1952, "I'd much rather get a law than organize a union." She thought it was wrong that workers should have to strike in order to achieve safe conditions, reasonable hours and subsistence wages. These seemed to her the responsibility of society. Besides, strikes were often costly, ineffective, violent, divisive to the community and, even when successful, beneficial to the few rather than the many. Contemplating the peaceful revolution accomplished by the commission, she became convinced that legislation was the better social tool.[34]

Chapter 11

➤➤×⤜⤜

Marriage to Paul C. Wilson. Her name. Women's suffrage. Mayor Mitchel's administration. The Maternity Center Association. Wilson's illness.

HER WORK for the Consumers' League and Factory Commission had sharpened her interest in politics, and in June 1912 on the invitation of a friend she went to Baltimore to watch the Democratic National Convention. Much of the time she spent with two other New Yorkers, Henry Bruère and Paul C. Wilson, economists interested in government. For a week they attended sessions together while Woodrow Wilson slowly overtook Champ Clark and on the forty-sixth ballot won the presidential nomination.[1]

Fifteen months later, on September 26, 1913, she married Paul Wilson in the chantry of Grace Church at Tenth Street and Broadway. No family or friends were present; they had concealed their plans and emotions from everyone.[2] Except for a few letters from mid-1911 and this week at the convention, how they met, where or when are unknown. Both were reserved by nature and, possibly because his subsequent ill health made the marriage difficult, neither confided the details of their courtship to anyone, not even in later life, not even to their daughter. The letters, however, suggest that his heart was the first to be touched, perhaps as early as the summer of 1911: "I wish I could . . . visit the places dear to you . . . God bless you, dear Frances," and "Goodnight, dear."[3]

Neither was young at the time of their marriage; she was thirty-three, and he, thirty-seven. He was of middle height, with thick, dark hair and a remarkable square head and features; he was also quiet and unaggressive, but with enthusiasms easily aroused. His manner and appearance seemed to Robert Moses to indicate a scholar or a lawyer.[4]

Perkins dressed for the wedding alone in her apartment at 164 Waverly Place and presumably walked to the church, which was close by. The Episcopal service was conducted by the Reverend Charles Lewis Slattery, a minister she admired, and the witnesses were strangers, two women collected for the purpose. Afterward she and Wilson left for a trip that was necessarily short, since on October 1 they were to move from their apartments into a small, two-story house they had rented at 121 Washington Place West. Also they were needed in their jobs: she in organizing support for the minimum wage recommendations of the Factory Investigating Commission, and he, as a member of the Bureau of Municipal Research, campaigning for a reform candidate for mayor.[5]

A native of Chicago, Wilson had studied for a year and a half at Dartmouth College and then transferred to the University of Chicago, from which he graduated in March 1902. With Henry Bruère, a young instructor who was his best friend, he worked briefly on a project for the McCormick Harvester Company, and in 1905 the two came to New York to join the staff of the Bureau of Municipal Research — Bruère as director and Wilson as an expert on budgets. There they gave courses on municipal administration and worked for a reform movement, the Fusion party. In the November 1913 elections it captured the city's administration, and the new mayor, John Purroy Mitchel, appointed Bruère his City Chamberlain and Wilson his Assistant Secretary. Since Wilson was one of Mitchel's close friends, the Wilson home on Washington Place (and especially a small, free-standing studio in its backyard) became a meeting place for the reformers. Overnight Perkins found herself at the center of city politics, not altogether a strange world but one in which Smith, Wagner and her Tammany friends began to appear as the enemy. She and Wilson had agreed, however, that their political activities would be separate.

Their life together was comfortable, for in addition to their salaries he had considerable money. They rented the house, they hired a German couple who lived in and they planned a six-month trip to Europe when their jobs were less pressing; meanwhile they frequently entertained. Her friend Agnes Leach remembered Wilson at this time an an exceptional host, handsome, interesting and in every way Perkins's "equal."[6]

Despite her independent life, it seemed natural to Perkins's friends that she should marry. She had always been sociable. At Mount Holyoke she had often invited a high school friend, William Piper, to come "over the Notch" from Amherst. In Worcester and Portland she had always entered social events with zest. She was fond of dancing (she first met Franklin D. Roosevelt at a tea dance) ; she liked people; she enjoyed her friends. That she should have found someone to love did not seem surprising.[7]

But the marriage announcement itself must have been a surprise, both because she had hardly mentioned Paul Wilson to friends outside New York, and because she and Wilson sent out a simple white card:

> PAUL C. WILSON and FRANCES PERKINS
> announce their marriage
> September 26, 1913 New York City

In an age when parents announced their daughter's engagement, when a wife took her husband's name, when couples after a wedding trip were "at home" to friends at a specified time and place, it was an odd announcement; it did not even include an address to which good wishes might be sent.

John A. Kingsbury, a member of the Committee on Safety, was one of the first to respond.

> October 1st 1913
>
> Dear Paul Wilson and Frances Perkins —
>   I take off my hat to Paul C. Wilson — I throw it in the air and hurrah for the man who has been fortunate enough to capture Frances Perkins! I don't know Paul Wilson anything like so well as I know Frances Perkins. Nevertheless, I have always entertained a very high opinion of him: now I know he must be a dandy, or Frances Perkins would never have had him! — I should like to be informed whether either of the names are to be changed? I trust this message will reach you at the address below.
>   With the very warmest congratulations, I am
>
> Sincerely yours,
> John A. Kingsbury

He addressed the letter to Mr. and Mrs. Paul C. Wilson, at Washington Place West.

On October 5 the Worcester *Sunday Telegram* announced the marriage but in a report with such curious mistakes — it gave her college as Smith — that presumably neither she nor her family had a hand in it. Once again there was no indication of where the couple would "make their home" or any biographical description of Wilson. It would seem as though she, who never missed writing a friend or classmate on a marriage, was shy about announcing her own. Perhaps she felt she was too old, at thirty-three, for the usual forms to be appropriate, or perhaps she consciously intended to minimize the importance of marriage.[8]

Years later, attempting to explain her attitude at the time, she said:

> There was a kind of New England pride in me. I wasn't very anxious to get married. To tell the truth, I was reluctant. I was no longer a child, but a grown woman. I hadn't wanted to marry. I liked life better in a single harness, and the older I grew the less likely I was to marry. Young girls marry at eighteen to twenty-two, and it doesn't much matter whom they pick. A girl, at that age, usually marries the first man she sees who gives her a thrill. That's that. It's over. She accepts the situation. Having passed that period without fatal commitments, for one reason or another, I was on the whole rather anxious not to marry.
>
> When I did, Pauline Goldmark lamented, "Oh, Frances, why did you marry? Oh dear, you were such a promising person. Why did you marry?" She felt I would be less interested in the social work movement and the Consumers' League.
>
> I remember replying, "It's hard to say, Pauline, but I thought I better marry and get it off my mind, because I was always being challenged by somebody who thought he should marry me or wanted to recommend the institution. Marriage was constantly put to me, and I spent so much time, in the course of a year, analyzing the reasons for and against it, I finally thought, 'I better marry. I know Paul Wilson well. I like him. I've known him for a considerable time. I enjoy his friends and company, and I might as well marry and get it off my mind.' "
>
> I remember Pauline saying, "That's a strange reason for marrying — to get it off your mind."[9]

Perhaps out of shyness Perkins implied less than the truth, for at the time at least she had been very much in love. In the weeks before her marriage she could hardly bear the separation from Wilson. From Maine, where she was vacationing, she wrote him almost every day, sometimes twice a day, sometimes by special delivery. One eight-page effusion about the ache of loneliness ended: "To think I write you like this!! I am a different woman. I am indeed."

He replied, "I feel you and your perfect love have power to make me see things anew . . . I want, I need to tell you everything. I must. I adore and worship you, beloved, dearly beloved." And she wrote of the joys before them "as we summon the courage to really know each other and as with spiritual daring we admit each other to the inner places."[10]

She had never before admitted anyone to her inner places; she intended the marriage to be complete and for life. She looked forward to children and to reducing the pace of her work. As her full-time, paid job for the Committee on Safety came to an end, she would replace it with volunteer work, two or three days a week.

She and Wilson agreed that she would retain her name for most purposes. In her work, she believed, it had attained some authority, which would be lost if she changed it. In addition, besides a strong feeling in much of the world that a married woman should not work but should put her husband's affairs first, there was a potential conflict in their political roles: how could she as Mrs. Wilson publicly attack the city's policy on fire prevention when Mr. Wilson was the mayor's Assistant Secretary? She would have greater freedom and effectiveness as Frances Perkins.

Looking back, she acknowledged that she also had acted from feminist ideas. "My generation was perhaps the first that openly and actively asserted — at least some of us did — the separateness of women and their personal independence in the family relationship. There was always talk about: should a man support his wife, should he give her an allowance, should everything he had be hers, or did she earn her keep as a housewife?" Several years earlier she had told Amy Peters's younger sister, who was about to marry, that it was "not right" for a woman, on marriage, to be forced to give up her individuality and change her name.

The world, however, clung to its old ways. Within two weeks of their marriage a reporter with a photographer at his side came to the house to question her about her name. Wilson, "a much franker person than I am and also much quicker to anger," was indignant, but she asked him to search for something upstairs, and he took the hint. To the reporter she said soothingly that of course she still took phone calls as Miss Perkins since many people as yet knew nothing of her marriage; the confusion would continue for only a short time. She had no idea, she said, of whether she approved of women keeping their maiden names; she had given it no thought. Eventually the reporter departed without a story or picture.[11]

She had a more difficult time with the Mount Holyoke alumnae office. Acting on its own, it began addressing mail to her as Mrs. Paul C. Wilson. She sent it an icy letter of correction. Months later it was still using her married name, and she returned an alumna form with the statement "Do not use husband's name either socially or professionally or legally." She omitted his name from the space provided, but someone at Mount Holyoke supplied it. On later forms she left no blanks but filled in "Married Name" with Frances Perkins.[12]

She was as firm with the Mutual Benefit Life Insurance Company of New Jersey. The company's lawyers, in preparing a policy in her name with Wilson as beneficiary, tried to "compromise" her with "Frances Perkins Wilson, alias Frances Perkins." She hired a lawyer, who demonstrated that there was no legal requirement for a woman to change her name on marriage; it was "nothing but a custom."[13]

All her life she helped women who wanted to make an issue of this point, providing them with a summary of her lawyer's memorandum and using her influence on stubborn institutions, such as the Department of State. Eventually the high position she attained in government was itself an effective example in resolving these disputes. "It is a matter of common knowledge," declared the Oklahoma Supreme Court in sustaining a woman's right to choose the name by which she will be known, "that at the present time there is a very distinguished woman holding an office in the cabinet of the President of the United States and transacting official business in a name other than her own married name."

Yet in purely social gatherings she was content with Mrs. Wilson and, stories to the contrary, when traveling with her husband she always registered in hotels as his wife. Not to do so she thought "absurd." It was only in the working and institutional world that she insisted on being Frances Perkins.

In her contribution to the Fourth Class Letter, in 1915, she tried to minimize the differences between her life and the lives of her Mount Holyoke classmates. She wrote less about her work and more about "trying to raise bulbs in a New York backyard" and of "a shack in the country on the edge of Long Island Sound" where she and her husband went on weekends, "winter and summer." That would be appreciated in New England, where friends assumed that life in New York was unbearable. Then, "I know that many of you believe in your hearts that I live in a sleeping car and let my husband eat delicatessen food out of a paper bag. No, really I don't. I have a comfortable though old-fashioned house, and there always appear to be plenty of competent professional household workers who want to take care of the house and me and my man. I've never been so comfortable on that side of life, although I never know what I'm going to have for dinner."

Still, the name rankled, even among friends. Once when she and Wilson were going to Portland, she telegraphed Amy Peters, now Mrs.

Eugene Nickerson, that they would be at the Eastland Hotel. Amy had been staying with her classmate Louise Gilman, one of Perk's best friends. The two called the Eastland and asked for Miss Frances Perkins. "No such person registered" was the reply. A few moments later they called again, asked for Mrs. Paul Wilson and were told, "She is expected." The conspirators took this evidence of inconsistency as a kind of victory over Perkins, and when they taxed her with it, she had once again to explain her position. Eventually her friends accepted it; her critics, all her life, used it as a club to beat her.[14]

The Factory Investigating Commission submitted its final report to the legislature in February 1915, and the work of the Committee on Safety began to wind down. Sometime early that spring she bore a child who "died shortly thereafter" — which was as much as she would ever say of the event; her feelings and thoughts she kept entirely to herself. Few if any of her friends in later life knew of the lost child, and even within the family Susanna's knowledge that the infant's death was deeply felt by its parents came more from her father than her mother.

As a result of the pregnancy, Perkins contracted septicemia and was forced to spend several months in bed. She kept up with her work by telephone, however, and in the final days of the session fellow lobby- ists, among them Pauline Goldmark, Robert Binkerd and Joseph Hammit, presented her committee's position on bills before the legis- lature.[15]

By fall she had recovered and was giving speeches again for women's suffrage, which was to be put before the voters (all men) in a refer- endum in November. For the first time the movement's leaders in New York City had organized the campaign to appeal to immigrants and workers, and leaflets were distributed and speeches delivered in twenty-four languages. The campaign's climax was a parade, in which Perkins marched, on October 23, 1915. About twenty-four thousand women (and two thousand men) dressed in the suffrage colors, yellow, blue and white, started at Washington Square and proceeded up Fifth Avenue to Fifty-ninth Street. Their divisions were led by 74 women on horseback and included 57 marching bands and 145 automobiles. Almost a quarter of a million people watched them and applauded. But in November the men of the state rejected votes for women by 748,332 to 553,348.

Nevertheless Perkins, who had marched in a state of exaltation, felt the campaign had been worthwhile. She was impressed by the solidar- ity and friendship that developed among women of all ages and backgrounds who found themselves working outside their homes in a common cause. She theorized later that the movement was a new experience for most women. Until then their friendships had formed only if chance had put them in the same class at school, or made them neighbors, or had given them children of the same age or husbands who were friends. Campaigning for a shared ideal, she believed, was, for the majority, a new experience, forging stronger emotional and intellectual ties than they had known. "Those people," she remarked once, with all the emphasis she could muster, "were the ones who stood by me when I was in trouble as a public officer many years later."[16]

The following February her father died at seventy-one after a short illness. He was buried in Maine in a small cemetery just a half mile down the road from the family home. Later that year his daughter Fanny again became pregnant, and on December 30, 1916, she gave birth to a girl, whom she named after a maternal ancestor, Susanna Winslow, wife of the second governor of the Plymouth colony. Both parents enjoyed the child; children, particularly when very young, always appealed to Perkins. But she still had her job for the Committee on Safety to finish, so she hired a nurse to help with the baby.

A few years before his death her father had become sole owner of the family property at Newcastle, and it now passed to her mother, who continued to go there every summer. A tradition developed that Fanny's younger sister, Ethel (who had married Frederic Harrington, a dentist in Worcester), would take her children there for July, and Fanny and Susanna would go down in August, sometimes staying into September. In this way another generation of children began to visit the old house and to play on the Damariscotta.

Throughout these summer months of separation Wilson would write regularly, almost daily, full of questions and worries about the baby. He longed for their return. One summer, after several weeks of being apart, he wrote to his beloved Frances, "I am so happy and glad that you will *soon* be close beside me. In my arms, in my eyes, seeing I cannot do anything so well without you. Your last letter was wonderful in its penetration and grasp. I adore you, I admire you, and rely upon you greatly. Your lover, Paul."[17]

In New York during the winter of 1916 the Wilsons did a great deal of entertaining, much of it connected with the city government. Wilson's position of Assistant Secretary was more important than the title suggests, for he not only carried out policy but helped to shape it. When the garment workers held a fourteen-week strike in the spring and summer of that year, his memoranda were the basis of Mitchel's actions, day by day, and placed the city government for almost the first time on the side of the workers.

In all such matters Perkins was careful to remain a bystander, but inevitably she heard sooner than the public that the administration was running into trouble with its reforms. Under Mitchel's leadership the quality of the city government, which had begun to rise with his predecessor, William J. Gaynor, continued to improve, and when Bruère proclaimed that his own office of City Chamberlain was obsolete and should be abolished, even foreign newspapers noted the administration's reforming attitude. But local bureaucrats and politicians took it ill.

Unfortunately, Mitchel's manner also offended them. He was a tall, steely-eyed, long-nosed man with a flaming temper — a passionately honest man whose intensity, even when he was calm, disturbed many. His grandfather, John Mitchel, had been a famous Irish patriot, but the mayor refused to be sentimental about Ireland or the Irish. Tammany men, who had been prepared to love him at the slightest wooing on his part, came to hate him. His honesty, energy and ability emphasized their laziness, ineptitude and small corruptions. By midsummer 1916, with elections due the following year, the opposition to him was stiffening rapidly.

Many reform strategies were planned in the Wilsons' house. The German couple would serve lunch, and the politicians would retire to the studio in the backyard to debate their problems. Even if a discussion began at the dinner table, Perkins was careful not to intrude. And when some individual, racked by a decision, poured out his anguish to her, she practiced listening, not speaking.

Wilson also offered their house to the mayor as a hideaway from City Hall. Mitchel suffered from prostrating migraine headaches and, when afflicted by one, he would retreat to Washington Place, where a bedroom was set aside for him. After several hours of rest he would usually recover and return to his office.

Of all the reformers and politicians who passed through the house Perkins became fondest of Wilson's friends, Bruère and his wife, Jane. Like Wilson, they were natives of Chicago, and Perkins discovered that they had many friends in common. Jane Bruère was an intellectual, articulate woman, with a highly diverting, modest manner of presenting her views. Bruère was an unusually competent economist and administrator. In the opinion of some of his friends he was considerably shrewder than Wilson and had a strong drive to know the right people and to make money. At the same time he had a vigorous social conscience. Eventually, as president of the Bowery Savings Bank, he achieved his financial and social ambitions while doing more than any other bank president for the city's poor.

With Mitchel's wife, Perkins found little in common. Olive was pretty and sweet but gave her husband little political support. She rarely appeared beside him in public; she preferred private dinner parties at the Vanderbilts'. "Not remotely worthy of him," was the judgment of one reformer, Robert Binkerd. Perkins was almost as censorious: "She enjoyed what money bought. She was not interested in politics." She wanted a comfortable, chic life filled with smart parties; "her attitudes were commonplace." It bored her to sit on a windy platform or in a hot auditorium while a politician took a thousand words to say what might be said in one. Revealing as much about herself as about Olive, Perkins said, "It is kind of grubby going around with politicians unless you happen to enjoy the human race in its many peculiar aspects."[18]

As the campaign for mayor developed in the autumn of 1917, it became extremely nasty. The reformers, led first by Gaynor and then by Mitchel, for eight years had excluded Tammany from patronage, and Murphy and his district leaders were determined to recapture the administration of the city. They found their most inflammatory issue in what they claimed was an attack on the Roman Catholic church.

The controversy began when Mitchel's Commissioner of Charities and Perkins's friend, John A. Kingsbury, filed charges against the secretary of the State Board of Charities. He alleged failure to maintain the state's minimum standards of health and safety in certain charitable institutions, Catholic and non-Catholic. The charges were against the state officer, not the charities, but they could be tested only by examining conditions in the institutions.

In the hearings there were claims and denials that the Catholic charities, mostly orphanages and hospitals run by nuns, were condoning mistreatment of children, spiriting witnesses out of town and attempting to block the investigation. Mitchel, himself a Catholic, steadily maintained that church institutions must be subject to examination like any others. Because of his stand, Murphy succeeded in turning many Catholics against him.

There was also testimony, admitted to be true, that the police on Kingsbury's orders had tapped the telephones of various institutions, Catholic and non-Catholic. Perkins, as she listened to the discussions in her home, was less and less in sympathy with Kingsbury. She felt he was pushing Mitchel too hard. He had become fanatical on the subject of institutional reform and was "unwilling to recognize that large objects, like the Roman Church, move slowly." From her own observation she was prepared to believe his stories about unsanitary conditions in the kitchens of Catholic institutions and of their meager and improper diet. But she recognized, too, that the archbishop, though he could instruct the Sisters of Charity on faith and morals, could not give them orders on how to run their kitchens. That had to be done by persuasion and education, which required time. Kingsbury, however, had "this fatal streak in him of no compromise."

Fanned by the newspapers, the vituperation on all sides mounted, and among the rank and file of the Democratic party, Mitchel effectively was vilified. On election day he and the reform movement went down in stunning defeat. In 1913 he had won 57 percent of the total vote; in 1917, 24 percent.

There were issues other than the Catholic charities. Mitchel was unlucky in the war, which the country had entered in April. From 1914 on he had supported the Allies, which had angered the Germans in the city and infuriated the British-baiting Irish. Ultimately, though, all issues reduced to a failure to build a popular base for the reform movement. Smith, as governor, would launch his reforms on such a wave of popular sentiment that if on occasion he took the unpopular side of a particular issue, he was able to ride out the storm and continue on course. Theodore Roosevelt summarized Mitchel's defeat in a phrase encompassing both Olive Mitchel and intricate politics: "Too much Fifth Avenue; too little First Avenue."[19]

So severe was the defeat that Mitchel took it, apparently, less as a political setback than as a permanent repudiation of himself and his values. Though he was almost forty and too old for service, he obtained an exemption to join the air force and, while training in Louisiana, died by falling from his plane into a swamp. Many who knew him believed that his death was not accidental; that he had jumped from the plane's cockpit, either because of a migraine headache or because of disappointment with himself, with Olive and with life.[20]

Mitchel's friends, Wilson among them, took his defeat and death very hard. Perkins grieved with them, but having seen social change brought about by many different methods, she did not believe that, because of one election, reform was at an end. In fact, when Patrick Joseph Hayes became Archbishop of New York in 1919, the church began a complete overhaul of its charities. She saw no need for Mitchel's "heart to have been broken." He was "too intense," too easily disappointed.[21]

Another result of the 1917 election was that, in a second statewide referendum, women won the vote in New York. Although the leaders of the suffrage movement, all middle-class women of native stock, had worked for the cause for generations, they succeeded only after campaigning effectively in the immigrant, working-class districts of the state's industrial cities. In rural upstate the referendum was defeated by 1500 votes; in New York City it won by 103,863. The spread of the movement apparently originated in the social changes brought about by the industrial revolution. Perhaps, as Jane Addams had argued, the modern city necessitated the women's vote because it absorbed so many of her interests: for a city woman to care properly for her family she needed a voice in the government that determined whether her home had pure water, fresh food, proper sanitation and adequate police and fire protection. Perkins, like most social workers, believed that once women got the vote they would take a great interest in social projects. The suffrage victory in New York, the country's most populous state, was widely taken as a sign that shortly women in all states would have the vote, probably by amendment of the federal Constitution.

By 1917 the Committee on Safety was all but dissolved, and one volunteer project Perkins undertook in its place reflected the new political emphasis on women. Immediately after the elections the Women's City Club established a program to educate women on the structure and procedures of city government. Perkins agreed to serve as director, but she quickly discovered that "when it came right down to it, the ladies didn't like to go to the Board of Estimate meetings, sit and listen to the dreary debates, follow the budget in great detail and become competent on it. They thought it would be fine for me to do all that and tell them what they thought." With an occasional brilliant exception, the women resisted education in city government, and after several months the project was dropped.[22]

For the same club, however, she soon took part in "the most successful piece of social work I have ever seen organized." The Maternity Center Association, a national voluntary group still in existence, was founded in 1918 with Perkins as executive secretary. Its purpose was to combat the extraordinarily high death rates of mothers and babies in the months surrounding birth.

From 1911 on, in an expanding program, a number of doctors, voluntary committees and the city's Health Department had discovered, by conducting surveys, that 40 percent of the infant deaths occurred in the first month after birth, that most deaths were caused by injuries or lack of care before or during birth and that most mothers received no prenatal instruction of any kind. Also, about 35 percent of deliveries were performed in a hospital; of the balance, at home, 30 percent were by midwives, 25 percent by general practitioners and 10 percent by obstetricians. As a result, in 1918 in the United States 9.2 mothers were dying for every thousand live births — the rate, of course, being much higher among the poor — whereas in sixteen other countries with comparable statistics the rate was considerably lower.

In September 1917 the Women's City Club opened the first Maternity Center in the city, at Hartley House in the Hell's Kitchen district. Expectant mothers were sought out and urged to visit the center to see a doctor, to receive nursing care and to learn from exhibits and demonstrations how to prepare for and take care of their babies. The center also provided a housekeeper service in which neighborhood women were employed to run the mother's home until she could safely do it herself again.

The project was so successful that the following April a group of nine, among them Perkins, founded the Maternity Center Association, to develop similar centers in each of ten zones covering all of Manhattan. Acting as the association's executive secretary, Perkins set out to create its administrative structure, integrating the work of its various committees, doctors, nurses and volunteers. She attended all meetings, prepared minutes, sent out notices, examined clinical techniques used in other cities, devised uniform records so that meaningful statistics could be kept, investigated the possibility of maternity insurance and helped to raise money.

The response from the community was extraordinary. Most of the women who worked in the centers as volunteers had been able to afford the best medical care for their own pregnancies and wanted passionately to make it available to all women. Perkins herself at this time had a small child; she also knew what it was to lose a baby and to be ill from the complications. Like the other volunteers, she felt a special responsibility for the association. Of her coworkers she said, "They were young women completely caught up in the operation of that basic emotion known as maternal feeling, which is very expansive. They felt, therefore, warm, sympathetic and tender toward every other child in the world." The association demonstrated, she believed, that if women could be drawn into public life, it might be conducted more humanely.

The support given the association by private citizens was possible only in a large city with a pool of private wealth and competent personnel. For rural areas and small towns, a national approach was formulated by Julia C. Lathrop, chief of the Children's Bureau in the federal Department of Labor. Beginning in 1918, each year she offered Congress a bill to extend maternal and child health services throughout the country. Congressmen showed little interest until the nineteenth amendment to the Constitution — the provision for women's suffrage — was declared ratified on August 26, 1920. Then pressure for the bill increased, with most of the leading women's groups actively supporting it. Just before Christmas of that year Florence Kelley spoke in its favor at a Senate hearing, giving what many people thought the most eloquent speech of her career, and in January the bill, known as the Sheppard-Towner Act, was passed.

Perkins's position as executive secretary to the Maternity Center Association was unsalaried and a step toward a less demanding working life. The hours were flexible and the routine relatively simple for an experienced administrator. Certainly when she accepted the position she had no idea of becoming a leader of social reform. "What social projects I did, which seem to have been successful, I took up because at the moment they moved me very deeply. They seemed right." And, in a sentence reminiscent of Mary Lyon and Mount Holyoke, she added, "Nobody else was there to do it, and I did it."

She was still planning to have "at least one more child" and to devote herself more to her family. As her committee jobs ended, she would not replace them.[23]

Sometime in the winter or spring of 1918, however, Wilson became ill in a way that perhaps neither he nor his wife ever clearly understood. Among his friends he had a reputation for drinking occasionally to excess, but apparently this was only a response to some deeper trouble, which now surfaced. "He suffered from an up and down illness," Perkins said later.

> It was always up and down. He was sometimes depressed, sometimes excited.
>
> The cycle was terribly irregular. From nineteen-eighteen on there were never anything but very short periods of reasonably comfortable accommodations to life. It was always something. But, of course, there are

degrees in that. Sometimes he was hospitalized, sometimes not. Sometimes he would go off on a little trip. Sometimes he would have an attendant who was called a secretary. There was great variety in the whole process.

The hospital, the trips and the attendants came later, in the 1930s. During the first ten years of his illness, until early in 1929, he managed to hold various jobs; the last, which he held the longest, was with the Equitable Life Assurance Society. But "whether he did anything that would be called competent or not," Perkins was never sure.

At the start neither of them expected him to be sick for long, and perhaps at first both thought of it as a physical rather than emotional or mental illness. It proved otherwise, and she developed a strong reserve about it. With most friends she did not discuss it or even mention it, and she has left no description of its first manifestations. But it was accompanied and perhaps brought on by an experience that reshaped their lives: just as she was reducing her career to become more of a mother and housewife, he lost all his money gambling in gold stocks.

> Then this accident occurred, and I saw it couldn't be done. I saw that I must get more work to do in nineteen eighteen. I had to hustle to find things to do that would see us through that crisis, because the money we thought we had also had disappeared. Part of the illness, really, had to do with the exaggerated use of money. That's just one of the accidents of life.

By nature and intent she pushed such accidents "into the background. I haven't brooded over them and had a Freudian collapse." She tried to take practical action.

They were not faced with immediate bankruptcy, and Wilson soon recovered enough to go to Washington and take a job with the Shipping Board. He had a small apartment in a house on I Street, which was owned by a friend of his father's, and she went down regularly to see him. At the time Bruère, who had a consultant's position with the U.S. Employment Service, also was frequently in Washington, and the three often ate together at the Shoreham Hotel. In the coming years Bruère was probably the only friend with whom she openly discussed Wilson's illness, and she constantly turned to him for advice.

Most of her friends knew little or nothing about it. Wilson, like the other reformers, was unemployed after Mitchel's defeat, and it doubtless seemed natural and patriotic that he should take a war job in Washington. Many men had taken such jobs, leaving wives at home, and in the general confusion few people noticed the domestic crises of friends.

As the months passed, however, Perkins gradually realized that she would have to take responsibility for the family's finances. The money lost could not be replaced, and Wilson's earnings in the future would be uncertain. She could hope that he would recover, but she could not count on it, and as she said, "That did make a difference."[24]

PART IV

Public Office

The New York State
Labor Department

Chapter 12

➤➤❮❮

Smith appoints her a member of the state's Industrial Commission.
Senator Frawley and how to dress. Initial reforms on the commission.

IN THE 1918 elections Smith ran for governor against the Republican
Charles S. Whitman, who was seeking a third term. It was the first
election in which women could vote, but not until late October did
the Independent Citizens' Committee for Smith create a Women's
Division to campaign among the many women's groups. Both Perkins
and Mary Dreier were members, but it was conceived and directed by
Belle Moskowitz, whom Perkins had introduced to Smith.[1]

The election was close. Smith had Tammany's enthusiastic support,
but outside New York City that was a liability. Upstate his Catholicism and his position against Prohibition were also against him. But at
the last minute he was aided by a subway accident in Brooklyn, which
killed ninety and which he was able to blame, with some justice, on
Whitman's appointments to the Public Service Commission. Outside
Manhattan and Brooklyn he lost by 132,480 votes, but in those two
boroughs his margin of 186,382 carried him into office.

On a Sunday in January, soon after Smith was inaugurated, Perkins
was in Washington with Wilson when she received a phone call from
Abram I. Elkus, who had been counsel for the Factory Investigating
Commission. In New York they frequently consulted on legislation
that the Consumers' League wanted, but now Elkus, who had been
chairman of the Independent Citizens' Committee for Smith, was
calling for the governor. Smith wanted to see her the next morning, if
that was possible. Elkus either didn't know or wouldn't say why, but
she suspected that Smith was ready to propose an amendment to the
child labor law. She had already discussed it with him and had
material prepared for drafting the bill. She would be in Albany by

noon, she told Elkus. Later that morning another call came — this time from Wagner, who had the same message.

"What do you suppose that means?" she asked Wilson. "Can it be just child labor?"

"Probably. But you'd better have your other recommendations in writing," he said. "He'll be getting his legislative program in order."

The next day in Albany, after she and Smith had exchanged greetings, she started to present her material on child labor. "We'll talk about that later," he said. "I've got something else." She sat back.

"I was thinkin'," he began. Then he asked abruptly, "How would you like to be a member of the Industrial Commission of the State of New York?"

The idea was so startling — in New York no woman had ever been appointed to anything but an advisory board, much less one of the Labor Department's top administrative posts — that the best she could manage was, "You mean it, Governor? You mean it?"

"Yeah," he said, "I was thinkin' of appointin' you."

The idea left her speechless. They were in the governor's small, inner office; big blue velvet curtains hung on the window. Without realizing that she was turning her back on him, she rose and went to the window. After a moment, having found a thought, she faced around and said, "Well, I think you ought to think it over."

"I've been thinkin' it over!" he said. "Furthermore, I asked you to come up. Don't you think I've thought about it?"

"Well, it's quite a surprise to me," she murmured.

"Didn't Elkus let on to you?"

She shook her head.

"I told him not to," Smith said, "but I thought he would."

"It's so astonishing," she said. "I just don't know. How did you get the idea of appointing me to this or to any public office? It's so unusual."

"I'll tell you," he replied, "because I've been thinkin' about it. In the first place, I think the Industrial Commission is in terrible condition. We brought all that out when we were making the investigation. I know you know about it because you have testified about it. You've studied the commission and the way it's organized and operated. I was thinkin' we've got to reform that, to turn it inside out and get it to be a good department.

"In the second place, I've been thinkin' over my situation since the election. Women have got the vote. It's the first time. Women are going to vote from now on." He looked up in a way she thought innocent and tentative, as if still not sure of his judgment. "I thought I ought to show some attention to women. I ought to bring women into the political picture in my administration. I thought about you."

"Why me?"

"I know a lot of women," he said. "Most of them in the Democratic party are the wives and sisters of political leaders. They're all right. They're nice women, but they don't know anything about things like this. They don't know anything about government. I didn't want to appoint somebody's sister or wife. That's kind of an insult to women, to appoint somebody just because she's related.

"Don't forget, I've known you a long time in Albany. I remembered that when you were appearing before committees, you had somethin' to say. You said it quick, you said it clear, and I could understand it. I knew, too, what you said was true — I could rely on it. When you got through, you sat down. That's more than most people can do. I thought the way you had appeared before committees, the way you had appeared before the Factory Commission, the way you could always make everybody on the committees understand what you said, the way you knew about the Industrial Commission and had ideas about it, would make you a good appointment. What's the matter with that?"

In her astonishment, however, she was still defensive. "You ought to give me time to think about this."

"Have you anything on your conscience," he pressed, "makin' you feel it wouldn't be right to be a public officer?"

She hadn't, but he sensed what was on her mind.

"Your husband won't object, will he?"

She didn't think so.

"I know Paul," he said. "He won't object. He's interested in public affairs. I think you better do it. I think it's the right thing for you to do, and I don't think you ought to delay long."

"Let me ask one person's advice," she suggested.

"Sure, but I think you might just as well tell me now you'll do it. Whose advice do you want?"

"I want to ask Mrs. Florence Kelley."

"Oh, you do!" he exclaimed. "What an idea! She'll say 'Glory be!' "

"I'm not so sure," Perkins remarked, her assurance beginning to return. "I think she finds a great distinction between people who work for the Consumers' League, who work for social betterment, and mere political administration."

"Say," he remarked, "there'd better not be any of that separation much longer if we're to get good government. If you girls are going to get what you want through legislation, there'd better not be any separation between social workers and the government."

She left thinking that she would take the job.[2]

The next day she found Florence Kelley, who was about to take a train, in the Pennsylvania Station. They had time for a cup of coffee, and Perkins began to recount her meeting with Smith. "Glory be to God!" Kelley broke in, her eyes filling with tears. "You don't mean it. I never thought I would live to see the day when someone we had trained, who knew about industrial conditions, cared about women, cared to have things right, would have the chance to be an administrative officer."[3]

Two days later, on January 15, Smith announced the appointment. Under the state's constitution it had to be confirmed by the Senate, which the Republicans controlled, 29 to 22. Smith, as he must have foreseen, would have a fight.

The first skirmish occurred at once, in his own office. The Attorney General insisted he could not make out the papers for the Senate in any name but Frances Perkins Wilson. She was married. Wilson was her name.

Smith called her and she spouted the legal argument her lawyer had used with the insurance company. "Sounds like common sense to me," Smith said. "The name by which you're generally known is the legal name." She heard him tell the Attorney General, "Send it in as Frances Perkins."

In the next four weeks manufacturers complained she was usurping a manufacturer's seat on the commission; labor officials that she was not a union member; men that she was not a man; and Senator George F. Thompson of Niagara that "agitation has been so closely linked with her name that she would not change it when she got married." In Worcester a newspaper with pride proclaimed: "Fanny Perkins, Former Worcester Girl, Gets $8000 Job and Starts a Rumpus." The envious begrudged her the money, said to be the highest salary any woman had earned in state government. But Smith stood firmly on her qualifications, which in the end proved decisive. On February 18, thirteen Republican senators joined the Democratic minority to confirm the appointment, 34–16.[4]

She had not intended to be a leader among women in government, but fate had made her one. And also her grandmother, who used to say, "If somebody opens a door for you, unexpectedly, without connivance on your part, walk right in and do the best you can. It's the Lord's will for you."[5]

She resigned her position at the Maternity Center Association, knowing that she would miss it and be missed, but in her circumstances glad to have a full-time job that paid so well. The government post took her for the first time into a world almost exclusively male. It was the world in which she would spend most of her career, often resented, sometimes slandered and once threatened with impeachment. For protection she had her technical competence and an unusually varied background of human experience.

She had learned one lesson she considered valuable for a woman in government from an extraordinary episode in 1913, when a Democratic Senate and Assembly had impeached a Democratic governor, William Sulzer. Murphy, the leader of Tammany, had put Sulzer into office, whereupon the governor, a stiff-necked man, tried to lead a crusade against "boss rule." The grounds of impeachment were that Sulzer had falsified his report of campaign expenditures. He was indeed guilty, but his guilt was not the reason he was impeached. The real issue was independence, and Perkins felt that the impeachment was actually the result of a personality ill matched to the job. She viewed history less in terms of impersonal forces than of personalities. As she said of it once, "Personality meets the situation, and these are the reactions."[6]

One day as the impeachment proceedings were getting under way, she was in Albany lobbying for factory bills with little success, since the legislators could talk only of Sulzer. Entering the Capitol from a side door after lunch, she saw coming down the hall Senator James J. Frawley, the chairman of the legislative committee investigating the governor. Frawley was a Tammany stalwart, a florid, rough man of ungrammatical language who liked to swathe his prominent stomach in a pink shirt, low-cut plaid waistcoat and two or three yards of gold chain. He was not an important senator or even a reputable one, but from trying to win his vote she was acquainted with him, and she wished him a good afternoon.

He gave a kind of gasp, as if she were a ghost, and clutched her hand. "Oh, Miss Perkins, we've done a terrible thing!"

"Senator?" His directness startled her.

"Oohh, it's a dreadful thing. Oohh, we're in a dreadful predicament." Pulling out his handkerchief he began to mop his face, and then to sob, holding fast to her hand all the time. "Oohh, that man. Oohh, that man. He's so stubborn. Oohh, we tried to save him. I tried to save him myself. All he must do is drop this business. We don't want to impeach him. No one wants to ruin him. This will ruin him, ruin him forever! Oohh, it's a terrible thing!" He wept.

"Now, Senator Frawley," she began. "I'm sure it's terrible, but . . ."

"We had to do it. He wouldn't give us any way out. He just wouldn't agree. He wouldn't give us any way out. Oohh, it's a dreadful thing."

While she was murmuring "I'm so sorry, so sorry," he announced, with a great sob, as if to justify his tears, "Every man's got a mother, you know." Then, releasing her hand, he continued down the hall and out the door.

At first she thought the incident comic and told it as a funny story. But soon she began to see much more than a joke in it. Why had Frawley revealed so much of himself to her, a near stranger? Because, she decided,

> I was a woman, and one he thought of as a good woman who would not make fun of him . . .
>
> I learned from this that the way men take women in political life is to associate them with motherhood. They know and respect their mothers — ninety-nine percent of them do. It's a primitive and primary attitude. I said to myself, "That's the way to get things done. So behave, so dress and so comport yourself that you remind them subconsciously of their mothers."

Until then her clothes had been in fashion: nothing extreme, but nothing odd. Now, for anything connected with her work, she dressed the part as carefully as any actress. She adopted as a kind of uniform a simple black dress with a bow of white at the throat, and almost invariably she wore a small dark tricorn hat, which she often kept on all day.

She had no doubt that she had discovered the right way to dress. "It has always worked. I have had so many demonstrations," she said when she was in her seventies.

> I became a judge in workmen's compensation, a new idea at the time, and I realized that some of the old lawyers and insurance company representatives, as well as the injured men, took it pretty hard. I tried to remind them of their mothers, and it worked. They could take justice at

the hands of a woman who reminded them of their mothers. They couldn't take justice from the hands of a fly-by-night.

I sort of sympathized with them. Many good and intelligent women do dress in ways that are very attractive and pretty, but don't particularly invite confidence in their common sense, integrity or sense of justice.[7]

No matter how staidly she dressed and comported herself, however, she could not be sure of her welcome at the State Industrial Commission. In the November 1915 fire at the Diamond Candy factory in Brooklyn, twelve persons had died and thirty-five had been injured. The subsequent investigation revealed that the commission's Factory Inspection Division kept inadequate records of its inspections, seldom checked to see if violations had been corrected and hardly ever prosecuted delinquent companies. Violations had been reported in the candy factory, few had been corrected and twelve workers had died, trapped on a fire escape or jumping from fifth-story windows.

As executive secretary of the Committee on Safety, Perkins had taken a leading role in arousing public opinion. She had prepared the seventy-three page *Statement to Governor Whitman,* in which she condemned the five commissioners as morally responsible for the deaths. In the reorganization of the Labor Department, following the Triangle fire, they had been given all the department's administrative, judicial and legislative power. They could, within limits, make additional regulations, exceptions or rules of inspection, and they had the power and duty to enforce them. In the *Statement* she wasted no time deploring the situation in general but went right after specific commissioners — "the individual members are to be judged by their conduct as supervising heads of their respective bureaus." Using their own testimony to condemn them, she asked the governor to appoint new commissioners in place of James M. Lynch, Louis Wiard and Edward P. Lyon. For the commission as a whole she used such phrases as "gross neglect," "inefficient" and "ignorant of its duties."[8]

As a result of the publicity the Chief Factory Inspector resigned, and more resignations were expected. When none followed, Perkins held a meeting of her supporting organizations and passed resolutions, which were sent to the newspapers, again demanding the retirement of Lynch, Wiard and Lyon. But in the end all five commissioners were reappointed by Governor Whitman.[9]

Before she took office in February 1919, Smith told her that he would use the special powers given the governor in the Moreland Act to name a "Moreland Act commissioner" charged with investigating the state Department of Labor. Her appointment to the Industrial Commission was merely the first step in a complete overhaul that would give greater effect to the new safety laws and regulations.[10]

She was to take the place of Wiard, whose term had ended with the new year. Another commissioner, Henry D. Sayer, had been appointed since the fire and presumably had no reason to dislike her. But with Lyon, Lynch and John Mitchell, the chairman, she felt awkward. How should she approach them? She consulted Abram Elkus, who advised, "Just go in boldly. Smile as though nothing had happened. Be polite to everybody. After all, they're politicians."

Nevertheless, as she entered the commission's main office at 230 Fifth Avenue, she felt "a little queer." But Elkus's advice proved sound.

With Mitchell, one of the great labor figures of the time, her relations soon became easy. A slight, wiry man with brown eyes and a dark complexion, he was almost fifty, ten years older than she. He had gone into the mines in 1882 at the age of twelve and at twenty-seven had led a strike with distinction. Before he joined the state Department of Labor in 1914, he had served as president of the United Mine Workers and vice-president of the AFL. His manner was quiet and modest, and he was good at working out compromises as well as scrupulous in keeping his end of a bargain once struck. Perkins went out of her way to keep him informed about what she was doing or hoped to do. Though Mitchell was a weak chairman, he did not resent the efforts of others to provide, through him, the kind of leadership the commission had lacked.

In Henry Sayer, a younger man, she found an ally. He came to talk to her as soon as he heard that she was in the office, and from him she began to learn how ineffectively the commission was still operating. The commissioners met only occasionally, and nothing controversial or embarrassing was ever discussed. "As to unfinished business," Sayer told her, "we have no clear category. Things just sort of lap over." The various bureaus and divisions, such as the Women's Bureau under Nelle Swartz, whom she knew well, were left to run themselves. In the main the commissioners confined their attention to approving settlements in workmen's compensation cases. Most of whatever else was accomplished was done by Sayer and Lynch.

With Lynch, a labor leader from Syracuse, she developed a working relationship but no trust. For each problem she had to approach him anew. He was too much of an individualist to create or comply with any overall policy and procedures. From day to day she was never sure whether she would have his cooperation.

Her most difficult relationship was with Edward P. Lyon of Brooklyn. Since he did not stop by her office to call on her, she called on him in his. She discovered an elderly man who had been president of the Brooklyn Young Men's Christian Association for twenty years and who had very hurt feelings. He protested that he took his duties on the commission seriously but that she had held him up before the world as a man who was irresponsible, ignorant and careless about human life.

After several meetings she decided that if they were to work together she would have to apologize. She was sorry for what she had said, she told him. She had made her charges in the heat of political battle, and she realized now that they were not proved. She had done him an injustice; she should never have suggested that his intentions were not good.

He for his part stated that no one felt worse than he about what had happened; it was just terrible. He had known nothing about factory inspection — he'd never even heard of it. (She held her peace as he explained that it had not been brought to his attention.) He was a lawyer, and he had given all his time to the legal problems of the Workmen's Compensation Act.

That was the great fault with the department, she concluded after several weeks. The commissioners had allowed workmen's compensation to dominate their attention. It was understandable: It is easy and pleasant to give away other people's money. No tension is involved. "It's a lovely thing to hold a hearing and make an award to a workman who obviously has been hurt."

Factory inspection, on the other hand, is tiresome work, technical and often contentious, for the factory owner must be forced to spend his money when he often would rather not. There is no lovely feeling about it. No owner is ever grateful to an inspector for reporting a violation; no worker, hat in hand, ever thanks a commissioner for a job well done.

Reorganizing the Factory Inspection Division was the obvious place to begin, and for the first few months she gave it most of her attention. She was fortunate in the Chief Inspector, Louis Havens, who had been appointed after the Diamond Candy fire. He admired her greatly, and thought her attacks on the commissioners had been fair and courageous. The two of them began to rotate the inspectors among districts in the state, to inspect off-schedule rather than on-, to improve the system of recording violations and to have regular meetings of inspectors around the state so that problems could be more quickly discovered and resolved.

Smith meanwhile had appointed Jeremiah O'Connor the Moreland

Act Commissioner to survey the Department of Labor, and O'Connor conducted an investigation that lasted several months. He uncovered some corruption in the Department's two largest divisions, workmen's compensation and factory inspection, but its greatest failing was revealed to be in work not done and opportunities not taken. For four years, despite the pressure of the Factory Investigating Commission, Governor Whitman's Republican administration had shown little interest in the department. The commissioners he appointed had done little with it. Now, stimulated by Smith, Perkins and O'Connor, they woke up and started to operate with energy and efficiency. The new laws, properly administered, began to achieve their purpose of aiding and safeguarding the state's workers.[11]

Chapter 13

➤➤➤❮❮❮

The strike at Rome, New York, June–August 1919.

EARLY IN JUNE 1919 in Rome, New York, some 4400 workers, about one sixth of the town's population and almost its entire labor force, went on strike. Most of the men were Italian immigrants who spoke little English. They were unorganized, without a strike fund or recognized leaders, but the strike lasted through June and into July. On July 14 they rioted, a mill owner was assaulted and the mayor asked the governor for the state police.[1]

Among her duties at the Industrial Commission Perkins was in charge of the Bureau of Mediation and Arbitration. A few days before the riot she had received a phone call from John Flynn, an organizer for the metal polishers' union. He was in Rome, and the situation seemed to him so critical that he thought she should come up herself. "You know me," he had said. "I wouldn't mislead you. The workers are right. Call Packy Downey, who has been up here for your commission."

Downey, a mediator for the bureau who worked out of Albany, had confirmed Flynn's report. The workers were opposing five companies, all manufacturers of copper in some form: tubing, wire sheathing, screening and boilers. The strikers wanted an eight-hour day and a raise in wages to the level that Connecticut copper companies were already paying. But as they were unorganized, they were unlikely to win, for the owners had refused to negotiate. Meanwhile the town's life was disrupted and violence, it seemed, inevitable.

She thought she should go. Several of the other commissioners believed it unnecessary, but Smith agreed with her that the presence of a commissioner might help. She arranged to take the night train on July 15, and she asked Downey to board it in Albany so that they could arrive in Rome together the next day. On the train, she learned from the Rome *Daily Sentinel* that some workers had attacked and knifed a mill owner, James A. Spargo, who had been rescued by others in the crowd. He was alleged to have fired a gun at the workers. He denied it, however, and no injuries were reported. Other mill owners also had been attacked. The *New York Times* reported that Governor Smith, at the request of the mayor of Rome, had sent the state police to "quell the riot."

The following morning the conductor tried to persuade her not to get off the train. "There's no way you can get into Rome," he insisted, "except across that bridge," and he pointed in the direction of a drawbridge over the barge canal. "They shot a man there yesterday, and they're shooting again now." He had orders, he said, not to let passengers off at Rome. When Downey sided with her, the trainman supported the conductor. The train stood in the station with closed doors while the argument continued, but finally a door opened and Perkins and Downey stepped down onto the empty platform.

The town's taxi driver was willing to try the bridge. He would put down the canvas top of his touring car so that they could stand and be seen. At the end of the bridge, he assured them, were workers with guns. He was full of Monday's riot and, while he folded and punched the canvas into place, he gave his version of it: how Spargo had called the workers dreadful, obscene names; how they had rushed his car and he had fired into the crowd, but miraculously no one was injured; how he had since disappeared and no one knew where he was, which was a good thing or there would be more shooting.

The driver pulled away smartly from the station, but on reaching the bridge he slowed to a triumphal pace. His passengers stood, and in the middle of the bridge he stopped. At the far end a crowd of workers blocked the road.

Downey, whom no one ever called anything but "Packy," was an elderly pixie whose good nature shone in his face. Smiling at the men, he made beckoning gestures and soon was recognized. A group of about twenty advanced. She saw rocks in their hands and, she believed, some half-concealed guns. "You all knows me," Packy said. "I'm the mediator from Albany. This is the Industrial Commissioner."

She made a little speech: she was there to represent the State Industrial Commission. Governor Smith had asked her to come. She had talked with John Flynn, and later in the day she wanted to talk with them, to hear what their problems were. Then she would talk with the employers.

At the familiar names the men stopped scowling and even began to smile. Plainly they had no ill will toward Flynn, Downey, herself or the governor. Waving the car ahead, they signaled to the others to open a lane, and she and Downey rode in state to Stanwix Hall, an old hotel close to the center of town.

In the next few days she talked with everyone she could. On the workers' side she dealt chiefly with Flynn, William Collins, a representative of the AFL, and John O'Connor, an organizer for the International Machinists Association. None of the three had an official position with any of the workers, yet because of their experience and fluency in English they functioned rather like counsel. They were not leaders — they could be repudiated at any moment — yet their advice was constantly sought and generally taken. Although each hoped eventually to win recruits for his union, their combined aim at the moment was to win something for the workers by bringing order out of chaos. There were too many groups of workers, each with its own leaders, for orderly bargaining.

Fortunately for her, the counsel for the majority of the employers was T. Harvey Ferris, a state senator whom she knew and who had supported her appointment to the commission. Throughout the strike she and Ferris frequently disagreed on what should be done, but they never doubted each other's good intentions. Nor, with one major exception on her part, did they conceal anything from each other. Though frequently protesting, he cooperated with her.

She had in fact more power than she used. As an Industrial Commissioner she could convene a hearing and subpoena witnesses and their records. This was never necessary. For the most part, the employers were genuinely upset over the strike's effect on the town and were anxious to settle it, though of course on their terms.

The employer she met most often was Percy Thomas, whose attitude was typical of the others. For him neither the money nor the hours were the main issue; privately he conceded that the Rome companies had fallen behind their competitors and should pay more. He was also ready, if necessary, for an eight-hour day. But he would not talk with a committee of his workers about their grievances or wages. To negotiate with a committee was to recognize a union, a long step toward "a closed shop," in which a company could hire only union members. For Thomas, it was too much. In such shops the company's power to choose who would enter its premises and handle its machinery had passed from it to the union. He would talk at any time to the workers individually, man to man, but he would not negotiate with their committees.

She tried to assure him that a closed shop was not always the result of collective bargaining and to explain why, with the rise of industry, the man-to-man relations of an older age no longer were serviceable. She pointed out that workers needed unions and collective bargaining to balance the economic power increasingly concentrated in a few owners. But Thomas came from an old family in Rome, and he saw the town, himself, the workers and their relations to their employers in terms that had once been true but were no longer.

To Perkins, an outsider, the town clearly was at a divide in its history. Since revolutionary days its chief industry besides agriculture had been metal manufacture: first iron and then, as the electrical age began to need wire, copper. In the old days a few local families had dominated the mills, which employed only several hundred people, most of them in some kind of craftwork. No one made a great deal of money. Everyone, workers and owners, had farms and common recreations, mostly hunting and fishing. The population was a stable mixture of old English and Dutch extraction.

In the twentieth century all this had changed; after the beginning of World War I, changed with astonishing speed. The price of manufactured copper shot up, and it was rumored that eleven men in Rome had become millionaires. The town had never known such wealth. Some of the rich continued to live in their grandfathers' simple houses, but others built new homes, which the county judge described to Perkins with indignation as "palaces, lady, palaces." And instead of the common recreations there was a country club where the rich played golf.

To work the mills, the owners had encouraged immigration, and within twenty years Rome's population had increased by 40 percent with most of the new people coming from southern Italy, unable to speak English.

As if in a single night the industrial age, with all its problems and new relationships, had overtaken the town, confusing everyone: workers, owners, Yankees and Italians. Almost no one knew any longer how to behave.

At the center of the confusion was the owner of the Spargo Wire Company, James A. Spargo. With remarkable unanimity everyone told her that Spargo was a terrible man, disagreeable and violent. He had come to Rome from Birmingham, England, thirty-four years earlier as a boy in his teens. He had joined an older brother in running a two-man wire shop and, overcoming several setbacks, had developed an important wire company. Yet his position among the town leaders was never quite accepted.

He was a strong, stocky man. When a committee of three workmen had attempted to present its demands to him he had knocked the men downstairs. Downey and Flynn saw it; they had coached the men on what to say and were waiting at the bottom of the stairs.

"Oh, it was terrible," Packy told her. "It stirred up this town so I thought they'd set fire to his place. But Johnny Flynn and I pacified them. We told them never to get angry or act drastic. Take another chance on it.

"So Johnny Flynn and I went with another man from Rome who didn't work in Spargo's place. We went up the stairs. I went first because I'm Irish and ain't afraid and had me credentials as an officer of the State of New York.

"Would you believe it" — Packy's eyes widened — "that wild man he came out and never looked for a minute at me credentials. He just started to swing on me. But I knew his habits. I ducked, and he got the fellow from Rome. Johnny, he was halfway down the stairs."

Later, with the help of John O'Connor, a group of Spargo's workers had sent him a proposal for an agreement. It had come back through the mail, torn in pieces, with a note: "Kiss my ass and go to hell."

That too had stirred up the town, and there was talk of prosecuting him for improper use of the mails. Privately, Percy Thomas expressed the greatest indignation to her: he and the other employers did not want to be associated with Spargo. They had their counsel, Senator Ferris, and Spargo had another. Publicly, of course, the employers would continue to present a united front in refusing to meet with any committee of workers.

All that had happened in mid-June. For a month the situation continued stable but unsatisfactory. Besides Downey's efforts for the state, a mediator from the federal Department of Labor tried to nudge the employers into a meeting with the workers. So did the mayor, H. Clayton Midlam, and the Chamber of Commerce, whose motto was "For Rome, Romans and Results." All failed. Meanwhile the town was losing more than $100,000 a week in wages, many workers were living on credit or taking jobs in Utica and some small businesses were already half-ruined. Then on Monday, July 14, came the attack on Spargo, the resignation of a number of special deputies on the police force and, at the mayor's request, the state police.

Founded only two years earlier, the state police had been used primarily in rural areas. This was the first time they had been called out for a strike. The entire force — roughly two hundred men organized in four companies — converged on Rome from Oneida, Batavia, Albany and White Plains. Some troopers arrived individually, but most came in groups and were applauded as they marched up the street. They established headquarters at the Rome jail, stabled their horses in the jail yard and bunked in the courthouse.

On the evening following the riot, they began to patrol the streets of East Rome, the Italian section. Their chief weapon was the horse. Whenever two or three men were seen together, they were ordered to separate and go home. If they did not, they were ridden down. The troopers then would chase them to their homes, riding the horses onto the porches and, on one occasion, into the building. Guns were confiscated, heads cracked and houses searched. By Wednesday morning, when Perkins arrived, the streets of East Rome were quiet, even deserted. But every house in town buzzed with anecdote, and fifty years later what most old-timers recalled of the strike were incidents involving the state police.

Still, the strike was no nearer settlement, and the enforced peace had its own dangers. In her first talk with John Flynn he took her into a small room off the hotel's main sitting room and closed the door before speaking. "Commissioner," he said, "I've got to tell you something. The governor must withdraw these state police. The workers are crazy, wild Eyetalians. I can't handle them. They're not Irishmen. Their blood is up. Real dynamite. That's what they say." He took her to see a worker, a man named Ludovicci, who said simply, "Lady, it will be bad. Mr. Johnny is right."

For the next four days she and Senator Ferris battled for the governor's support. She phoned Albany to urge him to withdraw the police; Ferris, to urge that he not withdraw them. There will be violence, she insisted, if they stay; violence, Ferris argued, if they go. Never, in her conversations with Smith, did she mention the dynamite; the only person she told was Downey. Though she had not seen it, she trusted Flynn and believed in its existence. To speak of it to anyone in authority, she felt, was certain to lead to its explosion, for an immediate effort would be made to seize it. While she talked to Smith and Ferris, Downey and the union organizers talked to the workers, urging them to be calm and insisting that "the Commissioner" was even now on the phone asking the governor to withdraw the police.

In the end she prevailed, perhaps because she and not Ferris offered Smith some plan for settling the strike. When Smith asked her how she would forestall the "rumpus" that Ferris predicted if the police left, she said, "I'll get the whole commission up here to hold hearings."

"They'll never come," Smith said doubtfully; yet she had given him something. She was able to cite him the law authorizing such a hearing, and at least it would force the employers into the same room with the workers. With fanfare Smith announced to the papers that a public hearing would probably be held if the manufacturers continued to refuse to confer with their workers. Then he ordered the state police to withdraw.

They left on Monday morning, after a week in the town. The people could see them go and hear the clop, clop of the horses growing fainter as the men rode up the street. They would remain on call in barracks in Oneida.

That night Ludovicci led her and Flynn to two homes in East Rome. In each, Ludovicci made a short speech in Italian. Then she said a few words, enough to show that she understood what he was saying and knew why they had come. He would begin by stating that he knew what they had in the cellar, and the lady — *la signora* — knew too. They must get rid of it. The lady had promised the governor that if he would withdraw the police, they would get rid of it. Now the police were gone and they must do their part. There were hesitations, but in each case the men, whose names she never knew, went down to their cellars and came up with sacks and suitcases. They carried these to the canal and dropped them in. One man wheeled his load in a baby carriage. She never knew how much dynamite there was or whether the men had disposed of it all.

The manufacturers continued to balk at meeting with the committees of workers, and the Industrial Commission convened its public hearing on Monday, August 4. Commissioners Mitchell, Lynch and Lyon came to Rome for the occasion. After his opening statement as chairman, Mitchell adjourned the hearing while the commissioners tried once more to settle the strike by conferences with workers and employers. But these, as always, broke down over the issue of recognizing any kind of organization among the workers. With regret Mitchell resumed the hearing at 9:00 A.M. on Wednesday.

The courthouse, facing a small square with benches and a statue of a local revolutionary hero, was in Greek Revival style with two-story Ionic columns at the front. In the large and rather featureless courtroom on the second floor the four commissioners sat shoulder to shoulder on a judge's dais designed for one. Several hundred persons occupied the seats for spectators, and at least another hundred stood along the back and side walls. By noon the heat was stifling, but all paid close attention to every witness and there were no disturbances.

By law the commission was authorized only to determine the cause of the strike; it had no power to enforce a settlement. During the morning and most of the afternoon it heard testimony by union organizers and the workers themselves on their wages, hours, conditions of work and attempts to negotiate with the employers. The stories were repetitious, yet moving; visible behind the cents an hour were the men and their families trying to break even. For many, the wartime weekly bonus had made the critical difference, and this had been cut.

The commissioners hoped that the workers' stories might move the employers to some concession. Four mill owners were present; the fifth, Spargo, had not been seen for days and was believed to be at a fishing camp in the Adirondacks. He was not even represented by counsel, and Mitchell read his offensive note to the workers into the record with plain disapproval.

Toward the close of the afternoon session Ferris replied for the four other employers. He ended by saying: "It appears that the cancellation of the war bonus was one of the immediate causes of the strike, and the idea of collective bargaining another. Wages have been lowered. I do not wish to take up any time, as we concede the causes of the strike and that wages should be readjusted according to those paid by our competitors."

He perhaps thought that conceding the causes of the strike and also a raise in wages would close the hearing. But the commissioners were determined that the employers should respond to the workers in their own words, not through the mouth of a lawyer. As Perkins observed later, there is a kind of denial of the workers' humanity when employers, "grown men who own factories, will not say for themselves what they think and will do but instead shut their mouths tight, look at the floor and get a lawyer to do their talking for them." In dealing with labor disputes over the years, it seemed to her that the violence in them often sprang from just such degradation of the workers, whether in their working conditions or during negotiations. Before adjourning for supper, therefore, Mitchell announced that the hearing would continue at 8:00 P.M., with the employers testifying.

This was what the workers had been waiting for. At eight o'clock the room was still more crowded, and hundreds stood outside in the square to hear by relay what had been said or done. Always the testimony came back to the same issue. When Percy Thomas of the Rome Manufacturing Company insisted that he would not meet with a committee of his own workmen, Mitchell observed in his kindly manner, "There are times in the interest of a community when someone should yield." Referring to Ferris, he pointed out, "You were represented just as these men want to be. They suggest that they send you a few of your own boys. We speak officially for the State of New York. We are not asking a great deal when we ask one to attempt to yield to his own judgment and try as best he can to compose the differences." But Thomas refused.

Herbert T. Dyett of the Rome Wire Company was asked why he would not meet a committee of workers. "Matter of pride," he answered. "What would keep you back?" "Logic." "Don't you ever intend to change your policy?" "We may some time."

Barton Haselton of the Rome Brass and Copper Company, when questioned, was even blunter. "Did you meet a committee?" "No." "Would you?" "No." "Why not ?" "Because I said 'No.' "

Where the first three employers had been belligerent, the fourth, Frank DeBisschop, was defeated. He ran the smallest shop, with only 135 employees, and acted as his own foreman. He had not cut back on wages, and his men had been the last to go on strike. Yet he had been attacked and beaten by the same crowd that knifed Spargo. A simpler man than his fellow employers, he was closer to ruin because of the strike. He had never refused to talk with his workers, but his actions were not the issue and could not affect the strike's resolution. When Perkins asked, "How do you think the strike can be settled?" he replied, "Possibly it will not be settled. This may be the end of the brass and copper industry in Rome."

It seemed possible. Nothing had broken the deadlock. Mitchell closed the hearing with a statement of the commission's disappointment "that its efforts have not met with a greater response from the manufacturers." They had not "met the wishes of the Commission in a spirit of cooperation." The next day, Thursday, the commissioners left for New York. The strike apparently would continue indefinitely.

Yet on Saturday Mayor Midlam, with the assistance of Downey, acting for the commission, started negotiations that led to a settlement on Monday. In the course of these negotiations the employers from the beginning dealt with committees of workmen. What caused the employers to change their position?

The only person to offer an explanation is Perkins, in her oral history, a series of tape-recorded interviews she made for Columbia University in the years 1951 through 1955. Other sources, including the Rome *Daily Sentinel,* simply leave the obvious question unanswered.

According to Perkins, shortly after she arrived in Rome, Flynn told her that a committee of Spargo's workers had received a letter from the mill owner, delivered from somewhere in the Adirondacks by a stranger passing through. In this letter Spargo told his workers, men and women, what he thought of them, in language far more vile than that of his single sentence note. Flynn had seen the letter and regretted that it had not been sent through the mail, for then unquestionably Spargo could be jailed for violating the postal laws. Flynn was full of indignation that "a grown man, an American" should write such a letter.

The next morning Perkins had a meeting with Ferris and the four employers to discuss what wages might be offered the workers. After lamenting that Spargo's continued absence made a general agreement more difficult, she remarked, "I understand there is a very interesting letter in circulation somewhere around town."

As she remembered it, "They all just looked as though they would die. I saw at once from their faces that they knew about it. I said, 'Of course I haven't seen it. I just heard a rumor. Rumors are rumors.' Silence fell upon them. I said to myself, 'This is true. These grown men . . . wouldn't be so paralyzed, wouldn't be struck dumb if they didn't know about them too.' I said no more about it, just passed it over, thinking I'd hold it for later."

When she came back for the commission's hearing on August 4, Flynn, who plainly had special contacts among the workers, gave her the letter. During one of the adjournments in the hearing she showed it to Mitchell and Lyon, leaving them alone in the room to read it. When she came back, Lyon, the good churchman, was "all the colors of the rainbow" and Mitchell was "white and explosive." She took it from them and put it back in her purse, explaining that she was under a pledge to use it only if absolutely necessary.

Later, when the four employers refused to meet a committee of workers and Mitchell had made his speech of regret, she whispered to him that the moment to use the letter had come. "Tell them you have to do this because the working people are so insulted. Tell them the workers are humans, should be treated like humans and allowed to negotiate with their employers. We are here to help them do that negotiating. After having explained that, tell them you are going to read the letter."

Mitchell was unsure, and they adjourned for a few minutes to discuss it. Lyon was aghast. "You can't read that. There are women in the audience."

"It was written to women as well as men," she reminded him, adding, "after all, I'm an official, and I have to stand it. I guess I can chaperone these girls."

Mitchell was inclined to read it.

When they returned to the courtroom, there was a sudden hush as Mitchell, looking very white, remained standing. He cleared his throat and said that a painful duty had come to him and that he had a communication he must read. But first he wanted to explain to the employers why he was reading it. He talked of how men can be insulted in their deepest natures. "These are workmen," he said. "They are human beings. God made them. They live here. They work here. They must be treated like human beings, and when they are not, the resentments that gather are terrible indeed. Because they have been so insulted, they are insistent upon having what they believe to be right and just and having it guaranteed by the State Industrial Commission. With this preface I think I must read — off the record — a letter [Perkins took it from her purse and handed it to him] which was received by a committee of workmen from the owner and proprietor of the Spargo Wire Company."

It was too much for Percy Thomas. Before Mitchell could get out the first sentence, Thomas was on his feet: "I wish to speak before you go further, for myself and my colleagues. We do not feel it is right that you should read the letter. We did not write it. I want you to know, Mr. Chairman, that none of us would ever have written such a letter. It was written by one of our colleagues. It is true that we are all in agreement and that we have spoken for him when we have said we would not negotiate with our workers. But in this matter we do not speak for him. We condemn him for having written such a letter."

On all sides the people broke into a cheer. "Oh, Percy! He's a man." Perkins could recall that phrase coming from somewhere out of the burst of applause. With a single instinctive act of decency Thomas had re-established a human relationship with his workers. Though the applause bewildered him, it also pleased him, and he went on to say that he thought an agreement could be reached.

Mitchell pressed the advantage. "You will reach an agreement with your workers?"

"Yes, sir, we will reach an agreement."

"Will you consult with a committee?"

"Yes, sir, we will consult with a committee."

The next day, after some preliminary meetings to set up the negotiations, the commissioners departed for New York. On Saturday the official negotiations began; in time they led to the settlement. And Spargo shortly after returned to Rome and accepted its terms.

A few days later, in discussing the strike with Governor Smith, Perkins told him of the dynamite that she had kept secret from him. "You had your nerve," he said. He meant it, and she took it, as a reproach. In retrospect she was not sure she had done right, not sure she had not betrayed his trust in her. She could only say that the situation was so unusual that no rules seemed to apply and that her silence seemed the best course to follow at the time.

Smith, too, perhaps, had second thoughts, for in his autobiography, *Up to Now,* he praised her work at Rome.

Chapter 14

-»>«<-

*She joins the Democratic party. The 1920 convention. Smith tem-
porarily loses the governorship. The Council on Immigrant Education. Reappointed to the Industrial Board. Administering the Workmen's Compensation Act.*

In SPITE OF Smith's remark that there should be no prejudices between
those in voluntary agencies who worked for social improvements and
those in public office, Perkins for a time apparently continued to think
of herself more as a Consumers' League representative on the Industrial Commission than as a Democratic office-holder. Her allegiance to
the party developed only gradually, and she required a sharp push
from Smith before she could acknowledge it fully to herself and to the
world.

The first party she joined, during her year in Philadelphia, was the
Socialist, and when she came to New York she transferred her membership and continued to pay dues through March 1912. She kept the
affiliation secret — her Republican father was "explosive" about
Eugene Debs — and perhaps her dues were no more than a private
protest against the excesses of capitalism, for the party's meetings and
members seemed to have played no role in her life. But party affiliation for women was somewhat academic until they had the right to
vote, which Perkins did not have until 1918, when she was thirty-eight
years old.[1]

The significant line of her developing allegiance to the Democrats
lay in her experience at work and in the struggle over power and
policy that split the Republicans in the summer of 1912. In June,
when she had been a spectator at the Democratic convention in
Baltimore, she had preferred Wilson to Clark because she felt he knew
more about the industrial problems of the cities. For the same reason,

when the Republicans convened in July she preferred Theodore Roosevelt to Taft. And when Roosevelt bolted the convention promising to found a Progressive party dedicated to the kind of social justice she advocated, her enthusiasm for him soared. In August, with the greatest excitement, she started for the Progressive convention in Chicago, but at Buffalo she received word of illness in her family and returned to the Newcastle farm.

There her Republican uncles were speaking of Roosevelt and his supporters as "scoundrels." When she attempted to reply, they ridiculed her arguments.

"How do you know he's a scoundrel?" she demanded in defense of Gifford Pinchot, one of Roosevelt's advisers.

"Look at his face," was their answer. "Look at his picture. You can tell by looking at him."

Eventually she lost her temper at their "elderly male logic," and after that summer she was never again in sympathy with the party to which her father and uncles were so strongly attached.

Later she felt fortunate that she had not reached Chicago and the Progressive Convention. Ten thousand people in the hall, after singing "Onward Christian Soldiers" and "The Battle Hymn of the Republic," had pledged themselves to Roosevelt's crusade and cut their ties with their regular party machines across the country. After his defeat and the party's quick decline many of them were left stranded, with no place in the Republican party during the 1920s or in the Democratic party in the 1930s. Because she was not at the convention to catch their enthusiasm, she had remained uncommitted, free to follow what was for her the more realistic course into the party of Smith, Wagner and Big Tim Sullivan.

Sometime about 1917 she said to friends who were discussing New York politics, "I think if I had the vote, I would be a Democrat."

To their laughter and exclamations about the evils of Tammany she replied, "All I know is this: When the Republicans are in power in this state, we don't get any social legislation at all. When the Democrats are in power, we make some progress."

"It was as naive as that. I only knew the state," she remarked years later. "I was much more aware of New York and of belonging to it than I was of belonging to the U.S.A., which perhaps is wrong and unpatriotic, but I honestly believe that's how people develop. You become responsible for a small area you can see. You gradually know the rest."[2]

In the 1918 elections, the first in which women could vote in New

York, she served on the Independent Citizens' Committee for Smith and actively campaigned for him. After he had won the governorship and appointed her to the Industrial Commission, he telephoned her one morning and asked her to come to his New York City "executive suite" in the Hotel Biltmore.

There several men were waiting in the main room to see the governor; a stenographer was typing in a bedroom; and Smith himself, his shirtsleeves rolled and his vest open, appeared in the doorway to another room as soon as she was announced. Puffing on a cigar, he apologized to the waiting men and asked her to come in.

"Take a chair," he said. "I want to talk to you about politics." Standing before her and hooking his thumbs into his galluses, he declared, "Commissioner, somebody told me you wasn't a Democrat."

For a moment she attempted to be roguish about it. But Smith was serious and her position weak, for technically the charge was true. She had registered as an independent even though she had campaigned for Smith. Apparently the Democratic leader of her district had discovered it.

She had not joined the party, she explained, because "that sort of ties your hands. Then you have to be for the Democrats even though on some occasion you might want to be for someone else."

Smith pulled up a chair. "I want to explain to you about that," he said.

That's the kind of a mistake a lot of good people are likely to make. They think they got something if they're independent. Commissioner, you ain't got anything by being independent.

In this country and in this state we got a representative form of government, and anybody can aspire to be elected to the Congress or to the legislature. Anyone can come forward and say he wants to be elected. Does he get any votes? No, Commissioner, he don't, not unless he has a crowd of people bound together in some way to support him and put him forward. It's kind of fresh for a man to recommend himself to the people. Some of his friends and acquaintances first ought to tell him he should be the candidate. That's what a political party is — a group of people who stand by each other.

The party's important. If you don't have a party organization, you won't continue to have a two-party system of government. If you don't have that, you'll have a kind of bedlam like they have in France — they never know who's in control. Nobody ever stands solid. Nobody ever stands firm. They can't make any progress through their government. Eventually they won't trust their government. That's what happens if the people don't stick around two or three rallying points. A party's a rallying point.

Suppose you got some good ideas. All right. You go to the party you belong to and you'll be listened to inside the party. They'll listen to your good ideas, about the administration or who ought to be appointed. You've got a group to whom you can really tell the truth, really lay it on the line. You can't go out and talk like that to the public because you just sound like a fool. There's nobody back of you. So when you get ready to announce your program, if your party is all set or even just a segment of it has okayed your program, then they put it before the state convention, or the county or the city convention. They're all for it, and they put it over. They make it popular. It doesn't seem like a one-man crank idea.

Let's say there's an ill-will fellow who owns more factories or has more money than he should who opposes it. They've got to listen to him because he's a member of the party too. But you've had your say inside the party and have got a big element that's for you. They won't let this other one rule the roost just because he's got lots of money. They've got lots of votes, and he needs them just as much as they need him.

Reminding her of the owners of the Huyler Candy Factory who had opposed the 54-hour bill for women, he said, "They thought they had it fixed, but they didn't, did they? That never happens if you have a good, well-organized party. But you need to be in it. Good people need to be in the party, not outside looking in. If they're inside, doing their full duty by the party, voting, getting out the vote, helping with the campaigns and making what they know available to everybody, then they have some influence. Then the party takes up a good and wise program."

She was not convinced. "I want to see who I'm going to vote for before I enroll."

Smith replied:

No. You got to enroll, first so that you can have something to say inside the party, and second so that there's a kind of promise of a vote.

I get nominated. I know I got four hundred thousand votes up to the Bronx line [the northern boundary of New York City]. I know that. I don't have to worry about that. They're mine. They're going to stand by me. That's the enrolled party vote.

I know I got to win more votes before I can be governor. I got to win some votes upstate, some in every county. I got to win more in New York City. But for sure, I've got four hundred thousand up to the Bronx line. That's what makes it possible for me to go out and campaign freely, honorably and effectively. I'm not worrying about these people down behind me. They're going to stand still. So I can go freely and make my representations in other parts of the state. I can say things upstate to interest the upstate voters even though they might not interest the New York City voters.

Upstate, too, I know how many votes the party's got in Buffalo, Rochester, Syracuse, Albany and in the counties. We know just what we got, so we're free to sit down and figure what those other voters we want to attract want to know about us, about our program and our candidates. We can't tell them anything that isn't true, but we can emphasize the things they're interested in. That's the way you attract the independent voter.

We couldn't do that if we were worrying about all these people down in New York. But we've got them. They stay hitched to the party. They stay with it through black and white, thick and thin, defeat and victory. That's what a party government is. That's why it's important for everybody who wants to accomplish anything in the political field, or by political means, to be in a party and stay there.

"These people who jump around from one party to another never accomplish anything." He mentioned several citizens who constantly wrote letters to the papers about what ought to be done. "Have any of them ever accomplished anything? No. You've accomplished more in a couple of years than they have in twenty by always being so independent. But you won't get far if you won't line up with a party so the Democrats know that you're a Democrat and that they can rely on you — to vote with them, to speak up for them and to help plan the party program."

She left, promising to enroll when the books were next opened, and thereafter she assumed what he had described as the "full duty" of a party member. She regularly attended the state Democratic conventions, campaigned in every election and wrote position papers for the party leaders on what she thought should be done. The Democratic party became her chosen instrument in the movement for social justice. And the choice made, never, in defeat or victory, did she waver in her allegiance. From that day forward she was — and everyone knew it — one of the four hundred thousand up to the Bronx line.[3]

In June 1920 she went to San Francisco for the Democratic National Convention, not as a delegate, but to meet what leaders she could, mix with the rank and file and talk up the kind of social legislation that Smith was introducing in New York. His program included several housing bills (passed only when he called the legislature back into special session), a bill to increase the quantity and reduce the price of milk (which the legislature defeated) and, in her field, many improvements in the substance and administration of the workmen's compensation law. On the way to San Francisco she stopped in Cleveland and Springfield, Illinois, to talk with state officials about their problems with compensation funds.

In the five years from 1914 to 1919, during which Theodore Roosevelt's Progressive party had decayed and died, the Democrats more than the Republicans had picked up the Progressives' ideas. It was not only Smith in New York who had borrowed from them; in Washington, Wilson had persuaded Congress to enact a workmen's compensation law for federal civil servants, a law excluding the products of child labor from interstate commerce and a law establishing an eight-hour day on interstate railways. As Secretary of War, he had appointed a liberal, Newton D. Baker, who was the president of the National Consumers' League; and as Associate Justice of the U.S. Supreme Court, he had appointed Louis D. Brandeis, a lawyer associated with causes to improve the lot of workers. The Democrats were becoming the party of social justice. "This is the way it will drift," Smith said to Perkins once. "This is the way it will go in modern times."

In San Francisco she had a good time talking to people, but the convention itself was rather dull. For her the brightest spot came early, when Bourke Cockran, a Tammany congressman, nominated Alfred E. Smith for President. The New York delegation burst into cheers, waved banners, yelled and stomped around the hall while a band played Irish songs and an old ditty, ever after associated with Smith, "The Sidewalks of New York." After the commotion died, Wilson's Assistant Secretary of the Navy, Franklin D. Roosevelt, seconded the nomination.

The real contest for the presidential nomination, however, was among Secretary of the Treasury William G. McAdoo, Attorney General A. Mitchell Palmer and the governor of Ohio, James M. Cox. By the tenth ballot Smith had dropped out, with most of the New York vote going to Cox. In the remaining three-man race Palmer, the most controversial candidate, ran a poor third. At last, on the forty-fourth ballot, Cox won. Roosevelt subsequently was nominated for Vice-President, and Smith gave the seconding speech. There was much courtesy between Roosevelt and the New York delegation but not much warmth. He was not popular with the local party.

To Perkins he seemed less arrogant than she remembered him in Albany. "He had a more amiable expression on his face. He mixed more with people, more chatting, more slaps on the back with odds and ends of people around the lobbies. When he rose to speak, he towered over the average person. He had a big voice and could make himself heard." Once when he was seeking to be recognized, he moved closer to the chairman by putting his hand on the back of a chair and vaulting over several empty rows. "It was the most wonderful athletic feat — very graceful and unstudied." Even more, she felt, it showed a strong personality; he was not going to be ignored. "Curiously, that very insistence of his gained him a lot of respect in that convention. An immediate following sprang up for him. He was somebody." Yet she still had reservations; she saw in him a "streak of vanity and insincerity."

The events of the convention, however, mattered little. It was a Republican year, and Harding and Coolidge overwhelmed Cox and Roosevelt, 16,152,200 to 9,147,353, while in New York Nathan L. Miller, a crusty, competent lawyer from Syracuse, defeated Smith for governor. Even in New York City Harding carried sixty-one out of sixty-two Assembly districts. Yet the vote for Smith in the state was astonishing. Though the Republican national ticket in New York ran 1,200,000 ahead of the Democrats, Smith ran 1,090,000 ahead of Cox and Roosevelt and lost to Miller by only 75,000 votes. It seemed clear that he would be re-elected governor in 1922 and would be a leading contender for the presidential nomination in 1924. Meanwhile he was out of a job and, lacking the money to remain idle, went to work for a friend's trucking company.[4]

Perkins, too, lost her job as a result of the election. In a general reorganization of the Labor Department early in Miller's term, all five commissioners submitted their resignations, and he appointed a new group to what was now called the Industrial Board. One of these was Rosalie Loew Whitney, a lawyer who had been the congressional chairman for the New York City Suffrage party and who now became the second woman to hold a position at this level in the state government.

At the commission Perkins went from office to office saying good-bye to the people she had worked with, whatever their rank. For her this was not merely good politics but in character. As she wanted to be greeted on her first day at work, so she wanted to bid good-bye on her last: the appropriate gesture helped to define the experience. If a colleague was in the field, she took the trouble to write. In his reply L. A. Howell, the Chief Factory Inspector, wrote that it was "the first letter" he had ever had from a departing commissioner.[5]

In mid-April she began work as executive secretary of a new organization, the Council on Immigrant Education. This was a project of the Merchants' Association, a group of businessmen who wanted to make New York a more rewarding city for its citizens not only commercially but spiritually, and the council they organized eventually included twenty-five immigrant church and community groups, such as the Polish Club of New York, the Jewish Welfare Board and the International Community Center. Its purpose was to assist immigrants of all nationalities to emerge from their ghettos and begin to participate in the city's life. Once again Perkins became the workhorse of a burgeoning organization, arranging meetings, keeping minutes, setting policy, implementing programs and speaking to immigrant, church and community groups.[6]

The job was less demanding and rewarding than others she had held, but she needed the money. Wilson was neither sick nor well. He was working at the Equitable Life Assurance Company, but she seems to have been uncertain of what he did, and the company has no record. It is possible that the job had little substance and was obtained or even created for him by Henry Bruère, who had a loyal affection for Wilson and many contacts in the financial and insurance world.[7]

Among old friends Wilson still seemed able to blossom with wit and wisdom; he was not yet the misty figure he became in the 1930s. He was good at cards and played regularly at a whist and bridge club, and at home he had strong opinions, which he would defend vigorously, particularly against Perkins. To Henry Bruère's daughter, Alison, Wilson in the 1920s was "a general without buttons"; he had ideas but no status or position from which to launch them.

In public, especially among Perkins's political acquaintances, he seemed to withdraw. To one of her friends he seemed, despite his height, a "mousy man with not much to say"; to two others, "rather an odd person"; and to one of her classmates, "a rather insignificant person, as he would be." A belief was emerging among her friends that he was the sacrifice on the altar of her career.[8]

Undoubtedly, without intending to, she contributed to the spread of that belief by her reluctance to mention his illness to anyone but Bruère. For many years only her closest friends realized how ill Wilson was. Agnes Leach, who remembered him as a charming host during

•

the Mitchel administration, recalled a dinner at the Wilsons' in the mid-1920s. She and her husband were the only guests. Perkins, trying to draw Wilson out, suggested that he show some work he had done to Henry Leach, who was editor of *Forum,* a monthly magazine of public affairs. Though Leach was interested, Wilson resisted all their urgings with a sullenness that was alarming. The evening was spoilt, and the Leaches left in dismay.[9]

Similarly, Perkins's reluctance to admit her financial position, however guardedly, to anyone but Bruère concealed from most of her friends, and certainly from all her acquaintances, the reality of her situation. Most persons saw clearly that she enjoyed her work. They were dimly aware of a husband in the background who had a job with some insurance company. But they had no idea of the need for her to work if the family was to stay in New York and lead a life resembling the one they had known. Leaving the city was not a real alternative; both she and Wilson were over forty, and he was almost unemployable. Where else could they go where she, a woman with highly specialized training, could get a better job?

Sometime after the loss of his money they moved from the house on Washington Place to an apartment at 308 West Ninety-fourth Street. They had a floor through with enough rooms to allow her mother to come for long visits in the winter. Pauline Goldmark lived on the same street, and several Columbia professors whom Perkins knew were in the neighborhood. They entertained much less, seldom more than two or four for dinner, and in place of the German couple and professional nurse she relied on part-time help. In a few years she was able to enroll Susanna in Birch Wathen, a progressive school close by. Life was simpler, and though she always consulted Wilson about plans, the decisions, more frequently, were hers.

Nothing in their lives could ever balance Wilson's loss of health, but in her jobs she continued to be fortunate. Each, even the position with the Council on Immigrant Education, helped to build for her a kind of constituency, so across the state she had standing with a variety of groups.

She had happened to arrive in New York in 1909, just as the mass of unorganized, immigrant workers began to form unions. In the turmoil, which lasted through 1916, and because of her jobs for the Consumers' League, the Committee on Safety and the Factory Investigating Commission, she worked with, or at least met, many of the emerging leaders. These were mostly Jewish immigrants, among them Sidney Hillman, Jacob Potofsky, David Dubinsky, Rose Schneiderman and Pauline Newman. The Irish (and to a lesser extent the German) immigrants of 1875 to 1895 had found their way to positions of leadership and power through politics. Now New York's Jews (and to a lesser extent its Italians) arriving between 1895 and 1915, did the same through their unions. Since her work involved both the legislature and the factories, she became known to all groups, and her work with the Council on Immigrant Education at least kept her name before them.[10]

In addition, through the board members of the Consumers' League, the Committee on Safety and the Maternity Center Association, she had also met many of the city's rich and professional leaders who were public-spirited. She was well acquainted with such persons as R. Fulton Cutting, Henry Morgenthau, Sr., Anne Morgan and Henry L. Stimson. Now through the council she met William H. Woodin, the president of the American Car and Foundry Company, who served as the liaison between the council and its parent, the Merchants' Association. She worked with him closely and came to admire him; twelve years later both would be in Roosevelt's cabinet, Woodin as Secretary of the Treasury.

By 1921 very few women in the state could match the breadth of her acquaintanceship. Smith could appoint her to the government with confidence that the appointment would have wide support. When he was re-elected governor in 1922 — she again had campaigned for him — he simply telephoned to inquire if she was ready to go back on the Industrial Commission. She agreed at once; it was the job she liked best.[11]

The department to which she returned had been reorganized in such a way that its executive functions were divided from those primarily legislative or judicial. In place of the five-member commission, which had combined the three functions, there was now a single Industrial Commissioner, responsible for the department's administration, and an Industrial Board with a chairman and two members (often still called "commissioners"), which handled the quasi-legislative and judicial work, such as preparing or revising regulatory codes for industries and hearing workmen's compensation cases. It was on this board that Perkins was to sit.

Both she and Smith had testified against the plan when it was before the legislature, but both, after working under the new structure, found it an improvement. The Industrial Commissioner, without need to consult the board, could keep the department's affairs moving. He hired the staff, assigned the work, prepared the budget and enforced the codes by inspection and prosecution. But he did not sit with the board, and though there was consultation back and forth, he had no voice in determining the codes or in deciding the workmen's compensation cases.

As Industrial Commissioner Smith appointed Bernard L. Shientag, who had been the assistant counsel to the Factory Investigating Commission. The board's chairman, whose term had four years to run, was John D. Higgens of Oswego. Perkins was prepared to dislike him, for she had been told he was "severe" and "an old stiff." Instead she found a friend for life. It was true that he had been born before the Civil War, that he dressed precisely and sported a small, sharp mustache; on first meeting he seemed fierce. She had not been on the board for two days, however, when she happened to make a lightly barbed remark and he instantly capped it. She discovered that he had a delicious sense of humor. "He saw funny things in everything that happened in life. So much so that we finally had to agree not to tell jokes, laugh and make little sallies at each other when the public was around."

Higgens's humor was philosophic and, fed by a classical education, deeply humanistic. He frankly preferred the nineteenth century to the twentieth. From his experiences in Oswego, both as its mayor for six years and as one of its leading employers for almost forty, he judged the nineteenth better if only because the extremes of rich and poor were not so great and the disasters befalling people less catastrophic. The twentieth century, he felt, needed humor and, if life for workers was to be livable, a department of labor. His attitude toward it was positive.[12]

That of the board's third member, Richard H. Curran, was at best ambivalent. He was a union official, a molder by trade, and best known for his years as secretary of the State Federation of Labor. He too was an old man, but he was not very bright and was often distracted by the effects of diabetes. Though Perkins found him personally "a good scout" who "meant to do right," he also was "completely uninterested in the operation of the Labor Department, in the Labor Law, in the Workmen's Compensation Law. He could hear a case in workmen's compensation, but he couldn't decide it because he wasn't interested enough in the law to follow it through and see where the law could help this particular man, or how it applied to this case."[13]

His lack of interest was shared by most leaders in the construction unions, which were the heart of the AFL. From the first efforts to pass workmen's compensation in 1910, they had been unenthusiastic about it or even actively opposed to it. When she had gone to union meetings to urge support for the bill, the leaders would almost invariably point out how much the union had recovered for some worker in a suit for injuries — and the amount was always far greater than the injured man was likely to receive under the proposed act. To which she would reply that the bill, by reducing the impact of such legal doctrines as contributory negligence, would make recovery much less difficult and therefore more frequent. Union members as well as others would benefit. But those in the unions, or at least most of their leaders, were doubtful: in theory, benefits for workers should be won by the unions, not granted by the state, or the unions would be weakened. In any event they cared nothing about the unorganized.[14]

George Meany, then of the plumbers' union, years later, when he was president of the AFL–CIO, summarized the attitude of the time.

> My union was a closed union, closed in the fact that it didn't take in new members. [Sons or other close relatives of members got the few openings.] When we had industrial work crop up that we felt that we should do, we made an effort, if we had any weight, any pressure, to get that work for our contractors. We would not work [put on pressure] directly. We [simply] wouldn't work for anyone but our own contractors. We didn't want [to organize] the people that were on the work, we merely wanted the work. So far as the people that were on the work were concerned, for our part they could drop dead.
>
> We even went so far that we wouldn't take clearance cards. We shut the union to other union members of our own craft from other cities. I am not bragging about it. I am not proud of it. I am telling you that is what we did.[15]

Though leaders of the craft unions constantly denied that their aim was to monopolize jobs for the benefit of their members, it often seemed their chief purpose. Only a few worked actively for anything broader. One was John Flynn, of the Rome strike, who introduced the first pension bill for workers' widows. He had heard Florence Kelley speak and, as he told Perkins, "Since then I see it! You got to have a law or there'll be lots of abuses of women, children and poor weak people who can't defend themselves because they haven't got a union." John O'Hanlon, the legislative representative of the State Federation of Labor, was another who had been impressed by Florence Kelley and saw a need for social or labor legislation. In supporting bills before the legislature he could not exceed his instructions, but his opinion carried weight within the federation.[16]

The public, on the other hand, supported the Workmen's Compensation Act. Soon after it was passed in 1910, the state's highest court declared it unconstitutional. In November 1913 the voters (still only men) approved an amendment to the constitution specifically designed to allow the act. The vote was 510,914 to 194,497, an enormous margin. In the first weeks of January the new legislature passed it, and by mid-1914 the administrative machinery to implement it had begun to function.[17]

With regard to accidents on the job, the act made a great change in the relationship between employer and employee. Under the common law a worker could recover damages for an injury only if he could show that the employer was negligent and that he, the worker, was not disqualified by any of three defenses: that his injury was caused, however slightly, by his own "contributory negligence," or by that of a fellow worker or was the result of a risk he had assumed in taking the job. Because of these defenses workers seldom won their suits, and the few who did often had to pay over the greater part of their damages to their lawyers.

Under the Workmen's Compensation Act, however, a worker who qualified did not have to prove negligence on his employer's part. Nor, usually, did he need a lawyer. He had only to prove his injury, and a referee from the Department of Labor would make an award based on the severity of the injury and the amount of the worker's weekly wage.

In the early years of the act, the loss of a thumb would allow a worker an award of two thirds of his weekly wage for a period of 60 weeks; for the loss of an eye, two thirds of his wage for 128 weeks. He received the money from his employer directly or from his employer's insurance company or from a state insurance fund; it depended on how the employer had chosen, with the state's approval, to guarantee his ability to make compensation payments.

Both employer and employee had gained and lost something under the plan. The employer lost all his common law defenses of the worker's contributory negligence, a fellow worker's negligence and the worker's assumption of the risk. He now had to pay for a worker's injury on the job regardless of fault, and he had to pay much more often. But he also, by and large, paid much less. For if the worker qualified for workmen's compensation, he was required to sue under the act, and it limited the amounts he could recover. The worker gave up the chance at the occasional huge award made by a jury or a settlement out of court, but he gained certainty. He now had only to prove his injury (assuming it was not willful), and he generally would receive his award promptly and without the need to hire a lawyer.

In the eighteenth and even the nineteenth century a workman injured on the job was an object of charity. In the twentieth, with the great increase in the use of machinery, the number and seriousness of accidents also greatly increased, and public opinion had gradually come to insist that industry rather than the individual workers should bear the cost of the accidents. A workmen's compensation act was the governmental response to that opinion. Actually, of course, the cost of the accidents was borne ultimately not by industry, but by the general public, because the companies included their costs in their prices, and the Department of Labor's costs were met by taxes. Workmen's compensation, by distributing the cost of an individual's disaster among the community, was a form of social insurance.

That idea appealed to Perkins, which may explain her success in administering the New York Act. At one conference in Washington she referred to insurance as the most brilliant achievement of the mind of man.[18] She did not expand on her statement, but insurance united two of her strongest interests, science and religion: science, in the technical precision of actuarial tables based on observed fact; and religion, in the acknowledgment that each man, when the community shares the cost of one's disaster, is his brother's keeper.

The administration of a workmen's compensation act requires a mixture of technical knowledge, legal reasoning and sympathy tempered by common sense. In a room on the second floor of the department's building at 124 East Twenty-eighth Street, Perkins, as a member of the Industrial Board, would hear appeals by either the worker or employer from the decisions of the board's referees. In 1921 a member of the department wrote a description of her at work:

. . . "A five dollar bill for Sloan's liniment?" she asked of the representative of an employer who was present to object to the employee's claim for reimbursement.

"And he sent you an insulting letter, with just a memorandum and no receipt from his druggist?"

Miss Perkins considered the matter and then, suppressing a little smile, dismissed it: "Well, why not pay the bill and have it over with? After all, it's only five dollars." She looked somewhat quizzically at the young man before her, who seemed all at once to feel he had been placed in a slightly ridiculous position.

A middle-aged colored man had been awarded compensation for the loss of an eye. The employer's representative was there to object on the ground that, after the accident and removal of the eye, the hospital records revealed a cataract on it.

"But the law makes an award for the loss of an eye," argued Miss Perkins patiently. "And there was an eye here, an eye with some vision, even if there was a cataract."

In another case she scanned X-ray photographs to reach a decision that the award for injury to a "one-eighth portion of the left ring finger" should stand despite the objection raised by the insurance carrier.

A young woman claimed compensation from a cabaret because an injury received as a dancer in its employ had caused a tumor to form on her thigh. She was reasoned with, and an order given for the cabaret manager to appear before the Commission [the Industrial Board] the following week.

"There are many people who come here," said Commissioner Perkins to the girl, "who are disabled for the performance of certain work — and they learn other trades or professions, and sometimes make more money at them than they did at their former work."

"But I had a profession; I don't know what else I could do!" faltered the young woman.

"And she was discharged," her mother insisted, "the manager himself said so — because she wasn't lively like the other girls — and how could she be with a tumor on her thigh — and —"

Miss Perkins listened patiently but stuck to her point that, looking to the future, if the daughter could not continue to dance, she could learn to do something else, a possibility which to all appearances neither the girl nor her mother had previously entertained.[19]

The chorus girl could apply for an award because the risks covered by the act had been steadily expanded. When first passed in 1914 the act had applied only to workmen in certain hazardous employments, but in 1918 "hazardous employments" was defined to include any employment in which "four or more workmen or operatives" were regularly engaged. In 1920 twenty-three occupational diseases, such as lead or benzol poisoning, were made grounds for an award. In 1924, after experience had shown that awards for the loss of a thumb or eye were too small relative to the maximum award for a fatal accident, they were increased by lengthening the periods in which the worker could receive two thirds of his wage: for a thumb, 60 to 75 weeks; for an eye, 128 to 160 weeks.

Not all the act's extensions originated in the legislature; many came from court decisions. In one of these Perkins became the moving force when she felt that a legal quirk was depriving a workman of his due.

A Finnish carpenter living in Brooklyn, Matti (Matthew) Lahti, had taken a job with Terry and Tench, a construction company, and been sent with a team of workers to repair a dock on Staten Island. In order to work around the piles at water level and to have a place to put their tools, he and a fellow worker constructed a small raft. Once, when Lahti was standing on it, a beam fell on his foot, injuring it seriously.

He was entitled to an award, ruled Perkins.

He was not, insisted the insurance company, and appealed the case. The insurance lawyer argued that since the injury occurred on the water the Workmen's Compensation Act did not apply. Admiralty law applied to accidents at sea; therefore Lahti must sue the ship on which the injury occurred — his raft — and look to the ship's owners — himself and his companion — for reimbursement.

To Perkins such an argument was ludicrous. A raft tied to a pier for the sole purpose of working on the pier was a part of the pier. The Appellate Division agreed with her, but the Court of Appeals, the state's highest court, reversed the decision. "The *locus* of the accident was maritime," Cardozo wrote for a unanimous court. "We do not stop to inquire whether the raft is to be classified as a boat, for however that question were to be answered, the territorial basis of jurisdiction would remain."

Perkins was not convinced, nor was Lahti. Again and again he came to her office, a blond, thin, washed-out-looking man. One day he asked, "Many times I come here. You make me an award. The next day I hear there is an appeal and I get no money. Why I get no money?"

She persuaded a reluctant state Attorney General to appeal the case to the U.S. Supreme Court. Because the deputy assigned to it seemed uninterested, she undertook to educate him on the law and made suggestions for his argument and brief. Thus lashed into performance, he was victorious: the court ruled that a raft tied to a dock, which is acknowledged to be an extension of the land, is also an extension of the land. Five years and one week after the injury, Lahti received his award, computed at twenty dollars a week for 205 weeks.

After several such cases — though not all of them reached the Supreme Court — she was invited out to dinner one night in Albany. The other guest was Cardozo, who had expressed a desire to meet her.[20]

To some persons, perhaps, Perkins seemed a busybody: shouldn't a member of the state's Department of Labor acquiesce in a decision by the state's highest court? To others she seemed the ideal public servant: she attempted always to administer the laws so that they benefited rather than oppressed the people of the state.

Though workmen's compensation in New York had originated in 1909 with Republicans, as a party — aside from some exceptions, such as Higgens — they soon began to oppose it. Not only did they fight any extensions of the act but, under Miller, they actually curtailed it. Smith, on the other hand, pushed for extensions, talked often and proudly of the Department of Labor and throughout the decade from 1918 to 1928 constantly increased his party's support among the workers. Perkins, as Smith's representative at safety conferences, State Federation of Labor conventions, Democratic State Conventions and the Department of Labor, was often the one with whom workers and their leaders came into contact. They discovered that she listened to their problems, studied them and devised remedies. They thought well of her. Eventually in the presidential election of 1928 the Democrats for the first time in many years outpolled the Republicans in the nation's twelve largest cities. Urban America, largely immigrant, industrial and, in 1920 and 1924, solidly Republican, had switched its allegiance. In that revolution, at least in New York, the country's most populous and industrial state, as Smith's lieutenant for labor Perkins had a part.[21]

Chapter 15

-»><«-

The 1924 convention: Smith loses the nomination and Roosevelt returns to politics. The Child Labor amendment: the cardinal's emissary and Florence Kelley call on Smith. Changes in settlement workers and among women. The improvements in labor legislation.

SINCE THE CIVIL WAR, the Democrats had won only four of the fourteen presidential elections — twice each with Cleveland and Wilson. And both men in their first terms had been helped into office by angry Republicans who had bolted their party, the Mugwumps in 1884 and the Bull Moose Progressives in 1912. And now, in 1924, the scandals of the Harding administration provided the Democrats with an issue likely to divide the Republicans.

The party however had a problem: it was sorely split on several questions and lacked an undisputed leader. The chief contenders for the nomination were William G. McAdoo, Wilson's son-in-law and Secretary of the Treasury, and Al Smith. Roughly speaking, McAdoo was the candidate of the South and West, and Smith of the Northeast; McAdoo of the countryside and smaller marketing cities, and Smith of the fewer but larger industrial cities. Though each controlled a large bloc of delegates, without some compromise neither seemed likely to attain the two-thirds majority necessary for the nomination.

The delegates assembled in New York at Madison Square Garden,[1] and for the first time their proceedings were carried to the country by radio. Hardly had the routine words of welcome faded on the air before listeners heard a bitter debate over the party platform. At issue was not Prohibition — though McAdoo was a dry and Smith a wet — but the party's attitude toward the Ku Klux Klan. After World War I, partly as a result of the intolerance and anxiety fostered by the war, the Klan had spread rapidly across the country, not only in the small towns but in many of the larger cities, particularly in Ohio, Indiana and Illinois. Though its active membership probably was never more than a million and a half, in much of the South and West its influence was felt at all levels of government and it was often estimated to have as many as four million members.

In general Klansmen wanted the country to continue as they imagined it had been before the war. Fundamentalism was a central thread in their program. They were distressed by the growth of the cities and the seeming decline in morality, displayed by short skirts, drinking, dirty books and dirty pictures. They were distressed, too, by the increasing political power of the larger cities, which seemed often to be controlled by blocs of immigrants. Klansmen wanted the country to end immigration, to reject the League of Nations and the World Court and to withdraw from Europe. They emphasized Americanism — defining Americans as white and Protestant.

At its best the Klan advocated a policy for the country, but that policy, by ignoring the rise of industry, looked to the past. At its worst it was a terrorist organization, assembling masked men under fiery crosses and preaching racial supremacy. Outside the South, however, in the 1920s its terrorism was aimed less at Negroes than at immigrant Catholics and Jews. At the convention its supporters' fears were symbolized by the signs prohibiting spitting and smoking in the galleries: they were in Italian and English. "Those bilingual signs," commented William Allen White, editor of the Emporia *Gazette,* "told a real story."

In the debate McAdoo's supporters argued for a plank that would condemn the Klan's principles without naming the organization — something innocuous, similar to what the Republicans had adopted at their convention two weeks earlier. Smith's supporters wanted a plank condemning the Klan by name. After a struggle that hardened prejudices in both camps as well as across the country, McAdoo's supporters won by the margin of a single vote.[2]

Later, during the balloting for the nomination, William Jennings Bryan, the great agrarian leader, came forward to speak on behalf of McAdoo. There were cries of "We don't want to hear him," and the galleries, packed by Tammany with Smith's supporters, hissed and booed so malevolently that extra police were summoned. Meanwhile Bryan, who had three times won the nomination, roared back at the galleries: "You do not represent the future of America!"[3]

By then compromise was no longer possible. On either side the struggle had become a crusade of self-righteousness: Smith's for an open America in which a Catholic or Jew could be nominated for President; McAdoo's for a clean America purged of big city corruption and bossism. Yet the Klan in all its actions was not so clean — nor Smith in all of his so pure. At one point a group of western delegates who were Catholics and supporters of McAdoo tried to break the deadlock by suggesting Senator Thomas J. Walsh as a compromise candidate. Walsh, the convention chairman and the man most responsible for uncovering the Teapot Dome scandal, was a Catholic. But Smith would not consider the idea; apparently he and only he was to be the first Catholic nominated for President by a major party.[4]

Still, after more than a week of balloting Smith and other minority candidates began to release their delegates; McAdoo retained his until the ninety-ninth ballot. Then the delegates coalesced behind John W. Davis, nominated on the hundred and third ballot. Bryan and McAdoo promptly announced that they would support the candidate. Smith did, too, but in a tasteless fashion. Asked to address the convention, to thunderous applause from the galleries he described his achievements in three terms as governor but scarcely mentioned Davis. Eventually Bryan's brother Charles was nominated for Vice-President. But by then the election had been lost. The convention was the most disastrous in a national party since the Democratic convention of 1860, when after fifty-seven ballots the party split in two, North and South.

For Perkins some of the political realities of national politics, such as the South's grip on the party machinery, came as a surprise. She had never before had a part in a convention, but now she was chairman of the platform committee of the Women's Democratic Union, campaigned with the Women's Division and, as a member of Smith's administration, had an aisle seat on the convention floor close by the steps to the platform. Though the convention did not open formally until June 24, starting in May she attended committee meetings, spoke before delegates and their wives, helped to entertain them and eventually, as the balloting continued week after week, took in as guests two women delegates from the West who were running short of money. As the weeks passed, she began to glimpse how Smith appeared to people outside the state.[5]

The idea of holding the convention in New York had originated with Murphy, and its accomplishment represented a triumph of intrigue. But after she saw the animosity of many of the delegates toward the city — they considered it the Gomorrah of America — she began to question Murphy's wisdom. Perhaps New York was not the best place to present Smith as a candidate. The behavior of the galleries clearly "sickened the delegates."

Yet it was Smith himself who was responsible for it. Murphy had died of a heart attack on April 25, and throughout the convention Smith was the real head of Tammany. He could have appealed for better behavior or changed the distribution of tickets, but even in his autobiography he had not a word of regret for the galleries.

Smith, or perhaps his closest advisers, Belle Moskowitz, Joseph M. Proskauer and Robert Moses, made a similar mistake on the issue of Prohibition. As window-dressing Smith had asked Franklin Roosevelt to take Murphy's post on the Democratic State Committee, but Roosevelt, who would be making his first convention appearance since his attack of polio, was allowed to do little. He prepared a statement for Smith in which the Prohibition issue was described as a "red herring." It had Smith say: "A temperate people are a happy and contented people, and to that end all my acts and words will bend." But Smith refused to use it; instead he repeated his demand for immediate repeal of the amendment or, failing that, modification of the Volstead Act to permit the sale of beer and light wine. His position was consistent and absolutely honest, but the bluntness of his statement was unnecessarily provoking to those who still favored Prohibition, the party's majority.[6]

Similarly, in being true to himself he was unable to dim his Broadway style, so dear to New Yorkers and so startling to others. One day some delegates from Kansas, a strong Prohibition state, stopped at Roosevelt's office to meet the candidate. Smith was at the christening of a friend's daughter, but eventually he appeared

> . . . entering like a breeze, in a swallowtail coat, a silk hat at a rakish angle and with the usual cigar in his mouth. "Hello, hello, my boy, and how's things?" he said, addressing Roosevelt. The latter introduced his callers as delegates from Kansas. "Hello, boys" said Smith, shaking hands. "Glad to see you. Y'know, the other day some boys were in from Wisconsin and I learned somethin'. I always thought Wisconsin was on this side of the lake. It's on the other side. Glad to know it. Glad to know more about the place where the good beer comes from."[7]

Aside from considerations about Smith's religion, it was possible for some to question his fitness for the presidency. He might be New York's favorite son, but what did he know about the country, about its farm problems or its international affairs? Perhaps more quickly than Smith, Perkins began to realize that if he was to move from the state to the national scene he would have to increase the range of his experience and modify the flamboyance of his style. She saw it was not enough to be a specialist in New York. He would have to learn "to carry water on both shoulders, as indeed nearly all candidates for the Presidency must do, except in situations of crisis and emergency."[8]

One Democrat to emerge from the convention with burnished reputation was Roosevelt, taken on at the last minute because of Murphy's death. Due to another death that year — that of Bourke Cockran, the great Tammany orator — Roosevelt was also selected to nominate Smith. He was not allowed to compose the speech, only to make additions (chiefly a plea for party unity) to a draft prepared by Proskauer. Wordsworth's famous phrase, "The Happy Warrior," always to be associated with Smith, was Proskauer's idea. Roosevelt protested that it was too poetic but was overruled.

The gravity of Roosevelt's condition and his courage in facing it was obvious in the convention hall. Everyone knew that he had lost the use of his legs three years earlier. Now the delegates saw him day by day as he haltingly made his way to his seat. He would arrive with his sixteen-year-old son James supporting his left arm, a crutch under his right and steel braces on either leg. After he was seated, his son would take the crutch and stand by to run errands or lend an arm.

On June 26, when it came time for the nomination, Roosevelt and James went down the aisle to the rear of the platform. At the top of the steps, he left his son, took a second crutch and started alone for the speaker's stand.

A hush came over the hall as the crowd watched him slowly lurching forward. His feet would drag; then he would advance a crutch and swing the feet forward in a circular, hitching wrench. The movements were awkward, ugly and plainly insecure. As he reached the speaker's stand, the convention cheered with relief and approval. He could not take his hand from the stand to wave, but throwing his head back he greeted the convention with a broad, brilliant smile.

From her seat Perkins could see that, as he spoke, his hand on the lectern never stopped trembling. Every cheer, every demonstration prolonged his agony of self-support. His voice, however, was always vigorous, clear and under control. With this speech for Smith, he proclaimed to the Democratic party that Roosevelt, who was crippled, who had almost died, was alive and re-entering politics.

While he was still speaking, Perkins realized that someone must cover his awkward movements as he left the stand. "I saw around him all those fat slob politicians — men — and I knew they wouldn't think of it." She whispered to the woman beside her, and as soon as he had finished they hurried onto the platform and stood in front of him as he turned to leave. It was a maneuver that afterward became routine; when he came to the end of a speech several people would appear on the platform — ostensibly to greet or congratulate him, but actually to provide a screen. For the purpose women were better than men; their skirts made more of a shield.[9]

In the election Coolidge defeated Davis, 15,725,016 to 8,385,586. A third party of farmers, socialists and labor unionists, led by Robert La Follette, polled 4,822,856. Most of these voters seem to have been Republicans though on the West Coast a sizable number might have voted for Smith if he had been nominated.

Instead he ran for governor of New York, easily defeating Theodore Roosevelt, Jr., and leading the Democratic national ticket within the state by more than a million votes. As a result, by the end of the year he emerged as an even stronger candidate for the next presidential nomination. Some of McAdoo's supporters, looking to 1928, began to shift their allegiance.[10]

Because they did not experience him directly, people outside the state found Smith's hold on New York mysterious. But few governors have been so successful in talking directly to the people, in seeming to be one of them while at the same time educating them on issues. In April 1925, when he was faced with probable defeat in the legislature on a complicated tax measure, he arranged a radio hook-up and for an hour and a half explained what he was trying to do. In closing he urged everyone to write to his or her representative in Albany. Letters and telegrams poured in on the legislators, and the bill passed. In the elections of 1927 nine constitutional amendments were presented to the voters. Smith told them in detail why he wanted all but Number 6 passed. Meanwhile the Republicans were urging that all nine be rejected. All but Number 6 passed.

His strength lay in his honesty of purpose and his ability to translate his experience of life into political programs that not only appealed to voters but worked well in administration. This talent, even genius, for government was the more extraordinary because he had had no formal education in law, accounting or political science; he had left school at the age of fourteen to help support his widowed mother and sister.

In 1911 he was speaking on a bill in the Assembly, or so the story goes, when a member asked leave to interrupt with the results of a crew race at Poughkeepsie. Cornell had won, and there was much joking about the positions of Yale, Columbia and other schools.

"Mr. Chairman," Smith called out, "if my old alma mater had been represented, we'd have won. Boats and boating were very necessary to my alma mater. We were, and I say it without boasting, strong on the water."

"What is your alma mater?" asked a member.

"F.F.M.," Smith replied. "I'm an old F.F.M. man."

"Where's that, Al?"

"Fulton Fish Market. That's where I got my higher education."[11]

In another speech in the Assembly, on his third inauguration as governor in January 1925, he spoke more seriously about his education: "This is the sixteenth time I have taken the Oath of Allegiance in this room. I have a deep and abiding affection for the Assembly Chamber. It has been my high school and my college; in fact the very foundation of everything I have attained was laid here."

Perkins, who had watched Smith transform what he had learned from factory tours into remedial legislation, felt his gift for leadership was

> . . . a translation of his capacity to love, to love personally and to extend that personal love which he had for individuals and his family to embrace thousands of other people whom he could actually feel to be his brothers and sisters and to feel with them and for them and sense how their backs ached and how their feet ached. And then he had the capacity to translate into practical action this love of his fellows. This would never seem either to him or to anyone else a pious pose. It was as natural as trying to pick up a child who has fallen in the street or to comfort an old woman who has lost her way in the city. But having had this sincere emotion, he had the skill and the instinct and the ability to translate it into a definite moral purpose. He knew it was a moral purpose rather than an economic purpose because he saw no economic advantage to him or to anybody else.[12]

In the winter of 1924–1925, Smith's Catholicism became a problem in politics in Albany. The question was the fate in New York of the proposed Child Labor amendment to the federal Constitution. Over it Smith clashed first with his church and then with Florence Kelley, who by the quarter century had herself become something of an institution in reform circles.

The amendment proposed to authorize Congress "to limit, regulate and prohibit the labor of persons under eighteen years of age" while reserving to the states their right to enact any child labor laws that did not conflict with federal legislation. Its supporters hoped that Congress would prohibit the employment of children in certain industries, such as mining and textiles, or at least set minimum standards of age, health and education for child labor.

An amendment seemed necessary because twice, in 1918 and 1922, the United States Supreme Court had declared federal laws regulating child labor unconstitutional because they were an invasion of the police power reserved to the states.[13] Yet leaving the problem to the states seemed unsatisfactory to reformers because few states would act. Those that did were likely to suffer for it; in Massachusetts, for example, textile companies were beginning to move their mills to southern states where labor was cheaper — often because it was child labor.

According to the census of 1920, more than a million children aged ten to sixteen were working. Roughly 60 percent of them were in agriculture, 17 percent in mining or manufacturing and 14 percent in trade or clerical positions. Child labor in agriculture was an explosive issue, and Congress had never attempted to regulate it. But the laws declared unconstitutional had concerned the 17 percent in mining and manufacturing — about two hundred thousand children. With regard to these it seemed clear that the people and Congress favored action.

Yet the amendment aroused opposition even among reformers. Some now favored action by the states, however slow. Others thought the timing poor: the Coolidge era with its emphasis on "normalcy" and business was hostile to reform legislation. Many, discouraged by the example of Prohibition, felt that a federal amendment was not the way to proceed, though the successful administration from 1916 to 1922 of the two invalid child labor laws suggested that the analogy was false.[14]

Employers almost without exception opposed the amendment. Alonzo B. See of the A. B. See Elevator Company in New York complained to Jane Addams, who forwarded his letter to Kelley, that ratification would keep boys from healthy labor, deprive them of "manliness and self-respect" and turn the country into "a vast kindergarten." The National Association of Manufacturers declared the idea bolshevik-inspired, an effort to nationalize children.[15]

At first the amendment seemed likely to have the full support of Catholic voters. Among its most articulate advocates were Senator Walsh of Montana and Father John A. Ryan, a priest who had a major role in determining the church's social programs. But William

Henry Cardinal O'Connell and the hierarchy in Massachusetts began to oppose it on the grounds that it interfered with parental discipline and attacked the sanctity of family life. In a letter to Archbishop Curley of Baltimore, the cardinal called the amendment "Soviet legislation." In a pastoral letter a few weeks before a state referendum on the amendment he urged priests to tell their parishioners to vote against it. The following month, November 1924, it was defeated, three to one.[16]

In trying to analyze what had gone wrong, supporters in the Child Labor Committee, Consumers' League, Women's Trade Union League, the Parents-Teachers Association and other organizations were unable to fix on any one cause. Many people seemed unable or unwilling to understand that the amendment would not prevent children from washing their supper dishes. Others, apparently, truly believed that the amendment was a communist idea. Some, possibly as a reaction to the war, seemed adverse to any form of national regulation. In Kansas the Republican sage, William Allen White, concluded, "We are in a slough of reaction. It is the height of folly to push humanitarian measures at this time and give their opponents the prestige of defeat."[17]

Even Florence Kelley began to despair. In a letter to Perkins the month after the Massachusetts vote, she asked, "Is there any living Democrat in this State, beside the Governor and the State Department of Labor, who is right on the Children's Amendment?" She worried about the New York legislature, which would convene in January. Would it pass the amendment? If the country's most powerful newspaper, Ralph Pulitzer's New York *World,* "owned and edited by 'liberal' Jews," joined Cardinal O'Connell "against the children," the amendment was lost, not only in New York but in the country.[18]

When Perkins was in Albany one day, Smith phoned and asked her to come to his office. After she arrived, to her surprise he seemed to have nothing to say. Then the secretary announced a cleric. Smith said to her, "You stay here. We'll go on with our conversation later. You don't need to say anything. Just stay here."

A clergyman of considerable rank and dignity entered. Smith introduced Perkins as a member of the Industrial Board, and she took a seat on the far side of the desk, a little apart from the others.

The man approached his subject directly, and it was Perkins's understanding from what he said that he spoke as a representative of Cardinal O'Connell. He'd come about the child labor amendment, to explain the church's objections. God had set up the family as the unit.

The family must control all of its members. Only so can we have a real society — a Christian society. The family must decide whether the child should work, where he should work, whether he is able to work and how much he should be paid. That is for the family to decide. It is not for the state to interfere in the sacred life of the family.

Smith listened, puffed his cigar and allowed the priest to finish without interruption. Then, after thanking him for speaking so directly, he said, "You know, Father, I'm a good Catholic."

"Oh, yes, indeed," said the priest. "We know that."

"I'm a good Catholic. I practice. I say my prayers, make confession, go to communion. You know that, Father."

"Oh, yes, we do."

"You know I love the church."

"Yes, we know you love the church."

"I know I owe a great deal to the church," said Smith. "I owe my character, my bringing up and my nature to the church. I'm very thankful and grateful."

The priest smiled the church's appreciation.

"But I want to tell you something, Father. You know I'm the governor of the State of New York."

"Oh, yes. That's a proud day for us."

"You know I have to think of the welfare of all the people in the State of New York, whether they're holy Catholics like you and me, or whether they're something else. I have to think about them and about their welfare."

"Oh, yes, of course, but the family is a sacred institution."

"I recognize that," Smith continued, "and I wouldn't do anything to break it up, but there are times when a father of a family dies and can't support his family. There's a great temptation to send the little children to work. There are times when a family doesn't even know about its sacred duty to protect the children. I've seen such families, Father, and I know it's something that can happen. I know there are an awful lot of children in this state who go to work when it isn't good for them and who go to work when it ruins their health for the rest of their lives. It deprives them of the freedom and happiness of childhood. I know that an awful lot of them are paid a wage so low that a grown person wouldn't take it. That's why they're hired. They're exploited, Father. I know that. I've seen them."

"Oh, yes, but we must rely upon God's goodness and the family."

"You know, Father, I understand the duty of the church. I under-

stand your duty. I understand the duty of the priests; I understand
the duty of the Holy Father. I'm bound to obey the Holy Father and
I'm bound to obey you in all matters of faith and morals. But there's
nothing in the law of the church that says I have to obey the church in
matters that are economic, social or political. No, Father. That's not
a part of the duty of the church to tell me that. I'm the governor of
the State of New York and I know more about these things than you
or any other priest can ever know because you don't have to deal with
it. I'm very grateful to you, Father, for telling me this. Any time you
come to me on a matter of faith or morals where I've been doing
wrong, you can be sure I'll go along with you, but this belongs to me.
This is the governor of the State of New York's duty and it belongs to
me. It doesn't belong to anybody else."

The priest coughed, stood up and shook hands. Smith showed him
out. When he returned, he was mopping his brow. "It took some
doing," he said.

"You did fine, Governor."

"You know," he said, "you have to tell them sometimes. He don't
mean any harm. If he knew what you and I know he couldn't talk like
that. How would he get to know? There's no way he can know."

She felt the story was not hers to tell, and she did not recount it
publicly until the autumn of 1957, in a lecture at Cornell. The
meeting, however, gave her absolute confidence in assuring others that
Smith would not be swayed on questions of government by pressure
from his church.[19]

Smith's certainty of his independence perhaps blinded him to the
doubts of others. He was well aware of prejudice, and in planning a
campaign in New York might say, "Better let those Protestant guys go
upstate to make the speech." In matters that he considered personal to
his practice of religion, however, he would make no concessions. He
kept a picture of the pope in his office. He knelt in public to kiss the
ring of a papal legate. As a prominent Catholic layman, in 1926 he
attended a Eucharistic Congress. When a Protestant fell in love with
his daughter Emily, he required the man to convert, then gave the
couple a sumptuous wedding, complete with a cardinal officiating and
a papal blessing brought by a special messenger. Many people found
it easy to doubt his independence from the church.[20]

For some reformers, among them Kelley, an Irish Protestant, his
tactical approach to the amendment excited doubts. Though he said
in his annual message to the legislature that he was in "hearty accord
with what is sought to be done" by the amendment, he recommended

that the legislators, instead of voting on it directly, submit it first to the people in a referendum. To its supporters this seemed a shove onto the course that had led to disaster in Massachusetts. Also it would force them to propagandize the entire electorate instead of its 225 representatives, and they lacked the money to do it effectively.[21]

Yet political reasons alone could account for Smith's action. He faced a legislature in which both chambers were controlled by Republicans, whereas the Democrats had a majority of the electorate. And only the previous year, with the Prohibition amendment in mind, he had argued that in the future any amendment to the federal Constitution should be submitted to the people rather than to their representatives in the state legislatures.

In March the state Senate voted in favor of the referendum, but the Assembly postponed any action on the amendment in the current session. About this time a despairing Kelley asked Perkins to arrange an interview for her with Smith.

She arrived breathing fire, as Perkins, who joined her in the governor's outer office, realized too late.

Like the priest, Kelley started right in. It was outrageous that the Assembly should delay in voting on the referendum. If the governor only would take an interest, the Assembly would act. "I don't like to say this to you," she said, shaking her finger at him, "but I know the Catholic church is opposing this. I fear that you have given in to the church on it."

Smith said angrily that he was not controlled by the Catholic church, nor would he be by some Protestant bigot.

"I'm not a bigot," she said. "I've always been in favor of child labor legislation. You know that."

"What you said now about the Catholic church interfering in the Assembly in my opinion is a mark of bigotry. I don't think they are, but if they are, they're doing it through the consciences of the individuals who are members. The only way you can combat that is to go to those individuals one by one and show them the reasonableness of your project. You can't do it by calling names."

Voices rose. Kelley's became shrill. Suddenly she said, "I see no further sense in this conversation. Good morning, Governor!"

"Good morning, Mrs. Kelley!"

Perkins said quietly to Smith, "I'll go out with Mrs. Kelley."

"Oh, Mrs. Kelley," she said in the hall. "What have you done? I know of my own knowledge, because I heard it, that the governor is *not* taking the position of the church, that the church has taken no authoritative or official position, though some of the clergy have. The governor has not given in to it, I know it."

"Why doesn't he interfere?"

"You can't interfere with everything in the Assembly. It's a matter of political strategy and timing. You have to get things along as you can."

But Kelley was not listening. Though she later voted for Smith, it is doubtful if she ever forgave him.[22]

Meanwhile, children in most of the states continued to work in the mines and mills. Ten years later two thirds of the states still had not ratified the amendment, though by January 1938, under the spur of the Depression, the number rose to twenty-eight of the forty-eight, most of them in the North and West. In the end the U.S. Supreme Court, by upholding the Fair Labor Standards Act of 1938, in which Perkins as U.S. Secretary of Labor had a part, simply reversed its decisions of 1918 and 1922. It ruled that Congress had had the power all along to regulate the employment of children when the products of their work were part of interstate commerce. At that moment the amendment became unnecessary.

The failure of the Child Labor amendment in the 1920s reflected a number of changing attitudes in the country, not least among the reformers themselves. When the vigorous, profoundly religious executive secretary of the Child Labor Committee, Owen Lovejoy, resigned in 1926, he was succeeded by cautious, colorless Wiley Swift, the candidate of the more conservative members. For Swift the crusading days of the committee had passed. "From now on," he wrote in 1927, "the movement will be more gradual and necessarily less spectacular. A little here and a little there is the way we shall inch up to better things." But when the Depression struck and child labor increased, he was eased aside in favor of a more aggressive leader.

A more lasting change overtook the settlement workers or, as they were more frequently being called, social workers. They might have been expected to provide the proposed amendment's strongest support, but many were apathetic. Throughout the 1920s a generation gap among them became visible, with Perkins, Kelley and most others born before 1895 on the dwindling side.

Before World War I the settlement houses had drawn their recruits chiefly from men and women with a strong sense of mission, generally with a religious basis. Many of them also had postgraduate degrees in fields related to their work. But after the war, or perhaps slightly before it, the younger settlement workers often lacked both. They reacted with embarrassment to the unabashed religious drive of their elders. At a meeting in 1930 Helen Phelan, head resident of Merrick House in Cleveland, said apologetically: "I am old-fashioned enough to have a religious motive for doing the thing I am doing. It is old-fashioned in these days, isn't it, to mention religion."

Without their elders' spirit of dedication, the new social workers disliked the idea of residency, of living in the community where they worked. More and more of them commuted from their own middle-class neighborhoods, and gradually their relationship with the people they sought to help shifted from that of neighbors working for the common good to the professional and client. In the 1920s much of the younger workers' time was taken up with establishing themselves as a profession: drawing up ethical codes, defining areas of work, setting standards for courses, schools and personnel. Vida Scudder, one of the founders of the College Settlement Association, characterized the difference between the new professionals and older amateurs as that "between a salaried clergy and the mendicant orders who had become fools for Christ." An observer, Abraham Epstein, wrote in 1928:

> No longer are the voices of the early Isaiahs heard in the demand of justice. Vital social reforms are left to languish and social workers as a group take but little interest in them. Except for campaign purposes social work no longer proclaims itself as pure altruism . . . It has lost its spiritual equilibrium and it has become too practical to be passionate . . . It speaks with the polished tongue of the financier through expert press agents and high pressure publicity. Instead of denouncing wrongs it has become merely amiable. Its only crusades are community chest drives which it conducts with the zip-zip of a successful team's cheerleader.

The younger social workers, in transforming themselves into a bureaucracy, produced no leaders of the stature of Jane Addams, Graham Taylor, Lillian Wald, Paul Kellogg or Florence Kelley. The older generation had blamed poverty on low wages and inhuman conditions; they had joined strikers on the picket lines or marched on city hall to demand better sanitation or housing. The new people, whose emphasis was increasingly on casework and whose fashionable concern was often with psychoanalysis instead of social agitation, tended to see poverty as a psychological problem, an inadequate "adjustment" to reality. They were inclined to concentrate on adjusting individuals to their environment rather than working for social legislation.[23]

In the coming decade, as Perkins continued to urge the ratification

of the child labor amendment, its opponents, labor officials and journalists would often refer to her as a "social worker." The imprecision
of the label faintly irritated her, for although she had done settlement
work and even social work, she was not a "social worker" as the term
was used then. She had never done casework, and the whole purpose
of her career was to improve "conditions" not "adjustment."[24]

In much the same way, she and those who had led the movement for
women's suffrage found themselves out of step with the succeeding
generation of educated, middle-class women. After the vote was won,
women returned home. What had been anticipated as a revolution in
their lives proved to be only a reform. By 1920 all over the country
the League of Women Voters had difficulty recruiting members. Most
women seemed to care only for home, husband and children.

The change of mood was often blamed on the war, though signs of it
appeared earlier. One college girl, speaking for her fellows, proclaimed, "We're not out to benefit society . . . or to make industry
safe. We're not going to suffer over how the other half lives." To
Virginia Gildersleeve, dean of Barnard, the college girl of the twenties
was characterized by "blasé indifference, self-indulgence and irresponsibility."

The symbol of the period was the flapper, whose cause, the "emanci-
pation" of women, meant cocktails, cigarettes and extramarital sex.
Yet, for all their talk, a greater percentage of the graduates of
women's colleges married and while in college proclaimed marriage
their chief aim in life. Perkins's Mount Holyoke class of 1902, of
which half, thirteen years after graduation, was unmarried and almost
half working, had a different point of view from the Class of 1915,
which thirteen years after its graduation reported itself two-thirds
married and only one-sixth working. As college enrollment had
swelled, the sense of obligation in a college education had disappeared.

Many colleges encouraged the change by introducing courses on
domestic science and by theorizing in reports and commencement
addresses that a woman's education should be different from a man's.
Mary Lyon, founding Mount Holyoke to give women the equivalent
of a Harvard or Yale education, would not have understood.[25]

In such an atmosphere Perkins, despite her remarkable career — on
January 1, 1926, Smith appointed her chairman of the Industrial
Board — was not an interesting figure to women. In New York State
in certain political, feminine and labor circles she was admired, and
Paul Kellogg commissioned articles from her for *Survey* and followed

her career with approving editorials. But the mass circulation magazines — *Ladies Home Journal, Good Housekeeping* and *Saturday Evening Post* — ignored her. Even the *Mount Holyoke Alumnae Quarterly* had only an occasional perfunctory note. Undoubtedly the lack of attention was agreeable to her, for she disliked personal publicity. But without the active support of women, new and major social legislation, such as the child labor amendment, almost everywhere stalled.

Perkins was eager to supplement the accident insurance of workmen's compensation with other insurance programs for retirement and unemployment, but such programs were too broad for the times. What improvements she and Smith could accomplish were in extending existing laws — workmen's compensation, for example — by amendment or court decision. The 54-hour law for women and minors in industry became a 48-hour law, though with many exemptions. The one-day-rest-in-seven law was extended to more industries, the number of factory inspectors was increased and the Bureau of Women in Industry, which had been abandoned, was restored. Though unspectacular, when taken all together the changes made a steady record of reform.

Her primary goal in those years, however, always eluded her. She wanted a minimum wage law, and if necessary would accept it only for women and minors as a start. She considered it the key to better industrial relations between labor and management. Not only was it the best protection for labor against overlong hours; it would also protect business from the cutthroat competition that led to the sweatshop. By lessening the desperation to make ends meet, felt by both labor and business, the law would drain much of the bitterness out of their relations. But even though Smith again and again recommended a minimum wage board, as had been first suggested by the Factory Investigating Commission, the legislature never would approve it. The temper of the decade was against it.[26]

Chapter 16

→»«←

The 1928 convention: Smith wins the nomination. Perkins campaigns for him in the South and in Missouri. Smith's defeat and the reasons.

PERKINS did not go to Houston for the 1928 Democratic convention. The winter had been hard; Wilson continued ill and her mother, while visiting her in the fall, had suffered a stroke and died. The place at Newcastle, now considerably reduced, was left to Perkins and her sister, and there were affairs to settle. In any event Smith seemed certain to be nominated; and at the conclusion of the first ballot he was. Roosevelt again gave the nominating speech.

The convention was broadcast, and she heard much of it across an airshaft from a neighbor's radio. Until then the old man had used earphones, but for the occasion he had bought a loudspeaker. Lying on her bed one hot night in June, she was amused to think that she was kept awake in New York "by the noise of the Democratic convention in Houston."[1]

Once the campaign began she was more active than ever before. Smith had persuaded Roosevelt to run for governor, and in New York the party worked for the two without preference. She made some speeches for the ticket, but her chief function was to accompany Roosevelt on tours of the upstate cities, introducing him to local labor leaders.

She was impressed by his stamina, his ability to conserve his strength until he needed it and his good humor. When everything went wrong and the scheduled stop at Oriskany Falls had to be canceled, he could abandon the prepared speech, with its paragraph on the battle monument, pull into the center of Skaneateles and greet the surprised people with a few impromptu remarks — all without agitation. It was a valuable talent, one that she felt he had developed since his illness:

"If you can't use your legs and they bring you milk when you wanted orange juice, you learn to say, 'That's all right,' and drink it."[2]

Later she went to Boston to speak for Smith. There was an audience of academic and professional people and she shared the platform with Senator Pat Harrison of Mississippi, the party's oratorical virtuoso. A droll, plump man with a broad accent, he made "a rip-roaring Democratic speech about free trade."

Her style was simpler, less finished but more specific. She said in effect: "This is what Al Smith has done in New York. These are the items in which he had a part. This is what I've seen him do, what I've been interested in, what I've been trying to promote. This is what he has done." Then, item by item, she described the law or administrative practice he had introduced to resolve a problem in factory safety, workmen's compensation, child labor, hours or wages.

The crowd applauded throughout, especially after her accounts of Smith's solutions to various problems. Felix Frankfurter, who was then teaching at Harvard Law School, came up to congratulate her. "Frances, you have given me a new idea about campaign speeches," he said. "I never heard one like that before. Obviously the people are interested in what a candidate has done for them. I never had thought of that before. You went through the program of the Consumers' League [he always associated her with the Consumers' League], and you showed that Al Smith as a political officer had moved in that direction. They like it and they're going to vote for him. It's a political discovery. I don't know whether you know that or not, but this is something for the Democratic party to remember."

She thought his remarks exaggerated — she had been giving the same speech in New York for years. Yet he planted in her mind the thought that the campaign, whether Smith won or lost, would bring his social program to the attention of the whole country for the first time. And to the people, it would be the Democratic program. Thus, to the traditional Democratic doctrines of free trade and states' rights, Smith and the party workers speaking for him were adding another: social legislation. That was something for the party to remember.

In Pittsburgh, Buffalo, Chicago and other northern cities she pitched her speech more to this point, while keeping to the simple style natural to her. In the large industrial cities her arguments seemed to make an impression. In the South and West, where there were fewer industries, people were less receptive; they seemed not so much opposed to the ideas as simply uninterested. She began to wonder if Smith could win.[3]

*

In Boston her aim had been to convert independents to Smith on the basis of his record. A month before the election she went on a southern tour with Irene Gibson, the wife of Charles Dana Gibson, the artist, for the purpose of reconciling Democrats to Smith's Catholicism. Irene Gibson was a Southerner; both she and Perkins were Protestants. The trip was arranged so that they spoke often in private homes and country clubs, and their speeches were correspondingly informal and anecdotal. As they went through Maryland, Virginia, North Carolina and Georgia, they developed a secondary purpose: to reconcile southern women to Smith's wife, Katie. Rumors were circulating that she was coarse, vulgar and given to drunken parties in nightclubs.

Katie, the daughter of an Irish contractor, had been raised in the Bronx and educated by nuns. Her life was her family. Undeniably she overate, and much of the fat went to her chin. To the taste of some, she overdressed. Perkins, a frequent overnight guest at the Executive Mansion, could not recall Katie taking a drink, even on the most likely occasions. Often, when Smith had worked late, he would invite anyone still in the Capitol back to the Executive Mansion for a snack. Katie would greet them, and Smith, putting his arm around her waist, would say, "How about a little music?" She would sit at the piano and play songs that had been popular when they were courting. While he sang, in a better than average baritone, the butler would bring refreshments: sandwiches and beer or ginger ale. Katie never took the beer, and no one who knew her could imagine her in a nightclub.

Gibson would describe her, tell how she'd first met her, how she had invited the Smiths to dinner, how they had behaved, and then close with a line that always brought a burst of applause: "Anyhow, I tell you he loves her."

Perkins would follow with a description of Smith and his religion: how he believed in God, believed that God would guide him and that it was his duty to follow God's laws. She would describe his mother, who had taught him his prayers, and often she would close with: "He says his prayers. I would rather have a man in the White House who says his prayers than one who doesn't pay any attention to religion."

The emotional style as well as the use of stock phrases was not congenial to Perkins, and though she occasionally attempted it for the party at labor conventions and on campaigns, she never had much success with it. Nevertheless, with the better educated people in the South she felt that perhaps she and Gibson had succeeded, if only because of party loyalty. But Maryland's Eastern Shore had been a shock. There the Klan was strong. The people repeated and believed stories of obscene practices in Catholic countries, and several times she had pointed out to her the estate that had been purchased for the pope, where he would take up residence as soon as Smith was elected. And in Atlanta there had been an attempt by fellow Democrats to break up the meeting.[4]

She returned to New York distressed and doubtful. Southern prejudice against Catholics was stronger than anything she had imagined, and it was complicated by Smith's stand on Prohibition. In the South as everywhere, there was much hypocrisy about Prohibition, but also much sincerity. Smith was foolish, perhaps, not to treat that sincerity with greater care.

In his speeches he drummed into audiences that he would work for repeal — the amendment had not succeeded in its purpose, liquor was everywhere and law and enforcement were corrupted. He was so blunt that he may have played into the hands of Republicans, who were suggesting that he wanted his will rather than the people's to prevail.

It was his style, though, to meet the problems head on. When the Ku Klux Klan lined the railway into Oklahoma City with burning crosses, he determined to speak out against intolerance. He gave the thirty thousand people in the auditorium a fine lecture, but it was words in the wind. The next night an evangelist preacher spoke in the same hall to the same number; his speech was "Al Smith and the Forces of Hell."[5]

Perkins did not speak in Oklahoma, but in the final weeks of October she made a tour of Missouri with Senator Harry Hawes and Mrs. Vanderbilt Webb, again for the purpose of reconciling Democrats to Smith. During her trip Smith himself arrived to speak in St. Louis, which had a large Catholic and immigrant population. Rapturous crowds gathered. Women tried to touch him; men held up their babies to be touched; many wept; others fainted. She wondered if the adulation wasn't too much; if it wouldn't offend Protestant tastes. Yet it seemed evident that he had won the people's devotion. Party workers traveling with Smith assured her that he had had similar receptions in many cities.

But St. Louis was not all of Missouri. While she and Aileen Webb were in Kansas City, they were invited to speak at a Democratic meeting in Independence. Senator Hawes advised them to accept but insisted on accompanying them. "They're a rough outfit," he explained, "and they're kind of wrought up."

What about? the women asked.

"Smith's religion. They don't like it."

As they drove there, he recounted the town's history as a post for outfitting wagon trains headed West. A great deal of organization went into a wagon train: building the wagons, hiring guides, gathering livestock and packing fodder and food to last for months. People from all over had come to Independence. A big trek of Mormons had passed through during a smallpox epidemic, and many had fallen sick and been left behind. Some had joined later wagon trains and gone West; some had stayed in Independence and their descendants were still there.

"You may see some," Hawes said. "They're mostly Democrats."

Perkins was always stirred by local history, and she found the senator's love for his state very appealing. He spoke its name with a caress, "Mizzoura," and drilled them in pronouncing it.

As they came to the center of town, she saw a banner advertising a "Speaking Tonight" at Memorial Hall — their meeting. She also saw some torn banners hanging limply from the lampposts.

"Some boys, I guess," said Hawes. "Just kids romping around."

In front of them, a man climbed a ladder and pulled down another banner.

"The same boys?" Perkins asked.

"Yeah," said the senator. "The same boys."

A crowd had gathered at the hall, overflowing the little lawn, the sidewalk and steps. Driving slowly through it, they got out at the back of the hall where, according to Perkins, the senator "sort of hustled us in." A man appeared and said, "It'll be all right, Senator." Hawes, looking relieved, led them to a room just off the stage, on which the curtain was drawn shut.

While the women sat down to wait, several men came, whispered to Hawes and took him away. Perkins got up and peeked through the curtain. Except for seven or eight people, the hall was empty. "Why, they haven't been able to get up a meeting!" she said.

She and Webb began to hear shouts in the street. In a moment, Hawes appeared. "There's an audience, all right, but they aren't allowed to come in," he said. "People are trying to stop them. Can you beat the nerve of that?" But he was sure the sheriff would be able to handle the crowd.

The hall soon did begin to fill. A band playing "Hail, Hail the Gang's All Here" and "The Sidewalks of New York" marched into the auditorium at the head of the reception committee. It kept playing until about twelve hundred people had been seated. Then the president of the Democratic club called the meeting to order and a Baptist minister prayed for the deliverance of all men from religious intolerance and bigotry.

Webb spoke first. She had been an ardent Prohibitionist, she said, and was thrilled when the amendment was adopted. But now she felt that it had failed, that the bootlegging and breakdown of law enforcement would not end until the Volstead Act was modified. The atmosphere was tense; there were shouts, boos and shushings, and she cut the speech short.

Perkins in turn attempted to make two points. First, she said that she had originally been a Republican, but that moral issues had led her to become a Democrat. In her work in New York she had noticed that Republican members who voted right on legislation were not returned to office, but Democratic members were. That decided her in favor of the Democratic party.

Second, she ventured on the touchy question of Tammany, which Westerners seemed to think was still as corrupt as in the days of Boss Tweed. Smith, she insisted, was a man who had never broken a promise. "He is not a boss but a leader. He even leads Tammany, though you people have heard that he doesn't. He rides Tammany, not Tammany him. And if he is elected President, he will keep his promise to give the American people the lowdown on what is taking place in their government." Throughout there was constant booing and shouting from the rear of the hall.

Finally Senator Hawes spoke, for more than an hour. He minimized Hoover's relief work abroad after the war and more recently at home during the previous year's floods. He called Hoover an international adventurer assuming the role of a Santa Claus with the American people's money, and he scolded the audience for its doubts about Smith. The louder the boos, the louder he roared. Perkins was filled with admiration: "He went right through with it. He had the most enormous, reverberating voice. He could holler, and although they were making a terrible noise out there, he out-hollered." Then the Baptist minister closed with a prayer and, since the meeting seemed about to break up into fist fights, the senator hustled them out the back and into the car.

Many years later in Washington she mentioned to Harry Truman, then a senator, that she had once been in Independence, and she described the meeting. He remembered it well: he'd been one of the men trying to arrange it. He had seen her for the first time that night.[6]

*

Perkins was back in New York by October 31, when Smith was to speak in Newark on his social and labor legislation. Because she had provided much of the material and he would speak on the radio, she went to Belle Moskowitz's house for the broadcast. She never would have a radio of her own; the perpetual noise of it, she said, made her nervous.

Moskowitz, whom Perkins had introduced to Smith in 1918, had become one of his important advisers. The much admired Reconstruction Commission of his first term had been her idea, as had many of the special citizens' committees in the campaigns, and though she never held any high official position, insiders knew that her influence was great. Between her and Perkins there were no pretenses about Smith or his chances.

Now as they heard him speaking from Newark, Perkins began to have misgivings over his strong New York accent: "raddio" for radio and "horspital" for hospital. He had always refused to change his pronunciation because to do so would be to deny his origins. But she knew it disturbed many people; she was constantly asked about "that awful whiskey voice of his!" Without really understanding the complaint she had defended his voice as natural to him. But after campaigning in other parts of the country she heard it afresh, and it sounded blurred and thick. Radio was not a good medium for him.[7]

She wondered, too, what people outside the big industrial cities would think as he described his programs. "Under my leadership the State of New York provided a forty-eight-hour week for women. It prohibited night work of women in industrial establishments. It prohibited the employment of women in dangerous occupations. It required restrooms in factories and mercantile buildings, and made many contributions by law to the health and comfort of women in industry." Most of the country, she feared, had no experience of the need for such laws and would reject a candidate proposing them. How strange to country people would be the idea of a government regulating the number of toilets or the hours of labor.

When Smith finished, Moskowitz said, "That was wonderful!"

"Belle," said Perkins, "I just don't think it will go in the country."

"You're quite mistaken, Frances. This is what the country is longing for."

But on November 6, Hoover defeated Smith, 21,392,190 to 15,016,443.

A week or so after the election, she saw Smith in his office in Albany. She was still chairman of the Industrial Board, and until January 1,

1929, he was still governor. "Sit down," he said, "and let's see what happened."

The religious prejudice was plain. As Smith remarked, "The time has not yet come when a man can say his beads in the White House."

Yet he felt there had been something more — a discrimination by class, at least among the party regulars outside the big cities. The time had not yet come, they agreed, "when a man from the city slums could be put into high office by the Democrats." The party sought the votes of the lower classes in the cities without fully accepting them as citizens, qualified, like the rest, to be President. Being raised on a farm was still the surest way to success in American politics.

Smith and those closest to him, in their soul-searching after the election, tended to brood on these prejudices to the exclusion of other reasons for his defeat, and they soon became embittered. Perkins did not, perhaps partly because, unlike most of them, she had roots outside New York. In 1928 a Maine farmer, after listening to her extol Smith's work as governor, had said: "Never heard of him. What happens in New York don't make no difference down here." That may have been ignorance or insularity, but it was not religious or class prejudice. Such jolts, on home ground, helped her perspective, even as campaigning in eleven states greatly enlarged it.[8]

Chapter 17

->->>-|<<-<-

Governor Roosevelt appoints her Industrial Commissioner. The new administration. Differences in working for Roosevelt and Smith. She disputes Hoover on unemployment figures. The Committee on Stabilization of Industry recommends unemployment insurance.

THOUGH PERKINS had suspected Smith might lose the election, neither she nor anyone else had imagined that, if he failed to carry New York, Roosevelt might win it. Yet after a close count requiring twelve days before his opponent would concede, Roosevelt defeated Albert Ottinger by 25,000 votes, half of 1 percent, whereas Smith trailed Hoover in the state by almost 150,000. The difference was mostly in the vote upstate, where Roosevelt apparently was aided by his Dutchess County background, his freedom from Tammany and, in some areas, by the fact that Ottinger was a Jew. Though it would be some time before everyone grasped the election's significance, it not only put Smith out of office in his own state but also out of power. Roosevelt succeeded to both.

Perkins did not expect to be affected by the change of administration. She knew, because Smith had told her, that he had recommended to Roosevelt that she be retained as chairman of the Industrial Board. He also had recommended that James Hamilton, the Industrial Commissioner, be replaced. Hamilton's appointment two years earlier had paid a political debt, and he had proved incompetent. She had absorbed much of his work, particularly in the preparation of the budget, but it was an unhappy, even unconstitutional, solution. The department's judicial and legislative duties, for which the board was responsible, were required by law to be separate from its administration, for which the commissioner was responsible. The situation was one to be quickly improved.[1]

In December, at Roosevelt's invitation, she went to Hyde Park, and while he drove her slowly over the back roads of the estate, they discussed the department and its problems. She was impressed by his grasp of them. He knew all about Hamilton and the budget as well as such details as the department's difficulties with the lawyer assigned to it by the state Attorney General. Some of his information he had from Smith, but he had also made inquiries on his own.

To her surprise he offered her, instead of the position as chairman of the board, the post of Industrial Commissioner, and she asked if he had discussed the change with Smith. He had, and seemed eager to repeat their conversation. Smith had said: "I don't think I would do that. I don't think the men will want to work under a woman. It's all right on the board because she doesn't have to direct them, but it's a big department, with a lot of men at the head of various enterprises. I don't think they'll like it."

She remembered that "Roosevelt laughed when he told me that," which she decided was "an expression of some kind of vanity that he was more broad-minded than Smith about such things." In the next few years she often heard him remark, "Al would never have thought of making a woman the head of the department." She concluded that in addition to his obvious desire to prove himself greater than his cousin, Theodore Roosevelt, he also felt a need, at least at the start, to prove himself greater than Al Smith. But in breaking down the prejudice against women she thought Smith, a decade earlier and with an Irish-Catholic background, had shown the greater courage.

Her appointment as Industrial Commissioner, Roosevelt said, would please the women who had worked for the party. She was less sure, but he said he had talked to his wife, Nancy Cook and Caroline O'Day. These were women he saw regularly, leaders of the Women's Division of the party. She was with them but not of them: her position in the state government, combined with her sex, gave her a unique role in campaigns and party politics.

She asked if he had consulted the political leaders around the state. "No," he said, "no," pulling at his lower lip. In the next few years she came to recognize this as an evasive gesture: perhaps he knew nothing about the matter, felt remiss or was not telling the truth. In this instance she had the feeling that the appointment was his own idea and that, except for Smith and the women, he had not discussed it with anyone.

When they parted, she thanked him but added: "Don't regard this as sewed up today. I won't say a word about it to anyone. In the next few weeks you'll get plenty of advice, and you'd better consult some leaders. If anyone says it's unwise to appoint me or will make trouble with the leaders, just disregard today. Telephone to say you are going to appoint James Jones. That'll be all right with me. I'm not going to tell anyone, so you're not sewed up."

He looked surprised. "That's very decent, I must say, but I'm not going to change my mind."[2]

She changed hers. Sometime later at home she composed a letter declining the position:

> . . . I regard the work of the Industrial Board which, as you know, exercises exclusively the judicial and legislative powers of the Department of Labor, as of even greater importance than the work of the Industrial Commissioner which is purely administrative.
>
> Even the best administration is effective in the lives of the workers of this State only during the brief tenure of office of a Commissioner with a talent for administration — while the decisions of the Industrial Board in compensation claims, in labor variations and in codes regulating especially hazardous industries, if soundly and liberally conceived, are permanent and continuing as beneficent influences on our industrial life for many years . . . Moreover, I believe that such talent as I may have for public service lies much more in the judicial and legislative work of the Department than in the administrative . . .[3]

Her colleagues, whether in the state or federal Departments of Labor, have generally confirmed her self-appraisal. As an administrator she was good, perhaps even more than good; as a judge or legislator she was quite extraordinary. She had a judicial temperament and a strong sense in all situations of what was fair. She was always open to new ideas and yet the moral purpose of the law, the welfare of mankind, was never overlooked. In any situation she could find her way to the most important principle.[4]

She did not mail the letter; it was in her papers at her death. She may have been influenced to accept the appointment because the annual salary of the Industrial Commissioner was $12,000 and of the Chairman of the Board only $8500. Wilson early that year had ceased work altogether and his health was more uncertain. Susanna was twelve, with school to finish and presumably college to attend. Perhaps Perkins recalled her grandmother's admonition to walk through any doors that were opened; forty-eight was young to start refusing opportunities.

After the appointment was announced, she saw Smith, and he said kindly, "That's all right. I'm sure you'll handle the problems in the best way."[5]

As the weeks passed, first Eleanor Roosevelt, then Caroline O'Day and several others, and finally, four years later, Mary Dewson all repeated to her what she had said to Roosevelt. He had told each how she had urged him not to feel "sewed up" if there was objection to her; how she'd promised not to speak of the appointment, and had not. Evidently he liked in her that she was not greedy for office, that she would not be quick to hold him to a promise and that she could keep her counsel. It was the foundation of a remarkable relationship.[6]

The change of administration in Albany was difficult. Smith from the moment of his defeat seemed to lose his touch not only in large affairs but also the smallest. In the weeks between the election and Roosevelt's inauguration he failed to remove himself and his family entirely out of the Executive Mansion, and at a small reception given by the Roosevelts just before the inauguration the family's trunks and bags were still in the halls. When Mrs. Smith went to get her coat to leave, the maids in the cloakroom burst into tears. Mrs. Smith also wept, and it was awkward. Perkins couldn't help thinking that the scene should have been played and finished earlier.

At the same reception Smith tried to advise Roosevelt on policy and personnel. He had already suggested that Robert Moses be kept as Secretary of State, and had been rebuffed; and now, as Perkins passed the side parlor where the two men were talking, she noticed that Roosevelt had a very artificial expression and was pulling at his lip.

Later he told her that Smith at that moment had been recommending Belle Moskowitz as secretary to the governor. Roosevelt was uncertain. "Do you know her well?"

"Very well."

"What do you think of her?"

"She's an able woman — extremely able. Personally I like her very much. She's always been a good friend to me. She's helpful, intelligent."

Roosevelt seemed anxious to talk about the appointment. He repeated Smith's praise of Moskowitz and then what Mrs. Roosevelt had said:

> Franklin, Mrs. Moskowitz is a very fine woman. I have worked with her in every campaign. I never worked with anybody that I liked to work with better. She's extremely competent, far-sighted, reliable. What

she says she'll do, she does. I think a great deal of her, and I think we are friends. But you have to decide, and decide now, whether you or Mrs. Moskowitz is going to be governor of this state. If she is your secretary, she will run you. It won't hurt you. It won't give you any pain. She will do it in such a way that you don't know it a good deal of the time. Everything will be arranged so subtly that when the matter comes to you it will be natural to decide to do the thing that she has already decided should be done. That is the way she works, the kind of person she is. She doesn't do it in any spirit of ill will. It's simply that her competence is so much greater than anybody else's that even with Al Smith, as much as she loves him, she ran him in that subtle way.

Perkins agreed: that was how Moskowitz worked, the kind of person she was.

Roosevelt asked how Smith had met her, and Perkins said that she had introduced her to him in 1918. Moskowitz had been working for the Republican governor, Charles S. Whitman, and in anger about something he had done, or not done, had determined to switch parties. The fact impressed Roosevelt. Several times he murmured, "So she was with Whitman and left Whitman to go to Al."

Suddenly he said, "Right at this moment, as I am now, I know I mustn't allow myself to be bossed, or I might get into the habit. It would be easy as I haven't my full strength." It was just a remark in passing, but eventually he decided against Moskowitz.[7]

Perkins one day tried to explain to Smith, whose feelings had been hurt, why she thought Roosevelt had rejected his advice. It was like a mother and a child, she said. At some point as the child grows, he must reject his mother's advice and start thinking for himself or he never will. The experience had been common among her friends. But as the words left her lips, she knew that they would mean nothing to Smith. He had never felt that way about his mother or imagined that anyone could.[8]

Perkins's new position raised some problems in her personal life. As chairman of the Industrial Board she had been able to schedule her work around the needs of her family. She could arrange to sit on workmen's compensation cases one day but not another, and if necessary she could write the decisions at home. But as Industrial Commissioner, the department's chief administrator, she would have to be in the office every day.

She debated whether she should live in Albany, though for both Wilson and Susanna it would be an unhappy move. When she raised the point with Roosevelt, he said, "I suppose you ought to. It's the seat of the government." For the winter, however, she did nothing, and by spring it was clear that so much of the department's work was in New York, where four fifths of the factories and workers were located, that it was reasonable to remain. She usually spent Monday and Tuesday in Albany and the rest of the week in New York. Often when she was in Albany, because the Roosevelts were hospitable, she stayed at the Executive Mansion.[9]

In November she moved her family to an old apartment house at 1239 Madison Avenue, on the northeast corner of Eighty-ninth Street. Except for an additional bathroom their apartment had the same number of rooms as before, but they were bigger and with a better exposure. She no longer was forced to listen to her neighbor's radio, and there was a doorman to take packages. For the next thirty-five years, though she sublet the apartment for long periods, she never took her furniture out of it, and in New York, for the family it was home.

Because of the job, however, she inevitably saw less of her husband and child. As far as Susanna was concerned, this may not have been all loss. Perkins, in the opinion of some of her friends, was not a "natural" mother (though very much a natural grandmother). She did not seem to know instinctively when to overlook a fault, when to let a child risk a mistake and when to interfere to prevent it.[10] And after Susanna ceased to be a child, Perkins had less fun with her. She once wrote a friend:

> I have to give you the advice I always give everybody. Enjoy your children while they are *little,* and never postpone the practice of companionship until they are, in your view, old enough to be companionable. At just the age when they are old enough to be companionable they begin to be tremendous individualists and interested only in themselves and their own generation. So do take the fun and education that parents get out of their children in the first ten years, and principally between one and six. As a matter of fact, I think that the most attractive age in a woman's life is three years.[11]

Susanna at twelve was already an individualist, a strong, healthy, gawky girl, a bit docile perhaps but full of warmth and artistically inclined. She had loved her first nurse, Nora Dowling, who had stayed with her until she was eight, but for the many governesses who succeeded she never developed any lasting affection. Some of her friends, as well as some of her mother's friends, thought she had a hard life, but given the need for Perkins to work there was no alternative.

A difficulty Perkins had with children and even adults was that the intensity of her attention could be overpowering. Adults sometimes complained that she was too "forceful"; children, suddenly subjected to a concentration of her attention on their half-articulated problems, sometimes burst into tears. Once when Susanna was a girl and driving in a pony cart with her father, they almost tipped over. As they turned into the lane by the Brick House, he suggested quietly that they not tell her mother about their close call, and Susanna willingly sacrificed the story.[12]

Coupled with Perkins's intensity was extraordinary energy. She needed little sleep and seemed able to make up any she had lost in the year by a single long session. On vacation in August she would go down to Maine with her family and for the first ten days or so would hardly get out of bed. The cooking would be done by a local woman, and Susanna or Wilson would carry meals up to her on a tray. Then she would begin to get up and around, and by the end of the month they would often be glad if she left a day early for a convention or meeting. Age seemed not to affect her; if anything, the more important her job, the more energy she developed.

One aspect of her new position that she did not relish was the additional publicity. Almost any speech now was reported, sometimes incorrectly. Speaking one day to the Brooklyn Parents' League, a group of middle-class women, she remarked that a part-time working mother added nothing to family income unless she earned at least $3500 a year, the cost of hiring assistants to replace her in the home. A reporter for the Brooklyn *Eagle* rephrased the remark to have her say that unless a woman with home responsibilities earned $3500 a year she was an economic failure. There was an immediate protest in the newspaper's letter column, and despite her effort to correct the misapprehension she was left portrayed as extremely limited in her view of the rewards of work or the reasons for it.[13]

Also the higher she rose in government the more obtrusive for many became the fact of her sex, though she tried to keep it irrelevant. At a lunch in her honor at the Hotel Astor, she began a speech to 900 representatives of business, labor, women and political groups by stating firmly: "I take it we are gathered not so much to celebrate Frances Perkins, the person, but as the symbol of an idea — the idea that social justice is possible in a great industrial community." From that line she never departed. Though she mentioned with gratitude men and women who had helped her to gain technical knowledge, she did not add that they had helped her to become the first woman in a governor's cabinet or that her career might be a symbol of lessening discrimination against women. Yet her letter of thanks to Mary W. Dewson, who arranged the lunch, suggests that a chief reason for it was her sex. Try as she would to ignore it, it was constantly thrust at her. When she was appointed U.S. Secretary of Labor, a reporter asked if being a woman was a handicap in government. "Only in climbing trees," she replied crisply.[14]

The lunch at the Astor and another given by the department's employees at the Hotel Commodore were evidence that her appointment was genuinely popular. The president of the State Federation of Labor, John Sullivan, stated that no appointment would have pleased labor more, and even her most bitter opponent, the secretary of a manufacturers' group called Associated Industries, wrote her privately, "I think on all matters affecting the Industries you are fair enough to give us an intelligent hearing [and] be open to conviction." She insisted always that she was not against industry and that labor legislation did not drive it to ruin or even out of the state. She frequently quoted a survey of the Merchants' Association, which concluded: "The fact remains that the industrial progress of New York State between 1925 and 1927, at least according to official statistics, has experienced a ratio of acceleration not accorded to any other manufacturing state."[15]

She told her audience at the Astor:

> Thus I come into office at a time when the industrialists of the state are ready to cooperate in any plans which, as they see them, are going to make for the economic and social welfare of the whole community.
>
> Now, what of the future? I regard the great mission of the Labor Department, as do all of us who are thinking about these matters, to be the prevention of robots. Whenever I see that picture which is becoming so familiar of the great mechanical man who does things automatically and can perform almost anything that a human being can perform, I confess to chills of horror lest we become like him. I repeat that we are committed to the belief that the human race is not destined for that kind of efficiency, but for an efficiency of the spirit and of the mind. If this robot-man can release us from chores like turning of switches — all right, let him release us! But let him release us to be human beings and let us not develop a race who are going to be patterned after him.
>
> For the realization of this aim we are going to need in this state both intelligence and education on the part of the people who are themselves the problem — that is, capital and labor.[16]

She always had faith in the common sense and good will of the American people: if they were presented with the facts of working conditions, they would want to correct what was wrong, to act morally. Upon the foundation of an informed citizenry a public official could enact a program of constructive reform. She had seen Smith do it.

In some respects she found Roosevelt more difficult to work with than Smith. Though both were intuitive in their approach to a problem — they would start with the conclusion they wanted and then search for facts and arguments to support it — Roosevelt's reasoning was more devious. Perhaps as a result he was more easily upset. Someone would go to him with a story, and "he would get all hot and bothered and telephone you that you ought to do this or that. You knew it was not wise, but you couldn't convince him on the phone. You had to go up and see him and have a talk." With Smith, "people would come in with a song and dance, and he would say 'Hmm,' and that was all."

Smith also was quicker to grasp the gist of a problem. She discovered that to plant an idea firmly in Roosevelt's mind she should go over it three times. She'd begin with a statement of the subject. "Now I want to tell you about the hazards of dust in materials that up to date we thought were nonexplosive."

"Such as what?"

"Such as the dust that comes from grinding aluminum."

"How can aluminum explode?"

Then she'd tell him. "There's been an explosion in a small aluminum plant, not in New York fortunately. The report on it is this. It seems to be the proportion of air to dust that does it. Any spark will set it off and sometimes it appears to be spontaneous."

The explosion would interest him, and he'd ask about the people injured, how many, how badly and what was being done for them. Then, after the story had brought him to the problem, she'd say: "Now, see here, I've told you about explosion hazards where there is dust. We've got to do something about it. I want to know if you'll support me." He'd agree to, and they would discuss the best way to achieve a new safety regulation: by a release to the newspapers, by a paragraph in his next speech or by a report to a legislative committee.

For Roosevelt, as for Smith, a problem was illuminated by its human side, and she tried always to have vivid examples of what underlay the statistics — three girls in textile mills in Rhode Island scalped when they knelt to pick up spools, because the guards on the flywheels did not extend underneath the table.

It was always better to talk to him than to phone or to write a memorandum. Smith had been excellent on the phone, but Roosevelt responded less to principles than to personalities, and these could be presented best in conversation. "You went to see So-and-so. Well, what'd the old cuss say?" She'd tell him, but she'd always bring him back to the principle.

Another person's later story, however, was apt to push her earlier one from his mind, and she finally made it a practice to have a long conference with him, about an hour, at least once every ten days. Like his wife, Eleanor, over the years Perkins developed an extraordinary skill in knowing when and how to bring something to Roosevelt's attention so that he would act on it.[17]

And yet her most important political act in his two terms as governor was taken in the heat of emotion and without consulting him. On January 22, 1930, on the front page of both the *New York Times* and *Herald Tribune* Hoover announced that the corner of the Depression had been turned; for the first time since the stock market crash in October 1929 the employment trend was up. His Secretary of Labor, James J. Davis, predicted that the present year "should see us well on the way to complete recovery."

The story angered Perkins, for she knew its basis was false. The data at the state's Bureau of Labor Statistics showed a steady decline in employment. All over the country men without jobs would be asked by their wives, children and in-laws, "Why can't you get a job when the President says others are working again?" It was cruel. She arrived in the office full of fire and determined to refute Hoover.

By early afternoon, working with the chief of her statistics bureau and confirming their surmises by a call to the chief of the federal bureau, she knew the source of the figures underlying the statement. Secretary Davis had by-passed his own statistics bureau, where the figures were discouraging, and had used figures from the U.S. Employment Service. These were up because every Christmas season the big department stores in the country hired extra help. Comparing these figures to those of November proved nothing; they had to be compared to a previous December.

Calling in reporters, she announced that Hoover's figures must be incorrect; the situation in New York, the country's greatest commercial state, was anything but better. "December was the worst month for unemployment since nineteen twenty-seven and the worst December since the records of the Department of Labor were started in nineteen fourteen. Figures so far for January indicate that unemployment will be greater in New York State than for any previous month in the last sixteen years."

After the reporters had gone, someone in the office said, "You certainly have your nerve to dispute the President of the United States."

"I don't see why," she said, "if he's wrong." But she realized she should have consulted Roosevelt first, and she called to explain, with apologies, what she had done.

He laughed. "I think that was bully; just wonderful. How did you have the nerve? I'm just as glad you didn't ask me, because if you had, I'd probably have told you not to do it. But you've done it now. The blood be on your hands. If you're not right, you'll get plenty of punishment from the country."

But anyone with eyes could look around a city and see that she was right. There was no spurt of new construction, no factories working overtime; more men, not fewer, were on street corners selling apples. A few girls behind notion counters for the holiday was not a turn for the better.

Thereafter on this point she hounded Hoover's administration. When in June Secretary of Commerce R. P. Lamont announced that unemployment was at only 3 percent, she pointed out he was using census rather than working population figures. "For instance seven cities in New York State with a population of 2,043,078 were accounted for as having 61,350 unemployed, or 3 percent. As only 40 percent of 2,043,078 or about 800,000 were employable, the percentage of unemployment in the seven New York cities was about 13 percent, or more than four times the percentage given out by the Secretary of Commerce." In August she described a cheerful statement by the federal Employment Service as "cruel and irresponsible at a time when the unemployed are reaching the end of their resources and when cities, states and private organizations are attempting to raise funds for relief next winter."

Soon, whenever a statement on unemployment was issued in Washington, labor leaders, state officials and newspaper editors would call her to check the figures against those of New York. She was invited to testify before the U.S. Senate's Commerce Committee on Senator Robert Wagner's bill for unemployment relief and later to give figures on unemployment in New York City and State to Senator La Follette's subcommittee. She became the most prominent state labor official in the country.[18]

But disputing Hoover did little to help the unemployed, and to do more she suggested to Roosevelt that he appoint a committee to seek ways of stabilizing employment by distributing it more evenly and effectively. No one, not she, Roosevelt or anyone else, envisaged how much worse the Depression would be in two years. No one yet was thinking in terms of relief, of direct state aid to the unemployed. On March 30, 1930, when Roosevelt announced a Committee on Stabilization of Industry for the Prevention of Unemployment, New York was the first state to take such a step.

The committee was largely her creation. The chairman was Henry Bruère, then a vice-president of the Bowery Savings Bank; the members were Maxwell S. Wheeler and Ernest Draper, businessmen from Buffalo and Brooklyn; John Sullivan, president of the State Federation of Labor; and Henry H. Stebbins, Jr., a labor official from Rochester. She was an ex officio member, and the headquarters were in the Department of Labor building at 124 East Twenty-eighth Street in New York. She and Bruère provided the leadership, and the Department of Labor provided much of the administrative and technical help.

The committee first sought to determine what methods factories in the state were presently using to stabilize employment, since what worked well for one might be recommended to another. The most common was to keep all employees working but on a reduced schedule of hours or days. In a few instances factories were even alternating shifts by weeks. As a temporary measure this reduction of hours was proving fairly successful; the employees received some income and the work force was held together. Another method favored by some firms was to bid low on contracts. But this was effective only for a short time, for as competing firms lost business, they too lowered their prices. Still other firms did what they could with manufacturing for inventory, soliciting advance orders and using employees for repair jobs ordinarily done by outside labor.

The committee held hearings around the state, inviting any who wished to testify, and often the testimony was pungent. A labor leader in Utica, for example, might rise and say, "We've got a lot of skunks here among the employers. They think they know everything. They like to see us sweating. They like to see a breadline."

She and Bruère developed a technique for blunting such barbs. While he presided, she would sit beside him making notes. After the last witness had spoken, he would ask her to sum up the testimony. She'd begin, "I think it is the sense of this meeting . . ." and in fifteen or twenty minutes summarize the ideas presented, leaving out the emotions. The committee never took a vote or promised any action. Its purpose was to educate itself and the community on the problems of unemployment and to stimulate people to attack them.

She and her assistants in the department set an example of what might be accomplished by reorganizing the state public employment offices. In January and February these had placed in jobs an average of 4800. In April they placed 8600; in May, 10,400; and in June, 7600. And the increase was achieved while the market for labor was steadily declining. In New York, in the clothing and fur trades, employers and employees set up joint insurance funds to relieve the most needy unemployed, and in Rochester a similar fund was started in the men's clothing industry. In Schenectady the General Electric Company, led by Gerard Swope, started a plan under which a worker, two weeks after being laid off, would receive for the next ten weeks an amount based on his wages.

The committee's final report, submitted on November 13, besides recommending methods for stabilizing employment within industries, also suggested a State Planning Board for increasing the size and effectiveness of public works programs. And, without using the term, it recommended some kind of unemployment insurance. If that could not be provided by the various industries for their workers, then it should be provided by the state. For in the words of the report, "The public conscience is not comfortable when good men anxious to work are unable to find employment to support themselves and their families."[19]

Chapter 18

-»>«<-

Roosevelt re-elected governor. Smith sulks. The Depression grows worse. The Committee on Stabilization's programs for combating unemployment. The Governors' Conference on it. She studies British unemployment insurance. Florence Kelley dies.

IN NOVEMBER 1930 Roosevelt was elected to his second term as governor in a stunning victory. For the first time in the century a Democratic candidate defeated a Republican in the counties outside New York City. Roosevelt came down to the Bronx line with a plurality of 167,784, to which he added a margin in the city of 557,217. In all, he defeated Charles H. Tuttle by 725,001.

Even if the larger number of voters and the more favorable times for the Democrats are discounted, Smith had never had such a victory, and it rankled. He still had not recovered his spirits after his defeat, which he now blamed entirely on prejudice against his religion. "As for running for office again — that's finished," he said. When friends would suggest that he should start planning for the 1932 presidential election, he would laugh and say, "What do you think I am? Another William Jennings Bryan?"[1]

Those closest to him — his political advisers, such as Moses, Proskauer and Moskowitz; his rich Irish-American friends; and the party's national chairman, John J. Raskob — chose to believe he was not serious. Those more distant were puzzled. His apparent indecision over whether to seek the nomination weakened his supporters, while those who opposed him remained firmly convinced that religion and Prohibition must not again be the issues. Smith, however, seemed unable to settle on any others.

Meanwhile, in his home state his misunderstandings with Roosevelt developed slowly into ill will, nurtured on each side by their lieutenants, Moskowitz and Moses for Smith and Louis Howe for Roosevelt. Perkins noticed that whenever Roosevelt had a speech referring to a program initiated by Smith, between drafting and delivery Smith's name would be deleted. She was sure it was done at the last moment by Howe.[2]

The conflicts gradually grew more direct. Smith wanted the national committee to take a forthright stand for repeal of Prohibition. He must have expected to be opposed by the Southerners on the committee, but not until the meeting to discuss the issue, held in March 1931, did he discover that Roosevelt had made an alliance with them to defeat his proposal. Roosevelt's move, purely as politics, was smart: it allowed him to evade the issue while ingratiating himself with the South at Smith's expense. But as an act between supposed friends, it was a cheap trick. Only about then did Smith's supporters begin to realize the extent to which Roosevelt had already begun a campaign against Smith for the presidential nomination in 1932.[3]

Fortunately for Perkins she was not in either man's inner circle of advisers. Moskowitz soon was referring to Roosevelt as *"your* governor" and trying to force her to say she was either for Roosevelt or for Smith. "I won't say that, Belle," Perkins would reply. "I'm for Roosevelt because I work for him. I like him. I think he's doing the right thing. He's supporting all the things I care about. I think the world of Al Smith for the same reasons."

Nevertheless, she thought Smith should not run for President in 1932, and said so to Moskowitz. He would split the party again, lead it to another defeat and reopen all his wounds. He could be governor again. "He's been governor," Moskowitz said. "But it's one of the greatest posts there is," said Perkins. Moskowitz thought senator might be better, but to Perkins that position would make little use of Smith's extraordinary administrative abilities or of his great love for the State of New York. "He's entitled to the presidential nomination," said Moskowitz. "The Democratic party owes it to him." Perkins knew that was also Smith's feeling, but she doubted it was shared by Democrats in the West and South.[4]

As the months passed, it became clear to her and others that she was being drawn into Roosevelt's camp simply by the performance of her duties. One time when she asked his permission to attack another of the Hoover administration's pronouncements about unemployment, he said, "Frances, this is the best politics you can do. Don't say anything about politics. Just be an outraged scientist and social worker." Yet she never lost Moskowitz's trust, perhaps because she had been so open about her feelings, or perhaps because her loyalty was clearly less to politicians than to social labor programs.[5]

Meanwhile, the Depression grew worse. Across the country the average number of bank failures per month was 54 in 1929, 112 in 1930, 192 in 1931, and 121 in 1932. In the same four years, as businesses failed or cut back, the estimated number of unemployed rose from 1,864,000 to 13,181,000. New York, the country's largest manufacturing state, had the largest share of the disaster. What it could mean to a city was revealed in annual surveys of Buffalo made by the state Department of Labor. It found that 6.2 percent of the men able and willing to work were wholly unemployed in November 1929, 17.2 in 1930, 24.3 in 1931, and 32.6 in 1932. In the same period the percentage of workers employed only part-time rose from 7.1 to 23.4. By November 1932, only 44 percent of the male workers in Buffalo had full-time employment.[6]

As men and women used up their savings, sold their possessions and began to lose their homes, they turned to the traditional sources of help, the churches, private agencies, counties and towns. New York City had a Municipal Lodging House for its homeless, which in 1931 provided 408,100 lodgings and 1,024,247 meals. In 1932 it provided 889,984 lodgings and 2,688,226 meals.

Perkins and the Department of Labor had only a slight role in the measures for relief, chiefly providing statistics. To the small extent the state government worked directly with the private agencies and towns, it acted through the Department of Charities, or, as it was renamed in 1929, of Social Welfare. But by mid-1931 many towns and agencies were reaching the end of their resources, and in August Roosevelt called the legislature into special session. In his message he declared that when men willing to work were unable to find jobs then modern society — "not as a matter of charity but as a matter of social duty" — had an obligation "to prevent the starvation or the dire want of its fellow men and women who try to maintain themselves but cannot."

The legislature responded by passing the Wicks Act, which created the Temporary Emergency Relief Administration, separate from the government's regular departments. With TERA, New York became the first state to put into operation the principle of state aid for relief. A young, relatively obscure social worker, Harry L. Hopkins, was appointed executive director, entering a field of work in which he later would take a leading part nationally. Perkins had known him slightly when he was the director of the New York Tuberculosis and Public

Health Association. In recent months she had seen more of him because Bruère, finding him practical and cooperative, frequently consulted him about the problems of unemployment and relief. Now, as she provided him with statistics and surveys, she saw him regularly and watched with admiration as he created an organization in a field that was wholly new.[7]

While Hopkins worked on temporary, emergency relief for the unemployed (the program eventually aided, at one time or another, about 40 percent of the state's population), she and the Committee on Stabilization of Employment continued to concentrate on long-range programs. Of these the more important were the expansion of public works, the improvements in the state employment agencies and the introduction of a system of unemployment insurance. All were included in the committee's report to the governor in November 1930, but by then its work had outstripped its recommendations.[8]

The committee had least impact on public works, for by mid-1930 almost everyone was ready to agree that these should be used as a balance for business depressions: When private construction began to lag, public construction should increase. Perkins had an example she often used before citizens' groups to explain the theory. If one hundred thousand construction workers became unemployed, they would be unable to buy any toasters for their families, and soon the toaster industry would begin to lay off workers. Thus, less production in toasters, hence less wages, hence less income, hence still fewer customers for other industries, so less production somewhere else — and the cycle began again. After the example she would restate the idea in more theoretical terms: prosperity in an industrial society depends on maintaining *mass* purchasing power. Or, in terms of toasters, if one family has $100,000 in surplus, it will still buy only one toaster, but if one hundred thousand families have a dollar in surplus, among them many thousands will buy toasters. Insufficient buying power, not insufficient capital, was aggravating the Depression.[9]

Any expansion of public works, however, faced a practical difficulty in 1930: most towns or counties by then found themselves with tax revenues so shrunken that they could not afford to increase the number of roads or bridges they repaired. Also, any new and large project in its first year employed only architects and engineers, doing little to improve mass purchasing power. What was needed, said the committee and many individuals, was a larger, richer governmental unit than town or county — the state — and planning in advance. Then when the need for a project was determined, the plans would be ready and approved and the construction workers could be hired at once. The state's Department of Public Works did what it could, but with more than a million unemployed in New York, increasing the number of men working on the state highways from 14,728 in 1930 to 19,383 in 1931 had little impact. The committee recommended a State Planning Board and more projects, but neither it nor the legislature was yet thinking in terms big enough for the problem.

Perkins's position in the government ensured that the committee's recommendations for improving the state's employment agencies would be pursued even before they could be presented. The committee in its report, therefore, was able to announce that the state's eleven employment centers had already been reorganized and had increased their placements. But the chief problem with the state agencies, aside from their inefficiency, was the lack of them. Throughout the 1920s the labor market was served predominantly by private agencies, which collected a fee from the worker. In 1930 there were 1036 private agencies in New York City and the state had only four. Even so New York State, with its eleven employment centers, was better off than most. Twenty-eight had none. But at best the private agencies were only a partial solution. Many handled only certain types of jobs, so a worker might have to travel miles (telephoning was still uncommon) to find an agency to serve him. And among private agencies there was almost no cross-referencing or system of referrals. The federal agencies, which had been created in World War I to resolve such problems, had been almost entirely disbanded. Wagner, who had been elected a senator from New York in 1927, constantly urged Congress to re-establish them. But when Congress passed his bill, Hoover vetoed it, and Secretary of Labor Doak reorganized the existing federal service without improving it. For New York the committee recommended that the location and personnel of the state agencies be improved, and Perkins sought and received larger appropriations to implement the recommendation. Connecting men with jobs was one way to limit or prevent a depression.[10]

Her major concern, however, was to advance a program for unemployment insurance. Yet Roosevelt at first, like many persons, seemed to confuse unemployment insurance with "the dole." The term applied to the British system of unemployment compensation, which had begun as a program of insurance but which, while retaining the trappings of insurance, had, in effect, been turned into a program of relief. Whenever she would start to talk of unemployment insurance, he would say, "I'm against the dole, Frances. Don't you get any dole in here!"[11]

The dole had its origin in Britain in 1911; an unemployment

insurance plan was started by the government for three industries in which employment was expected to fluctuate more or less regularly, building, engineering and shipbuilding. The plan, covering some three million workers, was run as a true insurance fund to which both workers and employers contributed. During World War I another million munition workers were brought into it. After the war ex-servicemen, when they left the armed forces, were allowed to receive weekly benefits but only for a limited period. Because jobs then were easy to find, the servicemen's use of benefits did little damage to the fund except as a precedent. Then in 1920 the government extended the coverage to almost all workers except domestics, agricultural laborers and civil servants. About twelve million workers now were under the plan, and the fund, still financed by contributions from both workers and employers, had as its sole purpose the providing of insurance against casual, short-term unemployment.

Events soon forced the plan awry. The experts had assumed an unemployment rate of 4 percent, or about half a million men a year drawing benefits for only a few months. But the impact of inventions and of the steady drop in export trade forced Britain through what was almost a new industrial revolution. Such traditional industries as coal or cotton manufacture were in decline, and others, such as the production of automobiles and internal combustion engines, were rising. Unemployment, particularly in the declining industries, passed 10 percent, and more than a million workers applied for benefits. When the periods for which they were covered ran out, the government continued the payments, calling them from 1921 to 1924 "un-covenanted benefits," from 1924 to 1928 "extended benefits" and after 1928 "transitional benefits" (and after 1934 by the most accurate term, "unemployment assistance"). After a few years of uncovenanted benefits the entire fund was exhausted, and the government replenished it with "loans." But as the unemployment continued severe (until World War II), the loans were never repaid. Except for the small amounts still being paid as an unemployment insurance tax by those working, the annual loans were subsidies taken from the general tax revenues. Unemployment insurance in Britain as early as 1921 for many workers had become unemployment relief.

There were several strange twists to the change. The relief, instead of being paid out by local town and county agencies under the Poor Law, which required proof of poverty, was now paid through labor exchanges not as a charity but under the guise, however misleading, of a contractual right. Because of the extremely uneven pattern of unemployment whole communities, like a coal town, might be on the dole, so no social stigma was attached to it. Whereas the victims of the first Industrial Revolution, lashed by hunger, finally had entered the frightful factories, Blake's "Satanic mills," the unemployed miner or cotton worker in the 1920s had a decent though old-fashioned house in a reasonably well-kept town. The dole made life bearable while he waited for the better times he was told were coming.

There was much in the situation to raise tempers. The British unions, strong in the declining industries and weak in the rising, demanded "Work or Maintenance." Workers in the rising industries, who were seldom unemployed, often felt they were being doubly taxed (unemployment insurance tax plus general taxes) to support men who, year after year, seldom did a day's work and refused to learn another trade. Undoubtedly the dole delayed the transfer of workers from declining to rising industries. Yet because of it the British may have muddled through an extremely difficult economic readjustment (for after World War II the huge numbers of unemployed did not reappear) and avoided a political revolution. But in the heat of discussion — especially by Americans, who had made only a superficial examination of the scheme and the underlying problems — what was frequently obscured was that unemployment insurance had not been tried and found wanting; it had for most recipients been turned into unemployment relief.[12]

Perkins thought the original concept was valid. Irregularity of employment was a constant problem in some industries, and it seemed fair to her that the industries rather than the individual workers should bear the burden. The British, she believed, had made a mistake at the start in limiting their plan to three industries. She wanted all the important industries to participate so that the insurance payments, by being available to a larger number of employees, would have a greater effect in stabilizing their mass purchasing power. Such a scheme would not cure the present depression, though it might help to cure it; its chief impact would be felt in the future, when it would serve as a first-line defense against a depression. But whenever she tried to discuss the idea with Roosevelt, he "threw out loud statements" against the dole. So she tried a different tack and set about educating him in unemployment insurance through other people.

There were plenty of learned articles on the subject, but she knew that he would respond more to a personal conversation than to a paper, and she invented reasons why members of the Committee on

Stabilization should see him. She took in Ernest Draper one day to describe how his company, which imported dates, had been able to cut down seasonal unemployment by storing the dates in refrigerated warehouses so that the packing could be extended over more months. Still there were slack periods, and if Draper did not mention unemployment insurance as a method of tiding workers over them, doubtless she did.

She arranged for Roosevelt to talk with Max Meyer, a leading clothier, with Edmund N. Huyck, who made Kenwood blankets in Poughkeepsie, and with John R. Adams of the Manning Paper Company in Troy. Each described the problem peculiar to his industry and what had been done and could be done to ease the irregularity of employment. Roosevelt discovered that he and Adams had friends in common, and he promptly invited the younger man and his wife, as well as Perkins, to dinner at the Executive Mansion. Much of a pleasant evening was passed in discussing the irregularity of employment and what might be done to ease it.

She told only Hopkins what she was doing; it seemed disloyal to Roosevelt to suggest he needed educating. But to Hopkins one day she said, "The governor doesn't know anything about industries or how they are conducted. He doesn't know what the clothing industry looks like, or the chemical or paper industries. He doesn't know about unemployment or what might be done about it." And she enlisted Hopkins in her campaign.[13]

Their efforts perhaps merely hurried Roosevelt to a conclusion he would, in time, have reached himself, but the acceleration in his thinking is impressive. In March 1930, when he appointed the Committee on Stabilization of Employment and announced its purposes, he did not mention unemployment insurance, and during that winter's legislative session he did nothing about it. Yet on June 30, in his address at the Governor's Conference at Salt Lake City, he became the first major political figure in the country to commit himself to unemployment insurance: "Some form of insurance seems to be the only answer." The country would come to unemployment insurance for irregularity of industrial employment "just as certainly as we have come to workmen's compensation for industrial injury." He pronounced himself firmly against the dole. The system was to be self-supporting and run on an actuarial basis.[14]

Perkins had drafted that part of his speech, but he had cut and softened it. As she listened to him on the radio, she was disappointed. But the next day she saw that his political sense had been more acute than hers. "He had toned it exactly right for absorption and approval by the governors. The fact that every newspaper played it as 'Governor Roosevelt Comes out for Unemployment Insurance' showed his power to gauge the public reaction. If he had been more emphatic, there would have been an immediate shying away by all except the already convinced."[15]

Once Roosevelt was persuaded of the soundness of the idea and perhaps sensed its political appeal, he began to hurry along with it. In September he urged Senator Wagner to include in the keynote address to the Democratic State Convention "suggestions for an immediate study of the broad subject of unemployment relief by a contributory system and not the dole methods." And acting on a suggestion of Perkins's he urged the convention delegates to pledge creation of a commission to study unemployment insurance and unemployment stabilization. The idea thus became part of the Democratic state platform in the election of 1930.

The Republicans in the state were against any form of compulsory insurance because experience in other countries had shown it was the first step toward the dole. The party instead pledged to encourage employers and workers voluntarily to lay aside a portion of income earned in good times for use in bad. This was also essentially the position of the AFL: it wanted unemployment solved by private industry, without state interference.[16]

To Perkins, Bruère and others on the Committee for Stabilization the job was larger and almost certainly more expensive than industry could undertake alone; more expensive perhaps than even a state could undertake alone. Within the committee they discussed the possibility of a compact with neighboring states, so that one large fund might cover an entire industrial region. No one then thought in terms of a federal law. There was little federal labor law in existence and most attempts to create some had been declared by the Supreme Court to be unconstitutional.

The committee suggested to Roosevelt that he call an interstate conference on unemployment. He took to the idea but with caution. He had Perkins check first with the labor commissioners in each state to see if the governors would be willing to come, and before publicly issuing the invitations he telephoned each governor himself.

The conference met in Albany on January 23 and 24, 1931, and in addition to Roosevelt for New York there were governors, their staffs or representatives from Massachusetts, Rhode Island, Connecticut, New Jersey, Pennsylvania and Ohio. The seven states contained about a third of the country's population and two thirds of its wealth. Probably on the recommendation of Bruère, Perkins hired Paul H. Douglas, later a senator from Illinois but then an economist at the University of Chicago, to organize a program of speakers. Most were limited to ten minutes with an equal period scheduled for the governors to ask questions. The subjects were public works, public employment exchanges, public unemployment relief and, by proportion in time of about five to one, unemployment insurance — or, as it was called, on Perkins's suggestion, "unemployment reserves" with "safeguards against the dole."[17]

As an educational device the conference succeeded. The technical experts and the governors educated each other, and the newspapers carried the ideas to the public. An increasing number of people began to think that unemployment insurance was a reasonable idea and could be adapted to American traditions. One result of the conference was a committee of the governors' representatives to continue studies on ways to develop such a program. Another was that Roosevelt appeared to the country as open to new ideas and willing to use them to attack the Depression.

That summer he sent Perkins to England to study the administration of the interlocked British system of public employment offices and unemployment compensation. She booked passage on the *Rotterdam,* reserving a stateroom for herself and a "companion." The line asked that her cabinmate be identified. She replied merely, "My companion is Susanna Wilson," without revealing their relationship. Perhaps because she was traveling as Miss Perkins she was reluctant to state it. The name was never entirely easy.[18]

At Kew, in a low building enclosing many acres, the British government kept the records of their unemployment compensation plan. Except for a few offices at the front the building was entirely filled with shelving, as in library stacks. On the shelves in boxes were record cards for every worker covered.

She had been led barely a yard down the first file when her instinct for fire regulation was jolted by the sight of cardboard boxes stacked row on row on wooden shelves. Another step and her instinct for accident prevention was aroused by the sight of an elderly woman seated atop a painter's ladder, writing. Beyond her there were more, and more, all on ladders. It hardly seemed possible, but each man or woman, most of them aged, had his own ladder and was either searching or adding to the records. "There they were, with their spectacles and notebooks, sitting high up in a cramped space, copying onto cards in ink and in longhand something they were reading out of the boxes."

Her guide explained: A worker applies for his weekly benefit in Liverpool. The office there writes here for his employment record, how many weeks coverage he's had, what he'd previously claimed as his trade, where he had worked in the past, what jobs he had been referred to and whether he had taken or refused them. All this was on his card, written in different hands because it was recorded at different times by different clerks. She spent several days at Kew finding out what worked well or poorly and collecting samples of all their forms.

"How about unemployment insurance?" Roosevelt asked her on her return. "Are you sold on it? Remember, I'm against the dole."

"We can never do it like the English," she said. "If we have to do it that way, we might as well give it up, because the American mind will just not grasp or cope with anything so complicated, so time-consuming and so inefficient as the record-keeping at Kew."

When she described the old ladies on ladders, he began to laugh, and the picture never left his mind. From then on, whenever unemployment insurance was discussed, he would make some quip about the ladders, until one day several years later she was able to reply, "That's all right. We've had Tom Watson's men at IBM at work on this for two years now. We are going to do it differently."

Nevertheless, some aspects of the British system she admired.

As you followed their operation through, you saw their government's extraordinary skill in handling a human situation. Here is a man who wants his unemployment compensation. He isn't entitled to it unless he has applied at the proper employment office for work, has made an effort to get work, and the office has been unable to provide him with work. He makes the statement. The person in charge listens, asks questions, scolds him a little if he hasn't been energetic about looking for work, and tells him he cannot lie back on his determination to be a plasterer and only a plasterer. The government will give him one week more; then he must take a job as a dish washer. He says "Yes, sir," and the official gives him a slip to take across the street to the unemployment insurance office where he gets his money. An adjudication has been made.

Eventually all those slips go to Kew and are recorded in that enormous building. The recording system seems to have nothing to do with the operation. That has always amazed me about the British. Whatever they do, no matter how complicated the record, the operation is very simple, much simpler than ours. The people are less conscious of the red tape than we are with our efficiency in which everything is reduced to forms and numbers — like 0257.1, which doesn't mean 0257.1 but some regulation. We create red tape and write letters so full of it that people don't know whether they are entitled to their money or not, or maybe just getting a brush-off.

"Why can't we get away with that here?" said Roosevelt. "I like the direct method of administration."

"Because the American people can't stand it. You've dealt with insurance companies. You know how many papers you must file, when a man dies, just to collect a claim."

"You've got to prove he's dead!"

"You've got to prove it at every level of American life. In England they'd believe you if you told them your husband was dead. All you need is the coroner's paper or a certificate from the parson who buried him. That wouldn't go with us. We'd suspect the parson was in a racket."[19]

That November in *Survey* she published her ideas for "an American plan" of unemployment insurance, based on her study of the British system. "I believe that industry should foot the bill," she said. "There is a certain theoretical justice in having each employee contribute directly, but practically it is a complicated scheme. All forms of social insurance should be kept impersonal." Using the Port of New York Authority as a model, she suggested an "insurance authority" of the seven industrial states that had attended the conference in Albany — New York, New Jersey, Pennsylvania, Ohio, Connecticut, Massachusetts and Rhode Island.

Even before she had left for England, the Interstate Commission for the Study of Unemployment Insurance, which had originated in that conference, had begun to meet, and in February 1932 it submitted its recommendations to the various governors. It proposed an insurance plan to which only employers would contribute, a benefit with a maximum rate of ten dollars a week or 50 percent of an employee's wage — whichever was lower, and a maximum benefit period of ten weeks a year. Roosevelt, who by now had consulted many experts on the subject, promptly forwarded the recommendations to the legislature. Perkins and others testified in support of the proposals, but the Republican majority voted merely to keep them under study. That year bills for unemployment insurance were introduced in seventeen states, but only Wisconsin adopted a plan.[20]

Roosevelt was eager to have another conference on unemployment in June, and Perkins and Bruère did the preliminary work for it. In the end, however, they advised against it. By the spring of 1932, with the party conventions and nominations for President only weeks away, the issue of unemployment and how to contain it had moved from the state to the national level.[21]

On February 17, 1932, at age seventy-four, Florence Kelley died. In her last ten years she had made little progress in abolishing child labor, reducing infant and maternal mortality or improving hours and wages for industrial workers. Speaking at a meeting of the Consumers' League in 1925 she had surmised that the early years were easier because the opposition had been less well organized. "That was before the National Association of Manufacturers and the National Industrial Conference Board and many other great national organizations for slowing the national pace had got their stride."

Yet it was never her nature to be discouraged. "Despise not the day of small things," she would say to league members as she prepared to lavish on an audience of twenty the same vigor and intensity with which she addressed two thousand.

Always she had tried to turn the public's attention to the reasons behind poverty and sickness among industrial workers. "Why," she asked, "do we *have* widows?" Because men by the thousands were killed in accidents at work and by industrial diseases — most of which could have been prevented. Always she believed that the public, if given the facts of the situation, eventually would force action to improve it.

Because for her a new law or amendment might save a worker's childhood, or arm or life, she was tireless in pursuit of her goals. Often, when a program seemed about to stall, she had turned to Perkins with a steely look and said, "Frances, you've got to do it!" And what might have been postponed or dropped was pushed ahead.

Perkins thought "the key to her tremendous drive" was her maternal feeling, which "was spread over all the children and helpless people of society." In the midst of an industrial world Kelley had "lived and worked like a missionary, no sacrifice too great, no effort too much."

As a child she had been greatly influenced by her Irish Protestant father, and doubtless from his side of the family she inherited her quick wit, sense of fun and fighting spirit. From her mother's Quaker relatives, perhaps, she inherited the implacable patience that finally overcomes: eleven years for the passage of New York's 54-hour bill.

In 1927 she had formally joined the Society of Friends, and a month after her death a meeting in her memory was held in the Friends

Meeting House at Fifteenth Street and Stuyvesant Square. Among those asked to speak was Perkins:

> There are many women in this audience today, whose first knowledge of Florence Kelley came when they were young women in college or in school, when she didn't find it too much trouble to journey on a night sleeper in the dead of winter to a small New England town where there was a little handful of girls studying economics or sociology who thought they would be glad to hear from her.
>
> She was willing to go into these little far corners where a handful of girls were students and tell them about the program which she was evolving for industrial and human and social justice. And that influence which she had over a whole generation was of extreme significance. She took a whole group of young people, formless in their aspirations, and molded their aspirations for social justice into some definite purpose, into a program that had meaning and that had experience and that had practicality back of it.

Though no one in March 1932 could foresee it, Kelley's ideas soon would receive a great push forward. She had often been forced to fight for them state by state. But in the next seven years many would be adopted by Congress and applied nationally.[22]

Chapter 19

-»»)«««-

*The 1932 convention. Roosevelt nominated and later elected. Wil-
son's health declines. The campaign for her appointment. Eleanor
Roosevelt. Molly Dewson. Perkins turns to her church for advice.
She outlines her programs to Roosevelt. She accepts the appointment.*

ON JULY 1, 1932, on the fourth ballot, the Democratic party in
convention in Chicago nominated Roosevelt for President. The nomination was not made unanimous because Smith, who had run second,
refused to ask his supporters to switch their votes. His poor sportsman-
ship did not seriously divide the party, for only the delegations from
New York, Connecticut and Massachusetts followed his lead, but it
lessened what was left of his political power and increased the bitterness between him and Roosevelt and among their supporters.

Perkins, who was not at the convention, had no part in Roosevelt's
campaign for the nomination beyond providing him with information
and ideas about the Depression. But perhaps because he made it the
overriding issue of the day, which for Smith was still Prohibition, she
had become an FRBC, For Roosevelt Before Chicago. On March 4,
1932, hopefully forecasting his inauguration, she had wired him, "This
day next year will be interesting." And he had replied, "I approve
your faith."[1]

The eight months from Roosevelt's nomination to his inauguration
were a difficult, unhappy time for her. Roosevelt's success in the
election meant that she faced the possibility of an appointment to a
President's cabinet and a consequent move to Washington just as her
husband's health began to deteriorate and he entered a sanitarium.
Wilson had stopped work at the Equitable Life Assurance Society
early in 1929 and for several years had succeeded in keeping his
drinking and alternate moods of elation and depression within man-

ageable limits. Their friends still occasionally included him in their activities, and the Roosevelts invited him several times to Hyde Park and at least once to a formal dinner at the Executive Mansion. But on such public occasions his charm and humor no longer came through. He was becoming a kind of nonperson, someone to be talked at rather than with. As a sensitive man he cannot have been unaware that socially he was failing his wife.[2]

Yet he was not without interest in her career. When she and Susanna returned from England in the summer of 1931, he was on the pier to greet them, and as was their family tradition for gaining attention in a crowd he waved his handkerchief slowly up and down rather than frantically side to side. As soon as they saw him, he held up a newspaper, pointed to it several times and put his finger to his lips. Perkins understood that the paper carried a story on which she should avoid comment. Sure enough, directly behind the immigration officers, reporters came aboard, found her on the boat deck and asked for a statement about some shakedowns uncovered in the workmen's compensation bureau.[3]

But some time in the next year Wilson's health gave way, and by January 1933 he had been in the Bloomingdale Sanitarium for several months. In the weeks when he was better, friends visited him; he played tennis and bridge, and sometimes came home on weekends. When he was worse, only Perkins saw him, usually on Saturday. By 1937 he was able to live outside the sanitarium for long stretches of time, and Perkins, who was then in Washington, found inns or boarding homes for him. At first he had a "secretary," a male nurse; later that was not necessary. Beginning about 1943, when he was sixty-six, his problems eased, and in the last ten years of life he found some peace and enjoyment.[4]

His treatment was expensive, and, as they had no insurance, the burden of it might have been expected to force a change in their style of living. The fact that it did not supports the belief of several of her friends that most of the medical bills were paid by someone else. Bruère, who was now relatively rich, may have been the source of help. He was the only person other than doctors with whom she discussed Wilson's illness, and he never wavered in his loyalty to his friend.[5]

With Wilson in a sanitarium Perkins's tone toward him changed: ". . . I hope, darling, that you are making a real effort at reaching the quiet and poise of which you are capable and which will convince everyone that you are as well as you feel. Do try my dear one." Or perhaps an earlier change only now became clear. They were never again equals in their life together. She allowed nothing to interfere with her weekly visit to him, but among her friends she ceased to mention him. For those who met her only at work, it was easy to forget that "Miss Perkins" was married.[6]

Many friends, she was aware, considered her to some extent responsible for Wilson's illness. Was she? He was thirty-seven when they married, and his first breakdown occurred in 1918, when she was sloughing off her career. Robert Moses, who had known them both at the time, thought in retrospect that Perkins, with her "strong woman-libber views," perhaps should not have married anyone, or at least not Wilson. "But once married she wasn't going to abandon him. She had standards." Agnes Leach felt that Perkins's strong "Yankee reserve" concealed a sense of guilt. After Wilson entered the sanitarium, she seemed "ashamed" of him and his illness. "She couldn't seem to accept it and to go on from there." Leach was inclined to think it a mistake for a husband and wife to work in the same field, but then added, "What of the Roosevelts?" Whatever Perkins herself may have thought she encased in her reserve and carried to the grave, undisclosed.[7]

Roosevelt was to take office in March (subsequent presidential inaugurations have been in January), and, following his election in November, the possibility of his appointing her Secretary of Labor began to agitate her life. She was eager for the post, yet appalled at the thought of breaking up the family's home in New York and of the publicity that would beat upon her, her husband and her child. She was over fifty, fully satisfied with her job as Industrial Commissioner and assured by Governor-elect Herbert H. Lehman that she would be reappointed. She could not make up her mind or sort her feelings, but her admirers pushed ahead anyway, certain that in the end she would not desert them.

Those close to Roosevelt received a clear signal to pass to others: he would like to appoint a woman to the cabinet; he would like her to be Frances Perkins. It all depended on the call for her around the country. Thus invited to create a ground swell, committees sprang up to solicit telegrams and letters from bankers, businessmen and labor groups. Social workers and women's groups almost without urging adopted resolutions and wrote letters. Agnes Leach, from 1925 to 1930 state chairman of the New York League of Women Voters and from 1930 a member of the State Health Commission, made sure that support was voiced around the state. Her husband, the editor of *Forum,* followed every speech on a lecture tour of the Midwest with a plea for letters, and in February published a call by Jane Addams for Perkins as Secretary. Meanwhile in Washington in December, Grace Abbott, head of the Children's Bureau, arranged a conference on the problems of children in the Depression and invited Perkins to be the main speaker. When she arrived in Washington, she discovered to her astonishment, that Abbott had also made arrangements for her to be photographed, interviewed and introduced to senators and congressmen on Capitol Hill.[8]

Then there was the friendship of the Roosevelts. Perkins had known neither well until he had been elected governor, and her friendship with Mrs. Roosevelt, whom she saw less often, was slower to develop and not so deep. She admired Mrs. Roosevelt's political skill in helping her husband at receptions, screening him from troublesome guests and bringing others up to him one at a time. She also liked her for herself: "She talked with another woman on the frankest, pleasantest terms. There wasn't any of this waiting for the men to come in after their coffee."[9]

They rode back and forth to Albany on the train together, and sometimes Mrs. Roosevelt appealed for help with a political lunch or dinner. If the Executive Mansion was filled with guests, they sometimes shared a bedroom, for Mrs. Roosevelt invariably gave up her own large room for a smaller one on the third floor. One night when they were upstairs preparing for bed, Perkins admired Mrs. Roosevelt's necklace. It had been given to her by her father, Mrs. Roosevelt said, and while she combed her hair, she spoke of how much he had meant to her and of how, after his early death, she had been passed from one relative to another. Sitting in bed she described her marriage, her problems with her mother-in-law and the lack of any home of her own. Perkins was moved, but she also later was startled when Mrs. Roosevelt published her story.

> It embarrassed me that she should put all that in a book to be read by everybody and anybody. I had kept it absolutely secret. Frankly, any candid picture embarrasses me. I don't care who writes it. I'm embarrassed by André Gide's candid revelations, not because they are revelations of peculiar sexual behavior, but because they tell all, which seems to me is not necessary. I think he could have dropped a curtain over all of his life. It was nobody's business. It was finished. Nobody asked him. He wasn't called to the stand to testify under oath. It embarrasses me to think that a human being, who has the rights of liberty, the basis of which is privacy, will so degrade himself as to expose his whole life and

thinking, to throw away the privacy which he's entitled to and which God gave him.

Perkins could never live, as the Roosevelts now did, exposing to the public for political purposes their life, their children, their home, his yachting, his dog, his stamp-collecting. There would never be a night when Perkins would reciprocate Mrs. Roosevelt's confidences. They were friends, but not intimate.[10]

In one respect, others noticed with amusement, between them there was an occasional touch of friction, caused by Perkins and gracefully absorbed by Mrs. Roosevelt. In conversation, when Perkins knew the subject, she could be blunt: "You are wrong on that, quite wrong." She often covered the attack with charm, but not always, and Mrs. Roosevelt, who was not used to such positive correction, did not like it.

But underneath the friction, some friends sensed, Mrs. Roosevelt was envious of Perkins. She envied the formal education that had led to an advanced degree and the training and experience in a single field that had produced a career. Perkins was on her own in a way that Mrs. Roosevelt longed to be but would not achieve until after Roosevelt's death. Perhaps, too, she envied the opportunity Perkins had, because of the training and position, to work with Roosevelt. A wife's position, even as First Lady, was something different. In the future she would dislike Perkins's biography, *The Roosevelt I Knew*, and when Agnes Leach asked why, she was evasive. Leach was left with the impression, however, that Mrs. Roosevelt felt the book was too exclusively about Roosevelt; her part in his career was not sufficiently valued.[11]

If Perkins was aware of this touch of envy, she did nothing to ease it. "I always knew him better than her," she would say. In later years, when journalists sometimes wrote that she was appointed or retained as Secretary of Labor only because of Mrs. Roosevelt, both denied it. "I don't even know if Roosevelt asked her advice," Perkins said. "If he did, she would have said, 'Whatever Mary Dewson says is all right.'"[12]

More than anyone else Mary W. Dewson, the director of the Women's Democratic National Campaign Committee, was the key to Perkins's appointment. She had come from Maine to New York after twelve years in Masachusetts as superintendent of parole for girls. Then for a time she had worked as research secretary for the National Consumers' League, consulting regularly with Perkins and Felix Frankfurter on the constitutionality of some of the league's programs. More recently she had proved a brilliant political organizer. Where patronage was concerned her initials, M. W. D., were said to stand for More Women Dewson. In Perkins, whom she liked, she had a woman qualified for a governmental post higher than any woman had yet achieved. Even before the election she had made up her mind that Perkins should be Roosevelt's Secretary of Labor.

By January "Molly" Dewson had begun to release trial balloons in the papers. Roosevelt would be reported to be considering Perkins for the position, and the story would start a flurry of comment. Most letters to Roosevelt or the papers were favorable. Many officials in the hierarchy of the AFL, however, were opposed to any nonunion member and particularly to a woman. But Dewson always would say, "Just can that. It doesn't count. That will always be the case. Franklin has told me that he thinks it would be a good idea to have a woman in the cabinet. So there we are. He's not afraid of those who don't want a woman."[13]

After one balloon Josephine Goldmark saw Perkins in the Cosmopolitan Club and said, "Frances, these little items in the newspaper are the most exciting thing in the world."

But that day family problems were uppermost in Perkins's mind. "Josephine, I'm not going to be Secretary of Labor. Just stop talking about it. Stop thinking about it. It is just something that you, as a Consumers' League person, think would be wonderful, but it wouldn't. It's not been offered and I don't believe it will be offered. If it were, I can't do it. It just isn't possible."[14]

Shortly after, on February 1, she sent Roosevelt a handwritten note:

> You are quoted as saying that the newspaper predictions on Cabinet posts are 80% wrong. I write to say that I honestly hope that what they've been printing about me is among the 80% of incorrect items.
>
> I've had my "kick" out of the gratifying letters etc. but for your own sake and that of the U.S.A. I think that someone straight from the ranks of some group of organized workers should be appointed — to establish firmly the principle that *labor is in the President's Councils.* John Frey of the Moulders Union or Ed. McGrady, Legislative Agent of the A.F. of L., are really *first* class people and would be a help to you and keep you realistically closely aware of the fundamental needs and aspirations of the workers. Administration is relatively unimportant in the Labor Department.

She went on to say that he was welcome to any ideas she might have without the necessity of appointing her to any post, and she touched lightly on her personal problems, which "might seriously impair" her usefulness.[15]

Roosevelt replied, she recalled, with a little squib on the back of a scratch pad, "Have considered your advice and don't agree." It was a response as vague as he had given to the AFL's Executive Council, which was urging the appointment of Daniel Tobin, head of the Teamsters' Union and treasurer of the AFL. Roosevelt was not yet ready to commit himself.[16]

Soon after Perkins's conversation with Josephine Goldmark and her note to Roosevelt, Dewson called on her. "Frances, we've got to straighten out a few things here." She said that she had gone on record as recommending Perkins for Secretary, she had Farley's agreement and she did not want to go further if she was to be turned down at the end.

"Well, Mary, it isn't you that's being turned down," said Perkins. "I don't think Roosevelt wants me."

"He'll be all right," said Dewson. "The Women's Division has something to say about these things. We did a lot to elect him. I know I did, and he knows I did. Anyhow I want you to do it."

She recited her reasons. Perkins had the training for the job, and from her work for the state and the Consumers' League she had a program for the country's industrial problems: unemployment insurance, minimum wages, maximum hours, safety programs and abolition of child labor. "You want all these things done. You've done them. You have the ideas, and you have no doubts. You can do it as nobody else can," she said. "What's more, you can get on with Roosevelt. He trusts you. He likes you."

She brushed aside Perkins's fears of Washington as a more complicated political scene — "You'll feel your way" — and dismissed the suggestion that Roosevelt could have the program if he appointed a man from the AFL. "Nobody else will do it. It's all very well to give Roosevelt a program, but he can't make a Secretary of Labor carry out your program. The program will spring from the Secretary of Labor."

Then she added, "You owe it to the women. You will probably have this chance, and you must step forward and do it." Otherwise "generations might pass" before a woman was asked again. "You mustn't say no. Too many people count on what you do. Too much hangs on it."

Dewson left reassured, but without the full guarantee she had sought.[17]

Still uncertain where duty lay, Perkins consulted an Episcopal bishop, Charles K. Gilbert. After reflecting on her question for two days, he wrote:

> If the nation were at war and faced with a crisis in which you could render service that no one else could render with the same measure of effectiveness, your decision could easily be made. You will agree, I am sure, that our present crisis is more grave than any that war has ever presented. God has fitted you by natural gifts and by experience for a service such as few others are competent to render and, as I see it, that service can mean great things for multitudes of distressed and bewildered people whom He wants helped. If we are to find a just and righteous way out of the problems which now seem to threaten our social security, the contribution you are equipped to make will be urgently needed.
>
> I am not thinking only of the Department which would be your special responsibility but of the influence you would have in the councils of the Administration. I know that your persuasiveness and your discerning judgment and your insistence upon the higher human values would make itself felt.
>
> I really believe that it is God's own call. If it is you can't refuse. I can appreciate the sacrifice that may be involved — for you personally and for those whose feelings you are bound to consider. Perhaps no one will know the price you have to pay for the privilege of rendering the difficult service that is demanded of you. Men will think only of the great distinction that comes with the high office to which you go. They will be quite unmindful of the fact that there would be no distinction in that office did it not carry with it a crushing burden or responsibility. But, if it is a job to which God has assigned you, what man thinks is of no consequence. And, if the assignment is His, He will help you to see it through; and He will take care of the domestic problems that may be presented.[18]

She decided to accept the appointment, while still half-hoping it would not be offered. The following week one of Roosevelt's secretaries telephoned: The governor would like to see her at his New York house at eight in the evening of February 22. She agreed and called Dewson, who said, "Sure, I know what it's all about. You do too. Don't be such a baby. Frances, you do the right thing. I'll murder you if you don't."[19]

Shortly before the appointed hour she presented herself at Roosevelt's house on Sixty-fifth Street. The entrance hall, which had once had a touch of elegance, had become a campsite for policemen, reporters and politicians. The chairs, table and even the floor were piled with coats, hats and briefcases. Someone had brought in some standing ashtrays, but ash was everywhere. The handsome oriental rug was rumpled and spotted with grime.

She was shown up to the main floor. To the front was Roosevelt's study, to the back a drawing room and, between, a small hall room in which she was asked to wait. A blond, bespectacled man, whom she did not recognize, was also waiting. From the cut of his clothes she thought perhaps he came from upstate — Syracuse or Buffalo — but she paid little mind to him, for she was absorbed in herself.

For the past month she had been dropping into her lower right-hand desk drawer notes on what she thought a Secretary of Labor should try to accomplish in the next four years. In preparation for the evening's appointment she had listed her ideas on a piece of scratch paper and done some research on the powers and duties of the department. Now, while the stocky, blond man had his interview, she reviewed her thoughts. Suddenly she was called in.

Roosevelt gave her a friendly greeting and, extending his hand toward the blond man, said, "Frances, do you know Harold?"

"Shall I just call him Harold or do you want to tell me his last name?"

"It's Ickes," he replied with a laugh. "Harold L. Ickes."

He was a Chicago lawyer and former stalwart of the Progressive party who had actively campaigned for Roosevelt, and he had just accepted the post of Secretary of the Interior. Other than Perkins he would be the only member of Roosevelt's cabinet to serve from its first to last day.

As soon as they were alone, Roosevelt said, "Did Molly Dewson tell you what I have in mind?"

"Well, I never know if Molly is speaking the truth, or just reflecting her own hopes and aspirations."

They joked a little back and forth, and then he said, "I really mean it, Frances. I think you'd be a good Secretary of Labor, and I'd like you to come along."

Thanking him for the honor, she questioned again whether he ought not to appoint an official from some labor union, preferably one from the AFL. Roosevelt replied that the time had come to consider all working people, organized and unorganized. He would stand on her record as Industrial Commissioner of New York. He wanted to accomplish for the nation what had been done for workers in New York.

Shifting her approach, she said that if she accepted the post she would want to pursue certain programs.

"Well, what?"

"I have written out a few notes," she said, producing her scratch paper. "I won't hold you to this. But I don't want to say yes to you unless you know what I'd like to do and are willing to have me go ahead and try." She doubted that he was as interested as she in some of the programs, and she intended to lay them before him unequivocally.

First on her list was some form of federal aid to the states for direct unemployment relief. Next, public works. These would provide some jobs, though not many. In conjunction with them there should be a law or constitutional amendment to prohibit child labor, both to keep the children in school and to save the jobs for adults. Also some laws on maximum hours and minimum wages, so that the adults would receive a living wage, enough to preserve health and allow them to share in community life.

"Can that be done constitutionally?" he asked. The Supreme Court decisions seemed to indicate it could not.

She was uncertain, but she repeated to him an idea that Felix Frankfurter, in connection with some Consumers' League projects, had described to her and Mary Dewson several weeks earlier. It was that the United States, in purchasing goods, whether paper clips or battleships, could stipulate in its contracts with the manufacturers what the minimum wage was to be. Private industry in bidding for the government contracts would have to accept the minimum wage.

Roosevelt was interested.

Her next idea was entirely her own. She pointed out that workmen's compensation had gradually spread over the country as one state had copied another. She wanted the federal Department of Labor to hold conferences and start programs to persuade the states to copy each other. The federal department could not order the sovereign State of Rhode Island to enact a law requiring sanitary facilities in factories, but it might be able to stimulate the state to create a labor department (it had none) and aid that new department with statistics, model statutes and technical advice.

"I don't know how you'll do it," said Roosevelt, "but it's all right. You have to invent the way to do these things. Don't expect too much help from me."

"All I expect from you," she said, "is that you call a governors' conference and that among the items mentioned will be some of these things that I have in mind. I'd like you to lay the path, to make it possible for the Secretary of Labor to approach the various state labor departments."

When she shifted the discussion to unemployment insurance and old age pensions, he broke in, "You know, Frances, I don't believe in the dole and I never will." But she insisted she meant true insurance plans. And then she talked of the need for a "well-developed, central public employment office, which really has money back of it. Senator Wagner," she said, "has a bill, and it's a very good bill." She suggested that they could start backing it at once.

Finally she mentioned the need to reorganize the Bureau of Labor Statistics. She would require his support "because it will cost money." She felt afterward that he had agreed promptly because he knew the country would back him: people were angry about Hoover's misleading figures on unemployment.

With regard to the Bureau of Immigration, she confessed that she didn't know what to recommend. She had read the Wickersham report on the bureau, been horrified by its account of illegal acts by some immigration inspectors and had been to talk to Wickersham. Obviously some sort of reform was needed.

"That's all right," Roosevelt said. "You can always do that."

With notes in hand, she said, "Are you sure you want these things done? Because you don't want me for Secretary of Labor if you don't."

"Yes. I'll back you. Is it all right?"

She realized that somebody else must be waiting, and thanking him again for the honor she accepted the post, asking only for a delay in any announcement until she had consulted her husband.

"Can you see him tomorrow?"

"Yes."

"All right. Let me know tomorrow night."[20]

As she rose to leave he said, referring to her program, "I suppose you are going to nag me about this forever." She took that to mean that he wanted her to nag him about it every now and then. "He wanted his conscience kept for him by somebody."[21]

The next day she went to the sanitarium. She was sure Wilson would accept her decision. "Nevertheless, the amenities between my husband and me were such that I would never dream of doing a thing that he hadn't been informed of and consulted about in advance."

He was in "a good, controlled mood. So we didn't have any emotional crisis over it. His only comment was, 'I can't go to Washington. I will not go to Washington! I'm not going to go under these circumstances.' I knew he couldn't go anyhow. He was too ill to go. But, of course, he didn't think of himself as being ill as I knew him to be. So he thought of it always as a project of our life together. He said, 'Where will I live?' "

She suggested that, as it would be better for Susanna not to change schools, they should keep their New York apartment. "That'll be home. I'll come up weekends."

"You promise you'll be up every weekend. You'll come up and see me every weekend?"[22]

She promised, and on February 28 Roosevelt announced the appointment. Green, president of the AFL, promptly denounced it, but on the whole, as her record was publicized throughout the country, the appointment was well received.

PART V

The United States Department of Labor

Chapter 20

⇢⇥⇠

The Bureau of Immigration and appointment of Daniel W. Mac-
Cormack as Commissioner. Relief and the Civilian Conservation
Corps. The conference with leaders of organized labor.

ON TAKING OFFICE as United States Secretary of Labor Perkins had no
order set for implementing her ideas on labor legislation, which perhaps was fortunate, for she discovered that the department's most
pressing problem was in the Bureau of Immigration. She had told
Roosevelt that it was the bureau most in need of reform and that she
was uncertain of what should be done. But she found there was no
time for indecision. Before leaving New York she had been warned
that special investigators in the Section 24 division of the bureau were
engaged in shakedowns of aliens, and after a day in office she was
convinced the charge was true.

A simple purge of the division's leaders was not possible because
they had recently been given the protection of the Civil Service Act.
So, on the suggestion of Robe Carl White, the First Assistant Secretary, she announced that as an economy measure during the Depression she would not request any additional appropriation for the
division; and because it had already overspent its budget, within the
month it was disbanded. She had found a neat exit from a difficult
situation. And in yet another respect her luck with the problem
continued to hold.[1]

Shortly after taking office she received a telephone call from an
acquaintance in New York, Daniel W. MacCormack, president of one
of the city's bigger banks, the Fiduciary Trust Company. Because his
colleagues had plans for the bank of which he disapproved, he was
resigning, and he wondered if she knew of a job in Washington for
which he might qualify. She asked him to take charge of the Bureau
of Immigration.

Colonel MacCormack, as he was known, had been born in Scotland in 1880 and brought to the United States by his parents at the age of nine. He attended colleges in Montreal, Aberdeen (Scotland) and Boston, and from 1912 to 1917 in Panama he had organized housing and supplies for the thousands of men digging the canal. During the war, as an army officer, he had unraveled the tangle of railroad cars bringing supplies to New York for convoy to France, and after the war, from 1922 to 1927, as a member of the American Finance Mission to Persia, he had reorganized that country's tax and transportation systems. In the process he became a hero to many Persians and also learned all there was to know about the growth and illegal distribution of opium. Back in New York he had turned banker and at fifty-two was a bank president. Few bureau chiefs in Washington could match the breadth of his experience, and Perkins was eager to have him reorganize both the Bureaus of Immigration and Naturalization, which together accounted for four fifths of the Department of Labor's money and personnel.

But there was a problem. The appointment of Commissioner General of Immigration was not hers to make but the President's, and traditionally the post went to a loyal party worker. Commissioners in the past had been defeated congressmen or men allied with immigrant or labor groups. MacCormack had no political connections. He was simply her personal choice. In such an appointment Farley's voice counted for as much or more than hers, and there was a "rule" requiring all federal appointees from New York City to have the approval of Edward J. Flynn, the Democratic leader in the Bronx.[2]

She probably spoke to Farley directly. At about this time she asked him for a six-month delay in replacing Robe Carl White with a Democrat as White was the only man in the department with enough knowledge of its affairs to help her to reorganize it. Farley agreed, and it seems likely that she won him over to MacCormack with a similar argument. She had already told Roosevelt privately of the corruption in the bureau, and in her memorandum for him on MacCormack, which would be seen by many in the White House, she did not mention it. She stressed qualities in MacCormack, however, that would be useful in a major bureaucratic reorganization: "A man of ingenuity and extremely practical as well as forceful in handling all administrative problems. . . . very successful in the handling of people . . . [with] a broad social point of view with regard to public policy . . . [with] a very significant success in semi-diplomatic dealings with nationals of several countries and in handling rather difficult international adjustments." Roosevelt was persuaded, Flynn's approval followed and on March 31 MacCormack took office.[3]

He served until his death by heart attack in January 1937 and proved as brilliant as Perkins had predicted. With his small mustache, military bearing and slight Scottish accent, he suggested a British Army officer. On the Mexican border he reorganized the immigration inspectors, who carried guns and resisted discipline, and though he extended their duties, at the same time he won their respect. They thought it a terrible shame that he had to work for a woman. He was equally successful with citizens' groups and congressional committees. He was always candid, clear in what he said and able to defuse the irrational hostility many people seemed to feel for aliens. He consulted constantly with Perkins, not out of fear or incompetence but because he was aware of the political difficulties immigration affairs could cause the department. Unlike Garsson and Doak, he and Perkins measured success by the absence of scare headlines about radical aliens, and his able, trustworthy administration of the department's largest bureau left her free to concentrate on labor and social programs.[4]

One day shortly after the inauguration Perkins had a phone call from Harry Hopkins. He and William Hodson, the executive director of the New York Welfare Council, had come to Washington with a plan for unemployment relief that they wanted to present to Roosevelt. But at the time thousands of people were mailing plans to officials in Washington or trying to present them in person, and the two men had been rebuffed by Roosevelt's secretary. So Hopkins called Perkins, insisting that she see them.

Her one free moment that day was at six, before a dinner conference at eight. She had just moved from the Willard Hotel to the Women's University Club, and she suggested they meet there. But at six every seat in the lobby and dining room was taken. She finally discovered a bench backed against the stairway and, borrowing a stool from the telephone operator, the three huddled under a curl in the stair while Hodson and Hopkins described their plan for relief on a national basis.

Both had experience in relief work, and their program seemed practical. She promised to discuss it with Roosevelt as well as to procure an appointment for them. But if the plan was adopted, who should administer it? They suggested six or eight names including their own, adding that either of them would be better than the others because of their experience and because the plan was theirs. But between themselves they had no preference.

In the next few days she arranged a meeting with Roosevelt, but it was not decisive. His mind at that moment was on other matters: the Emergency Banking Act and, to explain it to the country by radio, his first "fireside chat"; also an Economy Act, cutting federal salaries and pensions; and an act allowing wines and light beers until the Prohibition amendment could be repealed. In addition several bills on farm and financial matters were in preparation. Though relief for the industrial unemployed was constantly mentioned in cabinet meetings, especially by Perkins and Garner, priority throughout the spring went to agriculture. Crops would not wait for man, and Roosevelt and most of his advisers saw the country's agricultural problems as the key to recovery.[5]

Meanwhile Perkins met with three senators, Wagner, Robert La Follette, Jr., of Wisconsin and Edward P. Costigan of Colorado, and drafted a bill for unemployment relief on the principle of grants by the federal government to the states. Making use of the state organizations in existence seemed the quickest and most efficient way to aid the unemployed. This was the essence of the Hopkins-Hodson plan, but it was also the thinking of others. None of the ideas that underlay the various New Deal programs was the inspiration of any one person.

Early Tuesday morning, March 14, Perkins had breakfast with Raymond Moley, at the time one of Roosevelt's closest advisers. She outlined for him the senators' bill for unemployment relief and asked if Roosevelt was ready to think about it. Moley agreed to find out. She also pointed out to him some labor problems in a bill the President was considering, which would employ five hundred thousand men a year to work on conservation and public works projects. This was an idea that in one form or another he had been turning over in his mind for many months. Under the bill the men would receive housing, food and a dollar a day. For conservation projects the low wage, perhaps, was all very well, Perkins remarked, but "when it is applied to public works such as levee building [flood control], drainage works etc., it tends to bring down the price of free labor to the same level." Organized labor, she predicted, would object.

At nine that same morning Moley repeated the conversation to Roosevelt, who brushed aside the relief and public works part of it to describe still another variation of a conservation program: to take about 250,000 men from the cities and put them to work on federal land and in the national parks. He was full of the romance of the idea — city men discovering nature in the forests — and talked of sending a bill to Congress at once. Moley suggested that on Roosevelt's behalf he prepare a memorandum outlining the plan and circulate it to the Secretaries of Labor, War, Agriculture and the Interior. He thought it would give a chance to the Wagner–La Follette–Costigan group, through Perkins, to raise again the idea of grants-in-aid to the states for unemployment relief.

His maneuver worked smoothly. The next day the four Secretaries replied to Roosevelt that they had considered not only the conservation project, later called the Civilian Conservation Corps, but "the whole program of relief for industrial unemployment." "We are of the opinion," they said, "that there are three items to be considered in this program." These were the CCC, grants-in-aid to the states for relief and a public works program.[6]

On Thursday Roosevelt had a meeting to discuss the three programs with Perkins, La Follette, Costigan and Hopkins, who had come down again from New York. He was least enthusiastic about public works. He doubted there were enough worthwhile projects to allow it to have a significant part in a recovery program. But the group persuaded him to include a public works program with the other two in a message to Congress on relief, which he delivered on March 21. He asked for action first on the conservation project, and immediately after the message was read the Senate majority leader, Joseph T. Robinson, on behalf of himself and Wagner, introduced a bill to establish the Civilian Conservation Corps.

As Perkins had predicted, the leaders of organized labor promptly denounced it, in particular the dollar-a-day-wage provision. Perkins, whose department would be in charge of recruiting the men, was called to testify by the House and Senate committees sitting jointly. It was her first appearance as Secretary of Labor before any committee, and she confessed later to being "rattled" — partly because of the size of the room and the number of spectators, so much larger and more numerous than in Albany, but even more because of the speed with which the bill had been introduced. So many details were still vague. So much could be asked her for which she had no answer.

Yet to all who heard her she appeared at ease and in command of her subject. The administration, she said, regarded the bill as a relief measure. It expected most of the workers to be the young, unmarried men "who had been left out of calculation by most relief agencies." The dollar-a-day wage could not be compared to "sweatshop work" because the men would be given housing, clothing and food as well.

Enrollment would be voluntary. There would be no regimentation of labor, and she saw no reason why the dollar-a-day-wage scale should be adopted elsewhere.

The next day William Green, AFL president, testified. The bill "smacked of fascism, of Hitlerism, of a form of Sovietism." If it passed, Congress would go down in history "as a Congress that has established a dollar a day wage for the payment of labor on the public domain . . . The masses will lose sight of the relief feature, but they will remember this Congress determined that a dollar a day . . ." His testimony was carried by radio coast to coast.[7]

After Green had blasted Perkins's appointment as Secretary of Labor, as one of her first acts in Washington she had called on him. It was a private call, in his office; she did not announce it to the press and neither did he. She simply set out to show that she bore him no ill will, and he took it in that spirit. After his testimony on the CCC bill, Roosevelt said to her, "Now that you are all reconciled with Bill Green, you go sell him this idea that a dollar a day is good wages. Besides, it isn't wages at all. It is just relief."[8]

Probably she was only one of many who talked to Green; it was the cumulative effect that caused him to soften his opposition. On March 27 both houses received an amended bill in which, paradoxically, the President was given more discretionary power than he had originally asked but that power was defined in vaguer language. He was authorized simply to create and run the CCC "under such rules and regulations as he may prescribe, and by utilizing such existing departments or agencies as he may designate." Even the controversial dollar a day was omitted.

Some congressmen objected to the amount of power delegated to the executive branch, but their leaders urged the needs of the emergency. One important amendment was offered. The sole Negro congressman, Representative Oscar De Priest, Republican of Illinois, asked "that no discrimination shall be made on account of race, color, or creed . . . under the provisions of the Act." With this amendment the bill was passed; it was the administration's first act in the field of relief and social legislation. Roosevelt signed it on March 31, and on April 5 by executive order the Civilian Conservation Corps began its existence. On April 7 its first member was selected and enrolled.[9]

For Perkins, whose department was in charge of enrollment, the pace was a scramble. In discussing the proposed bill one day with Roosevelt, Ickes and Dern, the Secretary of War, she had asked how the men were to be selected. "Use your employment service," said Roosevelt.

"Mr. President, we haven't got any employment service," she said. "I told you only last week that what calls itself that is a fake. It doesn't work. I'm wiping it out."

"Make one," he said. "Create one. Create one just like that."

Later she said to him privately, "I'll have to get an awfully good man to run this at the Department of Labor level. Is that all right with you? Can I have anybody I want?"

"You can have anybody you want and can get. It doesn't matter who it is. Just get anybody and get it going. That's all I ask. Get it going quick."

She called W. Frank Persons, who from 1909 to 1917 had been superintendent of the Charity Organization Society in New York City. What brought him to mind now was his work in World War I as director of the Department of Civilian Relief of the American Red Cross. He had created a national organization for relief work almost overnight. She asked him to leave his job as executive vice-president of the American Association of Personal Finance Companies (a national trade association) and to work directly for the country's poor in the Department of Labor. He agreed, and within the first week in April they had reconstituted the U.S. Employment Service with Persons as director and created within it a division known as the National Re-Employment Service to recruit men for the CCC. Wherever possible the division would rely on local relief agencies already acquainted with young men in sufficient need to qualify for the corps. State directors were appointed as quickly as possible to coordinate the local agencies, and each state was given a quota to fill, based on its share of the national population. Like MacCormack, Persons would prove a happy choice for a difficult job.[10]

On the same day that Roosevelt signed the CCC bill, Perkins held a conference in her office of labor leaders and a few experts in other fields to discuss ideas for relieving unemployment. In February she had considered the possibility of such a conference but Green's denunciation of her appointment had made it seem awkward, and she had done nothing about it. Then suddenly the idea received impetus from outside.

On Saturday, March 11, as she was leaving for New York to pick up a bag of fresh clothes and to see her husband and child, she had been called on the phone by Dr. Leo Wolman, an economist in charge of statistics and research for the Amalgamated Clothing Workers. He said that Sidney Hillman, the union's president, and its other leaders were "restive" because "nothing is being done for labor."

She pointed out that the administration has been in office only six days.

"I know there hasn't been time to turn around, but they were so excited about the Democratic victory that they wanted something to happen. Hillman is the one who's upset. My advice to you is to do something quick — anything. It doesn't matter what it is. Just something that can be put in the paper. I know you can't have any serious labor legislation overnight. I know it takes time to do it, but they don't know that. Anyhow, Hillman wants to see you."

She was quite willing to see Hillman. She had some personal affairs in New York, she said, and would be returning to Washington on the Sunday midnight train. Could they meet in the station an hour earlier? Wolman agreed.

They gathered at the information booth and then moved to a bench in the waiting room. Hillman, thin and intense, trembled with excitement; Wolman was calm and practical. Hillman wanted some demonstration of the administration's interest in labor.

"What do you suggest?" she asked. "I can't bear to do just a showoff thing without substance. You know what the program is. I've told you both the suggestions I made to the President."

"That's a fine program," Hillman said, "but it'll take you most of a year to put it through."

"It'll take more than a year to put it through. After all, we're elected for four years."

"But the labor people can't wait! They've got to have something now. A signal. A symbol. A demonstration that the administration cares about labor. Why don't you call a conference of labor leaders?"

"What good will it do? You know that nothing can come out of it."

"Yes, but it will make them understand that something's being done!"

They talked it over, and on the train she decided Hillman was right. Organized labor needed some signal of the administration's concern for working people, though the substance of it would have to come later. But a conference at the Department of Labor when all the bureaus were in such disorder? It seemed impossible.

The next morning she consulted with some people in the department, chiefly Clara Beyer, head of the industrial division in the Children's Bureau. Her husband, Otto Beyer, was a labor-management consultant for several railroads, and the two of them knew personally many of the leaders in the national and international unions.

The question of which leaders to invite was complicated by union rivalries and politics. Hillman's union, the Amalgamated Clothing Workers of America, was not affiliated with the AFL, and he himself was disliked, even hated, by the federation's leaders because he had founded Amalgamated in 1914 by seceding from the United Garment Workers, an AFL union. Among trade union commandments was a prohibition against "dual unionism," two competing unions instead of one. To include Hillman in a conference with AFL leaders was unusual, even radical, and if successful might open a way for him to lead his union into the AFL.

It was almost as startling to invite David Dubinsky, whose International Ladies' Garment Workers' Union also was not affiliated with the AFL. Because its members were almost entirely women it had developed independently, but it had also developed as a "vertical" or "industrial" union, organizing all the workers in the shop, unskilled as well as skilled. All but a very few of the AFL unions were "horizontal" or "craft" unions, organizing only skilled workers. Their leaders distrusted the industrial unions, in which the unskilled often outnumbered and outvoted the skilled.

National politics also created complications. Construction unions controlled the AFL, and most of their leaders were Republicans. William "Big Bill" Hutcheson, head of the Carpenters, had been a member of Hoover's campaign committee. Perkins wanted the Republicans to come, or the purpose of the conference would be defeated. But she did not want them to dominate it and pass antiadministration resolutions. So she and Beyer tried to balance them with Democrats, such as George Berry of the Printers and Dan Tobin of the Teamsters. Martin Durkin of the Plumbers was a Republican; Dan Tracy of the Electrical Workers a Democrat.

Beyer suggested John L. Lewis of the Mine Workers. "He's a Republican, and always was, but he had some kind of falling-out with Hoover. I think he's just ripe to come and help us. He's under a cloud at the present — he used to have a big union, and it has shrunk — but he's still a man to be reckoned with."

The United Mine Workers was affiliated with the AFL, but Lewis himself was unpopular with its leaders. He wanted to be a member of its executive council, and they refused to elect him. But with an invitation list of more than seventy, there was no reason for omitting Lewis.

Perkins also invited several women, among them Agnes Nestor of the Glovemakers, Melinda Scott of the Hat-Trimmers and Rose Schneiderman of the Women's Trade Union League. Such recognition of women in labor was unusual, a reason Perkins was eager to include them, but she also knew she could count on their support. In addition she invited several labor experts in other fields: Monsignor John A. Ryan, William M. Leiserson and Sumner Slichter, an economist at the Harvard Business School.

After the invitations had gone out, Perkins and Beyer heard rumors of huddles and long-distance phone calls among the union leaders to find out who had been invited and who was accepting. Because there had never been a conference like it, some question about its purpose was inevitable. She had stated that she hoped they might agree on some first steps to recommend to the President for easing the unemployment problems of the Depression. As a lure she had implied that the President might see them, or at least a committee of them. About sixty-five persons accepted.

They met in the biggest space that could be put together in the old Labor building, the Secretary's office and the outer office, usually separated by double, sliding doors, now opened to make one room. As she recalled it, everyone was full of good wishes and greetings, but the AFL leaders cast "a big pickle eye on Hillman and Dubinsky" and Lewis was "less than happily welcomed."

She opened the conference with a statement of its purpose: the President wanted first on his agenda, she said, relief for the unemployed and then measures for the prevention of unemployment. Slichter followed her with a gloomy analysis of the country's economic situation, and after several more prepared speeches she asked for questions, promising "the freest kind of discussion." But she had difficulty persuading the labor leaders to speak.

Perhaps by the afternoon, she suggested, they could agree on a few ideas about what might be done, and a committee could take these to the President. They protested, however, that they would need a second day before reaching any conclusions. She had expected that: they wanted the evening to talk things over among themselves.

Finally George Berry of the Printers started the discussion. After lauding the President and praising Perkins for calling the conference, he began to describe the situation of the printers in his home state, Tennessee. They were out of work, their savings exhausted and the state's money for relief used up. He suggested that federal money be given to the states to help the people on relief. The others, describing the conditions in their trades and states, backed him. It became clear that organized labor would support a program of relief.

Their next idea surprised her: the unemployed should be allowed to sleep in public buildings. She thought it impractical. Hotels and dormitories are constructed differently from public buildings for good reasons. "You might expect the idea from a warm-hearted, not very scientific charity organization but not from really tough labor leaders." Meanwhile the room was rapidly heating up, and the men began to squirm on the small folding chairs the department had rented.

Dan Tobin of the Teamsters rose. He was a blustery, explosive type of man and was visibly hot and bothered. "Madam Secretary, this is no kind of place to hold a conference. This is a dreadful room. We can't do anything here. I move we adjourn and meet in the AFL building right after lunch." The AFL building had an auditorium and a large conference room.

"That won't be practical," she said. The Department of Labor people had to be available for phone calls. She herself was expecting a call from the President. Then bluntly she said that it was a terrible room, but it was a Department of Labor conference and it should be held in the department. She knew she couldn't accede to the suggestion. The country would think the AFL had captured the department.

To her astonishment Lewis came to her aid. The Secretary, he said, had made a very proper ruling. "Although unemployment has been a problem plaguing this country for many months, there have been no meetings called by the AFL in the AFL auditorium to solve this problem. The Secretary of Labor has asked us here to help her solve this problem about which she has an official duty. I think it extremely appropriate we should continue to meet here. It is the government that is calling this conference, and we should meet here in the government's rooms."

Berry, Hillman and a few others supported him, and the general discussion resumed. But after lunch Tobin did not reappear for several hours; cooling himself off, someone said, with a few beers. She was sympathetic. "The chairs were too small for the great big men that they were. It was a horrid place to meet."

At noon on the second day, when the discussion seemed at an end, she quickly summarized the ideas that had been presented. To Clara Beyer at the back of the room this summary, which was entirely improvised, was so well done that it won for Perkins the respect of many of the men who had been hostile to her. The conference had developed a ten-point program to present to the President:

1. unemployment relief by federal aid to the states
2. safeguards against relief's being used by employers to subsidize sweatshop wages

3. public works to stimulate the basic industries
4. abolition of child labor
5. the use of public buildings for education and other purposes for the unemployed
6. limitation of hours
7. higher wages
8. the possibility of industrial boards to set minimum wages in certain industries
9. the government in its contracts to specify that the Department of Labor could determine minimum wages and conditions of work [She had presented the conference with the idea that Frankfurter had given her and Mary Dewson.]
10. the right of workers to organize and to choose their own representatives

She appointed the committee to report the recommendations to the President. Even before the conference she had thought of making Tobin the chairman of it. He had been the AFL's candidate for Secretary of Labor and the one most put out by her appointment. She had discussed it with Green, saying, "Of course, you're the natural chairman, because you're the President of the AFL, but it occurred to me that we might at least give consideration to making Mr. Tobin the chairman. What do you think?"

"That would be a fine idea, Miss Perkins. That will help Dan. He likes to go and see the President, and it will help him out. He feels kind of bad now and that'll help."

So she made Tobin chairman of the committee, putting on it Lewis "just because of what he'd done," Berry, Hillman, Green and several more, including a woman. Then she took them over to see the President.

The recommendations were perhaps unexceptional, but their source, a conference in which almost all of organized labor and the Department of Labor were joined, was not. There had never been such a conference before, and if a signal to organized labor of the administration's concern was needed, the conference gave it.[11]

Chapter 21

-»»«-

Relief and the fight over Public Works. Senator Black's Thirty-hour bill. The National Industrial Recovery Act. Public works included. NRA and PWA separated. The appointment of Hugh Johnson to be director only of NRA.

TWO OF THE RECOMMENDATIONS on the labor leaders' list were federal aid to the states for unemployment relief and a public works program. Both had been requested by Roosevelt, along with the Civilian Conservation Corps, in his message to Congress on March 21. And in the following week Senators Wagner, La Follette and Costigan had introduced a bill to establish a Federal Emergency Relief Administration, FERA, to funnel federal money to the states. During April, while Congress conducted hearings on it, La Follette through Moley kept reminding Roosevelt that nothing had yet been done about public works. But whereas Roosevelt and his cabinet were in general agreement about the need and size of the relief program, they were divided over public works, and the presentation of a bill to Congress was constantly postponed. Meanwhile the relief bill advanced rapidly, and early in May Congress passed and Roosevelt signed it.[1]

The act appropriated $500 million for aid to the states in providing relief for the fifteen million people now estimated to need help in order to survive. Half the money was to be distributed to the states on the basis of one dollar for every three from all other public sources spent on relief during the preceding quarter-year. The scheme was adapted from the relief program in New York, in which counties, cities and towns had matched the state's contributions. The balance of the fund could be spent without such matching.

Perkins had taken both Hopkins and Hodson to see Roosevelt, and although he asked her opinion, she did not recommend one above the other. She thought Hopkins the more dynamic but Hodson the more skillful in handling people. Possibly because Hopkins pursued the job harder or because Roosevelt had seen more of him in New York, he was chosen. Roosevelt announced the appointment on May 22, and Hopkins began work at once, inheriting a small staff from the tiny Emergency Relief and Construction Administration set up under Hoover in 1932. By evening of the next day he had communicated with all the states and made grants to Colorado, Illinois, Iowa, Michigan, Mississippi, Ohio and Texas.[2]

A program for public works, however, continued to lag. In Congress Wagner insisted that it was the "keystone of recovery," the best way to stimulate business and reduce unemployment, and Senators Costigan, La Follette and Bronson Cutting of New Mexico introduced a bill for a $6 billion building program. Within the cabinet Perkins made herself the idea's chief proponent. She constantly raised the subject in meetings, mentioned it in speeches and had a bill drafted by her department's lawyers, which she presented to Roosevelt. Yet even though her efforts were supported by Ickes, Garner, Wallace and Dern, Roosevelt constantly put off a decision. As late as April 14 he was still telling reporters that he had not yet discussed it.

Within the administration the idea's leading opponent was Lewis M. Douglas, Director of the Budget. He feared that the proposed figure of $6 billion, more than ten times the amount appropriated for relief, would make it impossible to balance the budget for many years, and that would destroy the government's fiscal credit. Douglas, who had given up his congressional seat from Arizona to become budget director, was not a member of the cabinet though he was often invited to its meetings. But unlike cabinet members he had an appointment with Roosevelt every morning. His advantage drove Perkins nearly wild.

She recognized, however, that much of the opposition came from Roosevelt. He had never been enthusiastic about public works: he doubted there was a sufficient number of worthwhile projects to justify an expenditure of even a billion dollars. And behind the doubt lay a political problem: he had made conflicting promises in his campaign. In San Francisco he had said that the government's task was "distributing wealth and products more equitably . . . Every man has a right to life; and this means that he has also a right to make a comfortable living." Many people took this to mean that if private industry could not provide jobs at decent wages, then the government should — by public works.

But a month later in Pittsburgh he had charged Hoover's administration with "the most reckless and extravagant past that I have been able to discover in the statistical record of any peacetime Government anywhere, any time." He promised, if elected, "to reduce the cost of current Federal Government operations by 25 percent." He would move toward "the one sound foundation of permanent economic recovery — a complete and honest balancing of the Federal budget." The only reason for an exception would be "if starvation and dire need on the part of any of our citizens make necessary the appropriation of additional funds." Relief, not public works, could be the exception.

"This was one of the conflicts in Roosevelt's nature and thinking," Perkins wrote later. "He wanted a balanced budget, but he also wanted to do the right thing by his unemployed fellow citizens." In Roosevelt's first weeks in office this conflict, still unresolved, was projected from words into deeds. After the Emergency Banking Act he persuaded a reluctant Congress, as its second piece of major legislation, to cut veteran's pensions, congressional salaries, salaries of federal employees and departmental budgets — all to save the budget half a billion dollars. Yet eleven days later he approved the Civilian Conservation Corps, which was relief in an imaginative but very expensive form: not only were the corpsmen given food but also housing, clothing, transportation, training and a dollar a day.

Perkins had fewer hesitations than Roosevelt. Relief, soup for the starving, did little or nothing to stimulate industry and create jobs. If mass purchasing power was to be restored, then industry alone or combined with government must provide millions of jobs at good wages. If this threw the budget out of balance for several years and devalued the dollar at the grocery store, so be it. As a student of Simon Patten's who had continued her reading in economic theory, she believed that industry, with its enormous potential, if once revived could easily create the wealth to balance the budget.[3]

Douglas, on the other hand, believed that the government's first aim after granting relief should be to stabilize the value of the dollar. Not only economic recovery but civilization rested on fiscal credit. "To those who say, 'You must not cut the army, for instance,'" Douglas declared, "I say, which is more important? A national defense which is perfectly futile, if the credit of the government collapses, or an unimpaired credit of your government? For myself, I say 'An unimpaired credit of the government.' For it is upon that, that all human values of our people ultimately rest." He was not against a public works program in itself; he merely wanted it restricted to projects for which engineering plans already existed. Otherwise the projects would not come into being until long after the condition they were supposed to cure had passed. But that meant cutting the program down to less than a billion, a point at which those who believed in it felt it would do very little good.[4]

"The nearest the cabinet came to hard feelings," Perkins wrote later, "was over Douglas's ability to postpone action by the President on the public works bill." She felt he adopted a program of delay as a deliberate technique. Already Congress was sitting later into spring than usual, and sometime soon its special session to pass the emergency legislation would abruptly end. "The days were passing, and in those early months we counted two days a long time."[5]

The succession of events in the first months of Roosevelt's administration was very swift. Before Congress adjourned on June 15, it passed fifteen major laws, each with alarms and diversions. While Perkins was trying to advance the bill for public works, another bill aimed at reducing unemployment but based on a wholly different theory came up for debate in the Senate and was passed in only three days. Suddenly the administration was faced with the possibility of a program for economic recovery in which it had played no part and of which it disapproved.

The bill's sponsor was Senator Hugo L. Black, whom Roosevelt in 1937 would appoint to the Supreme Court. Black wanted to reduce unemployment by dividing the existing jobs among more workers. He proposed to achieve this by barring from interstate commerce any article made in an establishment in which the employees worked more than five days a week or six hours a day. He had deduced a theoretical relationship for the amount of production, size of market, number of jobs and total payroll and concluded that if hours of work in interstate commerce were limited to thirty a person, then six million more workers could have jobs. Often known as the Thirty-hour bill, it had excited considerable support across the country when Black had first introduced it in December 1932. At the hearings in January the AFL had come out for it strongly, Green even threatening a general strike if it did not pass. When the Senate Judiciary Committee reported on it favorably except for a reservation about its constitutionality, the pressure on the senators to act increased, and on April 6 they passed it, 53–30.

The bill had many obvious defects: it was almost certainly unconstitutional, under the child labor law precedent; it provided no minimum wage, and for many workers a drop from forty-eight hours to thirty hours of weekly pay would leave them destitute; dividing jobs without increasing wages did nothing to stimulate business or increase mass purchasing power; and in many industries the work was not divisible — not everyone could milk a cow or cut a diamond. If enacted, the bill would seriously dislocate industrial patterns and in many industries might force a drop in production, with workers again being laid off. The scheme, which Black proposed for a two-year trial, was too rigid. Yet even Wagner, who saw all its defects and was working feverishly on other plans for recovery, had voted for it rather than be recorded against it.

Its potential embarrassment for Roosevelt was even greater. After promising more action than Hoover he did not want to veto an effort, however impractical, to cure the Depression, and he wanted any scheme that was enacted to be associated more closely with his administration. Industrial unemployment was within the jurisdiction of the labor department, and he sent Perkins to testify at the bill's hearings before the House Committee on Labor. She was to be enthusiastic for the bill's general purpose, as who was not, but discouraging about its details. With luck its momentum might be stopped or it might at least be improved by amendments suggested by the administration.

The assignment was not merely a legislative feint for Perkins or, she felt, for Roosevelt. With proper amendments the bill might serve as one approach for attacking the Depression. "I endorse the principle of the thirty-hour week," she told the congressmen. The increasing use of machinery made shorter hours possible and necessary. But she favored a gradual reduction of hours rather than a sudden drop to thirty, and she thought some provision must be made for setting a minimum wage, at least in those industries where the reduction of hours would lower workers' pay to substandard levels. This meant some sort of government bureau to set the minimum wages and to enforce them, an idea labor leaders strongly opposed: any minimum wage, they said, would soon become the maximum. Nevertheless the House committee was sufficiently impressed with her ideas to request a bill incorporating them.

She hastily put one together in the labor department and sent it over to the committee. Its chief features were a relaxation of the antitrust laws to stimulate business by allowing industries to unite against unfair trade practices; a power in the Secretary of Labor to limit a company's production when it was working excessively long hours to undercut competitors; and minimum wage boards for industries in which workers were unfairly compensated or paid too little to subsist. What she hoped to inject into the Black bill was flexibility for the extreme case or the needs of special industries or areas. What most labor leaders saw was a minimum wage set by the government; and most businessmen, the possibility of government control of production. They communicated their shock to the newspapers, and the stories talked of her "bid for unlimited power" and her attempt to inject "Sovietism" into American business. The headlines described her as a potential "Czar of Industry" and economic "Dictator." "Please remember," she urged reporters, "that the Black bill is limited to two years." But her explanations, though reasonable, never wholly quelled the agitation.

On April 25 just before she was going to testify again before the House committee, Roosevelt telephoned her. Ishbel MacDonald, the daughter of the British prime minister, was at the White House, and Mrs. Roosevelt had suggested they attend the hearing. "Do you mind?" Roosevelt asked. Of course she did not mind, but their presence compounded the confusion of the hearing. Ishbel MacDonald was much in the news, and for a First Lady to attend a congressional hearing was unprecedented. Four hundred men and women jammed into the hearing room as Klieg lights baked the air and movie cameras whirred. It was the sort of experience Perkins found "trying."

Nevertheless the *New York Times* reported that she was "serene and composed" and "replied to a barrage of questions in crisp, incisive sentences." She offered evidence of the severity of the Depression with statistics on the decline of railroad freight-car loadings. She pointed out that merely spreading the work would not increase purchasing power. She insisted that some kind of minimum wage control was necessary and asked for flexibility in determining the number of hours a plant's employees might work. She suggested that boards of three members might make the decisions.

She was followed by Green, speaking for the unions of the AFL, most of them craft unions, since at this time not many factory workers were organized. He was unalterably opposed to any minimum wage, except for women and children, and was willing to concede flexibility in hours only because it was the administration's policy. To ensure that as many union representatives as possible be available for appointment to the boards he proposed an amendment: "Workers . . . shall not be denied by their employer the free exercise of the right to belong to a *bona fide* labor organization and to collectively bargain for their wages through their own chosen representatives." It was a theme that Lewis of the United Mine Workers had introduced at the Senate hearings in January.

Representatives of industry vigorously opposed all the amendments as well as the Black bill. They foresaw chaos in the sudden limitation of hours and, perhaps even more terrifying, the specter of government control. By May 10, when the committee issued its report, no one was interested in it. Roosevelt had decided that the endorsement of industry was necessary for any recovery bill and ten days earlier had withdrawn the administration's support from both the Black bill and the Perkins amendments. Along with the committee's report they were buried in the House Rules Committee while Congress awaited the substitute bill that Roosevelt promised.[6]

The administration's bill, the National Industrial Recovery Act, was put together in late April and early May from several drafts developed independently by different groups. One day at a cabinet meeting early in April, when either Perkins or perhaps Farley or Ickes had again raised the question of public works, Douglas had said, "Mr. President, I have heard in the last few days of a plan being worked out here in Washington. It is so far-reaching, so compelling, so thoughtful, that it takes in every economic factor. I am positive, if it can be developed, that it will do for our economic system in a very short time what could never be done by the public works scheme. It will make all this unnecessary."

When Perkins asked for some details, Douglas replied that the authors of the plan were not yet ready to reveal it. As soon as they were, he would report on the details. And that ended the discussion of public works at that meeting.[7]

The plan, which was soon uncovered, was primarily the work of Hugh S. Johnson and Donald R. Richberg. Johnson, a retired cavalry general who continued to use his title, worked for Bernard Baruch's enterprises. Richberg, a former partner of Ickes's in Chicago, was counsel for several railroad unions and had helped to draft the Railway Labor Act of 1926. Their idea, not very different from what Perkins had suggested, was to stimulate industry by suspending for several years some of the prohibitions of the antitrust laws. Representatives from each industry were to be called together by the government to formulate codes to regulate the industries, especially in their hours and wages. At that time Perkins, like many other officials, was receiving hundreds of letters from businessmen desperately asking for help in stabilizing wages.[8] The Johnson-Richberg plan would allow industry to set the ground rules within which the game of competition was to be played, and it included penalties for those who would not abide by the rules. It also included a relatively small public works program.

Within the government another group led by the Assistant Secretary of Commerce, John Dickinson, and one of Roosevelt's advisers, Rexford G. Tugwell, had developed a similar plan, though with a different scheme for enforcement. It was typical of Roosevelt's methods of working that each group should have thought it had his mandate for the job and been astonished to discover that he had also assigned it to others. Within the administration he had given the responsibility for industrial recovery to both the Departments of Labor and of Commerce, and yet one day he had also asked Moley to devise a recovery plan. And Moley, who was already overburdened, had delegated the job to Johnson. As a system of statecraft, Roosevelt's method ensured a good harvest of ideas, but it often frustrated workers by wasting their time and talent in duplication.

In this instance there was still a fourth group, which originated in Wagner's office, developing a similar plan, though with important additions: a strong public works program and a guarantee that labor should have the right to organize and to bargain collectively. Besides the usual arguments for public works, this group stressed one more: the projects could be used as a way of stimulating business for industries that agreed to regulate themselves. If, for example, the brick manufacturers formulated a code but had no customers, then the government could start projects that used bricks. The argument for the labor clause was that unions tended to keep wages up, hours down and working conditions safe — all purposes of the plan. The most cutthroat competition, worsening all three, invariably came from those industries or low-cost areas that kept unions out. The pattern in the steel industry or much of the South was that anyone who joined a union lost his job. If such industries or areas were to have the benefit of the codes, then their workers should be allowed to join unions and bargain collectively.

When the Perkins substitute for the Black bill clearly failed to win support around the country, Roosevelt hurriedly asked the three other groups and their technical advisers to combine on a single bill. There were many conferences, in some of which industrial and labor leaders participated, and much passionate argument. Though perhaps most of the discussion was on the system of codes, its principle at least was accepted by everyone, and by the industrialists with enthusiasm. There was more direct opposition to the public works program and the labor clause. For the latter Wagner was the champion, supported within the administration by Perkins and publicly by the labor leaders. For public works Perkins was the leader, with strong support in the Senate from Wagner, Costigan, Cutting and La Follette. Within the administration Douglas continued to be her major opponent and Roosevelt remained undecided.

In an effort to reach a decision Roosevelt asked Douglas, Ickes, Dern, Wallace and Perkins to meet in the White House on a Saturday afternoon, April 29, when they would have time to drive the discussion to a conclusion. Also present was Charles E. Wyzanski, Jr., the Solicitor of the Labor Department, who had drafted a bill according to Perkins's directions. Ickes recorded in his *Diary:*

> After going over the draft of the bill which called for an appropriation of $5 billion, the President asked what public works there were that would call for the expenditure of such a large sum. Miss Perkins then produced a list prepared by some association of contractors and architects covering the entire country. The President at once turned to the proposals for the State of New York.
>
> I had never before seen the President critical in perhaps a captious way, but he proceeded to rip that list to pieces and Miss Perkins was, in effect, put on trial, although she was not responsible for the list but simply presented it as a suggestion brought in by others. The President was perfectly nice about it all, but I got the impression that he had begun to feel the nervous strain resulting from the extra pressure he has been under as a result of the foreign representatives being here during the last ten days. There was no opportunity to go to Miss Perkins's rescue, much as I wanted to once or twice, not that she needed it, as she was perfectly able to handle it herself, but once or twice I did feel a bit sorry for her. I felt, however, that it would be better all around if the President got out of his system whatever he had in it. In the end we got around to a discussion of the subject matter of the bill and made considerable progress.[9]

Ickes, like Perkins, believed in public works and wanted an appropriation of five billion. A report by the Construction League of America — almost certainly the report Perkins presented at the meeting — estimated that three billions' worth of projects could be started in four or five months. In a press conference in mid-April she had listed some: roads, sewage systems, low-cost housing, bathrooms, telephone and light poles leading to farms. She had amazed reporters by pointing out that despite the nation's fame for bathtubs 30 percent of the people in cities and 90 percent of those in rural areas had none, and 60 percent of the incorporated towns and villages had insufficient sewer systems to permit tubs. She envisaged an almost limitless opportunity "to modernize America" while "offering labor a fairly continuous employment."[10]

Nevertheless by the end of the meeting the figure for a public works program had been reduced to one billion. Wyzanski, the labor department's Solicitor, who, though only twenty-six, was more fiscally conservative than Ickes, Wallace or Perkins, was privately pleased. He wrote his parents that night:

> The President handled the situation excellently. He had Douglas talk about the budget — Douglas is charming, has real brains and is the soundest man I've met in Washington. I think he is first rate. Then the President asked to see a list of the proposed projects. He took the New York part, went through the whole list, commented on each project and showed a remarkable knowledge of every single item. It was a masterly demonstration and he convinced everyone how unsound most of the projects were . . . I felt much greater confidence in the President than I had expected [Wyzanski had voted for Hoover], and Douglas was the real backbone of the conference.[11]

But Perkins, who had greater experience than Wyzanski, was delighted. For the first time Douglas had presented his views where they could be answered. "We had as hot a debate as I ever heard in cabinet," and the advocates of public works had won their principle. The size of the appropriation was the least part of it.[12]

No one recorded just which arguments convinced Roosevelt, but it seems likely that two, both political and very possibly left unstated, were persuasive. Douglas's position, however logical and appealing in its basic human experience — balance income with outgo, or bankruptcy follows — was too reminiscent of Hoover's reluctance to use the government to fight the Depression. Roosevelt by temperament and political conviction was committed to action. Also, if he followed Douglas, he would be outnumbered and outflanked: too many of his cabinet and members of Congress were for a public works program. He could perhaps persuade the cabinet members to give up the idea and to hold their peace, but he could not stop Wagner, La Follette, Cutting or Costigan from introducing a public works bill in the Senate. When that happened, what position could he take that would not be weaker than including some provision for a program in his own bill for industrial recovery?

Another reason for Perkins's delight was that Roosevelt had agreed that public works should be part of a single bill for industrial recovery. There were some in Congress who did not want to suspend the antitrust laws even in part and others who did not want to appropriate money for public works. Either program presented alone was less likely to pass. Douglas had argued for separate bills.

In the following two weeks the single omnibus bill, the National Industrial Recovery Act, was put in final form. Roosevelt planned a message to Congress on May 17 in which he would call for it, and immediately afterward Wagner would introduce it. Title I of the bill would allow certain agreements within industries, and Title II would set up a public works administration.

On the Friday before May 17 Perkins discovered to her dismay that in the bill's latest draft public works had been dropped. She traced the change to the Budget Bureau. "I was very angry then and thought this wasn't on the level. I called Wagner and found that Wagner didn't know that it was out either." She telephoned Douglas, who said, "Yes, I spoke to the President. I think the President thinks it's better to have the public works program a separate bill."

After hanging up, she sat for a time "and gave it a good think." Then she telephoned Roosevelt, saying that a matter of great importance with regard to the recovery act had come up and she needed to see him for at least half an hour. "I'm awfully busy," he said, but when she insisted, he suggested Saturday afternoon right after lunch. Then she telephoned Marvin McIntyre, Roosevelt's appointments secretary, to ask when Douglas was scheduled to see the President on Saturday. Though the question made her uncomfortable, she was relieved to hear that his appointment was in the morning.

She took Wyzanski with her in case there were to be changes made in the bill, and shortly after two o'clock they were shown into Roosevelt's study. She explained the situation about the two titles, briefly rehearsed Roosevelt's stand over the years in favor of public works and closed by saying, "We've got to lock the presses *now*. If Douglas hears about this before the bill goes in on Monday morning, he will do all he can to upset it. I want to tell you that Title II is out of the draft now. Do you want it put back or not? Wagner wants it back. You do believe me, don't you? If you want to verify it, I know where you can reach him by telephone."

"I don't want to verify it," Roosevelt said. "I know you'll tell me what Wagner says." He began to question Wyzanski on the bill's administrative provisions, and she recognized that he was giving himself time to think. He also was interested in discovering what sort of fellow Wyzanski was, so young and yet so highly recommended by Felix Frankfurter and Judges Learned and Augustus Hand. To Perkins's ear Wyzanski answered all questions "briefly, clearly, pleasantly, persuasively," and finally Roosevelt said, "All right, put it in the bill and tell Wagner."

She had checked in advance where Wagner would be, and suggested they call him at once. Roosevelt waved her to the phone. "I'm here in the President's study," she said to Wagner. "I've consulted with him about this public works title going in with the NRA bill. He says he wants the public works section attached."

Roosevelt took the phone. "Hello Bob. I think that's right, don't you? Frances says that she thinks it's best and I think it's the right thing, don't you, Bob?"

After Wagner made some comments, the conference ended. Everyone understood that Roosevelt had committed himself beyond recall.

As she and Wyzanski drove away, he said, "This really is a most revealing thing. I've studied law. I've studied political science. I never could have conceived that important matters were settled like this, but this is the way government operates apparently."

She always felt uncomfortable about the episode. "I don't like to deal with a man that way. I would have liked either to have had Douglas beaten in an open fight and stay beaten — that's what I really would have liked — or I would have preferred to have him beat me. Then I would have taken the next step, which was to get the public works bill introduced separately."[13]

Though Douglas eventually would resign over Roosevelt's failure to balance the budget, in recollecting years later the birth of the public works program he did not feel that Perkins had gone behind his back or treated him unfairly. His appointments were generally in the early morning, so hers almost inevitably had to follow. He did not believe that Roosevelt was "deceitful." Roosevelt wanted to be liked, so he tended to agree, or at least not show disagreement with whomever he was talking to. He may not always have remembered what he had promised this or that person. He was a man of the present, not the past or even the future. Decisions were made because of today's problem for today's reasons.[14]

On May 17 Roosevelt sent his message to Congress asking for a National Industrial Recovery Act in two parts. Title I would suspend certain provisions of the antitrust laws in order to encourage industry-wide codes on wages and hours. Imbedded in it as Section 7 (a) was a guarantee of labor's right to organize and bargain collectively. Title II was a public works program with an appropriation of $3.3 billion. Congressional pressure had forced Roosevelt to raise his $1 billion figure.

Debate in the Senate began on June 7 and focused almost entirely on the antitrust questions. A week later the bill had passed both houses and on June 16, the day after Congress adjourned, Roosevelt signed it. Under Title I, NRA, the National Recovery Administration, came into existence; and under Title II, PWA, the Public Works Administration.

Whoever administered the National Industrial Recovery Act would have a position of tremendous power. Everyone saw that even before the act was passed. Not only would he have $3.3 billion to spend, but through the National Recovery Administration he would also have the deciding voice in many aspects of industrial production. In mid-May, as soon as the bill was introduced, speculation began on whom Roosevelt might appoint.

The man most often mentioned was General Hugh S. Johnson. Perkins had met him at one of the early planning sessions, which she had attended as Roosevelt's representative. It had been a hot day, and Johnson had been in shirtsleeves. As the discussion turned to legal questions, "he squirmed in his chair like a restless child." He ran his hand through his hair; he got up and walked around; he was disgusted, he said, with "poppycock discussions." Several times he interrupted the lawyers, "You don't seem to realize that people in this country are starving. You don't seem to realize that industry has gone to pot. You don't seem to realize that there isn't any industry in this country unless we stimulate it, unless we start it. You don't seem to realize that these things are important and that this law stuff doesn't matter. You're just talking about things that are of no account. We've got to *do* this."[15]

Since he seemed the leader of the group, she made an effort to see more of him. She had just moved from the Women's University Club into a small house in Georgetown, which she had rented with a friend, Mary Rumsey, who had a lively interest in government. Both enjoyed people and encouraged friends to drop in after dinner for conversation. Among those who came most often was Hugh Johnson, sometimes alone, sometimes with his wife, who seemed bewildered and even unhappy in the hurly-burly of Washington.

As Perkins saw more of him, she found him "an erratic person, but

with streaks of genius." He had a remarkable gift for exciting people
to work, not just by exhortation but by the practicality and, sometimes, brilliance of his ideas. But he took advice hard and often
became mulish when it was offered. His face would flush, his hair
would become tousled and his silences sullen. He assumed, as the act
progressed through Congress, that he would be appointed its administrator. "I think this is the way to do it," he would say. Or, "I'm
planning that." He even began to recruit a staff. No one knew the
extent to which Roosevelt had encouraged him, but other men from
time to time were also rumored to be likely candidates.[16]

One evening Bernard Baruch dropped in at the Rumsey-Perkins
house. A number of people were there, and in a moment when the
others were talking excitedly he took Perkins aside, placed her near his
good ear and asked quietly, "Is there anything at all to this rumor that
the President is going to appoint Hugh as the head of this new
plan?"

"I haven't asked the President outright," she said, "but I think
that's what's going to happen."

"You'd better interpose. Hugh isn't fit to be the head of that."

She made no effort to hide her shock: Baruch was supposed to be
Johnson's friend and backer. "He's been my number three man for
years," said Baruch. "I think he's a good number three man, maybe a
number two man, but he's not a number one man. He's dangerous
and unstable. He gets nervous and sometimes goes away for days
without notice. I'm fond of him, but do tell the President to be
careful. Hugh needs a firm hand."

"Why don't you tell the President?" she said. "You're the one who
knows this. I don't know this."

Baruch had a personal reason why he could not call on the President. "Please believe that. But you go. You must intervene. It's your
duty."

On reflection she decided to bear the message, and the next time she
saw Roosevelt, she said: "Baruch came to my house the other night. I
thought he came to make a call, but I discovered that he came to say
something in particular. This is what he said. I'm going to hand it on
to you because he asked me to."

Roosevelt was upset and immediately began to question her about
Johnson. "I've only known him these few weeks," she said. "He's
slightly unstable at times. That I can see. But he's a driver and
able."

Then, referring to the NRA part of the bill, she said, "It's going to

take a queer temperament to do the job. A good, flat-footed administrator would never walk into it." Roosevelt agreed, and though they
discussed several others, she left feeling that Johnson would be appointed. Roosevelt had asked her, however, to keep a close eye on
Johnson, and now in her house or at committee meetings she began to
watch him carefully.[17]

He was excitable, his temper at times was short and excessive in its
emphasis and on occasion he drank too much. A few years earlier, she
discovered, drink had been a serious problem, which he supposedly
now had in hand. She was also disturbed by some of his ideas on how
to run the program.

He seemed to think, for example, that he could set a code for an
industry simply by meeting with the executives of the companies
involved. She felt that it must be done in public hearings, at which
anyone could make objections, present facts or suggest modifications.
She had in mind representatives of labor and the public.

"I can't see it," he would say. "I think this is crazy, Frances. Why,
we'll spend all our time on public hearings."

"It's wrong not to do it," she'd argue. "We're operating a democracy here. You don't pass a bill in Congress that affects people's lives
without a public hearing on it. You're going to adopt a code which will
affect thousands of people's lives. You must have a public hearing on it.
Congress has delegated this authority to you."

"Oh, it's a crazy idea," he'd insist. "If I can't decide it, then let the
President appoint somebody else. If I'm not good enough, if I don't
know enough . . ."

"But, Hugh, nobody knows enough. The whole idea is that in a
society such as ours no one man is good enough, wise enough, imaginative enough, farseeing enough, to adopt rigid regulations which affect
the lives of thousands of people. We must, as public officers, submit
ourselves humbly to the concept that in the apparatus of a public
hearing there lies the safety for the people to protest, to suggest or to
cooperate — whichever they wish to do. If they don't cooperate, it'll
be a failure. You know that."[18]

She was a difficult opponent, for she had thought deeply about the
principles and problems of administrative law. It was a truism that
with the growth of an industrial society administrative law had bur-
geoned. No one needed a license from the state to drive a horse and
carriage, but an automobile, yes. And the number of regulations
about the granting of that license was steadily growing. From the time
that she had worked on the Factory Investigating Commission she had

been constantly reminded by angry citizens and their lawyers of just how burdensome and unfair regulations could be. In administering the Workmen's Compensation Act she had seen how a person's rights could be violated — an unnecessary medical examination required or an irrelevant fact used to deny a benefit. She had become aware of the limits and dangers of administrative law and sensitive to the need for due process at every point of a government's contact with its citizens. It was a reason she had been so appalled by the Immigration Bureau's treatment of citizens and aliens under Doak's administration. When she had discussed that problem with George Wickersham, he had been so impressed with her understanding of it that he had invited her to address the American Law Institute on the need for due process in administrative law. Though she never thought of herself as such, she had become an expert on the subject.[19] And some of Johnson's ideas about how he might administer the codes disturbed her.

She began to worry also over his ability to direct the public works side of the bill. There was a great deal of money to be spent. She had no doubt of his honesty, but with thousands of contracts to be awarded each would offer a chance for a cut or kickback. Would he have the patience to read them and to check the accountants' figures? His genius, she felt, was for "splurging enthusiasm," not for detail.

A day or two before the bill was passed she went to Roosevelt again. "You've practically decided that you're going to appoint Johnson."

"I haven't quite decided. I'm sure he thinks so, and many other people do, but it isn't settled. If you think it's wrong, I'll consider something else."

"No, I don't think it's wrong, but I don't think you ought to put him in charge of Title II, which is the public works section."

"Why not?"

She described her fears, suggesting that he consult someone else. Marvin McIntyre had seen a lot of Johnson, and he was called in. When the question was explained to him, he said, "She's absolutely right, boss. Hugh is an easy mark for any grafter in the U.S.A. He doesn't know the difference. I don't know what he would do. He would throw those public works around to please anybody and to get him off his back."

Roosevelt said, "Why didn't you tell me that before, Mac?"

"You didn't ask me, and it's not my business to tell you."

They all laughed, and after McIntyre had gone, Perkins said, "Consult somebody else."

"No," said Roosevelt, "I really believe you're right, but, oh Lord, how will I break this to Hugh?"

"Surely he's not a fool. You can tell him that's what you think you'll do."

"Who'll I put in charge of public works?"

She suggested Clarence Dykstra who was making a reputation as city manager of Cincinnati, but Roosevelt wanted him for another job. After he had rejected several other names, she said, "Well, there's one thing you could do, and it would serve at least as a stopgap." He might appoint a cabinet officer, and she suggested Harold Ickes. She did not know him well, but she was impressed with his "punctilious, fussy scrutiny of detail." She had noticed that within the Department of the Interior he pursued "every little ripple of irregularity." He seemed the sort of man needed for a public works program. Johnson could have the NRA, which as a new concept in American life would require a great deal of promotion.

The bill passed on June 15, and the following day, Friday, there was a cabinet meeting at 2:00 P.M. Roosevelt asked her to come to the White House shortly before lunch. He had decided, he said, to appoint Johnson the head of NRA and Ickes the head of public works.

When she asked if he had talked with Ickes, he said no, and pulled at his lower lip. She knew he felt remiss.

"I think you ought to speak to Ickes," she said.

"How can I? Hugh doesn't know yet."

"You haven't told Hugh?"

"No."

"Oh, Mr. President!"

"I thought it would be better and he would be less hurt if we did it in an atmosphere of glory and praise."

"Yes. Perhaps."

"I can't talk to Ickes. Somebody will find out."

"But it's only a few hours now."

"Well, I don't know," he said.

"Let me talk to Ickes."

"I don't know. How am I going to tell Hugh?"

"I don't know," she said.

"Can't you think of some way that would make it seem glorious?"

She considered Johnson a vain man, who would be pleased by any mark of special attention, and she suggested that he be invited to attend the closing minutes of the cabinet meeting. Roosevelt could give a speech, with Johnson present, full of praise for what he had done to create the National Industrial Recovery Act and announcing that he was to be its administrator. "Then after all the praise say that because of the utterly remote connection of Title I and Title II you think it will be better and a relief for him to take this terrible administration of public works off his shoulders, not administering Title II with Title I. It's a double job of contraries, and you have decided to place this in the jurisdiction of one of the cabinet officers. Then appoint Ickes." Half an hour before the meeting she would telephone Ickes so that he wouldn't be taken by surprise.

Roosevelt agreed and had McIntyre alert Johnson to be at the White House for the close of the cabinet meeting. Then at one-thirty Perkins called Ickes. After recounting to him the reasons why Johnson would be appointed administrator only of the NRA part of the bill, she went on to say that the President was going to appoint him, Ickes, the administrator of public works. "The hell he is!" said Ickes. "He should talk to me." She apologized for Roosevelt, who had a foreign dignitary for lunch and could not make the call himself. The problem was Johnson. She begged Ickes, no matter what he thought of the idea, to keep it to himself until after the meeting was over, until Johnson had accepted the fact that he would not administer both parts of the act. "Then you can go to the President and tell him anything you want. If it's wrong for you to administer it, if you know just cause why you should not, then you can be the temporary holder of it. Then the President can appoint somebody else next week or the week after, but you hold it temporarily."

An hour later in the cabinet room of the White House office wing they listened to Roosevelt discourse on the National Industrial Recovery Act. He briefly described its purpose, and stated that he would sign it that afternoon and appoint General Johnson its administrator. Then he turned to its administrative provisions. The public works program could be handled independently: he had consulted the Attorney General. Cummings in a few sentences gave the reasons. Perhaps, Roosevelt said, it would be wiser to keep the two parts of the act separate. Either was a big job and public works, with its huge expenditures, would need close attention. What did the cabinet think? His own position was already clear. Dern, who as governor of Utah had had experience with a public works program, and Farley both spoke strongly in favor of keeping public works separate. No one mentioned Johnson.

"I think that's what I'll do," Roosevelt said. "Johnson's here. I asked him to come over. I wanted to present him to you."

Johnson was brought in, introduced and seated beside Roosevelt, who began to shower him with praise for his contribution to the creation and passage of the act. Then, as Perkins later recalled,

Roosevelt began to discuss the administrator's job. He said to Johnson that he had discussed it with his cabinet colleagues and that "we" had come to the conclusion that the NRA part would be "so enormous" and take so much of the administrator's time that "he ought to be relieved of any responsibility for public works," which after all was "just an ordinary, routine" program. And therefore, Roosevelt concluded, he had decided to have that part administered separately.

Johnson's color turned from his normal light tan to deep red and, finally, to purple. Meanwhile Roosevelt cheerfully rattled on. He was going to announce something no one else knew. He was appointing "that fellow down there," pointing at Ickes, to administer public works. A laugh went round the table. Ickes said, "This is rather sudden, Mr. President," and made a few more remarks, enough perhaps to cover Johnson's immediate embarrassment. Almost immediately Roosevelt declared the meeting over.

Perkins could see that Johnson was "just about wild." Roosevelt, who was making his preparations to leave the room, said nothing to him. The other men quickly disappeared. None spoke to Johnson.

Perkins walked beside Roosevelt briefly as he was wheeled from the room. "Hugh is about crazy," she said. He was still sitting in his chair, muttering, "I don't know why. I don't know why."

"Stick with him, Frances," said Roosevelt. "Don't let him talk to the press. Get him over it."

She went back to Johnson. "This is fine, Hugh," she said. "Now you can get to work right away on all these plans." But he only muttered, "I don't know why."

She offered to drive him back to his office. She had something she wanted to discuss with him. Leading him down a back stair to avoid the press, she drove around the city with him while he struggled with his emotions.

He was beside himself. He swore. "Then he would go into a great deep melancholy, saying 'The President has disgraced me. I can't do anything. If he doesn't believe in me, why doesn't he get somebody else?' "

"He does believe in you," she would insist. "He thinks you're a genius. He thinks you've got lots of qualities. You've got the drive and leadership for this great, new enterprise that has never been done before. Public works is nothing."

After an hour of driving around the city, she took him to the airport to board a plane for Chicago, where he would announce the birth of the National Recovery Administration before a convention of businessmen. Bad weather forced him down at Pittsburgh, so he addressed the convention by radio. The NRA was started, driven by a man of action.[20]

Before her appointment Perkins had presented Roosevelt with a list of objectives she thought his administration should pursue in the fight against industrial unemployment. A month later in Washington, as a result of a conference she had convened, labor leaders had presented him with a similar list, including an important addition: some guarantee of the right of workers to organize, choose representatives and bargain collectively. Though in office only three and a half months, the administration, together with Congress, had enacted many of the suggested programs. There was relief for the unemployed, both in the Civilian Conservation Corps and Hopkins's Federal Emergency Relief Administration. As parts of a National Industrial Recovery Act there was a large public works program and the promise of a system of industrial regulation through codes that would shorten hours, raise wages and abolish child labor in interstate commerce. There was also, in Section 7 (a) of the act, a guarantee of labor's right to organize. Though it was still too soon to tell whether the gap between a bill's passage and the achievement of its purpose could be bridged, the ccountry as a whole was deeply stirred and excited by the government's drive and leadership.

Chapter 22

※※※

Pressures of the job. Social life and sharing a house with Mary Rumsey. Spiritual life and the St. Bede Lectures. Slights because of sex. Her difficulties with the press and questions about its role.

WHEN CONGRESS ADJOURNED on June 15, 1933, its special session had lasted just a hundred days, and the fifteen major bills it had passed represented a burst of legislative activity greater than any in the country's history. Besides the measures to stimulate industry, reduce employment and provide relief, there were others equally important for agriculture, banking and the issuing of securities. There was also the Tennessee Valley Authority Act, providing for the conservation and development of a river valley winding through three states. In ordinary times the passage of that act alone would have made the session memorable.

In this period Roosevelt sent fifteen messages to Congress, had a hand in the passage of all the major laws, delivered ten speeches, held press conferences and cabinet meetings twice a week, talked with foreign heads of state and sponsored an international conference. His energy, mastery of various bills and political skill in advancing them took almost everyone by surprise. "The truth is," one of his advisers noted, "F.D. really loves the appurtenances of the job. He savors completely the romance and significance of each experience."[1]

For others, too, the Hundred Days were exhilarating, but they could also be exhausting and even terrifying. Charles Wyzanski had not been in Washington a day when Perkins took him to the White House for a discussion of public works. When it ended, Roosevelt said to him, "Have on my desk tomorrow morning a draft of a bill carrying out this idea." As Wyzanski recalled the moment: "I never could be so scared again."

Yet the pace increased. At times he felt surrounded by chaos and panic. Perkins as Secretary of Labor seemed a "natural point of approach for a large number of crazy people," most of them with plans for ending the Depression. "The President also seemed to have thought she was the normal receptacle for crackpot suggestions." Some of the ideas he examined were "so preposterous" he began to think they were "nightmares." Even the more routine work came "in great masses," and he had "no notion at all how to handle these problems and decide them so quickly."

Alone in his apartment he agonized over the job's magnitude and his inadequacy. During the first weeks he was hardly able to sleep three hours a night. Before a month had passed, he offered his resignation. "Miss Perkins was a steady individual at this point, much steadier than I." She telephoned Frankfurter, who called Wyzanski, urging him to be patient. Frankfurter also called Justice Brandeis, and the seventy-six-year-old Justice invited the young lawyer to dinner.

Encouraged by his elders, Wyzanski stayed on. He bought rubber stamps with his name and distributed them to his assistants. He concluded gradually that, though the job was indeed too big for him, most jobs in Washington were too big for those attempting them. "The whole question is whether you somehow or other adjust yourself to the difficulties which the immensity of the task presents."[2]

Perkins, too, suffered from the pressure. In addition to the problems of the office, she had to find a home. Ilo Wallace had installed the Wallaces in the Wardman Park Hotel, where she had found a housekeeping apartment with big closets. But Perkins, single in Washington and with a family in New York, had no time to assess closets, and Mary Rumsey's imaginative proposal that they share a house in Georgetown had come as a stroke of good fortune.

Rumsey was a woman whose background, training and talents joined to produce an extraordinary person. She was the daughter of E. H. Harriman, the railroad magnate, and after graduating from Barnard, where, like Perkins at Mount Holyoke, she had majored in science, she had served for a time as her father's secretary. The experience had given her a strong grasp of business and finance without blunting her interest in art and, more especially, in people.

Her husband, Charles Cary Rumsey, who had died in an automobile accident in 1922, had been a sculptor. His statue of Pizzaro, the conquistador, had been a feature of the San Francisco Fair celebrating the opening of the Panama Canal in 1915, and bronze castings of it later were mounted in Chile and Spain. He also had been a ranking polo player, and she had shared his interest in horses. After his death, among her other activities she kept up their farm at Middleburg, Virginia, where she rode with the hunt, fattened cattle for market and held office in several agricultural societies.

She and Perkins had met in New York in 1918 when Rumsey became a director of the Maternity Center Association, and their friendship had continued. Both were executive with a strong sense of social responsibility and, faced with the depression, the instinct of both was to take action, either personally or through the government. Rumsey had entered political circles by supporting Al Smith in 1928 and later Roosevelt, and with Roosevelt's election and the mounting excitement of the Hundred Days she was eager to have a base in Washington, to share in the play of ideas and perhaps even to have a part in the administration. Eventually she would be appointed chairman of the NRA Consumers' Advisory Council, but first she had suggested to Perkins that they share a house. And she had found a small octagon house in Georgetown for which she provided the furniture and staff while agreeing, at Perkins's insistence, that the daily running expenses be shared.

Though the arrangement stretched Perkins's finances to the limit, it suited her. Because of the staff, she had no duties in running the house, and frequent small dinner parties were possible. Since both she and Rumsey had homes and families elsewhere there was much coming and going, and they as often entertained separately as together. But they had no disagreements over people. Both liked all sorts and mixed them together: old and young, famous and unknown, politicians and artists. Jo Davidson, the sculptor; Margaret Bourke White, the photographer; George Russell, the Irish poet; Starling Burgess, the yacht designer; a folk singer who collected ballads in the Appalachians; a man from Maine who vied with Perkins in reciting stories in Maine dialect — when mixed with the likes of Baruch, Johnson, Will Rogers, Eleanor Roosevelt or Douglas MacArthur, they could produce an exciting evening.[3]

Nevertheless, Perkins felt the need for some other balance to the pressures of her position and found it in her religion. Though other Episcopal churches were closer, she crossed the city to St. James, at 222 Eighth Street, N.E., where the services were Anglo-Catholic, or high-church. The rector, Alfred Q. Plank, was a tertiary of the Anglican Order of St. Francis, and he served at Mass rather than communion, heard confession if asked — Perkins confessed — and was called Father by his parishioners. Though he conducted a Protestant service, he surrounded it with much of the color and ritual of Catholicism. Perkins found his services and personality satisfying, and she recommended him to Wallace. The two cabinet officers soon were familiar figures in the church — the Wallaces always sitting halfway back on the left of the aisle, and Perkins a little more forward on the right.

Sometime in the midst of the Hundred Days she talked with Plank about the demands of her job, for unlike Roosevelt she did not enjoy all its appurtenances. The publicity was hard to bear, the separation from her family worrisome, and as much as anyone she feared failure, doubly so as she knew a defeat for her, a sudden or forced resignation, would be a defeat for all women.[4]

Plank suggested that she refresh her spirit from time to time by visits to a small community of Episcopal nuns in Catonsville, Maryland, south of Baltimore. All Saints Convent consisted of fourteen Sisters living in a fieldstone dormitory with a bell tower and a simple church at one end. A quarter of a mile away, at the entrance to the grounds, was another building, which the nuns operated as a convalescent home for babies preparing for or recovering from the "blue baby" operation. Midway between the two was a small cottage for their chaplain and any overnight male visitor; female guests were lodged in the main building. The community was at the end of a country road and, except for a field stretched between the buildings, was surrounded by woods. To the west, amid trees, the land dropped steeply to the Patapsco River.

Perkins could reach the convent in an hour by train to Baltimore and then a taxi, and she made her first visit in April or early May. She found the experience rewarding, and returned at least once a month, often in the middle of the week. She would go for a day or half day, staying overnight. She would attend the schedule of prayer, seven services with the first at 6:00 A.M. and the last at 8:30 P.M., and in the hours between she might walk, study in the library, cut dead blossoms from the lilacs or pray. The Sisters soon noticed that she spent much of her time in prayer. She told the Reverend Mother that she was the Secretary of Labor and the other Sisters soon were aware of it, "because we are a family." But she always registered and was addressed as Mrs. Wilson. The other women who, like herself, came for spiritual refreshment never knew her by any other name.[5]

She told no one in the department where she went except her secretary, Jay. Even with close friends she seldom talked of the convent or mentioned it in letters. It was not simply an escape from the shoptalk of Washington, for she liked to discuss with Reverend Mother Laura the concepts behind social legislation. Nor was it simply an escape from a male-dominated society, for in Rumsey and such women in her department as Grace Abbott, Katharine Lenroot and Clara Beyer she had feminine companions of similar backgrounds.

The closest she came to a statement about part of what she found there is in a letter to a friend who had just had an operation for cancer of the throat and who, while learning a new method of speaking, was required to live in silence.

> I sometimes go for a rest for a few days at a Convent near Baltimore where they keep the rule of silence which is imposed on visitors as well as Sisters for all but two hours of the day. I have discovered the rule of silence is one of the most beautiful things in the world. It gives one time for so many, many ideas and occupations. It also preserves one from the temptation of the idle word, the fresh remark, the wisecrack, the angry challenge, the hot-tempered reaction, the argument about nothing, the foolish question, the unnecessary noise of the human clack-clack. It is really quite remarkable what it does for one.[6]

But there was more. As a young settlement worker in Chicago she had listened on a snowy day to friends arguing about the reasons for finding a poor man a good pair of shoes. One had said, "Because his feet are cold"; the other, "For Jesus' sake." At the time she had thought the difference in reasons unimportant; the result was the same. Now she began to think the difference was crucial.

The better reason for attempting social or industrial reform was "for Jesus' sake," because a merely humanitarian urge, however strong, would not last. "The poor aren't grateful in the long run, and quarrels come up." Among her friends and colleagues she could see that many of the humanitarians had grown discouraged and quit the struggle. Her conclusion would be supported years later by an analysis of the careers of more than a hundred reformers, not including her own, whose lives spanned both the Progressive and New Deal eras. Those who had continued active throughout were those who had most directly experienced the mass misery of the poor in the country's great industrial cities and those who had a religious basis for their work.[7]

In 1948, not long after she had resigned as Secretary of Labor, she put her thoughts on religion into three lectures and possibly for the first time crystallized what until then had been instinctive. Entitled "The Christian in the World" and delivered to the parishioners of St. Thomas Episcopal Church in New York, the lectures are her most direct statement of the values underlying her twelve years of work as Secretary of Labor.

She believed that "man is a creature made by God," who endowed him with "the power to love" God and other men. As a result God and not man is at "the center of the universe," and in any conflict between divine and manmade law God's law takes precedence. Another result is that because of God's love "man has infinite worth," and "the part of Christians in all this is to see that the state does care about what happens to the individual and doesn't say — 'Oh, well, it can't be helped.' "

She told the parishioners how a member of the immigration bureau had observed these rules. One day shortly after she took office, she had received a call from Ellis Island. A social worker had discovered a woman about to be deported, was upset by what seemed an injustice and asked Perkins to intercede. Perkins sent for the file.

The woman was a Canadian who had crossed the border to marry. She lived peacefully with her husband and had three children. A disgruntled neighbor — "and it is nearly always that" — called the Immigration Service. The woman was perfectly open with the officers: Yes, she was born on the other side. No, she had no papers. Sure, she had entered illegally. Off she was sent to Ellis Island to be deported, while three small children waited at home alone, for her husband was in the hospital with a broken back.

Perkins summoned the Second Assistant Secretary, William W. Husband, who in one post or another had worked on immigration matters for thirty-one years. After reviewing the facts he said, "She's clearly deportable; that's all within the law."

"It is ridiculous," she said. "Can't you think of something?"

"Well, I'll try."

Two hours later he was back. "What have you done?" she asked.

"Nothing. As a matter of fact, perhaps that is better. You get into controversies with officials all down the line when you start to take action. We can just remand her back to the station in the town where she lives for further questioning. Then she won't be on Ellis Island. She will be home where she belongs. After that we can take our time. You see how it works out. It will be all right."

She had been pleased, and praised him. "I have been in public life a long time," he said, "and I have learned that man must so administer the laws of men that the laws of God will have a chance to operate, too."[8]

Perkins assured the parishioners that she was not suggesting that bureaucrats take the law into their own hands but only that they be aware of God's laws and be eager to apply them. To those who worked closely with her, her success in implementing her belief was her most extraordinary quality. Some called it her "standards," others her "religion" and still others her ability to pick out the largest principle entangled in an issue. But whatever the term, it represented an active moral conscience.[9]

For her the Incarnation, God becoming man in Jesus, was "the great and mighty principle upon which we rely for our understanding of man's function in a Christian society and of what a Christian society ought to be." Man's destiny, she said, was "to know, love and serve God, and finally, to be joined with him in eternity." A Christian society would be one in which there was "a pattern of social coopera- tion and social justice" expressed in legal, economic and social rela- tionships. It would also be one in which men helped each other by service toward a better understanding of God.

Her emphasis on a "Christian" society provoked a question from a Unitarian: "Instead of wishing to create a Christian society, why not say a 'decent' society, recognizing the noble aspirations of the Hebrew prophets and those like Gandhi who belong to quite alien faiths?"

She was completely ready to agree to that. All she wanted was a society in which "people of all kinds of faiths who believed in God could cooperate."

She told of a labor leader (Sidney Hillman, but she did not name him), "not a Christian himself," who had agreed that she might appoint an arbitrator in dispute between his unions and its employers. He asked her, "Who are you going to appoint?"

"You are not supposed to ask me that."

"I don't want to know the name of the person, but I would like to know something about him."

"What do you want to know?"

"Arbitration is very tricky," he had said. "I would like to be sure that the arbitrator has some kind of religion and believes he must answer to God for what he does. Because this concerns the lives and the welfare of my people, and if he has only got to answer to you and to the President and to the Congress, well, that is not enough."

A "decent" or "Christian" society posed no problem to her. Throughout her career, in Albany as well as Washington, she worked happily with Catholics, Jews, Unitarians and people of whatever faith. She cared for the conscience, not the label.[10]

The pressures of the job came in many forms, some the result of attitudes unconsciously held and therefore relentlessly applied. A congressman told a reporter that he admired her ability to testify before a committee but "wouldn't want to be married to her." Hugh Johnson, in a much quoted remark, announced she was the best *man* in the cabinet. Would he have said Ickes or Wallace was the best *woman?* Following a dinner given by the Woodins, at which she and five other cabinet members and their wives were the guests, Ickes recorded in his *Diary:* "After dinner the men, all of us being members of the Cabinet, went upstairs to smoke and have our coffee. This gave us an opportunity to talk about important national matters."[11]

Other slights because of her sex were more open. The Gridiron Club, a press group that admitted only men to membership, gave a dinner to which all cabinet members but Perkins were invited. Mrs. Roosevelt chose that same night to give a dinner at the White House in her honor, and the affair survived a moment of distress when Senator Hattie Caraway of Arkansas was bitten by a White House dog, the only male present.[12]

The protocol of official occasions offered a problem for which she insisted on her solution. By State Department rule any Secretary of a department represented in the cabinet ranked ahead of any Secretary's wife. Thus Perkins, though Secretary of the lowest-ranking department, ranked ahead of all her colleagues' wives. The protocol officer, who advised the White House and others how to seat a formal dinner, wanted to follow the rule. Perkins did not. Hoover's administration had been demeaned by an alleged feud over precedence between Dolly Gann, the Vice-President's sister and official hostess, and Alice Longworth, the wife of the Speaker of the House. Though the feud, if it truly occurred, was between the men for "the honor of the office," the press reported it as a catfight between women. To avoid any possibility of such silliness in Roosevelt's administration Perkins insisted that she would rank as the wife of the Secretary of Labor, the lowest of the cabinet wives. Except for the protocol officer, apparently no one objected.[13]

Still, she preferred formality for large parties where guests were unacquainted, and at small dinners she enjoyed separating from the men for coffee. It varied the pace of the evening and gave women who were friends a chance to exchange views.[14] Whatever Ickes may have thought privately about the levels to which conversations with women might rise, in working hours he dealt with her as an equal. The social attitudes were familiar pinpricks. A new and far greater problem for her was the attitude of the press, and her first example of it came the day after she assumed office.

In her press conference in New York before leaving for Washington she had asked reporters not to exploit her husband and child, but almost the first story in the *Times* was just the sort of human-interest feature about her daughter that she had hoped to prevent. Susanna's dog, Balto, a small, stub-tailed Irish terrier, had run out of the apartment in New York and been returned by a fireman, who had traced the owner through the dog's license. In making the most of the incident — eleven paragraphs and large headlines — the *Times* trumpeted that Susanna Wilson was the daughter of Miss Perkins, Secretary of Labor; that since Miss Perkins had gone to Washington, Susanna, who apparently lacked a father, lived with "a maid" at 1239 Madison Avenue, in an apartment on the fourth floor; and that her small dog, Balto, was extremely friendly with strangers.

Only a year earlier the kidnaping of the Lindbergh baby had caused a sensation, and the crime suddenly had become common. All over the country parents who were even slightly prominent or rich were anxiously warning their children not to speak to strangers, not to reply if spoken to and under no circumstances whatever to enter a stranger's car. The *Times* story, stressing the parents' absence and revealing the child's name, the dog's name, the dog's disposition and the apartment's street address and floor, would strike many parents as malicious journalism.[15]

Perkins worried about her daughter's safety. In January 1932, she had complained to a reporter for the *Herald Tribune* who had mentioned Susanna in a feature article: "You have told the school which she attended and that is one of the secrets which I have guarded with my life. You have heard of kidnapping and you must know that I have plenty of enemies."[16]

In talking of enemies — persons capable of violence — she was not overdramatic. As New York's Industrial Commissioner, administering workmen's compensation, she sometimes had made awards that, justifiably or not, caused bitterness. One bizarre case involved a man who had been hit on the head by a bucket and partially lost his reason. The insurance company paid for his broken bones, but, despite Perkins's ruling, refused to pay for his mental injury. On appeal it argued that the man all his life had been mentally inferior. He understood that Perkins had made the award, and he knew that he had not received the money; therefore, he seems to have reasoned, she must have it, on her person. So he appeared at her office with a knife — to have the money or to cut her throat. Her secretary insisted she had left for the day; in fact, she was in the washroom. As she emerged, the man was slashing the throat of the insurance company's agent, who had come for an appointment. She caught the agent as he fell while the man fled down the hall. (Later, the man was caught and the agent recovered.)

Another time she was in a courtroom listening to a compensation argument when the witness, a workman, lost control of himself, rose and, cursing the insurance company's agent, began to walk toward him. Sensing that the workman had a gun, she moved behind him, knocked his right arm in the air and kept it up until the guard reached them.[17]

She made light of such events. In April 1933, in connection with a speech she was to deliver in Philadelphia, she began to receive letters threatening her life. She dismissed them publicly as the work of "a crank" and kept her engagement, though with a police guard. For herself she found it easy to be unconcerned, but not for her husband or child. Her staff in Washington soon observed that the quickest way to make her flush with anger was to show her an article in which they were mentioned.[18]

Generally such articles originated outside the regular Washington press corps; its members never questioned her about her husband. For that kindness she was extremely grateful and believed, apparently with reason, that Mrs. Roosevelt had described Wilson's illness to White House reporters, who had circulated the account among others. At any large press conference, however, there was always the chance that some new or visiting reporter would raise the subject, and Perkins continually was nervous.[19]

Her first two large conferences, in which she described the reorganization of the department and discussed the extent of the Depression and plans for reversing it, went extremely well. Yet Bess Furman of the Associated Press, who thought them "masterly and revealing previews of the whole New Deal economic overturn," noticed that "the rank and file" of the press were thrown off by Perkins's reliance on statistics. "They were not yet oriented to the fact that news would move on a socioeconomic front."[20]

Most of them, like Sidney Skolsky, who had a syndicated column, wanted gossipy, human-interest stories. After discussing her eating habits he reported that "she sleeps in a twin bed, wears an old-fashioned nightgown and kicks the blankets off." Perkins felt that the Washington press corps "had come to feel that news was property, their property, and it should be manufactured for them." Furman indirectly confirmed that attitude in a comment on the "fantastic distortions" of the Dolly Gann–Alice Longworth feud: "They did not deserve this of the press, for they were two first-class news sources. They did not hide behind social secretaries or unpublished telephone numbers." The implication was clear for someone like Perkins, who refused to list her home phone number and cherished her after-office privacy. In Furman's words, "the press retaliated."

In an article for *Fortune* in 1941 Perkins wrote, "I was wrong in not understanding that when reporters come to a press conference they had to go away with news, that their jobs depended on getting news." The remark was for publication and did not represent her true feelings. In fact, she thought "the intrusion of this purely commercial element into the affairs of government" ought to be stopped. It too often interfered with government. About some program that was rumored she might be asked, "Have you consulted Secretary Ickes about this?" If she answered no, then the headline would read "Perkins refuses to consult Ickes," and he would be offended. If she said yes, then she would be asked what he had said, when he may have wished not to be quoted. Either way the development of a program to present to Congress was made more difficult. Even good ideas sounded half-baked when exposed prematurely.[21]

The time for questions, she felt, was after the bill had been presented to Congress and before or during the hearings on it. Then the ideas had been formed and put in order, and representatives of the government and public, after a chance to think, could give their views. The stories then could be based on public fact — the bill proposes . . . or William Green testified — rather than on private supposition — if the government introduces a bill on food it seems likely that labor will . . .

She blamed Roosevelt for introducing the press into governmental affairs at a point she considered too early. His regular press conferences were "a great mistake." They had led the press to confuse its right to print its views with an imaginary right to know whatever "went through the mind of a public official," to know "what was happening before it happened."[22] As a result the demands of the press on cabinet and other administrative officers greatly increased, and their work — the governing of the country — became more and more entangled in gossip, rumor, leaks to the press and what was coming to be known as public relations. It was a field in which she performed with little skill and almost at once took a terrible fall.

On May 22, 1933, she went to Brooklyn to speak to the Girl's Work Section of the New York City Welfare Council. Most of the girls

worked in shoe factories, and she attempted to explain how the proposed NRA codes might help them by building up mass purchasing
power in other parts of the country. As an impromptu example she
said that "the whole of the South of this country is an untapped
market for shoes." If, for the first time in almost a generation, southern textile workers could be paid decent wages, then they would be in
the market for shoes made in Brooklyn. "A social revolution can take
place if you put shoes on the people of the South."

A public relations man for the council wrote a story on the meeting
for the *Herald Tribune,* basing it on the impromptu example. When
Perkins read it the next day, she winced. The following day, after
southern papers had picked it up, the avalanche fell. In Montgomery,
Alabama, a paper proposed a Wear Shoes Week; in Birmingham, an
editor imagined "the extraordinary appearance" at a meeting of the
Rotary Club "if every member came actually wearing shoes." Letters
poured in to the White House and Department of Labor, and not all
were in good humor. When she went to Atlanta seven months later to
make her first speech in the South, bands serenaded her with "All
God's Chilluns Got Shoes," the governor in his introduction twitted
her on her gaffe, and on every occasion she had to apologize and
explain, again and again. On the whole, Southerners, without forgetting, were willing to forgive, but the power and readiness of the press
to escalate a minor remark into a regional issue was quite clear.[23]

Basically, however, her relations with the press were poor because of
a difference between her and most reporters in temperament. At the
extremes of human nature are those who will kill to achieve publicity
and those who will kill to preserve privacy. Scattered between are the
great majority, with many more yearning for privacy than is generally
realized because the newspapers seldom concern themselves with those
who refuse to be interviewed or to have their picture taken. Perkins
was never violent, but at least once she turned on a photographer who
had flashed his bulb in her face and in a fury demanded his plate.[24]

Reporters blamed the difficulty on her "sense of privacy," an impre-
cise term and in her case somewhat misleading. She did not seclude
herself from others; she enjoyed people. Though she cultivated an
interior, spiritual life, for years she had been a public figure, addressing conventions, leading crusades and campaigning across the country.
Except for short-term reasons, she was never reluctant to discuss her
work. Quite the contrary; she wanted the whole country to talk about
unemployment insurance and workmen's compensation.

The difficulty arose when the reporters' questions became personal or when she feared they might. "When I was a child I was so shy that I couldn't walk into the public library to ask for a book or go into a store to buy a spool of thread. Since I have been the Secretary of Labor I have rediscovered that shyness. I do not like personal publicity."[25]

It was her misfortune to arrive in Washington at a time when all the means for publicity were increasing — radio, moving pictures, telephones and speedier press runs. She also served in an administration that made far greater use of publicity than any before. Roosevelt's two secretaries, Stephen Early and Marvin McIntyre, were both former reporters. So was his assistant, Louis Howe, and all three were experts at planting or generating stories in the press. Ickes constantly leaked news to the columnist, Drew Pearson, and Garner to congressmen and senators. Eleanor Roosevelt broke precedent as First Lady by writing articles and a column and holding her own press conferences. But above all there was Roosevelt himself, who reveled in publicity. Chiefly because of him, by 1934 the United Press wires were carrying three times as much Washington news as in 1930, and one quarter of all Associated Press news was originating in Washington.

Despite the exciting legislation of the Hundred Days much of the increase in news was fluff, what a later generation might call "image-building" stories. Perkins, determined to keep her personal and family life private, had very little part in it yet suffered its results in her press conferences. Reporters are by nature curious, and good reporters are very curious. What most of them sought in their questions and interviews was some touch of human interest to exploit, for they knew that only one reader in a thousand would struggle through a serious discussion of NRA. Their questions tended, therefore, to press beyond the subject to the personalities involved. What did she feel about General Johnson? Was it true they had disagreed over the textile code?

She, on her side, was always trying to keep the personalities out of the discussion so that the concepts might be clearer and could be judged on their merits. Her efforts must have struck many reporters as quibbling. They were apt to couch their questions and later their stories in terms that were close to clichés: "Do you think that hardhearted employers will pay the tax?" She was always insisting that not all employers were "hardhearted," or aliens "undesirable" or the poor "idle." She thought that kind of talk interfered with clear thinking; the reporters knew, consciously or not, that in a story or headline such puffs of prejudice titillated readers and sold newspapers. Part of her "sense of privacy" was an intellectual integrity about the way she would use words and present issues.

In her personal dealings she had the same kind of integrity. She could never understand, for example, why the reporters at the White House allowed Roosevelt to address them by their first names. Couldn't they see what he was doing and why? The suggestion of intimacy was quite false. Since he insisted on "Mr. President," when he addressed a reporter as Bob rather than Mr. Jones, he had not lessened but increased the distance between them. And he had increased his power: an appeal, "Now, Bob . . ." was harder to resist. For an illusion of intimacy the reporters had sacrificed some independence. As the years passed, a growing number of them began to think they had indeed been taken into camp by a master of public relations.

Perkins did not practice such tricks, and neither did Al Smith, so it was not a question of a career passed in appointive rather than elective offices. Yet most reporters thought her cold and unapproachable. They did not see that her formality was part of her honest dealing. At a time when public relations, personal publicity and advertising — people bearing false witness to their use of cigarettes and soap — was greatly on the increase, her kind of integrity was judged old-fashioned and treated with impatience.

For the first few months her press image was good, even excellent; then gradually it deteriorated as most of reporters became dissatisfied with her. There were always exceptions with whom she talked freely, especially Louis Stark of the *New York Times,* Fred Perkins of the Scripps-Howard chain and Bess Furman and Ruth Cowan of the Associated Press.

Much of the difficulty was beyond her control. As the New Deal progressed, some papers began to oppose its labor and industrial policies and found her a convenient target. The attack was political but often couched in antifeminist terms. Among the most critical were the Hearst papers, the Chicago *Tribune,* the Baltimore *Sun* and eventually the Scripps-Howard papers. Her most constant detractors among writers, and syndicated columnists were George Creel, Marquis Childs and Westbrook Pegler.[26]

In 1935 in an effort to improve her image she hired a public relations officer for the department, James V. Fitzgerald, who had been a reporter for the New York *World.* Later he had worked for the New York and the national Democratic committees. In the unanimous opinion of her staff he was a disaster: "a real flat tire." He liked to play golf but was otherwise lazy. He spurned public relations. He would tell her of persons whose publicity was built up: "They haven't got anything else. They wouldn't need publicity if they had anything else."

Though members of her staff urged her to replace him, she never did. Later she recognized the reason; his advice "fell in with my own temperament." He would prepare her for a press conference by stressing all the questions she feared. By the time the reporters had gathered in her office she was thoroughly ill at ease. From behind her desk, with her hat on and Fitzgerald at her side, she would attempt to give the exact truth and no more. Her conferences soon were reputed to be the dullest in town.

By 1941 *Time* reported that "of all the game in the Roosevelt preserve, Secretary of Labor Perkins has been the most frequently chased and most savagely harried." Publicity was a problem she never resolved. She simply suffered through it.[27]

Chapter 23

-»><«-

Reorganizing the department. The divisions of immigration, children, women, employment offices, conciliation and labor statistics. Patronage problems with the AFL and Congress.

IN HER REORGANZIATION of the labor department Perkins aimed at greater efficiency, an objective with several facets. Policy was one: she wanted to be able to propose programs for the consideration of the President and Congress that would be factually sound and easy to administer. That required a staff capable of giving her good advice. She also wanted a department that could translate an approved policy into effective action; that required good administrators. The two talents were not always joined in one person. Another facet was coordination of work between her department and another, and that required good will. On her resignation in 1945, a compliment paid her by James Byrnes was that she had not indulged in jurisdictional disputes. She had often been willing for others, even in other departments, to do the job and have the credit.[1] Lastly, she sought to stir department members at all levels to do their best or, in the jargon of political science, "to liberate the energies of the operating units."[2] Liberation, however, often disrupted orderly administration when a person in one bureau, excited by a fresh idea, trod on the toe of a colleague in another. As Perkins's talents lay mainly in policy and liberation, orderliness in the department's procedures sometimes suffered.

In several respects, even after the dissolution of Section 24, the department's reorganization continued to be most apparent in the Bureau of Immigration. Because of the constantly decreasing number of aliens, she combined the immigration and naturalization services into a single bureau under MacCormack at a saving of $85,080 in annual salaries for fifty-nine positions. All new positions resulting from the merger were filled on a merit basis from persons already in the two services, allowing some of the more incompetent to be retired.[3]

In December Ervin F. Brown, Doak's nephew and a member of Section 24, was tried in New York on charges of accepting four bribes ($600, a watch, a camera and a lap robe) to obtain a reduction and, finally, cancellation of a criminal alien's bond. The case ended in a hung jury, but in others involving fraud in the granting of naturalization papers the government was more successful: 37 private citizens, 12 government employees and 151 aliens were convicted; 13 government men were dismissed for malfeasance and 5 resigned rather than face charges. Typically, Perkins and MacCormack made little of the scandal, and their work in correcting it went almost unnoticed.[4]

On policy they had a double program: to simplify the immigration laws, which were a maze of technicalities often producing cruel and ludicrous results, and to treat aliens in a manner worthy of the dignity and professed humanity of the United States. MacCormack spoke to groups around the country on the facts about aliens: by 1935 there were only 4.9 million (with 1.5 million in the process of naturalization), not the rumored 6 to 20 million; only 100,000 to 200,000 in the country illegally, not 3.5 to 10 million; and only 250 to 500 seamen entering illegally each year, not 250,000 to 500,000.

He had many examples of the cruelty of the laws: a Mexican "who had lived many years in this country and has an American-born family" waded across the Rio Grande while fishing. His return to the American side was held to constitute an illegal entry, and he was deported.

A Russian girl fled to Manchuria. There she met an American woman who agreed to finance her medical studies in the United States. Later, the woman withdrew her support, and the girl had to leave school. She married an American farmer. They had an American-born child

and were living happily in California when we instituted deportation proceedings because she had not maintained her student status. We cannot permit her to remain, and they cannot finance the journey to Manchuria and return. If they could do so, she would be immediately readmitted [as the wife of an American citizen].

So little discretion was allowed under the law that not even the President could excuse the girl the formality of returning to Manchuria. In cases like that of the Mexican, in which the family's breadwinner was deported, often the wife and children were forced onto the state's relief rolls until he could be readmitted.[5]

Perkins and MacCormack reversed Doak's policy for the bureau. While continuing and even increasing the deportation of criminal aliens (largely because of improved means of capture, like two-way radios), they held back wherever they could on the deportations of aliens of good character who had failed in some technicality of the law. At the same time, with the support of a few congressmen, they tried to persuade Congress to simplify the laws and allow greater discretion in their administration, but without success. Meanwhile they tightened procedures within the bureau, forbidding agents without warrants to arrest any aliens except those caught in the act of entering the country illegally. As a result the total number of aliens apprehended and deported began to decline.

The change in policy was entirely Perkins and MacCormack's: there was little impetus for it in Congress or the White House. Roosevelt was always distressed by her reports of hardship cases, but in spite of his legal training he had little interest in the concept of due process. He cared about votes, but aliens had no votes, which was also their weakness in Congress. On the other hand many citizens, especially lawyers who had dealings with the bureau, thought the change in policy and procedures "one of the brightest chapters in the development of American administrative law." But as the number of deportations dropped from roughly nineteen thousand a year under Doak to nine thousand a year under Perkins, she knew she might be storing up trouble. In the midst of a depression, when many people looked for scapegoats, a charge of coddling aliens could always arouse some citizens to anger.[6]

For a time Perkins also considered consolidating the children's and women's bureaus. There seemed a chance to improve coordination and by saving money on some programs to release it for others. She had the idea only vaguely in mind when she discussed it with Grace Abbott of the Children's Bureau, but was more specific with Mary Anderson, chief of the smaller Women's Bureau. They quickly convinced her that it was a bad idea, but the response of each was characteristic and, in the end, significant for their bureaus.

After a day or two of thought Abbott sent up a short memo stating that consolidation would be "a serious mistake" and offering a few quick reasons. She treated the idea as of little importance — any mind at work has some bad ideas — and apparently soon forgot about it.[7]

But to Anderson the idea was "a real shock" and "the memory of it made things difficult for me from then on." She began to think Perkins had little interest in the Women's Bureau and to feel personally excluded: "There were many new people brought into the department who had very close contacts with the secretary, and I gradually found I did not have the entrée to her that I had hoped to have."[8]

Neither Abbott nor her assistant, Katharine Lenroot, who succeeded her as chief in 1934, shared those feelings, though both had been in the department even longer than Anderson. Lenroot in fact thought access to Perkins remarkably open and used it to keep the affairs of the Children's Bureau to the fore at a time when they might easily have been pushed to one side. To some extent the bureau chiefs competed for the Secretary's attention and support, and in that competition Anderson came in last.[9]

Her friend and fellow trade-unionist Pauline Newman, who had known both Anderson and Perkins since 1912, thought their relations were "polite but strained" because of "a lack of kinship." Anderson was an immigrant from Sweden who, on arriving in the country at sixteen, had worked as a domestic and later in the garment and shoe industries. From 1905 to 1919 she had been the sole woman member of the national executive board of the Boot and Shoe Workers' Union, and from 1910 a national organizer for the Women's Trade Union League. In 1920 she had been appointed the first chief of the newly created Women's Bureau. To Newman, the lack of communication between Anderson and Perkins was a result of differences in education and mental habits. Anderson was "limited" and "lacked curiosity." She constantly surprised Newman, who was herself an immigrant, from Lithuania, by how little she had learned of her adopted country's history. Yet she was a brave, honorable woman, and "Perkins was not about to fire her or jostle her from the Women's Bureau."

Unlike the Children's Bureau, however, which in the New Deal period expanded its functions, staff and appropriations, the Women's Bureau merely continued its regular programs, chiefly statistics and conferences on the need for a minimum wage and the interpretation of women's problems to the public. Much good work was done, but the greatest gains for women came through the more generalized work of other bureaus. In her autobiography Anderson blames Perkins for this and prefers Doak as a secretary. Although almost no one else saw the situation as Anderson did, unquestionably Perkins had an administrative failure with the Women's Bureau.[10]

She had another with her personal secretary, Frances Jurkowitz, or Jay. Faced with reorganizing a department in a time of crisis Perkins asked Jay, who had been with her in Albany, to come to Washington. When Jay agreed, abandoning home and friends in New York, a relationship started between the two in which Jay offered all her loyalty and extraordinary competence to Perkins, who accepted both and with them a sense of guilt. So long as she lived, Perkins worried that she had done wrong in absorbing Jay's life so completely.

The problem with Jay, which became important only in Washington, was that she was no respecter of persons and could be extremely brusque. She allowed Senator Pat Harrison, whom she must not have recognized, to wait a long time before Perkins saw him. Word of the incident was soon all over Washington. And within the department Jay constantly bruised people's feelings. Perkins recognized the problem; many people advised her of it. But she could never bring herself to transfer Jay to a less vital position. Too much loyalty on both sides was involved.[11]

Where there was less, she was capable of firing a person, even a bureau chief, if she believed him incompetent or likely to be disloyal to the administration. On both counts, as soon as she took office she fired John McAlpin, whom Doak had appointed director of the U.S. Employment Service. She intended to wind down the service, which was thoroughly discredited, and to revive it only after Wagner's bill had passed Congress. The Wagner-Peyser Act, as it was known, proposed to grant federal funds to the 23 states that had 192 employment centers in 120 cities if they raised their standards of personnel and service; it also would aid the other 25 states to create such agencies if they would adopt similar standards. Wagner, Perkins and most students of employment services believed in state and local administration. But six weeks before the act was passed on June 6, because of the start of the Civilian Conservation Corps she had to create a temporary National Re-Employment Service, hire a director for it and begin at once to recruit men for the corps from all 48 states.[12]

She had persuaded W. Frank Persons to take the job, and though on occasion she may have rued the day he came to mind, she never doubted he was a fine appointment. He was a self-made man, a carpenter, who had worked his way through Cornell College in Mount Vernon, Iowa, and Harvard Law School. Thereafter he had worked for various charitable groups, including the Red Cross, and finally became an industrial relations expert. He had a vivid style of speech, was an excellent administrator and a wholly honest man. It was the last that occasionally caused her difficulty.

In Georgia the state director of selection for the CCC enrolled only white men though Negroes totaled 36 percent of the state's population and an even higher percentage of its unemployed. Persons promptly reminded the director that the enabling act stated: "That in employing citizens for the purpose of this Act, no discrimination shall be made on account of race, color and creed." After two weeks during which he saw no improvement, he telephoned the state's governor, Eugene Talmadge. Toward the end of their conversation he said that the governor would order his state director to start enrolling Negroes, or *all* recruiting in Georgia would be stopped. Talmadge reluctantly agreed, and some Negroes were enrolled.

The issue was complicated by the local customs of the time, relations between the federal and state governments and divided jurisdiction within the program. The labor department was responsible only for recruiting. The army ran the camps, and the corps's director, Robert Fechner, had control of the policy. He was faced constantly, as often in the North as in the South, with local objections to Negro camps (they were not integrated), and in only a few instances could he place them on federal property. When the issue finally boiled up to Roosevelt, he called it "political dynamite," asked that his name "be not drawn into the discussion" and acquiesced completely in the restrictions on Negro enrollment. (In its nine years, at a time when Negroes were roughly 10 percent of the country's population, the CCC enrolled about 2.5 million men of which almost two hundred thousand were Negroes.)

In the situation Perkins allowed Persons to express his views to a point where everyone in the program's administration was constantly reminded that discrimination in enrollment was illegal. But as soon as he reached a point where she thought he might cause the President embarrassment, she silenced him: "I prefer that this letter be not sent to Mr. Fechner." Her department would not differ with the President over policy. If the American people did not like the Roosevelt administration, in 1936 they could elect another man President.[13]

In administering the Wagner-Peyser Act she and Persons had no differences, but unfortunately their policy angered a number of labor leaders and congressmen. Because political patronage in appointments had contributed to the failure of Doak's reorganization of the U.S. Employment Service, in all early drafts of the act Wagner had provided civil service classification for the positions. But the House Labor Committee had deleted the provision. So Perkins, with Person's full support, by administrative order established a merit system for advancement and required at least a high school degree for the highest posts, which disqualified many labor leaders. She and Persons also refused to make political appointments if the candidate was not qualified, which was often. The level of competence in the service rose, and as a result more unemployed were placed in jobs. But many congressmen and union leaders felt cheated of patronage.[14]

In an effort to meet their complaints she recommended to Roosevelt that Turner W. Battle be appointed Assistant to the Secretary of Labor. Battle, a thirty-five-year-old naval aviator, bore one of the great names of the South and was sponsored by Senator Robert Reynolds of North Carolina. He was a tall, friendly, back-slapping man whose overwhelming interest was airplanes, and if allowed, he would talk all day about flying. In regard to labor problems, however, a colleague described him as a man who "just didn't know anything." Perkins used him mainly to represent her at unimportant committee meetings.[15]

If his appointment soothed the North Carolina delegation in Washington, it did little to satisfy those from other states, and the problem of patronage continued to plague her, most seriously, for a time, in the reorganization of the Conciliation Service. Under the legislation creating the Department of Labor the Secretary was given the power "to act as mediator and to appoint Commissioners of Conciliation whenever in his judgment the interests of industrial peace may require it to be done." A conciliator, even if he was the Secretary, had no power to force the parties to a settlement or to enforce any agreement; he could offer only to help them negotiate. When Perkins took office the service was handling about a thousand cases a year. It consisted of an office staff of six and thirty-five conciliators, most of them retired union officials used on a part-time basis. Because the work required no technical training, the unions, and particularly AFL officials in Washington, looked on it as a way to give a retired colleague a little prestige and extra money.

The men, most of them overweight from muscles turned to fat, were neither unwilling nor unable, but they had gotten into the habit of not doing much. Perkins would go to Hugh Kerwin, the director of the service since its founding in 1917, and ask, "Where's Jones?"

"He went to Philadelphia on that strike."

"What does he say about it?"

"I haven't heard from him."

"Hasn't he reported to you?"

"Well, no, no. He's up there. He's doing what he can."

It was impossible to be angry with Kerwin. He was, in Wyzanski's words, "a wonderfully amiable, nice Mr. Chips." He liked to tell stories, but they were "never malicious" and always intended "to help you in a situation." He was beloved by all the conciliators. But there came a day when, to satisfy a congressional inquiry, Perkins wanted to find out what some conciliator was doing and, since there was no report, she said to Kerwin, "Get him on the phone."

"I don't know how to reach him."

"You know what hotel he's staying in."

"Well, you know he lives nearby there."

"The payroll clerk has that. Call up his home and see if they know where he is."

After she had talked to a few startled wives, the men began to leave word where they could be reached. Not soon enough, however. She made a ruling that they had to make daily reports. "But I soon let up on that because I found they didn't write very well." She was not unsympathetic.

> You get home to your hotel room at ten or twelve o'clock at night after a day spent wrestling with a strike and you're in no condition to make an orderly report. What's more, nothing has happened. But I required weekly reports, and in writing. It nearly killed them . . . Also, I made Kerwin use a telephone and talk with his conciliators at least three times a week.

At the same time, in order to help him with the new procedure, she gave him a better file clerk and a topnotch secretary. She wanted to keep him as head of the service "because he was highly regarded by the trade unions" and because as a conciliator he himself "was awfully good." She also soon discovered that, though he could never have written a manual of procedure, he had a real talent for teaching others with his stories.

He enjoyed the quickened pace of the work. One day after the system of weekly reports had started, he came to her office: "Why we never had anything like this. It's just wonderful. I really know what they're doing now. Your idea that I call them three times a week is fine, because I often find them in a problem that they don't know how to handle, and I can nearly always tell them what to do."

If the work of the world is done by ordinary people the way God made them, as Perkins believed, then the art of administration is to learn how to use them. She showed Kerwin how by some administrative procedure he could spread himself over the country, and in a few years he had expanded the work of his conciliators by about a third without increasing their number.[16]

But against congressmen who thought that they should control appointments in the service or even that all conciliators hired during Republican administrations should be replaced, the amiable Kerwin was no help. Fortunately she received strong support from the First Assistant Secretary, Edward F. McGrady, a short, soft-spoken man of rather dark complexion, more Italian than Irish in appearance. In January 1934 he reported to her:

> While at the Capitol yesterday, I visited a number of Congressmen who have been friends of mine over a long period of years. I discussed with them the complaints on patronage that the Democratic members might take up at the Caucus that was to be held that night. I explained to them, "That as far as the Department of Labor was concerned there were very few positions that did not come under Civil Service. While it was true that the positions of Labor Conciliators were not under Civil Service, these positions should not be thrown on the political pie counter, because they carried with them grave responsibilities that affected the well-being of thousands of workers, as well as peace of mind of the employers. Practically all of these conciliators are trained men with long experience and splendid records of accomplishment.
>
> "Furthermore, if there was any criticism to make as far as the Bureau of Conciliation was concerned, I was responsible and not the Secretary of Labor. This Bureau is directly under my supervision and I have protested against disrupting our staff by the appointment of inexperienced and untried people."[17]

McGrady's backing was impressive in that he was himself a former AFL official and primarily a political appointee. Before succeeding Robe Carl White in the number two position in the department he had been the AFL's legislative assistant for fifteen years, and to some extent his appointment had been Roosevelt's sop to the federation for denying it the top post.

He had been one of the two labor men, however, whom Perkins had recommended to Roosevelt for Secretary, possibly because he favored improving hours and conditions of work by legislation as well as by union negotiation. Yet even though she had described him as "really *first* class," when he started work for her she was distrustful, fearing his allegiance would be to the AFL rather than to the department. When this proved untrue, all hesitation vanished, and she relied on him greatly, especially as a trouble-shooter in conciliation work. His defense of merit appointments in the bureau, in the main, was success-

ful: though the positions were not protected by civil service requirements, he was able to persuade most congressmen not to force the
issue. But he couldn't completely assuage their sense of grievance. On
patronage, Congress as a whole always resented Perkins.[18]

That resentment was aggravated for some by her competence as a
witness. Any good cabinet officer will know more about his department than the average congressman, who must hold in mind a general
knowledge of all departments. This frequently creates a tension at
hearings, for if the administrator's answers are too quick or too sure
those asking the questions will begin to look foolish. Perkins was
always polite, but the circumstances sometimes accentuated her tendency to lecture, and the legislators' feelings probably were not
soothed by the advice given them publicly in the Baltimore *Sun* and
Washington *Evening Star:*

> Call it a day, boys; call it a day. The lady is better than you are and
> we should not be a bit surprised if higher compliments could be paid
> her. What's more, she is not afraid of you. And that makes an awful
> combination. A woman smarter than a man is something to get on
> guard about. But a woman smarter than a man and also not afraid of a
> man, well, good night![19]

Even within the cabinet, after a year of self-discipline, her tendency
to lecture came to the fore and sometimes irritated members. Ickes
filled his *Diary* with brilliantly worded complaints about her talks on
labor problems: "her usual long recital about what might have happened but did not and probably would not." Yet his attitude toward
her was always ambivalent: she talked too much but "is interesting
and has ideas." Moreover, in his *Diary* he used the word "feminine"
so often as a pejorative, he suggests that along with boredom much of
his irritation was the result of sexual prejudice: he could hardly bear
to have a woman's opinion count for as much or more than his.[20]

The last division of her department to be reorganized, the Bureau
of Labor Statistics, was potentially the most important because its
surveys and statistics provided the basic material for many of the
studies in other bureaus and departments. For example, over 90
percent of the preliminary information on wages and employment
used by the planning and statistics division of Johnson's National
Recovery Administration came from the bureau or, as it was frequently called, the BLS.[21]

Like the U.S. Employment Service by the end of Hoover's administration the BLS was a discredited organization, though unfairly so. Much of the public held it responsible for the figures periodically announced by Hoover or Doak as evidence that unemployment was declining and the Depression coming to an end. In fact the bureau's commissioner, Ethelbert Stewart, an old stubborn statistician with a striking resemblance to Mark Twain, had frequently informed Doak that the government's figures were being misused. On one occasion when reporters came to him to check an optimistic announcement, in their presence he telephoned Doak to say that the bureau's data did not support the government's claim.

His reward was to be rebuked by Doak at a press conference and to be omitted by Hoover in July 1932 from the list of officials continued in office though overage. His appointment was to have run for an additional eighteen months, and he told reporters, "I have had a tin can tied to the end of my coat tail."

Unfortunately for him his forced retirement took place just as the Democrats nominated Roosevelt for President and Roosevelt flew to Chicago to address the convention. Stewart's story, often so shortened as to be unclear, was buried on the back pages. In New York Perkins saw it. "Greatly distressed at your retirement," she telegraphed him. "Anything I can do to help prevent it?" But she was too late. Stewart was neatly hanged in obscurity and his voice silenced. Hoover did not appoint anyone to replace him and the bureau drifted.[22]

Stewart had written Roosevelt urging Perkins as Secretary of Labor, and shortly after she took office he called on her. Because of his age it seems unlikely that he hoped to be reappointed, but in any event Perkins had other ideas. Stewart had been commissioner for twelve years and toward the end of his term the bureau had grown out of date. There were many new ideas about collecting statistics, their use and interpretation, and she was eager to raise the bureau to a new level of competence.[23]

Since the post was a presidential appointment, she procured Roosevelt's agreement before proceeding. Then she asked the American Statistical Association to appoint several committees to examine all the bureau's indexes, such as the Wholesale Price Index, and to recommend improvements. She also asked the association to submit a list of statisticians and economists qualified for the post, promising that Roosevelt would choose from among them. At the same time she promised Roosevelt that she would have on the list some candidates who were sympathetic to the administration's ideas.

After several months the association's committees began to report.

Fanny Perkins at age 4

At Mt. Holyoke as a Junior

Paul C. Wilson in 1912–13, the winter before he and Frances Perkins were married

Frances Perkins on an inspection tour for the Factory Investigation
Commission, c. 1911.

With Susanna, aged 5 months, May 5, 1917. *Columbia University Libraries*

Her mother, Susan Perkins, at the side door of the Brick House and dressed to go calling, c. 1923. *Mary S. Piper*

Al Smith with Governor Roosevelt in Albany, 1929

January 1931, the month of the Governor's Conference on Unemployment which she organized for Roosevelt in Albany. With her are two New York State employers, Max Meyer of New York City and Maxwell Wheeler of Buffalo

William N. Doak at the White House to pay his respects to
President Hoover following his appointment as Secretary of
Labor, November 29, 1930. *Photo Trends*

Mary Harriman Rumsey, 1934. *Photo Trends*

Clara M. Beyer, Associate Director of the Division of Labor Standards for eleven years with Perkins, 1934–45

Isador Lubin, Commissioner of Labor Statistics, 1933–40

Gerard D. Reilly, Solicitor of the labor department, 1937–41

Charles E. Wyzanski, Jr., Solicitor of the labor department, 1933–35

President Roosevelt signing the Social Security bill, August 4, 1935. Standing, left to right: Senator Robert F. Wagner (D. — New York); Senator Robert M. LaFolette, Jr. (Prog. — Wisc.); Senator Augustine Lonergan (D. — Conn.); Secretary of Labor Frances Perkins; Senator William H. King (D. — Utah); Congressman David J. Lewis (D. — Md.); and Senator Joseph F. Guffey (D. — Penn.).

Wide World Photo

With William Green of the AFL and John L. Lewis of the CIO.
Photo Trends

Roosevelt, after a vacation, returns to Washington and is met by four of his cabinet: left to right, Secretary of War Harry H. Woodring, Secretary of Commerce Daniel A. Roper, Secretary of State Cordell Hull, and Secretary of Labor Frances Perkins. *Photo Trends*

With Senator Robert F. Wagner at a dinner on March 3, 1938, to celebrate the 25th anniversary of the U.S. Department of Labor

At the House Judiciary Committee hearing on the Resolution of Impeachment against her, February 8, 1939. Immediately on her right is Gerard Reilly, the Solicitor of the labor department. The other man at her table is the official reporter (stenographer) of the hearing. Reilly is looking directly at the Chairman of the Committee (not in the picture) seated in the center of a semicircular dais. The four committee members visible are the most junior members of the majority (Democratic) side: left to right, Edward E. Creal (Ken.), William T. Byrne (N.Y.), Sam C. Massingale (Okl.), and James M. Barnes (Ill.). The men at the large table are newspaper reporters and two clerks or investigators for the House UnAmerican Affairs Committee. Perkins has just submitted her written statement to the Chairman who shortly thereafter dismissed the reporters and closed the hearing. *Photo Trends*

Paul Wilson, c. 1950. *Columbia University Libraries*

Susanna Coggeshall, c. 1962. *Walker Evans*

All Saints Convent, Catonsville, Maryland. The chapel and bell tower to the left. *All Saints Convent*

At a reception at Cornell. *Telluride Association*

At age 83, at a dinner on March 4, 1963, celebrating the 50th anniversary of the U.S. Department of Labor. She is illustrating for President Kennedy the size of the cockroaches she found in her predecessor's desk when she took office as Secretary in March 1933

One, on examining the Cost of Living Index, had discovered that among the items listed as priced every six months in order to determine an average family's budget were high button shoes and women's muslin underwear. In fact neither had been priced for years because they were no longer part of an average family's clothing. But she knew that the high button shoes would amuse Roosevelt, and she promptly relayed the story to him as an example of why a revision was necessary.[24]

From the list of candidates for commissioner she picked Isador Lubin. When she offered him the post, she told him that he had been chosen because she thought he would remember that statistics were not numbers but people coping or failing to cope with the buffetings of life. She evidently stressed the point to Roosevelt, for he later repeated it to Lubin. It was not unimportant. The Commissioner of Labor Statistics was a statistician collecting and recording facts, which are represented by figures; he was also an economist interpreting the figures for the Secretary of Labor and others in the government, including the President. He was, or should be, an important economic adviser to the administration. Hoover's disaster with the American public was in part the result of his refusal to listen to his commissioner and his inclination to divorce the figures from the humanity behind them.

At the time of his appointment Lubin was thirty-seven. He had been born in Worcester and worked in his father's retail clothing business while putting himself through Clark University. Yet he and Perkins in what proved a long friendship never talked of Worcester; their interests were firmly in the present. Not until after her death did he discover that they both had graduated from Worcester Classical High School.

While working for his father Lubin had been sent out frequently to talk to those who were delinquent in their bills, mostly workers. He found the cause was almost invariably that the mill or factory had laid off the family's breadwinner, and there was no money in the house. The irregularity of industrial employment impressed him deeply, and the problems of labor and industry soon became his chief concern.

He did graduate work on a fellowship at the University of Missouri, studied and for a time lived with Thorstein Veblen, taught at the University of Michigan and then, in the late 1920s, through the Brookings Institution, was drawn into government work. In the 1932 campaign he wrote speeches for Wagner, and his appointment reinforced Perkins's good relations with the senator.[25]

Lubin was wholeheartedly in favor of the investigation that Perkins had started of the bureau's indexes because he knew he could use the Statistical Association's reports as a lever to secure additional staff and funds. And during the New Deal period the bureau's appropriations doubled and its staff tripled as its reports grew more sophisticated and timely. In the case of the Employment and Payroll Index, for example, whereas in 1933 70,000 establishments voluntarily (the BLS had no power to require reports) reported employment and payrolls for 4.5 million employees in manufacturing, by 1941 147,000 establishments were reporting for 10.5 million workers, approximately one half of these employed in manufacturing. The Cost of Living Index was completely revised and put on a quarterly instead of a semiannual basis. Food items were priced and published every two weeks. Such changes in every aspect of the bureau's work constituted a revolution, and far more than before management, labor and the government began to rely on the bureau's figures.[26]

Perkins and Lubin worked well together. Neither was an economic theorist with a closed system that could be put in a book. They were pragmatists — try this, try that — with a strong respect for facts. They also developed an affection for each other.

In 1936 Lubin's wife died in childbirth. He had left the hospital after her caesarean delivery believing both mother and child were well. He was called back an hour later and learned that his wife had died of internal bleeding. Someone in the hospital telephoned Perkins, who sent Turner Battle to take Lubin back to Battle's apartment and stay with him. When she was able to get there almost her first words were, "I stopped at a church and said a prayer for Ann." Recalling the incident years later, Lubin turned to gaze out the window and said quietly, "When you needed her, she was always there."

Besides adding his technical competence to the bureau he helped Perkins in other ways. In part because he could work extremely fast he had time to be friendly. He liked the people in his bureau, knew them by first name and went around to see them. He had no pretense and was rather boyish-looking, short, with bright brown eyes and ears that stuck out. Not only in his bureau but wherever he touched in the department, morale rose.

He had a rule that anyone in the BLS should immediately answer a question from a congressman or reporter, but for information only, not publication. He himself saw scores of reporters and had a flair for the kind of presentation they liked. He kept several triangular stands in his office on which he displayed large charts of the various indexes. One reporter called them "fever charts of the country's economic health." As Lubin explained them, it seemed as if right there, in that office, the country's heart was visibly beating. To some extent he offset Perkins's poor relations with the press.

Similarly he helped her with members of Congress. Like McGrady, he knew many personally, and he also had an extraordinary gift for explaining technical matters so that the slowest layman could follow the argument without any feeling of inferiority.[27]

The team Perkins put together to administer the department was one of the best in Washington. Most observers saw that and were impressed. Yet two important groups remained hostile. Labor officials, perhaps noting how McGrady as First Assistant Secretary had a role to play in the Conciliation Service between her and Kerwin, were always urging her to add more assistants between herself and the other bureau chiefs. The department was expanding, they would argue; therefore it was reasonable that she have more assistants. "But what will these people do?" she would say. She didn't want a layer of people between herself and the bureau chiefs, and she always refused.[28]

Also, many party stalwarts had objections. Wyzanski, MacCormack and Persons had no record of work for the party. Was it for this that good Democrats had waited twelve years to recapture the administration? Worse still, at a lower level the immigration bureau and the employment and conciliation services, all traditionally open for patronage, had been closed. When the House early in 1934 refused to pass an amendment on the Employment Service appropriation bill, McGrady investigated and reported to Perkins that congressmen ascribed the defeat "primarily to the pique on the part of many members because they did not secure patronage in the employment service."

For years the Department of Labor, as the newest and weakest of the executive departments, had been the dumping ground of political patronage. There was a price to pay for raising its efficiency.[29]

Chapter 24

➤➤)《◄-

PWA projects. An NRA code for steel and her visit to the mills. Long-shoremen's strike on the Pacific Coast. She argues with Hull and Cummings. Johnson's outburst at the strikers. She is accused of favoring communists.

IN BOTH PARTS of the National Industrial Recovery Act Perkins had a role. Once the Public Works Administration under Ickes began to function it moved of its own momentum: project selected, contract awarded, work begun and, in time, a post office in a small town or the Triborough Bridge in New York. But at the start the type of project to be undertaken had still to be determined, and at a meeting on June 29 of the Special Board of Public Works Perkins spoke forcefully in favor of socially useful projects — sewers, housing and schools — even though as a result so-called federal money would be spent on local rather than federal installations. She thought it "ridiculous" to build army posts or even immigration detention stations. "It does nothing to improve the standard of living for the people, the taxpayers of the country."

"It does something to put people back to work," said Rexford Tugwell.

"Oh, yes, if we are as badly off as that — I mean if there is no construction to be found in the United States which will raise the standard of living, we will put men to work on building handsome stone walls around private estates. I would be for that if we had exhausted everything else." Doubtless she was only articulating the thoughts of most of the Special Board, but at that meeting it became the policy of the Public Works Administration in selecting projects to keep in mind their social utility.[1]

A more difficult question of policy arose over the hiring of workers for the projects. The Special Board had proposed that all workers be hired from the federal employment offices that Perkins and Frank Persons were setting up, wherever possible in conjunction with state offices already existing. Perkins reported to the board, however, that the proposal had "created consternation in the hearts of organized labor." The AFL was strongly opposed to using the government's employment service. It feared that the agencies, with their lists of skilled workers, would supplant union headquarters as the hiring hall. To cope with the objection, at the board's request Perkins formed a Labor Advisory Board with Lubin as chairman. But then, as Ickes wrote later,

> organized labor began to make demands upon PWA for special consideration. It became apparent that the organizations were not thinking of the great mass of laboring people who might be benefitted by a public works program, but merely of the union worker . . . At first the unions insisted that all workers should be employed through their agencies; we were willing to go so far only as to allow their offices to be used for the hiring of union labor alone. An agreement to this effect carried a proviso that "in the event qualified workers are not furnished by the union locals within forty-eight hours after the request is filed by the employer, such labor may be chosen from lists of qualified workers submitted by local employment agencies designated by the United States Employment Service."[2]

Thus union workers, about one tenth of the labor force, were given first chance at the jobs, which was a powerful spur to nonunion workers to join the union. It was the sort of special favor for a special interest group that angered many people at the administration. Perkins was not distressed by it; unions were one way of improving hours, wages and conditions. But she continued to focus her department's attention on the nine tenths of the working force that was not organized.[3]

In the administration of the other part of the National Industrial Recovery Act, the NRA under Hugh S. Johnson, Perkins often represented labor, organized or not, during the formation of the codes. With the resources of her department, economists, statisticians and lawyers, she was better equipped than most unions, or even the AFL, to present the workers' side of a complicated, technical issue.

In the steel industry, for example, there had once been a powerful AFL union, the Amalgamated Association of Iron, Steel and Tin Workers. But in the famous Homestead strike of 1892 Henry Clay

Frick, the general manager of the Carnegie Steel Company (later part of the consolidation forming the United States Steel Corporation), had succeeded in all but destroying it. When the skilled workers of Homestead, Pennsylvania — members of the union — had declined a proposed cut in wages and were supported in their stand by the rest of the labor force, Frick had closed the mills and refused to negotiate further. Meanwhile he had already hired 300 Pinkerton men armed with Winchester rifles to protect the plant. As they approached Homestead, towed up the Monongahela River on two barges, they and the workers exchanged shots, and after an all-day battle in which ten were killed, the Pinkerton force surrendered, was put on a train and was shipped out of town. Six days later at Frick's request the state's governor sent in 8000 of the militia, and Homestead was put under martial law. Frick reopened the plant and started importing non-union workers, whom he had begun to hire even before the wage negotiations had failed. Four months later, when the union leaders officially capitulated, some 2000 strikebreakers held the majority of the jobs and only 800 of the original Homestead working force of nearly 4000 were reinstated.

Fifteen years later the Pittsburgh Survey revealed the condition of the steelworkers: whereas coal miners with a union were receiving $2.36 for an eight-hour day, the majority of unskilled steelworkers were averaging $1.42 for a twelve-hour day in a seven-day week. Throughout the years, in the face of the hostility of the steel companies, the old steel union managed to survive, but at a cost of not functioning. By 1933 it represented only ten thousand out of five hundred thousand workers, and its leaders were old men with bitter memories. In the formulation of a code for the industry the job of representing the unorganized workers, and to some extent even the union men, was taken up by Perkins and her staff.

She wanted the workers to feel consulted, however, and before the first public hearing on a code drafted primarily by the industrial leaders she started a tour of three of the most accessible mills: U. S. Steel's plants at McKeesport and Homestead, both close to Pittsburgh, and Bethlehem Steel's new plant at Sparrows Point, near Baltimore. She planned to visit the mills, meet separately with the supervisors and men so that the men could talk freely, visit some workers' homes and talk with the wives and explain to one and all what the government was trying to accomplish with the code. Though she would see only a small percent of the half-million work force, through reports of her visits in the local papers she might reach more.

As the mills were private property and she had no right to enter them, she asked the company presidents, Myron Taylor and Eugene Grace, to invite her, as part of the code's preparation, to inspect the mills and to talk with the workers. In each case there was a pause and then acquiescence. At the plants, on orders from the top, anything she asked to do was made possible.

At McKeesport the visit was uneventful. She took with her several reporters for Pittsburgh papers and was interested to discover that none had ever been inside a steel mill. The making of steel is a dangerous process, and visitors understandably are discouraged. But for the city's most important business to be able to operate beyond the bounds of any public scrutiny was an indication of its overwhelming power in the community.

The workers and their wives with whom she talked were quite uncritical. The idea that the government wanted to put a floor under wages was "wonderful," and almost anything Perkins proposed was "just fine."

At Homestead, after touring the mill, on the invitation of the town's burgess (the chief executive officer) she spoke and answered questions in the town hall. The workers were not very articulate. The discussion turned mostly on whether the maximum hours should be forty-four a week and the minimum wage $.40 an hour. Most of the mills were operating at less than half their capacity and employing men on eight-hour shifts on a share-the-work plan. For some men the problem was long hours, but for most it was a low wage, caused primarily by the irregularity of work.

At the end of the meeting as she was thanking the burgess for the use of the hall, sounds of a disturbance came up the stair. A reporter whispered to her that a number of workers had been excluded and were gathered outside the building. Turning to the burgess she asked if she could have the hall for a few minutes more.

"No, no," he said, his face darkening, "you've had enough. These men are no good. They're undesirable reds. I know them well. They just want to make trouble."

Perhaps so, she thought, but as a public official she had a duty to hear all citizens. After bidding the burgess good-bye she went downstairs and discovered several hundred angry people in the street. Then, as she described it later, standing on the building's steps, she said:

> "My friends, I am so sorry that you were not able to get into the hall. It was very crowded, but perhaps we can hear what you have to say right here."

By this time the Burgess, two secretaries, and the police appeared, shouting, "You can't talk here! You are not permitted to make a speech here — there is a rule against making a speech here."

The men on the sidewalk were tense with interest, wondering what I would do next.

There was a park across the way. "All right — I am sorry. We will go over to the public park."

Immediately the red-faced Burgess and his police were at my side. "You can't do that, there is an ordinance against holding meetings in a public park."

I protested, "This is just a hearing, not a meeting; it won't be long, only a few minutes."

The Burgess kept reiterating that they were "undesirable Reds," although they looked like everybody else to me.

As I hesitated, my eye caught sight of the American flag flying over a building on the opposite side of the square. Ah, I thought, that must be the post office, and I remembered that federal buildings in any locality are under the jurisdiction of the federal government. I did not know the politics of the postmaster, but I was an officer of the federal government and I must have some rights there.

To the crowd I said, "We will go to the post office. There is the American flag."

It was almost closing time. I have never forgotten that postmaster and his assistance. I had only a moment to explain matters to him. Nothing very dramatic happened. The people filed in, and the employees hung around to enjoy the meeting. We stood in the long corridor lined with postal cages. Somebody got me a chair, and I stood on it and made a brief speech about the steel code. I asked if anybody wanted to speak. Twenty or thirty men did. They said they were greatly pleased with the idea. They said they wished the government would free them from the domination of the steel trust. One man spoke about philosophic and economic principles. A few denounced the community. I invited the most vocal and obstreperous of the speakers to come to Washington and promised that he would have an opportunity to appear at the public hearing. We ended the meeting with hand-shaking and expressions of rejoicing that the New Deal wasn't afraid of the steel trust.

The story was picked up by the papers, and though the bad judgment was entirely the burgess's own, the steel companies bore its burden.

The McKeesport and Homestead plants were relatively old, but the Bethlehem plant at Sparrows Point was new. An experienced factory inspector, she was excited by the safety precautions, the sanitary facilities and cafeteria. It was a splendid example of what industry could do.

While there she had a meeting with about twenty workers in a private room and she asked:

"Do you want a union? I am told you don't want a union. Can you speak freely? Do you feel like speaking freely to me?"

One of the men said, "Yeah, I think it's all right. The Superintendent here is a decent man. If he said this is private, he's got no spies in here. I'll tell you how I feel. We work here without a union. We got on all right until this unemployment came. We had good jobs. There wasn't much dissatisfaction about the wages or the hours. They were all right. But, of course, there are lots of fights all the time. I think we ought to have a union, but the company don't, so none of us are going to kill ourselves to have it."

One by one they spoke up. Some felt no need of a union; others, that it would be a good thing. A union, they said, gave men a sense of independence; they didn't have to take everything from the boss; they could ask questions, make suggestions and say what was on their mind.

Sometime later Eugene Grace asked her, "What did they say? You must have asked them about unions."

"A mixed report," she told him. They weren't going to fight the company over a union, but they did see some values in it and, she added, "Perhaps you'll see that some day yourself, Mr. Grace."[4]

At the hearing she was the first to testify, and she declared that the industry in its proposed code "did not rise to the opportunity" of ruling out the seven-day week or the twelve-hour day. The permissible hours were almost always too long and the wages too low. She wanted the wording of the prohibition against child labor strengthened so that enforcement would be easier, and she wanted a prohibition against the use of labor spies. She suggested that if the industry was to be excused in part from the antitrust laws in order to stimulate business, then it should adopt a new policy toward its profits. Traditionally in bad years dividends were continued to stockholders out of surplus reserves. Some reserves should be set up for payments in bad times to workers.

She made a partisan statement for labor, but in the circumstances she and the industry's leaders considered that her function. They were willing to negotiate with her for labor because she represented the government, and without the government's approval they would have no code. The tiny steel union they simply ignored.[5]

Two weeks later Perkins held a meeting in her office to reconcile the few differences remaining and to obtain a statement from representatives of the employers, workers and government that the code met their approval and that they would operate in accord with it. She invited the chief executives from six steel companies, among them Taylor and Grace, and also William Green, who had recently been designated "labor adviser to the NRA." To her astonishment, when the steel executives arrived

> most of them did not permit themselves to be introduced to Mr. Green. They backed away into a corner, like frightened boys . . . I found they had expected to see only me and economists of the Department of Labor. They did not see how they could meet with the president of the A.F. of L. . . . If it were known that they had sat down in the same room with William Green and talked with him, it would ruin their long-time position against labor organization in their industry.
>
> "But," I argued with them, "Mr. Green doesn't represent the steelworkers. He is not a steelworker. I will tell you what he is going to say."
>
> I gave them a copy of his prepared remarks. He was to make a laudatory statement regarding the NRA and to give his full approval to the proposed steel code.
>
> No, that would not do. They were still afraid that it would become known in the steel industry towns that they had spoken to Mr. Green of the A.F. of L. This backing and filling went on for almost three-quarters of an hour. The difficulty penetrated to Green. I apologized to him. He was courtesy itself. In the end, however, he left in a huff.
>
> As the great barons of steel filed out, still looking solemn and sorrowful, I could not resist the temptation to tell them that their behavior had surprised me and that I felt as though I had entertained eleven-year-old boys at their first party rather than men to whom the most important industry in the United States had been committed.

To Perkins, "it was the most embarrassing social experience of my life. I had never met people who did not know how, with hypocrisy perhaps but with an outward surface of correct politeness, to say how do you do even to people they detested."

She also saw in the incident a touch of the blindness afflicting many employers about the provisions of the NRA codes. Under the National Industrial Recovery Act all codes were required to include the act's Section 7 (a), which provided that "employees shall have the right to organize and bargain collectively through representatives of their own choosing." To Perkins, for the steel executives to approve a code with such a statement and yet refuse to meet with Green was a contradiction. But "they didn't think all that applied to them. Their idea was that their workers didn't want to belong to a union. They were sure of that."

Four days later the last disagreements had been adjusted and Roosevelt signed the code. In a statement for the press Johnson as head of NRA explained its terms. It postulated a forty-hour week. Steel, with its furnaces that cannot be turned off or on by a switch, was a difficult industry to regulate. As soon as production in the mills reached 60 percent of capacity then the maximum hours for all but executives would be eight per day. Wages had already been rasied and were estimated to exceed an average of $.40 an hour. In return for these concessions to labor the industry was allowed to combine to set prices and to divide the market.[6]

Compared to steel the country's maritime industry was relatively unimportant. In the 1930s its gross receipts were less than one half of 1 percent of the national income, and at all ports in all categories of jobs it employed only about three hundred thousand men. Many were in unions, but because these were divided among ports as well as by craft, they were small and weak. Yet a strike called by one in May 1934 developed in two months into what is probably still the most extensive strike in American history.[7]

It originated among the longshoremen on the West Coast. Of the industry's three hundred thousand workers about half were longshoremen, but, distributed among seaports and inland waterways, in any one city they were few, about thirty-five hundred in San Francisco and only twelve thousand on the coast. Nevertheless, by withholding their labor they could inflict considerable damage on the economy, and because the country took a patriotic pride in its merchant marine, their strikes were always highly visible.

And there was something more. Like coal miners, sailors and longshoremen have a special niche in the labor movement of every country. The miners tend to form cohesive unions and as individuals to be politically conservative with a strong religious or philosophic streak — perhaps because they work in the dark and in constant danger. Sailors and longshoremen, on the other hand, tend to form relatively undisciplined unions and to hold radical political views — perhaps because of their proverbial lack of roots. Discouraged or bored with life, a longshoreman will ship out to another port or a seaman will take a spell ashore. And with groups of either a grievance typically will produce a work stoppage rather than a strike. A few longshoremen complaining, say, about the crane operator will stream out of the ship's hold onto the pier, discuss their complaint noisily for a few hours and then, often after only a token adjustment, return to work. The Pacific Coast strike of 1934 was something quite different.

Employers and workers alike had expected to have a shipping code, and in November 1933 after a public hearing one was drafted. But Roosevelt never signed it, apparently because it would have violated certain shipping rights confirmed to other nations by treaties. In San Francisco, however, largely as a result of the longshoremen's excitement over the guarantees of Section 7 (a), an independent union had sprung up among them where none had existed since a strike in 1919.

In the interim the shipping companies had prevented one from forming through a method of hiring called "the shapeup." Regardless of weather, the longshoremen would gather on the Embarcadero at six every morning, or whenever a ship came in, and a company foreman would hire the men he needed. Only those were chosen whose dues were paid up to "the Blue Book," a union that the companies controlled and that seldom pressed a grievance or asked a higher wage. The shapeup inevitably led to favoritism and kickbacks, and as there were always more workers than jobs, those who objected were not hired. They were forced into other work or, as times worsened, onto relief.

Under the protection of the National Industrial Recovery Act an independent union formed, calling itself a local of the International Longshoremen's Association but operating very much on its own. Its primary aim was to control hiring by having it done through a union hiring hall. A company foreman would ask for so many workers of a particular category, and the union would designate them, rotating the jobs among the workers. To work at all, a man would have to join the union.

Employers opposed the idea, and at the hearing on the proposed code, as a possible compromise the Department of Labor's representative suggested that the government run the hiring halls, which could be subsidized in each port by the union and the shipping companies. But the union, convinced that control of the hiring hall was its best and perhaps only way to survive, opposed the plan, which was soon pushed aside along with the inactive code.

Thereafter the union and shipping companies negotiated fitfully until in February at a union convention in San Francisco ILA delegates from twenty-four West Coast ports voted to poll members on the need to strike. The result was 6616 in favor and 619 opposed, and the date was set for March 23. At Roosevelt's request it was delayed, but when a mediation board appointed by him failed to work out a settlement, the strike began on May 9. Four days later in San Francisco, and soon after in Seattle, Oakland and Los Angeles, the Teamsters' local unions voted not to truck merchandise to and from the docks. On May 15 for the first time in the industry's history no freighter sailed from a Pacific port.

That same day the governors of California, Oregon and Washington appealed to the federal government for help, and Perkins sent out McGrady as a conciliator. But even before he arrived, the sailors, firemen, cooks and stewards had joined the longshoremen, and within a week the masters, mates, pilots and engineers had also walked out. The longshore strike had become a maritime strike.

The employers attempted to keep the ships moving with strikebreakers. They offered the Blue Book wages and overtime plus $1.50 a day, meals and lodging, and about a thousand men signed up: out-of-work carpenters, plumbers, farmers, lawyers and even a doctor. The largest group comprised football players from the University of California at Berkeley, recruited for the job by their coach. Many of the men were lodged in a liner turned into a boardinghouse, a "scab's paradise." High-ranking strikebreakers had private staterooms, a boy regularly changed the linen, the food was good and there were two movies aboard every night and boxing once a week. The only danger lay in crossing the Embarcadero where the longshoremen had pickets. If a scab was caught, he either had his teeth kicked out or his leg laid across a curb and broken. In the first sixty days there were 150 such cases.

The maritime workers' solidarity, so unusual for the waterfront, was dramatically confirmed after six weeks when they elected as chairman of their joint strike committee a man sure to impress the shipowners as a symbol of defiance. Harry Bridges had been almost unknown before the strike, but in the months leading up to it he had proved himself a smart, aggressive leader. He was an Australian, a seaman who had arrived in San Francisco in 1920, shipped out several times and then become a longshoreman, married and had a child. He was an alien, in the country legally. He was not a communist, but he associated with communists, often followed their advice and believed in the inevitability of class war. He deeply felt the injustice of the longshoremen's situation, and he had a sharp tongue for expounding it. With his election to lead the strike, the shipowners became convinced that the dispute was primarily political. As the president of the American-

Hawaiian Line put it: the strike "went beyond the aims of the usual accepted labor leadership. It was to get power. To get control, on the part of the Communist Party."

The shipowners were not alone in their view. Most business groups and newspaper publishers agreed with them, and even McGrady, after an effort to mediate had foundered on the longshoremen's intransigence, stated publicly: "San Francisco ought to be informed of the hold of the Red element on the situation. A strong radical element within the ranks of the longshoremen seems to want no settlement of this strike." The Department of Labor started an investigation of Bridges through its immigration inspectors, but the report confirmed that he was in the country legally and that there was no direct evidence that he was a communist.

Meanwhile control of the shipowners' position passed to the Industrial Association, a larger group of merchants, which was determined to "open the port. The group planned to move the merchandise from the piers into the city by using scab truckers, and at first it succeeded. Then on July 5 came Bloody Thursday.

For six weeks the shipowners and newspapers had characterized the longshoremen to the public as radicals led by a communist. But when the Industrial Association used strikebreakers on the Teamsters' Union, an established, conservative member of the AFL, and the newspapers began to imply that the truckers, too, were a bunch of reds, the policy boomeranged. The ranks of the longshoremen's supporters swelled, and on Bloody Thursday, in the fighting between the strikers and police, two men were killed, thirty were treated for bullet wounds and forty-three for club, gas or stone injuries. The next morning the governor called out the National Guard.

The following Monday fifteen thousand workers, almost four times the number of longshoremen, marched in honor of the dead while thousands more lined the streets. Sympathy in the city swung to the strikers. There had been talk of a general strike, and in union locals the rank and file, often disregarding their leaders, voted in favor of it. On Saturday at a meeting of the San Francisco Labor Council, it became official, confirming the general work stoppage, which had already begun to spread. Yet Bridges, though appointed to the fifty-man strike committee, was defeated for the post of vice-chairman by a conservative ferryman, 262 to 203. Though the radicals had brought about the general strike, the conservatives were going to lead it, and one of their first acts was to order the Bakery and Milk Wagon Drivers to continue making deliveries.

The printers' union, which had just signed a new contract, did not strike, and the newspapers continued to appear. The fact was significant, for the publishers now became the dominant figures on the employers' side. On the invitation of John Francis Neylan, Hearst's representative in San Francisco, they met and agreed, in Neylan's words, that they had "a responsibility to protect our community from Communism." To that end they created a committee that was to pass on all editorials and news stories about the strike, and the *Chronicle,* for example, was prohibited from publishing an interview with Bridges. From then on the San Francisco papers presented the strike as an attempted revolution by communists.

In Washington among members of the administration there was a crescendo of agitation. Roosevelt was vacationing on the U.S.S. *Houston,* proceeding from Norfolk via the canal to Hawaii. At his last cabinet meeting he had put Perkins in charge of problems arising from the strike, but she had a difficult time retaining control of the administration's response when officials on the West Coast began to bombard its members with warnings of catastrophe. From San Francisco Senator Hiram Johnson, the day after the strike vote, telegraphed Ickes, asking him to advise the Secretary of Labor: "Here is revolution not only in the making but with the initial actuality . . . Already a food shortage exists. Unless a miracle happens, Monday will bring discomfort, possible disaster and actual want. . . . The President's Mediation Board has failed through no fault on its part. Obviously Washington doesn't understand a general strike." Unless Roosevelt personally intervened, Johnson foresaw the "possible ruin of the Pacific Coast."[8]

Perkins was determined that Roosevelt should not intervene: the grievances on either side were not of a sort he could settle with a quick decision. But on the day following the strike vote, after she had been up most of the night talking to people in California, she received a call from Cordell Hull. In Roosevelt's absence Hull, who had remained in Washington, was the Acting President, and he wanted to discuss the situation in San Francisco.

His tone of voice revealed at once that he was genuinely disturbed, and she tried to cheer him with some optimistic observations: it wasn't a true general strike; the unions had made no preparations; there was no strike fund. It was a demonstration of sympathy for the longshoremen that would be over in a few days and the men, or most of them, back at work.

"I have been talking to the Attorney General," Hull said, "and we think it is very serious. We think that we should do something. I am, after all, Acting President, and I think I should take some severe and drastic steps immediately."

Her brain reeled. What could they be thinking of? What was there except the regular army? "I think perhaps I'd better come over and confer with you and the Attorney General and give you at firsthand some of our reports."

"Very well," he said. "I am in the Attorney General's office."

She hurried over to the Department of Justice and found Hull and Homer Cummings in the library, looking up precedents. "If they had been acting parts in a play, they couldn't have put on faces more appropriate to spell to the audience total disaster, total defeat of themselves and the end of the world."

Cummings had found a definition of a general strike, which he read aloud. It was to the effect that when a large number of unions, embracing all the major activities in a community, struck simultaneously to force an unwilling community to meet their demands, then the strike was a general strike because its essential purpose was to overthrow the ordinary procedures of government. "This exactly describes what is happening in San Francisco today," he said.

"It does *not* describe what is happening in San Francisco today," she said. "I think my information is correct and comes from sources more direct than any that you could have."

"My information comes from the district and United States attorneys."

"I suppose," she said, "that the United States attorneys are well-to-do gentlemen who live on the Hill and have offices in downtown San Francisco. I doubt if they are in close touch with the bakery wagon drivers, street car operators or the printers."

"But the town is tied up. Nothing is moving. Everyone is in great distress."

She changed her tack, asking where he had found his definition of a general strike.

"I'm reading from a book on labor and labor unions by P. Tecumseh Sherman."

"Do you know who P. Tecumseh Sherman is?"

"I do not. But I gather from the title page that he has been a professor at Cornell University and Commissioner of Labor Statistics of the State of New York; your state, Miss Perkins."

"He was commissioner about 1886. He's long since dead."

She was exaggerating: Sherman had been commissioner from 1905 to 1907, and he was still alive. But she was correct in pointing out that he had been active when unions were weak and few, and his definition was an academic's fantasy. The general strike in England in 1926, which had familiarized the term, was very different from what was taking place in San Francisco. In England the unions had prepared over the winter for a long strike. A fund had been built up, enough to support workers and their families for a considerable time. The purpose was clear. But in San Francisco there was no strike fund, no planned, coordinated pattern; only a sudden demonstration of sympathy. "It's pure accident that so many went out," she said. "They'll be back without the effort of anybody in just a day or two. What else can we do anyhow, except try to persuade them to go back?"

Hull began to read a legal opinion on the President's powers when local government has broken down. The police in San Francisco, he had heard, had been unable to keep the street cars running because workers had massed in front of them. "When the police are not able to keep the ordinary processes of life operating, surely one can say that local law and order has broken down." The federal government had an army post, the Presidio, in San Francisco. "I think federal troops should be sent in there to break this up."

"How would they break it up, Mr. Secretary?"

"By military means."

"You mean, force men to get on the bakery wagons; force them to drive them?"

"Or drive them themselves, with armed guards, so that if any group of bakery wagon drivers attempts to stop them, they can be . . ."

"Shot at?"

"Yes, shot at."

"Wouldn't that be a rather serious situation?"

"It's a very serious situation to have local government break down."

She returned to her argument that the workers had no intent to overthrow the government. She cited her sources: McGrady, immigration officers, labor officials, individual newspaper reporters and citizens. All had reported that the mass of workers had no grievance. There were no demands. It was not a strike but a demonstration, and was controlled by the conservative union leaders, not by Bridges.

Cummings said, "I don't think you see this in a serious enough light."

Mr. Cummings, I think I do. I see the military moving in from the Presidio. After your message, in an hour they will be under way. There will be all kinds of truck and motor vehicles. The soldiers will be fully armed and will undertake to operate the service activities of the city. It will create resentment, and all the trade unions not yet out will go out. It will create perfectly frightful resentment. What's more, you know San Francisco. It's a big, up-and-coming American city. Its citizens won't take this lying down. They'll gather in crowds to hoot and jeer at the soldiers driving a bakery wagon through the streets. You know what'll happen. The soldiers will fire. Somebody will get hurt. The mob will attack. A lot of soldiers will come in mass formation. There will be some regular shooting, and a lot of people will drop in the streets. I call *that* very serious.

I call it serious for us to use troops against American citizens who as yet haven't done anything except inconvenience the community. Sure they've inconvenienced people, but they haven't committed murder. They haven't rioted. They haven't interfered with the U.S. Mails, which was the excuse in the Pullman strike when Cleveland used the army. But there is no such thing here, only some inconvenience to the householders and businessmen.

I cannot tell you how serious it would be, politically, morally and for the basic labor-industry and labor-government relationships of the country, if we were to do this. What's more, if the cabinet does this while the President is out of the country, imagine the bedlam and trouble he'll be in!

Then she played her last card: "I will have to make it a matter of record that I demand, I insist, that you send a message to the President by naval communications telling him what you propose to do and get an answer from him authorizing it."[9]

On that they parted, and she hurried to the White House, hoping to get her message off before theirs. In the past few days cables representing every point of view had been sent to Roosevelt. She knew that his assistant, Louis Howe, felt as strongly as she, or even more strongly, that Roosevelt should not become involved. She thought that perhaps he should return to the country; Howe wanted him to continue to Hawaii. Any change of course, Howe felt, would only convince the press and country that a major crisis was at hand. It also would "put the President right in the middle of an obligation to settle whatever is wrong out there. He's in no position to do that. He can't do it, because he can't take the time. He shouldn't do it anyhow." Perkins agreed entirely, and she was delighted when Howe sent off his own cable to the *Houston*.[10]

She thought Roosevelt's reply, received on Monday, was almost perfect. "It settled nothing, but nothing better could have happened than to have the President settle nothing." There was "a sop to Cummings and Hull, in that I was told to consult with them about how to keep the food supply going. That meant they hadn't been ignored." There were complicated directions for her, which in their irrelevancy left her a free hand. And the problem of preferring one cabinet officer over another was neatly sidestepped by his statement: "I am inclined to think after Howe's radio today it is at present best for me not to consider changing my itinerary."[11]

Whatever its internal dissensions the administration in Washington managed to speak with one voice, but at a critical moment one of its members on the West Coast lost control of his emotions. General Johnson was on a tour to tout the NRA, and his alma mater, the University of California, had invited him to speak in the Greek Theater at Berkeley. By chance the occasion fell on the second day of the general strike, and as Johnson was the highest-ranking federal official in the area, a large crowd turned out to hear him.

He began in an unexceptional manner, describing the changes being wrought in the country by the New Deal. He talked of Section 7 (a), guaranteeing the workers' right to organize and bargain collectively, and suggested that "if the shipping industry does not fully and freely accord these rights, then on its head will lie every ounce of responsibility for whatever may happen here."

The judgment was stern, perhaps even unfair, but delivered in an even tone and predictable: it was the administration's position. When Johnson shifted to the workers, however, what were evidently very deep emotions began to overwhelm him. "There is another and worse side of the story," he said, his raspy voice rising. "You people are living out here under the stress of a general strike." His face reddened and he began to pound the lectern.

> A general strike is a threat to the community. It is a menace to government. It is civil war.
> When the means of food supply — milk to children, necessities of life to the whole people — are threatened, that is bloody insurrection . . . This ugly thing is a blow at the flag of our common country and it has got to stop.
> I lived in this community for many years and I know it. If the Federal Government did not act, this people would act, and it would act to wipe out this subversive element as you clean off a chalk mark on a blackboard with a wet sponge.[12]

In the West in the 1930s this was an invitation to the people to take the law into their own hands, which some had already begun to do. Now, with the federal government apparently extending its blessing, more followed suit, and in San Francisco and eleven other northern

Californian towns vigilante committees raided communist meeting halls, smashed property and beat up communists and persons merely suspected of communism. The newspapers ran photographs of the destruction, with captions and stories expressing delight.

Meanwhile Johnson had been scheduled the day after his speech to meet with John P. McLaughlin, the secretary of the San Francisco Teamsters' Union. Before reporters and photographers Johnson was to appeal to the unions to call off the strike in return for his promise to attempt to resolve the issues. McLaughlin was to agree, and conceivably, as a way out of the strike, which clearly had swung public sympathy away from the workers, the unions might follow his lead. But Johnson arrived drunk, and violently attacked labor. Two days later in Los Angeles he denounced Bridges by innuendo:

> I think it is about time for an America First campaign on this subject. I do not know the accuracy of the statement and I have no means to check it, but it has been said to me with at least the circumstances of verity that if the jobs of aliens and non-declarants were given to citizens and the former were deported, the unemployment and destitution problems of the United States would be reduced by at least one-third.
>
> That sounds like a pretty harsh remedy. But so is the distress of our own people harsh. I do not suggest such a move, but I do suggest that any alien who pretends to lead an economic group of our people in the direction of strike and bloodshed has no place here and should be no more tolerated than an armed enemy under a foreign flag.[13]

By the third day the strike began to peter out, and the mayor of San Francisco refused a request from employers to ask the governor to declare martial law. By the end of the week it was officially over, and both the longshoremen and shipowners, under pressure from unions and employers, had agreed to arbitrate all their differences. In October the National Longshoremen's Board, appointed by Roosevelt from recommendations given him by Perkins, handed down its decision. On the crucial issue it ruled: "The hiring of all longshoremen shall be through halls maintained and operated jointly," but "the dispatcher shall be selected by the International Longshoremen's Association." Though nonunion men were to be included among those registered and sent out to work, the right to select the dispatcher ensured the union's existence.

In the months and years thereafter Perkins more than anyone else in the administration reaped the results of Johnson's oratory and the anticommunist campaign of the newspapers. The hysteria that they had inflated out of people's latent fears and insecurities continued among many groups. The San Francisco Merchants' Committee, for example, in announcing a campaign against radicalism, stated that one of its goals was "to register, fingerprint and photograph all persons over eighteen" — citizens as well as aliens.

In mid-August, when the California American Legion gathered in San Francisco for its state convention, its leaders announced that their primary purpose was to combat communism in the schools and to censure Perkins for her failure to deport radical aliens. "The attack on Secretary Perkins," reported the *Chronicle,* "is the most open and determined made on a member of the Administration since Roosevelt assumed office."

She responded with a long telegram to McGrady, who as a member of the National Longshoremen's Board was still in the city. She recited the action taken in the most controversial cases, pointing out that often the aliens, though in custody, could not be deported because Russia would not accept them. McGrady published the telegram and arranged for it to be read to the legion's resolutions committee, which softened the proposed resolution of censure. On the floor, where she was defended by legionnaires who were union men, it was softened still further; it became a request that the Department of Labor ask for the cooperation of the Department of Justice in the investigation and deportation of aliens. But for almost a week her alleged laxity in deporting aliens was one of the top news stories on the West Coast.[14]

In March 1935 she became the first woman to deliver the Charter Day Address at the University of California. To an audience in the Greek Theater she discoursed on "The Status of Labor in Modern Society," insisting that labor must be free to organize, bargain and manage its own affairs. America does not want "a peon class, no matter how well fed." It was a partisan speech and according to the *Chronicle* "ripples of laughter greeted occasional barbed words directed at critics of the administration." On the same day she, Jane Addams and Herbert Hoover received honorary degrees, and at a reception one man who came through the receiving line, upon reaching Perkins, announced vehemently, his arms rigid at his sides, "I will *not* shake hands with a communist!" The president of the university, Gordon Sproul, glared at him; Perkins said nothing.

On that same trip Clara Beyer, who as a graduate of the university had accompanied Perkins to Berkeley, was assured by a classmate that

Perkins had not deported Bridges during the strike because both were communists and she was secretly married to him. No evidence to the contrary would be considered; passion had closed an educated mind.

The intensity of feeling was not confined to the West Coast. In St. George's Church in New York only three weeks later Perkins explained to an audience of ministers and laymen the provisions of the proposed Social Security Act. In the question period a young woman stated: "Karl Marx's *Manifesto,* page 30, proposes the same program of unemployment insurance and old age pensions that you have just outlined. How can you support such a program when you know that it is the same as Marx's?"

"I am supporting it," Perkins said, "because I'd rather see it a reality than on page 30."

Later the same woman said, "Doesn't Madam Perkins know that we are not going to be sovietized if it takes my life to prevent it?" And another asked if the social security program would benefit aliens who "ought to be deported." At the evening's end they and others of their opinion opposed a vote of thanks to Perkins for her address.[15]

Much of the feeling would have attached to anyone in her position: the Secretary of Labor was in charge of immigration and had the duty to defend labor's rights. But the criticism often took the line that a two-fisted man would stand up more to labor, or that she coddled aliens because of her soft, woman's heart. In one respect she differed from all others in the administration, and that alone sometimes seemed enough to cause those with a fear or a grudge to peck at her.[16]

Chapter 25

➤➤➤❮❮❮

Her book, People at Work. *Johnson's difficulties with drink and Miss Robinson. Johnson fired. The* Schechter *"sick-chicken" case. NRA expires.*

HER FAMILY LIFE continued broken by distance and Wilson's ill health. She was not able to visit him regularly, as she had promised, but she went to White Plains when she could and wrote to him frequently — often hurried, intense notes: *"Try for calm and peace and constructive, easy, relaxed living.* You'll soon do it my dear love."[1] But he was unable to make consistent progress.

One day her college classmate "Gilly" Rounds, with her husband, Raymond, visited Wilson at the sanitarium. That day his spirits were up, and the three had a pleasant afternoon. As he walked with them to the gate to say good-bye, he pulled a newspaper clipping from his coat pocket and said with pride, "Have you seen what Frances is doing in Washington?"[2]

Sometimes on weekends Susanna came down to join her, and occasionally they would go with Rumsey to the farm in Middleburg, where the generous hospitality was mixed with riding and other country sports. Often there were as many guests and family as in Washington, and with those who were absent Rumsey kept in touch by phone. On Sunday mornings sometimes she would use Susanna as a secretary and instruct her in the art of placing long-distance calls, a skill Perkins considered of doubtful value in a young girl.

Meanwhile, in New York during the week, Susanna lived with a schoolmate's family and in the spring of 1934 graduated from the Brearley School and was accepted at Bryn Mawr College. With maturity came mobility, and in the summer, besides spending August at the Brick House in Maine, she visited friends in New York and Vermont. The family, an acquaintance remarked, "all lived separate lives."[3]

The choice of Bryn Mawr rather than Mount Holyoke was mostly the result of a friendship, shared by Susanna and her mother, with a dynamic, articulate woman, Gertrude Ely, who lived in the town of Bryn Mawr and was a booster of the college. Also, Bryn Mawr was closer to Washington. Though Perkins remained devoted to Mount Holyoke and in June was elected to its Board of Trustees, she never felt that Susanna must follow her there. In the family there was always the sense that Perkins's career while admirable was perhaps not desirable, and in any event was too unique to be repeated.

In the late spring of 1934 Perkins published her first book, *People at Work*. A friend who was a journalist, Martha Bensley Bruère (married to Henry Bruère's elder brother, Robert), had suggested it, proposing to stitch together a number of Perkins's articles and speeches. The result was so dismal, however, that with the aid of people in the publishing house and labor department Perkins reconstructed it into a book of nine chapters, of which about half were devoted to a historical sketch of labor from Colonial times to the Depression. The balance discussed the Department of Labor's role in the government and the administration's efforts to increase employment and wages through its public works program and NRA codes. Though Martha Bruère received half the royalties, her name did not appear in the book, and Perkins almost lost a friend.[4]

Sales were poor; the reviewers polite but bored: "The historical development is readable and in order, if not profound. The facts obviously have been carefully verified." But too much of it was about the past when the chief interest in the author was her power to shape the future.[5] Still, *People at Work* was no worse than any of the other paste-up books that members of the administration rushed into print, and it at least presented clearly some of her ideas.

Her New England background shone through, lighting her approach to most problems. Americans resolved their differences, she said, "by talking things out together." Originally, in the town meeting; later, as the community expanded and relationships grew more complicated, in secular and church groups, such as the Consumers' League and Charity Organization Societies. "These discussion centers are the actual birth places of public opinion — they are where the American mind, harnessed to the American will, goes constructively and critically to work."[6]

She herself, in tackling any problem, invariably would suggest a conference of those concerned. In labor disputes she was always trying to get the parties together to talk, and she had almost endless patience in allowing them to disagree, so long as they continued to talk. Others with less patience, and perhaps also with a less firm belief in the efficacy of talking things out, thought her reluctant, even afraid, to use power. But her reluctance sprang not from a woman's supposed weakness but from a conscious and profound distaste for government by decree.

Her belief in a political system based on talking things out was reinforced by her belief that in the field of economics the time of rugged individualism was past and a more cooperative society emerging. She cited the testimony of employers, workers and experts at the hearings for the textile code: "They had all come to a point where they saw the need of mutual restraint and mutually desirable practices."[7] The Depression had accelerated the change by causing people to question a system that produced so much misery.

She acknowledged that the change required employers to relinquish power and did not suggest that they would do it voluntarily. In the 1932 election the people had voted for what they called a "New Deal," and "by that they meant apparently exactly what the term meant in its original card playing sense, a different arrangement of trumps and aces in different hands."[8]

The winning cards were the government's programs under the National Industrial Recovery Act, which, while attempting to stimulate the economy, created new rights for workers. "Every willing worker has a right to a job,"[9] she proclaimed, and along with it went the right to decent wages, hours and eventually some insurance against the irregularity of employment. Society, through the government, had a duty to enforce these rights for the workers. And the reason — she had no doubt of it — was that truly all men are their brothers' keepers.

At this point the book failed. It is imbued with her concept of what constituted moral behavior, to which she felt the great majority of people were drawn. But, characteristically, she never identified the sources of her morality, for that would have required that she discuss her religious beliefs. She would not do that in public, and the book lacks its essence.

Many reviewers sensed that something was missing but, knowing nothing of her religious life, could not identify it. One, who saw in unions the paramount, even sole, issue in the field of labor, thought she understood and was scathing:

> While she is giving case-histories of workers who have benefited by the NIRA, a three-cornered struggle is proceeding in the basic industries among the Government, the employers, and the workers, with the

Government receding steadily from its attempt to guarantee the autonomy of the workers. This struggle, and not the collective conscience of collective discussion, Federal employment exchanges, public works, or a "sense of brotherhood and cooperation," is the vital issue in the field of labor at the moment. Miss Perkins ignores it.[10]

As regards the book, the judgment was fair: Perkins did not discuss unions and their role. But as the longshoremen's strike was about to demonstrate under dramatic circumstances, neither she nor Roosevelt would align the government's power against an emerging union. Their objective, as it appeared to one shipowner, "was to increase the power of organized labor . . . Labor was given all the breaks."[11]

The critic's remarks represented a point of view, best articulated by Senator Wagner, that the *only* road to social justice, at least for workers in the larger industries, was through organization and collective bargaining:

The development of a partnership between industry and labor in the solution of national problems is the indispensable complement to political democracy. And that leads us to this all-important truth: there can no more be democratic self-government in industry without workers participating therein, than there could be democratic government in politics without workers having the right to vote . . . That is why the right to bargain collectively is at the bottom of social justice for the worker, as well as the sensible conduct of business affairs. The denial or observance of this right means the difference between despotism and democracy.[12]

Perkins did not disagree: America does not want "a peon class, no matter how well fed." But there was a difference in emphasis. She had less confidence than Wagner in the union movement as an instrument of social justice, perhaps because she was more conscious of the large groups, such as women, that it generally excluded. Even by 1936 the AFL claimed as members only 3.5 million workers out of what it considered "an organizable number of approximately 39 million," less than 10 percent even excluding the allegedly unorganizable — the domestic, agricultural and small shop workers. In the coming years Wagner, though always aware of the millions of unorganized workers, would continue to be a specialist in organized labor; she, with her conception of the labor department as the department of all workers, would emphasize legislation of wider scope.[13] His great achievement in 1935 would be the National Labor Relations Act, which would go far beyond Section 7 (a) of the NIRA in its effort to provide effective protection for the rights of workers to organize and bargain collectively. In the same year she would have a leading role in the passage of the Social Security Act, which gave some economic security to a larger, more general group of workers. Both acts would follow, and to some immeasurable extent be assisted in their passage by, the disappearance from the scene of Johnson and the NRA; the former largely through his own actions and the latter mainly by decision of the U.S. Supreme Court.

Johnson's difficulties with drink did not become apparent until eight or nine months after his appointment as administrator of the National Recovery Administration, and by then he had complicated the problem by developing a liaison with his secretary, Frances Robinson. As he traveled around the country negotiating the industrial codes and exhorting everyone to support them, "Robbie" was always at his side and Mrs. Johnson was in Virginia. Gradually a number of people realized that his secretary had become his mistress.

It was a difficult situation for anyone to deal with, partly because there was some good in it. Not only was Robinson a superlative secretary, she was extremely clever at covering for Johnson when he was drunk. If someone called, she might say he was in conference and that she would try to slip him a note. After a time she would call back and say, "The general has sent out a note which reads . . ." The caller would feel that he had reached Johnson personally, and the decision, which in fact was entirely Robinson's, was almost always sound.

Even within Johnson's family the situation was not black and white. The marriage between Johnson and his wife had been deteriorating for some time, and their son, Pat, who worked in the NRA (and preserved the traditional spelling of the family name, Johnston), saw that an attempt to force his parents together would not resolve their problems. He tried instead to support both in their increasingly separate lives, and he became an ally of Robinson, whom he liked, as both struggled to keep his father sober. Plainly no one would benefit if Johnson's career in government ended in noisy, drunken disaster.[14]

Because people close to Johnson worked hard to minimize his problems, they were partially concealed. But when, in September 1933, he had been about to depart for New York to lead a huge NRA rally, a leader of a women's group had telephoned the White House, reached McIntyre and warned him that no one wanted "that Robinson woman" in New York. McIntyre reported the conversation to Roosevelt, who sent for Perkins.

When she arrived in his office, he said, "What am I going to do, Frances? They're up in arms in New York. They don't want this Robinson girl. Robbie, you call her, don't you?"

"Yes."

"They don't want her there with Johnson."

"She shouldn't go. I've been saying for weeks that she shouldn't go. I've told her that she ought not to go on these expeditions with the general and certainly not be photographed. It was bound to lead to gossip."

"Well, the gossips are on it," he said. "What do you think?"

"If she's got to be there, let her go by train. Let her go to the NRA office but not to the reviewing stand. If he needs her, let her be in his office. The only thing that she does is to keep him from drinking. You know that, don't you?"

"Does she?" he said. "Does he drink too much?"

"You must have heard it by this time."

"Yes, but it's not too much, is it?"

"No, but sometimes it's in public. Anyway Ed McGrady can do that job."

"Frances, tell her not to go. Tell her *not* to go to New York. They don't want her, and you tell her."

"Mr. President, what a job!"

He had McIntyre check with Johnson's office, which reported that the general and Miss Robinson had left for the airport.

"Take a White House car," Roosevelt said. "They have no speed limits. Go out to the airport and get her off that plane."

"Why don't you send McIntyre?" she said.

McIntyre threw up his hands. "I wouldn't go under any circumstances."

"You're a woman," Roosevelt said. "You'll know how to say it to her.

"She'll take it better from a man."

"No, you go."

As she left, he called through the door, "Do it in a nice way."

So, to the sound of sirens screaming, she went to the airport, all the time hoping the plane would have gone. But it was on the airstrip, and no one had boarded.

She succeeded in getting Robinson alone and explained the problem, urging her to follow Johnson by train. After a moment's thought Robinson said, "I guess you're right, but I won't tell the general until just before the plane goes. I'll tell him I'm telephoning." She waited in a phone booth, apparently talking, until the plane was about to leave. Then she rushed out on the airstrip and told Johnson that something had come up at the office and she would have to follow later. He was distressed but not irate. Like the general's son, Perkins found much to admire in Robinson.[15]

But despite everyone's efforts Johnson's drinking grew worse, probably because the NRA moved into a phase for which his talents were ill suited. He was superb at arousing the country to pull itself up by its bootstraps, to try the system of codes and to abide by the agreements for minimum wages and maximum hours. "We Do Our Part" was the motto of the NRA's symbol, the blue eagle, which code observers were entitled to display, and Johnson made it exciting to be part of the movement. "It was as though the community rose from the dead," Perkins wrote later, and she gave much of the credit for the miracle to Johnson.[16]

But after the codes were set up and the NRA became a regulatory agency, he was less effective. He lacked the capacity to create an administrative organization, to place a man here, another there, telling each what to do and how the lines of authority would run between them. He was too dramatic in his view of himself and of events surrounding him. Roosevelt complained of him to Perkins, "He begins in the middle in telling a story. It's exciting and interesting, but I don't actually know, when he gets through, what he's doing." In an effort to keep track Roosevelt appointed a cabinet committee to oversee Johnson and the NRA. Perkins and Ickes were its most faithful members. Johnson hated the committee.[17]

His assistant, Robert K. Straus, thought part of Johnson's problems with the NRA originated in the separation of the public works program from the codes. Johnson never ceased to be bitter about it, and he was left with too little to absorb his extraordinary energy. As a result he threw himself even harder into the creation of codes, even for the smallest industries, even for the fishhook industry.

When Perkins read the code for that, she went to him. "Really, you mustn't go into this type of thing. You mustn't spend time, money, energy on a thing like this. It doesn't matter."

"They want it," he said. "This is part of the general atmosphere. We urge everybody to have a code. We urge every workingman to be sure that he's working under a code. Now these little industries come in and want to get their codes. They've got a good code and want to know why we can't approve it." But the multitude of codes, finally 750, interfered with the administration of those in the big, important industries. There was not enough time, money and energy to police them all.[18]

And there was another difficulty, of which Johnson had been warned even before the act was passed. At Straus's suggestion the two had called on Brandeis, who, after listening to Johnson describe the theory of the codes, had said, "It won't work. You will never be able to get the men to administer it."

This proved true. The men Johnson recruited to administer the codes were constantly seduced by the possibility of a good job in the industries they were regulating. Too often the codes were weakly enforced, with the victims usually the workers.[19]

Under Section 7 (a) of the act, included in every code, they had the right to organize and bargain collectively, but their attempts were often resisted by their employers. Frequently the result was a strike, which slowed production and delayed economic recovery. Johnson's temperament on such occasions was likely to betray him. Every inclination of his passionate nature and training as an army officer led him to rush into the situation and condemn the workers — as he had done in San Francisco. Or if he held back, then Perkins should not. As she described it, "He would draw himself up, scowling and throwing out his chest, and say to protesters, 'The Secretary of Labor will issue the necessary orders, tell you what you are to do and what the employer is to do.' " But, she added, "There was no such power in the office of the Secretary of Labor, nor should there be." In his book he quoted her with disapproval as saying, "The trouble with Hugh is that he thinks a strike is something to settle." He never grasped her point.[20]

His approach put him into conflict not only with Perkins but also with Senator Wagner, who felt that the NRA was not stimulating industry fast enough chiefly because the workers in their efforts to organize were not adequately protected. The only punishment the Compliance Division of the NRA could impose directly on employers who interfered with workers' organizing was to take away the blue eagle insignia. Wagner proposed to submit a bill to Congress early in 1934 to create a Labor Board armed with subpoena powers and authority to enforce its orders directly through the federal district courts. He wanted the board to be a permanent, independent, regulatory agency like the Federal Trade Commission. Johnson wanted the board in the NRA, where he could control it. Perkins thought it should be in the Labor Department.[21]

In their meetings to decide where the board should be located, Johnson's dizziness with drink became frighteningly apparent. He had long periods of blankness, his eyes often were glazed and frequently, from meeting to meeting, he could not remember what he had agreed to. Finally he went to the Walter Reed Army Hospital. At a meeting there with Perkins and Wagner he was irrational.[22]

Wagner went ahead and introduced his bill, the Labor Disputes Act of 1934, which was not passed. Johnson after several weeks in the hospital returned to his post, where his subordinates continued trying to protect him. And Perkins one day received a visit from Straus.

He, Pat Johnston and several others in the NRA, hoping they were acting in Johnson's best interest, had decided that someone should ask Roosevelt to order him to take a vacation. A spate of photographs of him and Robinson had stirred them to act, and they hoped that Roosevelt, for whom Johnson had an extravagant reverence, would succeed where they had failed. Through Straus they asked Perkins, as the general's friend in the cabinet, to bear the message.

She acted promptly, and Roosevelt did his best. But Johnson refused to leave his post and on returning to his office wrote Straus a note that, not unkindly, revealed that he had discovered and disapproved of the conspiracy.[23]

Perkins on her own went to Baruch. After edging up to the seriousness of Johnson's drinking, she discovered that Baruch was quite familiar with it: Johnson had a long history of drinking. She asked Baruch why, in discussing Johnson's appointment with her, he hadn't specified the disability instead of merely characterizing Johnson as a "number three man."

"He was in one of the sobering-off periods," Baruch said. "Maybe he was going to straighten out forever. I didn't like to tell you he was a drunkard."

"It would have been more effective if you had," she said, "but it was too late anyway."

She asked Baruch to take Johnson back into his organization, but with lots of fanfare for the press so the job would not seem a demotion.

Baruch shook his head. "Frances, when people have held high public office, such as Hugh has, something happens to them. They swell up, and they can never slip back into the same old job and the same old relationship. Hugh's got so swell-headed now that he sometimes won't even talk to me on the telephone."

She suggested that perhaps Johnson feared to reveal that he had been drinking.

"No, I know the difference," said Baruch. "He's got too big for me. My organization could never absorb him. He's learned publicity, too, which he never knew before. He's tasted the tempting but poisonous cup of publicity. It makes a difference. He never again can be just a plain fellow working in Baruch's organization. He's now the great General Hugh Johnson on the blue eagle."

At Baruch's suggestion she went to Walter Chrysler, another of Johnson's friends, but Chrysler's response and his reasons for it were the same. The experience left her "kind of sad." Here were two rich men, each claiming to be Johnson's friend, "and they wouldn't do something to save his face."

Sometime later she went back to Roosevelt, who by then was aware of many more incidents of Johnson's drinking and was anxious to ease him out of the administration, but in a nice way. Johnson's enthusiasm for his job was very appealing and aroused in almost everyone a desire not to hurt him. Then, too, as far as he had gone, he had done a good job with the NRA, and he would also be the first official of high position to leave the administration. Roosevelt proposed to appoint him the head of a commission to examine the progress of economic recovery in Europe. "Does it seem logical to you?" he asked. "Do you think it would please Hugh?" She thought it might.

That night Roosevelt talked by phone with Baruch, who agreed to press Johnson to take the job and to offer him assistance in recruiting a topnotch staff. When Roosevelt discussed it with Johnson, he felt he was persuasive, and later telephoned Perkins that everything was going "to work out all right." But Johnson, after a day's consideration and despite the urging of Baruch and Perkins, turned it down. His plain duty, he told Perkins, was to stay at his post in the NRA. Its counsel, Donald Richberg, could do the job in Europe almost as well, and "Richberg can't do the things I can do for the NRA."[24]

Richberg, the number two man in NRA affairs, was constantly proposing reorganizations that would increase his power. With reason Johnson distrusted him. Yet everyone agreed some sort of reorganization was necessary, and in it Johnson's role inevitably would be lessened, if only because of his drinking and Robinson — though he of course never considered either a matter to be taken into account. He saw only a conspiracy by Richberg and others to supplant him.

Among those others, because of disagreements over policies, he began to count Perkins. "Organization of both Industry and Labor to the ultimate," he once wrote, "is the only way to meet the serious economic problems with which we are faced." He foresaw continued regulation of production, fixing of prices and a permanent NRA, which would absorb the labor and commerce departments and reach into almost every phase of the country's government.[25]

To Perkins the vision was sinister. He had given her a book on the theories of Mussolini's corporate state, and though she was no expert on Italian affairs, she knew that under Mussolini a combination of the state and big business had gradually stripped consumers and workers of all defenses against exploitation. She thought that the NRA should continue to be a temporary agency and that the exemptions from the antitrust laws granted to business should be repealed as soon as the country's economy had revived. She began to wonder if Johnson "understood the democratic process" and whether he might "be moving by emotion and indirection toward a dangerous pattern." In discussions of the reorganization of the NRA she frequently opposed his ideas. This philosophic difference was picked up by the newspapers and fairly presented as a struggle over the future direction of the NRA. But it was not the immediate reason she was eager for him to resign.

Roosevelt decided to try again. McIntyre, who had few thoughts about the philosophy of the NRA, pressed him hard on the hazard of Johnson to the administration. What would voters think if they learned that the President had countenanced a mistress for Johnson at the public's expense and weeks at Walter Reed to dry out from his binges?

One afternoon Roosevelt said to Perkins, "I've just got to tell Hugh somehow or other that he has to go. It's worse than I thought, Frances. I hear from other people that it's worse than you said." She realized then that, like Baruch, she had tempered the wind to the shorn lamb, and she urged Roosevelt to be firm.

It was August, a Friday afternoon, and she had Roosevelt's permission to disappear for a week's vacation. She was going to visit friends in Cooperstown, New York, and Susanna would be there. On the way, Sunday morning in New York, she bought a Washington paper and read that Johnson had seen the President the previous afternoon. On leaving the White House and being asked by reporters if he intended to resign, he had said, "My feet are nailed to the floor for the present. I am not going to resign."

Perkins continued to Cooperstown. Whatever had happened was not her concern.

She arrived in the late afternoon. The White House had been calling, and she reached McIntyre, who said the President wanted her in his office Monday morning at ten o'clock. He implied that the reason was Johnson. To make the night train from New York, she would have to start back within the hour.

Because the executive wing was being refurbished, the President's office that summer was in the center of the White House, in the Blue Room. On one side, in the Red Room, were the stenographers, and on the other, in the Green Room, Early and McIntyre. As Perkins entered, she said, "McIntyre, what *is* this?"

He claimed not to know, but Richberg and Johnson had also been asked for ten o'clock.

"A pretty mess," she said. "What happened the day the President saw Johnson?"

"The President *thinks* he told him he wanted him to go. But you saw what Johnson told the press. I guess that's why he wants you all here."

She didn't like the picture at all. "Did anybody mention to the President that it was putting me in a bad spot?"

"That's his lookout, and yours." She got no sympathy from McIntyre.

Richberg came in, and received similar answers to his questions.

Then Johnson entered. He looked ill, she thought; very red in the face, puffy but sober. They shook hands. Johnson gave Richberg a mean look. "What are you doing here?"

"I was asked to come at ten o'clock."

Johnson seemed surprised. Almost immediately they were shown into the Blue Room.

Roosevelt was at his desk with his back to the windows. She saw at once that he had steeled himself for the meeting. He sat very straight, with no word or smile for any of them. To relieve the tension she said, "Well, Mr. President, I have had a beautiful vacation in Cooperstown." A slight scowl appeared between his eyebrows. "Sit down," he said.

While they were arranging themselves before the desk, he kept his eyes from theirs. "General Johnson," he began, "I have asked you to come today and I have asked Miss Perkins and Mr. Richberg to come today because I think we have been misunderstanding each other. I have asked you, General Johnson, to go on a mission to Europe in order to report to me on its economic recovery. That report would throw some light on our own situation and our own planning. You first indicated to me that you were willing to go."

Perkins studied her shoe. She felt that Roosevelt's approach, before witnesses, was wrong with a sensitive, vain man like Johnson.

"I want to ask you once more," Roosevelt went on, "if you are willing to go, because I would like to send you. I would like to put you at the head of this mission. You can put anybody else on the mission you want. Will you go?"

"No. I told you, Mr. President, I would not go. I will stay here and do my duty by NRA."

"Then we must move on to the second item," said Roosevelt. "I think you have misunderstood me, General Johnson, although I tried to make myself clear the other day. If you don't wish to go to Europe, I think you should resign at once. Frankly you have become a problem. I can't discuss it much further, but I think you should resign immediately."

Turning to Perkins, he said, "You understood what I said, didn't you, Miss Perkins?"

"Yes, sir."

"You understood what I said, Mr. Richberg?"

"Yes, sir."

Johnson rose. "Very well, Mr. President. I understand what you say. I'm a good soldier. I do what I am asked by my commander in chief. That's all there is to it, unless you want some further conversation with these two."

"Nothing more, General."

Johnson said good-bye and walked out. As Perkins and Richberg rose, Roosevelt asked them to wait. With a nod she darted into the Green Room to ask McIntyre to take Johnson out a private entrance and avoid the press.

When she re-entered the Blue Room, Richberg was still looking solemn and embarrassed, but Roosevelt was visibly relaxing. "Why in the world," she said to him, "did you send for me and Richberg?"

"I knew I had to have witnesses," Roosevelt said. "Hugh would not understand or believe that I was asking him to resign unless I had witnesses, and I didn't know anybody but you two whom I could safely have as witnesses. Johnson thinks a good deal of both of you. He trusts you. You're both close-mouthed. You won't tell the world about this. Yet you can testify that I did tell him to resign. You can tell him if he asks you, because I expect that he'll be confused again by tonight and not knew whether he's been told to stay with his feet nailed down, or to go."

Johnson's resignation technically was not submitted until a month later, but his power in the NRA ended that day. And so did his friendship with Perkins. She regretted the fact, but thought it entirely understandable and felt no resentment toward Johnson, even when he vilified her in his book, *The Blue Eagle from Egg to Earth*.[26]

She thought it was one of Roosevelt's illusions that he could handle people well, and with Johnson she considered he had made a serious psychological mistake. He had thought "in his manlike fashion" that

Johnson would prefer as witnesses people who knew him well; but if Roosevelt "had been a woman, he would have known that the one thing a person cannot endure is to be humiliated before the members of his family or before his friends — particularly if one of them is a woman." Her career was built on the premise that in daily work there was no essential difference between men and women, but this episode drew from her one of her very rare statements of a difference: women know more than men about humiliation.[27]

In his message to Congress on February 20, 1935, Roosevelt requested a two-year extension of the National Industrial Recovery Act. Without it, in June the enabling act for the NRA would expire. His message summarized the agency's new direction: codes would be fewer, simpler and more strictly enforced. Their goals of establishing minimum standards of fair competition and decent hours and wages for labor were still not wholly achieved. The administration of the agency was settling down and becoming more effective.

Then on Monday, May 27, 1935, the United States Supreme Court announced three decisions, all unanimous, all against executive or congressional New Deal measures. One struck down the Frazier-Lemke Act for its method of relieving farm debtors, another rebuked the President for forcing a member of the Federal Trade Commission from office for inadequate cause and the third, the *Schechter,* or "sick-chicken," case, involved the NRA. The Schechter brothers, poultry jobbers in Brooklyn, had been charged with violating the Live Poultry Code on several counts, including selling diseased chickens and ignoring wage and hour regulations. On two grounds the Court ruled that a constitutional basis for the prosecution was lacking: the NIRA's delegation of legislative power, wrote Cardozo, was "delegation running riot," and the Schechters were not engaged in interstate commerce; hence the federal government had no authority to regulate working conditions in their plant.

For many in the administration the day of the three decisions was Black Monday, the day when "nine old men" gave the New Deal its greatest setback. If the federal government lacked the power to prevent the sale of sick chickens, how could it hope to combat the Depression? Throughout the government the assumption quickly spread that the NRA was finished.

Perkins felt differently. As she studied the decision, she thought its application was relatively narrow. The Schechters had a small business, but steel, coal and the big industries still qualified as interstate

commerce. Wyzanski, too, thought much of the NRA could be sal-
vaged. After a conference in her office with some of the administration's leading lawyers, who agreed with her view, she requested an
appointment with the President and was told to come right over: the
Attorney General was with him.

Cummings, who had already seen Roosevelt once about the decision,
believed that it completely undercut the NRA and had told as much
to the press. Against him, she, who was not a lawyer, had little chance,
and sensing that she had already lost the argument she indulged
herself for a few minutes in disliking Cummings's physical features.
He was tall, and his shoulders stooped slightly even when he was
sitting. He was bald, with a long nose pinched halfway down by a
small pince-nez of half lenses. Ordinarily she liked Cummings but
that day she was irritated by his constant peering at her over the lenses
and then down through them to read some paper. His attitude was
"poppa-knows-best." "He wasn't willing even to listen to what I
thought. He was just being elderly and stubborn."

He damned the entire court. The decision was "absolutely unnecessary." It was "in line with their old-fashioned, their archaic, their
reactionary decisions in the old *Hammer* v. *Dagenhart* case and in all
the other cases we have taken up. This is all you can expect of the
Supreme Court."

As she watched Roosevelt's face, she began to suspect he was relieved
that the NRA "could be washed up and we perhaps could return to
normal ways. I think the President had a sense that it was getting so
big, so sprawling, so involved that no one could ever manage it." But
if he felt relief, he concealed it from the country.[28]

Several days later at a carefully staged press conference he gave
reporters his opinion of the decision. In an eighty-five-minute mono-
logue, talking without notes and in a serious, courteous tone, he
reviewed the history of the interstate commerce clause and concluded
that the Court had reverted to a "horse-and-buggy" definition of it.
By their decision, he said, the Court's nine members had stripped the
federal government of its power to deal with contemporary social and
economic problems; the destruction of the NRA was the most important ruling since the Dred Scott case, which had precipitated the Civil
War. It was an impressive intellectual performance, particularly to
those present, but learned secondhand from the newspapers it stirred
little support around the country.

In June the NRA expired, but parts of its codes were already before
Congress in bills such as Wagner's Labor Relations Act and the Guffey

Act, which by declaring coal a public utility in effect would re-enact the bituminous coal code. There was also the administration's Social Security Act, which would provide the country's industrial workers with some measure of economic security.

Chapter 26

-»)«-

Unemployment and old age insurance: the Social Security Act.

IN HER CONFERENCE with Roosevelt before accepting her post Perkins
had included among her goals unemployment and old age insurance.
In the years after World War I groups had lobbied for both, bills for
them had been presented in several state legislatures, and in the U.S.
Senate in 1930 Wagner had introduced an unemployment insurance
bill, though it had not reached a vote. But since the Governors'
Conference in 1930 when Roosevelt, using a draft by Perkins, had said
that "the only answer" to irregularity of employment seems to be
"some form of insurance," he had been the chief political figure
associated with the idea of unemployment insurance. His commitment
to it, as well as to some form of old age or retirement insurance,
seemed firm.

During the Hundred Days of the New Deal Congress, neither he nor
she had time to further insurance plans, but in the winter of 1934 she
had an unemployment insurance bill drafted in the labor department.
It followed a suggestion of Justice Brandeis's that seemed likely to
meet any constitutional test: A federal payroll tax would be levied on
employers with a provision for rebate (technically a tax-offset) to the
extent the employer contributed to an unemployment reserve fund
established by his state. Presumably the states, preferring to keep the
money rather than to pass it to the federal government, would rush to
create systems of unemployment insurance. At the time only Wisconsin had one.

"It is probably our only chance in twenty-five years to get a bill like
this,"[1] Perkins told Roosevelt. Wagner introduced it in the Senate
and David J. Lewis of Maryland in the House. Yet in spite of
Roosevelt's endorsement, it did not advance: public interest at the

moment was on relief for the old, focused on a scheme called the Townsend Plan; and the experts on unemployment insurance were in shrill disagreement over whether the states should allow employers to set up their own reserve funds (the Wisconsin plan) or be required to pool them in a state fund (a proposed Ohio plan). "Do please telephone the Chief Performer [Wagner] on the Hill," Perkins nagged Roosevelt. "This must come out of committee and pass." But Roosevelt himself began to doubt some details of the bill and, at the same time, thought that the country was ready for a more comprehensive scheme, which might include old age, health and disability insurance.

On June 8, after conferences with Wagner, Perkins and others, he sent a special message to Congress in which, after discussing housing and natural resources, he said:

> Next winter we may well undertake the great task of furthering the security of the citizen and his family through social insurance.
>
> This is not an untried experiment. Lessons of experience are available from States, from industries, and from many nations of the civilized world. The various types of social insurance are interrelated; and I think it is difficult to attempt to solve them piecemeal. Hence, I am looking for a sound means which I can recommend to provide at once security against several of the great disturbing factors in life — especially those which relate to unemployment and old age. I believe there should be a maximum of cooperation between States and the Federal Government. I believe that the funds necessary to provide this insurance should be raised by contribution rather than by an increase in general taxation. Above all, I am convinced that social insurance should be national in scope, although the several States should meet at least a large portion of the cost of management, leaving to the Federal Government the responsibility of investing, maintaining and safeguarding the funds constituting the necessary insurance reserves.

The Wagner-Lewis bill, everyone understood, would be allowed to die in committee and a more comprehensive bill presented in January 1935 at the opening of the next Congress.

In discussing the project with Roosevelt, Perkins suggested that he might want to put a committee of cabinet members in charge. "He saw at once that a program developed by a committee of the cabinet would be under his control" and asked her to be its chairman. She questioned whether some other cabinet member, not so closely identified with social insurance, might not be better.

"No, no," he said. "You care about this thing. You believe in it.

Therefore I know you will put your back to it more than anyone else, and you will drive it through."[2]

On June 29, after she, Hopkins and Arthur Altmeyer, the Second Assistant Secretary of Labor, had worked out the organization, Roosevelt by executive order appointed a Committee on Economic Security.[3] Perkins was named chairman, and members were Secretary of the Treasury Morgenthau, Attorney General Cummings, Secretary of Agriculture Wallace and, the only noncabinet member, Federal Emergency Relief Administrator Hopkins. The order stated: "The Committee shall study problems relating to the economic security of individuals and shall report to the President not later than December 1, 1934, its recommendations concerning proposals which in its judgment will promote greater economic security." It also announced two subordinate agencies, to be appointed later, a Technical Board and an Advisory Council. The board was to be composed of members of the government who could give the committee technical advice, and the council of private citizens who might assist the committee in "all matters coming within the scope of its investigations." The post of executive director was created to direct and coordinate the work.

Altmeyer, who had drafted the order and soon was appointed chairman of the Technical Board, had become Second Assistant Secretary of Labor only a few weeks earlier, and while he held the post the Social Security Act (as it became known the following year) was his major responsibility. After the act passed, he was appointed one of the three members of the Social Security Board and then from 1937 to 1953 served as its chairman.

He was a good administrator, very methodical. Though a touch dogmatic, he had a sense of humor, which he often concealed, perhaps out of shyness. People did not warm up to him quickly, but those who worked with him became fond of him. He had a saying, "A successful administrator ought to be about as interesting as spinach — cold spinach," and he cultivated a cool, colorless façade not altogether in character.

Perkins had met him in the past at conferences on labor legislation, admired his work in Wisconsin and had persuaded him to join the NRA in a position where he would enforce the labor standards in the various industry codes. Seven months later, on the suggestion of Mary Dewson and apparently with the Social Security Act in mind, she asked him to join the Labor Department. Altmeyer felt that he was chosen because his "experience had been acquired in a state noted for its progressive social legislation."[4]

The same reasoning was probably behind her selection, as executive director of the committee, of Edwin E. Witte, the chairman of the department of economics at the University of Wisconsin. Witte in later life often referred to himself as "a government man," one whose career was spent entirely in a state government, a state university or the federal government. In Wisconsin, in various posts, he had drafted or administered many of the state's labor laws, and like Perkins had visited Europe in 1931 to study social insurance and relief institutions. An academic expert with much practical experience, he was warm, open and friendly; people took to him instantly. Lubin, who served on the Technical Board, thought him an excellent chairman: "Everyone got heard; no one for too long." In the best sense he was a politician, which was fortunate, because before the Social Security Act became law he had to negotiate with many of the country's most powerful interest groups.[5]

He came to Washington in late July, and in his first meeting with Perkins she defined the committee's job as twofold: to prepare (1) a comprehensive report embracing all phases of economic security and (2) an immediate legislative program of items to be presented to the next Congress. His job would be to carry out the policy that the committee would make, its decisions presumably following what Roosevelt had stated as desirable in his message to Congress: emphasis on unemployment and old age insurance; funds for each to be raised by contribution (a tax imposed only on those participating in the plan) rather than by an increase in general taxes; and all programs to be national in scope but with maximum cooperation between the state and federal governments.[6]

In both its comprehensive report and the immediate program for Congress, the committee soon fell behind schedule. August and much of September passed before Witte could assemble a staff. Many of the specialists he wanted could not come to Washington immediately or could come only part-time. By agreement with Perkins he did not ask several of the most distinguished because they were so committed to particular views of social insurance that they seemed unlikely to be able to consider all views impartially. But though the reason was obvious, some feelings were hurt.[7]

Of the committee's two subsidiary groups the Technical Board, drawn from experts already in government posts, was easily set up, but the Advisory Council was not, mainly because it lacked a concept. Should it be large or small? Render advice privately or by public report? Meet regularly with the committee or once in a national conference? Initially it was to be small, seven or nine, and to meet frequently and in private with the committee. But in late October, when Roosevelt came to make the appointments from a list prepared by Perkins and Altmeyer, the original plan no longer seemed feasible. Too many important representatives of industry and the public would have to be omitted if a balance between labor, industry and the public was to be maintained. Roosevelt appointed a council of twenty, which under pressure from social workers and the Catholic church was soon enlarged to twenty-three. But as events would show, the policy of inclusion adopted for the council could no more assure support for the committee's proposals than that of exclusion adopted for the staff.[8]

One policy question within the committee, fundamental to both its comprehensive report and immediate program for Congress, emerged almost at once. Hopkins wanted relief and social insurance of all kinds to be merged. Under his proposal any citizen on proof of unemployment, old age or ill health, regardless of need, could receive payments from the government. Although these might be called insurance benefits, they would come out of the general tax revenues. There would be no insurance fund to which the qualifying citizen had paid a premium in the form of a tax. The program, by moving large sums of money from the rich minority, which paid federal taxes, to the poor majority, which did not, would redistribute income on a national scale. To Perkins it was "a pretty extreme point of view for a country which had not had a social insurance system or a relief program before."

She and Hopkins went to Roosevelt to argue the issue, and "although Hopkins was eloquent, the President at once saw that this would be the very thing he had been saying he was against for years — the dole."

Hopkins pointed out that the unemployment insurance payments contemplated in any system then being discussed would not be adequate to support a family whose breadwinner was long out of work. The family would then have to turn to public assistance, relief.

Perkins agreed; that had always been understood. But surveys of the unemployed showed that by far the largest number had had intermittent employment. If at the start of the Depression they had been able to draw unemployment insurance benefits, even in small weekly amounts, their continuing expenditures would have cushioned the decline of business by preserving a market for the production of goods — thereby reducing the number of unemployed. Further, though the weekly payments might be small, if they came at the start of unemployment, they would sustain savings and credit, stave off evictions and tide a family over occasional periods of unemployment. In practical family budgeting and peace of mind the payments would have worth beyond their cash value.

She did not care, as Roosevelt did, whether the worker as well as the employer contributed, that is, paid a tax, to the fund. That to her was "sentimental" and only increased the administrative difficulties; what mattered was that a worker in a particular industry should have a right to some support from that industry if he was laid off for two or three months. Roosevelt saw a financial reason for workers' contributions: the workers would have a greater stake in the fiscal credit of the government. He also saw a political reason: a later administration of different persuasion would find it harder to repeal the program if millions of workers had a paid-up "contractual" right to benefits. But as opposed to Hopkins both saw the insurance plan as something separate from relief.[9]

It is not surprising that their views tended to agree: they had been working together on forms of social insurance for six years. The pattern of their thinking, which provided the framework for the Social Security Act, is clearest in the protection for old age after retirement. It is a three-tier system. At top is a private sector: annuities for those who can afford them. In the middle, old age insurance run by the government. It is nationwide and compulsory; premiums are collected in the form of taxes, and a citizen at sixty-five if retired from work or at seventy-two in any event begins to receive his benefit, regardless of need; his right to it is contractual. At bottom is old age assistance, relief, paid out of general tax revenues but only to those in need; poverty must be shown. In unemployment compensation: at top, in effect, is having a job; in the middle, unemployment insurance; and at bottom, relief. As Roosevelt once explained it to Altmeyer, if a worker exhausted his unemployment insurance (so much per week for so many weeks) and was still unemployed, he should automatically be given a green ticket, which would entitle him to some form of relief. (Altmeyer, with his mind for detail, wondered why Roosevelt made the ticket green!) [10]

The Social Security Act, as it finally was passed, contained ten programs, though most people associate "social security" with only one, old age or retirement insurance. Of the ten only two, old age and unemployment insurance, were not direct relief (old age assistance, pensions for the blind or aid to dependent children) or grants-in-aid to the states or to the U.S. Public Health Service.[11] The insurance schemes, however, caused the most controversy. There had always been some sort of assistance or relief for the poor and handicapped, whether provided by town, county or state. The federal government was merely a new agent implementing an old concept. But the insurance schemes, national and compulsory, were new concepts, with implications for almost every American family and many of the country's social institutions.

Though Hopkins had lost the decision on the type of economic security program the country should have, he continued after Perkins to be the most faithful and interested member of the committee. At its meetings Cummings was always represented by a substitute under orders to follow Perkins on questions of policy. Wallace and Morgenthau often came personally; Wallace tended to be more interested in the relief programs, because they solved immediate problems, and Morgenthau in the insurance schemes. Beside these committee members, Witte, Altmeyer and Thomas H. Eliot, the Assistant Solicitor who would eventually have to draft the bill, attended regularly. The meetings were held in Perkins's office, usually during the lunch hour, and she would have Jay send in sandwiches. Perhaps because of the preponderance of men, Jay continually produced meat sandwiches — to the distress of Wallace, who was on a vegetarian diet.[12]

One of the first casualties of the committee's decisions on policy was health insurance. In mid-August Perkins gave a radio address on the general purposes of the committee and touched briefly on the need for some sort of health insurance. The reaction from much of the medical profession was a cry of rage. Roosevelt was deluged with protesting telegrams, and the *Journal of the American Medical Association* in an editorial stated that the committee would try to push a compulsory health insurance plan through Congress without even consulting the profession. In fact, several doctors were preparing a report for the committee and had plans, soon realized, for the appointment of a Medical Advisory Committee. Yet despite efforts to placate the doctors, the furor continued, and the committee soon excluded from its program for Congress any proposal for health insurance. So strong was the opposition of much of the profession that during the hearings on the Social Security bill even a reference to a future study of health insurance was deleted at the request of members of the House. When the committee sent its report to Roosevelt, however, it stated: "Although we realize that a difference of opinion exists as to the advisability of establishing compulsory health insurance, we are convinced, after reviewing experience in this country and abroad, that the compulsory feature is essential to the accomplishment of the end in view."

In an accompanying letter Perkins suggested that the report "not be made public" until the Social Security bill then before Congress had been passed. And Roosevelt, who doubtless had reached the same conclusion, never released it.[13]

The committee's problems with old age or retirement insurance were of a different sort. One of the first issues to arise was whether the insurance, which would cover workers in every state, should consist of a single federal system or of forty-eight state systems in cooperation with the federal government. Aside from the question, which loomed large, of the constitutionality of a federal system, Perkins favored a state-federal system. She was always, in everything, "a states-righter." She had worked in a state government for twelve years, had seen it operate successfully a system of accident insurance (workmen's compensation) and believed in keeping the administration of such programs close to the people. Hopkins, with less experience of state government and as administrator of federal relief in constant battle with several of the states, strongly favored a federal system. Witte and Altmeyer, because of their Wisconsin experience, supported Perkins. But most important: Roosevelt, as he had stated in his message of June 8, wanted "a maximum of cooperation between States and the Federal Government."[14]

Nevertheless the committee recommended and Congress eventually created for old age insurance a purely federal system, the only one of the act's ten programs to have it. The reason was technical. The actuaries who reported to the committee on the problems involved were unanimous in advising the federal system. As Altmeyer later summarized it: the "mobility of workers made it impossible to estimate the future age composition of the working population of each state or the length of time that individual workers would be working in a particular state before retiring. These estimates needed to be reasonably accurate in order to determine future costs." Even if the states could be persuaded to adopt uniform systems and to transfer the workers' records, wage credits and contributions paid from state to state, the administrative difficulties were appalling. Like everyone else Perkins was soon convinced intellectually of the necessity of a federal system, but emotionally the decision went against the grain. Throughout the fall she muttered to herself about it.[15]

In all phases of the committee's work publicity was a problem. Perkins, Witte and Altmeyer had no flair for it, and Fitzgerald, who as the department's information officer handled the committee's news releases, was of little help. In retrospect Witte concluded that their failure to develop "a real publicity service" was "a serious mistake."[16] He was thinking then of countering "sources hostile to the committee's programs," but some of its greatest difficulties were produced by its friends and one, involving old age insurance, by two of its staff.

Because the committee was spending more time on unemployment than on old age insurance, Barbara N. Armstrong and J. Douglas Brown, two professors who had come from the University of California and Princeton to work on old age insurance, began to feel that their subject was being slighted, even in danger of not being included in the program to be sent to Congress. Suddenly in mid-November, after the President's speech at the National Conference on Economic Security, they saw a chance to bring it to the fore.

The conference was an effort by the committee to educate the public through news reports on the various types of relief and insurance that might be sent to Congress. Roosevelt's speech, initially drafted by Witte but revised by Perkins and Altmeyer, devoted several paragraphs to the necessity of providing security for old age, both immediately by relief and in the future by insurance. Then in a sentence soon to be unduly emphasized he said, "I do not know whether this is the time for any federal legislation on old age security." Immediately following, referring indirectly to the Townsend Plan, he said, "Organizations promoting fantastic schemes have aroused hopes that cannot possibly be fulfilled. Through their activities they increased the difficulties of getting sound legislation, but I hope," he concluded, "that in time we may be able to provide security for the aged — a sound and uniform system which will provide true security."

To the committee and to most of its staff and those at the conference, which had a round-table discussion on old age security, the statement did not imply that a program to help the aged had been dropped, merely that its details were undecided. Several newspapers, however, reported that old age security, both relief and insurance, had been rejected. The stories raised a political storm.

Some reporters and editors perhaps reached that interpretation independently, but thirty-eight years later Brown confessed that he and Armstrong had called a friend in the Scripps-Howard chain and deliberately started a false interpretation across the country in order to arouse passions for old age insurance.[17]

Roosevelt was dismayed by the repercussions and called Perkins, who promptly issued a statement that the interpretation was unjustified. Two days later Roosevelt declared to the National Conference of Mayors that he would include both old age security and unemployment insurance in his recommendations to Congress. But the story would not die. The *New York Times* published a column by Arthur Krock, unchecked by him with any of the principals, that Witte had written the fateful sentence and that Perkins was furious. Not only was the story unfair to Witte, but it suggested serious disagreements among him, Perkins and Roosevelt where there were none. She wanted to refute it, but Witte persuaded her to let it pass. When one day he asked Armstrong and Brown if they knew of any reason why there had been such an extraordinary response to the President's speech, he did not receive a straight answer.[18]

The imbroglio over old age insurance was symptomatic of a general difficulty with the staff. Though every specialist on being hired had agreed to subordinate his personal views to those of the committee and the President, in practice many could not. Professors and other experts without government experience took offense when their ideas were not followed. They complained, they sulked, they intrigued. They also had standards of perfection for their work quite out of step with the pace of government, and only a few had their major reports finished in time to assist the committee. As a result the comprehensive report never came into being in any useful form. Eventually in 1937 a summary of the staff's reports was published, but during 1935 when Congress held hearings on the Social Security Act, few reports were ready and those only in typescript. Witte furnished a list of these to congressional committee members, but none was ever requested. Probably even members of the committee only glanced at them. Yet much of the staff's short-term work was indispensable, and Witte doubted if a less specialized staff could have done better.[19]

The Advisory Council had many of the same difficulties as the staff, though here most of the issues centered on unemployment insurance. The twenty-three members divided roughly into four groups: representatives of labor, industry, social work and the public. Among them were Raymond Moley, Mary Dewson and Grace Abbott, who had just resigned as chief of the Children's Bureau to take a post at the University of Chicago. On Perkins's recommendation Roosevelt appointed as chairman Frank P. Graham, president of the University of North Carolina; she thought it best not to have in the post a representative of either labor or industry. But the most important member of the council proved to be one of her own selection, Paul Kellogg, the editor of *Survey*, who was elected vice-chairman at the first meeting. Since 1907, when he had directed the Pittsburgh Survey, he had

sought to introduce some reason and humanity into industrial relations, and now he saw a chance.[20]

In late April he had been the moving force behind an open letter
from reform leaders asking the administration to move faster with its
social legislation, and on April 27 he and a small delegation had met
with Roosevelt for three quarters of an hour. Soon after, he wrote
Perkins that they all had been charmed by Roosevelt and delighted
with "his project of a blanket scheme of social insurance from the
cradle to the grave." It would include every kind of social insurance,
even health, and Kellogg saw in it a chance to "do in a year what
might otherwise take a generation." And he added, "The President
said that you and he did not wholly agree in the matter — you
favoring a bite at a time and he the whole cherry."[21]

Perhaps Kellogg, misled by his own enthusiasm, misconstrued
Roosevelt's offhand remarks as a firm political program, for he poured
into the council greater intensity than its advisory role could contain.
In no time at all he was organizing support within it less to advise the
administration than to bind it, by votes in the council, to a particular
course of action. On one such occasion Abbott, with far greater
experience of government, lost her temper and moved that the meeting be ended.[22]

Later Perkins wrote him:

> The exact number of votes for a certain proposition is of little signifi-
> cance so far as the Committee on Economic Security is concerned. After
> all, the Committee was the body of responsible government officials
> whose duty it was to make recommendations to the President concerning
> questions of policy. Therefore, all of the opinions of the members of the
> Advisory Council and of members of the staff regardless of whether they
> were majority or minority opinions were equally helpful but not con-
> clusive.[23]

Kellogg's points were not unimportant, but one at least had been
decided before the council began its deliberations. Like Hopkins, he
wanted to use general tax revenues as well as the special taxes on
employers and workers to fund payments to the unemployed, in effect
merging the insurance scheme with relief. But unlike Hopkins, he
would not abide by Roosevelt's decision. He kept writing and talking
in public about the inadequacy of the proposed unemployment benefits without acknowledging the size of the complementary work relief
program. As a result rather than explaining the proposed economic
security program he appeared constantly to be attacking it.[24]

Another important issue was whether unemployment insurance

should be a purely federal or federal-state program. Because the administrative difficulties were less than in old age insurance and because the federal-state program seemed more likely to be held constitutional, the committee eventually followed Roosevelt's inclination – and recommended to him, and he in turn to Congress, a federal-state scheme based on the tax-offset plan of the Wagner-Lewis bill. Kellogg favored another plan with tougher standards for the states and more federal control, and by 1955, after twenty years' experience of unemployment insurance, almost everyone agreed that Kellogg's plan would have been the better. But at the time the Social Security Act was before Congress, its members clearly favored less rather than more federal control and had no intention of following Kellogg's views. His trumpeting of them at the hearings merely allowed the act's opponents to go about the country claiming that even a long-time advocate of social insurance disapproved of the bill.

Perkins pled with him to see the committee's limited program as "an adequate *beginning.*" He replied that, though "standards can be raised later," without what he considered to be the minimum "there is no beginning at all."[25]

Looking back, Witte thought the committee should have followed Frankfurter's suggestion to forget all about the council and substitute for it a governors' conference at which Roosevelt would explain to representatives of the states the federal-state aspects of the program he was about to submit to Congress. Perkins, partly as a result of her experience with the council, adopted as a principle of administration: Never appoint a committee to offer advice on a general subject; limit it to a specific question submitted by a responsible official to whom the report must be made. As she once lamented, I have "been stung enough times to know that whenever you let people give advice on anything that occurs to them, they'll give you some advice you jolly well can't afford to have, and they'll give it publicly."[26]

But if much went wrong in the committee's organization and procedures, more went right. To have the committee composed of cabinet members and Hopkins proved extremely useful. There were rumblings of opposition in the legal and economic staffs of the Treasury Department and Department of Agriculture, but because of the special relationship of the cabinet officers to the President, Perkins was able to quell these revolts and keep the report unanimous.[27]

Another blessing of the committee's small size was the speed with which it could function. The scheduled date for its report to the

President, for inclusion in his opening message to Congress, was December 1. But the delays prevented Witte from having the first draft ready until December 15, and even then the Advisory Council's report had not been received. On the night of either December 22 or 23 the committee met at the Perkins-Rumsey house to settle on the wording of its report. Perkins greeted the members at the door, locked it behind them, led them into the dining room, where for "provisions" she put a single bottle of whiskey on the table, and for six hours she, Hopkins, Wallace, Witte, Altmeyer and Josephine Roche sitting in for Morgenthau went over every word of the draft so that Witte could put it into final form for the committee to sign.[28]

Then on the afternoon of December 24 Perkins and Hopkins with the draft as their basis made an oral presentation of the report to Roosevelt. After several hours' discussion he accepted all of its recommendations and proposed to deliver them to Congress in a special message within ten days after the session opened.[29]

On the afternoon of January 16, the day before the special message, he called Perkins to his office. He had discovered in the tables of the old age insurance program that in 1965 the benefits would begin to tap the general tax revenues. Why? She explained: If workers who reached retirement age in the early years of the program were to receive even a small benefit, they would have to be paid partly out of current taxes paid into the fund by employers and younger workers. Then when the younger workers reached retirement age the fund would not have enough money on hand to pay the benefits to which they were entitled. The money would have to come from the general tax revenues, but it probably would not cost the government any more than in the earlier years because as more and more workers qualified for old age insurance, fewer and fewer would need old age assistance. The insurance program would gradually liquidate much of the need for the relief program.

It was a compromise with Hopkins's idea of combining the two, but it offered several advantages. A smaller reserve fund would be needed, and the initial tax rate, imposed equally on employer and worker, could be kept lower. The program would be less of a drag on business, at a time when they were trying to stimulate it, and would take less money out of circulation.

Roosevelt would have none of it. The program was to operate on true insurance principles. The report and accompanying bill were changed to leave the plan's details open, and in the hearings Morgenthau presented the details of a wholly self-supporting old age insurance system. The tax rate would start at 2 instead of 1 percent and rise to 6 in twelve years instead of 5 in twenty. The reserve fund would eventually total $47 billion instead of $15 billion.[30]

The figures disturbed many, and the leading members of the House Ways and Means Committee reported to Roosevelt that old age insurance was endangering the passage of the entire bill. Could they vote on its parts separately? Roosevelt was adamant: the bill was to be treated as a whole and old age insurance kept in it.

Witte considered this one of the crucial decisions in the bill's history. Though it reflected the view of the cabinet committee, its circumstances made it peculiarly Roosevelt's decision. If the measure had been presented in separate bills, Witte believed, of the ten programs only old age assistance, relief, would have passed.

Nevertheless, in both the House and the Senate many important changes were made during the hearings. Agricultural and domestic workers were dropped from both insurance plans, also workers for charitable, educational and religious institutions. The latter sometimes received pensions from their institutions, but the agricultural and domestic workers had no protection. Yet traditionally they were exempted from labor legislation, and Congress saw no reason to antagonize farmers and housewives with servants. The unemployment insurance program, in addition, was changed: instead of applying to employers of four or more for thirteen weeks of the year, it applied to employers of ten or more for twenty weeks. This was done to exempt canneries.

Several of the programs had difficulties over the matter of federal standards. In old age assistance, in which the federal government was to pay 50 percent of whatever relief a state gave to its old and needy, the state was to be required to furnish sufficient assistance "when added to the income of the aged recipient" in order to provide "a reasonable subsistence compatible with decency and health." Senator Harry Byrd of Virginia led the attack, and it quickly became apparent that many Southern legislators feared the provision would allow the federal government to interfere with the manner in which the southern states treated Negroes — an obstacle unforeseen by the committee or its staff. The provision was deleted.

Another stating that the administrative methods of the states must be satisfactory to the federal government was qualified by adding "other than those relating to selection, tenure of office and compensation of personnel." The leading member of the House committee, Fred M. Vinson of Kentucky, who later became Chief Justice of the

United States, gave the reason: "No damned social workers are going to come into my State to tell our people whom they shall hire." He meant Perkins and Frank Persons. In the U.S. Employment Service offices and in making grants to the state systems they required the personnel to be selected on a merit basis.

Perkins's resistance to the patronage demands of Congress haunted the bill. As submitted, it proposed that a Social Insurance Board be created in the Department of Labor to administer the two insurance plans and to have Hopkins's FERA administer old age relief and aid to dependent children (grants to mothers). Instead, Congress created an independent Social Security Board to administer all four programs. Though arguments could be made as to why that was sensible, Altmeyer felt that the chief reasons were a general distrust of the Department of Labor as too prolabor and a personal dislike of Perkins: "She was a woman and an articulate, intelligent woman at that . . . [and] not sufficiently amenable to patronage needs."

Altmeyer himself, as a member of the new board, soon felt the force of the problem when Vinson requested a job for a man whom Altmeyer felt was "wholly unqualified." Confronted by Vinson in a congressional corridor and asked pointblank if he would appoint the man, Altmeyer took refuge in saying that he would act "as my conscience dictated." Vinson pushed him against the wall, waved a fist in his face and shouted that he, too, had a conscience. With fifteen million unemployed the pressure for jobs was unrelenting, and like Perkins, Altmeyer discovered that most problems of patronage arose not with Farley or the Democratic National Committee but with Congress.[31]

The bill's progress in Congress was extremely slow. The press, which was favorable at first, gradually turned against it, led by the *New York Times*. In a story that it published in its Sunday editorial section it reported that the committee had slighted the advice of experts, disregarded the report of the Advisory Council and, "except for the old age assistance" part of the bill, had produced "a debacle." Perkins and Witte were presented as bumbling bureaucrats who had refused to allow the experts to prepare a better law.[32]

In Congress the major obstacle was the Senate Finance Committee, which conducted the hearings. A large number of its members were Southerners, several were extremely conservative and the chairman was Pat Harrison, who, in Witte's words, "felt rather edgewise toward Secretary Perkins." Nonetheless he was a loyal member of the administration, an able parliamentarian and on many occasions delayed or advanced a vote in order to take advantage of circumstances. If he had been "less adroit," Witte believed, the bill might not have passed.

Throughout the hearings, and the debates that followed, Perkins continued to be the bill's chief advocate. She spoke for it constantly, over the radio and before groups of all sizes, and she organized a small but influential campaign for its support.[33] The House passed its version of the bill in April, 371–33, but the lopsided majority did not truly reflect the struggle before the Ways and Means Committee. Similarly the Senate's vote in June, 77–6, was deceptive. Then the Conference Committee to reconcile the two versions was unable to agree on how to handle an amendment, and throughout July the bill seemed unlikely to pass. Eventually the Conference Committee decided to recommend it for passage without the amendment, which a special committee would present to Congress at the next session. (In fact, by then interest had waned, and the amendment was not presented.) Finally, on August 8 and 9, the House and Senate accepted the conference report, in both instances without a roll-call vote, and the long struggle ended in drabbest routine. Three days later, to celebrate the occasion, Perkins gave a small dinner for members of the Committee on Economic Security and a few congressional leaders who had worked hard for the bill's passage.[34]

On August 14 the bill went to the White House for Roosevelt to sign. As Perkins was leaving her office for the ceremony, she was called to the phone. It was her husband's nurse in New York. Wilson had disappeared. He was probably in no danger, but alone in the city he could easily become disoriented and upset. Her instinct was to rush to be with him, but on this of all days her absence at the White House would bring the press down on them. She went to the signing, posed for the usual pictures and went directly to the station. In New York with the help of others she found him, unharmed.[35]

Chapter 27

-->>><<<--

Rumsey dies. The Federal Art Project. A new building for the Department of Labor. AFL conventions. Smith and the Liberty League. Roosevelt re-elected. His demagoguery.

ONE DAY while the Committee on Economic Security was preparing its report for Roosevelt, Perkins received word from Middleburg that in the hunt that morning Mary Rumsey's horse had fallen and rolled on her. She was badly injured and while in the hospital contracted pneumonia and a month later died.[1] Perkins lost a friend and a way of life.

A frequent guest at their house that winter had been George Russell, the Irish poet, and one evening during a lively discussion of property versus personal rights he had scribbled:

> How would they think on, with what shame
> All that fierce talk of Thine and Mine,
> If the true Master made His claim
> The world he fashioned so divine.
> What could they answer did He say,
> "When did I give my world away?"[2]

Her social life was never again so casually brilliant. What she could do in conjunction with Rumsey she had neither the time nor the means to sustain alone. She soon moved from Georgetown to 2326 California Street, into the house of a couple who were in England. Perhaps because the furnishings were mostly theirs, she seemed to many friends to be more perched than settled. She still entertained on occasion, but the guests now were seldom more than two or three, old friends or office colleagues. Though she remained influential in government circles, her position as a Washington figure declined.[3]

She continued, however, to care for artistic people and their problems and within the administration supported the government's program of relief for artists. She may even have had a small but significant role, in the autumn of 1933, in starting the program.

She first heard of it from the artist George Biddle, who in May had written to Roosevelt suggesting that artists be hired to decorate the new Department of Justice building with murals. The idea had appealed to Roosevelt, but during the summer it became mired in committee reports and seemed unlikely to advance.

Meanwhile Susanna returned from visiting a friend in Vermont and began to plague Perkins about the plight of artists. Alfred Barr, the director of the Museum of Modern Art in New York, was a neighbor of Susanna's friend, Jane Perry, and he had stuffed the girls' minds with ideas of what the government could do, if only it would. Susanna in turn, with all the intensity of a convert, spouted her new knowledge to her mother. "She annoyed me so much with it," Perkins later recalled, "that I finally listened. I remember that she told me — and she must have gotten this from Barr — that the public buildings of America were dreary and gloomy and that artists could decorate their walls. Then the buildings would be interesting and cheerful and make people happy as they entered."

After brooding on the idea for several weeks Perkins promised to speak to Roosevelt. She apparently decided that the key to the plan was Morgenthau, who as Secretary of the Treasury was responsible for money spent on public buildings, for she raised the subject with Roosevelt on a day when Morgenthau had the next appointment. As she expected, Roosevelt instinctively responded to the plight of artists. He had no knowledge of art, but he saw the human waste in requiring artists to dig ditches for relief when there was artistic work that could be done.

While Perkins was fanning Roosevelt's enthusiasm for the project, Morgenthau entered. "Henry, we've got a brand-new idea," said Roosevelt brightly. "A lot of artists are out of work. You've got the Office of Procurement. Let it hire these people and put them to work at painting pictures on public buildings." Enjoying Morgenthau's surprise, Roosevelt rattled on. "There's Boulder Dam. We can cover that all over with sculptures."

"Sounds kind of crazy to me," said Morgenthau.

"Anyhow, Henry," said Roosevelt, "look into it." And Morgenthau, who took directions literally, looked into it. Soon, in conjunction with Hopkins's Civil Works Administration, what had started with Biddle emerged as a practical program.

Perkins's part in it was finished, but when the Corcoran Gallery in April and May of 1934 held an exhibition of works commissioned by the Public Works of Art Project, she not only went but later borrowed 130 of the oil paintings to decorate the long corridors of the new Department of Labor building at Fourteenth Street and Constitution Avenue.[4]

The move to the new building, in January 1935, greatly changed the daily life of the department. Just as its programs and personnel were expanding, it was able to move out of an old, dirty, cramped building into one that was clean, spacious and partly air-conditioned. It was fashionable among Democrats to deplore the design, approved by Hoover's administration, as too palatial. In fact, all the space was soon filled, and the conference rooms and auditorium were constantly used.

Naturally there were unexpected problems. From the street to Perkins's office in the southwest corner of the third floor there was a private elevator. Perkins never used it, so neither she nor her secretaries thought of it immediately when one day strange, muffled cries for help penetrated her office. Eventually they discovered Hopkins in the car, stuck between floors.[5]

She always used the main entrance and public elevators, because she wanted to be seen by as many of the department as possible and to see them. But that too had its dangers. One day a college student, hired as a messenger for the summer, turned a corner in the corridor at full speed and knocked her flat. She was badly shaken and he was appalled, but she managed to thank him as he helped her up.[6]

The move raised new problems with the press. The reporters demanded free office space in the building, and she refused it on the ground that the government should not subsidize profitable, commercial enterprises in this fashion. When, on McIntyre's advice, she finally assigned the press a room, the reporters complained that it was on the first not the third floor and demanded free telephones. She thought they ought to use the public phones in the corridor or provide their own, particularly as many of their calls were merely to arrange for lunch or dinner.

Eventually they got the phones, and meanwhile one of them had "retaliated" with a story about her washroom. The architects had put into the Secretary's office suite a small washroom and shower stall lined with beige tiles. The reporter described it as a bathroom with pink tiles, implying that it was large and designed to her personal taste. A taxpayer in a letter to the *New York Times* demanded, "Why can't Miss Perkins bathe at home?" and concluded, "Even New Dealers, who are supposed to be for the Forgotten Man, have swelled heads regarding personal perquisites."[7]

She simply could not win with the press. Over the years one of its most troublesome, and inaccurate, stories was a one-sentence filler that editors occasionally inserted to make their columns even: "Miss Frances Perkins, United States Secretary of Labor, is a collector of old patchwork quilts." Each time it appeared she would be deluged with letters, often from the desperately poor offering to sell her the family quilt, or even with quilts sent on approval. The story originated apparently in a chance remark made at a New York State Fair when she was Industrial Commissioner. In this terse form it lived for years; in January 1939 she received twenty-two letters offering her quilts.[8]

As Industrial Commissioner she had always enjoyed the State Fair; she liked the display of people's work and the visiting among friends. As Secretary of Labor she had no comparable event. The one that might have been somewhat similar, the annual AFL convention, was devoted entirely to union politics. Her role in it was small and uncongenial, and she did not perform it well.

In Roosevelt's first term she was asked each year to address the convention and in her speech would review what the administration had done for workers. The speech was thoroughly political, and Roosevelt always examined it in advance. For the 1934 convention she proposed to say, in the midst of a discussion of the need for unemployment insurance, "The immense and still inadequate relief fund which we have had to establish has been a true dole and has cost us far more and given our people far less security than the British unemployment insurance system." Roosevelt wanted the sentence deleted because "our relief is not a dole," and he disliked the comparison to the British system.[9]

Each year the convention was held in a different city, Washington, San Francisco, Atlantic City or Tampa, and always in the largest convention hall. She was an excellent speaker on the radio or in smaller auditoriums, where she could pitch her voice to the back rows without amplification. But in the large convention halls she was at a disadvantage. The amplification was unkind to her voice, and the atmosphere called for broad gestures and overstatement, which was not her style.

In addition she was not among friends. The leaders of the construction unions, who dominated the AFL's executive council, were the men least reconciled to her appointment. "We regard that as our department," said Green in 1935, and his audience understood him to mean organized labor's department. Also, at the time, her interests and theirs were different. Under the protection of the NRA codes their energies were almost entirely devoted to organizing unions. Legislation such as the Social Security Act had little interest for them. Not until almost the end of World War II would they establish social security staffs and begin to care deeply about social insurance.[10] Meanwhile her speeches on what had been accomplished were delivered to an audience whose interest was elsewhere. She did her best, but the speeches rang with a false heartiness.

At the 1935 convention at Atlantic City an event with the greatest consequences for herself and the country took place. Led by John L. Lewis, a number of union leaders proposed that the AFL attempt to organize workers in the mass production industries by industries rather than by craft. A man working with a hammer and nails in a steel mill would belong to a steel union rather than to a carpenters' union. The idea was heresy to the leaders of the construction unions, which were organized by craft. But as Lewis pointed out to the convention, the craft unions had failed to organize the mass production workers. Under the NRA the great increases in union membership had been in mining and the needle trade, both of which were organized industrially, not by craft. The delegates, however, turned down his motion by a vote of 18,024 to 10,933.

Later when Big Bill Hutcheson of the carpenters' union asked from the floor that all discussion of industrial unionism be ruled out of order, Lewis protested and walked up the aisle to confer with him. Hutcheson rose, there were angry words and suddenly Lewis hit him in the face. As the men grappled and fell to the floor, pandemonium broke out in the hall.

It was the start of a split in the labor movement, deeper and more permanent than any in the past. Out of it, by the 1936 convention, would emerge the Committee for Industrial Organization, six unions with 828,000 of the AFL's 3,308,000 members. In the next twenty years factories, the press and legislative halls would resound with strife as the two groups fought each other for the allegiance of workers. It would prove both a disaster and a spur for the union movement, and a terrible thorn in the side of the administration.

It also delayed longer than might otherwise have been the case warmer support from unions for the kind of social legislation, like a minimum wage law, that Perkins still hoped to introduce. For after the split in labor's ranks the frantic rival organizing and union-raiding took even more of the leaders' attention, and what she was attempting often seemed peripheral. Probably the opinion held of her by Jacob Potofsky, Hillman's lieutenant, was typical of most union officials. Asked if she was a good Secretary of Labor, he concluded:

> She wasn't dynamic enough to leave an imprint in my recollections . . . I want to be fair about it. I think she has made some excellent speeches when she appeared before our convention, and she was doing a certain amount of pioneering . . . But somehow you had a feeling that she was a social worker basically and not a dynamic Secretary of Labor.

Asked to state the distinction between a social worker and a labor leader, Potofsky said:

> Well, one is the do-gooder, and the other one is the more dynamic person who will make decisions and do a number of other things that will bring results directly and indirectly — through strikes and other means. The social worker would be more the soft type who would just try to appease and settle things in a nice way . . . We respected her, but there wasn't that dynamism in her that excited my imagination. My imagination was much more excited by people like Phil Murray and John L. Lewis [11]

As Roosevelt's first term drew to an end and he began to seek a second, to Perkins's distress his chief opposition within the party continued to be Al Smith; and the fighting between them became almost as brutal as between Lewis and Hutcheson. Smith, through his power in New York, blocked a scheme by which Roosevelt hoped to appoint one of his stalwarts, Edward J. Flynn, to the U.S. Senate.[12] To retaliate, Roosevelt tried to force Robert Moses from the Triborough Authority by cutting off PWA funds to build the bridge. Amid complete news coverage the plan failed, and Roosevelt was caught withholding relief funds — jobs for the unemployed and bread for the hungry — for his personal whims.

Smith thereupon joined the recently formed American Liberty League, whose main purpose was to deny Roosevelt a second term. The members were mostly rich or distinguished Democrats: John W. Davis, Governor Ritchie of Maryland, former Governor Ely of Massachusetts, John J. Raskob, Jouett Shouse and others. Davis spoke often on constitutional themes, the limitations of federal power and the rights of property and contract. "A planned economy," he warned, was "inimical to human liberty and destructive of American ideals."

The league's speakers and pamphlets suggested that Roosevelt was leading a subtle revolution to transform the government from a republican to a communist model. The climax of their campaign came five months before the convention as Smith addressed an audience of two thousand of the country's richest people gathered in the Mayflower Hotel in Washington. "There can only be one capital," he cried to the diamonds and furs. "Washington or Moscow." The speech and audience seemed out of character, and he failed to stir the country. Six months later, when the Democrats nominated Roosevelt, Smith walked out of the convention and soon after publicly announced that for President he would vote for the Republican candidate, Alfred Landon. By then his position on the national scene was that of a conservative or reactionary without any votes to command, and he was soon forgotten.

"I really don't know what happened to Al," Perkins said later. But over the years she continued to see him. He had an office in the Empire State Building, which he was managing, and when she went to New York, she often would make an appointment with him, always telling Roosevelt first to avoid any tale-bearing by others.[13]

She could not understand why Smith objected to the New Deal; so much of its social and labor legislation was only an extension of his own programs in New York. The Factory Investigating Commission had recommended a minimum wage law. Why was it wrong in the NRA? None of the common explanations of his behavior — new and richer friends, personal bitterness, natural conservatism — satisfied her.

Possibly because she had seen Smith's more liberal side when she worked for social and labor legislation in New York, she had overestimated his liberalism in other areas. He had always been fiscally conservative and strong for states rights, but in the Harding-Coolidge years these characteristics had been less important. Also, having left public office before the Depression began, he lacked the experience of one remedy after another failing for lack of scope, power or funds. And so, perhaps, was less ready to try exceptional remedies. Wagner in his visits with Smith would sometimes argue these points until both men were screaming; Perkins seems to have sought less heated subjects. Unable to fathom his problems but devoted to him, she never let too long go by without a visit or a letter.[14]

Her own position in the country at the time was high. Though the Patriotic Order Sons of America wanted her investigated for "laxity" in enforcing immigration laws, her mail showed that many people

admired her work, most of all in social security. She may have been
reluctant to be photographed or featured in news stories, but she was
well known from her radio speeches. In a secret ballot officials of the
Washington radio stations voted her one of the nation's five best
political speakers. On a basis of audience appeal and technical perfection these were, in order, Roosevelt, Hugh Johnson, Senator William
E. Borah, Henry Wallace and Perkins. She was admired for her ability
to ad-lib and because she was "logical and to the point, appealing to
men as well as women." Her mail after each speech came from all
parts of the country.

Inevitably she had a special significance for women, and in a poll of
the 1935 graduating class of the New Jersey College for Women she
was voted the woman most admired in contemporary life. Such acco-
lades perhaps meant little, but they drew attention to the Department
of Labor and helped to make it an exciting place to work. The
following year, when she delivered a radio speech from Paris, Jay
wrote the next day describing those who had listened. She added, "We
were all elated, too, over your having been voted the most prominent
woman in the world. We sort of felt it put a feather in our caps."[15]

That same year much of the excitement at the Democratic National
Convention in Philadelphia was generated by women. There was no
question that Roosevelt and Garner would be renominated, but
whereas at the Republican convention there had been only 60 women
delegates, here there were 219. In addition 302 alternates were
women. The Associated Press reported that the Women's Division
headquarters were as large as Farley's reception room combined with
Garner's headquarters and the party's publicity room. For the first
time women were included in the platform committee and eight were
appointed vice-chairmen of the national committee. Mary Dewson, in
sole charge once again of the Women's Division of the Campaign
Committee, was chiefly responsible for the women's advance, though
in Eleanor Roosevelt she had an important ally. Also Farley and the
President were sympathetic and, if pressured, generally would respond.

To keep the pressure on during the week-long convention, Dewson
started every morning with a breakfast rally for the women delegates.
At one of these Perkins received an ovation when, departing from her
prepared speech, she paid tribute to Mrs. Roosevelt:

> There is a woman Democrat who is not at this political convention be-
> cause she is detained by social conventions. But she has not shown her-
> self to be restricted by the usual conventions, realizing that she had a

great talent, and was responsible for its use on behalf of the people.

Her talent was an unusual ability and capacity to love the human race, and to hear, learn and understand its troubles, miseries, wants and aspirations.

She has therefore gone out through the length and breadth of the land, in the face of unfavorable criticism, not only to meet the people of the country personally as a friend, but also to utilize that contact, and make herself a channel through which their need, their hopes, their desire could be carried directly to places where solutions could be found to their problems. She has been gallant, courageous, intelligent and wise.

Many women in this country when they vote for Franklin D. Roosevelt will also be thinking with a choke in the throat of Eleanor Roosevelt![16]

The climax of the convention came Saturday night with Roosevelt's acceptance speech in Franklin Field. Though the weather in the early evening was bad, more than one hundred thousand gathered in the stadium to hear him, and when he arrived, in a bit of Roosevelt luck, the weather cleared. Perkins was on the speaker's platform, next to Dewson.

He began on a note of unity, thanking members of his own and other parties for their unselfish, nonpartisan efforts to overcome the Depression. "In our strength we rose together, rallied our energies together, applied the old rules of common sense, and together survived." But all was not well with the country. Though political tyranny had been defeated in 1776, economic tyranny now threatened Americans.

It was natural and perhaps human that the privileged princes of these new economic dynasties, thirsting for power, reached out for control over Government itself. They created a new despotism and wrapped it in the robes of legal sanction . . . The royalists of the economic order have conceded that political freedom was the business of the Government, but they have maintained that economic slavery was nobody's business. They granted that the Government could protect the citizen in his right to vote, but they denied that the Government could do anything to protect the citizen in his right to work and his right to live . . . These economic royalists complain that we seek to overthrow the institutions of America. What they really complain of is that we seek to take away their power.

The crowd roared its approval, but Perkins was distressed by the phrase "economic royalists." She murmured to Dewson, "This is going to be used against him." Dewson disagreed.[17]

"There is a mysterious cycle in human events," Roosevelt continued. "To some generations much is given. Of other generations much is expected. This generation of Americans has a rendezvous with destiny." A clamorous roar swept the stadium, overwhelming his final words, that along with his audience he was "enlisted for the duration of the war."

Perkins's premonition soon proved correct. It was not only the "privileged princes" of wealth who felt singled out for disapproval. Among her friends were widows living on trust funds, and she had to explain to them that they were not what Roosevelt meant by "economic royalists." They had no individual control over an industry, over thousands of jobs. They merely lived off the profits that far-sighted fathers and husbands had provided for them. Similarly, among her artistic friends were several who earned large amounts by commissions or royalties, and they too felt condemned.[18] The phrase troubled people, especially as Roosevelt always seemed willing to push its unpleasant connotations still further.

Before he arrived at Forbes Field in Pittsburgh to make a campaign speech, his advance men warmed up the crowd. State Senator Warren R. Roberts recited the names of the local rich — Mellon, Grundy, Pew and Rockefeller — waiting after each for the crowd to shout its disapproval. The next speaker was the state's governor, George H. Earle, who used the same technique. Between each name, wrote a reporter, the governor

> was forced to pause as the crowd vented its scorn on its enemies, like the whine of the hurricane before it strikes. He stood, smiling and confident, enjoying the tempest he had produced. (Again, you could almost hear the swish of the guillotine blade as it fell.)
>
> The mob was whipped into a frenzy ready for the deliverer.
>
> He entered in an open car. It might have been the chariot of a Roman Emperor.
>
> They drowned him with paeans of joy.[19]

A few days later Roosevelt delivered the campaign's concluding speech in New York, to a packed house in Madison Square Garden. The crowd was constantly on its feet, its explosive cheers punctuating the sentences. "We had to struggle with the old enemies of peace — business and financial monopoly, speculation, reckless banking, class antagonism, sectionalism, war profiteering. *They* had begun to consider the Government of the United States as a mere appendage to their own affairs. And we know now that Government by organized *money* is just as dangerous as Government by organized *mob*."

His voice became harder. "Never before in all our history have these forces been so united against one candidate as they stand today. They are unanimous in their *hate* for *me — and I welcome their hatred.*" The applause, according to the *New York Times,* came in "roars which rose and fell like the sound of waves pounding in the surf."

Dropping to a gentler tone, he continued, "I should like to have it said of my first Administration that in it the forces of selfishness and of lust for power met their *match.*" Over the cheers he went on: "I should like to have it said . . ." but excited cheers were already overpowering his words. He paused and cried, "Wait a moment!"; then, "I should like to have it said of my second Administration that in it these forces met their *master.*" The crowd's roar was like thunder, and most of what followed — statements about improving working conditions, cheaper electricity and aid to farmers — was ignored, and perhaps in the din not even heard.

Many people found his performance distressing, in particular members of the old Progressive party, some of whom had been campaigning for social justice before Roosevelt had entered the New York legislature. By and large they supported such programs as social security, relief and the TVA. But they disliked his public relations posturing, his cult of himself as a hero, his constant and divisive appeals to interest groups and his language of class warfare.[20] It was the age of dictators, and to take the public's general feelings of insecurity, distill them into a hatred and focus them on a small minority was a totalitarian technique.

Perkins knew that he was tarring that minority with too broad a brush. In New York City she belonged to the Fortnightly, a large group of the politically minded wives and sisters of the minority he condemned. At a meeting in April 1936, she had been delighted by the amount of understanding and support voiced for the New Deal policies.[21]

One day, when the opportunity offered, she told Roosevelt of her friends, also his friends, who were deeply disturbed by his phrase "economic royalists." They thought it an attack, she said, on anyone who had some money, who perhaps had worked hard, been thrifty and saved.

He laughed. "Of course, they did not know what I had in mind, but perhaps it was a lucky choice of words. Anyhow, I don't think people ought to be *too* rich."

She never knew what he meant by "too rich," and she doubted if he did. It was not important. She disliked his demagoguery, but she was sure he had no program to dispossess the rich, and she felt he was by temperament incapable of being a dictator. "Despite his shortcomings," she wrote in *The Roosevelt I Knew*, "I, on the whole, respect the methods he used to handle his problems and develop his strength."[22]

Out of loyalty to Roosevelt she seldom discussed the facets of his character she did not admire. But they were there, and even his incredible victory in the election — he carried every state except Maine and Vermont — did not stampede her judgment. She continued to be able to gaze on him with affection without sacrificing the independence of her view.

Chapter 28

-»)«<-

A president for Mount Holyoke.

IN THE YEARS 1935, 1936 and 1937 Perkins as a trustee of Mount Holyoke became embroiled in a controversy that left her badly shaken. Almost nothing she experienced in government stirred her so deeply. At issue was the presidency of Mount Holyoke. Who should succeed Miss Woolley?

In January 1901, when Perkins was in her junior year, Mary Woolley came to Mount Holyoke from the Biblical Literature Department at Wellesley. In the years following, while keeping dormitories, classrooms and money in balance, she expanded student enrollment from 550 to 1017, the faculty from 54 to 123 and the endowment from $586,723 to $4,676,887. It was a notable achievement, and in 1931 President Hoover appointed her to the American delegation — the only woman member — to the Disarmament Conference in Geneva. Though these duties took her away from the college for almost nine months, Mount Holyoke and many women's groups felt honored. Finding a successor, everyone agreed, would not be easy.

Perkins was not appointed to the trustees' Committee on the Succession to the Presidency; she was too busy, and others were more active in the field of education. But her classmate Rowena K. Keyes was one of the two women appointed to the five-member committee (later expanded to nine, five men and four women). Perkins's first intimation of trouble was a letter in January 1935 from Keyes:

This is to ask you to help me . . . I am the only one on the committee who believes heartily that if a really suitable woman for the position can be found, she should be preferred to a man. We all agree that we must first look over possibilities among both men and women, but the others either waveringly or (in the case of the very emphatic Mr. Kendall) strongly prefer the idea of a man . . . Mr. Kendall's arguments emphasize the following ideas: 1. We need some strong professors to replace the many soon to retire, and a man can get better ones, especially men. 2. A man with a nice wife would give social tone which the faculty has lacked. 3. A man can be a good pal with men outside (raising money, I suppose). Some of these seem to me to have some force, but I contend that the answer is always that for the essential ones a really *good* woman would be as efficient.[1]

Rowena Keyes was an English teacher at the Julia Richman High School in New York and, as Perkins well knew, not nearly as emphatic a personality as Henry P. Kendall. She answered at once, which was unusual for her, and at length. She was wholeheartedly for a woman, and in response to Keyes's ideas on qualifications she added some of her own: "We should try to get a woman of the world with worldly experience, and that is more often denied to . . . great scholars because of the necessity of attaching themselves so completely to academic life. I don't mean . . . that scholarship is a handicap, but merely that I don't think it should be particularly emphasized." She favored an older woman, close to fifty. About fifteen or twenty years, she thought, was as long as anyone could bring fresh ideas to the job. Also, "in this Mid-Century where women need very much to learn to respond to leadership of other women, a college aided by a vigorous and inspiring woman is one of the ways in which they can learn."[2] Part of education for girls was to see women in positions of prestige and power.

Thereafter she tried to stay abreast of events. She made a greater effort to attend trustees' meetings and placed herself firmly in the ranks of those who wanted a woman. Wellesley had recently installed as president Mildred McAfee; Mount Holyoke surely could find a woman of the same high quality. "It has to be a woman," she wrote Keyes in November. "I don't quite see the sense in conducting a college for 100 years if it and others like it don't produce at least one female capable of running such an institution."[3] The new president would be installed in 1937, a hundred years after Mary Lyon had founded the college. It was inconceivable that the centennial should be marked by a man becoming president.

But she was in Washington absorbed in her work, while the search was being conducted by others based mostly in Boston. As a result, late in May 1936 she was "simply stunned" to receive a letter from the chairman of the board, Alva Morrison, stating that the committee had unanimously decided to nominate a man for the position — Dr. Roswell G. Ham, associate professor of English at Yale. Three women had refused the committee's offer of the presidency; Ham was prepared to accept.[4] He enclosed a description of Ham. In almost the same mail came a letter from Keyes, to which she instantly replied.

> I really never for a moment doubted the ability of the Committee to find a suitable woman . . . There are so many in the academic field to whom this particular position would be a chance to demonstrate the great capacities they have . . . The job makes the person, I think, if the person is at all good, and certainly nothing about Dr. Ham seems very impressive to me. Apparently just a pleasant person with a good scholarly . . . record. I think the fact that women's colleges are more and more inviting men to teach . . . and hold executive positions without much protest from the women professors makes it even less likely that women will be able to demonstrate in advance their capacities for this kind of work.[5]

She would definitely be at South Hadley for commencement and the June 6 trustees' meeting, when the committee would present its recommendation to the full board.

Before leaving she received another startling letter, this one from Woolley and addressed to all trustees. The president reported that she had only just been informed of the committee's intention to propose a man for the presidency and "in loyalty to the cause of the advancement of women, I protest."[6]

Although the letter from Keyes seemed to warn of "a scrap" at the trustees' meeting, it seems unlikely that Perkins arrived at the college with any idea of what was about to happen or of the atmosphere in which the trustees' meeting would be conducted. The usual procedure in electing a trustee, which was being followed for the election of the president, was for the board to receive the nomination at one meeting and vote on it at the next. But in this instance the chairman had scheduled the nomination and election for the same meeting. Several trustees present complained of the haste, but their motion for delay was defeated. Six of the twenty-four were absent. Arrangements had been made for them to vote, however, and they voted, four to two, against the nomination of Ham. These votes would not have changed the outcome of the election, but it seems odd that they were solicited; under the by-laws they were void because cast by absent trustees. Were those four who voted against Ham deliberately misled? The influence of their presence and possible arguments prevented? Who distributed the newspapers' announcements of Ham's appointment before the board had voted? On the record available, a considerable array of fact and opinion, there was foul play by some of the trustees, but until their successors make the entire record available, it is best not to apportion blame. Possibly with so many participants now dead, the truth will never be known.[7]

A committee of the faculty, five women and a man, had requested to address the board. Each spoke briefly in favor of delay. In a recent poll of their colleagues on the question "Do you prefer a woman as President?" eighty-seven had answered yes; eleven no and eight, in effect, "the best person regardless of sex."

After the faculty's representatives Woolley spoke. "No expression of opinion should have greater weight than that of the faculty . . . No opportunity has been given for an alumnae vote on the question of choice between a man and a woman, but judging from the individual comments from all sections of the country, it is reasonable to assume that a large majority of alumnae prefer a woman."

Her talk had an effect, and on the insistence of Perkins and another graduate trustee she was invited to address the board again in the afternoon. This time when she finished, two men proposed delay. A graduate trustee rose, however, and began a verbal attack on Woolley. "Stop that sneering," said another woman, "and sit down!"

In the silence that followed Woolley said, "This Board of Trustees should know that the way in which this action towards the election of a man is being taken is more worthy of Hitler than of the United States of America!" She concluded by reciting calmly her judgment of what had been done to women by the methods of a few trustees, women as well as men.

Perkins escorted her home. When she left the president's house to return to the meeting, Woolley was sunk in a chair at the dining room table, her shoulders forward, her head resting on her hands. The final vote to extend an invitation to Ham was fourteen to four, two more than the necessary two thirds of the trustees present. Apparently a delegation to offer him the post was unnecessary. It had been offered and accepted even before the meeting. Of the four trustees present who voted against Ham, one was Perkins and the others were a woman and two men. Rowena Keyes, who as one of the selection committee had recommended Ham to the board, also voted for his election. Just when and why she changed her position is not known.[8]

The announcement of his appointment was released at once, throwing the alumnae gathered for commencement into successive states of disbelief, consternation and, in some cases, fury. The same passions that had marred the board meeting now flowed through the alumnae, except in almost reverse proportions. A small minority — there was

plainly a response to individual personalities as the blocs formed —
began to defend the board's majority. Another small minority moved
steadily toward action to overturn the decision. In the center, pulled
this way and that by each new fact or friend's opinion, was the
majority. "Consider for a moment," wrote one graduate to the trustees "what you ask us to believe: that the only women fitted to fill Miss
Woolley's position were the three who refused it; and that the qualifications of a man who has had no experience in such a position
transcend those of all other women candidates. It is not credible."[9]

As the summer progressed, the number of protesting letters increased, addressed to the Board of Trustees, to Perkins personally and
to Woolley. Perkins was a natural focus for them: she was on the
board, was thought to have power and had been reported widely as
voting against a man. Some newspaper editorials charged her with
inconsistency: she held a man's job on a basis of supposed merit while
wishing to deny a man a job on the basis of sex. She asked the editor
of the *Alumnae Quarterly* for space in its August issue to state her
views. The request was refused with the excuse that the editor wished
to avoid controversy. A similar request from Woolley was also refused,
but the decision later was reversed. The issue opened with an article
by Alva Morrison, chairman of the board. With bland statements
about the committee's "long and sometimes discouraging" search for a
new president, he evaded the issues, and the turmoil continued.[10]

By midautumn it was clear that the board was forcing its choice on a
disapproving president, faculty and sizable portion of alumnae. The
students marched with torches to support Ham, but as one said later,
"It was not a considered opinion, just an easy, safe way to be against
the administration and faculty."[11]

The key to the situation lay in the uncommitted alumnae. If any of
several protest groups could unearth hard evidence of deceit, then
almost certainly the alumnae would force the board to back down,
regardless of feelings or reputations. If not, the appointment, however
much regretted, would be allowed to stand. No one considered Ham
responsible for the situation; equally, no one bothered to dispute that
the board in allowing it to develop had been incompetent.

In defense of the board's majority Morrison circulated among trustees and selected alumnae excerpts from a letter of the dean of Smith
College, Marjorie Hope Nicolson, to a leader of one of the protest
groups.

As you undoubtedly know, I was one of the three women to whom
the Presidency was offered. There was absolutely nothing in my situa-

tion to prohibit my accepting the offer . . . I know nothing about the
reasons for the other two women; but I feel sure that they were free
agents as was I . . . For your committee to suggest that the invitations
were a mere empty gesture to three women who could not and would
not accept is to take away from us the pleasure and the recognition we
all must have felt from the invitation. Your committee in its zeal for the
recognition of women has gone far to suggest that at least three women
were not recognized on their merits, but were merely chosen as convenient figureheads . . . I cannot let pass this opportunity to say to you
and your committee that your trustees — men and women — put every
possible pressure upon me to accept the position. Far from feeling at
that time that they wanted a man for president, they offered every in-
ducement to secure a woman. Mr. Morrison was particularly insistent;
and had he had his way, a woman would today be the next president of
Mount Holyoke. I met many of your trustees and was impressed with
their sincerity, their ardor and their conviction. It is only just to them
that I say to your committee that your report misrepresents the attitude
of those trustees in the period in which I was in contact with them. I
found only one of them who definitely preferred a man for president;
and his reasons were sincere and cogent. I felt no prejudice in him; if
I had accepted the offer, he would have welcomed me heartily. The
others, including Mr. Morrison, all laid stress on their desire to find a
woman.[12]

But there was to be no certainty. Perkins received a letter from
Marion Park, the president of Bryn Mawr.

> I think you know all my mind on the subjects of the presidencies of the
> women's colleges and of Miss Woolley's character and position, and the
> impression made on me by Mr. Morrison and Mrs. Maguire when in the
> course of their investigations they wrote me and later visited Bryn Mawr.
> Dean Schenck of the French Department who was interviewed by them
> and later by Mr. Kendall, Mr. Cheney and Miss Keyes confirmed my
> impression that these members of the Committee at least set out to find a
> man and with the possible exception of Miss Nicolson did not recom-
> mend women who could accept the position at South Hadley.[13]

Park's letter reached the Department of Labor the day after Perkins
left for Paris to attend meetings of the International Labor Organization. Though Jay promptly forwarded it, Perkins could do nothing
about it in Europe. As one alumna later described Perkins's role in
the controversy, "She protested, but not soon enough or hard enough
to affect the outcome — in which case she might have done better not
to protest at all."[14] She had accepted the honor of election to the

board and, when the crisis arose, lacked the time to do the work. Her knowledge of her ineffectiveness only deepened her misery over what was happening.

During the winter one protesting group, the Committee of 100, in an effort to uncover facts rather than opinions to present to the alumnae, began an investigation of the board's treasurer and Finance Committee. This was off the issue and a kind of blackmail, and apparently after explosions of temper all around, everyone drew back from it.[15] The answer sought was not in open ledgers but in the minds of the committee appointed by the board to find Woolley's successor. Had its nine members conspired to lull everyone into expecting a woman and then moved so fast with a man that all protest was too late? The suspicion was never laid.

Perkins went to the Centennial in May 1937 and gave a dull speech entitled "The Role of the College Woman in the Community." Her heart was not in it. Just before going she had written her classmate Gilly Rounds:

> I wrote somebody that I would not give any money to a fund for Mount Holyoke College; that I would give my money for scholarships, fellowships and endowments to institutions that give opportunity for women . . . There are lots of first-class colleges that are offering both education and professional opportunities to women, and I think it is a mistake for the alumnae to turn their hard-earned money over to a college whose trustees have no faith in an educated woman. I have advised Betty [Mrs. Owen Roberts, a classmate] not to give . . . I also advised everybody else who asked my advice not to give . . . Thanks for the news about Rowena [apparently an academic advancement]. I am writing her a *perfunctory* letter of congratulation. She behaved like quite a rotter on the matter of the President, and I don't think she is entitled to the hearty and earnest support of her old associates.[16]

It was all very uncharacteristic, evidence that Mount Holyoke, as she had experienced it, was the fount of her identity and career. When Felix Frankfurter wrote her on her resignation as Secretary of Labor, she replied, "It is all right with me. I didn't come here to work for the press anyway. I came to work for God, F. D. R. and the millions of forgotten, plain, common working men."[17] F. D. R. came later in her life, but God, the workingmen and the sense of mission, together with its possibility for a woman, were all discovered at Mount Holyoke. The selection of Ham seemed a repudiation of all that Mary Lyon had attempted and the college attained.

She did not attend his installation; "official obligations" kept her away. In the next few years she barely managed to be civil to him. When he wrote requesting her vote to change the name of the Department of Botany to the Department of Plant Science, she refused it. "I don't think the name hampers the scholarship in that field." Plant science, she wrote, smacked of departments and courses like domestic science, which lacked toughness and discipline. "All of these have opened the door to absurdities in content of courses, to dilution of the intellectual discipline and to prevocational specialization, which I think is not only unnecessary but positively out of place in a college like Mount Holyoke which still strives to educate rather than to entertain and train."[18]

By her final meeting before leaving the board, in May 1944, she was making an effort once again to be constructive, and toward the meeting's end made a statement about what she thought the college should be doing.

> Those who come to Mount Holyoke should have a real desire for an education, and the College should not try to attract more students on a cheaper basis of intellectual activity, but fewer students for a better purpose. The drift toward a free elective sytem has run its course. The choice offered is too broad and there are too many courses, each subject split into too many sub-divisions. There should be a return to emphasis on culture as opposed to vocation. Culture may be the thing that turns out to save mankind.
>
> Those subjects should be studied which have a relation to life, such as the Classics — those subjects which discipline the mind and give us our cultural background. In the serious state of the world's moral, intellectual and spiritual development, it must be recognized that women will have to carry on the cultural life of the nation.
>
> At Mount Holyoke, as well as in other women's colleges, there should be a determination to make for a leadership devoted to a Christian point of view. Private morals and private tastes have suffered in this country, but no indoctrination is given in this subject. Theology used to be called Queen of Science. The meaning of religion is the support of faith in things which are eternal and true in life, and the religious life should be a part of the life of a community. Young people should be trained not only to think but to know the things that have been discovered by those who have devoted a lifetime to it. We should be a leader in this field still to be reopened.[19]

Her classmate Josephine Bolding had warned the trustees early in the succession controversy, "When once the precedent is established of placing a man at the head of a women's college, it is rarely broken."[20] Perkins lived to see Ham succeeded in 1957 by Richard G. Gettell (succeeded in 1969 by David B. Truman, the current president). Her relations with her classmates continued close and in her last years grew still warmer. Her relations with the college, though she continued to support it, were never again so close.

Chapter 29

→»×«←

The Public Contracts Act. Wagner's National Labor Relations Act.
"The G— D— Labor Board." Court-packing. The Fair Labor
Standards Act. Its administration.

FOR PERKINS there was little difference between Roosevelt's first and second terms; her objectives, discussed with him at the start, remained the same. There now existed relief under Hopkins, public works under Ickes and unemployment and old age insurance under the Social Security Board. And for a time under the NRA codes there had been provisions for minimum wage and maximum hours. Though the Supreme Court by its decision in the *Schechter* case had seemingly ruled the entire NRA concept unconstitutional, she did not abandon the objectives. Within a fortnight she had announced, the "people of the United States may not be expected to give up the philosophy of fair play and cooperation simply because that philosophy has not yet found adequate legal expression."[1]

The problem was pressing. Immediately after the Court's decision, for example, the War Department suspended all code restrictions in advertising for bids on supplies. Many companies construed this to be an invitation to cut prices by lowering wages and increasing hours. Roosevelt was furious with the government's purchasing agents,[2] and she kept him aroused by continually reporting instances in which manufacturers were beginning once again to sweat labor and thereby undermine the nation's recovery by reducing mass purchasing power.

Even before the *Schechter* decision Perkins had asked the department's lawyers to prepare two bills that might be used in place of the NRA's codes. One was a general bill authorizing the federal government under certain conditions to set wage and hour standards in an industry;[3] the other, a bill covering only government or public contracts, which was more likely to be constitutional. It was based on Frankfurter's suggestion that the federal government had power under the Constitution to determine the working conditions under which goods purchased were manufactured.

In one of her conferences with Roosevelt on the impending fate of the NRA she said, "Never mind, I have something up my sleeve."

"What have you got?"

"Two bills which do everything you and I think important under NRA. I have them locked in the lower left-hand drawer of my desk against an emergency."

He threw back his head and laughed. "There's New England caution for you!"

"But you and I agreed in February 1933 that putting a floor under wages and a ceiling over hours was essential," she said. "We've explored the NRA. It is fine, but if it doesn't work or breaks down, we have to be prepared for something else."

When in May 1935 the Court's decision doomed the NRA, she was ready with the public contracts bill, eventually known as the Walsh-Healey or Public Contracts Act. Though Congress did not pass it until June 1936, it was in time for Roosevelt to use in his campaign as an earnest to workers on the party's platform pledge to establish "a floor under wages and a ceiling upon hours."[4]

The act provided that goods and services bought by the government in quantities over $10,000 must be manufactured under certain conditions: an eight-hour day and forty-hour week (with overtime at higher wages), no child or convict labor, prescribed safety and health standards and a minimum wage set by the Secretary of Labor in accordance with the "prevailing minimum wage" in the particular industry or similar industries "currently operating in the locality." It was estimated that the act would apply annually to about 30 percent of the government's contracts, with a purchase value of about $400 million.[5]

It was applied slowly. It did not become effective until three months after passage, and initially Congress made no appropriation for its administration. Perkins assigned only temporary personnel to it until September 1937, when she established within the department a Public Contracts Division and persuaded L. Metcalfe Walling, director of the Rhode Island Department of Labor, to be its administrator. The delay perhaps was useful; it gave manufacturers and the government's agents time to become familiar with the concept. The idea that the government might set the conditions under which goods purchased were to be manufactured, rather than merely accepting the lowest bid, was still very strange. Also, the act for the first time introduced federal inspectors into factories.[6]

Walling started with a force of only ten field investigators, which was expanded, by the year 1940 to 1941, to forty. They inspected not on complaint but by selection, and about 50 percent of the manufacturers inspected were found to be violating the law, though often in small ways. The inspectors themselves settled cases of underpayment of wages of $50 or less, and the department settled 90 percent of all wage collection cases by correspondence, without recourse to a formal complaint and hearing. By June 30, 1941, the division had caused $449,000 to be paid to workers for violations of the overtime provision and $80,000 for violations of the minimum wage provision. The sums were small, but the fact of the government's interest loomed large.[7]

In cases where a wage determination seemed necessary, Walling as the division's administrator would start with an informal meeting of representatives of the industry and its workers to define the industry's scope and its wage structure. Then a public hearing would be held before a Public Contracts Board at which anyone could give his opinion or offer factual evidence. Finally the board would make its recommendations to the Secretary, who almost always accepted them.[8]

As far as possible, however, wage determinations were avoided. In the five years from 1937 to 1941 there were only forty-two, but some were important. The case that tested the act's validity, *Perkins* v. *Lukens Steel Company,* arose out of a determination in the steel industry. The Supreme Court ruled that the company had no standing to challenge the determination since it did not invade or threaten any of the company's legal rights. The federal government had unrestricted power to produce its own supplies, to determine with whom it would deal and to fix the terms and conditions upon which it would make purchases. Particularly satisfying to Walling and Perkins was the Court's approval of their procedures to ensure administrative due process. These had been based for the most part on the procedures used for factory inspection and regulation in New York.[9]

The act's impact was difficult to gauge. In November 1939 Walling estimated that 20 percent of those employed in manufacturing or two million workers had benefited directly. In the manufacture of tags the government rate probably had little effect because the government purchased relatively few tags. But in the aviation industry, where it was the chief client, it set the minimum rate for the entire industry. When the steel companies went on a general forty-hour week, because the continuous nature of their operations made it impossible to segregate government contract work, other industries were affected. Much of the act's impact was educational: in part because of it the idea of a basic forty-hour week, after which overtime begins, seeped into the national conscience.[10]

In the 1935 session of Congress, in which Perkins first caused the Public Contracts bill to be introduced, Senator Wagner introduced a revision of his Labor Disputes bill of 1934, only this time he consulted neither Perkins nor Roosevelt. The National Labor Relations bill was entirely Wagner's, in concept, drafting and presentation. In this period, with his legislative staff, led first by Simon H. Rifkind and then by Leon H. Keyserling, he had a small, specialized labor department of his own.

The quality of his staff's work was high, possibly the highest of any in Congress, and contributed greatly to the solidity of Wagner's reputation. In urban and industrial affairs he was the acknowledged congressional leader, and so secure was his position with the voters of New York and with union leaders and members across the country that he could, when he chose, operate quite independently of Roosevelt.[11]

He played his senatorial role with flair. "He is a widower," wrote a columnist, "lives in the most exclusive hotel in Washington, and is active socially. He is immaculately groomed at all times, is short — a bit rotund — has iron gray hair and is in perpetual good humor." He was "Bob" to friends and admirers and extremely popular with the press. Yet he was a disappointing subject for reporters. As one concluded, "Wagner does not put on a good show."

Like Perkins he relied on facts for his speeches, had no real or contrived eccentricities to exploit and refused to play to the galleries. He was not without vanity. He had left a position on the New York Supreme Court partly because "the work is accompanied by no public acclaim." But perhaps because senator was the highest post in the federal government to which he as an immigrant could aspire, in Congress he was all work — quiet, patient, persistent and effective. During Roosevelt's first two terms in his chosen field he was, as Perkins named him, "the Chief Performer on the Hill."[12]

Her relations with him and his staff were good and were strengthened by Lubin, who before becoming Commissioner of Labor Statistics had frequently worked with Wagner and Rifkind. Though she never felt the personal sympathy for Wagner that warmed her relations with Roosevelt and Smith, and although he plainly preferred women in the

home or in a chorus line, each respected the other's technical competence and good intentions.[13]

Like her Public Contracts bill Wagner's National Labor Relations
bill had a limited purpose: to strengthen the workers' rights to form
unions and to bargain collectively. The alleged constitutional sanction for the bill was that interstate commerce would then flow more
freely and abundantly. If unions could form free of opposition from
employers, there would be greater industrial peace. If any union on a
showing that it represented a majority of the workers in the plant or
industry was given the right to bargain for all the workers, that too
would improve the chances for industrial peace. Through the collective bargaining of the unions thus formed, wages would rise, mass
purchasing power increase and interstate commerce benefit. These
ends, the bill stated, are "declared to be the policy of the United
States."

To achieve them the bill proscribed certain actions as "unfair labor
practice[s] for an employer." These were simply any act that interfered with or discriminated against men trying to form a union, or any
refusal to bargain with a union representing a majority of the workers.
No unfair labor practices were listed for workers; Wagner's bill was
nakedly special-interest legislation, just as tariffs, for example, aid
certain industries but not others. The history of labor relations under
the NRA had convinced Wagner that the balance of power was still
too much in favor of employers. In the San Francisco longshoremen's
strike they had systematically fired all union organizers, hired scabs to
replace striking workers and steadfastly refused to bargain with the
union. Industrial peace, said Wagner, "rests upon freedom, not restraint; upon equality, not subservience; upon cooperation, not domination." More protection for workers was needed.[14]

The bill proposed a three-member National Labor Relations Board
to rule on workers' complaints of coercion by employers or their
refusal to bargain or to hold elections in plants to determine if a
union had enrolled a majority of the workers. It would have the
power of subpoena and direct access to the federal courts for restrain-
ing orders. More than anything else the lack of these powers of
enforcement had undermined the various boards appointed by Roosevelt to carry out the provisions of Section 7 (a).

Neither Perkins nor Roosevelt liked the bill: it was too one-sided.
Politically, for him it would be a sharp break with business. In his
program for national recovery, the NRA, which was still before the
Supreme Court, was an effort to cooperate with business; this would be

an attempt to coerce it. Philosophically, he and Perkins wanted to use the government's power to preserve a choice for the worker: to join a union or not. The bill, by allowing a majority to bargain for *all* workers in a plant or industry, might force large minorities to be represented by a union they distrusted. In most cases, because their only effective recourse would be to join it, the government's power would be used to drive some unwilling workers into unions.[15]

The majority rule also cut another way. In times past many unions representing only a minority of workers had won contracts. For this bill's purposes such unions would have no standing. Further, the proposed board would have the power to decide whether "the unit appropriate for the purposes of collective bargaining shall be the employer unit, craft unit, plant unit, or subdivision thereof." This meant that the government rather than the union would decide a union's jurisdiction. When Perkins pointed out the effect of these provisions to labor leaders, they were uninterested. Later, after the CIO had split labor's ranks, many AFL leaders bitterly regretted them.[16]

Lastly, both Perkins and Roosevelt wanted the proposed board placed in the Department of Labor. Boards established outside the executive departments often ignored the administration's general policies and sometimes even countered them. But Wagner and others insisted that the Labor Department would be considered prolabor, and the board could better maintain impartiality as an independent agency.[17]

Without any support from Roosevelt the bill passed the Senate and only when it seemed likely to pass the House did he endorse it. Even then, according to Perkins, he acted reluctantly and only to avoid a serious break with labor leaders. Eleven days later the Supreme Court delivered its decision in the *Schechter* case, and suddenly the only measure immediately available to protect the workers' right to organize was Wagner's bill. Interest in it quickened. In the House at Perkins's request an effort was made to put the board in the Labor Department but was defeated. On July 5, 1935, the National Labor Relations Act, or simply "the Wagner Act," became law.[18]

Largely because of its protection union membership began to grow rapidly, aided also by the increasing aggressiveness of workers, the competition between the CIO and AFL and the advent of World War II, when a government contract became more important to a company than resisting the organization of its workers. In the ten years from 1935 to 1945 union membership swelled from roughly 3.3 million to 14 million, or about 40 percent of the industrial working force. And the significance was greater even than the numbers. Before 1936 there were few unions in heavy industry; they were concentrated in the needle trades, coal mining, printing, public utilities, railroads and building construction. But in these years the heavy industries — steel, rubber, automobiles — were successfully invaded. Cities such as Pittsburgh, Akron and Detroit, famous as antiunion strongholds, became centers of the union movement.

The act's National Labor Relations Board in this decade held roughly twenty-four thousand elections in which six million workers voted to determine collective bargaining units. The CIO won 40 percent of the elections, the AFL 33.4 percent, independent unions 10.5 percent, and in the balance, 16.1 percent, no bargaining unit was selected. On complaints of discrimination against union members about three hundred thousand workers were reinstated with back pay of $9 million. The board, it should be remembered, had nothing to do with wages and hours, only the rights to organize and to bargain collectively.[19]

From the moment the act was passed, much of the responsibility for making it work fell on Roosevelt and Perkins. The three members of the board were to be appointed by the President with the advice and consent of the Senate. Finding the three persons was Perkins's job, and it proved extremely difficult. No one suitable wanted to serve. Finally she persuaded J. Warren Madden, the dean of the University of Pittsburgh law school, to be chairman and Edwin S. Smith and John M. Carmody to be members. Over the years there was a considerable turnover in the three positions, partly because the jobs were so thankless. Someone always was furious with the board.[20]

The situations that came before it were often very tangled. In a typical factory there might be a small AFL union of skilled workers that had a two-year contract with the employer. The CIO would organize the unskilled workers, demand an election and, with a majority of the workers enrolled, would be declared by the board to be the plant's bargaining unit. When the employer bargained with the CIO, as he was required by law to do, the AFL workers struck, alleging a violation of their contract. Angry employers and often angry workers' representatives would storm into Perkins's office demanding that she do something. In October 1938 *Fortune* reflected the feelings of many with an article entitled "The G—— D——Labor Board."[21]

Perkins's experience with the act confirmed her opinion that the board would have aroused less criticism, and done a better job, if it had been placed in the labor department. In an established organization the procedures would have been more settled and the collective experience of administration greater.[22] Though she and Roosevelt tried to instill "more statesmanship" in the board, their efforts generally were rebuffed. One instance involved the employer's right to free speech.[23]

The board in a series of decisions was ruling that an employer in person, through newspaper advertisements or by hand bills could not urge his employees to vote against a union. Given the employer's position, said the board, words even without actions could be coercive.

Roosevelt asked her to tell Madden that he must modify the rule. It was too embarrassing politically. People simply did not understand why a man, even an employer, couldn't say what he thought.

She spoke to Madden, but "he was very firm and very judicial." It was his business, he said, and not the Secretary of Labor's.

"Yes, but it's the President's business, too."

"No indeed, it is not. It is the business of the National Labor Relations Board. We are created by an act of Congress, and we are charged with doing certain things and using our judgment with regard to certain matters which are laid down in the law. The President has no right to interfere."

Unable to move Madden, she tried Edwin Smith. He had been Commissioner of Labor in Massachusetts, and she felt he would understand the problems of administration, the need to find some way of easing the law's impact without nullifying its intent. That was part of the art of government. Smith, who had been active in state Democratic politics, would understand political responsibility to the top executive. "Can't you manage it?" she said. "Can't you get the third member with you on this and raise the question?"

To her surprise Smith announced, "There are great concepts at stake. If we lose this concept that these men have a right to organize and reorganize and organize again any way they please, completely free from any influence of their employer, of public opinion or of the government, then we will have lost everything for them." His lecture continued in a style so uncharacteristic of him that she began to wonder if he was spouting someone else's ideas. The board, he said, "is absolute authority in this matter. Nobody can modify it and nobody has anything to say about it."[24]

Wagner came to see her. "Really, you shouldn't be doing this."

"I'm not doing it on my own," she said. "But as the Secretary of Labor in the President's Cabinet, it is my duty to assist him in every operation that in any way touches upon labor matters. Therefore it's my duty to convey to Madden and the Board this idea of the President's."

"But the President shouldn't have such ideas," said Wagner. "He shouldn't think about this. It is a judicial matter."

Two historians of the board, however, have stated bluntly that to consider its work primarily judicial is "a grave misconception of its functions." About 80 percent of its work was administrative: informal investigations, negotiations and settlements in the field by agents operating out of regional offices. Board members and Wagner dealing with great concepts in Washington might forget this, but people elsewhere did not; they addressed their angry letters to Roosevelt, not to Chief Justice Hughes.[25]

She tried to persuade Madden to soften other rules, but always he refused.

Roosevelt grew angry and proposed to fire him. Perkins now found herself allied with Wagner. Madden had left a good job in Pittsburgh; he deserved better than a humiliating discharge. While Roosevelt grumbled, she delayed action until a position became vacant on the Court of Claims, to which Madden was retired. Then she persuaded Harry A. Millis, chairman of the economics department at the University of Chicago, to become chairman of the board. He softened some of the rules, though not much. The board, Perkins wrote in *The Roosevelt I Knew,* "remained wholly independent" and from his point of view "wholly unpredictable."[26]

As Secretary of Labor she publicly defended the act and opposed amendments that would have introduced the government still further into union affairs. At the same time, at the AFL conventions of 1940 and 1941 she spoke pointedly about the responsibility of union leaders to their rank and file and to the public. By responsibility she meant faithful adherence to contracts, public accounting of funds, abandonment of coercive practices and peaceful adjustments of interunion differences. Failure to clean house, she warned, would inevitably bring government regulation.[27]

It arrived in 1943, over her opposition and Roosevelt's veto, with the Smith-Connally Act, and still more came in 1947, after she had left office, with the Taft-Hartley Act. She regretted the reaction and blamed the Wagner Act. It had pushed the pendulum of government favor too far toward the unions, and the reaction was correspondingly severe. Labor would have been better served, she felt, if the unions had been left more to themselves and allowed to develop more slowly.[28]

*

Shortly after Roosevelt's re-election in 1936, when the Public Contracts and Wagner acts were already operative, he asked Perkins for the second of the two bills she had been holding in reserve in case the NRA should be declared unconstitutional. She sent it over to the White House and was given to understand that it would be one of the administration's principal bills for the 1937 Congress.

This première version of the Fair Labor Standards Act contemplated a procedure under which a minimum wage board could be appointed by the Secretary of Labor whenever wages below subsistence levels were discovered in an industry. Subsistence level in an area would be determined by reference to the cost of living figures collected by the Bureau of Labor Statistics. The wage board would conduct public hearings and recommend to the Secretary of Labor an appropriate minimum wage for the industry. It also, after investigation and public hearings, might recommend a maximum work week (not including overtime), but in no event could the maximum hours be fixed at more than forty-eight a week. The bill also allowed some discretion in fixing the roles of overtime pay.

The Public Contracts Act, with its wage and hour provisions, applied only to manufacturers doing business with the government. A Fair Labor Standards Act would apply to all manufacturers whose products, by crossing state lines, entered interstate commerce. Potentially the group was much larger. But the bill's concept seemed less likely to be held constitutional because in 1918 the Supreme Court in *Hammer* v. *Dagenhart* had ruled that Congress did not have the power to ban from interstate commerce the goods of manufacturers who employed children under fourteen or permitted those from fourteen to sixteen to be employed more than eight hours a day. That decision was still controlling, and the current Court through similar decisions had recently struck down a series of New Deal measures. Whether the trend of its decisions might ever be reversed was much discussed.

Roosevelt's answer to the seemingly hostile Court was a bill touching its membership: For every justice who failed to retire from the Court within six months after reaching seventy, the President would be empowered to appoint a new justice up to a total of six. The bill's ostensible purpose was to help the Court meet its calendar; its real purpose, as everyone understood, was to ensure a favorable majority for Roosevelt. If he could appoint even two additional Justices, his legislation would probably be upheld by 6–5 decisions; and he conceivably might be able to appoint as many as six. He had not mentioned court reform in his campaign, and except for the Attorney General he did not discuss the bill with cabinet members or congressional leaders until he revealed it to them at a joint meeting on February 5, 1937. That same day, before there could be any serious discussion of it, he sent it to Congress.

The "court-packing" bill, as it was promptly called, aroused intense opposition, even among his most loyal supporters. As the fight over it developed, he sent word to Perkins that the Fair Labor Standards bill would have to be delayed.[29]

Publicly cabinet members supported Roosevelt on the Court bill or remained silent. Perkins was among the latter. At a cabinet meeting a year earlier, in which Roosevelt had talked enthusiastically of seeking a confrontation with the Court, she had advised against it. Ickes recorded in his *Diary:*

> The only member of the Cabinet who expressed a contrary view on this matter was Miss Perkins, but I suppose that was to be expected of a woman. Apparently she thinks that we ought to pussyfoot on the Supreme Court issue and not present anything, if possible, that is likely to elicit adverse opinion.[30]

Perkins read the Court's opinions carefully and in the autumn of 1936 she thought she began to detect in them a change in at least one Justice's thinking: Owen Roberts apparently was becoming more consistently liberal in his views. She knew him personally — he was married to her college classmate Elizabeth Rogers — and some of his remarks in conversation reinforced her belief.[31] If she was correct and if, as rumored, some of the more conservative Justices were about to retire, Roosevelt soon would have a clear majority on the Court. For these reasons she considered his bill to be the wrong bill at the wrong time. He also had presented it badly. He had conceived it in secrecy, introduced it like a blow in the face and based it on grounds of efficiency, which were immediately proved spurious. His methods and language suggested that he was eager not only to reform the Court but to humiliate it. Friends asked her whether Roosevelt was not seeking to change the constitutional balance between the judiciary and the executive. Was he not, perhaps, aiming at freedom from restraint, at dictatorship?

At the time presumably her answer was no. Fifteen years later in her oral history she returned to the question. The bill, she was certain, had originated with Attorney General Cummings, and she doubted whether either he or Roosevelt had understood its implications. Cummings's failure she ascribed to lack of imagination; Roosevelt's to lack of attention. Following the *Schechter* decision Cummings had pushed Roosevelt, she felt, into a position "which, if Roosevelt had been a better lawyer himself, he wouldn't have been pushed into." Once in the fight Roosevelt's vanity took over, and he was unable to admit a mistake.

After blaming Cummings, however, she added, "I don't exonerate Roosevelt in this . . . He was nudged along into a situation which I can't say he was unwilling to be put into. There was a certain willingness on his part . . ." She thought him "too lazy" to aim at dictatorship. He hated decisions "and he postponed them. He temporized with them. He gave evidences of conflict with himself, showing that when he had the power, he couldn't put on the screws." She seemed to think it a matter of temperament rather than principles, and she did not think the question foolish.[32]

She noticed that although Roosevelt was more effective than Al Smith on the large stage — campaigning across the country and over the radio — at close quarters he was often less. Those who worked with Smith invariably came to love him and to trust him. Of those who worked with Roosevelt many were thrown off by his methods and rather slippery charm. He was a more complicated man than Smith, and she recognized a dark side to his character.[33]

By May 1937 much of Roosevelt's support for the court bill had faded as the Court by several decisions upheld the kind of social and labor legislation it had previously been striking down. The first, confirming a state minimum wage law, was a 5–4 decision in which Roberts joined the former minority. The decision had been reached, though not announced, before the court bill was made known. In April the Wagner Act was upheld, and in May followed two decisions upholding the tax basis of the unemployment and old age insurance parts of the Social Security Act. When these were announced, Thomas Eliot, who had drafted the act, rushed to Perkins's office with a bottle of champagne, and, using paper cups, they celebrated.[34]

Roosevelt continued, however, to put pressure on Congress to pass his bill. In states where senators were not supporting it he held up judicial appointments. Garner, who as Vice-President was President of the Senate, was so disgusted that he withdrew to Texas in order not to have to work for the bill. Eventually, in a defeat for Roosevelt, it was recommitted to the Senate's Judiciary Committee and allowed to die. Meanwhile he had returned to the Fair Labor Standards bill partly on the assumption, which soon proved wrong, that it would be popular in Congress and would reunite a divided party.

The bill had been redrafted primarily to insert some language that might increase the likelihood of its being held constitutional and to add a child labor clause. The proposed child labor amendment to the Constitution authorizing Congress to act in that field was still eight states short of the thirty-six needed for adoption, and a clause in the bill might achieve much the same end. Goods of manufacturers employing children under sixteen or working older children more than eight hours a day would be barred from interstate commerce.[35]

On May 24, 1937, Roosevelt sent the bill to Congress, where it was introduced in both the House and the Senate. "A self-supporting and self-respecting democracy," he said in his message, "can plead no justification for the existence of child labor, no economic reason for chiseling workers' wages or stretching workers' hours." This redrafted version of the bill would enable Congress to set statutory minimum wages and maximum hours with a five-member Fair Labor Standards Board empowered to raise the standards.

In the hearings Perkins testified against statutory standards set by Congress. She favored action by wage boards that could "go into the thing more in detail over a longer period of time" and set a minimum wage for each industry as evidence indicated. She continually argued for administrative flexibility, but on that point almost everyone was against her. Green for the AFL, while faintly endorsing the bill, expressed labor's dogma that "the minimum tends to become the maximum"; southern legislators feared that the South's low wage scale would be raised, depriving the region of an advantage over the North; and there was some distrust or dislike of her personally. Senator Harrison remarked, "If the measure is passed, that Madam is going to have a good deal to say in its administration. And to be perfectly frank . . . that is one among many reasons that I am not for this legislation." Another, which he discussed at length, was her "shoes" speech of four years earlier. When Congress adjourned in August the bill had passed the Senate but was still pending in the House.[36]

Roosevelt, however, was not quitting. He had pledged action, and the country was in a recession. Figures from the Bureau of Labor Statistics revealed that the downward spiral had begun again. Without the NRA codes most workers had no protection. He called the Congress back into special session in November: "The exploitation of child labor and the undercutting of wages and the stretching of the hours of the poorest paid workers in periods of business recession has a serious effect on buying power."

Meanwhile the AFL in its October convention had repudiated its former lukewarm endorsement of the bill, and several of its more conservative leaders publicly condemned it. Wages should be left to collective bargaining. The only labor leader wholeheartedly for it was Hillman, whose clothing workers were constantly threatened by competition from sweatshops. But again Congress adjourned without passing the bill.

Roosevelt still would not give up. When Congress reconvened in January 1938, he urged immediate action on the wage and hour bill: "We are seeking only, of course, to end starvation wages and intolerable hours. More desirable wages are, and should continue to be, the product of collective bargaining."

What with changes to meet objections, the bill had grown bulky and now stretched to almost forty printed pages. "Can't it be boiled down to two?" Roosevelt asked Perkins. He thought part of its difficulty was simply its length.[37]

She gave it to Gerard D. Reilly, the current Solicitor of Labor, and he compressed the gist of it into ten pages. This version was then introduced by Mary T. Norton, chairman of the House Labor Committee. The AFL was still opposed, and through a congressman submitted a very restricted bill, which divided support. A labor leader explained the federation's stand to Reilly: "If you give them something for nothing, they won't join the union."[38]

As the debate progressed, various amendments and substitute bills were offered, and at one moment the AFL and the National Association of Manufacturers were united in opposition. On May 3, however, Senator Claude Pepper of Florida, who had supported the administration's efforts, won a spectacular primary victory in a campaign that had turned on the bill. When Lister Hill of Alabama also won a primary election on the same issue, many legislators heard the voice of the people. The long struggle was at an end. The following month the House and Senate agreed on a compromise bill, which Roosevelt signed on June 25.

"Everybody claimed credit for it," wrote Perkins in *The Roosevelt I Knew*. "The AFL said it was their bill and their contribution. The CIO claimed full credit for its passage. I cannot remember whether the President and I claimed credit, but we always thought we had done it. Certainly he gave a sigh of relief as he signed it. 'That's that,' he said."[39]

Reilly, who saw them working together on it, was impressed by their relationship. She could reach him by phone whenever she wanted, and "on some of his suggestions that she didn't think were sound she didn't have to say much before he'd back off." Roosevelt handled the political end of it, but she "kept it in the boiler" of his mind and "was a good deal of the push behind it."[40]

The act as finally passed allowed less administrative discretion than she would have liked. Congress set the basic standards: a minimum wage of $.25 an hour rising to $.40 in seven years, and a forty-four-hour week dropping to forty in three years. A Wage and Hour Division was created within the Department of Labor, to be headed by an administrator appointed by the President. The administrator was authorized to appoint committees for individual industries, but these could recommend an increase in wages only up to $.40. More important, the administrator had full power to investigate any manufacturer and to enforce standards through the courts.

The Bureau of Labor Statistics estimated that in September 1938, when the act became operative, roughly eleven million workers and 250,000 employers were covered. Of the workers, about 300,000 receiving less than $.25 an hour and 1,384,000 working more than forty-four hours a week would be affected immediately. A year later, when the minimum wage rose to $.30 and the maximum hours dropped to forty-two, an additional three million workers would benefit.[41]

For the post of administrator Perkins submitted a list of four or five persons from which Roosevelt selected Elmer F. Andrews, who had succeeded Perkins as Industrial Commissioner of New York.[42] It seemed a logical choice, but Andrews, with the aid of an assistant, Paul Sifton, and a personal secretary, Eugenia Pope, began to make an empire of the division. He planned personnel, publicity and legal offices, insulated from the department, and he told the Acting Director of the Budget, Daniel W. Bell, that he would present the division's budget directly, not through the department. On October 10 he delivered a memorandum on his position to Perkins.

Within three days she had arranged a meeting of herself, Reilly and Bell with Roosevelt, and the four reviewed the legal basis for channels of authority. "That is enough," said Roosevelt, "the division is in the Department of Labor."

Perkins went down a list of the division's functions: accounts, audits, purchase of supplies, guard duties, assignment of rooms and so on. To all of them Roosevelt said, "Same thing; the Department of Labor will provide all that. Life is too short to have rival organizations."

She emerged with a memorandum for Andrews describing exactly how the division was to operate.[43] But egged on by Sifton and Pope,

Andrews continued to dream of empire. He squandered money, apparently expecting to be given more by special appropriation.

By the summer of 1939 Perkins was anxiously searching for a successor. Both she and Roosevelt hoped Andrews would resign, and she attempted to find another place for him in the government. But he either did not or would not understand. So, one day after Perkins returned from a meeting with Roosevelt, she asked Gladys Burch, one of her secretaries, to summon Andrews, Sifton and Pope. As they arrived, Burch showed each into Perkins's office, and each emerged red in the face and fired.[44] The division finished out its fiscal year in a kind of receivership, and a second administrator was appointed, Colonel Philip B. Fleming of the Army Corps of Engineers.

Recommending him to Roosevelt, Perkins said:

> I don't think anyone else can straighten it out so well. The advantage of a military man is that he has a safe secure post to which to return and no one, therefore, can ruin him by threats, political or otherwise. Moreover, he is trained to administration and executive work and isn't emotional about it. He is accustomed to getting things done the quickest and cheapest way. Col. Fleming, in addition to the usual military equipment, is a man who has had excellent experience and an excellent record in civilian administrative work. He got on well with labor and with contractors. He is not a vain or dominant personality but just hews the way to the line and gets the work done. He was always very cooperative in taking the suggestions of civilians who had particular experience. In addition, a military man is under your authority. *You can tell him to take the job and he has to.*[45]

The last was important because the civilians she had approached had all refused the job.

The appointment of a military man to a civilian post aroused some letters of protest,[46] but Fleming soon demonstrated his good qualities and the division began to function smoothly. Though the great majority of employers voluntarily complied with the act's provisions, a constant stream of complaints flowed into the division. An inspection and enforcement system was slowly built, and in 1941, with roughly twelve hundred inspectors in the field, the division made 48,449 investigations resulting in approximately 19,000 establishments paying $10 million in additional wages to their employees.

Lubin, watching from the Bureau of Labor Statistics, was impressed. The act was "probably the most vital social legislation" in the country's history, both in "its philosophical basis" and in numbers affected:

"every worker in interstate commerce in the United States." Its enforcement was very open to bribery or inefficiency, but because of the procedures Perkins and her subordinates instituted, and because of the kind of people they were, there was none. In such circumstances to put "into effect a nationwide system of administration" without a scandal somewhere was "proof that she was a genius in a way."[47]

The act was particularly dear to all those who had worked for so many years to abolish child labor. The Supreme Court, in holding it constitutional in 1941,[48] simply overruled *Hammer* v. *Dagenhart,* and the movement for a constitutional amendment to end child labor came to a halt. To be sure, the act did not cover children in agriculture, and those of migratory workers in particular were still exploited. But throughout the land factory employment of children under sixteen was prohibited. In changing people's attitudes to make that achievement possible no individual had a greater part than Perkins's former chief, Florence Kelley.

The act was the last of Roosevelt's New Deal measures. Congress had grown increasingly hostile to both his methods and programs. Because of the court-packing scheme a bill to reorganize the executive branch of the government was attacked as another of his efforts to extend his power. It barely passed the Senate — even Wagner voted against it — and it failed in the House, 204–196, with 108 Democrats deserting their party. It was the worst defeat Roosevelt was ever to suffer in the House, and he compounded the disaster the following fall by intervening in local elections in an attempt to purge the party of those who opposed him. His action suggested to many a totalitarian view of the party and was resented. In every case but one the voters rejected his candidate, and he was widely considered to have put himself on the wrong side of a moral question.[49]

The record on his programs was mixed. In 1939, after six years of farm subsidies to limit production, the cotton carryover was three million bales greater than in 1932. "Only the war rescued the New Deal farm program from disaster," concluded one historian.[50] In the industrial area the NRA, public works and relief had not prevented another depression. Between September 1937 and April 1938 four million workers were laid off and the steel industry lost two thirds of its business. Much remedial legislation, however, was not yet fully effective. Unions were still organizing under the Wagner Act. The old age and unemployment insurance plans of the Social Security Act were only just beginning to make payments, and the wage and hour standards of the Public Contracts and Fair Labor Standards acts to be enforced. The country seemed prepared to wait, perhaps because the Republicans offered nothing better. Though the Congress would not pass any more of Roosevelt's reforming legislation, neither would it allow what had been passed to be repealed or even greatly amended. The New Deal ended without having solved the country's economic problems, yet some of its achievements, particularly in the field of labor, seemed solid.

Chapter 30

Susanna married. Al Smith. Whispers about Perkins. The sit-down strike. A public relations disaster. Falsehood and truth of her relations with communists.

EARLY IN Susanna's junior year she left Bryn Mawr to work in Washington as an assistant at the Phillips Gallery. Though her mother disagreed, Susanna thought the experience would be more worthwhile than finishing the college course. At the same time she became engaged to David M. Hare, a son of one of Perkins's friends on the board of the Maternity Center Association in New York.

Perkins liked Hare, but she opposed the engagement, though not to the point of alienating the couple. After much persuasion, she announced it on December 30, 1936, Susanna's twentieth birthday. Hare was three months younger, and Perkins's chief objection to their marriage was their youth, not only in years but, as it seemed to her, in maturity.

She did her best to delay the wedding and succeeded for a year, but after Susanna came of age Perkins capitulated and began to make plans. Although their apartment at 1239 Madison Avenue was sublet, they were still a New York family, and the service would be at the Church of the Resurrection with a reception afterward at the Cosmopolitan Club. Wilson, who had left the sanitarium the year before and was boarding in North Carolina, would give the bride away in the church and act as host at the reception. Unlike their own wedding, Susanna's would be entirely conventional.

Perkins enjoyed keeping track of the lists of guests — who responded, who sent gifts, who planned to attend — and the event, on March 12, 1938, moved her. She wrote a friend: "Getting a daughter married takes one back to the beginnings of things, and old forgotten,

half-completed affections, intentions, purposes, hopes and disappointments. The emotional upheaval that mothers go through on such an
occasion is undoubtedly a helpful purge, but it is extremely difficult."

Susanna and her husband soon left for Santa Fe, where he started to
prepare a book of photographs on the Pueblo Indians. Perkins on
cross-country trips managed occasionally to stop for a night's visit and
in her letters mixed news of the CIO and AFL with descriptions of
hats and suits and admonitions to "look after your hair."[1]

That year, or perhaps the next, before going to New York one day
Perkins mentioned to Roosevelt that she had an appointment with Al
Smith. Usually Roosevelt would ask her to relay some polite but
empty message, but this time he said, "You're very good, aren't you.
You keep up that friendship."

"I'm fond of him," she said. "I don't like him to feel he's got no
friends of the old crowd."

"Tell Al," said Roosevelt, "that I think a lot of him and am grateful
to him. I wish he would come down and see me. I honestly mean
that."

When she repeated his words in New York, Smith said, "Humph,
you think he means it?"

She did.

"I might come," said Smith. "When do you think I should?"

They talked a bit more, and soon after, on his way south, Smith
called at the White House.

Though Roosevelt's secretary, Grace Tully, thought a warm relationship was re-established, to Perkins the breach was only "nearly
healed." Amenities between the men had been restored, but Roosevelt
found no use for Smith's talents. The waste saddened her: "It was just
one of those historical tragedies."[2]

This period of Susanna's marriage and Smith's meeting with Roosevelt coincided with one of the most difficult for Perkins in her government work. She often had been attacked for the legislation she
advanced, and the fact did not disturb her: the criticism generally was
honest difference of opinion. In the years 1937 through 1939, however,
she was subjected in addition to something quite different. First in a
whispering campaign and then openly in Congress she was accused of
disloyalty to the country. Not only were an increasing number of
speeches, cartoons and editorials directed more at her person than her

programs, but eventually in Congress a resolution was introduced to impeach her. In the twelve years of Roosevelt's administration that happened to no other member of his cabinet.

The whispering campaign seems to have begun on the West Coast during the 1934 longshoremen's strike. Stories began to circulate that she was somehow related to the union leader, Harry Bridges, and was protecting him. As the stories slipped eastward, they took on an anti-Semitic cast. Her sister, Ethel, was visited one day in Worcester by a genealogist who, in tracing the Perkins line back to the seventeenth-century immigrants from England and Scotland, asked about the possibility of a Jewish ancestor. No chance, said Ethel, for in those days "there were no Jews in New England."[3]

It seems likely that the genealogist was a man named Robert Edward Edmondson, or someone working for him, for the following year, 1935, he published a sheet alleging that Roosevelt's administration was dominated by Jews, many of whom were foreign-born and communists. The six most important were shown on a Star of David; they were Frankfurter, Brandeis, Baruch, Henry Morgenthau, Jr., Edward A. Filene and Perkins. There was also a description of her taken from a pamphlet of the American Vigilante Intelligence Federation of Chicago: "Frances Perkins says she was born in Boston April 10, 1882. There is no record of her birth in the Boston Register for 1882. Her husband's name is given as Paul Wilson. The only record of marriage of Paul Wilson was at Newton, Mass., in 1910, when he married Matilda *Watski*. Secretary Perkins gave Emma Goldman (*Communist*) permission to enter the U.S. *Secretary Perkins has decreased alien deportation 60 percent.*"[4]

The sheet was widely distributed and stirred up considerable animosity against the six, particularly Perkins, either because she was the best known or the most vulnerable. It was true that as the Secretary in charge of immigration she had admitted Emma Goldman to the country on a three-month visitor's permit. But "Red Emma" by 1934 had the unique distinction of having been deported from the Soviet Union as well as the United States, and was living in Canada, old, harmless and longing to visit home. It was also true, or almost, that Perkins had cut the deportation of aliens by 60 (actually 55) percent, and there were reasons. But those who wrote angry or inquiring letters cared little about these decisions. What aroused them was the idea of deception: Why didn't she live with her husband or use his name? Why couldn't she produce evidence of her birth?

The marriage at Newton, of course, was not hers. Nevertheless for several years the clerk there confirmed to those who wrote that a marriage was recorded in 1910 between a Paul Wilson and a Matilda Watski. As soon as he realized the reason for the inquiries, he asked Perkins for the facts of her marriage so that he could disseminate them. But meanwhile, as the campaign of vilification began to concentrate on Perkins, there was a large mailing by someone in which people were sent copies of the Wilson-Watski record as evidence that she was not the person she claimed.[5]

Her birth date was the worst confusion. She *did* say that she was born in 1882, when in fact she was born in 1880. She made the mistake at least as early as 1923 on a Mount Holyoke alumnae form and in the years thereafter apparently came to believe it. But because it was the wrong year, the Boston Registrar reported to all who inquired, including her, that there was no record of her birth in 1882. She tried to establish the year through the testimony of her mother's surviving friends, but their memories were failing and they could not agree on the winter of her mother's pregnancy.[6]

In April 1936, therefore, after a Mrs. Wagner MacMillan of New York had asked in a pleasant letter for the facts of her ancestry, birth and marriage, Perkins wrote a detailed reply, which she also offered to newspapers. After describing her family's origins she said, "There were no Jews in my ancestry. If I were a Jew, I would make no secret of it. On the contrary I would be proud to acknowledge it." And she gave the wrong birth date and correct marriage record.

A number of newspapers published the statement, but it appeared only once and not everyone saw it. Friends still occasionally sent her evidence that an organized whispering campaign continued, but probably its stew of half-truths and lies would have cooled if events had not heightened the feelings of insecurity and fear throughout the country.[7]

In September 1937 an economic recession began that carried through 1937 and 1938 and eased significantly only as the country started to supply the Allies in World War II. It was not so severe as the 1930–1933 Depression — there were only ten million unemployed, and many alleviating programs existed — but Roosevelt had boasted in 1935 that "we are coming ba k soundly because we planned it that way." Now the boast proved hollow, and discontent rose.[8]

At the same time the number of strikes greatly increased, and Perkins, whose department included the Conciliation Bureau, was personally involved in several of the most prolonged and difficult.

There was another on the West Coast, with Bridges again the leader, but this time there was far less violence and bombast. More important for the country, labor and Perkins was the "sit-down" strike of a relatively small union, the United Automobile Workers, against the huge General Motors Corporation.

The strike began in the final days of 1936, when workers in several plants put down their tools but refused to leave the buildings. The immediate cause varied from plant to plant, but the underlying reason was a refusal by General Motors to bargain with the union. The United Automobile Workers had about thirty thousand members, less than a fifth of the work force but enough to stop production if the men were not replaced by scabs. Until the previous summer the union had been a member of the AFL. Now it was independent, though closely backed by the CIO.

The sit-down technique had been used before, chiefly by rubber workers in Akron, Ohio, but never on such a scale. It caught the country's imagination, and everyone's attention focused on Flint, Michigan, where the strike centered. The company cut off the heat in the plants — the outdoor temperature was 16° — but the workers stayed in; food and other supplies were brought regularly through the picket line. When the police tried to rush Fisher Body Plant No. 2, they were met by a hail of coffee mugs, pop bottles and automobile hinges. When they returned with tear gas, the strikers held them off with water from the plant's fire hoses.

Discipline within the plants was good, and though a great deal of glass was shattered, none of the company's machinery was damaged. But the potential for damage was enormous, and the strikers clearly were guilty of trespass and perhaps something more since they were denying the owners of the machinery the use of it. When the police failed, many people felt the state militia should be mobilized to clear the plants. But the state's governor, Frank Murphy, delayed because, as he said one night on the phone to Perkins, "My God, it seems an awful thing to shoot people for — trespass!"[9]

Murphy as governor was the key to the situation; Perkins was peripheral. He in Michigan sought to maintain order in the automobile towns while trying to persuade the men to leave the plants; she in Washington tried to bring together company and union officials to negotiate an agreement. But Alfred P. Sloan, Jr., the president of General Motors, though sometimes seeming to be ready to meet with union leaders, always in the end refused, insisting that the plants be evacuated first. After one of his on-again-off-again performances

Perkins in a press conference denounced his attitude as "legalistic." He was like a homeowner, she said, who refuses to talk to the owner of a car parked on the front lawn until it has been removed. "It is a procedure which brings no one any good."

"The American people," she went on, "do not expect them [General Motors] to sulk in their tents because they feel that the sit-down strike is illegal. There was a time when picketing was considered illegal and before that strikes of any kind were illegal. The legality of the sit-down strike has yet to be determined."

A reporter thereupon asked if the sit-down strike was not generally regarded as illegal. She said that she had never heard of any court decision on the point. "Anyway it is of no importance whether the sit-down strikes are legal as compared to the obligation to discuss the problem." Prosecuting workers for trespass, as Sloan proposed, would never resolve their grievances; agreeing to allow them to bargain collectively would instantly end the trespass. The problem, as she perceived it, required a moral choice between conflicting values. "This is a challenge which the American people must face if General Motors will not."

Asked if she spoke for the President, she said no, and perhaps for that reason her remarks for the most part were buried toward the end of the reporters' stories. But after a day or two they reappeared in editorials and columns all over the country, quoted generally with indignation. She was portrayed as having said that until the Supreme Court declared otherwise the sit-down technique was legal and that the rights of private property came second to the right of workers to organize. Protests poured in on the department. It was the "shoes" speech again, only now on a national scale. Among her talents, unquestionably, was an ability to make a statement that could be turned against her.[10]

Within the cabinet her position cost her the admiration of Garner. At a meeting in which she was summing up the situation and possible lines of action, Garner burst out, "You don't think the employers should meet them while they're in the factories, do you?"

"Yes," she said. "I see no reason why they shouldn't. What good is it going to do to stick it out? If people are mad, they'll get madder. If they've made a mistake, they'll make the mistake harder. I think the employers could solve this right now by meeting a committee. If it goes on much longer, they may not be able to solve it just by meeting a committee."

But to Garner, the workers had seized the company's property, and the law was clear. Why didn't Murphy do something? Why didn't he get out the troops and enforce the law?

Perkins interrupted to say, "They have not attempted to assert ownership, and no court of law would hold that they have seized it, because they have done nothing with it. It's still there. It's unharmed, and it's there."

Though Garner leaned forward, his hand behind his ear, she felt he was too angry to hear what she had said.

"These labor men have been too much coddled," he said. "Hugh Johnson had these same automobile workers right here in the White House a couple of years ago. They were laying down the law as to what they would have. Hugh Johnson encouraged them. The Secretary of Labor here deals with them when they come in. Now she says they're not going to be pushed out of these factories."

"I did not say they're not going to be pushed out. If Governor Murphy wants to push them out, he can. It's up to him."

"Why doesn't he do it? Why don't you tell him to do it?"

Roosevelt interposed. "We haven't yet reached the point where the President tells the governors of sovereign states what they are to do inside their own states." He made a few jokes and promised Garner that, if Murphy asked for help, "you can be sure we'll give it to him." But Garner was not convinced and later broke with Roosevelt over the issue.[11]

Perkins and Roosevelt, on the other hand, had a perfect understanding on it. He was constantly urged to act, or at the very least to say that the strike was reprehensible, and in resisting the pressure he more than once called on her firmness of mind.

"They're pressing me very hard," he said one time. "What do you think I'd better do?"

"Well, do you think it's reprehensible?"

"Yes, I do. Don't you?"

"Yes, I do. But after you've said it's reprehensible, then what? What do we do next? I'll say to you that it's reprehensible, and you say to me that its reprehensible. So long as we say it only to each other, we don't have to do anything. But once you say it to the country, then what?"

"That's what I don't know."

"My advice is not to call it intolerable or reprehensible or illegal unless we have a course of action to put immediately into effect."

He agreed. Though the strike had now idled 112,000 of the company's 170,000 workers, it was still a local not a national disorder, and it was still for the governor not the President to determine whether order was being kept and how best to ensure it.

"What *can* we do?" Roosevelt asked.

"Well, what do you think we can do?" And then to tease him — "You're a lawyer."

"Ah," he said, "stop your nonsense."[12]

They made no pronouncements. She sent McGrady to Michigan to assist Murphy while she kept trying to bring the company and labor leaders together in Washington. Every night by phone she and Murphy would go over the day's events and coordinate their next efforts. Meanwhile John L. Lewis made a tactical blunder by publicly calling on Roosevelt to support labor now in payment for labor's support in the previous election; but Lewis was rescued by Sloan, who angered just as many people by walking out of a meeting Perkins had arranged.

Following that incident she had another public relations disaster. A young reporter for the *New York Times,* Cyrus Sulzberger, called her at home at 2:00 A.M. She was asleep but, awakened by the phone's ring and fearing some disaster in the family, she picked it up. When she discovered who was calling, because he was an acquaintance of Susanna's and someone she knew socially, she did not cut him off. In his story the next day he stated:

> When reached after midnight, Miss Perkins seemed almost on the verge of tears. The strain of her constant endeavors, day and night for two weeks, to get the two sides together at a conference table was apparent in her voice as she exclaimed: "It seems that all of my work has gone to waste." At first reluctant to talk . . .[13]

The damage was in the tears. No one who knew her believed them for a moment. But the story was widely copied, one of its variations being that she had run to Roosevelt beseeching him to punish Sloan, and Roosevelt had said, "Frances, this is a democracy, not a tyranny of tears." To millions who did not know her, she was presented as a weak woman overwhelmed by the pressures of her job.

Some observers thought differently. After the strike was settled in February, with General Motors agreeing to recognize the union, Jay Franklin, a columnist for the Washington *Star* wrote:

> No man could have done any better in acting as a buffer between President Roosevelt and the sit-down strike situation in which his foes desired to entangle him. There were a few spiteful passages in the press about

her "tearfulness" and "feminine hysteria," but the little lady with the three-cornered hat took them calmly while the ball — or buck — passed to Gov. Frank Murphy . . . This was partly because it would have been disastrous for Mr. Roosevelt to appear to pay his political debt to Mr. Lewis at the point of a pistol . . . This, I submit, is shrewd if thankless politics.[14]

Though the American people accepted the moral "challenge" on just the terms in which she put it, deciding again and again in these five years that the rights of labor should prevail over those of property, the cost to her was very great. Few in the country understood the limitations of her office. Sloan could walk out on a negotiation because she had no power to compel him to attend. Similarly she had no power to force a worker to pick up his tools and work. Yet with the country in bad times many of the strikes, especially the jurisdictional battles between the AFL and CIO, often seemed as much against the community as against an industry, and understandably the ordinary citizen vented his frustration on the Secretary of Labor.

Her own frustration led her into two uncharacteristic acts. On the phone, within the hearing of others, she lost her temper at Sloan when he backed out of a meeting after giving his word to come. Under the torrent of her anger he kept repeating, "You can't talk like that to me! I'm worth seventy million dollars, and I made it all myself." Morally, she told him, he was "a rotter," and forecast that his money would not save his soul.

She also wrote Senator Joseph Robinson and asked that Congress grant her subpoena powers so that she could force Sloan or Lewis to attend meetings with their records. Her proposal was favored by CIO leaders but opposed by the AFL, and nothing came of it. Congress was not about to grant her the power, and she herself in a day or two may have regretted the request. It seems to have been the only time, not in war, that she thought the government should have more than informal, noncompulsory powers to mediate strikes.[15]

Her efforts to keep the government and forcible solutions out of labor affairs was little appreciated by labor leaders. Guiding a nation through a period of enormous union expansion and greatly increased collective bargaining would have been job enough for any Secretary, but in addition she faced a split in labor's ranks. Though she favored neither side, both criticized her, and because the CIO at the time was the more radical and successful, the complaints of the more conservative AFL were particularly bitter and damaging. Farley reported to Roosevelt after the party's 1938 election defeats:

The supposed influence of the CIO on the administration — I say "supposed" advisedly — had its effect, particularly with farmers and small businessmen. This is especially so because Frances Perkins is being tied in with the CIO. I don't say she is, but that's the impression.[16]

The mere size and speed of union growth was enough to alarm many people. Less than a month after a union had organized the largest company of the automobile industry, another led by Lewis and Philip Murray won recognition without a strike from the United States Steel Corporation. In 1935 unions of all kinds had an estimated 3,300,000 members; in 1938, 5,944,000; in 1941, 8,339,000; and the unions themselves often claimed figures considerably higher.[17] For membership drives in the big industries Lewis and the unions of the CIO pledged funds in the millions of dollars. A new power had emerged in the country, and to those who were not its beneficiaries it often seemed hostile. Senator Wagner could talk of industrial democracy, but the man in the street could see that the leadership never changed. Lewis, Hillman or Hutcheson were never voted out of office. They were monarchs for life, ruthless and absolute; and dominating them all was Lewis, the most ruthless and absolute, who according to the AFL was favored by Perkins.

Lewis's rise to the top of his union in the 1920s had been accompanied by violence and fraud, and in the 1930s he sometimes employed communists as organizers or in executive positions. Foremost among these was Lee Pressman, general counsel for the CIO. Perkins did not know Pressman's private beliefs or purposes, but through direct observation and reports of her staff she became aware that he constantly defeated efforts to heal the labor split or even to advance wage and hour programs. Often at the end of a conference, just as everyone seemed ready to agree, he would throw the subject into new turmoil with fresh objections. From her experience in New York she recognized this as a communist technique, and one day after listening to Clara Beyer describe a conference that, because of Pressman, had ended in frustration she called Lewis. Bluntly stating the problem, she said that in the future Pressman would not be accepted at the department as a representative of the CIO; Lewis would have to send someone else.

He did. But the country knew nothing of her action. Many continued to believe that she favored the CIO and, along with it, communists. To those who knew her such suspicions were as ridiculous as the charge of tears. But to millions of others they seemed confirmed when she was accused of delaying the deportation of Harry Bridges. Suddenly in mid-1938 the slanders of the whispering campaign and her alleged softness for communist labor leaders began to reinforce each other and build from an annoyance and slight injustice into a movement to drive her from office.[18]

Chapter 31

→≫≪←

She postpones the Bridges hearing. Resolution of impeachment against her. The Landis report on Bridges. The whispers grow louder.

As AN AFTERMATH of the 1934 longshoremen's strike Perkins had requested immigration officers in San Francisco to investigate Bridges, and they had reported that they could find no evidence "that he is in any manner connected with the Communist Party or with any radical organization." The San Francisco police, after an independent investigation, agreed, and the FBI had no evidence against him. But he was an alien, with left-wing views, and the leader of an important union. He was constantly accused of communism, frequently in conjunction with a demand that Perkins deport him.[1]

In the autumn of 1937 some evidence appeared. Four witnesses stated under oath to immigration officials in Portland and Seattle that in those cities they had seen Bridges participating in Communist party activities. Perkins sent the department's Solicitor, Gerard Reilly, to the coast to investigate. The evidence was unusual for a deportation case: none of it came from statements made by Bridges or from documents he had prepared or circulated. Nevertheless, on March 2, 1937, the department began a proceeding to deport him and scheduled the hearing for April 25.[2]

But on April 6 the Fifth Circuit Court of Appeals in New Orleans announced its decision in *Kessler* v. *Strecker,* a similar case. Strecker, a Polish immigrant, had joined the Communit party in 1932, quit it after three and a half months and then applied for citizenship. But as soon as he admitted membership in the party, which he freely did, the immigration bureau stopped his naturalization proceedings and began to deport him. The Fifth Circuit Court, to which he appealed, ruled in his favor, refusing "to assume and find that merely because Strecker joined the Communit Party of America, he is an advocate of, or belongs to, a party which advocates the overthrow by force and violence of the government of the United States."[3]

The decision, when taken with two recent rulings by the U.S. Supreme Court, created a conflict in the administration of the deportation laws, and the Solicitor General on Perkins's request agreed to appeal it. As it stood, it cut to the heart of the Bridges case, for other than his unproved membership in the party the department had no evidence that he advocated the violent overthrow of the government. If the Supreme Court, which agreed to hear the *Strecker* case, upheld it, then whether the department succeeded or failed in proving Bridges a member of the Communist party was immaterial: without something more he could not be deported. So Perkins, after consulting with Reilly, postponed the Bridges hearing, as well as eleven other deportation cases similarly affected, until after the Supreme Court ruled in the *Strecker* case.[4]

In such circumstances this was common administrative practice; it prevented the waste of money on useless litigation. And it did not alter the rights of either the country or Bridges. If in the meantime he acted in some way to overthrow the government by force, on the new evidence he could be arrested, tried and, if found guilty, deported.

Later one of her critics suggested that she should have proceeded with the Bridges hearing "as though the *Strecker* case had not occurred," and if the decision went against him, let him appeal it. She felt that such a course was "an abuse of executive power." Any administrative official had a duty to take judicial decisions into account "before subjecting other persons to punitive action and putting them to the expense of a prolonged and hard defense of themselves."[5]

Because the postponement was routine and seemed so obviously sensible, she foresaw no danger in it. But the following month the House of Representatives approved the formation of a special Committee on Un-American Activities, with Congressman Martin Dies as chairman. Dies was a tall, blond Texan who had come to the House in 1931 and not yet made a name for himself. He held the committee's first public hearing in mid-August, and in the first few days witnesses branded as communist no less than 640 organizations, 483 newspapers and 280 labor unions. Dies was on the front page of almost every newspaper, and their readers, many of them still victims of bad times, seemed almost ready to believe in conspiracies against them.[6]

On August 30 Dies released an open letter to the papers stating that "deportation proceedings against Harry Bridges should be commenced without any further delay." In her reply Perkins pointed out that a proceeding was under way and the hearing merely postponed. She also described the *Strecker* case and its bearing on the Bridges hearing. The following week Dies announced he would call her to testify, and two days later he told reporters during an interview in Texas that, if she did not enforce the law under which Bridges was "clearly deportable," she might face a move to impeach her. She repeated the reasons for postponing the hearing and refused to comment on the threat of impeachment.[7]

In October two men connected with the California American Legion testified that Bridges was a communist and protected by Perkins. That same week Dies, in two national broadcasts, one from the Herald Tribune Forum, told the country: "The responsibility for this breakdown in the enforcement of our deportation laws must be laid at the door of Secretary Perkins. The conclusion is inescapable that Secretary Perkins and those around her are not in sympathy with the deportation of radical aliens." He did not mention the *Strecker* case.[8]

Dies also aimed his attack at Frank Murphy, who that November faced a gubernatorial election. Though both were Democrats, just before the election Dies called to testify before the committee a number of Michigan officials, including several police officers, a Republican judge and a Republican city manager. They accused Murphy of working with communist elements in the CIO and of "treasonable action" in not using force to dislodge sit-down strikers. Murphy was anxious to rebut the testimony, but the party strategists thought it would be more effective for Roosevelt to reply. In a carefully worded statement at a press conference he defended Murphy's handling of the strike and regretted that the committee should allow itself to be used "in a flagrantly unfair and un-American attempt to influence an election." Dies retorted that the President had been "wholly misinformed" and was relying on "prejudiced sources." Murphy lost a close election and at first blamed the defeat on his actions in the sit-down strike. Later, and perhaps more accurately, he ascribed it to the recession.[9]

Dies continued to attack Perkins. In another letter released to the press he accused her of deceiving the Department of Justice about the facts of the *Strecker* case with the aim of delaying the Bridges hearing. A month later he urged Ickes, Hopkins and Perkins to resign.

The truth is that Secretary Ickes, like Mr. Hopkins and Secretary Perkins, brought with him to Washington when he was appointed Secretary his many radical associates. These satellites range in political insanity from Socialist to Communist . . . [and] have been consistent in only one line of policy — the promotion of class hatred. While they fortunately comprise only a small minority . . . they have succeeded in spreading their venom far beyond the confines of their departments and in securing passage of certain legislation bearing their unmistakable imprint.[10]

As Perkins had advanced more legislation than either Ickes or Hopkins, the attack seemed aimed primarily at her. Finally, as the new year began, the committee filed its report, stating among other charges that there was no justification for not proceeding with the Bridges hearing.

Over a period of four months Perkins found the unremitting attack hard to withstand. She began to receive hate mail, all of it depressing, most of it repetitive. An Irish-American in Massachusetts was one of the few to defame her with style:

One charge is admitted. Your shame for your husband. Perhaps you have good reason. No decent Jewess would refuse to bear her husband's name, and a faithful Irish wife would scorn to masquerade as a maiden. Why do you love to deceive . . . In the seclusion of your boudoir — free from the irritating influence of your lawful husband — sipping your cognac and sucking your cigaret, you may calmly reflect on the harm that your injudicious acts have done to President Roosevelt.[11]

Often more moving was the anguish of those who wrote because they saw falsehood squeezing out truth. Though the California American Legion denied that the witnesses spoke on its behalf and suggested their testimony had been bought by the Industrial Association of San Francisco, the story was obliterated by the space given to the Legion's national commander, who joined Dies in his charges. A telegram of protest at Dies's speech was read at the Forum the next day, but the applause it elicited did not erase the impact of his national broadcast. Now whenever Perkins addressed groups on social security or wage and hours, almost always someone would rise to say, "This may be off the subject, but are you a communist?" Or, perhaps, "Is your daughter married to Harry Bridges?"[12]

She reminded herself constantly of her grandmother's rule that in the midst of social disaster "all are to act as though nothing had happened." She continued to meet every engagement and struggled to treat the most personal questions as reasonable. Almost invariably, if she could manage a soft, attentive answer, her questioner's antagonism would drain away. But she found the self-control exhausting and increasingly turned to prayer to achieve it.[13]

Disarming critics one at a time, however, was no answer when Dies was raising them up by the thousands, and she looked for ways to reach more people. An old acquaintance, Wilfrid Parsons, dean of the Graduate School at Georgetown University, lectured frequently in the Midwest and requested a statement on the law and facts of the Bridges case that he could use in answering questions. With Reilly's aid she prepared one and sent it not only to Parsons but to friends, correspondents and newspaper editors. In it she included — rare for her — a short, personal credo:

> Communism has no place in American life. I am not an expert on Communist teaching but the concept of a dictatorship of the proletariat and the contempt for Christian ethics, concepts reiterated in communist literature, are contrary to all my beliefs, devoted as I have always been to the democratic principles of our own Constitution with the protection of individual liberties, freedom of religious worship and freedom of speech guaranteed to us by the Bill of Rights.[14]

At the same time she prepared a more detailed statement for Mary T. Norton, chairman of the House Committee on Labor, to present to the House in answer to the criticism of the Dies Committee's report. At her own expense she had three thousand copies of it reprinted from the *Congressional Record* and distributed to influential people. But whatever good this might have accomplished was negated on January 24, when a Republican member of the Dies Committee, Congressman J. Parnell Thomas of New Jersey, introduced a resolution demanding the impeachment of Perkins, Reilly and James L. Houghteling, Commissioner of the Immigration and Naturalization Service. The other two were her subordinates, and the charge — conspiracy to avoid enforcing the deportation laws against Harry Bridges — was primarily directed at her. Across the country in the following days the headlines referred to the Perkins impeachment.[15]

She never saw any reason why Thomas rather than Dies introduced the resolution and always considered Dies its architect. She saw no rational explanation for his motives, "nothing to be gained for him politically." He was a congressman from Texas, and "they didn't know me or care there." She was not concerned with oil or agriculture, and few of his constituents with shipping and commerce. The seeming irrationality of the attack made it only the more disturbing.[16]

To her, he seemed obsessed with the idea of aliens' being undesirable. In 1932 he began his career in Congress with a bill (passed only by the House) to expel all alien communists. Then in 1935 he made several alarming speeches about the number of aliens entering the country illegally, reporting, for example, that one hundred thousand seamen each year jumped ship to enter when in fact the number for 1933 was 664 and for 1934, 972. And apparently by a mistake in calculation he branded five hundred thousand children born of Mexican parents in the United States, and therefore citizens, as illegal entries.[17]

Perkins wondered if the obsession was in some way an aftereffect of the Civil War. "He came, after all, from that part of Texas which was part of the deep South, and he cherished those strange hidden feelings of the defeated . . . He was a grandson of the Civil War, had grown up in a small town, haunted by poverty and by social changes that had come about by the abolition of slavery." She and the recent immigrants, perhaps, represented the triumphant, industrial North against which he subconsciously struck back.[18]

In this period, when almost every morning the papers reported some new condemnation of her and even the *New York Times* abandoned her with an ambiguous editorial, she felt like some early Christian in an arena where a faceless leader called to the crowd, "Shall we save this woman? Or ruin her?" Thumbs up, thumbs down — on a gust of passion. To preserve her balance she started going to church every morning.

Her temptation, she realized, was not so much a retreat from principle as a search for shelter in the name of privacy. She must face the crowd, keep on with her schedule and take all questions from the floor. "You do what is your duty to do and then act as if nothing had happened, as grandmother said."[19]

One morning at the church Father Plank asked how she was getting on. At first she said merely, "Very well, thank you"; but then, "I find that I have great difficulty in praying for my enemies. It is very difficult. I grow confused."

He suggested that she pray for them not by name but by categories; first large, then small. "Pray for those persons who despitefully use all other persons; pray for those who bear false witness against all other persons. Then pray for those who despitefully use you or bear false witness against you. Don't mention them by name. Eventually you will move over that point and be able to do it."

She worked at it. When Dies went to the hospital for several weeks, she sent him a book and a personal note hoping he would soon recover. His wife wrote a graceful note in reply.[20]

The Judiciary Committee seemed to her to move very slowly on the resolution. She was impatient to testify, but the chairman, Hatton M. Sumners, seemed reluctant to call her. He was a Texan, an expert on constitutional law and a specialist on impeachments. The only picture in his office was a portrait of Benjamin F. Butler because Butler had managed the impeachment of Andrew Johnson in 1868. In 1933 and 1936 Sumners had managed the impeachment of two federal judges, one of whom had been removed.[21]

She phoned him several times about an appearance and gradually realized that as a chivalrous Southerner he was trying to save her, a woman, from an unpleasant experience. But she wanted a public hearing. Sumners consulted the committee, and to her disappointment it voted to have the hearing private. When she told Reilly, he laughed. "They don't want to face it themselves. They know there's nothing to this." He thought her unnecessarily nervous about the outcome: She was right in her position, and the Democrats controlled both the committee and the House.[22]

Among others with that view was Eleanor Roosevelt, who replied to Anne Hyde Choate, a friend she shared with Perkins:

> I realize that Frances is under a strain and I wish she could take it more lightly because I think it is purely a political attack, and in public life women must accustom themselves to these things in the way that men have. She is alone, and I wish that the women of this country, particularly in the organizations, could be induced to realize what the true story is on the whole Bridges question. Frances has it and, it seems to me, could give it to the heads of the different organizations if they would only request it. Then their backing could be made vocal. At present, many of the Federation of Women's Clubs members, who met down here, are down on Frances because they believe she is a Communist. When you get women started along those lines they are like sheep. They think Dies is doing a wonderful job and do not realize that he is doing something to make himself personally popular with the sole idea of being candidate for President, and Miss Perkins was the easiest victim.
>
> Frances does not know how to get on with newspaper people and neither has she a secretary who can do it.[23]

There was much truth in what Reilly and Mrs. Roosevelt had to say, but neither was at the center of the storm. Conceivably politics could work against Perkins. Sumners had been an outstanding opponent of Roosevelt's court-packing scheme, and Congress at the moment would pass nothing the President proposed and seemed tired of him personally. History was filled with instances in which a king in order to survive had sacrificed an unpopular minister. Perkins had no illusions that Roosevelt, if hard-pressed, would act differently.

On February 8 she appeared as a voluntary witness before the House Judiciary Committee. Reilly had testified the previous day and reported that it was a rather impromptu affair. But for her — "the accused," in the language of the proceeding — reporters, photographers and the full committee of twenty-five were present.

When she and Reilly, who, as the department's Solicitor, was allowed to accompany her, were summoned from the committee's anteroom, they were led through a door that opened into a long room. At its end was a curved, paneled dais, on which sat the committee members at their desks, watching her as she entered. Below them was a large table for reporters and photographers and a smaller one for herself and Reilly. As her eye took in the distance to it, she turned to him and said, "Do you remember the priest who walked beside Joan of Arc when she went to the stake?" The picture had flashed in her mind, and in that moment she felt she had experienced a mystical communion. "I had a sense of the Lord Jesus looking after his people and walking beside them."

Reilly, who was taller, looked down and said softly, "Oh, yes." For the first time he understood how profoundly shaken she had been by the experience of the previous six months.

The moment passed, and when Reilly smiled she felt they were "like children whispering in school" and with lighter heart moved forward to the table.

Sumners conducted the hearing with great formality. Before it began he permitted her to distribute copies of her prepared statement to reporters and allowed photographers to take her picture; then he declared the hearing closed and dismissed the press. He began with an opening statement to which she replied, thanking the committee for its courtesy and sense of fair play in allowing her to appear. She asked if she could read her statement on the background of the Bridges case. Permission was granted, and though once or twice a committee member started to interrupt, Sumners always ruled that the question must wait until she had finished.

She had prepared the statement with Reilly and Wyzanski, who had come down from Boston. It was divided into three parts: a brief summary of the principles by which she tried to enforce the immigration laws, and analyses of the *Bridges* and the *Strecker* cases. Much of what she had to say was technical, the reason the committee had allowed Reilly to accompany her. But she never needed to refer to him. She had been well coached and had it all in mind.

The question period was difficult. Almost every member had at least one query, and some were couched in terms that indicated shaking wrath and indignation. Sumners, however, never let the hearing slip from his control. He folded his fingers in front of him and contemplated procedure. He wrinkled his brow and considered requests to be heard. He raised his hand slightly, and a member would lower his voice.

But the tension was there. Congressman Earl C. Michener of Michigan began softly: "You have given us reasons that I am bound to respect, and I recognize that you had an administrative right to do this, but you don't convince me" — by now he was shouting — "that Bridges is not an undesirable alien and should not be out of the country."

She had not tried to convince him that Bridges was not an undesirable alien; she had tried only to explain and defend the procedure by which that fact might be established. But the distinction had not penetrated his mind. With him she had failed. It seemed to her "a long, long morning."

After she was dismissed Sumner's secretary asked her to wait in the anteroom: the chairman wished to speak with her. When he came out he complimented her on a good appearance; he had not expected her to be able to think so quickly or reply in such detail without constantly having to refer to papers or counsel. She thanked him, but refrained from adding that she did not always do as well in her own department, where there was less pressure.[24]

After that there was nothing to do but wait. The committee continued to hear testimony, to examine the report of the Dies Committee and to study the relevant judicial cases. Finally on March 24 it reported to the House that "after careful consideration of all the evidence in this case, this Committee is unanimous in its opinion that sufficient facts have not been presented or adduced to warrant the interposition of the constitutional powers of impeachment by the House." On receiving this unanimous report the House tabled the resolution.

Unfortunately for Perkins the action was taken on an undebated motion without any mention of her name, and many reporters and probably even members of the House missed the significance of what was happening. Still worse for Perkins, the ten Republican members of the Judiciary Committee had added to its report a short section entitled "Additional Views." The section was not a minority report, because "we are in general agreement with the findings." Yet the ten members felt that Perkins and her subordinates had been "lenient and indulgent to Harry Bridges," and they concluded, "This course of conduct which we condemn does not justify impeachment, but it does call for the official and public disapproval of this Committee."[25]

They never carried their call for "official and public disapproval" any further, so that it remained in a gray area of something more than a private statement and something less than an official demand for censure, which might have been debated and upheld or defeated. On its face it was not a vote of the House or even of a committee of the House. Yet five days later Congressman Thomas, in a national broadcast on the *Bridges* case, without once referring to the committee's unanimous opinion that there were no grounds for impeachment, quoted only the "Additional Views," of which he said: "This strong censure was made by a large membership of the Judiciary Committee of the House of Representatives, and by this censure the official acts of the Secretary of Labor and her associates have at least been officially condemned." From that lie Perkins was never able wholly to clear her name.

Two days later Senator James M. Mead of New York, on the same radio network at approximately the same hour, tried to counter the slander. But he was a colorless man; the facts he had to present were complicated and his speech was not very effective.[26] The real trouble lay in the press. As soon as the committee's report was announced, it no longer saw any story in the Perkins impeachment resolution. Congressman John A. Martin of Colorado, who had never met Perkins and had no appointees in her department, took the floor of the House to say:

> After months of nation-wide publicizing of unjust and unfounded charges against a public official, the final result is heralded by no blare of trumpets and is scarcely brought to the notice of the public, which for months and months has been fed with promises that a national public official would be shown to have been guilty of high crimes and misdemeanors . . . it is to be regretted that a case which thundered so long in the index has dwindled to almost less than a whisper in the text . . . The word "finis" has been written on this abortive attempt to destroy the first woman ever to have the honor of a seat in the Cabinet. In the interest of history the report should be exhumed from the tomb of a million forgotten documents and embalmed in the imperishable pages of the *Congressional Record*. I deem it a privilege to perform that service.

Though he failed to stir much editorial interest, Perkins was grateful and had twenty-five thousand copies of the speech printed. The Democratic National Committee distributed twenty thousand, the

Department of Labor the rest. After the six-month barrage of adverse publicity it was not much, but it was something.[27]

Meanwhile, on April 17, the Supreme Court decided the *Strecker* case, ruling that an alien who, after entering the country, becomes a member of the Communist party "is not deportable on that ground if at the time of his arrest his membership has ceased." It was clear now what the immigration bureau must prove in order to find Bridges deportable: not only that he was a member of the Communit party at some time but that he was a member on March 2, 1938, when the warrant for his arrest was issued.[28]

To conduct the hearing Perkins sought someone distinguished, without ties to labor or industry on the West Coast or to the labor department, and she selected James M. Landis, dean of the Harvard Law School, who was a specialist in administrative law. Before going to the law school he had been chairman for two years of the Securities and Exchange Commission. Everyone, even the California Hearst papers, seemed to think she had chosen well.

Throughout the summer Landis presided over a well-publicized hearing on Angel Island in San Francisco Bay. The government called thirty-two witnesses, the defense twenty-nine. The transcript ran to 7724 pages, and after the hearing both sides submitted briefs. Finally, on December 28, 1939, Landis delivered his report to Perkins. He found Bridges's aims to be "energetically radical" but "proof fails to establish that the methods he seeks to realize them are other than those that the framework of democratic and constitutional government permits." Then, after a discussion of the judicial definition of "affiliation," he concluded, "the evidence therefore establishes neither that Harry R. Bridges is a member of nor affiliated with the Communist party of the United States of America."

As soon as the report in summary was published, Landis began to receive hate mail. "I had thousands of letters on the decision, maybe one in fifty complimenting me on it. The other forty-nine would be addressed to: 'You Goddamned Communist,' 'You Goddamned Jew,' 'You so-and-so' et cetera." Two years later, after the United States had entered the war, he was appointed director of the Office of Civilian Defense. In Congress Representative Leland M. Ford of California commented that although "Dean Landis is very 'pink,' you would have a hard time getting somebody 'pinker,' but, nevertheless, we might have had Madam Perkins, with whose record you are all familiar."[29]

Even after the immigration bureau was shifted from the labor department to the Department of Justice, in June 1940, she was never altogether free of the Bridges case, and its effects sometimes overtook her in curious places. In April 1941 the director of the FBI, J. Edgar Hoover, testified to the House Appropriations Committee that "practically the whole [Landis] proceeding was not conducted in accordance with law because none of the witnesses were really testifying under a legally administered oath." Hoover was wholly mistaken, but perhaps not everyone realized that when they saw him quoted and his view adopted by the committee in its report to the House. The following month at a convention of the Episcopal diocese of New York, late on the final day, when most of the delegates had left, a resolution was suddenly introduced and passed calling for her resignation. In the newspapers it became the day's major story about the convention. Its immediate cause was the wave of strikes in defense industries, and it asked the President to appoint a new Secretary of "unimpeachable patriotism."[30]

Later that year the myth of her Russian-Jewish ancestry again began to circulate. A magazine, the *American Citizen,* published it, and the editor, Dewey McKinley Taft, refused to publish a retraction though furnished with a correct genealogy and marriage record. A congressman, Phillip A. Bennett of Missouri, referred in a speech in the House to "Frances (Wadski) Perkins" and to "her native Russia." The whispering campaign had now been dignified by congressional statement. Bennett went on to say, "Surrounded as she is by Communists . . ." She asked him to correct the *Congressional Record* because it "becomes history," and he did amend what he had said about her birth, marriage and "native Russia," but not about her being "surrounded by Communists."[31]

Unquestionably the continuing suspicion and slander decreased her effectiveness. Possibly by 1940 no legislation with which she was closely associated, such as unemployment insurance or the minimum wage law, could have passed Congress. Yet, paradoxically, the more she was abused the greater seemed to grow the number of those who admired her. They were in all walks of life, of varying amounts of education and in every section of the country. In their letters they often revealed a clear perception of what she was trying to achieve and of her difficulties. In the midst of the impeachment proceeding a Mrs. Arthur Solbert wrote and in a sentence perfectly stated the ideal for which Perkins strove:

> I am not a worker but a farmer housewife, but I realize that our problems are identical; namely, a decent standard of living, an education for

our children and a little leisure time to study, reflect and express those things that make Life a little fuller, richer and better for all of us.

By others her integrity was increasingly appreciated. On her resignation in 1945 the secretary-treasurer of the Sailor's Union of the Pacific, Harry Lundeberg, wrote:

Our organization is sorry to see you leave the Department of Labor. We feel that during your regime you acted squarely and did everything possible to lighten the burden of working people.

"Acted squarely." That was how she tried to act with all persons, high or low, left or right. There was never a change of course simply because the wind of favor had shifted.

Fortunately for her, she was by nature optimistic. Her reaction to the following was quite predictable. From Albert Lea, Minnesota, P. J. McMullan wrote:

I have been asked to talk before a group of men in about two weeks and assigned the subject "Why Perkins should be ousted from the cabinet." Just why I was given this subject I do not know. I have never been able to make myself think this is the thing to do, and I have decided to double cross them and give a speech that will convince them that you are the most valuable member of the cabinet.

I lack some data for this speech and while I do not expect that you have the time to send this, will you be so kind as to have some member of your force forward some material that I can use and believe me it will be greatly appreciated.

Off went the material. As long as others continued the battle with such good cheer, she had not time for sulking.[32]

Chapter 32

-->>|<<--

The National Conferences for Labor Legislation and the Division of Labor Standards. The International Labor Organization. Roosevelt and the 1940 convention. Her reasons against and for a third term. She attempts to resign.

A PROJECT Perkins had discussed with Roosevelt before accepting her appointment was the use of the federal labor department to stimulate those of the states. Workmen's compensation was gradually spreading by imitation from state to state, and she believed that if a forum could be established in which the state officials and labor leaders could meet and exchange ideas, other insurance, safety and inspection programs might also pass from state to state. Roosevelt was interested but promised no help; she would have to invent and promote the program herself.

In the spring of 1933 she was too busy with other matters — immigration, the CCC, NRA — to do more than mention the idea occasionally. But in July she and her staff organized a conference in Washington for members of the sixteen state labor boards that had minimum wage laws to administer. Seven of the states had only just passed such laws, and for many of the administrators the problems were new and the kind of help that the federal department could give in preparing and using data was often not understood.[1]

Spurred by the meeting's success, she and the staff planned a two-day National Conference for Labor Legislation to meet in Washington on February 14 and 15, 1934. To it she invited the governor of each state or his representative, the Commissioner of Labor of every state having such an officer and, from each state, one or more representatives of organized labor, as designated by the governor. Delegates from thirty-nine states attended.

In her welcoming address she said that the problems of labor legislation were now national as well as state concerns, but "the fundamental power to make regulations with regard to welfare . . . lies with the sovereign states." She offered them the use of the federal department's resources for research and reporting. "In no sense of the word is the Department of Labor attempting to dictate what the States should be doing."[2]

Though that theme was repeated throughout the conference, for the first day at least the delegates remained unconvinced. They were defensive about themselves and their states, cautious in their remarks from the floor and ready to protest at the first sign of anything being put over on them. Perkins was not surprised. As New York's Industrial Commissioner she had considered the federal department remote, ill informed and interfering.[3]

She was surprised, however, by a failure in the program. She had asked Paul Douglas, still a university professor, and Abraham Epstein, an expert on unemployment insurance, to speak on various approaches to it. Douglas gave a brilliant account of why he favored a state-fund system of unemployment reserves (the Ohio plan) over the individual plant-fund system (the Wisconsin plan). But when he finished and Perkins asked for some delegate to state the opposite view, there was silence. An air of resentment hung over the hall.

Epstein's speech, though equally good, also ended badly. He analyzed reasons why the New York State Federation of Labor had switched its support from the plant- to the state-fund system, and before he had finished he sounded as if he were officially announcing the federation's views. Its president, Emanuel Koveleski, rose and said bluntly, "Mr. Epstein does not speak for the New York State Federation of Labor. We appreciate his cooperation, but he does not represent us or speak for us."

The experts had failed to gauge the audience and evidently struck many delegates as academic and arrogant. Perkins, too, had misjudged in thinking that any state or labor official, with more on his mind than employment insurance, would publicly question Douglas or Epstein. The experts were too articulate. Besides, Douglas's analysis, in its academic purity, was somewhat irrelevant to the battle over unemployment reserves as it was fought in a state legislature. More than the abstract virtues of either system, what counted were the personalities, power and prestige of the backers.[4]

But in other respects the conference seemed worthwhile, and Perkins decided to repeat it another year, though without such high-powered speakers. She would emphasize the practical problems of the state labor departments. To that end in mid-July she created within the department a Division of Labor Standards. It was "to be a service agency, a rallying point for the efforts of interested persons and organizations, state departments of labor and federal government departments." A primary aim would be to promote uniformity of labor legislation among the states.[5]

Though Clara Beyer of the Children's Bureau did most of the preliminary work in setting up the division, Perkins told her that as the first woman Secretary she could not appoint a woman to lead it. She would bring down Verne A. Zimmer from New York, for twenty-one years a member of the state's Labor Department and an expert on workmen's compensation. He would have the title and salary of director and work mostly on compensation. Beyer, as assistant director, would work on everything but compensation and have almost equal power and prestige.[6]

The man and woman thus yoked together were very different. Zimmer, short, chunky and with close-cropped white hair, was an average man: he had humane feelings, was easy-tempered and proud of his children. Beyond high school, he had little formal education; most of what he knew he had learned on the job. Beyer, on the other hand, was a trained economist, a graduate of the University of California who had taught at Bryn Mawr. She also had served as secretary of the minimum wage board in the District of Columbia and executive secretary of the New York Consumers' League. She had a husband, three sons and energy enough for an additional full-time job. Where Zimmer was lovable, Beyer was, or could be, formidable. Yet between them they made Perkins's unlikely arrangement succeed — in large part, said Beyer later, because Zimmer "was pleasant and really interested in workmen's compensation."[7]

They began by establishing contact with state labor law administrators, state union leaders and groups and individuals working for labor legislation. In January and March of 1935 they held regional conferences in Nashville and San Francisco on labor law and social security problems. Martin P. Durkin, the Director of Labor in Illinois, who had attended the Nashville conference as an auditor, promptly asked his governor to "advise Miss Perkins to the effect that a similar regional conference could be held with profit to all concerned in this state."

Before another regional conference was held, however, a second national conference met in October 1935 in Asheville, North Carolina.

The state's Commissioner of Labor, A. L. Fletcher, in thanking Perkins for her presence and "evident sincerity of purpose," touched on a difficulty of labor in the South.

I think that some of your assistants, and possibly you, as well, are at a loss to understand the attitude of organized labor toward the Department of Labor in this state. Accustomed to looking upon elected Labor leaders as spokesmen for Labor in most states, you think the same situation exists in North Carolina. I would like to talk to you about this sometime, and I do invite you to look into the situation from an unbiased point of view. All of our industrialists and all of our politicians can't be wrong.

Throughout most of the South, because of an unhappy history of labor relations, there was a strong sense of organized labor against all and all against organized labor. A function of these conferences, consciously undertaken, was to ease that confrontation by bringing union and government officials together in circumstances in which they would not be opposed but working for a common end, such as better safety standards. But any easing of tension, as Fletcher's remarks suggested, would take time.

He went on, however, to say, "You are the first Secretary of Labor to show an interest in state departments of labor. No secretary before you has made any effort to build them up or solve their problems. For this I am truly grateful." Other delegates agreed, for they passed a resolution suggesting that the national conferences be held annually. Twenty months had intervened between the first and second; only thirteen between the second and third. When the delegates gathered in Washington, D.C., on November 9, 1936, five states that at the time of the first conference had lacked departments of labor now had them: Alabama, Kentucky, Louisiana, Rhode Island and South Carolina. All had been assisted in setting up their administrations by the Division of Labor Standards.

In several other states existing departments were reorganized. Joseph M. Tone, Connecticut's Commissioner of Labor, a machinist by trade and former union official, confessed to Zimmer that at the first conference he had understood hardly a word. But he was interested, and also a politician of great charm. He persuaded talented people to join his department, and he and they turned it into one of the country's best. "He could sell anything," said Beyer, "even ideas to a legislature, so great was his charm."[8]

Sometimes there were failures. Alerted by Beyer, Perkins one day

called the Labor Commissioner of Tennessee, W. E. Jacobs, to warn
him of a bill in the state legislature that would strip his department of
much of its power. Jacobs replied that he was getting old and no
longer cared. He had taken the post "to sit in the shade." Unfortunately for the workers of Tennessee, the agency that received the
power had little interest in exercising it.[9]

Besides help with administrative and legislative problems the division also began to offer the states a Factory Inspectors' Training
Course. The first was held in 1936 at the Johns Hopkins University in
Baltimore with inspectors drawn from four states. The second, in
1937, at the request of Durkin was at the University of Illinois in
Chicago. Inspectors from five states attended, and subsequently more
courses were offered throughout the country. Usually they ran two
weeks and were aimed principally at the detection, appraisal and
correction of health and safety hazards. There were lectures on types
of hazards — fire, machine and disease — and others with such titles as
"How to Approach Management in Promoting Continuing Health
and Safety Programs." There were inspections of factories with discussions afterward of how and what to report, and there was even an
occasional demonstration. In the Illinois course the lecture on dust
explosions was punctuated by a blast arranged by the local office of the
United States Department of Agriculture. By 1938 the division had
developed and published a factory inspector's manual adapted to the
needs of any state.

Later it also produced a suggested "standard of qualifications for
factory inspectors," which it mailed to all governors and state labor
administrators. The response was not always reported, but in Alabama the governor picked up the phone and conferred with his labor
commissioner: they adopted the standards. Then they asked the division to send a safety engineer to help them train a new group of
inspectors.

Because of Zimmer's extraordinary grasp of workmen's compensation, it was a major subject at every conference. By June 1939 more
than half the country's workers were still not covered by state programs, and only twenty-two states offered insurance against occupational disease. Zimmer constantly tried to cajole and lead state
administrators into improving their programs, and sought to help
them achieve uniformity between states so that employers in one were
not more taxed than those in another.

In the field of occupational disease, among the division's projects
were two that attracted national attention. The first, in 1936, fol-

lowed "the Gauley Bridge disaster." Workers drilling a tunnel through rock for a hydroelectric power plant at Gauley Bridge, West Virginia, inhaled the dust and began to complain of shortness of breath; eventually 1500 were disabled and 476 died. The dust, it was discovered, had a high silica content, which scarred the lung tissues. The division organized a series of conferences on silicosis that brought together medical experts and engineering technicians, and they were able to devise methods to reduce the danger. These were relayed to the states and also projected in a film, *Stop Silicosis,* which was shown to workers and employers all over the country.

The other project was a report in 1940 by Dr. Alice Hamilton, medical adviser of the division's Safety and Health Unit, on the dangers of chemical poisoning in the making of rayon. The industry fought the investigation even to the extent, in one case, of attempting to mislead the investigating team by switching cadavers, but fortunately only one of the two had an appendectomy scar. The report confirmed what workers claimed — exposure to carbon disulphide caused illness and sometimes insanity — and regulations followed.[10]

Zimmer also proclaimed a special interest in labor organizations, for "the active aid and driving force of organized labor is always needed" to put through "any substantial program of labor legislation." The division had a "special duty" to "interpret or explain the effects of proposed legislation" to union leaders, and for a conference of the New England State Federations of Labor, for example, it provided a comparative analysis, with graphic charts, of the five states' existing and proposed labor laws. On the whole, however, the unions used the division less than the state administrators.[11]

To the extent she could, Perkins participated at every level of the division's programs, particularly those involving the state administrators. As a former factory inspector she was interested in the training courses, and would try to appear at least once, to make an address or to hand out the certificates. At the regional conferences on labor legislation she generally was present for at least one full day, and she presided over every national conference, as an observer remarked, "joyfully and indefatigably."[12]

She always had a Greeting to the delegates signed by Roosevelt, and would give it, a presidential autograph, to the delegate who had come the furthest. She had ribbons to award the state administrators for legislation enacted during the year: red for minimum wage, blue for maximum hours, green for child labor and so on. The commissioner from Pennsylvania one year covered his chest with ribbons, but as he and everyone else knew, he was a cheerful fraud: the legislature had withheld the money to enforce the laws. The give-and-take among the delegates over the years became extraordinary. Though their membership changed slightly, as governors left office, they developed a sense of unity from their common aim, so they could discuss the most touchy issues — discrimination against Negroes or the qualifications of state administrators — without tempers rising.

They considered Perkins the author of the program's success. At the fifth national conference Tone, too much of a politician not to have tested the response to his plan before embarking on it, suddenly produced a three-part resolution: it praised Perkins for "her resourcefulness, wisdom and energy in creating this institution"; asked that the institution be made "a permanent agency" for bringing together state, union and federal labor leaders; and requested that copies of the resolution be sent to "the President of the United States and to the Governors and Governors-elect of all States here represented."

She was at home in this work and among friends with these people as in almost no other activity she pursued as Secretary. Because of it she could constantly delight and amaze them. To close a conference Beyer told her once, "Oh, just say something funny." From the podium Perkins regretted to the delegates and guests that she had nothing funny to say. Instead she would read them some "doodles" she claimed to have picked out of the delegates' scrapbaskets. Then for thirty minutes, her eye roving over the auditorium, she improvised the opinions of twenty or more of the best-known delegates about the programs, about herself and the staff and about each other. Everything she said was warm, humorous and apt.

She never bored her friends by playing the actress, but they soon discovered that she had the ability to turn on a performance whenever she wished. These were never "scenes" but typically, as here, at one remove from herself. She would tell the delegates what they thought of each other, not what she thought of them. But to some extent her sense of privacy and decorum kept her always on stage. South Carolina's Commissioner of Labor, Sydney Gamble, once told her staff of his excitement at discovering that she was on the same train as he and in the same sleeping car. Now surely, as she emerged from her berth, he would see her without her tricorn hat. In the morning he waited. He saw her hand reach out to push aside the curtain, and there she was — ankles crossed, hand characteristically at her belt buckle and hat in place — smiling at him.

It is difficult to assess the importance of the program as part of the

New Deal administration. Students of the labor department have ranked it high, but many of the more famous biographers and historians of the period have ignored it altogether, possibly because there are so few traces of it in the White House, in Congress or in newspaper headlines. Yet plainly for many workers the improvements in their working conditions were more often the result of state than of federal laws. William L. Connolly, Rhode Island's Director of Labor, in an impassioned letter to Roosevelt in January 1945 was willing to attribute "all" the improvements in Rhode Island to "the fine manner in which the Secretary of Labor has conducted her department." Perkins was more cautious. But she thought the program was extremely important. The conferences, with their supporting services, "have probably done as much for the working people of the United States, by and large, as any one thing that we ever did."

Connolly's letter to Roosevelt accompanied still another resolution of a national conference expressing the hope that "these conferences will continue." By January 1945 it was evident that Perkins must soon retire, and many delegates feared her departure would signal the end of the conferences. In fact her successors kept them going for another ten years, but they steadily deteriorated. A spark was missing. Perhaps they truly were personal to her — among her successors only Durkin matched her background in the problems of state administrators — but also the great improvement in the state labor departments may have obviated the need for the conferences. If so, they had been brilliantly improvised for the needs of their time.[13]

Another project that she conceived and promoted on her own was the adherence of the United States to the International Labor Organization. It was a possibility she had often considered, and she had not mentioned it to Roosevelt in New York only for lack of time. When she raised it later in Washington, he approved and left it to her.

In *The Roosevelt I Knew* she describes how on his advice she first approached the Secretary of State and then, with Hull's support, all the principal members of the Senate Committee on Foreign Relations. She called on them all personally. Wyzanski drafted a resolution for her that a senator might introduce in Congress and that, if passed, would authorize the President to apply for membership in the ILO. Because of the Senate's fight with President Wilson over the League of Nations, any move to join an international organization was likely to raise opposition, and she was careful not to hurry the senators. But from time to time she would telephone, and one by one they began to respond. Senator Hiram Johnson said, "I have analyzed the proposals, and I believe that is perfectly possible — in fact, a good idea — for the United States to adhere to this *one* organization. It is quite clear to me that in adhering to the International Labor Organization the United States does not commit itself to the League of Nations in any way and that the two are quite separate institutions."

Others reached the same conclusion. In June 1934 the resolution was introduced and passed by the House, 236–110, and by the Senate — she had done her job well — unanimously. On August 20 Roosevelt, acting for the United States, accepted the ILO's invitation to become a member.[14]

Like the League of Nations the ILO was conceived at the Paris Peace Conference following World War I, but was created an independent body. The conference delegates appointed a special Commission on International Labor Legislation, with Samuel Gompers as chairman, and it decided to set up a permanent organization for the improvement of labor standards. The first International Labor Conference was held in Washington, D.C., in 1919, but thereafter, because of the fight over the league, the United States participated in ILO programs only to exchange information.

Among international organizations of the time the ILO's structure was unique and to many people exciting. At its conferences and in its Governing Body, three groups were represented: governments, organized workers and organized employers. A member state at a conference was allowed four delegates: two representing the government and one each from labor and employer groups. It occasionally happened that the latter two voted against their state's delegates, and in such cases the voice of the people seemed to be directly heard. Sometimes, despite a state's desire to keep a problem closeted, the delegates could force it to be aired.

The organization's purpose was to gather information in order to arrive at certain standards of working conditions that it would then attempt to enforce by obtaining agreements among the states. When the standard covered great numbers of workers, say on maximum hours, the states generally ignored it; when it covered a few, such as establishing the minimum age of fifteen years for children employed at sea, they often enforced it. But among the more industrial countries, like the United States, similar standards usually were already in force, so that little seemed to have been gained.

The fact continually threatened the appropriations to support the country's membership in the ILO. In a debate in the House in 1936 Congressman Robert L. Bacon of New York said:

We questioned the different people who came before our committee as to concrete results. They gave us page after page of testimony full of beautiful ideas for the future, but our committee has not been able to find any one actual concrete good that has yet come out of our membership in this organization.[15]

Others frequently were harsher in their denunciations. The appropriations were small, however, and, in the main, were passed as requested. Actually, by 1936, the United States had received a concrete benefit. In setting up its programs under the Social Security Act, it had been able to use the skills of André Tixier and Oswald Stein, two ILO experts on social insurance plans. But concrete results were among the less important benefits of membership in the ILO. Though Perkins could be intensely practical, as in the program with state labor administrators, she also valued intangibles such as exposure and discussion.

As a kind of postgraduate school on world problems, the ILO was extremely good. At its conferences and committee meetings delegates from the United States were exposed to labor problems different from or more intensified than those at home, and they heard the policies of their unions and government discussed from a different perspective. Undoubtedly John G. Winant's experience in the ILO, as Assistant Director from 1935 to 1936 and from 1937 to 1938 and as Director from 1938 to 1941, made him a more effective ambassador to Great Britain in the years 1941 to 1946. By education and background he might have been expected to succeed with Churchill and the Tories. He arrived in London, however, with contacts also among the trade unionists and the Labour party, and throughout the crucial war years was able to represent the United States to all the British people.

Over the years Perkins worked steadily to strengthen the ILO and the country's contribution to it. Others in the labor department took it equally seriously, but many of the union and business delegates did not. A conference was often merely an excuse for a European junket. She tried to weed out the frivolous, but even when for political reasons she could not, she was never discouraged. Any lasting government, she believed, is government by persuasion not coercion, and persuasion means talk: introducing people to ideas and slowly moving them from the less good to the better.

She once wrote in an *Annual Report* to Congress,

In a successful democracy there must be a certain minimum unity of purpose and some contribution from the citizens as a whole to the idea and practice of the general welfare. Where the lives of millions of per-

sons are involved, as is true where the wage earners of the United States
of America are concerned, there must necessarily be a multiple of complications, sharp differences of opinion, friction at many points. Always,
however, there remains the permanent idea that through understanding
of the human problems involved, a sane and sensible adjustment can be
created.[16]

She was incurably democratic. Whether at Albany, Washington or
Geneva she wanted to involve people and excite them to solve their
problems. There was no change in her as she moved from state to
national to international labor problems; on all levels she approached
them in the same way. What was extraordinary was how far she had
been able to carry her eagerness for social justice. She told Wyzanski
once that as a young woman she had hoped one day to be a delegate to
the ILO. The idealism of it had always appealed to her. He thought,
too, that "like many people in her generation she tended to think that
foreign affairs were more important than domestic." It was part of the
complexity of her character that she who was so practical was also such
an idealist, and that she who was such a vigorous Secretary of Labor,
so domestically concerned, should be so interested in international
labor problems.

From 1938 on, as Roosevelt's second term came to an end, without
saying so publicly he began to maneuver for a third. No President had
ever had a third term, and at the convention in Chicago in 1940
Farley, who saw much good in that tradition, ran against him for the
nomination. Garner, representing some conservative Democrats, also
opposed him. Roosevelt's mainstay was the New Deal liberal wing of
the party, led by such men as Hopkins, Ickes, Hillman and Thomas G.
Corcoran.

Both before and during the convention Perkins supported Roosevelt, but about the wisdom of the third term she privately had doubts.
She had not questioned him in 1938 about the attempted purge of the
party's conservatives, and in 1940 she never asked him outright,
"Would you refuse the nomination?" It was "too blunt a question to
ask a friend." But from his evasive replies to her "sallies in that
direction" and from conversations with Farley and others, she became
aware of the guile with which he was approaching the convention and
the ill will he was storing up for himself.[17]

She thought a third term for any President was bad "on principle"
because it impeded growth and change. If those who have held office

for eight years continue for another four, then the younger people, "who ought to be out hustling for votes, get a sort of numbed feeling that it has all been arranged, all done. The ardor peters out." Within the executive departments "if you stay on, you're going to keep the people you've appointed. You like them. They're doing all right. But if you go out, they'll resign. The new man will make new appointments. Politically, it's a good thing to have a turnover."[18]

The principle fitted her feelings of the moment. Regardless of which Democrat was nominated or who won the election, she intended immediately after it to resign. Of all the programs she had discussed with Roosevelt before coming to Washington only health insurance had not been enacted. She did not believe the New Deal had resolved all the problems of the Depression, but at least for urban and industrial workers, her particular charges, "a great deal had been done to take the edge off it."[19]

One day in 1937, as she later wrote to a friend, she had happened to be in an employment office and heard a woman "raise hell" with the clerk "because her unemployment compensation check had not been delivered on time." In the sound of that woman's voice, claiming a right, not asking a charity, Perkins felt the "fulfillment" of her life's work. When in June 1940 she read in a newspaper that the Republican party in convention had adopted all the social security programs in its platform, she burst out to the man beside her, "God's holy name be praised! No matter who gets elected we've won." In that "we" was not only the New Deal but Al Smith, Florence Kelley and every other man and woman who had fought for industrial and social insurance programs back to Theodore Roosevelt and the Progressive party. So she approached the question of a third term for Franklin Roosevelt in an autumnal mood. He and his cabinet had had their eight years; it was time to retire.[20]

Yet after September 1939, when the war in Europe began, she gradually concluded that Roosevelt's nomination was inevitable and necessary. Inevitable because he wanted it and from his position in the White House could have it, and necessary because no other Democrat had his national constituency or his ability in a crisis. By April or May 1940, though he was still concealing his intentions, she felt he had settled the question in his own mind. If she said to him of some action that had to be postponed, "We'll do it next year; you know who will be President," he would no longer contradict her, but smile. That spring, they even discussed whom he wanted for Vice-President. She favored Wallace, but Roosevelt was undecided.[21]

At the convention in Chicago in mid-July, Perkins was appalled by the bitterness of many of the delegates. Roosevelt still had not declared himself in the running. He wanted the delegates to draft him, unanimously, without a ballot. He was to be the indispensable leader called back into service. His supporters argued that at the polls a draft would offset the prejudice against the third term, but to many the idea seemed born of vanity. Why not a ballot? Wasn't that the American way? When Mayor Edward Kelly of Chicago tried to whoop up a spontaneous draft with his opening address, the delegates refused to be stampeded. Meanwhile Roosevelt's lieutenants, led by Hopkins, were pressuring candidates to withdraw and delegates to switch their votes. Because they were lobbying for an incumbent President likely to be reelected, their threats over patronage were sharp and bitterly resented. During a speech by Senator Alben Barkley there was another effort to stir the delegates to demand Roosevelt by acclamation. From all over the auditorium came a roar of "We want Roosevelt," though very few delegates seemed to be shouting. Soon it was discovered that Mayor Kelly had secreted a man in the cellar to lead the chants over a hidden amplification system. It was a totalitarian technique, and because Roosevelt had deliberately selected Chicago for the convention so that Kelly would be in control, even Perkins held him responsible. "That was a mistake, I think, from the point of view of the people of the United States."[22]

When the first and only ballot was counted, the tactics seemed even more sordid because so unnecessary. Of the 1100 votes, Roosevelt received 946½ or 86 percent, Farley received 72½, Garner 61, Millard Tydings 9½ and Hull 5½. Farley, putting the party first, promptly moved that the rules be suspended and Roosevelt be nominated by acclamation. The delegates made very clear, however, that the cheering and applause that followed were for Farley, not Roosevelt.

The rancor distressed Perkins, and she took seriously the suggestion of a reporter that she telephone Roosevelt to urge him to come to Chicago in order to heal party wounds. After consulting Dewson and several others she put through the call.

"Absolutely no," Roosevelt said. "I'll have to promise this and that. They'll begin to trade with me. I must not be in a position where I'm going to be traded with."

"The situation is very bad," she said. "Just as sour as it can be."

He suggested his wife might go. "Eleanor is pretty good about this kind of thing. You call her. If she says no, tell her to see what I say, but don't tell her that you've talked to me." Then he asked about the nominations for Vice-President.

"No clear pattern is evolving yet," she said. "Everybody would like to know who you want, but you haven't declared yourself. Everything is absolutely open. Candidates are lining up."

"What do you think?"

"There's just no way of knowing. I think you will have to indicate somehow or other who you want."

They started to discuss the possibilities, and he mentioned Wallace: "Frances, don't you think he'd be good?" While she murmured agreement, he recited Wallace's good qualities. At one point he confessed, "I should have decided long ago." If he ever had, she felt he had truly forgotten previous considerations and was starting afresh with her as a sounding board. Finally he said, "Yes, I think Wallace will be all right."

"Do you want to say that you want Wallace?"

He again went over the candidates, again concluding, "I think Henry Wallace is the one."

"Well, that's fine. How are you going to put it over?"

He told her to tell Hopkins and "then telephone Eleanor."[23]

Perkins was always astonished that "the Wallace decision" was made "like that," on the phone, to her, not ordinarily one of Roosevelt's political lieutenants. Yet "that was the way he often talked to me about things, when he knew it was wrong not to have decided before. To most of the men he would have talked to he wouldn't have said, 'I ought to have decided long ago,' but he could say that to me without humiliation."

Arthur Krock of the *New York Times* said of them, "He knew she was his most loyal friend — that she was probably the only person around him who had no ax of any kind to grind. She would tell him what she thought. If she disapproved she would say so. But she would do it gently." After twelve years of working together they had a relationship of trust and tenderness.[24]

The nomination of Wallace for Vice-President went extremely hard. In waiting so long to declare whom he wanted Roosevelt had encouraged some seventeen candidates to enter the field. Then suddenly he sent Hopkins, Byrnes and others onto the floor to pass the word for Wallace. His move embarrassed the candidates and, when he backed it with a threat to decline the nomination for President if he could not have the man of his choice, it infuriated the delegates. They did not want Wallace. Until 1928 he had been a Republican; his close association with the New Deal did little to balance the ticket; he had no political constituency of his own. Roosevelt's maneuver struck many as an act of arrogance.

Amid confusion and anger fifteen of the candidates withdrew, leaving only Wallace and William Bankhead of Alabama, Speaker of the House. Before the balloting Eleanor Roosevelt was brought to the podium. Over what to many seemed an act of low politics she attempted to put a gloss of patriotism. If the President felt that the strain of a third term might be too much for any man and that Wallace was the man who could carry on best in a time of crisis, then the President should be allowed the help of the man he wanted. The delegates, she urged, should sink all personal interests in the interests of the country. The delegates listened in silence. After she finished, the balloting began.

It started badly for Wallace, but the votes were the least of it. The delegates had not felt free to express their anger at Roosevelt, the President, but there was nothing to hold them back from Wallace. Perkins, on the platform, had experienced nothing like it. At every mention of Wallace's name there were catcalls, boos, hisses and denunciations screamed from the floor. Wallace had been led to believe that the nomination would go smoothly and had arrived early to sit at the back of the platform with his acceptance speech in his pocket.

Perkins saw him. "His mouth was half-open, in that unbelieving half-openness. He was stooped a bit forward, listening, but his eyes were way off. I could have spoken to him, and I'm sure he would not have heard me. He had a face of utter, blank suffering." She moved to sit in front of him, to shield him from the delegates.

From there she could see Ilo Wallace, beside Mrs. Roosevelt, closer to the front of the platform. She was "reeling. You could see it. Her brain was reeling inside her head. The antagonism was crushing. I remember seeing Mrs. Roosevelt take her hand."[25]

For more than an hour the balloting continued, and at the end Wallace was nominated by a slight majority, 627 of the 1100 votes. Farley had no doubt that Mrs. Roosevelt's appearance had saved the day for Roosevelt. No part of it was saved by anyone for the Wallaces. As he came forward to make his acceptance speech, Hopkins harshly advised him not to show himself, and he was hustled out.[26]

After the convention Farley resigned as national chairman and declined to manage Roosevelt's campaign. He later wrote that the convention showed Roosevelt to be "a master of political rough-and-tumble with no holds barred," but he also made plain his disgust at the amount of deceit that Roosevelt had used to divide and overwhelm any possible opposition. Farley had been warned by Al Smith "never to rely on Roosevelt's word," but he was by nature trusting and had found the advice hard to follow. His disappointments with Roosevelt, which during twelve years had steadily increased, were most often over Roosevelt's failures as a human being.[27]

Perkins saw those failings, and when she could she protected others from them by nudging Roosevelt to make a phone call or write a letter.[28] But, in the end, she was more forgiving than Farley because she saw another quality in Roosevelt that she felt uniquely fitted him to be President. "He would have flashes of almost clairvoyant knowledge and understanding of a terrific variety of matters that didn't seem to have any particular relationship to each other. He couldn't always hold that or verbalize on it, but sometimes he could. Sometimes he could act on it."

Musicians reportedly have such flashes, in which they see or hear the structure of an entire symphony or opera: where it will go fast, where slow, the orchestral color here, there. A problem of composition then becomes a matter of getting enough of it onto paper before the flash fades, so that the overall form is clear. Later, missing parts, where the flash was weak or memory failed, can be constructed by schoolbook rules.

"In Roosevelt this aptitude for knowing all kinds of diverse things at once in a flash did not stay. It would come and then it would go. It would stay only a minute or two; sometimes long enough to solve the problem, sometimes only enough to give him a hunch. Sometimes it would disappear."

The talent would be useful in any period, but its application is particularly obvious in wartime, when every facet of a country's life must be directed to a single end. After four years as governor and eight as President, Roosevelt presumably had gained experience in using his talent, but also the approach of war gave him an extraordinary opportunity to display it. As a peacetime leader in the Depression he was only moderately successful. His two administrations had not solved the country's economic problems. But as a wartime leader in the four years from 1940 through 1943, mobilizing the country for war and leading it to a point where victory was assured, he was brilliant. There were evidently many, many times when he truly could see it all: men, guns, ships, food, the enemy, the Allies, the war aims and finally the peace.

But such a talent raises its own problems. A day later he often could not recall what had been so clear the day before. Perkins might try to remind him: "But you said yesterday . . ."

"No, I think you are mistaken," he would say.

But she knew he had said it. She had written it down, and there were others who had heard it. Such "a peculiar mentality," she felt, "made it almost impossible for people to become an intimate, trusting, trustworthy friend." Too often they felt deceived or even betrayed.[29]

Farley, she considered, was a supremely decent man. Throughout her papers she extols his honesty, kindness, modesty and lack of guile. She ranked him very high as a human being and also as a public servant. He was one of the three men most helpful to her in settling strikes; he constantly assisted her in recruiting good men, even of doubtful party allegiance, for government posts; and he was wise about what might be accomplished and how to go about it. She saw his personality as intensely practical and almost wholly without intuition.[30]

Hopkins, on the other hand, she knew could be arrogant, cynical, ungrateful, self-centered — almost anything bad. At the same time he was extremely intuitive. In the 1940 convention, she believed, he had almost as much cause as Farley to feel misled by Roosevelt. But his reaction was different. He had "a sympathy toward the man who could see so much.

"If Roosevelt had been a less clairvoyant person, less able to see so many things and so many facets of everything, he wouldn't have had so hard a time with himself. He would have stuck to a few simple principles and followed through, just doing these things because this was the way people behaved. But he could see all kinds of other things creeping up, things that were not in the conventional pattern. Therefore, he suffered more intellectually and spiritually in that post, and in the decisions he had to make, than a person with a less diverse, less sensitive and less understanding mind."

Hopkins saw that, she felt, and was drawn to Roosevelt because of it. Hopkins "was able to feel what Roosevelt meant, even when the expression was unclear. Also, I think, by his intuitive capacities, he saw Roosevelt's historical position and the importance of having Roosevelt desire and attempt to do the right and best thing." In the attempt, because Roosevelt had neither the time nor the talent for administration, he needed help "to translate" the right and best thing "into terms in which other people could cooperate." Hopkins "developed an extraordinary talent, which none of us supposed he had, of designing operations. I mean operations at the political level as well as at the level of action, of finance and so on."[31]

To keep Roosevelt's extraordinary talent in the country's service in wartime seemed to her more important than changing the administration or disciplining him for his personal failings. In her support there was personal loyalty and party chauvinism for she was always a good friend and Democrat, but there was also considered judgment.

Perkins, however, intended to resign, and after the election, in which Roosevelt defeated Willkie 27,243,466 to 22,304,755, she spoke to him about it, recommending for her post Daniel W. Tracy, the Assistant Secretary. Tracy, before entering the department in 1940, had been president of the International Brotherhood of Electrical Workers, an AFL union, and she had a high regard for him. Doubtless the CIO would complain, but its opposition should not be insurmountable in wartime.

After several weeks in which Roosevelt had not reached a decision, she raised the subject again.

"I haven't had time to think of it," he said.

After rumors of her retirement had appeared in the papers, and been denied, she went to Eleanor Roosevelt.

"See here, you see the President more often than I."

"But I don't get a chance to talk to him."

"You can make a chance. Find out when he's going to act on my resignation. If he's not absolutely unwilling, let me know." She had several opportunities for jobs, she explained, and they might not stay open forever.

In about a week she had a note from Mrs. Roosevelt. "I have talked to him about it, and the answer is no, absolutely no."

Perkins telephoned. "What does that mean?"

"That's it," said Mrs. Roosevelt. "He's got to think about the war, the appropriate diplomacy, the foreign problems and all that. He just can't put his mind on a new person operating in your field. You do understand each other. That's that. It can't be done."

"That doesn't mean forever, does it?"

"I suppose not, but that's what he feels for the present."

A few days later, after a cabinet meeting, Roosevelt said to her, "Did you hear from my Mrs.?"

"Yes, it's bright of you to communicate with me like that."

"Well, I meant to tell you myself, but the more I thought of it, the more I didn't see how I was going to do it. Really, it's personal, I suppose. I know who you are, what you are, what you'll do, what you won't do. You know me. You see lots of things that most people don't see. You keep me guarded against a lot of things that no new man walking in here would protect me from."

"Dan would do it."

"Oh, I couldn't say anything with Dan sitting there. You know I couldn't." He looked up at her.

She began to laugh. No talk about her age, or finances or ideas. Just a personal appeal in a time of crisis. She stayed on.[32]

Chapter 33

-->>|<<--

Preparing for war. She opposes fingerprinting. The Bureau of Immigration transferred. The War Manpower Commission. Preserving Labor Standards. The War Labor Board. The fight over the Cost of Living Index.

IN LATER YEARS, when Perkins was lecturing at Cornell, she was sometimes urged to discuss her role in wartime. She seldom would, dismissing it as routine administration: "hundreds of hours spent in straightening out tangles." The more interesting time, she was sure, was the period of developing ideas and programs, the years with Smith and Roosevelt as governors and Roosevelt's first two terms as President.[1]

Though she was right, her wartime role was more interesting than she allowed. She had no part in the military decisions, and even on the home front she and the labor department were less important than before. Yet she was not without influence and, where she could, she used it to prevent or delay regimentation. The country fought a total war against totalitarian governments while itself maintaining to a remarkable degree its traditional open society, and in that achievement Perkins had a part.

Wyzanski, who admired her enough to judge her by the highest standards, once remarked, "She was not a great thinker. I suspect she did not read books on the theory of government and society. Her instincts, however, were supremely good, and I doubt if on any major issue she was wrong." Often, as the war put society and government under stress, people's instincts became more visible. Often they were about all anyone had to bring to the solution of sudden, new problems.[2]

On September 4, 1939, immediately after Germany invaded Poland,

Roosevelt asked the cabinet to discuss the wisdom and necessity of declaring a national emergency, which by law would give him extraordinary powers. Perkins wrote him the next day.

I had never given the matter any thought since 1933, and I apologize for being unprepared to state my point of view promptly . . .

I recall that in 1933 Moley and General Johnson urged you to declare an emergency, and I recall your clear, quick, vigorous statement that the people never intended a merely difficult and complicated situation to be used to invoke such far-reaching powers over them and that you thought the real reason for not doing it was that the cure was likely to be worse than the disease and damage those who used the powers, as well as those who were affected by them.

That was a sound piece of spontaneous, denunciative reaction to those who love efficiency and thoroughness and expedition for its own sake.

The same situation is here now as I see it. There is no national emergency in the sense in which it was intended. We are not attacked by enemies or famine or pestilence, and we are not at war. The [emergency] powers given to the Executive branch are very broad and far-reaching — reaching to civil rights and restriction of personal freedom, as well as power over industrial enterprises, transportation, etc.

The people of the United States are stunned today. They may sometime feel that they ought to join in this war but not now certainly. I think the declaration of emergency as suggested by the War Department would frighten them and at this time interfere with that national unity which is growing and to which you appealed so splendidly on the radio . . .

I would trust *you* with all of them [the powers] at any time for you are instinctively a Democrat and habituated like most Americans of political experience to parliamentary government. But I know you will have to delegate many of these powers in detail to others, and we shall have wiretapping and raids and searches, etc., by small well-meaning subordinates, and the American people won't like it because our national objective won't seem clearly to make all that sort of thing a lesser evil.

Moreover, others will come after your term — twenty years hence perhaps — who, realizing from such an experience in 1939 how much can be done by this method, may use and invoke it for selfish or unworthy purpose. They might even pull the election machinery up after them.[3]

Roosevelt doubtless received similar advice from others, for he held off declaring a national emergency until May 27, 1941, using the interim months to present a Selective Service (conscription) Act to Congress, to establish the lend-lease program for Britain and to build as best he could a sense of national purpose and unity. In June 1940 he appointed two Republicans, Henry L. Stimson and Frank Knox, to be Secretaries of War and of the Navy, and later he employed the party's leader, Willkie, on a mission to England.

Cabinet meetings in these months became a kind of graduate course in the economic, military and political hazards facing the country. Roosevelt clearly was preparing the cabinet for the likelihood, even certainty, that the United States would be drawn into the war. Often he would look down the table and say, "Frances, you know a battleship is not the worst thing in the world."

After two or three such occasions she spoke up. "Mr. President, I'm not a pacifist. Please get that into your mind. I'm not a pacifist at all. I don't sit around wishing for war, but I know what it is. I know that the human race is likely to have it from time to time, and that if it is going to occur, you'd better be well prepared to come out on top. I think the things we care about should come out on top." But he continued to do it, at first to her amusement and then to her annoyance. She resented it as a piece of stereotyped thinking about women.[4]

Meanwhile, having "things we care about come out on top" embroiled her in a continuing argument with J. Edgar Hoover, director of the FBI. He wanted all aliens, over whom she had jurisdiction, fingerprinted. Further, if he could obtain the necessary legislation, he wanted all citizens fingerprinted. He wanted to start a government dossier on every person in the United States.

The idea disturbed her belief that privacy is the basis of liberty. It also offended her religious belief in the sanctity of the individual; it was a step toward treating people like cattle. In reforming the immigration bureau with MacCormack she had seen examples of how easily good intentions had become illegal raids, and official behavior brutal. The FBI was an agency for dealing with criminals, and the attitude of its agents toward citizens inevitably would be that of the police toward criminals. But Roosevelt, whose need for privacy seemed as small as hers was great, was inclined to back Hoover, and in March 1939 he suggested that all Americans should voluntarily submit to fingerprinting. A few days later newspapers published a picture of Hoover taking the fingerprints of Vice-President Garner.[5]

In a meeting with Perkins one day Hoover tried to state for her some benefit the millions of noncriminal citizens might receive from fingerprinting. "Think of the number of fine citizens," he said, "who die of heart attacks and train wrecks and who are not identified for months. We could send cards to their families."

"Mr. Hoover," she said, "isn't it enough that his Maker would immediately recognize him?"

She was quite serious: that was the important consequence of death.

A few hours or even days saved in notifying relatives could not justify the government's keeping tabs on every citizen. Even in regard to aliens she steadily resisted fingerprinting for noncriminals.[6]

The war resolved the issue. For several years she had been urging Roosevelt to transfer the immigration bureau, whose problems so little concerned labor, to the Department of the Interior. Instead, one night in May 1940, he called her at home to say that the growing problem with spies and saboteurs had decided him to transfer it to the Department of Justice. What did she think? "Under ordinary circumstances," she said, "I think that's a bad place for it." Immigration and naturalization should not be associated with criminality but should "be treated as one of the humanitarian functions of the government." But in wartime perhaps the Department of Justice was reasonable. The proposed reorganization was announced the next day and soon passed by Congress, which required that all aliens now be registered and fingerprinted.[7]

Because of the Bridges case the transfer came at a difficult time for Perkins. During the debate in the House, John Taber of New York said, "We are going to vote for this reorganization plan because the President has not the patriotism nor the courage to remove the Secretary of Labor, a notorious incompetent, and one who for the last seven years has steadily and steadfastly refused to enforce the Immigration Law." Fortunately, as she once observed, "Roosevelt did not find anything embarrassing because you were called names," and also, despite the virulence of some of the attacks by political and labor leaders, she was not without support among the rank and file. After one election Roosevelt said to her, "I notice that we haven't lost the labor vote or the women's vote on your account."[8]

Nevertheless, though the transfer to the Department of Justice was not a repudiation of her policies in peacetime, the new wartime regulations, such as registering and fingerprinting aliens and tightening border controls, made it appear so. As a result, her reform of the bureau under MacCormack and his successor, James L. Houghteling, was all but unnoticed in the editorial and congressional cackle of glee at her seeming chastisement.[9]

Far more serious, however, was the removal of her voice from those advising Roosevelt on questions touching the treatment of aliens and even of citizens. In February 1942 a horror of the kind she had warned him against took place. Egged on by small-minded, well-meaning subordinates — mostly army officers, not Hoover — Roosevelt signed Executive Order 9066, by which one hundred and ten thousand

Pacific Coast residents of Japanese ancestry, two thirds of them United States citizens, were interned in concentration camps for the duration of the war. The incarceration was brutally done and was justified on the ground that all people of Japanese ancestry were potentially disloyal. But at the war's end the record did not disclose a single case of Japanese disloyalty or sabotage. It was the sort of act on Roosevelt's part from which Perkins, with her emphasis on procedure and due process, might have saved him. At the time she kept her opinion of it to herself, and never, even in later years, discussed it publicly; privately she thought it "very wrong."[10]

On the Monday morning after the Japanese air strike on Pearl Harbor, Perkins had "an instinct" to be in her office early in order to see as many members of the department as possible. "It was the same instinct you have with members of your own family when they are in trouble. You want to see them right away." At noon Roosevelt was to go before Congress to ask for a declaration of war; meanwhile everyone was in a state of grief, confusion and alarm. Though the cabinet had met the previous night, Perkins knew very little more than anyone else of what had happened or was going to happen, but in the department "they would feel that I must know more." She ought to be available to them.

As she entered the building, she stationed the chauffeur by the elevator to tell others arriving that she was in her office and would be glad to see anyone who cared to come up. Many came directly, and the big room and outer offices were soon filled. Passing among her colleagues, workers in all grades, she could be only vaguely assuring: "We will find the strength to meet this." But words that morning were less important than the strength each seemed to draw from the presence of others.

She discovered that many the night before, learning that she was at the White House, had come to the department to be at their desks in case something had to be done. In the past year, in preparation for partial or total war, each bureau had begun to develop plans — for the evacuation of children, for example — but few of these were coordinated, nor had priorities among them been determined. With these needs in mind, she scheduled a meeting in the afternoon with the bureau chiefs so that they could start reorienting the department's programs.[11]

When Roosevelt on a vaster scale did the same with the government's entire executive branch, he chose not to make the Secretary of

Labor a powerful War Labor Administrator, as had been done in World War I. Instead, he by-passed Perkins and the department by creating temporary agencies, such as a War Labor Board to handle the important labor disputes and a War Manpower Commission to coordinate the work of all agencies dealing with manpower. He had a number of reasons for the policy.

Temporary agencies were a way of overcoming apathy. A man, important in a community where the war was little understood, could be invited to Washington, offered a job with title and powers and, if he accepted (as almost all did), his neighbors at home quickly became more interested in the war effort. For an administration entering its third term this was also a method of infusing itself with new blood. Further, if a temporary agency failed in its purpose or abused its power, it could be quickly disbanded and another with different powers and personnel substituted. This easy end to a bureaucratic group was always useful and might become particularly so at the war's end.

With these reasons Perkins both publicly and privately agreed, urging only that whenever possible the new agencies should use existing services rather than creating their own. When a wage stabilization board was being considered, for instance, she was prepared for the board to make policy but wanted it to gather its information and effect its decisions through the labor department's bureaus. "Please don't forget," she wrote Samuel Rosenman at the White House, "that the Department of Labor has the only existing machinery through which this job can be done in the area of disputes, and that to build up new machinery would be complicated, expensive and full of antagonisms." But she wasn't always successful in preventing a temporary agency from creating duplicate machinery.[12]

In addition to the publicly stated reasons for the new agencies, however, there were others, at least with regard to her department, which neither she nor Roosevelt could be expected to mention. After the Bridges case she was too controversial to be used in a prominent position in the war effort. Also she was a woman, and for that reason alone both she and Roosevelt were receiving letters protesting her continued appointment in wartime. Women as often as men wrote in, and one, in a letter to Perkins, added, "I am far from rich, but I do have something, and I'd be glad to contribute what I could until you were able to find something else."[13]

For Roosevelt the protests over Perkins's sex would be harder to meet in 1940 than in 1933, when she had brought special skills to the problems of the Depression, and they would be avoided altogether by the establishment of temporary agencies outside her department. So throughout the war she sat on boards as a member but not the chairman; she created commissions and staffed them with others; she provided the agencies with all kinds of technical assistance from the department's bureaus; and quietly, from her position in the background, she spent hundreds of hours unsnarling bureaucratic tangles. She was less in the news, but that suited her.

One temporary agency whose creation she steadily opposed was a commission to direct the flow of men, and perhaps women, into factories and onto farms as well as into the armed forces. Some of Roosevelt's advisers, particularly Harold Smith, Director of the Budget, and some of the military, were impressed with Britain's program of "national service," under which all men and women over eighteen and under sixty-five were registered and, when needed, assigned by the government to a war job. At a time when men were being taken involuntarily into the armed forces, the idea of an industrial and agricultural draft seemed to many people logical and fair.

Smith thought a similar program in the United States would help to resolve conflicts among the armed forces, industry and agriculture over the supply of men. In addition, a manpower commission might allocate workers among industries, preferring the essential to the nonessential. Some of the military saw it as a way of ensuring supplies by guaranteeing contractors a labor force that could neither strike nor quit.

For that reason labor leaders, always opposed to the conscription of labor, were against it. They also feared the assignment of nonunion workers to union jobs, which might erode a union's foothold in a plant. As many people pointed out, the British example was based on several conditions that did not prevail in the United States: the country was relatively small, its people homogeneous and the possibility of its defeat quite clear to everyone. Also the British labor leader Ernest Bevin, who was administering the program, had the trust of all the British people to an extent inconceivable of any of the squabbling CIO or AFL leaders.[14]

Perkins opposed such total mobilization as "about as destructive of our conception of a free society as possible" and not to be used until absolutely necessary. In the spring of 1940 the country still had 8.5 million unemployed, and even at the close of 1942 there were still more than a million. The following year many peacetime industries, no longer producing, were releasing workers for wartime jobs, and women by the hundreds of thousands each month began to take jobs. Ultimately 6.5 to 7 million joined the labor force, most of them married, with children over sixteen. Even so, whereas in Britain, by the summer of 1941, 49 percent of its labor force was engaged in war work, in the United States, by 1944, the figure was only 40 percent, including those in the armed services. To the war's end Perkins argued that there was still no need for a program of total mobilization.[15]

She felt that "the way to run the country in wartime is to let the people move and follow their own good sense, stopping them only when they do something that is either ridiculous for themselves or against the public interest." Most problems could be met by utilizing "all that we know about social, political, economic and patriotic incentives to lure people into doing what we want them to do."

Roosevelt, pulled this way and that by the conflict among his advisers, finally in April 1942 created the War Manpower Commission and appointed Paul V. McNutt its director. But its powers were considerably less than those of its British model, for it was to operate on a voluntary basis without legal sanctions.

On it were representatives of almost every agency with an interest in manpower: the Army, Navy, Selective Service Board, War Production Board and so many more that its meetings were often unwieldy. At these Perkins and General Lewis B. Hershey, director of Selective Service, frequently spoke out against proposals that seemed likely to lead to unnecessary regimentation. She once described Hershey, meaning to be complimentary, as "one of those flatfooted people who knows his business and does it. He's moderately humanitarian, but he isn't sick of it. He believes in letting people do about what they want to do, giving them some guide lines."[16]

That was her view: Let the workers sort themselves into the new jobs. In her oral history she offered an example. When the supplies for making lampshades were diverted into war industries, and the lampshade workers came on the labor market,

> it was a terrible mistake to try to move hordes of workers to where you wanted them by decree. That's what these nice, logical people like Harold Smith had assumed would be done. That was what McNutt thought could be done. You can't do that. The people who make lampshades on East Thirty-first in a little hole in the wall cannot be made to go over to Jersey City where there was a great munitions plant. In the first place, they can't get there. The old man liked to work on East Thirty-first

Street because it was near where he lived. You didn't have to bother about such people. They all found jobs. The less you did, the better. The more you tried to make them go somewhere, the more trouble you had. We were in a period of expanding employment. All they had to do to get a job was to read the "help wanted" ads and take their pick. People didn't like having the factory where they made lampshades closed. There were all kinds of personal reasons why they preferred to work where they did. But, when that job was no longer, they found themselves another job.

But there were others on the commission who thought, for example, that the newspapers should stop printing help wanted ads. Let the workers be forced to go to the U.S. Employment Service, which would refer them to a war job, only to a war job. The idea had logic but seemed to Perkins ill adapted to human nature, even to the extent that it was practiced voluntarily by the Employment Service officials.

She was in an employment office in Chicago one day when a worker, taking her for a manager, angrily said, "That fellow won't tell me what I want to know. He keeps telling me he has a job in the powder mill. I don't want to work in the powder mill. I'm a mechanic. I want to work in a mechanic's job. Doesn't he know of any jobs for mechanics?" She investigated, and there were mechanics' jobs available, though not in essential industries. And another man happily went to the powder mill.[17]

In November 1942 she read in the paper that Roosevelt, whom she had been seeing less frequently, had said in a press conference that he was thinking of registering all women between fourteen and sixty-five. She wrote him a letter, pointing out that an "occupational registration" of all males had produced thirty-nine million questionnaires, but as Congress had not appropriated any funds for their analysis, little good had come of them. Registering women probably would add another forty million questionnaires to the pile, without adding greatly to the knowledge that most women were housewives. The estimate was that in 1943 about three million women would join the labor force and another three million in 1944. These could be hired through regular channels. "Whenever the Employment Service has advertised for 50 or 500 women for real jobs, they have had more than enough turn up." She concluded, "I recommend against the general registration of women for two reasons: 1. That it is not necessary, and 2. Because it will cause excitement and confusion and give to some 40-odd million women and the men of their families the idea that (a) they are going to be forced into something; (b) and even worse that they are immediately needed and are immediately going to be called to serve their country."[18]

At the war's end some seven million women had entered the labor force in their own time, in their own way and without the expense and agitation of a general registration. Ironically, although Perkins continued to be criticized as a radical, she was playing the part of a conservative.

Another area in which this was true was the preservation of labor standards. During the months before Pearl Harbor a number of defense contractors complained that state and federal laws on hours and wages were decreasing the speed of production. Beneath the patriotism, however, sometimes lurked self-interest. The crux of many objections was the forty-hour week, after which the employer was required to pay his workers at a rate of time and a half. Some employers, rather than hire more workers from the millions of unemployed for the overtime periods, apparently sought to work those already employed for extra hours at regular rates.

Misled, perhaps, by these employers or blinded by their own patriotism, the Secretaries of War and of the Navy as well as the director of the Office of Production Management immediately after Pearl Harbor telegraphed the governors of the states urging the relaxation and even the suspension of many of the state laws. Not one of the gentlemen, Stimson, Knox or William Knudsen, thought to consult first with the lady most concerned.

But this was an area in which Roosevelt trusted completely in Perkins, or, as she more modestly phrased it in *The Roosevelt I Knew,* he "saw the peril as soon as it was called to his attention." Her subsequent telegram to the governors began "The War and Navy Departments have assured me that they have not requested any blanket suspension of state laws" and went on to state that machinery was being devised "to confine exemptions to specific cases where required for war production." That machinery was set up in the department's Division of Labor Standards.[19]

A conference was called in January for representatives of the War, Navy and Labor Departments and labor commissioners from the chief industrial states, and at its conclusion Perkins issued a statement, in which the War and Navy Departments concurred, confirming the basic principles of the forty-hour week, eight-hour day and six-day week. Experience consistently had demonstrated that longer hours and lack of one day's rest in seven soon reduced a worker's efficiency and impeded production.[20]

Yet many people with no experience of factories seemed unable to grasp the issues, and their confusion and sometimes anger often surfaced in the newspapers. Some editors apparently thought that the forty-hour week was an absolute limitation, not realizing that in many factories the young and strong regularly worked longer. Others, even on the *New York Times* and the Washington *Star,* seemed to think the cost of overtime restricted production, forgetting that the typical war goods contract was either for a "lump sum," in which case an employer had included the costs in his negotiated figure, or a "cost plus," in which case he was guaranteed a profit over costs.[21] But as one working woman put it in a letter to Roosevelt and Perkins:

It has taken labor a long time to get decent working hours for the men, and labor is willing to work to the limit of its strength but not at the expense of the health of the men and not for nothing. The government is paying the employers in defense works grand money, and if the "little" man has earned it, he wants to be paid for what he has to sweat for.

Perkins called another conference in December 1942 to review the basic principles and, again, they were confirmed. Only in mid-1943, after the pool of unemployed had been drained, was the basic work week in federal acts raised from forty to forty-eight hours. There were also many temporary variations under the wartime powers of the governors and the President, but no fundamental changes. The country emerged from the war with its basic labor standards intact, and as Perkins happily observed, "proved clearly by the record that the standards for labor protection make for efficiency."[22]

Always her role was in the background. In the year before Pearl Harbor, when strikes threatened defense production, she suggested a National Defense Mediation Board, which Roosevelt created by executive order in March 1941. It had eleven members, representatives of labor, management and the public, with Clarence Dykstra as chairman, succeeded in mid-June by William H. Davis.

By August the board was beginning to founder on the question of the union shop, and in mid-October it broke apart when the issue became central in a dispute between the United States Steel Corporation and the United Mineworkers Union, led by John L. Lewis. About fifty-three thousand men worked in "captive mines" owned by the steel company, and about twenty-five hundred of them were not union members. Lewis asked the board to require these twenty-five hundred to join the union or be fired. The board refused, 9 to 2, stating that a union shop was a matter for collective bargaining and that the government should not be used to force men into a union against their will — whereupon the two CIO members and their five alternates all promptly resigned from the board. Roosevelt refused their resignations, but to no avail. The men refused to serve, and except for its administrative duties the board ceased to function.

Meanwhile, on Lewis's orders, the workers at the captive mines resumed their strike, and two hundred thousand more at other mines joined them. With war threatening, the steel industry was all but shut down. Roosevelt declared that the government would not order a union shop, insisted that negotiations continue and made preparations to seize the mines if no agreement could be reached — but no one could foresee clearly how the government would mine the coal.

Then suddenly and unexpectedly, on November 22, the strike was called off. Lewis had agreed to binding arbitration of the issue by a three-man tribunal composed of himself, Benjamin Fairless, the president of the company, and John R. Steelman, whom Perkins had personally hired for the labor department and steadily advanced in the Conciliation Service.

It was generally believed, and perhaps proved by events, that Roosevelt and not Lewis had given in, for Steelman was known to favor a union shop. Roosevelt through Perkins must have known that, and the tribunal's vote was as expected, 2 to 1 for Lewis. Perkins nowhere discusses her part in this maneuver, and such silence with her is often a sign of distress. Because of the crisis Lewis had been able to force from the government what he could not win at the bargaining table, and the administration to many people seemed all too willing to sacrifice individual rights to a group interest.

With the National Mediation Board no longer functioning, Perkins saw no alternative but to create another with slightly different personnel and powers. In wartime there had to be some agency superior to the Conciliation Service for averting strikes. If the Secretary of Labor could say to a union "I will certify this case to the board," then most unions would continue to work because the dispute had been promised special handling. For some, accepting a decision from the board might be only a device for saving face, but for most it was a recognition that the times demanded some sacrifices of everyone. As the first board began to crumble, she insisted to representatives of both labor and management: "No matter what you do, another board will be created. It has to be. There is no other way to handle this situation."[23]

Davis, the board's chairman, had suggested: "You might as well let it go. We're all so mad now — everybody is stirred up — that it might be a good idea to let the board die and rest in peace for a few weeks. I agree that the President will have to create something else, but the fact that this board has died will make a more amiable disposition. The labor leaders will miss it when they find they haven't got it, and the employers know in their hearts that they need something like it. Let it go."[24]

In Eleanor Roosevelt's opinion Perkins was "at her best" in these months as, "quietly and with infinite patience," she went about creating a new board to serve as a final court of appeals for wartime labor disputes. She planned to have it emerge from a conference of labor and management on wartime labor relations, and in preparing for the conference she met again and again with individuals and groups in an attempt to enlarge the areas of agreement. The national defeat at Pearl Harbor impressed others with the need for a new board, and ten days later twelve representatives of industry and twelve of labor, six each from the CIO and AFL, convened in Washington as the War-Labor Conference and stayed in session for a week. The two moderators were Davis and Senator Elbert D. Thomas, chairman of the Senate Labor Committee. Perkins herself refused to preside because "labor would resent it if I did not rule in their favor, and the employers certainly would resent it if I did." And she invited Thomas because she wanted a legislator at the conference who might take some responsibility for the decisions and be able to explain them to Congress.

At the end of their sessions the conference members had agreed on this much: There would be no strikes and no lockouts for the duration of the war. Disputes would be settled by collective bargaining with the aid, if necessary, of the Conciliation Service. All matters on which they could not agree would be referred to a board to be appointed by the President, and they agreed to be bound by its decisions. All matters, that is, but one.

The exception was the union shop. The employers insisted that no dispute involving a union shop could be referred to the board, and the labor leaders were determined to refuse such a limitation. Despite the efforts of herself and the two moderators, neither side would compromise, and on this point the conference adjourned without agreement.[25]

When she told Roosevelt, he said, "We can't expect perfection. I'll accept the three important points they *have* agreed on with thanks. I'll promise to appoint the board promptly." He paused suggestively. "We'll let the board make its own rules and regulations and determine its jurisdiction." On January 12, 1942, by executive order he established a National War Labor Board of twelve members, four each to represent labor, industry and the public, and appointed Davis chairman.

Until Congress gave it some statutory sanctions the following year, the board's power to enforce its decisions rested entirely on what was no more than a pledge between twelve union and twelve business leaders. Yet almost all others on both sides held themselves bound by what Perkins called "this proxy promise," and throughout the war the average number of working days lost in strikes was about $3/10$ of 1 percent a year, or perhaps one day per worker per four years. When anyone wrote to Perkins complaining of any work stoppage at all in wartime, she was always prompt to point out with statistics that, though "some rigid system" might be worked out, "free American workmen" were continuing to outproduce "all the world's bound or frozen labor."[26]

On the thorny problem of the union shop, the board was able to work out, as Roosevelt had hoped, a compromise called "the mainte- nance of membership" principle. Unions would not seek either a closed or union shop in their negotiations, but union members or those who subsequently joined the union would be required to keep up their membership for the life of the contract or be subject to dismissal. Once the principle was agreed upon, it was consistently upheld throughout the war and eventually applied to some three million workers, or 20 percent of those covered by collective bargain- ing agreements.[27]

But in another aspect of wartime labor relations, wage stabilization, the board was less fortunate, and because its decisions were based upon the Cost of Living Index, the Bureau of Labor Statistics, like some helpless target vessel, was slowly drawn into the line of fire. The trouble started in April 1942 when the board established a measure, the Little Steel formula, for settling wage disputes. Increases would be allowed to the extent that the cost of living index showed a rise in prices since January 1941. As the price of clothing, food, rent and transportation rose, labor leaders increasingly focused their attention on the Cost of Living Index. Was it keeping pace?

The bureau itself under Acting Commissioner Ford Hinrichs

(Lubin, though still sometimes consulted, was on loan to the White House) asked the same question, and Perkins, as she had done in 1933, asked the American Statistical Association to appoint a committee to review the index. In October 1943 the committee reported: The index was a trustworthy measure of price changes, and many of the criticisms of it arose from attempts to use it "for purposes to which it is not adapted."

The index was limited in what it could measure, and its name for many people was misleading. It did not record the cost of living in the sense that most people understood the phrase but only the change in prices of certain consumer goods, chiefly food, clothing and rent. If a worker, in order to be closer to his new job, took a new apartment at a higher rent (often the only one available), his cost of living had increased but was not reflected in the index. Or if, after the Depression years of eating hamburger, now with good wages he occasionally ate steak, the rise in the price of hamburger, recorded in the index, did not reflect the rise in his out-of-pocket expenses. Many increases were forced on workers because of wartime shortages. No grocers or butchers offered sales when everything could be sold at top price, and secondhand items were often unobtainable. Union leaders stressed that the index was lagging on the cost of living, and in the sense in which they understood the phrase, it was.

To meet their complaints Roosevelt, in late October 1943, appointed a Presidential Committee of five from the War Labor Board to examine the situation. Perkins wanted its hearings to be open, so that the BLS staff could explain the index to the public, but Davis, the committee's chairman, thought that might only increase the confusion. He also ruled against having a BLS representative attend all the committee's sessions in order to answer any questions. Partly as a result, when Hinrichs and Aryness Joy Wickens, who was in direct charge of the index, testified before the committee, the atmosphere was slightly inquisitorial, not the best for explanations of complicated matters.

Hinrichs was an extremely competent statistician, but he lacked Lubin's gift for clear explanation. After he had talked for about half an hour, Wickens thought George Meany and R. J. Thomas, the two labor members of the committee, were growing confused and angry, but whenever she interrupted in an effort to answer their questions more clearly, beneath the table Hinrichs would give her ankle a kick. He was the Acting Commissioner and it was to be his show.

In the following weeks Meany and Thomas had their union statis-

ticians prepare a report, which, without a warning to anyone, they
released to the press. It was more of a political attack than a statistical
analysis. The BLS was accused of consciously rigging its figures to
hold the index, and labor's wages, down, and the union statisticians,
using their own tables, showed that prices had risen 43.5 percent from
January 1941 to December 1943 whereas the BLS index showed only a
23.4 percent rise.

What the report really offered was an alternative index with a
different basis for measuring the rise in the cost of living. Whether it
should be used for that purpose was a political not a statistical decision, to be made in the White House and Congress, not in the BLS.
Meany was attempting to change a national policy by attacking a
technical agency and its information. His charges that the BLS was
consciously rigging figures against labor were not likely to stand up.

He returned to them again, however, at a meeting in June between
the BLS and union statisticians to review the bureau's index and its
problems. Meany asked to appear and, once again without warning,
distributed his speech to the press. It was an hour of personal attack
on the staff of the BLS. Hinrichs, who was present and presiding, was
"a bureaucratic monkey on a stick who moves up and down in conformity with the dictates of administration wage policy." And on the
BLS as a whole: "There are sharp indications that, the price control
policy of the government having failed to keep living costs down, the
Administration decided the next best thing to do was to keep down
the cost of living index. In this policy the Bureau of Labor Statistics
obsequiously acquiesced. We are led to the inescapable conclusion
that the bureau has become identified with an effort to freeze wages, to
the extent that it is no longer a free agency of statistical research."

Later that month a technical committee, appointed by Davis to
examine the index, made its report to the Presidential Committee.
The BLS had done a competent, honest job in its price index work.
The three members of the technical committee, led by Wesley C.
Mitchell, probably the most distinguished person in the field, concluded that the margin for error in the BLS index was probably
between 2.5 and 4 points rather than the 20 points claimed by the
union statisticians.

The bureau emerged from the controversy far stronger than it went
in. Its statistics had a claim to be the most investigated in the world
and its staff the most frequently complimented. The improvement in
its national reputation from the Hoover years of the Depression was
striking, and in that achievement Perkins, Lubin, Hinrichs and

Wickens all had a share. The circumstances of their victory, however, drained it of pleasure, and ultimately Meany's rancor, passed on to others in labor circles, would have a part in denying both Hinrichs and Wickens the bureau's top post, though both were qualified.[28]

For Perkins the controversy was typical of much of her work in the war. The hours of discussion had produced no legislation; no one was better off because of them; without climax the controversy one day simply began to fade as another emerged. A succession of such problems was just routine administration, and in later years she could not imagine anyone wanting to hear about it.

Chapter 34

※※

*Roosevelt's health. The Equal Rights Amendment. She tries to resign.
Roosevelt's fourth inauguration. His death. Her talk with Eleanor
Roosevelt. Her successor, Secretary Schwellenbach.*

Roosevelt's decision to seek a fourth term bothered Perkins less than his decision to seek a third. All the reasons connected with the war seemed stronger in 1944 than in 1940, and Dewey far less than Willkie seemed a suitable alternative. Toward the end of Dewey's campaign she wrote a friend: "He is running for President of the United States, a great office, implying great power, great wisdom, and a deep knowl edge of public and international policy, and he is running for it the way a District Attorney would try to trap a criminal. It is very disheartening. It makes one ashamed."[1]

She apparently knew little of Roosevelt's ill health and nothing of his weakened heart. She saw him less often and for shorter periods, and though he was visibly aging he still seemed sound. Eleanor Roosevelt, her most likely source of the truth, was herself deceived. As early as April 1944 the White House physician, Vice Admiral Ross McIntire, began systematically lying to everyone about the President's condition, and perhaps because the war was going well the press did not seriously challenge him.

There remains a question about those who saw Roosevelt with some regularity during this period, among them cabinet officers, his wife and daughter, Grace Tully, Edwin Watson, Stephen Early and Harry Hopkins. Some of these at least saw his fainting fits, trembling hands and slack jaw, and yet said nothing. What was their responsibility to him and to the American people? How was their behavior any different from the palace guard that surrounded, say, Mussolini and kept his physical decline from the Italian people. Seemingly not at all — except that in the United States there was a free press. The fundamental responsibility for the deception would seem to rest with the doctors who concealed the medical facts and the press that chose not to pursue them.

In her biography, *The Roosevelt I Knew,* Perkins states that the first time she became alarmed about his health was at the cabinet meeting the day before his fourth inauguration: "I still think he had been well until that time." During the campaign she had dismissed the photographs of him as carefully selected by the Republican press to show him at his worst, and in the weeks before the convention she had seen nothing to cause her to doubt his fitness, at sixty-two, for another term.[2]

She had no official role at the convention, but during it and the months preceding she worked to keep the party from endorsing an amendment to the Constitution that would prohibit any discrimination because of sex. Since 1923, when such an equal rights amendment had first been proposed by the small but vocal National Women's party, it had divided women's groups. Florence Kelley, after supporting the idea as the natural sequel to the women's suffrage amendment, had reluctantly turned against it as a threat to legal protections for women such as maternity aid, mothers' pensions and industrial regulations. Throughout the 1920s she made opposition to the amendment a regular part of Consumers' League work while continuing to fight for measures to end specific discriminations. In the same period Mary Anderson of the Women's Bureau also steadily opposed the amendment, as did the League of Women Voters. Perkins by nature and experience was with the majority: the National Women's party was "a little handful of women fighting for a theory."[3]

The amendment came to the fore during the war because of the large number of women entering the work force. Suddenly working women, the majority of them married and with children, were everywhere. Industry, the press and government praised them, and unions, though keeping them often under disabilities, began to accept them. At the same time, however, the press carried stories of children penned in basement corrals or exiled for hours to the neighborhood movies. A social worker in the San Fernando Valley counted forty-five infants locked in cars in a single war-plant parking lot, and the number of child-neglect cases in Norfolk, Virginia, tripled.

The issue of child care centers financed by federal, state and local governments exposed the general confusion in the country over what was meant by equality between sexes and the duties of motherhood. A program of child care centers would have been protective legislation for women, and yet Perkins, Anderson and Katharine Lenroot of the

Children's Bureau were against it. A "mother's primary duty is to her home and children," a Children's Bureau bulletin declared. "This duty is one she cannot lay aside, no matter what the emergency." Conversely many women who favored the amendment also favored child care centers, though in doing so they seemed to seek the kind of protective legislation they condemned as discriminatory. The debate was hot and without conclusion beyond the obvious fact that Congress, state legislatures and most communities were not prepared even in wartime to encourage young mothers to leave their homes. On this point Perkins was in step with her times.[4]

Months before the convention her opposition to the amendment exposed her to the wrath of a friend, Jane Grant, founder of the Lucy Stone League, which battled for the right of married women to work, vote, travel and campaign under their maiden names. Though Perkins was the outstanding Lucy Stoner of her day, Grant wrote in an article, "Confessions of a Feminist":

> Annoying to a budding feminist, were those anti-suffragettes who, by keeping their fences nicely mended while their fellow females were scrapping for the vote, were now in positions of power . . . [This] group is led today by Secretary of Labor Frances Perkins; Mary Anderson . . . and others who proclaim that "women must assume equal responsibility with men" but turn thumbs down on proposals for real equality.[5]

The tone was misleading, for after a subsequent exchange of letters in which neither changed her views, Grant closed with "I disagree with you but always respect you," and ten years later she was again asking for advice on how to persuade the State Department to issue passports in maiden names. But she correctly identified Perkins as a leader of the amendment's opposition.[6]

In the weeks preceding the convention, for the most part Perkins acted through others "because I thought it would be more seemly not to appear to be organized within the administration." But to Florence A. Armstrong, the chairman of the National Women's party, she put her views directly:

> It is with great regret that some of us recognize that the small group of women in the National Women's Party who were in favor of suffrage and who worked with us for suffrage, should have taken this doctrinaire position which makes more difficult the passage and maintenance of legislation aimed to improve the conditions of their working sisters, which was one of the primary reasons why many women wanted to vote and many wanted to have them vote.

A constant argument of the National Women's party was that protective legislation, such as limiting hours or prohibiting night work, often deprived women of jobs. And in some cases that plainly was true. But a survey of the effects of such legislation by the Women's Bureau in 1928 had shown that 98 percent of women benefited from it, and only 2 percent suffered. Ever since the passage of the 54-hour bill in the New York legislature Perkins had chosen to work for the good of the greater number, and she continued to do so now.

When the convention opened, she spoke against the amendment before the resolutions committee and also on the floor. In the end, however, she and her side were defeated. "No comment," she told reporters.[7] That year both national parties in their platforms promised to seek an equal rights amendment, though neither acted to redeem the pledge. The Senate in 1946 approved one, 38–35, 26 votes short of the two-thirds majority required. Not until 1972, twenty-six years later, would the Senate pass an amendment not crippled by exceptions and send it to the states for ratification.

By then the need of working women for special legislative protection had declined and with it some of the fear that the amendment would wipe out whatever protection women had. After the U.S. Supreme Court in 1941 held the Fair Labor Standards Act constitutional, the idea that government was a proper instrument for regulating the hours and wages of men and women, treated alike, steadily gained ground. Also unions less often opposed social legislation, and by admitting more women protected more by collective bargaining. And, most important, the women's liberation movement grew and grew, but by the time it was well under way, Perkins had died.

After Roosevelt defeated Dewey, Perkins again suggested to him that he accept her resignation, and this time he agreed, asking only that she wait until inauguration day, January 20, 1945, when he would announce it together with the appointment of her successor. But just as four years earlier, whenever she tried to discuss a successor with him, he put her off.

Meanwhile, as she described in *The Roosevelt I Knew:*

> I had told the people immediately around me in the Department of Labor so that they could be making their own plans. I packed my books and papers. Carpets were cleaned and chairs reupholstered. Everything was in readiness for a successor.
>
> Here it was the eve of Inauguration Day. I felt something must be done, because we had agreed upon that date. I had sent him a note in

the morning to remind him to tell the other members of the cabinet that this was my last meeting. It was a little courtesy he had observed when other cabinet officers retired. I felt he would make a nice little speech, the other members of the cabinet would comment on our long association, all the amenities would be observed and we would part in friendly fashion. He did nothing of the kind, so I asked to see him after cabinet. Several of us wanted to see him. Since we always waited in order of our rank, I was last, for the Secretary of Labor is the lowest ranking officer of the cabinet, not because of his subject matter but because the office was created last.

We had been in session almost two hours. It was four o'clock. The change in his appearance was marked. As I sat down beside him I had a sense of his enormous fatigue. He had the pallor, the deep gray color, of a man who had been long ill. He looked like an invalid who has been allowed to see guests for the first time and the guests had stayed too long. In a hospital a nurse would have put her arm behind him and lowered him down onto his pillow. But he was sitting in an office chair. He supported his head with his hand as though it were too much to hold it up. His lips were blue. His hand shook. I hated to press him, but I had to.

"Don't you think," I said, "I had better get Early [his press secretary] to announce my resignation right now? I'll go in and write out the announcement."

"No," he said. "Frances, you can't go now. You mustn't put this on me now. I just can't be bothered now. I can't think of anybody else, and I can't get used to anybody else. Not now! Do stay there and don't say anything. You are all right."

Then he said beautiful words which I shall always think of as our parting; he said them in a voice filled with exhaustion, and I knew that it was an effort for him to speak and that he was saying something he felt.

"Frances, you have done awfully well. I know what you have been through. I know what you have accomplished. Thank you."

He put his hand over mine and gripped it. There were tears in our eyes.

It was all the reward that I could have ever have asked — to know that he had recognized the storms and trials I had faced in developing our program, to know that he appreciated the program and thought well of it, and that he was grateful.

I could not say more, although I felt, intellectually and logically, that I ought to have insisted that the resignation go through. I could not insist. I felt I must stand by until this pressure and strain were over. I felt it would pass. When he came back, and if the war load lightened a little, the question could be opened again.[8]

The next day was the inauguration, held at the White House, where it would be least tiring. He looked better than on the previous afternoon, but just before taking the oath he said to her, "Frances, I can't do it," to which she replied, "Mr. President, you must."

His speech was short, a plea for patience and faith, based on a recollection from boyhood.

> I remember that my old schoolmaster said, in days that seemed to us then to be secure and untroubled: "Things in life will not always run smoothly. Sometimes we will be rising toward the heights — then all will seem to reverse itself and start downward. The great fact to remember is that the trend of civilization itself is forever upward; that a line drawn through the middle of the peaks and valleys of the centuries always has an upward trend.

During the reception he began to look so ill that people became alarmed. Mrs. Woodrow Wilson frightened Perkins further by saying, "He looks exactly as my husband did when he went into his decline."

"Don't say that to another soul," said Perkins. "He has a great and terrible job to do, and he's got to do it, even if it kills him."[9]

Two days later Roosevelt left secretly for the Crimea and the meeting at Yalta with Churchill and Stalin. Two and a half months later, on April 12, as evening fell, he was dead.

After the ceremonies in Washington and Hyde Park, Perkins went to the White House one day to spend an hour with Eleanor Roosevelt. The walls were bare, the books packed, the furniture tagged. Other people were moving about the rooms, but they found a bench at the end of a hall and sat there "like two school girls and talked about FD."

She had not come to console Mrs. Roosevelt on the loss of a faithful husband. She knew the story of Lucy Rutherford and probably also that Roosevelt, behind his wife's back, had continued to see Mrs. Rutherford. They talked of Roosevelt the leader, by whose loss they both were devasted.

Perkins had tried to find "a sense of compensation" through prayer, but his physical presence was still too much with her. She longed to have "a good laugh with him over the confusions of the human race," or even more to watch him "put his subtle and delicate hand into the mess of human passions and jealousies and bring out some kind of voluntary and creative order." As she wrote a friend: "You remember Plato said once that creation is the victory of persuasion, not the victory of force. I always thought FD was an extraordinary illustration of that."

Mrs. Roosevelt, though she wept, felt a stronger sense of compensation: Roosevelt's spirit would continue to work with all the spiritual forces in the world that made for peace, order and righteousness. Released from his person by death, he might be able to accomplish more for mankind.

That seemed to Perkins a highly personal, vigorous version of the communion of saints and, overwhelmed by her sense of loss, she doubted. For the moment she clung to the memory of Roosevelt's most wonderful trait. "FD was never disappointed. If things went wrong, he took another tack." The battle for peace, order and righteousness went on.

She left the White House comforted and inspired. Eleanor Roosevelt was "a great person really." Everything she had said and done in the last weeks was "almost perfect." Since Perkins thought no human could be perfect, she could give no higher praise.[10]

Soon after Truman became President, Perkins offered him her resignation, but he asked her and others in the cabinet to stay on for the time being. Then only a few weeks later, in May, his secretary requested her, Secretary of Agriculture Claude Wickard and Attorney General Francis Biddle to submit letters of resignation immediately, to be effective July 1. Biddle was offended at receiving the message from a secretary and even suggested that they protest on the ground that the abruptness and lack of cause cast a slur on their records. But neither she nor Wickard would join him. She thought it entirely reasonable that Truman should want his own cabinet, and though she would have preferred a call direct from him, she continued to have cordial relations with him.[11]

Her successor was to be Lewis B. Schwellenbach, a former senator from Washington and for the last six years a federal judge in Spokane. She remembered him as a pleasant man and, recalling her difficulties in succeeding Doak in the office, looked forward to easing Schwellenbach's succession. As soon as his appointment was announced, she wired him in Washington, offering her congratulations and cooperation in the transfer of power.

In June she wrote, suggesting that she could meet him at the airport or train, offering him the use of one of the department's cars and asking if she could make any hotel reservations for him or his party. His replies were so short they seemed almost cold, and one with information about his train was signed only by his secretary. She continued, however, to prepare memoranda for him on matters pending, postponed a decision on the Relief and Rehabilitation Act until he could give his opinion on it and refused in her last week to upgrade personnel because to do so required transferring funds among bureaus.

Meanwhile a Recognition Dinner in her honor was held at the Mayflower Hotel on June 27. Among the sponsors were some of her oldest acquaintances, Mary Woolley, Mary Dreier, Rabbi Stephen B. Wise, Agnes Leach and Henry Morgenthau, Sr. The speakers were William Green for the AFL, Philip Murray for the CIO, Mary T. Norton from the House, Wagner from the Senate and Eric Johnston for the U.S. Chamber of Commerce. Green made such a graceful speech that in her closing remarks she set the audience laughing with the observation that it seemed as though, after twelve years of her administration, just as she was about to retire, labor had finally become reconciled to her appointment.[12]

Several days later she went to the railroad station to meet Schwellenbach, taking both department cars and intending to turn one over to him. To her distress, when she greeted him and his wife and secretary on the platform, he "seemed utterly astonished that I should be at the station to meet them."

In the car as they drove to his hotel she realized that, while she talked about the department, he talked mostly about his small dog, Ginger, which he held on his lap. He took it everywhere with him, he said. She offered to make arrangements for Schwellenbach's swearing-in, but he said that he was thinking of asking some senatorial friend to administer the oath. By then he was so plainly evading her questions that she asked no more.

His attitude upset her. "I mean, I was a Democrat. I wasn't an enemy. If he had been a Republican taking office, I might have understood it — that there was party enmity — although as far as I was concerned, there would not have been." At the department, when staff members asked her about details of Schwellenbach's plans, she had to confess she did not know.

On Saturday, June 30, he was sworn in at the Capitol by his friend Sherman Minton, a former senator from Indiana and now a federal judge. Perkins was present, but the newspaper accounts of the ceremony were given mostly to an announcement by Schwellenbach of the department's need for a complete reorganization. By then it was clear to members of the department that he meant to disassociate himself from Perkins. Though both were Democrats, though the Social Security Act and Fair Labor Standards Act were among the glories of the New Deal, he evidently did not account her an honorable predecessor.

Later that day one of the staff pointed out to her that Schwellenbach's swearing-in was not effective. Minton did not qualify under the pertinent statute as a person authorized to administer the oath. She left word therefore that when Schwellenbach arrived at the department, before he signed any papers, he should be sworn in again as quietly as possible, "in order not to humiliate him." And on July 2 he was officially sworn in by James Dodson, the Chief Clerk, with only Gladys Burch, one of Perkins's former secretaries, as a witness.

Soon after, Schwellenbach called in the department's bureau heads and addressed them, beginning, "I don't know anything good about you." When he finished, no one could think of anything to say.

He also issued to the entire department a General Order No. 1, which he gave to the press. The Washington *Evening Star* put it on the front page:

> July 2, 1945
>
> I am issuing this order now before any specific instance arises, so as not to subject anyone to embarrassment. Perhaps because my previous experience has been in the legislative and judicial branches of the Government, I am particularly sensitive to the importance of this question.
>
> I must insist that in this Department there is given full recognition to the fact it is the function of this Department to execute the laws. The duty of an officer in this Department is to accept the laws as Congress has written them and as the Courts have interpreted them. The fact that he may think the Congress should have written, or the Courts should have interpreted a law differently in no case justifies him in ignoring or attempting to circumvent the law. I will expect full cooperation on this policy.
>
> /s/ Lewis B. Schwellenbach

It was his judgment on the Perkins administration. The staff was alternately outraged and puzzled. In his first press conference he had announced a major reorganization of the department, to be completed within "the next thirty days" — an administrative impossibility. He had talked of asking labor to be the reorganization's "advisor as well as its advocate" and to give "direct assistance." Two weeks later he announced that the statistical work in the Bureau of Labor Statistics was very poor, "too academic." In view of the controversy with labor leaders over the cost of living index, Acting Commissioner Ford Hinrichs offered his resignation. Schwellenbach, however, said he had been misunderstood and misquoted by the press, and persuaded Hinrichs to remain.

In September he issued a statement affirming confidence in the bureau and announcing that henceforth the Cost of Living Index would be named the Consumers' Price Index for Moderate Income Families in Large Cities. Because the title was more accurate, it was an improvement; but the change was a flourish, not a matter of substance.

It gradually became clear that in Schwellenbach's years away from Washington he had lost touch with government affairs and on his return had accepted as true the views of the department's most partisan congressional and labor critics. But as the months passed he frequently found, as in the BLS controversy, that the other side of the argument was more convincing. In a Christmas speech to the staff he confessed that he had found "many dedicated people at work in the department." It was as close, perhaps, as a proud man could come to an apology.

Perkins, enjoying a summer in Maine, ignored the department and its affairs. Truman had agreed to send her in October as a government representative to the International Labor Organization meeting in Paris. Beyond that her break with the department was complete.

Still in another sense she would never be free of it. She would always be Miss Perkins, the first woman in the cabinet, and as so many people had observed, in such an unlikely post. In the years after the war, as Schwellenbach and his successor, Maurice J. Tobin, struggled with strike after strike, she often thought of those editorial writers who had been so sure that a two-fisted man was all that was needed. And "I would laugh and laugh and laugh."[13]

PART VI

After Sixty-Five

Chapter 35

➤➤≪≪

Susanna. The Roosevelt I Knew. *Her changing ideas. The Civil Service Commission. Wilson's death. She moves to New York and starts a new career.*

AFTER TWELVE YEARS of cabinet office Perkins was happy on vacation, but she had no intention of retiring from the world of work. Her health was good, she was sixty-five (she thought she was sixty-three) and she believed in work. It was the surest source of health and happiness, which "usually evade you if you seek them."[1]

Her cabinet salary had been $15,000 a year, from which she had been able to save very little. Besides herself, she supported Wilson and sometimes paid bills for Susanna, who had separated from David Hare in 1943. That year the family's medical expenses rose to $6000, and even so she gave $1500 to charities. Always, regardless of how her income rose or fell, she tithed.[2]

Beyond her salary — her ability to work — her financial assets were small: an apartment in New York, whose rent she covered by frequently subletting; a half-interest (her sister held the other half) in an untilled farm in Maine with a house more than a hundred years old; a house in Washington, which she had recently bought with a large mortgage; and about $200 a year income from stocks and a savings account. All turned into cash, they would not have carried her far.

More valuable were her name, her association with Roosevelt and her ability to lecture. She also had the admiration of Truman, who had suggested she take a post in his administration. For the moment, however, she went to Newcastle with Susanna and planned a visit to the Fallonsby Inn in North Sutton, New Hampshire, where Wilson was spending the summer.[3]

*

Her relations with Susanna at the time were troubled. Susanna, twenty-nine and recently divorced, was developing a personality of her own, and Perkins at sixty-five was not ready to accept it. She still had strong ideas of the kind of person Susanna should be, and she was used to dominating.

It may be that anyone who works for long in high public office risks becoming defective as a human being. Certainly the choice has consequences. In 1933, when Perkins went to Washington, Susanna was sixteen, and they seldom thereafter shared a home. Much of what the average parent does for a child, Perkins for lack of time did through her secretary, Jay. When Susanna got in some scrapes at Bryn Mawr, Jay was sent to act for Perkins. Predictably, relations between Susanna and Jay were sometimes prickly.

Perkins's letters to Susanna were frequently dictated to Jay, and they often have the tone of an office memorandum: "I appreciate your desire to know something about the state of the Nation; and only regret that you haven't been reading the newspaper. I have now subscribed for the New York Times for you." But a child of any age wants to be loved, not administered like a bureau in the labor department.

The occasional short cuts for efficiency can harden into an attitude: "Susanna and David are back from the West . . . Susy, for the first time in her life, turned out to be a real friend, standing by and doing errands nobly." The busy public official expects support, forgetting that in the office it is partly bought by offering subordinates wages, power or prestige. But in a family it must be earned, at least in part, by imaginative attention to the problems of others. Though that takes time, there is no substitute.

Among Perkins's most loyal supporters in the department, with the exception of Reilly, Susanna had a reputation for being a trouble to her mother. Years later many still spoke of her with recollected disapproval. Among Perkins's friends in New York, however, sympathy often flowed the other way. Perkins was acknowledged to be bossy, and on her resignation her friend Margaret Poole wrote her: "What are you going to do now, and have you the house in Washington? I do hope that will be a success, for Susanna needs you more — these young things should have their chance."[4]

Another chance for Susanna was how Perkins regarded her daughter's divorce. In Santa Fe Susanna and her husband had led a harumscarum life, which, in Perkins's opinion, had offered Susanna insufficient stability. With Wilson's problems constantly before her, she was always fearful that Susanna might have inherited a tendency to emotional instability. So she was glad to have Hare pass from the scene and hopefully set about assisting Susanna to restructure her life.[5]

In the case of a friend, Nannie Burgess, Perkins's approach to the problems of divorce had been characteristically disciplined and practical. One day on entering the Burgess house she had found Nannie, the fourth wife of Starling Burgess, the yacht designer, weeping on the sofa. Life was over. Starling was divorcing her for a girl thirty years younger who could read Greek poetry and navigate. Perkins, looking down, had said: "Get up from there. Stop crying. Go wash your face. Then go to early communion every Sunday for a year and then see how you feel." Later she added, "It's only your pride that's been hurt," and in retrospect Nannie Burgess decided that both the prescription and the diagnosis were correct.[6]

The same approach was less successful with Susanna. Her husband, too, had left her for another woman, but she was much more deeply wounded. For a number of years, to friends "she seemed just to float and dream, and life was purposeless."

Meanwhile some of her mother's practical suggestions and arrangements were helpful and others not. Perkins had found an apartment for Susanna in New York as well as a roommate, Miranda Masocco, one of Susanna's Santa Fe friends. But then one day she sent instructions from Washington on how Susanna and Masocco should dress for a reception she was attending in New York for Princess Juliana of Holland. Masocco wore a simple black dress and pearls as requested, but Susanna appeared in a watermelon skirt with green top, Capezio shoes tied up to the knees, her hair piled on her head with a huge red rose and another huge red rose on a black velvet ribbon around her neck. For just a second Perkins lost her self-control, and her face registered shock.

As Masocco listened to the arguments between mother and daughter, she was constantly amazed at "the mixture of affection, hot words and total misunderstanding." The difficulty seemed less one of different generations than of genuinely different personalities. Both were warm, enthusiastic and highly articulate. But where Perkins approached humanity through politics, Susanna approached it through art. For Perkins success was generally the result of careful calculation and compromise; for Susanna, of bold assertion. Perkins urged conformity in choice of dress, friends and way of life; Susanna sought adventure. Be practical, said Perkins, but Susanna could not. And often when her father was present, he would support her in her efforts to be herself.

Ultimately Perkins counseled caution: Don't ever reveal all of yourself. Don't let anyone in too close — not into your secret places — or you will be hurt. Susanna sometimes wondered if her mother had ever revealed all of herself to anyone, even to her husband.

One gift of value that Perkins daily gave her daughter was privacy. She still steadfastly refused to discuss her family with the press or to be photographed with either member, and away from the glare and confusion of publicity Susanna was able to work her way out of an unhappy divorce and back to ordinary life. By 1948, helped by her job at the Metropolitan Museum of Art, she had developed a life and identity for herself that gave her and her friends satisfaction. In 1953 in Margaret Poole's apartment she married an artist, Calvert Coggeshall, and the following year they had a son. From the day he was born, Perkins lavished affection on him. Being a grandmother was a relationship at which she was superb.

Susanna once observed of her relations with her mother that their difficulty was not too little love on her mother's part but too much. If only her mother had been able to have five or six children, then her powerful maternal drive would have spread over many instead of concentrating on one. In a small family her extraordinary energy was almost a curse.[7]

As the two, in July 1945, traveled north to Maine for Perkins's first long vacation in many years, her friends, like Margaret Poole, wondered where that energy would be focused next. For none could imagine her retiring.

Her first project was all but forced on her by a friend who was a literary agent, George Bye of New York. Within weeks of Roosevelt's death Bye had suggested that she write a biography of Roosevelt, and though she refused — she felt she had neither the time nor the talent for writing — Bye kept calling and coming to see her. He had interested the Viking Press in the idea, but the editors, hoping to have the first biography on the market, wanted the manuscript by May 1, 1946, for publication that fall. When Perkins sailed in September 1945 for the October meeting of the ILO in Paris, she had again refused. Time was too short.

She went first to England, and in London an agent of Bye and Viking's promptly appeared at her hotel with a contract. Susanna was with her and urged her to go ahead with the book. "Oh, do it,

Mother. Don't be so stupid. Just do it!" Perkins allowed herself to be persuaded, signed the contract and thought no more about it until she returned to Washington just before Christmas. By then May 1 seemed very close, and she lamented "the irresponsibility of the young," always so "willing to urge their parents to crucify themselves."

She had four months in which to produce a biography of Roosevelt and, with a sense of "running a terrible race with the wolves just behind," she hired several typists and a research assistant and began to write. After several weeks of hard work she had next to nothing, and she began to panic. She bought a recording machine and started to talk her memories. Now the words came too easily; around the room were piles and piles of typed sheets, which refused to coalesce into a book. In despair she called Bye: "At first I couldn't write enough; now I can't stop. And it's terrific — there's so much of it, redundant, overlapping, repetitive. I can't clean it out. I haven't got that kind of mind. I can't remember what I said in Chapter Two."

He recommended an editor and suggested an acquaintance, Howard Taubman, just out of the army and about to rejoin the *New York Times* as a music critic. Taubman was not yet settled down, said Bye, and in need of money; a short-term job at good pay would appeal to him. She eagerly agreed, yet with regret. The addition of still another to her staff would consume almost her entire advance of $20,000. Unless the book was a big success, she would have a financial as well as a literary disaster.

Taubman arrived in Washington in late April and for three weeks, in her house at 2127 Leroy Place, worked day and night to fashion a book. He thought her material excellent but her organization and style terrible. At a book's length her flow of thought had proved circular, and she was unable to impose on it any beginning, middle or end. Taubman began with an outline — The Man, The State, The Nation, The World — and into the categories he fitted her material, demanding more where needed.

Every night sitting in bed she would talk into the recorder, and in the morning the spools would be on the floor outside her door. A typist would come in early, take them to a large room on the top floor and start transcribing them. Taubman would arrive, review the previous day's work and have an interview with her, after which she would disappear to do her research before again dictating into the small hours of the night. He was impressed by her ability at sixty-six to stick at the job and turn out the work.

Her memory was extraordinarily good, particularly for detail, but her sense of which detail was interesting was very uncertain. And he was constantly surprised that she could be so brilliant in anecdote or conversation and so poor in writing. She seemed to need the riposte of conversation, or at least the physical presence of an audience, to sharpen her diction and sense of form. At the end of three weeks, on May 15, they turned in a typescript of 196,000 words, which Taubman thought was still "too windy." The publishers agreed, and in two more weeks of work in New York he reduced it by a third.

What emerged, *The Roosevelt I Knew,* was Perkins's book in material, tone, approach, sense of proportion and perspective. But the writing was entirely Taubman's, and her friends instantly saw the presence of another's hand. After the first excerpt appeared in *Collier's,* Henry Bruère sent her his sigh of relief in a letter from a summer hotel. "I took the magazine and hurried to the back end of the porch, drew up another chair to screen me from the boarders, and read it. And it is beautiful. You've done it, you've hit it — it's all right."

Despite the odd and hasty collaboration it is still one of the best biographies of Roosevelt, and at the time, with the field to itself, it was a popular success. Editions soon were published in England, France, Germany and Austria, and Perkins began to feel better about it. She gradually perceived the quality of Taubman's work and later confessed, "I've never been grateful enough to him." But the book's success did not incline her to pursue a literary career: "I was exhausted at the end of it."

One thing it gave her that almost thirty years of public service had not. After paying all her expenses, taxes and the costs of repairing the houses in Washington and Newcastle, she was able to set aside in stocks and bonds about $25,000. The amount would have been almost double if either her agent or publisher had thought to advise her of the tax laws regarding literary works, but apparently no one expected the book to be so successful. It continued to pay royalties for years, however, and these plus the income from her holdings gave her, for the first time since 1918, an annual income of several thousand dollars above what she earned. Roosevelt surely would have been pleased.[8]

One of the book's extraordinary qualities is that it is so entirely about Roosevelt and so little about Perkins, but the virtue entails a loss. During the twelve years of his administration her ideas about some of the programs of the New Deal and of their impact on American life began to change. The book conceals the fact, except perhaps by implication, but in a few of her letters and remarks to friends she clearly, if only momentarily, revealed her feelings.

The most profound change concerned her attitude toward the government's welfare programs: what it could and should do for citizens. Her loyalty to the social insurance programs never wavered, or to the public works program of capital construction in time of recession. But by 1939 she had doubts about the administration — not the principle — of the relief programs under Hopkins.

By then unemployment was about half what it had been in 1933, yet the appropriation for fiscal year 1939 was the largest in the program's history. Roosevelt, who had been cutting down on relief, had spectacularly reversed his policy in an election year to ask for the appropriation, and Hopkins had made his remark: "We will spend and spend, tax and tax, and elect and elect."[9] At some point in this period Perkins's instinct turned against the administration of a relief program that seemed more and more to be politically motivated.

She never changed her belief that the government should allow no one to starve, but she was distressed that some people on relief, doing little or no work, should live as well, or almost as well, as some of her self-sufficient, hard-working neighbors in Maine. Federal control was perhaps too remote to be effective. Aryness Joy Wickens in the Bureau of Labor Statistics thought Perkins in this period seemed "to take a position directed toward less big government and more work by private sources of all kinds." It was just the reverse of the position she had held at the start of the Depression and for the twenty years before it.[10]

As a young reformer, apparently before World War I and possibly following a meeting with Edward Devine of the Charity Organization Society, she had written herself a memorandum.

Private Charity

Has it come to stay? Idea of Devine's that no state can be conceived where charity and relief not needed. C.O.S. leaders are planning for permanent organization investment.

Fail to see futility and anomaly of *private* charity. Should be public perhaps under private watch dog supervision.

Better idea of charity as a temporary phase to be abolished as soon as possible. In social work things should appear in reality opposite.[11]

Though the final sentence is unclear, the others convey an idea, beginning to gain support at the turn of the century, that the churches, organized religion, had failed and were bound to fail in alleviating the mass misery of an industrial society. Government, it was argued, must assume the job. But by March 1944 Perkins was writing a friend:

> Although I am quite sure that I started my reformer's life with the conviction that if I could build enough model tenements and make factories perfectly sanitary and safe, reduce the hours of labor to a level of comfort and raise wages at least to the subsistence standards of the ordinary New England farmer, that there would automatically flow out of that situation a population whose moral, cultural, spiritual as well as physical levels would be well-nigh perfect, God has granted me a life long enough to realize that that is not necessarily true and that systematic approaches to the reforms of the individual have to be made from another angle.[12]

In the philosophic argument over the welfare role of the churches it is often said that the underlying motive of government welfare programs is social justice; of the churches, charity. Some enthusiasts for social justice even argue that charity hinders justice; that it is not based on equality and is therefore undemocratic; that it presupposes a superiority in those with more who give to those with less.

Others answer that this is a perverted view of charity. True charity is done for the Lord's sake, in whose eyes all persons are equal.[13] Sometime during the mid-1930s Perkins evidently moved toward a belief that what the government can and should do is limited. Even economic security cannot be guaranteed to everyone from the cradle to the grave, for some people will consistently waste the assistance given them. Also, filling material needs is not the whole problem; there are psychological and spiritual needs that no government program can or should fulfill. In her experience these were best met by religion. In government her enthusiasm remained strongest for such programs as the insurance schemes and public works, which had limited, specific aims.

Ideas like these were not popular with liberal Democrats in the last decade of her life, 1955 to 1965, and may have contributed to the very modest position as a sage that she was accorded within the party.

In her conversations with Truman he had asked her what post she would like in his administration, and she had suggested a position on the Social Security Board. The act was "the measure nearest to my heart," and though Congress had denied her the administration of the unemployment and old age insurance programs, she had never ceased to watch over them, speak on their behalf and urge their improvement. But apparently no position came open, or perhaps there was objection; in any event, on September 12, 1946, Truman appointed her to the Civil Service Commission.[14]

The next day her two fellow commissioners, Harry B. Mitchell and Arthur S. Flemming, called to congratulate her and the commission on her appointment, and she took office the following month under pleasant circumstances. On her resignation seven years later she confessed that, unlike her years in the Labor Department, she "wasn't stimulated all the time," but it was also a relief not to be "always handling fire and bombshells."[15]

The principle infusing all her work was that "the Commission is not a Consistory imposing *punishment* . . . It is concerned only with the question as to whether the applicant is a *suitable* person for the post for which he applies." She opposed any questions on applications or examinations not directly related to suitability and any prying into an employee's private affairs so long as he conducted his personal life in a manner not to discredit the public service.[16]

In her first speech she told an audience of government personnel workers that the answer she would give to some of the medical questions on a civil service application form was "none of your business." She saw no reason for the government to classify the physical defects and minor ailments of its employees. "The less we have beyond first-aid rooms in Government the better. The Government under no condition should have a case history of any employee." The trend, however, was the other way, though without her opposition it might have been stronger.[17]

She had no confidence in the government's ability or desire to keep confidential any information, however personal or tentative. Once when a professor protested that she surely was exaggerating the dangers of misuse, she looked at him as though he were a benighted sophomore and said, "Don't forget: I was the Secretary of Labor during the Harry Bridges case."[18]

Because the government was contracting in the years after the war, more than a million employees lost their jobs, and among them, in competition for the remaining posts, there was much tattling on each other. Her judicial temperament and her experience with the New York Workmen's Compensation Act were useful in helping her to sift legitimate charges from gossip. One case in which the witnesses hurled complaints at each other drew only a quiet comment: "A typical confused human situation."[19]

The case that upset her most, if the intensity and number of her penciled notes are a measure, concerned a Washington policeman and a woman working for the government. The policeman asked the woman to perform on him what has sometimes been considered an unnatural sex act. Later the man felt remorse and confessed the act to his priest, who imposed a religious penance. The priest also advised the man to report the woman to her superiors, which the man did after receiving a promise that his name would not be used. Charges were made against the woman and her case came before the commission.

Perkins was disgusted by the act and thought the man's moral character was so "degraded" that, as a policeman, with the right to enter people's homes, he was "a threat to the community." But she was still more upset that the commission should accept evidence from a source who refused to be identified. Again and again she urged her fellow commissioners to report the man to his superiors so that he, too, might be dismissed. But they refused: he had been promised immunity. She interviewed the man, pointing out that for a mutual, private act, which he had made public, the woman would lose both job and reputation while he would retain both. To her astonishment he could see no injustice in what was happening. His reasoning was as mysterious to her as hers to him. She was defeated.[20]

All her experience in government only strengthened her belief in the right to privacy as a basic human right, the basis of liberty. It is society's loss that she never put her thoughts into a public statement, for she might have articulated the feelings of many. Once, after an article in *Collier's* more on her personality than her deeds, she wrote a friend: "When I read these articles about myself, I always say to Miss Jay, 'Don't let anybody look at me in my coffin.' I have the same sense of their peering underneath the drawn shades into one's private home."[21]

The public's right to know, to know everything, was a kind of voyeurism. What did it matter that she kept a private phone, could not live as did Eleanor Roosevelt or had difficulty admiring Anna Rosenberg? Or that she slept in a single bed, wore a nightgown and kicked the blankets off? When reporters broadcast such facts, she felt pawed and peered at. A sense of privacy for her had nothing to do with a feeling of superiority to others and much to do with a feeling of shame. Also with integrity: People who continually tell all waste their integrity and soon have none; they become creatures of image-building, with nothing firm behind the façade. More fundamentally yet, it had to do with religion. God gave everyone a unique personality, and privacy to protect it. An invasion or waste of privacy was a kind of disrespect for the Deity.

Predictably, when Sam Rayburn as Speaker of the House ruled against having television cameras and radio microphones at House committee hearings, she wrote him a fervent letter of approval. Testifying on complicated legislation was difficult enough without being blinded by Klieg lights. And "there is no reason why the general public should enter at that level. The records are available for history, and there is something very bad about expecting these serious hearings to furnish entertainment for the American people, which is just about what they do."[22]

Though television in subsequent years brought American government into the home, it also narrowed the group from which the country could draw its leaders. For if some public officials reveled in personal publicity, others like Perkins did not, and under the impact of television the latter were even less inclined than before to enter public service. Would Perkins under today's conditions accept a cabinet appointment? It seems doubtful.

In 1951, while Perkins was still a Civil Service Commissioner, Wilson came to live with her. It was his first appearance in Washington, but she introduced him to very few people. He was seventy-five and, as she wrote to Susanna, "not confused" but also "neither well nor ill."

He rose, took a short walk every morning, sat in the garden in the afternoon and between times rested. He had little interest in anything, not even in reading, which he used to enjoy greatly. To a friend she described him as "without passion." His presence chafed her because he was so dependent: one day when she went to New York "he nearly cried." Yet her letters to Susanna about him, written without the intervention of Jay, are among her warmest.

Sometimes he exasperated her. Though his eyesight was failing, he refused to go to an oculist, and "I think he believes himself unable to write although I can't figure it out because he *can* do whatever he wants." She tried to find a housekeeper or nurse so that she would be less tied down. But the older women she hired were always quitting in order not "to lose" their social security. Perkins couldn't understand it. "Queer psychology," she wrote to Susanna when yet another left. "She seems to feel that she *can't* work — she must get the $42 a month even if she goes naked in order to live without working."

Sometimes, with temporary help, she was able to get away, and then as if in reproach Wilson would do better. "He had no ill turns, took to drinking tea, coffee and ginger ale, which was an expansion of his diet, and saw a number of people and apparently had a good time. However, as soon as I got home, he started eating as little as possible and not feeling able to see anybody."[23]

Some years later, after Wilson had died and she was on the faculty at Cornell, she saw a colleague, Leonard Adams, struggling to help a wife who showed many of the same symptoms as had Wilson and who also required medical, hospital and nursing care. To help him she broke her rule of silence and in the course of several conversations revealed some of what she had been able, and unable, to do for her husband.

Wilson's behavior, so obviously damaging to himself as well as to her, had always been a puzzlement. She had never been able to discover any pattern in it, and neither he nor any professional to whom she had turned for advice had been able to explain it. Were the cause and its aggravation entirely in the individual whose behavior was so inexplicable, or were they in the marriage relationship that was the responsibility of both? At his death her perplexities, doubts and self-questions were still unresolved.

She said, in effect, "We all suffer. We must all bear these burdens. Even they are lifted in time." The experience, in Adams's opinion, had left her spirit bruised but not broken, for she had learned to find satisfactory experiences in other ways. Possibly the need to work in order to meet expenses had been her salvation, but from the way she talked of her husband, Adams felt, it would be unfair to consider him a sacrifice to her career.

On December 31, 1952, Wilson died, and Perkins buried him in Maine in the family plot in the Glidden cemetery, just an easy walk up the road from the Brick House. By the time of his death not many knew him, but from Mary Dreier in Florida she received a note that evidently moved her. Dreier recalled Wilson "as one of the most gallant young men in John Purroy Mitchel's cabinet with their dreams of public service shattered by the loss of the man they trusted and loved," and Perkins replied, "It is good to remember that now after all these years."[24]

When Eisenhower became President in 1953, she offered him her resignation from the Civil Service Commission. He accepted it, and because she still could not imagine retirement, she looked for work. Recently she had received a number of invitations to lecture, of which the most attractive was from the University of Illinois. For $2000 she would be required to hold twelve seminar meetings on the labor department and labor movement during the New Deal and give one university lecture, "The Roosevelt I Knew." The lecture held no terrors for her, but a seminar was different. If she could make a success of it, she could continue to be entirely self-supporting and independent.

She collected background data from the Bureau of Labor Statistics, worked it carefully into her topics and arrived on the campus at Urbana, eager to charm the faculty and students. So well did she succeed that, when the student body had changed, she was asked back. As word of her success passed around the academic community, more engagements followed, and at seventy-three she had started a new career.

But as the months passed she grew lonely, or thought she did. Perhaps it was partly the sudden absence of Wilson or the disappearance of Susanna into another marriage or merely that the house now seemed too large for her needs. In her phrase, she had never "cracked" Washington as she had New York, and in the spring of 1955 she decided to move back. She would be closer to Susanna and her grandchild, to friends like Agnes Leach, Rose Schneiderman and Margaret Poole, and to Maine and her Mount Holyoke classmates, scattered for the most part through New England. She would miss Washington, but she could come down.

The move was more difficult emotionally than she had anticipated. The house at Leroy Place had been her home for ten years, and she had been in Washington for twenty-two. She was more used to it than she realized. In New York her apartment at 1239 Madison Avenue was sublet, and for the time being she would stay with Margaret Poole. And when she began to count, many friends in New York were dead, but the people she had worked with in Washington were younger and still around.

She began to think she had made a mistake. She asked Reilly, who was acting as her attorney in the sale of the house, to offer to return the deposit, but the purchaser refused to cancel the contract. To Reilly's amusement she suggested that perhaps he could find some infirmity in the contract he had drawn, but he could not. She had to go through with it.

When all was packed and stowed in the van and the house was broom-clean for the purchaser, he drove her to the station. As he watched her depart, alone, for the first time she seemed old and without spark.[25]

Chapter 36

->>|<<-

Visiting professor at Cornell. Her name. First woman in Telluride
House. Her biography of Al Smith. Death, burial and her tombstone.

WITH NEW YORK as her base, Perkins continued to lecture at universities around the country. In the city she rented a room in Margaret Poole's apartment at 139 East Sixty-sixth Street, leaving her own, at 1239 Madison Avenue for Susanna's family. Space, comfort and familiar possessions around her were never necessary for Perkins. At times during the war she had lived in Washington in a single room at the Hay-Adams Hotel and even shared a single bedroom apartment with Nannie Burgess.

But in her first months in New York after leaving Washington her spirits did not rise. She had accepted invitations to lecture in Europe in the early spring, at the Salzburg Seminar and the University of Bologna, and she wondered aloud to Margaret Poole if she was up to it. She had suffered for years from hardening of the arteries, which produced high blood pressure, and she was supposed to take digitalis every day. But when she was working, she frequently forgot or skipped it. Now for the first time she began to talk to Poole about her health. Poole suggested a physical checkup and recommended her doctor, Margaret Janeway.

Just before the appointment Poole called Janeway to say that Perkins's blood pressure seemed no worse than in other years and that the problem might be more psychological than physical, brought on by the move from Washington and the start of a new career. In any event she was sure Perkins would be happier working, if she was up to it, than being in retirement. When Janeway found nothing unexpected in the tests, partly on Poole's recommendation she urged Perkins to go ahead with her plans. The lectures at Salzburg and Bologna were a great success, and Janeway, who continued to see Perkins regularly, never again saw her in doubt about what she would do.[1]

In May 1955 Perkins had delivered a lecture entitled "The Future Responsibilities of the American Labor Movement" at Cornell, in Ithaca, New York, and in the months following a few of the faculty of the university's School of Industrial and Labor Relations conceived the idea of asking her to join them as a visiting professor. The arrangement could be informal so that she might continue to lecture elsewhere, but at Cornell she would be a faculty member with continuing responsibilities to the students rather than an expert brought in for a day or a week. There are a number of other schools of industrial and labor relations in the country, but the one at Cornell is the largest, and the faculty there had the imagination to see first what only later became obvious to others: Perkins with her long background in the federal and New York labor departments should be at Cornell.[2]

Before recommending her appointment to the university, the school's dean, Martin P. Catherwood, checked with universities at which she had lectured, and the reports were all favorable. The most interesting to him, however, came from an individual. Catherwood, who at the time was also State Commissioner of Commerce, attended many meetings of businessmen around the state. At these, whenever Perkins's name was mentioned, all the businessmen would ridicule her with jokes and stories — except the secretary of Associated Industries of New York State, Mark A. Daly. Yet he as the paid lobbyist of business had steadily opposed almost every reform she had supported in the 1920s. When Catherwood asked why he should be the only one to defend her, Daly replied that he was the only one who knew her, and gave a warm account of her integrity, open-mindedness and fairness.[3]

With his reports in hand, Catherwood went to Deane Malott, the university's president. Malott later confessed that, on hearing the name Frances Perkins, his heart sank. He thought of the aura of radicalism surrounding her and of his conservative trustees. And he thought of academic freedom, swallowed hard and agreed to make the appointment.

Later, after one of her first lectures, he was standing beside her when a young woman, a reporter for the college paper, asked her: "What *is* your real name? What should we call you?"

"Miss Perkins."

"But you are married and have a child."

"Oh, indeed, I'm a grandmother. But" — with a smile — "*Miss* Perkins."

The reporter plainly was puzzled by the odd mixture of age, conservative clothing and novel idea; Malott and others on the faculty were charmed.[4]

The substance of Perkins's lectures and seminars was less important than the authority she brought to them. Many of the students had not been born in 1935, and once an innocent admonished her, "But in the United States we have always had social security." She, on the other hand, had entered college in the nineteenth century, reached thirty-seven before the country entered World War I and was fifty-three before she went to Washington. With her vivid memory for detail she could make real for others Chicago as it was before 1910, Jane Addams and the settlement houses, the Triangle fire, Smith and Wagner in the New York legislature and Roosevelt in the White House.

In December 1957 in a university lecture on Smith she not only brought him alive in his accent, clothes and gestures, but made of his development from boy in the fish market to national leader an inspiring example of what a man can do, for himself and for others. At the end an excited audience rose to its feet and gave her an ovation.[5]

In telling Agnes Leach about it in New York she revealed more of herself than she intended. "It really was a standing ovation," she said, "for I asked the man next to me."

With sharpness born of affection Leach said, "Frances, how much can you see?"

"Well, I can't see the back rows at all."

Only a few weeks earlier Dr. Janeway had discovered that Perkins was losing her sight when a flustered Perkins had fumbled badly in searching through her purse. In familiar surroundings, Leach's room or Janeway's office, Perkins moved with confident gestures, concealing how little she saw. She suffered with degeneration of the fundus of both eyes, and though Janeway sent her to several specialists, none could help her except by prescribing stronger and stronger eyeglasses.[6]

At Cornell the administration kept renewing her contract on an informal basis, paying her almost $7500 a year, which she supplemented by lecturing elsewhere. Even at eighty she lived on less than she earned, and her capital, augmented by additions and inflation, by 1960 was worth about $100,000. Five years later, at her death, it had doubled, all of it amassed after she was sixty-five.[7]

Apparently it gave her no sense of security, and because she did not feel rich she continued to assume that she was poor. The few times that she went to a hospital she insisted on the cheapest room and fretted whenever a nurse appeared. To insure enough on her death for her grandson's education, she denied herself small luxuries that she could easily have afforded. But the habits of a lifetime were not to be changed. She continued to live frugally and took to carrying all her insurance policies and a copy of her will in her handbag, so that when she died she would be prepared and not "cause anyone any trouble."[8]

In the spring of 1960 she received an extraordinary invitation. The twenty-seven members of the Telluride Association at Cornell, all men, invited her to be a guest in residence in their house on the campus. Since the members, both college and graduate students, all held fellowships awarded by the association on a basis of intellectual ability, they were or had a claim to be among the intellectual elite of the university. The invitation therefore was complimentary; it was also unprecedented in that no woman had ever lived in the house (though many have since).[9]

The invitation was carefully launched. The members asked Perkins, Professor Maurice Neufeld and his wife, Hinda, to dinner one Sunday afternoon. The Neufelds, who were to drive Perkins to and from the Residential Club, where she lived, were told of the invitation in advance and asked to urge her to accept it. Neufeld pointed out that Perkins, a very private person, might not choose to discuss the invitation with third parties. The Telluride committee agreed that was likely but nevertheless wanted the Neufelds to be part of the grand strategy.

Sometime during the lunch a spokesman quietly issued the invitation. On the drive back to the Residential Club Perkins chatted. While she sat in the Neufelds' car before getting out, she began to reminisce about her grandmother. Suddenly she said, "Do you know what those boys at Telluride have done?"

"No," came the chorus.

"They have asked me to come and live with them. I feel like a bride! What shall I do?"

But even before the Neufelds could speak, it was evident she had already decided to accept.[10]

Her time at Cornell now became, if possible, even happier. As Susanna observed, the relationship with the students and faculty was the one at which she was best, close without being intimate. She had no housekeeping duties, yet had a house in which to give parties; and she thrived on the intellectual stimulation. Not since she had shared a house with Mary Rumsey had she had such a good time.

She was able to do wonderful things for the Telluride students, such as persuading Farley and Wallace each to come up for a weekend of seminars. She resurrected their flower garden, gave them Maine lobster dinners, taught them how to give sherry parties and simply by her presence improved their dress. They in turn improved hers: after the move to Telluride House she dressed with a noticeably greater flair.

On the campus she shared with the historian Dexter Perkins (no relation) a remarkable surge of affection from the students. Her duties were not burdensome, and she had time for everyone, in the classroom or on the sidewalk. She never preached, but by her manners she reminded many that the formalities of life can be pleasant, not stiff, and can open rather than close a way for communication. She also brought to the campus a unique distinction. When she entered a small reception for former President Truman, he walked across the room and kissed her, explaining in the most easy, natural way that besides his mother, wife and daughter he kissed only Miss Perkins.[11]

Her happiness suffused all her activities. She had not always been a popular president of her class at Mount Holyoke; at one time her classmates had been alarmed by her ideas and later a little bored with her greatness, which kept her so much in Washington. But now she had time, and presided over the reunions with gaiety and a deep sense of thanks. After the sixtieth, in 1962, one classmate wrote, "You are the focal point that has held us all together," and another called her the "polished cornerstone." Whatever she now gave back to class she felt was less than she had received from it and from Mount Holyoke.[12]

In her work she had one disappointment. She planned — and it was part of her agreement with Cornell — to write a biography of Smith, *The Al Smith I Knew.* She believed passionately that much of Roosevelt's New Deal legislation, particularly the industrial and labor legislation, had its origins in Smith's years as speaker of the Assembly and governor of New York. Roosevelt had not been a member of the Factory Investigating Commission and in those early years had not been active in social and industrial reform. It was to his credit that, coming to it later, he had been able to pick it up and carry it further, but she was eager that justice be done to Smith.

She started work, uncovered new material about his ancestry — he was not the son of Irish immigrants but a quarter each of English, Irish, German and Italian — and then was blocked by his relations with Roosevelt. She understood Roosevelt. In the preamble to her biography of him she said he "was not a simple man . . . He was the most complicated human being I ever knew . . ." Yet she could reveal him as almost no one else could, because she understood how complicated she herself was and how she, like him, deliberately created part of that complexity. The simpler character of Smith eluded her.[13]

Still, friends at Cornell noticed that she reserved her "purest admiration" for Smith. Though in conversation she never compared the two men directly; it was inherent in all she said. His family life was more attractive, his concern for individuals greater and his vanity less. His background and what he had made of himself were more exciting. For her who had worked so much with immigrants, with the urban and industrial poor, Smith was the new American, the future; Roosevelt the old and the past. Smith also far less often, if ever, used words and pictures to deceive.[14]

Of Roosevelt in her biography she makes the ringing assertion: "It is my final testimony that he *never let me down.*" But it follows a statement, a brilliant statement, of how to work with a man who is likely to let you down. And in the book she ignores his deceptions of the American people about his health, his family relations, and some of his speeches, such as those in Boston and New York during the third-term campaign, in which he was at best evasive and at worst lying. Smith did not make such speeches.[15]

It was Smith's break with Roosevelt's New Deal policies that she could not understand. So many of them were merely extensions of Smith's policies. She could not accept Robert Moses's explanation in terms of ordinary human political and social jealousies. At a meeting of the American Historical Association in 1960 she suggested that by psychology hidden motives can be revealed. Smith, she said, was rejected by the American people in 1928, and therefore he resented Roosevelt, who was subsequently accepted, became obsessed with the idea that Roosevelt disliked him and invented reasons for disliking Roosevelt.

Moses thought all such "psychological abracadabra is nonsense." There was resentment, of course, as well as differing personalities. But in retrospect, "if their respective friends, advisers and kitchen cabinets had been a little less fanatical, at least some of these differences might have been reconciled."[16]

That was her opinion until she started her biography of Smith. Then she began to feel that something more must have happened to sour relations between the two men, some episode of which she and Moses were unaware. Again and again she went to Albany or New York to interview persons close to Smith and to Roosevelt. But she was never able to uncover an event that brought the break between the men into focus.[17]

Sensing that she could not finish the book alone, she one day invited

Howard Taubman to meet her at the Cosmopolitan Club for tea. He had not seen her for many years, and when she entered the large, main room on the second floor, he was astonished at the aged, bent woman who walked slowly toward him. Once seated, with the infirmities of age no longer operating, her face and eyes snapped with vitality, but when she rose to depart, the mantle of age again dropped around her.

Taubman could not help her. He was busy, and her book was largely notes. For a time it seemed as if Daniel Patrick Moynihan, who was then Assistant Secretary of Labor, might collaborate with her, but his work soon became too pressing. She was defeated by age. To an editor at Houghton Mifflin she confessed, "I can no longer call up the reserves of energy I once could." After her death the material was used by Matthew and Hannah Josephson in *Al Smith: Hero of the Cities, A Political Portrait Drawing upon the Papers of Frances Perkins.*[18]

In the winter of 1964–1965 her health declined sharply. By now she was very fragile and almost blind. In New York between familiar landmarks, Hunter College or Lenox Hill Hospital, she counted the streets; at Cornell her notes were written in letters an inch high. For the first time she failed to make a contribution to the intellectual life of the university, and it seemed as though at eighty-five some kind of retirement would be forced on her. She could not imagine living with either her sister or daughter, and the winters in Maine were too severe for her to live there alone. The most likely alternative, although she seems never to have discussed it with anyone, was to stay with some friend in New York.

In the spring she went to Washington, saw old friends and went on retreat at All Saints Convent. Back in New York, staying in her room at Margaret Poole's apartment, she went to the ballet with Anne Hyde Choate. That night Fonteyn and Nureyev were dancing, but Perkins saw none of it. Yet the evening was pleasant: Choate was one of her oldest and most intimate friends.

The next day she felt ill and called Dr. Janeway. Her ankles were swollen and her heart enlarged, and she was admitted to the Midtown Hospital. About twenty-four hours later she had the first of several strokes and soon passed into a coma. She died on May 14, 1965.[19]

The community in which she had the most friends was Cornell, and they organized a memorial service at the University's Episcopal

Church preceded by a tribute delivered by Neufeld. "The Frances Perkins we knew appeared among us out of history," he began, and then recalled for them how the historical figure had gradually revealed her extraordinary, vibrant personality: her courage at seventy-five in establishing a new career in a new community, her extraordinary gift for friendship, her sense of formality and of privacy and her religious spirit, from which "emerged her sense of duty and inner discipline, pleasantly muted but nerve-deep, which increased with the years and formed the central core of her character."

In New York at the Church of the Resurrection there was a funeral service attended by those of her friends who survived and her colleagues in Albany and Washington. "Be ye stedfast," the minister recited from First Corinthians, "unmoveable, always abounding in the work of the Lord, forasmuch as ye know that your labour is not vain in the Lord." It was the passage on which Perkins had talked at the final class prayer meeting in June 1902, as she and her classmates prepared to leave Mount Holyoke for their work in the world. From its first words the class had taken its motto, and without it, Perkins once wrote, "I never feel a funeral is legal."

With a high-church Requiem Mass this was the service for Frances Perkins, first woman in the cabinet, Industrial Commissioner of New York and U.S. Secretary of Labor, and it was done with all the color and ritual she liked for such occasions. The men at Telluride House had asked what they could do, and at Susanna's suggestion eight of them served as pallbearers. When the moment came, they raised the coffin shoulder high, and Perkins departed the church and the world in style, carried by eight personal friends.

After the service Agnes Leach and Martha Whitney walked slowly up the slight rise toward Park Avenue. Whitney, a large, heavy woman, said, "If I'd known it was going to be so long, I don't think I'd have come. I'm not feeling very well today."

"Yes you would," said Leach. "For Frances."

"Well, yes I would," said Whitney.

As they paused on the corner, they were overtaken by Anne Hyde Choate.

"That service was just like Frances!" said Leach.

"Of course," said Choate. "She arranged for every word of it. Years ago!" It was true. As early as 1945 Perkins had written complete instructions to the rector.[20]

Later she was buried in the family plot in Newcastle. To the left is Wilson; to the right her parents. The service, as became a country cemetery, was simple, and in time Susanna put up a simple stone to match her father's. On it she had carved, as Perkins had requested, a Christian symbol and

FRANCES PERKINS WILSON

1880–1965

SECRETARY OF LABOR OF U.S.A.

1933–1945

Appendices

Notes

Bibliography

Index

Appendix A

Simon N. Patten, 1852–1917, and Frances Perkins

PATTEN'S INFLUENCE on the economic and social thinking of the country was exercised only in part from his position as professor of Political Economy at the University of Pennsylvania. Directly and through former students he had a hand in several institutions in New York that also strongly influenced the way social ideas throughout the country were developed.

Chief among these, as described in the text, was the Charity Organization Society, whose general secretary, Edward T. Devine, had earned a doctor's degree under Patten. Another was Columbia University, where Samuel M. Lindsay, a former student and now professor of Social Welfare, presented Patten's ideas. In 1905 Devine and Lindsay arranged for him to deliver at the School of Philanthropy the lectures that became the chapters of his most famous book, *The New Basis of Civilization* (1907). In addition two of the three original directors of the New York Bureau of Municipal Research, founded in 1907, also earned doctor's degrees under Patten, and their students carried his ideas into the governments of many cities across the country.

At the University of Pennsylvania Graduate School of Arts and Sciences, Perkins had taken Patten's course on Political Economy and came to know him personally. In recommending her for a fellowship in New York he also recommended her to Lindsay, whom she came to know personally. When she became secretary of the New York City Consumers' League she worked in the same building as Devine and in close association with him. Eventually she married a member of the staff of the Bureau of Municipal Research. Despite the move from Philadelphia to New York, therefore, she remained in a circle in which Patten's ideas were constantly discussed, probed and, for the most part, accepted. In her writings she describes him as "a very original mind" and singles him out as the man who more than any other influenced her generation in the fields of economics and sociology (see Frances Perkins, Oral History, Columbia University, Bk. 1, pp. 36–37, 65; Bk. 3, p. 557; and her book *People at Work,* p. 125).

Patten never constructed his ideas, which are described briefly in the text, into a completed system in which all contradictions were resolved and implications pursued to their conclusions. He had no plan, other than gradual education, by which men would transform themselves from rugged, self-centered individualists into cooperating citizens, and he shied away from any comprehensive program for redistributing the wealth. Nevertheless some of his ideas and their applications were stated clearly. In charitable work he wanted professional workers to replace volunteers, and in place of alms privately bestowed, often on individuals, he wanted governmental programs based on taxation to aid masses of people. Inevitably anyone putting Patten's ideas into practice worked to expand the government's role into areas traditionally left to individuals and private charity.

He believed, and Perkins seems to have followed him in this, that industry had created so much wealth that there was more than enough for everyone's subsistence. Therefore a better distribution of it would be possible without stirring a violent reaction. Those who had more would be willing through taxes to give up part to those with less because only when society was healthy in all its groups could it be truly healthy in any one.

Not everyone believed that there was such wealth. Perkins's friend and fellow lobbyist in Albany, Robert Binkerd, said of her: "Frances was the author of this legislation [fire prevention bills] . . . She was an awfully nice person. She had a heart as big as a balloon. She was animated by nothing except the most decent, generous ideas about helping her fellow human beings. She didn't know anything about economics and she didn't know where all the money to do all these things was to come from." (Robert Binkerd, Oral History, Columbia, p. 38)

In *The Roosevelt I Knew,* p. 273, as if in answer to Binkerd, she quotes Jesse Jones telling President Roosevelt, "If we can get the national income up to 90 billion in the next year or two . . . we don't have to give another thought to the budget. It will balance without the slightest difficulty . . . What we have discovered is that the national income grows by economic movement. The taxing power of the government applied to those truly economic processes of buying and selling and hiring and manufacturing and paying wages and spending the wages will make for a taxable income sufficient to get us out of this hole without any damage to our program." In short, increasing national income was the answer.

That was in 1938, and Perkins seems to have believed always in the dollars and cents side of the argument, but about its spiritual side she began to have doubts (see Chapter 35). She had assumed, as Patten had taught, that if only enough housing, schools and unemployment insurance were available, a healthy, happy people would necessarily follow. But something more seemed often to be needed. Patten had given religion a low place in his schemes; she gave it a high one and was not afraid to speak of God, sin and the devil.

But she had never been a true disciple; she had always thought for herself. At a meeting in 1930 she told the American Academy of Political and Social Science, "Dr. Simon Patten . . . undertook my economic education a good many years ago, and . . . after a couple of years at it he said to me frankly one day, 'Frances, I think you are a person of action; I advise you to go no further with these academic studies but to get out and satisfy your restless spirit by doing something about it.' And so, with that advice, my education ceased."

Appendix B

Roosevelt and the 54-Hour Bill

DID ROOSEVELT aid the bill's passage with a filibuster on birds? The question is not unimportant, for the alleged filibuster later appeared as the chief prop to a claim by his admirers that his record on labor legislation even as a state senator was good. Perkins, as quoted in the text, thought it was bad.

The problem carries over to his years as governor, 1928 to 1932, when she claims that she and others set out to educate him about industrial problems and the possible solutions by legislation. Plainly this claim gains or loses strength conversely to the strength of the first.

The historian who has examined the question most closely is Alfred B. Rollins, Jr., in his article "Franklin Roosevelt's Introduction to Labor" (*Labor History*, Vol. 3, pp. 3–18, Winter 1962). I have pushed his research a little further, chiefly in the examination of contemporary newspaper accounts of the debate.

There is no doubt that Roosevelt voted for the 54-hour bill: the *Senate Journal* records his vote. Unfortunately it does not record speeches or speakers, so there is no official record of what he said or even whether he spoke.

None of the following newspapers that reported the bill's passage mention him; those with an asterisk describe the Sullivans' being called back from the night boat: New York *Herald**, New York *World,* New York *Tribune**, *New York Times,* Albany *Knickerbocker Press**, *Daily Argus**, Albany *Evening Journal**, and Poughkeepsie *Daily Eagle.* The Poughkeepsie *Evening Enterprise* on April 1, 1912, had an editorial on the splendid record of Senator Roosevelt but no mention of a filibuster. Leroy Scott in his article "Behind the Rail," published within three months of the event, does not mention him.

The first reference, apparently, to any kind of a role for Roosevelt occurs in an extemporaneous speech he made in New York City during his gubernatorial campaign in 1928: "One of the first measures that we started in nineteen-eleven was the fifty-four-hour law for women and children in industry." But as Rollins shows, Roosevelt had replied evasively to Perkins in June 1911 when she had asked for his support.

Later, in June 1929, in a speech on old age security to the Women's Trade Union League, he talked of "our bitter struggle and eventual triumph for a shorter working day," and of his "standing shoulder to shoulder" with the women. During this period, Rollins concluded, Roosevelt was trying to exaggerate a rather poor record on labor legislation into something better.

On February 5, 1933, in a feature article on Perkins, the Worcester *Sunday Telegram* stated that the "President-elect of the United States led the filibuster when the bill lacked 'two votes' of passage, while Miss Perkins hurried to the telephone" to call back the Sullivans.

The anecdote could not have come from Perkins, but nothing in the article suggests that the unidentified reporter had talked with her. It might have been taken from Roosevelt's speeches or from an authorized biographical sketch that may have been used as the basis for press releases. This "Sketch of F. D. Roosevelt for Text Book," which according to Rollins was prepared about this time and is in the Roosevelt Library, mentions the filibuster but without birds.

They make their first appearance in an article by Louis Howe for the *Saturday Evening Post,* February 25, 1933, "The Winner." Howe ascribes every step in the bill's passage to Roosevelt's leadership and does not mention Perkins at all. He describes the speech on birds at length, but almost nothing he says of the bill's passage jibes with either the *Senate Journal's* record or the contemporary news reports. On what can be checked, Howe wrote not exaggerations but lies.

Still, because of the lack of an official record, there is always the possibility that Roosevelt on the motion to reconsider spoke for his full five minutes in explanation of his vote and spoke on birds.

After Howe's article the story was picked up by other reporters and reprinted. Later, Roosevelt historians began to use it as evidence of his good record on labor legislation. Frank Freidel, writing before Rollins, tells it at length in his first volume on Roosevelt, and James MacGregor Burns, also before Rollins, tells it in passing.

The story evidently bothered Perkins, for she once asked Roosevelt directly whether he had voted for the 54-hour bill. He replied that he had, but made no mention of a filibuster. Possibly between friends, face to face, he spoke the truth. She remembered his performance as so poor, however, that she was still not convinced. For it was after this conversation that she had an assistant look up the record. (Frances Perkins, Oral History, Columbia, Bk. 1, p. 206)

Notes

In addition to the abbreviations used for manuscript collections explained in the first section of the Bibliography, the following are used for persons.

FP   Frances Perkins
PCW   her husband, Paul Caldwell Wilson
SWC   their daughter, Susanna Wilson Coggeshall
AES   Alfred E. Smith
FDR   Franklin D. Roosevelt
ER   Eleanor Roosevelt
PUK   Paul U. Kellogg, editor of *Survey*
GM   the author

Full titles for the works cited are given in the Bibliography.

Chapter 1

(pages 3–14)

1. Congratulations from women's groups and low echelon labor leaders: FDR Library, OF File 15, Labor Dept. Misc. 1933–38.
2. Green's blast, e.g., *New York Times,* New York *Herald Tribune,* Philadelphia *Ledger,* all March 2, 1933. Press conference, e.g., *New York Times,* New York *Herald Tribune,* March 3, 1933. Schoolmarmish, e.g. interviews by GM with Gladys Burch, Agnes Leach, Charles E. Wyzanski, Jr.
3. Letter to FP, May 27, 1945, from Margaret Poole, FPP, Columbia.
4. FPOHC, Bk. 3, pp. 650–54.
5. FPOHC, Bk. 4, pp. 1–23; on Farley, Bk. 4, pp. 80–81, also Bk. 7, pp. 485–509. Interviews by GM with SWC and Ilo Wallace.
6. FPOHC, Bk. 4, pp. 23–30. On the speech, Rosenman, *Working with Roosevelt,* pp. 90–91. On Hoover and Mellon, Schwarz, *Interregnum of Despair,* p. 89. On FDR's admiration of his own speeches, Tully, *F.D.R. My Boss,* p. 97.
7. FPOHC, Bk. 4, pp. 31–95. Lenroot, OH, Columbia, p. 64. FP seems mistaken in some details in her account, such as LeHand and an usher

finding Susanna. Both Ilo Wallace and SWC agreed (interviews by GM) that it was Ilo Wallace. Also in FP, *TRIK*, p. 152, she has the wrong date for the swearing in. Cf. Farley, *Jim Farley's Story*, p. 37, and Furman, *Washington By-line*, pp. 148–151; New York *Herald Tribune*, March 5, 1933, 1:2, and White House Ushers Diary, FDR Library.

Chapter 2

(*pages 15–22*)

1. FDR Library, Usher's Diary, 1933.
2. FPOHC, Bk. 3, pp. 639–40; interview by GM with SWC.
3. Her name and title: Speech to Pen and Brush Club, April 19, 1945, FPP, Columbia; FPOHC, Bk. 4, pp. 184–97, 372–73; the story in the *New York Times,* March 6, 1933, 14:3, based allegedly on her remarks to people at the White House reception the day before suggests that she had independently reached Rainey's conclusion. FP denies the account given in Roosevelt and Hickok, *Ladies of Courage,* p. 190 — "Call me Madam" — FPOHC, Bk. 4, p. 373. She preferred the Madam pronounced with the accent on the first syllable and spelt without the final *e,* interview by GM with Lubin. Also FP letter to PUK, March 8, 1933, requesting "Madam Secretary," PUK Papers. Hugh S. Johnson, after his break with her, continually referred to her satirically as "Mme. Perkins," to the extent that it was noted in an editorial in The Springfield *Republican,* January 4, 1937.
4. FPOHC, Bk. 4, pp. 217–28.
5. On Doak, favorable: Roger W. Babson, *Washington and the Depression, including the Career of W. N. Doak,* Chap. 6, pp. 89–108; hostile: "One of Mr. Hoover's Friends," by Robert S. Allen in the *American Mercury,* January 1932, Vol. 25, No. 97, p. 53. "The Wickersham Report": National Commission on Law Observance and Enforcement, 5th Report, Vol. 2, on the Enforcement of the Deportation Laws of the United States, particularly Chaps. 2 and 3, "The System in Operation" and "Objectional Features and Proposed Remedies." On Employment Service: "Instead of a System!" by Ruth M. Kellogg, *Survey Graphic,* March 1933, Vol. 22, No. 3, p. 165. On Bureau of Labor Statistics, see Chap. 23, this book, on Ethelbert Stewart. Also interview with Clara Beyer by Dr. Jonathan Grossman and interview by GM with Gladys Burch. On need to overhaul the department: letter of K. C. Adams, United Mine Workers official, to FP, January 30, 1933, and of FP to Barrows Matthews, November 15, 1932, both in FPP, Columbia.
6. FPOHC, Bk. 4, pp. 95–125, 388.
7. The identity of the New York policeman, Lt. Newman, is obscure. She refers to him several times and in different contexts, without giving a first name. The New York City Police Department in 1972 was unable to trace him. The speed with which she dismantled the Section 24 group on taking up her post suggests that someone had tipped her off on what she would find before she left for Washington. Besides FPOHC, Bk. 4, pp. 112–20, 183, 208, also FP correspondence with Leo P. Brophy and James Dodson, April 1952–January 1953, FPP, Columbia.
8. For an account of Grace Abbott, the movement to make her Secretary of

Labor, and the White House Conference on Child Health and Protection, November 19–22, 1930, see Furman, *Washington By-line,* pp. 69–82. Documents on Campaign for Abbott, CMB Papers, folders 116–24. Perkins was the chief speaker at a National Consumers' League meeting that sent a resolution to Hoover in support of Abbott.

9. FP first tells this story in "Eight Years as Madame Secretary," *Fortune,* September 1941. Later in FPOHC (1951–55), Bk. 4, p. 112.

Chapter 3

(pages 23–30)

1. FPOHC, Bk. 4, pp. 125–27, 138; the cafeteria, FPOHC, Bk. 8, p. 911. Isador Lubin, who helped to draft the ruling, stated that it was consciously made as the right thing to do. Interview by GM with Lubin.

2. This conversation with Robe Carl White and those following start at FPOHC, Bk. 4, pp. 127, 205, 210, 215; with Gompers, p. 136; with payroll clerk, p. 144.

3. Herring, *Public Administration,* p. 286.

4. Doak on radical aliens. See *New York Times Index,* 1931 and 1932. In 1932, March 25, 2:4; April 22, 1:4; October 29, 10:3; November 29, 1:5.

5. Commissioner of Immigration D. W. MacCormack testifying before Subcommittee of House Committee on Appropriations — Department of Labor Appropriation Bill for 1936 — p. 89.

6. Section 24. In this and the next chapter I have followed FP's account, FPOHC, Bk. 4, pp. 205–34, though I have not been able to substantiate every one of her statements from other sources. In my search, however, I discovered nothing to contradict her account and so much to confirm it that I feel she is not only correct in substance but in detail.

   The number of persons said to be in the section varies, apparently depending on whether certain executive posts were included. But it was at least 87 and perhaps 93. See *New York Times* report, March 22, 1933, 3:1, of FP's first press conference and a memorandum on Section 24, April 19, 1934 in FPP, Columbia, under J. A. Shaw.

   Evidence of the section's activities and her response to them is scattered through her papers. In FPP, Columbia, the chief items are: An extremely long "Report of Activities of Section 24 Officers, 1930–1932" (presently filed under Subject — Civil Service Commission). Though unsigned it was evidently prepared by someone within or with access to the department. Two unsigned memoranda, March 6 and March 10, 1933, on the section's finances. A "Notes handed to the Commissioner General [D. W. MacCormack] by Miss Perkins when he came into office," no date but probably late April 1933 (Biographic Material). Memorandum, June 9, 1933, from D. W. MacCormack to FP on activities of Doak's nephew, Ervin F. Brown, as a special investigator (Documents, Li-Mad). For a history of the prosecution of Brown, see *New York Times* stories, December 1933. Letter of FP, March 15, 1933, to all district directors announcing the termination of Section 24 (under Irving F. Wixon). Also letters under Judge Charles F. Amidon, John F. Maragon, Allan C. Devaney and James E. Dodson.

In FPP, Connecticut, the chief items are: a memorandum, March 9, 1933, prepared within the department on her powers to act; another prepared anonymously by someone almost certainly within the Bureau of Immigration and sent to FP, March 13, 1933, through Helen Lathrop; letter to FP, March 21, 1933, from District Director S. D. Smith of Salt Lake City in response to her letter to all District Directors, see Wixon, above; letter of congratulation to FP, March 22, 1933 (almost certainly in response to the newspaper reports on that day following her first press conference on March 21, 1933), from former Commissioner of Immigration at Ellis Island, Benjamin M. Day. All the above in a folder marked "Perkins VII, Papers relating to the Immigration and Naturalization Service during Miss Perkins's term as Secretary of Labor." Also see speech by D. W. MacCormack, January 29, 1934, in "Perkins III, MacCormack addresses, 1933, 1934."

Also executive orders 6028, 6061 and 6067 in February and March 1933 and interview by GM with Gladys Burch, who was a typist in the bureau at the time.

FP summarized the evidence in a letter to Congressman John Taber, May 27, 1940, copies of which she sent to 58 congressmen and senators: "We [FP and MacCormack] were confronted on the threshold of our duties with not only certain undesirable situations of administration which had been denounced by The Wickersham Committee appointed by President Hoover, but by clear evidence of corruption in certain offices." FPP, Columbia.

7. FPOHC, Bk. 4, pp. 144–47.
8. *New York Times,* March 7, 1933, 24:1

Chapter 4

(pages 31–38)

1. FPOHC, Bk. 4, pp. 154–80. On the cabinet room, Rosenman, *Working with Roosevelt,* pp. 1–2; on Garner, Henry Bruère, OH, Columbia, p. 139; on Mrs. Garner, Furman, *Washington By-line,* pp. 97–98.
2. Memorandum on FP's interview with Murray Garsson, entitled "Notes handed the Commissioner General by Miss Perkins when he came into office," FPP, Columbia.
3. FPOHC, Bk. 4, pp. 182, 216, 249–50.
4. *New York Times* March 22, 1933, 3:1; Cf. Furman, *Washington By-line,* p. 162, and Washington State Labor News analysis of discharges, March 24, 1933, FDR Library, OF 15, Labor Dept. 15D.
5. FPOHC, Bk. 4, pp. 229–33. On the Garssons: Thomas H. Eliot, who began work as Assistant Solicitor in the spring of 1933, recalled that a private detective was hired to guard FP's office after it showed signs of having been entered and files searched. At the time everyone assumed the culprit was Murray Garsson. Interview by GM with Eliot. In 1947 the two Garssons and former Congressman Andrew J. May were convicted of defrauding the federal government. May had taken bribes from the Garssons to use his congressional influence on behalf of their com-

mercial enterprises. Indictment, *New York Times,* January 24, 1947, 1:5; conviction, July 4, 1947, 1:4. See also *The Chemical Warfare Service: From Laboratory to Field,* pp. 361–67, by Leo/ Brophy et al. Letter of Brophy to FP, April 15, 1952, and her reply, May 8, 1952; FP to James Dodson, January 19, 1953, and his reply, February 11, 1953. All in FPP, Columbia.

6. Letter to FP from Helen Lathrop, March 13, 1933, with attached memorandum, FPP, Connecticut, Perkins VII; FPOHC, Bk. 4, p. 213.

7. Letter FP to district directors: see letter to Irving F. Wixon, March 15, 1933, FPP, Columbia. Letter of S. D. Smith, district director, to FP, March 21, 1933, also letter of Benjamin M. Day to FP; both in FPP, Connecticut, Perkins VII. Also letter to Judge Charles F. Amidon to FP, July 20, 1933, FPP, Columbia.

8. FPOHC, Bk. 4, pp. 213, 209.

Chapter 5

(pages 41–51)

For the descriptions of the family and its life at the Brick House in Newcastle, Maine, in addition to the memories of FP in her papers and oral history I have relied particularly on correspondence with Leroy Ford, a grandson of Mrs. Perkins's elder sister after whom FP was named, and with Mary E. Piper, the wife of William S. Piper, FP's oldest school friend; also on correspondence and interviews with Vira Peters Towle, younger sister of FP's college roommate Amy Peters; and on family records in the possession of SWC. For the description of Mount Holyoke and the life of its students in the first decade of the century, besides the records at the college, I have relied particultrly on the memory, pictures and documents of Vira Peters Towle.

1. Birth certificate No. 5896 in year 1880, Registry Division, City of Boston. Baptized, June 12, 1887, at Plymouth Congregational Church (later by merger Chestnut Street Congregational Church), Worcester; copy in FPP, Coggeshall.

2. Cushman, *The History of Ancient Sheepscot and Newcastle;* F. W. Perkins obituary, Worcester *Sunday Telegram,* February 27, 1916; FPOHC, Bk. 1, p. 214.

3. On her grandmother's influence: FP letter to Gertrude Ely, January 26, 1945, and to Edith O'Dell Black, December 8, 1944, both in FPP, Columbia. Also FPOHC, Bk. 1, p. 241; Bk. 2, p. 671; Bk. 3, pp. 312–13, 649, 651; Bk. 6, p. 484; Bk. 7, p. 314; and "Tape 13" (transcribed) of "Lectures during 1957," FPP, Cornell.

4. FPOHC, Bk. 3, pp. 310–13.

5. FPOHC, Bk. 2, p. 246; cf. FPP, Coggeshall, AES, Chap. 2, p. 35.

6. F. W. Perkins obituary, note 2; feature article on FP, Worcester *Sunday Telegram,* February 5, 1933. FPOHC, Bk. 1, pp. 183–84, 343, 176, 2–3. In FPP, Coggeshall, AES, Chap. 2, pp. 39–40, she describes the atmosphere of the Smith home and adds, "So like my own Victorian bringing up." She implies she repeatedly was admonished not to cross her legs "because

it's not ladylike." Letters to GM from Leroy Ford and Mary Piper; interviews with Vira Peters Towle and SWC.

7. Interview by GM with Isador Lubin, who attended the school; FPOHC, Bk. 1, p. 180.

8. FPOHC, Bk. 3, p. 354.

9. FPOHC, Bk. 3, p. 356; interview by GM with SWC; FP, "Eight Years as Madame Secretary," *Fortune*. Feature article on FP, Worcester *Telegram*, Magazine Section, January 13, 1929; Holyoke *Daily Transcript*, Mount Holyoke College Centennial Supplement, 1837–1937, May 7, 1937, p. 2 (Vira Peters Towle collection) ; Feature article Worcester *Sunday Telegram*, February 5, 1933.

10. *Mount Holyoke Alumnae Quarterly*, April 1929: interview on her appointment as Industrial Commissioner of New York; FPP, Mount Holyoke, release on her appointment as U.S. Secretary of Labor, c. March 1, 1933. Feature articles in Worcester newpaper, and Holyoke *Daily Transcript*, note 9, FPOHC, Bk. 1, pp. 5, 269. Interview by GM with Vira Peters Towle. College transcript and Class Book of 1902.

11. FPP, Mount Holyoke, release on FP's appointment and Holyoke *Daily Transcript*, Centennial Supplement, note 10.

12. FPP, Mount Holyoke, Report of the fiftieth reunion of Class of 1902.

13. *The Life of Mary Lyon* by Beth Bradford Gilchrist (Houghton Mifflin, Boston, 1910). Gilchrist was a college classmate of FP. *The Letters of Emily Dickinson*, ed. by Thomas H. Johnson (Cambridge, Harvard University Press, 1958) : ED to brother Austin, October 21, 1847 and see, to Austin, February 17, 1848. Holyoke *Daily Transcript*, Centennial Supplement, note 9, has an unsigned article on ED at the college, with lurid stories of her "flagrant disobedience," but they are not supported by evidence. Letter to FP from Julia Prindle Nelson, February 25, 1933, quoting Mary Lyon. FPP, Columbia.

14. FPP, Mount Holyoke, Class Book, 1902.

15. Interview by GM with Agnes Leach.

16. Interview by GM with Vira Peters Towle.

17. FPOHC, Bk. 1, pp. 3, 22–23; also FP speech to Query, January 20, 1953, in FPP, Coggeshall. Query was a New York society, located near Washington Square, of women with independent minds. Many worked in professions. Perkins was a member from about 1917, when the society was founded, until her death in 1965. She spoke before it on several occasions and was devoted to its members and ideals.

18. Interview by GM with Vira Peters Towle.

Chapter 6

(*pages 52–62*)

1. *Mount Holyoke Alumnae Quarterly*, April 1929: interview on her appointment as Industrial Commissioner of New York. FPP, Mount Holyoke, the Fourth Class Letter of 1902 records that, by 1915, of the class, 61 were married, 59 unmarried and 5 unmarried "at last account"; of those working, 24 were teachers, 5 secretaries, 3 missionaries, 3 professional musicians and 7 others in various pursuits; of those affirming

political affiliations (many did not yet have the vote), 30 were Republicans, 14 Progressives, 4 Independents, 3 Democrats and 1 Socialist; and 52 were suffragists, 14 antisufffragists and 15 indifferent or undecided.

2. Influence of Florence Kelley: FP letter to PUK, August 2, 1945, PUK Papers. Also FPOHC, Bk. 2, p. 260, FP article "My Job," *Survey*, March 15, 1929, and FP speech at a memorial meeting in honor of Florence Kelley at the Friends Meeting House in New York City, March 16, 1932, quoted in Goldmark, *Impatient Crusader*, p. 61. Recording Kelley at Mount Holyoke: *The Mount Holyoke*, Vol. 11, No. 7, p. 382, March 1902, and Kelley's report, which emphasizes the importance of Prof. Soule, National Consumers' League *Third Annual Report for Year Ending March 4, 1902*, pp. 24, 31. At the time there was a ferment of social consciousness at the college, *The Mount Holyoke*, Vol. 11, No. 8, p. 434, April 1902, and on March 10, 1902, the College Settlement Association was founded. See also Cole, *A Hundred Years of Mount Holyoke College*, pp. 250, 268.

3. Goldmark, *Impatient Crusader*, pp. 72, 41, 6, 62. "Always in black," FDR Library, Dewson Papers. Mary Dewson to Ramona T. Mattson, April 1, 1954, quoted in Chambers, *Seedtime of Reform*, p. 5.

4. FPOHC, Bk. 1, pp. 4–6; also FP speech to Query (see Chap. 3, note 17) January 20, 1953, FPP, Coggeshall. On COS, Smith and Zietz, *American Social Welfare Institutions*, pp. 43–45.

5. FPP, Mount Holyoke, First Class Letter of 1902; interview by GM with Vira Peters Towle.

6. First Class Letter, note 5; FP speech to Query, note 4. Feature article, Worcester *Sunday Telegram*, February 5, 1933. Letter to FP, n.d., from Mrs. A. L. Stebbins (Harriet Hazen), FPP, Columbia. *Mount Holyoke Alumnae Quarterly*, April 1929. Letter to FP, December 1, 1902, from S. P. Willard of Bacon Academy, and letter to FP, March 4, 1904, from James F. Butterworth of Monson Academy, both in FPP, Columbia.

7. Interview by GM with Vira Peters Towle, and FPOHC, Bk. 4, p. 84; Bk. 2, p. 173.

8. On Lake Forest and Ferry Hall: Arpee, *Lake Forest Illinois, History and Reminiscences, 1861–1961* (Lake Forest, Lakeside Press, 1963); also letters and interview by GM with Arpee. Letters to FP from Elizabeth Cramer McClure, September 30, 1935, and from Mrs. T. J. Bolster, February 9, 1933, both students of FP at the school; letters in FPP, Columbia. Confirmation, Church of the Holy Spirit, Parish Register, Vol. 2, p. 84. Letter to FP, October 23, 1940, from Rev. A. G. Richards, who had presented her for confirmation, FPP, Columbia.

9. Interview by GM with Graham Taylor's daughter, Lea Demarest Taylor, who has the register.

10. On ritual. FPOHC, Bk. 3, pp. 415–25; Bk. 4, pp. 9, 71; and cf. Bk. 7, p. 42 and Bk. 8, p. 853. Letter to FP from Helen Reid, August 6, 1948, FPP, Columbia. Interview by GM with Vira Peters Towle.

11. On settlement houses. Chambers, *Seedtime of Reform;* Davis, *Spearheads of Reform;* Smith and Zietz, *American Social Welfare Institutions;* Trolander, *Settlement Houses and the Great Depression.* For a description of a political-religious fight over improving schools in which Jane

Addams was defeated by John Powers, the Irish Catholic boss of the nineteenth ward, see *Spearheads of Reform*, pp. 151–62.

12. Josephson, *Sidney Hillman*, p. 43.
13. FPOHC, Bk. 1, pp. 12–13; FP letter to Mrs. Graham R. Taylor, September 3, 1942, FPP, Columbia.
14. FPP, Mount Holyoke, Second Class Letter of 1902.

Chapter 7

(pages 63–75)

1. FPOHC, Bk. 1, pp. 10–17.
2. Davis, *Spearheads for Reform*, p. 106. See also F. Ray Marshall, *The Negro and Organized Labor*, or his essay, "Unions and the Black Community," in Brody (ed.), *The American Labor Movement*.
3. FPOHC, Bk. 1, p. 270.
4. FP, St. Bede's Lecture #1, "A Christian Order of Society," pp. 6–8, January 26, 1948, FPP, Columbia. The two men whom she identifies in the lecture only by first name are almost certainly Allen Burns and Robert Hunter, both of whom had distinguished careers in social work.
5. The estimate of her Ferry Hall salary is by Edward Arpee, historian of Lake Forest Academy. It is possible that FP from age 21 to 46 received a small income from a great-uncle's "family trust." She mentions it in a letter to C. E. Wyzanski, Jr., July 14, 1949, CEW Papers, but she may have invented it as an example of what she hoped to create. In her immediate family there is no memory or record of such a trust.
6. Mrs. Lydia A. Coonley Ward, Malvina and Susanna Shanklin (later Mrs. Waldo Brown). FPOHC, Bk. 1, p. 365.
7. Smith and Zietz, *American Social Welfare Institutions*, p. 231; Chambers, *Seedtime of Reform*, p. 92; *Alumni Register of New York School of Philanthropy, 1898–1911*, showing that summer sessions began in 1898, winter sessions in 1903.
8. FPOHC, Bk. 1, pp. 18–37, 63–68, 79. Her Socialist party membership card was issued by a New York City district, but written on it is "Transferred from Philadelphia, Pa., December 1909." The card has stamps showing dues paid through March 1912.
9. *The Pittsburgh Survey*, 6 vols, published by the New York Charity Organization Society and the Russell Sage Foundation. Quotations taken from the various reports. Chambers, *Paul U. Kellogg and the Survey*, pp. 36–46. For a modern view of Pittsburgh data, see Brody, *Steelworkers in America;* same, p. 159, "The impact of the Pittsburgh Survey was quiet but profound. The facts uncovered gradually spread beyond the limited audience of *Survey* subscribers concerned with social service."
10. Chambers, *PUK and the Survey*, p. 48. Cf. FPOHC, Bk. 1, p. 60.
11. FPOHC, Bk. 1, pp. 187–88, 211–14. Cf. Goldmark, *Impatient Crusader*, p. 99: "Mrs. Kelley basically distrusted Mr. Roosevelt. She thoroughly condemned his policy of the 'Big Stick.' She never for gave his actions in seizing Panama."
12. FP, St. Bede's Lecture #2, "The Vocation of the Laity," p. 49, February 2, 1948, FPP, Columbia.

13. See the Introductory Essay by Daniel M. Fox to his edition of Patten's *The New Basis of Civilization*. Also Appendix A of this book.
14. FPOHC, Bk. 1, pp. 37–38. *Bulletin of New York School of Philanthropy,* Vol. IV, No. 2, October 1910, pp. 9 ff. FPP Mount Holyoke, Third Class Letter of 1902.
15. On art and literature, 1910–1917. FP speech to Pen and Brush Club, April 19, 1945, FPP, Coggeshall. FPOHC, Bk. 1, pp. 342–85; Bk. 4, pp. 515–20. There are drafts of stories and plays in FPP, Coggeshall. FP letter to PUK's widow, Helen Hall, November 5, 1958, PUK, Papers. Mark Schorer, *Sinclair Lewis* (New York, McGraw-Hill, 1961), pp. 191–93. FP wrote Schorer a letter describing her life in New York.
16. FP's master's essay: on file in Special Collections Library, Columbia, in Columbia University Theses, 1910, Vol. 18, Political Science, P-R.
17. Transcript of her work at Columbia and the New York School of Philanthropy on file in the Records Division at Columbia.
18. Letters to FP from Helen Phelps Stokes, April 21 and 28, 1910, FPP, Columbia. FPOHC, Bk. 1, p. 37. She tentatively had been offered a job at $1200 the previous year by the New York State Commission of Immigration. See letter to FP from Frances A. Kellor, commission treasurer, who had hired her for the job in Philadelphia. Though the letter has no date, it clearly was written no later than the spring of 1909. FPP, Columbia.
19. FP speech to Query, Jaunary 20, 1953, FPP, Coggeshall; see Chap. 5, note 17.

Chapter 8

(*pages 76–90*)
1. FP speech at memorial service for Kelley, *New York Times,* March 17, 1932, and FP article, "My Recollections of Florence Kelley."
2. Goldmark, *Impatient Crusader,* Chap. 13.
3. FP transcript, Columbia, Records Division. Adelphi College, *Catalog, 1911–1912,* and also *General Catalog, 1896–1916,* p. 11. She taught nine students a full year course entitled "Introduction to Sociology," which was "designed to afford a synthetic view of social phenomena, and to furnish the student with a scientific method for the study of ordinary human association and fundamental social problems."
4. Factory Investigating Commission, *Preliminary Report, 1912,* Vol. 2, p. 310.
5. FPOHC, Bk. 1, pp. 41, 55. Cf. Dubofsky, *When Workers Organize,* p. 29, on typical AFL leaders in New York City.
6. FPOHC, Bk. 1, p. 115. She says the fire was caused by an explosion of lacquer. I have followed the *New York Times* and other papers in ascribing it to gasoline. *New York Times,* November 27 and 28, 1910, 1:1. For two days the fire story pushed the opening of the new Pennsylvania Railroad Station out of the lead column, despite crowds there of 100,000 and record-breaking train runs because of new tunnels under the Hudson River.
7. FPOHC, Bk. 1, pp. 175–203, entitled "Woman's Suffrage"; quotations,

pp. 191, 179. FPP, Mount Holyoke, Fourth Class Letter (1915) of 1902: of 126 reporting, 52 were suffragists, 14 against and 15 indifferent or undecided.

8. FPP, Coggeshall, AES, Chap. 1, pp. 1–4, 34–36. Cf. Binkerd, OH, Columbia, p. 31: Smith's "most outstanding characteristic and the one for which I loved him most was his utter honesty as to purpose."

9. Huthmacher, *Wagner,* pp. 27–28, citing among others, Binkerd OH, Columbia, p. 59.

10. FPOHC, Bk. 1, pp. 86–94.

11. FPOHC, Bk. 1, pp. 99–101; also FPP, Coggeshall, AES, Chap. 4, pp. 34–37.

12. On the Triangle fire. FPOHC, Bk. 1, pp. 120–38; also FPP, Coggeshall, AES, Chap. 5, pp. 1–20; Martha Bensley Bruère, "The Triangle Fire," in *Life and Labor,* Vol. 1, No. 5, May 1911, pp. 137–41 (an eyewitness account in the monthly magazine of The National Women's Trade Union League). Schneiderman's speech, *New York Times,* April 3, 1911, 3:6. Stein, *The Triangle Fire,* throughout (the most authoritative account), J. William Gillette, MA essay for Columbia, "Welfare State Trail Blazer," Chap. 1, "Disaster."

13. FPOHC, Bk. 1, p. 138; FPP, Coggeshall, AES, Chap. 5, pp. 21–25, cf. p. 143. H. F. J. Porter, "The Fire Bills," *Survey,* Vol. 29, p. 730, February 22, 1913, has an account of the meeting with the governor.

14. FPOHC, Bk. 1, p. 165; FPP, Coggeshall AES, Chap. 5, pp. 90–97. *New York Times* obituary of Stewart Browne, "He Heckled City Boards," August 5, 1973, 17:3.

15. Huthmacher, *Wagner,* p. 10; Stein, *The Triangle Fire,* p. 220.

Chapter 9

(*pages 91–100*)

1. FP as a lobbyist, the "burning eyes," interview by GM with Isador Lubin.

2. FPOHC, Bk. 1, pp. 98–105.

3. On the passage of the bill. My account is a reconstruction based on the sources that follow. The story has often been told. What is new here, based on FP's oral history and unfinished Smith biography, is the description of Wagner's role. I have followed her account of it because I think several of his actions, such as the ruling in favor of a "closed call," are reasonable only if he had the motives she attributes to him. The great majority of the quotations are from FP's accounts; a few are from Leroy Scott's; I have invented none.

   In FPOHC she ascribes the advice to accept the amended bill to Joseph Hammitt; in FPP, Columbia, AES, to Smith. I have followed the former because it was closer to the event and more reasonable. It seems the sort of advice one lobbyist might give another, and *not* the sort of advice, since it led to a Tammany defeat in the Senate, that might be given by the Tammany leader in the Assembly. Also, it may be human that, in her old age, when she was preparing a book on Smith, she associated events with him that, in fact, occurred with others.

Note: the legislative journals mentioned below record only motions and roll calls, not debates.

Metropolitan Magazine, July 12, p. 19, "Behind the Rail, Being the Story of a Woman Lobbyist," by Leroy Scott. It is the source of Sullivan's public remarks. FPOHC, Bk. 1, pp. 106–14; Bk. 2, pp. 293–94; FPP, Coggeshall, AES, Chap. 5, pp. 151–53; FP, *TRIK,* pp. 13–14; New York State Senate *Journal, 1912,* pp. 1085, 1375–77; New York State Assembly *Journal, 1912,* pp. 1298, 2149–51; Clerk's Manual 1912 of Rules, Forms and Laws for the Regulation of Business in the Senate and Assembly of the State of New York. *New York Times,* March 30, 1912, 1:1.

On Big Tim Sullivan: FPOHC, Bk. 1, pp. 225–26. Kenneth S. Davis, in *FDR: The Beckoning of Destiny,* p. 268, tells more than most historians about Big Tim: "He had abandoned (though providing financially for) his wife, had fathered at least two illegitimate children, had contracted what then was euphemistically called a 'social disease,' and would a few months hence be confined to a mental institution, suffering from paresis." Then in a footnote Davis adds: "Hopelessly insane, he escaped from the mental institution one night in late August, 1913, stumbled onto some New Haven railroad tracks, and was there killed by a freight train. His mangled body lay in the public morgue for thirteen days before it was identified, and then by accident, though he had long been one of the best-known men in New York City."

4. FPOHC, Bk. 1, p. 114.
5. Interview by GM with Agnes Leach; confirmed by all others interviewed. Letter to FP from PUK, May 9, 1934, PUK Papers, on the strategy for passing what became the Social Security Act. "The President said that you and he did not wholly agree in the matter — you favoring a bite at a time and he the whole cherry."
6. FPOHC, Bk. 1, p. 237; letter to FP, April 27, 1912, from New York Bindery Women's Union, Elizabeth Curran, secretary, FPP, Columbia. State of New York, *Public Papers of John A. Dix, Governor, 1912,* pp. 229–30. His memorandum on the approved bill, in which he urged the candy and textile industries to seek exemptions similar to that of the canners. For Pauline Goldmark's indignation, see New York City Consumers' League, *Annual Report for 1912,* p. 34.
7. FPOHC, Bk. 1, pp. 367–68. In mentioning Leroy Scott's article, and incorrectly placing it in *Collier's,* she states: "He referred to The MacManus as the 'devil's deputy from Hell's Kitchen.' Mr. MacManus didn't like it. It was a very amusing article. It was almost modern in its terrific overwriting and dramatism, but Mr. Scott was just earning his living." He was one of a number of her literary friends. See FPOHC, Bk. 1, pp. 362–84.
8. FP, *TRIK,* pp. 11, 14; FPOHC, Bk. 1, pp. 239–40. Her low opinion of FDR was shared by two other lobbyists in Albany at the time, Robert S. Binkerd and Laurence A. Tanzer. Both men thought him an opportunist, even unprincipled, Binkerd, OH, Columbia, p. 28; Tanzer, OH, Columbia, p. 58. On FDR's vote: FPOHC, Bk. 1, p. 206; and alleged filibuster, Freidel, *FDR,* Vol. 1, p. 122, citing Louis Howe, "The Winner," *Saturday Evening Post,* February 25, 1933, pp. 7, 48; Burns, *Roosevelt,*

Lion and the Fox, p. 42; Sidney Skolsky, "Tintypes," a column for News Syndicate Co., dated March 24, 1933, FPP, Columbia. See Appendix B.
9. FP, *TRIK*, pp. 24–25.

Chapter 10

(pages 103–121)

For the notes in this chapter the Factory Investigating Commission is abbreviated to FIC.

1. Letter to FP, May 6, 1912, from John A. Kingsbury, secretary of the Committee on Safety. On the committee's purpose, Kingsbury letter; FPP, Coggeshall, AES, Chap. 5, p. 145; *New York Times* editorial, April 14, 1911. FPOHC, Bk. 1, pp. 385–88, 282.
2. On which commissioners went on inspections: FPP, Coggeshall, AES, Chap. 5, p. 106; also Dreier's memory in 1960, Chap. 5, p. 35. The FIC in four reports (13 vols.) published a record of 62 of its inspections, meetings. and hearings. There were many more. An analysis of the 62, though in some instances only those asking questions can be identified, shows that Wagner attended 59, Dreier 57, Phillips 52, Smith and Jackson 37, Hamilton 22, Gompers 21, Dowling (and McGuire after latter's resignation) 13 and Brentano 10. Smith's figure probably is too low. There are a number of meetings at which he seems to have been present but allowed Wagner as chairman to ask questions for them both. The figures, though imperfect, perhaps confirm Smith's observation that a commission of legislators — with the brilliant exception of Dreier — would work harder than one made up of "the finest people." On Dreier, FPP, Coggeshall, AES, Chap. 5, p. 34; on Gompers, FPOHC, Bk. 1, pp. 318–19.
3. On her tie to the FIC: letter of FP, July 27, 1925, to Augusta W. Hinshaw, FPP, Columbia, and see Hinshaw's "Story of Frances Perkins," *Century*, September 1927. But the fact is extremely blurred. Smith, governor in January 1923, in announcing her appointment to the Industrial Board, stated, ". . . she acted as investigator and director of Investigation for the State Factory Investigating Commissions . . . [and] acting as a representative of the Committee on Safety, she also urged the passage of new Labor Laws . . ." The FIC Reports, however, do not list her among the commission's personnel. See FPOHC, Bk. 1, pp. 385–88.
4. FIC, *Preliminary Report, 1912*, Vol. 1, pp. 15, 22, 23. For the FIC throughout, Gillette's thesis, "Welfare State Trail Blazer." For her enthusiastic comments on three of the experts, Professor Ira Wolfson of the Engineering School, Columbia; F. J. T. Stewart, National Board of Underwriters; and Robert D. Kohn, American Institute of Architects (she greatly admired his design of Temple Emanu-El at Fifth Avenue and Sixty-fifth Street in New York City); FPP, Coggeshall, AES, Chap. 5, pp. 76, 144, 150. Also, index refs. on them in FPOHC, Bk. 1, and "My Job" by FP, *Survey*, March 15, 1929.
5. The candy factory, the two-story building and the pearl button factory: FPP, Coggeshall, AES, Chap. 5, pp. 106–116, 120.

6. FIC, *Third Report, 1914,* Vol. 3, pp. 546, 564; Vol. 4, p. 1463.

7. *Survey,* Vol. 29, p. 732, February 22, 1913. In this issue, p. 730, the FIC's former fire expert, H. F. J. Porter, criticized its proposals for not being drastic enough. To FP he was an idealist and difficult, but knowledgeable, FPOHC, Bk. 1, pp. 134–37.

8. Dreier-Dowling. FPOHC, Bk. 1, pp. 166–67, and with more tension suggested, FPP, Coggeshall, AES, Chap. 5, p. 74.

9. FIC, *Preliminary Report, 1912,* Vol. 1, p. 815.

10. *New York Times,* March 31, 1914, 15:5.

11. Binghamton fire: FIC, *Third Report, 1914,* Vol. 1, p. 62, and Appendix VII, p. 661. Diamond Candy fire, *New York Times,* November 7, 1915, 1:8, also known as the Williamsburg fire.

12. FIC, *Preliminary Report, 1912,* Vol. 2, pp. 216–17, the commission's third hearing and FPP, Coggeshall, AES, Chap. 5, p. 102. Language of latter version used. See Smith, *Up To Now,* p. 93. Of the 85 inspectors only 15, by law, could be women, FIC, *Preliminary Report, 1912,* Vol. 1, p. 60.

13. FIC, *Preliminary Report, 1912,* Vol. 1, p. 36; *Second Report, 1913,* Vol. 1, p. 304. See New York City Consumer's League, *Annual Report for 1913,* pp. 30–32. The FIC's bill was based in part on Wisconsin's experience with a similar industrial board, as explained to FIC by John R. Commons, FIC, *Preliminary Report, 1912,* Vol. 1, p. 23. *New York Times,* February 20, 1913, 7:6, and Oswald Garrison Villard, *Prophets True and False* (New York, Knopf, 1928), pp. 11–12, "epoch-making in their improvement of labor conditions."

14. FPOHC, Bk. 1, pp. 311–15; Bk. 2, pp. 479–81. See Lombardi, *Labor's Voice in the Cabinet,* pp. 75–95; Herring, *Public Administration and the Public Interest,* Chap. 17, "Providing Services for Labor."

15. The number of women and children and the canners' argument: FIC, *Second Report, 1913,* Vol. 1, pp. 143–45, 127. In 1912 the commission's inspectors reported discovering 1355 children under sixteen employed in canneries, of which 1259 were in the outside sheds as opposed to the factory proper. Of these 942 were under fourteen, 141 under ten and 30 under seven. For employment of children in New York City, see New York City Consumers' League, *Annual Report for 1910,* p. 16.

16. Visit to the pea cannery: FPP, Coggeshall, AES, ch. 5, 123–29. In FP, *TRIK,* 22, she mentions "an unannounced visit to a Cattaraugus County cannery." Perhaps she meant this visit in Cayuga County. The visit, "unannounced," seems also to have been unscheduled — not accompanied by the FIC's lawyers and stenographers. Doubtless there were many of these.

17. FPP, Coggeshall, AES, Chap. 5, p. 62.

18. FIC, *Second Report, 1913,* Vol. 1, pp. 143–47.

19. Huthmacher, *Wagner,* p. 6, citing interview with Dreier, p. 1962.

20. Smith, *Up To Now,* p. 95. Chamberlin had graduated from Vassar in 1909, FIC, *Second Report, 1913,* Vol. 3, p. 1005. The official report of the event, as might be expected, is less dramatic than Smith's memory of it. Chamberlin's testimony, however, is horrifying.

21. FIC, *Second Report, 1913,* Vol. 1, p. 170.

22. Smith, *Up To Now,* p. 96.

23. FIC, *Third Report, 1914,* Vol. 1, pp. v, 67. For this project the FIC created an advisory committee of 35 members, among whom were FP, Pauline Goldmark, Paul U. Kellogg, Lillian D. Wald and Edward T. Devine. This year, for the FIC, FP was also in charge of an investigation of fire hazards in mercantile establishments.
24. Wages. New York City Consumers' League, *Annual Report for 1913,* pp. 17–22; *Annual Report for 1915,* pp. 8–10.
25. FIC, *Second Report, 1913,* Vol. 4, pp. 1576–82.
26. Goldmark, *Impatient Crusader,* pp. 132–42. The eight states were California, Colorado, Minnesota, Nebraska, Oregon, Utah, Washington and Wisconsin.
27. FIC, *Fourth Report, 1915,* Vol. 1, p. 73.
28. FP on Smith and organized labor: FPP, Coggeshall, AES, Chap. 5, carbon "C", pp. 25–28. Smith, *Up To Now,* pp. 97–98.
29. FIC, *Fourth Report, 1915,* Vol. 1, pp. 76–83.
30. Huthmacher, *Wagner,* pp. 12–13.
31. FPP, Coggeshall, AES, Chap. 5, pp. 129–38. Cf. Smith's remarks in his annual message to the legislature, January 1928, reprinted in *The Industrial Bulletin,* Vol. 7, No. 4, p. 108, January 1928.
32. On Smith's ability to learn from others: FPOHC, Bk. 1, p. 428; Bk. 2, p. 232. "He read a book:" The remark exists in versions. In FPOHC, Bk. 1, p. 431, the Tammany man says it, apparently during the 1920s, to Alexander Sachs, who promptly repeats it to her. This seems the most likely version and was used by the Josephsons in *Al Smith,* p. 102. Unfortunately, she repeats the story in FPOHC, Bk. 3, p. 323, setting it in 1944, on Smith's death, and it is said by one Tammany man to another and is overheard by Isador Lubin, who has no memory of it (interview with GM). This seems the least likely version, as Lubin was seldom, if ever, in New York in 1944 and never in a Tammany gathering. Finally in FPP, Coggeshall, AES, Chap. 5, carbon "C", p. 5, the Tammany man says it directly to her: "He read a book, and that book was the people he met in the Factory Investigating Commission that taught him an awful lot." The time is again in the 1920s, on an election night while she and other Democrats are awaiting the returns.
33. FP, *TRIK,* pp. 22–23, 17.
34. FPOHC, Bk. 1, pp. 57–58.

Chapter 11

(pages 122–137)

1. FPOHC, Bk. 1, p. 212.
2. Register of Grace Church, Vol. 7C, p. 62. Letter of PCW to his mother, September 20, 1913, FPP, Coggeshall: "On Sept. 26th Frances Perkins and I are to be married at Grace Church, no one to be present, no one knows this yet, not even the man who must perform the ceremony . . . Frances and I know each other thoroughly and believe we can make each other happy . . ."
3. Letters PCW to FP, August 14 and 22, 1911, FPP, Coggeshall.
4. Interview by GM with Robert Moses.
5. FPOHC, Bk. 1, pp. 276–79. The story she tells of being asked to recom-

mend clemency for the proprietors of the Triangle Shirtwaist Company must be confused, for they did not go to jail because of the fire. The circumstances of the wedding, however, suggest that she did, indeed, dress alone. She told her daughter that the witnesses were "chance people" (interview by GM with SWC), and I have been unable to discover any other reference to them.

6. On Wilson: interviews by GM with Robert Moses and Agnes Leach; FPOHC, Bk. 1, pp. 243–44, 257, 273, 285; transcripts from Dartmouth and Chicago. *Bureau of Municipal Research: Purposes and Methods,* 1909, lists Bruère on the executive staff and PCW as an investigator and accountant.

7. Letter to GM from Mary E. (Mrs. William S.) Piper, Sr.; interview by GM with Vira Peters Towle; FP, *TRIK,* p. 9; feature article, Worcester *Sunday Telegram,* February 5, 1933; FPOHC, Bk. 1, p. 363.

8. FPP, Mount Holyoke, has an announcement of the marriage. Letter to FP and PCW from John Kingsbury, October 1, 1913, FPP, Columbia. Worcester *Sunday Telegram,* October 5, 1913.

9. FPOHC, Bk. 1, pp. 245–47; Bk. 8, p. 133, on being "as clear as mud and awfully amiable" on certain occasions.

10. Quotations: FP special delivery letter to PCW, September 5, 1913, PCW to FP, September 8, 1913, and FP to PCW, September 9, 1913, all in FPP, Coggeshall.

11. FPOHC, Bk. 1, pp. 244–48, 275–76; interview with Vira Peters Towle.

12. FPP, Mount Holyoke, letter FP to alumnae secretary, May 22, 1914, and forms filed December 5, 1914, March 15, 1918 and December 1, 1923.

13. FPOHC, Bk. 1, pp. 251–53; FP letter to Ruth Hale, September 4, 1918, FPP, Columbia.

14. On her name. *Huff* v. *State Board of Election,* 168 Oklahoma Reports 277. FPOHC, Bk. 1, pp. 254–55. In general: Letter of Turner W. Battle, Assistant to the Secretary of Labor, to Judge L. N. Neuenfelt (Dearborn, Michigan), July 27, 1935, explaining legal position underlying FP's use of her maiden name, FPP, NA, Women General, p. 82. Memorandum prepared in labor department, July 26, 1935 (presumably to accompany preceding), FPP, Columbia. Letter from Mary Anderson, Chief of Women's Bureau, to FP, October 21, 1938, on passport regulations prohibiting use of a married woman's maiden name, FPP, NA, Women's Bureau 1938, 81. Letter FP to S. P. Breckinridge, November 8, 1941, and letter to FP from Jane Grant, June 12, 1953, both in FPP, Columbia. Interview by GM with Vira Peters Towle.

15. FPOHC, Bk. 1, pp. 385–88, 280–82.

16. FPOHC, Bk. 1, pp. 189–202. On friendship among the suffragists: FP was not the only woman to reach this conclusion. The feminist Charlotte Perkins Gilman (no relation) suggested it as a new field for fiction in *The Man-Made World* (New York, Charlton Co., 1911), p. 104: ". . . the inter-relation of women with women — a thing we could never write about before because we never had it before: except in harems and convents."

17. Obituary of F. W. Perkins, Worcester *Sunday Telegram,* February 27, 1916. SWC, birth certificate; born at the New York Nursery and Child's hospital. Her name, letter FP to Margaret Leahy, June 5, 1924, FPP,

Columbia. FPOHC, Bk. 1, p. 274. Letter PCW to FP, September 19, 1917, FPP, Coggeshall.

18. On FP and the Mitchel administration: FPOHC, Bk. 1, pp. 243–342, specifically, pp. 255, 273, 283–94. On the close relationship between Mitchel and PCW: PCW's work can be seen in the Mitchel Papers at the New York City Municipal Archives. Though most of it was routine — answering letters, setting up meetings etc. — it sometimes flared into importance, as in the labor disputes in the garment industry in the summer of 1916. Mitchel Papers, Subject File 1914–1917, S (part 2)-T (Part 1), Folder entitled "Strikes and Lockouts — Garment Industry — Mitchel 1915–1916." Some of PCW's work is quoted or cited in Dubofsky, *When Workers Organize,* pp. 95–97, 184–85. Also interview by GM with Robert Moses and letter from Mary Dreier to FP, January 5, 1953, following PCW's death: ". . . I remember him as one of the most gallant young men in John Purroy Mitchel's cabinet"; FPP, Columbia. On Olive Mitchel, FPOHC, Bk. 1, pp. 264–67; Robert S. Binkerd, OH, Columbia, p. 14.

19. FPOHC, Bk. 1, pp. 258–64. Allan Nevins and John A. Krout eds. *The Greater City, New York, 1898–1948,* (New York: Columbia University Press, 1948), pp. 88–89. Eda Amberg and William H. Allen, *Civic Lessons from Mayor Mitchel's Defeat* (New York: Institute for Public Service, April 1921), pp. 24–25. On all aspects of the Mitchel administration: Edwin R. Lewinson, *John Purroy Mitchel, The Boy Mayor of New York* (New York: Astra Books, 1965).

20. *New York Times,* July 7, 1918, 1:1, and other articles on Mitchel throughout the issue. Robert S. Binkerd, OH, Columbia, p. 14. Lewinson, *Mitchel,* p. 255, believes that conscious suicide "can be easily dismissed."

21. FPOHC, Bk. 1, pp. 259, 286–87.

22. Women's City Club. FPOHC, Bk. 1, pp. 399–401.

23. Maternity Center Association. FPOHC, Bk. 1, pp. 401–12. Records at MCA, 48 East Ninety-second St., New York, New York 10028, FP letters to John B. Andrews, December 11, 1918, February 5, 1919, JBA Papers. FP's belief in the humanizing effect of women on public life parallels — I could find no evidence that it derived from — Charlotte Perkins Gilman's belief that "the distinctly feminine or maternal impulses are far more nearly in line with human progress than are those of the male." Gilman, *The Man-Made World* (note 16, above), p. 235. On the federal program: Goldmark, *Impatient Crusader,* pp. 105–109. Possibly on the organization of the Maternity Center in April 1918, or sometime later, FP began to receive a salary. The center has no evidence, and FP states only that she was not paid for her work in 1917. If she was paid, her salary was probably small; charities typically did not pay well for part-time, professional work. FPOHC, Bk. 1, pp. 407, 268; and "one more child," Bk. 3, p. 642.

24. Wilson's illness. FPOHC, Bk. 3, pp. 638–44; Bk. 1, pp. 412, 436; Bk. 4, p. 2. Interviews by GM with Robert Moses, SWC, Gerard Reilly and Leonard Adams. On Bruère for advice, FPOHC, Bk. 1, p. 435; letter FP to Bruère, September 29, 1934, FPP, Columbia. In view of PCW's subsequent ill health perhaps his frequent references in his letters of 1914 and

later years to the presence or absence of a headache is significant, e.g. PCW to FP, April 26, 1914, "I am most well. No headache." FPP, Coggeshall.

Chapter 12
(pages 141–150)

1. FPOHC, Bk. 2, pp. 208–19.
2. FPOHC, Bk. 1, pp. 435–43.
3. FPOHC, Bk. 1, pp. 443–44; Bk. 3, pp. 296, 650.
4. FPOHC, Bk. 1, pp. 253, 432–35. FPP, Mount Holyoke, has 5 newspaper clippings (unidentified), all dealing with her appointment. *New York Times*, February 19, 1919. Letter of Albert de Roode to Ansley Wilcox, January 28, 1919, and letters of T. Harvey Ferris to FP, January 17 and 22, 1919: ". . . while I do not doubt that you still read *The New Republic* and *Survey*, I am perfectly willing to take a chance upon your sound common sense." All in FPP, Columbia.
5. FPOHC, Bk. 3, p. 649.
6. On Sulzer's impeachment, FPOHC, Bk. 1, pp. 217–25; Huthmacher, *Wagner*, pp. 26–27; Josephsons, *Al Smith*, 149–53; Jacob A. Friedman, *The Impeachment of Governor William Sulzer* (New York, Columbia University Press, 1939). "Personality meets the situation," FPOHC Bk. 3, p. 225; Bk. 1, pp. 168–69: "I can never believe in these 'forces' — economic, political or anything else. I think that fifty people with a determination to do something right can start forces that have their strength largely because of the moral appeal of what it is they're recommending."
7. FPOHC, Bk. 1, pp. 227–33.
8. *A Statement addressed to Hon. Charles S. Whitman, Governor, upon the failure of The Industrial Commission to enforce the labor law with particular reference to The Fire In Diamond Factory, Williamsburg, Brooklyn, on November 6, 1915*, pp. 2–3.
9. *New York Times*, January 4, 1916, 6:2; January 16, 1916, II, 5:2; February 5, 1916, 7:3.
10. FPOHC, Bk. 2, p. 4.
11. FPOHC, Bk. 2, pp. 6–35, 104–108. *The Bulletin* (of the State Industrial Commission), Vol. 4, No. 6, p. 113, March 1919, had a full-page interview with FP entitled "Miss Perkins Tells Plans." But she was careful and told very little. Her assignments on the commission were: Mediation and Arbitration, Sanitary and Safety Devices, Statistics and Information, and Variations on New Construction. The next year Sanitary and Safety Devices were replaced by Women in Industry. In announcing her appointment *The Bulletin*, above, p. 101, stated, "She has a special interest in the welfare of women."

Chapter 13
(pages 151–162)

1. The story of the strike at Rome, with all quotations from FPOHC or contemporary sources, is reconstructed from FPOHC, Bk. 2, pp. 109–42,

191–206. Rome *Daily Sentinel,* June 4 to August 18, 1919. Transcript of
the Public Hearing of the State Industrial Commission held at the Court
House in Rome, August 4 to 6, 1919, FPP, Columbia. State Department
of Labor, *The Bulletin,* Vol. 4, No. 11, August 1919, pp. 201–209, 219, including an editorial description and partial transcript of the hearing, all
unsigned but almost certainly by the editor, Willard A. Marakle, who was
present. State Department of Labor *Annual Report* of the Industrial
Commission for year ending June 30, 1920. History of the Wire Business
of the Spargo Wire Company, given GM by James A. Spargo, Jr. Interviews by GM with Spargo, Robert M. Lake, Anthony Gualtieri, Alfred
and Katherine Santoro. Letter to FP from W. G. Levison, February 10,
1933, FPP, Columbia.

On Spargo's rough language. The obscene letter has disappeared, but
to those who knew Spargo its one-time existence seemed highly likely.
Robert M. Lake, former executive vice-president of Revere Copper and
Brass Co., heard the following story from his father who had it direct
from Spargo: sometime in the 1930s, when FP was Secretary of Labor, she
wrote Spargo asking for some information. He replied, "I have received
your letter and used it to wipe my ass."

For background of the town: Isaac F. Marcosson, *Industrial Main
Street, The Story of Rome — The Copper City* (New York, Dodd Mead,
1953), but ignore its description of the strike, pp. 79–80: "fomented by
communists and the I.W.W. . . . the strikers declared a Soviet Republic
of Rome" etc. Though some IWW literature was seized by the state
police, there was little of it and no IWW leadership. Any prolonged
strike will attract some radical talkers and literature. The evidence is
overwhelming that this was a local strike brought on by local wages,
hours and working conditions. On the change in the town's way of life:
the introduction of country clubs and the use of lawyers to speak for the
employers, FPOHC, Bk. 6, pp. 78, 81–82. FPOHC, Bk. 2, p. 205 and
Smith, *Up to Now,* pp. 177–78.

Chapter 14

(pages 163–179)

1. FP's Socialist party card, FPP, Coggeshall. FP's comments on some socialists, FPOHC, Bk. 2, pp. 164–69: "The Socialist party didn't amount
   to a row of pins in those days."
2. FPOHC, Bk. 1, pp. 210–15.
3. FPOHC, Bk. 2, pp. 36–48, 63, 227, 236, 556.
4. FPOHC, Bk. 2, pp. 66–74. On Smith's nomination, pp. 289–91.
5. Letter to FP from L. A. Howell, April 19, 1921; Cf. from V. F. Holland,
   July 6, 1945 and from Thomas Finn, February 3, 1955; all in FPP, Columbia. When she left the U.S. Department of Labor she shook hands
   with every employee in the department, some 7000 persons. According
   to the Washington *Evening Star,* June 27 and June 28, 1945, B1:5 and
   A2:2, it took four hours.
6. Two letters of FP to John B. Andrews, secretary of the American Association for Labor Legislation, give an idea of the work, in JBA Papers.
   FPOHC, Bk. 2, p. 93; Bk. 3, p. 270. The Merchants' Association was

founded and incorporated in 1897. In 1941 it changed its name to the Commerce and Industry Association of New York, Inc.

7. On the need to work. FPOHC, Bk. 2, p. 170; Bk. 3, pp. 640–44. The idea of a "made-up" job for PCW was suggested by Robert Moses; when put to Agnes Leach, she thought it entirely possible. Interviews by GM.

8. FPOHC, Bk. 3, p. 641. Interviews by GM with Alison Bruère Carnahan, Robert Moses, Mary V. Marvin. Letter to GM from Mary E. Piper and letter from Florence P. Holding to Vira Peters Towle.

9. Interview by GM with Agnes Leach. A larger dinner in return by the Leaches, with literary people whom they thought would interest PCW, went no better. On some of these occasions he would drink too much.

10. This point is well displayed in Dubofsky, *When Workers Organize,* Chap. 1; FPOHC, Bk. 2, p. 94. Cf. Yellowitz, *Labor and the Progressive Movement in New York State, 1897–1916.*

11. E.g. FPP, Mount Holyoke, Fifth Class Letter (1924) of 1902, p. 64, letter of Charlotte Swinnerton Drake, living in Buffalo: "I see Frances Perkins' face regularly in the paper." On her first appointment in 1919 *The Bulletin* (of the State Industrial Commission), Vol. 4, No. 6, p. 101, March 1919, omitted a detailed description of her because she was "too well known to need extended comment." FPOHC, Bk. 2, pp. 170, 174. *The Industrial Bulletin,* Vol. 2, No. 4, pp. 83, 88, January 1923. Smith submitted her name to the Senate on January 15; she was confirmed and started work on Jan. 27.

12. On Higgens, FPOHC, Bk. 2, pp. 171–74; *The Bulletin,* Vol. 6, No. 7, p. 123, April 1921.

13. On Curran, *The Bulletin,* Vol. 6, No. 8 and 9, pp. 141, 144, May and June 1921; FPOHC, Bk. 2, pp. 171, 502.

14. FPOHC, Bk. 1, pp. 59–60.

15. Goulden, *Meany,* p. 20. Cf. FPOHC, Bk. 1, p. 161, on Matthew Woll and the photoengravers union.

16. FPOHC, Bk. 2, pp. 497, 501.

17. On Workmen's Compensation Act. Throughout this section I found most useful Henry D. Sayer's *Workmen's Compensation in New York: Its Development and Operations* (New York, Commerce and Industry Association, 1953); the National Industrial Conference Board's *The Workmen's Compensation Problem in New York State* (New York, National Industrial Conference Board, 1927); and Governor Smith's annual message to the legislature for January 1928, of which the part concerning the Department of Labor was published in *The Industrial Bulletin,* Vol. 7, No. 4, January 1928, pp. 108–11. This contains the clearest list of amendments to the act. FPOHC, Bk. 2, pp. 178–86, 384–459.

Also, a series of articles, some in a popular style, on the department's administration of the act. All were originally speeches by the Industrial Commissioner, James Hamilton, and were then published in *The Industrial Bulletin,* Vol. 6, No. 5, p. 128, February 1927 (organization of the department); Vol. 6, No. 6, p. 152, March 1927 (administering the act); Vol. 7, No. 1, p. 4, October 1927 (attitude of workers to accident prevention); Vol. 7, No. 2, p. 44, November 1927 (compensation and physicians); Vol. 7, No. 8, p. 240, May 1928 (benefits of state fund); Vol. 7, No. 11, p. 332, August 1928 (on state fund).

   The act originated in New York with a Legislative Commission appointed in 1909 on the recommendation of Republican Governor Charles E. Hughes, which, according to Sayer, above, p. 4, "stemmed from a message to Congress by President Theodore Roosevelt in 1908 with reference to railroad workers and governmental workers." Chairman of the Legislative Commission was State Senator J. Mayhew Wainwright, who appears briefly in the story of the 54-hour Bill. Sayer is the man who served on the Industrial Commission with Perkins, 1919–1921. After the reorganization he served as the Industrial Commissioner until the appointment of Bernard L. Shientag.

18. Sayer, above, p. 73; cf. FPOHC, Bk. 2, p. 478.
19. *The Bulletin,* Vol. 6, No. 4, p. 64, January 1921. I have tightened the writing, mostly by cutting out laudatory terms similar to the two "patiently"'s left in.
20. The legal history of *Matter of Lahti* v. *Terry and Tench Co.* can be found in: Department Reports of the State of New York, Vol. 31, p. 209, 1924; 211 Appellate Division p. 825, affirmed without opinion; 240 New York Reports 292; 269 U.S. Supreme Court Reports 548, on certiorari; 273 U.S. Supreme Court Reports 639, reversed without opinion (October 11, 1926). FPOHC, Bk. 2, pp. 178–86, 386. Also the section on workmen's compensation, Bk. 2, pp. 384–459, in which she discusses a case expanding the term "in the course of employment," and allowed an award to the widow of a common law marriage, p. 388; also the institution of referee's conferences to make decisions uniform, p. 384, and the schedule of occupational diseases, p. 400. Also, FP letter to John B. Andrews, April 1, 1925 on the unfortunate, technical turn Appellate Division decisions were taking, and the correspondence with him and others in the American Association of Labor Legislation discussing cases and what might be done. Finally, letters indicating her support for a federal Maritime Compensation bill, March 16 and 18, 1926. All in JBA Papers.

   In her account of the *Lahti* case she describes, FPOHC, Bk. 2, pp. 185–86, persuading Henry L. Stimson to argue the case in the U.S. Supreme Court. The Court report does not mention him, and his law firm, Winthrop, Stimson, Putnam & Roberts, has no record of such a case. Evidently her memory here misled her. Cardozo, FPOHC, Bk. 2, p. 386.

21. Smith's attitude toward workmen's compensation, FPOHC, Bk. 2, pp. 399, 469. Her high standing with workers in New York: better evidence than the testimony of union officials is Farley's judgment, reported by Ickes, that she had "a lot of value" in the state for the 1936 presidential campaign. Her constituency was the rank-and-file worker. Ickes, *Diary,* Bk. 1, p. 632. The shift in vote: Lubell, *The Future of American Politics,* p. 34.

Chapter 15

(pages 180–195)

1. This was the Madison Square Garden between Madison and Fourth avenues at Twenty-sixth and Twenty-seventh streets. On the convention floor were about 3000 delegates and alternates; in the boxes and galleries,

about 9000 spectators. The most detailed account of the convention is in *Politics: The Citizens' Business,* by William Allen White (New York, Macmillan, 1924).

2. On the Klan, *The Ku Klux Klan in the City, 1915–1930,* by Kenneth T. Jackson (New York, Oxford University Press, 1967), pp. 15, 18–23, 236 and 252. The bilingual signs, White, *Politics,* p. 79. The single vote, 542–3/20 to 541–3/20, *Official Proceedings of Democratic National Convention — 1924,* p. 333. At the time of the vote it apparently seemed slightly less close. The *New York Times,* July 1, 1924, reported it as 546.15 to 541.85, and White, above, p. 77, as a margin of four.

3. Official Proceedings, above, pp. 533–36. Bryan's remark is quoted by Handlin, *Al Smith,* p. 123, but without citation. I could not find it in any account of the exchanges between Bryan and the galleries, but it is an apt summary of them. Claude G. Bowers, *My Life* (New York, Simon & Schuster, 1962), pp. 113–24, has a good description of the convention: "Finally, when the galleries resembled those of the French Convention in the period of the Revolution, Senator Walsh, finding it impossible to restore something of the dignity of a deliberate body, expressed his willingness to adjourn the convention to another city."

4. Smith, *Up to Now,* p. 285. His daughter, Emily Smith Warner, in *The Happy Warrior,* p. 161, could bring herself to say only: "As a matter of practical politics it may be that the demonstration was somewhat too enthusiastic especially where the galleries were concerned." FP, much more critical, FPOHC, Bk. 2, pp. 306–307: "sickened the delegates." She came to believe that holding the 1924 convention in New York was "undoubtedly a mistake" and adversely affected his 1928 campaign. FPP, Coggeshall, AES, folder entitled "The 1928 Campaign for President", pp. 1–3.

The qualification of "a major party" is necessary because in 1872 a splinter group of southern Democrats, unhappy with Horace Greeley as the party's candidate, formed the Independent Democratic Party and nominated Charles O'Conor, an outstanding New York City lawyer, a Catholic and son of an Irish immigrant. Throughout the Civil War O'Conor had defended slavery as "necessary and beneficent," and after the war had volunteered to defend Jefferson Davis, president of the Confederacy. Over O'Conor's objections his name was put on the ballot and without campaigning he received 29,408 votes, .45 percent of those cast.

5. On FP's part in the convention, FPOHC, Bk. 2, pp. 303, 311–13, 318, 320. Her preconvention speeches, *New York Times* May 20, 1924, 23:5 and June 13, 1924, 21:6.

6. Rollins, *Roosevelt and Howe,* p. 214, citing FDR Library, Group XVI (the 1924 campaign). Rollins also quotes Smith's outspoken letter in favor of repeal, which appeared in *New York Times,* June 9, 1924.

7. Bowers, *My Life,* p. 177, see note 3, above.

8. FPP, Coggeshall, AES, Chap. 1, p. 13.

9. FPOHC, Bk. 2, pp. 325–28, 565; "Those fat slob politicians," p. 326. Elliot Roosevelt, *An Untold Story,* pp. 208–09. Davis, *FDR: The Beckoning of Destiny,* pp. 749–53, citing Proskauer, *A Segment of My Times,*

pp. 50–51. On Smith's three closest advisers, Emily Smith Warner, *The Happy Warrior*, p. 152.

10. Among those switching, Bernard Baruch and Thomas L. Chadbourne. Handlin, *Al Smith*, 124–25, without citation.

11. Josephsons, *Al Smith*, p. 88.

12. FPP, Coggeshall, AES, Chap. 5, p. 141. FPOHC, Bk. 3, p. 319: "it was a moral question with him" (Smith).

13. *Hammer* v. *Dagenhart*, 247 U.S. pp. 529–35, 1918; *Bailey* v. *Drexel Furniture Company*, 259 U.S. p. 20, 1922.

14. Chambers, *Seedtime of Reform*, Chap. 2; Goldmark, *Impatient Crusader*, Chap. 7; Grace Abbott, "Federal Regulation of Child Labor, 1906–1938," *Social Service Review*, Vol. 13, No. 3, pp. 409–30; Courtenay Dinwiddie, "The Present Status of Child Labor," *Social Service Review*, Vol. 13, No. 3, pp. 431–39; Jeremy Felt, *Hostages of Fortune: Child Labor Reform in New York State* (Syracuse, Syracuse University Press, 1965), pp. 204–13.

15. Chambers, *Seedtime of Reform*, p. 38, citing National Consumers' League (Manuscript Division of the Library of Congress) Box 10. On NAM, Chambers, above, p. 40.

16. Wayman, Dorothy G. *Cardinal O'Connell of Boston* (New York, Farrar Straus, 1955), pp. 220–21, citing archives of Catholic University of America.

17. Chambers, *Seedtime*, p. 43, citing statement in *Woman Citizen*, February 21, 1925, p. 10.

18. Chambers, *Seedtime*, pp. 42–43, citing Kelley to FP, National Consumers' League, above, Box 11.

19. FP recounts the story three times: FPOHC, Bk. 2, pp. 252–59, the chief source of the text's version; in her lecture at Cornell, Autumn 1957, on "Al Smith as I Knew Him," FPP, Cornell; and in her unfinished biography of Smith, FPP, Coggeshall, AES, Chap. 5, carbon "C", pp. 17–18. The identity of the clergyman is uncertain. In FPOHC it is Cardinal O'Connell, but in the other two it is merely an emissary from the cardinal. The Albany newspapers have no report of the cardinal's visiting Smith at this time, nor do the archives of the Boston archdiocese.

20. FPOHC, Bk. 2, p. 251.

21. Chambers, *Seedtime*, p. 43. Goldmark, *Impatient Crusader*, p. 119, where Kelley's board of directors refused to support a petition campaign as too expensive.

22. FPOHC, Bk. 2, pp. 260–63. Goldmark, *Impatient Crusader*, p. 118, states that "Even Governor Alfred E. Smith of New York turned against the amendment when the position of his church became clear." Lash, *Eleanor and Franklin*, p. 312, has an account of Smith's interview with Kelley in which Eleanor Roosevelt takes Kelley to Smith, who admits to ER that he has been influenced by his church. It seems more likely, however, that Kelley would turn to FP for entry to Smith and most unlikely that FP would invent a story in which Kelley shows up so poorly.

23. Chambers, *Seedtime of Reform*, Chap. 5, "The Settlements in Service to Their Neighbors"; on Wiley Swift, p. 46; on Helen Phelan, p. 148; on Vida Scudder, p. 123; all with citations. Smith and Zeitz, *American Social Welfare Institutions*, p. 73, and on Abraham Epstein, p. 100, with cita-

tion. Also, Chambers, above, pp. 93–98. Chafe, *The American Woman,* Chap. 4, "Women in the Professions"; Lubove, *The Struggle for Social Security, 1900–1935;* and Trolander, *Settlement Houses and the Great Depression,* who offers as a reason for the change the rise of the Community Chest concept which put conservative businessmen in control of the distribution of funds.

24. Interview by GM with Gerard Reilly.

25. Chafe, *The American Woman,* pp. 92–93, with citations.

26. The best summary of what was accomplished is in Smith's annual message to the legislature in January 1928. The part concerning the Labor Department was published in *The Industrial Bulletin,* Vol. 7, no. 4, pp. 108–11. It is not known whether Smith, Perkins or the two jointly wrote it, but it is a remarkable summary of their common experience starting with the Factory Investigating Commission. "As Vice-Chairman . . . I became convinced that it was not only the right, but the duty, of the State to see to it that its working men, and women and children were properly protected . . . I became convinced that legislation for the betterment of working conditions was in no sense class legislation and was not designed to benefit any one particular group . . . With these principles in mind . . . I became Governor . . ." On minimum wage the key to better industrial relations, FP to Alice Cook; interview by GM with Cook.

Chapter 16
(pages 196–203)

1. FPOHC, Bk. 2, pp. 561–62. Her mother died October 28, 1927.

2. FPOHC, Bk. 2, pp. 563–65.

3. FPOHC, Bk. 2, pp. 626–35.

4. Southern tour, FPOHC, Bk. 2, pp. 577–622. On Katie Smith, Bk. 2, pp. 590–95. FP thought Mrs. Smith rather overdressed and spoke to Moskowitz about it, but nothing was done for fear of hurting the feelings of Governor and Mrs. Smith. On the musical evenings, Bk. 2, pp. 266–68.

5. Oklahoma City. Josephsons, *Al Smith,* pp. 380–87. Charles Michelson, *The Ghost Talks* (New York, Putnam's, 1944), p. 155: "The sidewalks-of-New York personality was the base of many sneers by his enemies, so he exaggerated the East Side twang, paraded the brown derby, and interlarded his address with 'raddio' and similar Gothamic variations." Michelson accompanied Smith as a speech writer.

6. Missouri trip, FPOHC, Bk. 2, pp. 638–79. FPP, Coggeshall, AES, folder "The 1928 Campaign for President," pp. 49–53. *The Independence Examiner,* Monday, October 22, 1928, reporting the meeting from Saturday night, October 20. Correspondence with Sue Gentry, a former reporter for the *Examiner,* about the city and hall as they were in 1928. Interview by GM with Aileen (Mrs. Vanderbilt) Webb.

FP in her account of the meeting, FPOHC, states that tomatoes and eggs were thrown at the speakers, that a tomato hit Hawes in the chest and that others landed in "the suburbs" of herself and Aileen Webb as each spoke. Webb confirmed the account in all respects except for the tomatoes, saying quietly: "I think if tomatoes and eggs had been thrown at us, I would remember it, don't you?" I do. Also the newspaper account, from which the gist of the three speeches has been taken, does not report any barrage of vegetables. There had been a meeting of "Hoover Democrats" in the hall that afternoon at which the speaker had warned of the danger of Tammany's taking over the national government, and the election was portrayed as "a struggle between the forces of evil and the forces of good for control of the government."

7. On Smith's speech from Newark, which FP mistakenly reports to have been from Helena, Montana, FPOHC, Bk. 2, pp. 575–77.

8. Reasons for Smith's defeat. FPOHC, Bk. 2, pp. 698–702; Bk. 3, p. 334. The Maine farmer, FPP, Coggeshall, AES, folder "1928 Campaign," p. 18. The folder contains a draft of a chapter for her biography of Smith, and the draft consists of 65 consecutive typewritten pages, double-spaced, and an insert on the southern tour of 11 pages, double-spaced. In preparing it she evidently wrote a number of persons requesting their opinions on the campaign, and she quotes from the replies of Sam Rayburn and of Henry Wallace. Though plainly not in final form the draft is clean copy, and her ideas clearly presented. These are, in summary: Smith's role in the 1924 convention was badly handled and his final speech one of his poorest. The effect hurt him in 1928. The prejudices against him because of his religion, city origin and accent were very great. The reputation of Tammany was against him. His stand against Prohibition was too strong. He was not well known outside New York. He knew little about the country. He treated rural people, even those from other cities than New York, as "hicks," demanding that they accept his prejudices though he rejected theirs. The appointment of John J. Raskob, a Catholic, to be chairman of the Democratic National Committee was a mistake. Hoover was a good candidate and a good "exit" for those not wanting to vote for Smith. Adulation of Smith by Catholics was overdone. Prosperity hurt him. He knew nothing about the federal government. There was genuine opposition to his social legislation. See also p. 29 of FP's speech on Smith at Cornell, Autumn 1957, FPP, Cornell.

Chapter 17

(pages 204–216)

1. FP, *TRIK*, p. 54; FPOHC, Bk. 2, pp. 174–78, 351; interview by GM with Robert Moses, Hamilton was "a joke, a left-over Tammany hack."

2. FP, *TRIK*, pp. 55–66; FPOHC, Bk. 2, pp. 719–26; on Smith's greater courage, p. 722, on FDR's trick with his lip, p. 725, and Bk. 3, p. 8.

3. FP to FDR, n.d., and probably never sent, FPP, Columbia.

4. Interviews by GM with Moses and Perkins's colleagues in the federal department. For an example of her good administration in New York, Bellush, *Franklin D. Roosevelt as Governor of New York*, p. 313, fn. 4.

5. FPOHC, Bk. 2, p. 727.

6. FP, *TRIK*, p. 58; FPOHC, Bk. 2, p. 727.

7. FPOHC, Bk. 3, pp. 5–25. I have not been able to fix the reception at which these scenes took place. The most likely was on the afternoon of

December 31, 1928. During the transition there were several such opportunities, see Albany *Knickerbocker Press* for January 2, 1929. The rift over policy between the two men was quickly reported, Albany *Knickerbocker Press*, January 12, 1929. Cf. Freidel, *FDR, The Triumph*, p. 17, citing interviews with FP in May 1953.

8. FPOHC, Bk. 3, p. 78.

9. FPOHC, Bk. 2, p. 727; interview by GM with Robert Moses.

10. Interviews by GM with Agnes Leach and Nannie Glidden. Also SWC's contemporaries.

11. FP letter to Bethsabe (Mrs. Harry) Pederson, October 27, 1944, FPP, Columbia.

12. "Forceful," interviews by GM with Isador Lubin and Agnes Leach; pony cart, interview by GM with SWC.

13. FP letter to editor of Brooklyn *Eagle*, April 7, 1930, FPP, Columbia.

14. FP letter to Mary Dewson, February 16, 1929, FPP, Columbia. "Climbing trees." The remark has been so widely requoted its first appearance seems lost.

15. Leter to FP from Mark Daly, January 16, 1929, FPP, Columbia. *Greater New York*, weekly bulletin of Merchants' Association, June 19, 1929, with concluding statement quoted in *The Industrial Bulletin*, Vol. 8, No. 10, p. 667, July 1929.

16. The speech (probably cut) was published as "My Job" in *Survey*, Vol. 61, No. 12, pp. 733–75, March 15, 1929.

17. On working with Smith, FPOHC, Bk. 2, pp. 729–31; other differences between Smith and FDR, Bk. 2, pp. 226–27; Bk. 3, p. 343; the aluminum dust and hour's conference, Bk. 3, pp. 212–22. Her skill in dealing with FDR, C. E. Wyzanski, Jr., letter to GM and interview by GM with Gerard Reilly.

18. FP, *TRIK*, pp. 95–97; FPOHC, Bk. 3, pp. 452–57. An interesting description of the "Social Consequences of Business Depression" within a family's life was given by Jane Addams in a radio address, October 24, 1931, of which a transcript is in FPP, Columbia. *New York Times* stories (only a few of many) disputing Hoover's administration on figures are January 23, 1930; June 28, 1930; August 25, 1932.

19. FPOHC, Bk. 3, pp. 139–81. "Stabilization of Employment," *The Industrial Bulletin* Vol. 9, No. 9, pp. 251–52, 272, June 1930. Report of Governor's Committee on Stabilization of Industry for the Prevention of Unemployment, November 13, 1930, in *Public Papers of Governor Roosevelt, 1930* pp. 589–601. See also Schneider and Deutsch, *History of Public Welfare in New York*, pp. 297–98, and Bellush, *Franklin D. Roosevelt as Governor of New York*, pp. 128–32.

Chapter 18

(pages 217–230)

1. O'Connor, *The First Hurrah*, pp. 237, 247; Handlin, *Al Smith*, p. 145; Josephsons, *Al Smith*, p. 431.

2. FPOHC, Bk. 3, pp. 341, 69.

3. See Freidel, *FDR, The Triumph,* pp. 178–82, which offers evidence that FDR had "done all that politeness required of him" in trying to notify Smith. See also in Freidel, above, Mencken's epitaph for Smith quoted at 311.

4. FPOHC, Bk. 3, pp. 68, 77, 275, 307, 332–35.

5. FPOHC, Bk. 3, p. 457. Cf. Bk. 3, p. 294.

6. Schneider and Deutsch, *History of Public Welfare in New York,* Chap. 16, pp. 293–316; Bellush, *Franklin D. Roosevelt as Governor,* Chaps. 6 and 8; Freidel, *FDR, The Triumph.* The statistics on Buffalo were published in the Department of Labor's Special Bulletins Nos. 163, 167, 172, 179.

7. FPOHC, Bk. 3, pp. 131–39, 165–66, 202–11.

8. Relief not a labor department job, FPOHC, Bk. 3, p. 210. Report of Governor's Committee on Stabilization of Industry for Prevention of Unemployment, November 13, 1930, *Public Papers of Governor Roosevelt, 1930,* pp. 589–601.

9. Her constant theme, perhaps best expressed in her speech "The Social Security Act," delivered over CBS on Labor Day, September 2, 1935, *Vital Speeches, I* (1935), pp. 792–94, and reprinted in Leuchtenburg, *The New Deal.*

10. Report to Governor FDR of an Analysis of Appropriations for and Expenditures by the Department of Labor, by FP and the Director of the Budget, Lyon Co., Albany, 1932. A Digest of the Full Report Submitted to FP, State Industrial Commissioner, by the Advisory Committee on Employment Problems, circa January 1931. On improving employment offices, see correspondence FP and John B. Andrews, June 1929–April 1930, JBA Papers.

11. FPOHC, Bk. 3, p. 175.

12. On British system. A. J. P. Taylor, *English History, 1914–1945* (London: Oxford University Press, 1965). FPOHC, Bk. 3, pp. 172–75.

13. FPOHC, Bk. 3, pp. 170–76; FP, *TRIK,* 93–94; FP lecture at Cornell, November 5, 1957, on origin and passage of Social Security Act, FPP, Cornell (typescript in FPP, Columbia); FP article "Unemployment Insurance, An American Plan," *Survey,* November 1931.

14. FDR speech quoted in Bernstein's *Lean Years,* p. 492.

15. FP, *TRIK,* p. 107.

16. Bellush, *Franklin D. Roosevelt as Governor,* pp. 162, 182–84.

17. FP, *TRIK,* pp. 103–104; FPOHC, Bk. 3, pp. 181–82; FP lecture at Cornell, November 5, 1957 on origin and passage of Social Security Act, FPP, Cornell (typescript at FPP, Columbia). See Members and Agenda of Conference. Public Papers of Governor Roosevelt, 1931, pp. 530–33.

18. Exchange between FP and Holland-American Line, February 28 and March 6, 1931, FPP, Columbia.

19. On Kew, FPOHC, Bk. 3, pp. 250–59. Her report to FDR, October 23, 1931, is in the form of a letter, FPP, Columbia and also FPP, Radcliffe, folder 864. Cf. FDR on advantages of direct administration to Arthur Altmeyer in latter's *Formative Years of Social Security,* p. 12.

20. FP, "Unemployment Insurance, An American Plan," *Survey,* November 1931. Digest of Report of Interstate Commission for Study on Unemploy-

ment Insurance; together with Roosevelt's statement on it, February 15, 1932. See *Public Papers of Governor Roosevelt, 1932,* pp. 467–69.

21. Freidel, *FDR, The Triumph,* p. 227, with citations.

22. Goldmark, *Impatient Crusader,* pp. 205–10, 3; FP, "My Job," *Survey,* March 15, 1929; FP, "My Recollections of Florence Kelley," *Social Service Review,* March 1954; FP's memorial address, quoted in Goldmark, above, p. 60. Accounts of memorial meeting, *New York Times,* March 17, 1932, 24:3; New York *Herald Tribune,* March 17, 1932, 17:7. Other speakers were Newton Baker, Secretary of War under Wilson and president of the National Consumers' League, 1915–23; Dr. Alice Hamilton, Harvard School of Public Health; Dr. W. E. B. Du Bois, editor of *Crisis;* and Dr. Harry W. Laidler, executive director of the League for Industrial Democracy. For a list of persons trained by Kelley who later entered public service, see "Fifty Years — The National Consumers' League" by Josephine Goldmark, *Survey,* Vol. 85, December 1949, p. 674.

Chapter 19

(pages 231–242)

1. Telegram FP to FDR and reply, *F.D.R., His Personal Letters, 1928–1945,* ed. by Elliott Roosevelt (New York, Duell, Sloan, 1950), p. 262.

2. Interviews GM with Robert Moses, Mary Marvin, Agnes Leach and Helene P. Gans.

3. FPOHC, Bk. 3, pp. 259–60.

4. FPOHC, Bk. 3, pp. 518, 560, 562, 608, 638–44; interviews by GM with SWC and Leonard Adams. The following letters, all in FPP, Columbia: FP to Henry Bruère, September 29, 1934, to Gertrude Light, July 22, 1935, to Mrs. Arthur Bullard, May 1, 1937, to Mrs. Arthur Brintnall, September 15, 1937, to PCW, May 27, 1943, to Mrs. Elma Macrae, November 10, 1944, to PCW, June 27, 1945, from Mrs. Everett Jordan, January 14, 1953, to same, February 10, 1953.

5. FP told Leonard Adams (see Chap. 35 of this book) that she had no insurance. Interview by GM with Moses, who was certain Bruère had "bailed out" PCW financially two or three times. Agnes Leach had not heard of it but thought it quite likely. She was sure FP had been helped by several women and when asked for names instantly said Eleanor Roosevelt and Caroline O'Day. According to Leach the women were proud of the position FP had reached and were not going to let her fail for lack of a few hundred or thousand dollars. Independently of Leach, Pauline Newman thought it likely that Caroline O'Day had helped FP financially.

6. FP to PCW, n.d., but in a group of letters dated by PCW "1934," FPP, Coggeshall. To Helene P. Gans, "FP *never* seemed married, not even in 1917," which was before his illness; interview with GM.

7. Interviews by GM with Robert Moses, Agnes Leach.

8. Henry Leach's promotion of FP on his tour was cleared first with FDR, interview by GM with Agnes Leach. The conference called by Grace Abbott, *New York Times,* December 11, 1932, 12:2, and interview by GM with Clara Beyer, who helped to organize it. Also, all in FPP, Columbia,

letters to FP from Harold Fields, February 7, 1933, from Lillian Wald, November 16, 1932 and from such labor officials as Claude E. Connally, Parke P. Deans, William R. Henry, Wiliam E. Hunter, Ethelbert Stewart and David I. White.

9. FPOHC, Bk. 3, pp. 3–4, 266.
10. FPOHC, Bk. 3, pp. 530–43, on Gide, p. 540.
11. Interviews by GM with Agnes Leach and Mary Marvin. Cf. FPOHC, Bk. 3, p. 291. Lash, in *Eleanor: The Years Alone*, p. 59, states that ER thought the third installment of the book as it appeared in *Collier's* "gave an inaccurate account of Franklin's third-term decision and failed to do justice to the president's background in economics."
12. FPOHC, Bk. 2, p. 170 "knew him better," and pp. 85, 87; Bk. 3, p. 543, "Dewson says." ER also denied any part in the appointment in *This I Remember*, p. 5, and *Ladies of Courage*, p. 277.
13. FPOHC, Bk. 3, p. 545.
14. FPOHC, Bk. 3, p. 517.
15. FPOHC, Bk. 3, p. 519 and *F.D.R., His Personal Letters*, above, p. 316.
16. FPOHC, Bk. 3, p. 524, and Taft, *The AF of L from Death of Gompers to the Merger*, p. 453.
17. FPOHC, Bk. 3, p. 517, 521–26, 543. In a letter to Mrs. Carrie Chapman Catt, June 11, 1945, FPP, Columbia, FP wrote, ". . . the overwhelming argument and thought which made me do it in the end in spite of personal difficulties was the realization that the door might not be opened to a woman again for a long, long time, and that I had a kind of duty to other women to walk in and sit down on the chair that was offered, and so establish the right of others long hence and far-distant in geography to sit in the high seats." Mrs. Catt, 1859–1947, was a leader of the national and international suffrage movement. In the same letter FP states, "I would rather have your approval than that of anyone else in the world, unless it could have been by chance of longevity that Jane Addams and Florence Kelley coud have lived till now."
18. Letter to FP from Bishop Charles K. Gilbert, February 11, 1933, FPP, Columbia. He was not altogether impartial as he was a member of a committee formed to urge for appointment; see letter to FP from Harold Fields, February 7, 1933, FPP, Columbia. The committee among others included Lillian Wald, Mary Simkhovitch and Joseph P. Chamberlain.
19. FPOHC, Bk. 3, pp. 569–70.
20. FPOHC, Bk. 3, pp. 570–607; FP, *TRIK*, 150–52; FP, speech to Pen and Brush Club, April 19, 1945, FPP, Coggeshall.
21. FP lecture at Cornell, November 5, 1957, on origin and passage of Social Security Act, FPP, Cornell (typescript in FPP, Columbia).
22. FPOHC, Bk. 3, pp. 608, 638–40.

Chapter 20

(pages 245–256)

1. For citations on the foregoing, see notes, Chaps. 1–4.
2. Description of MacCormack, FPOHC, Bk. 4, pp. 259–74. Also, MacMahon and Millet, *Federal Administrators*, p. 425, with fn. on "rule" for federal appointments from New York City.

3. Speaking to Farley, FPOHC, Bk. 4, p. 241; memorandum, FP to FDR recommending MacCormack, March 15, 1933, FDR Library, OF 15, Labor Dept. 15D.

4. The fullest collection of papers concerning MacCormack is in FPP, Connecticut. On his excellence, e.g. letter from Robert J. Caldwell, banker, internationalist and foreign relief administrator, to FDR, November 15, 1936, FDR Library, OF 15, Labor Dept. 15D; letter from Charles F. Amidon, U.S. District Judge, July 20, 1933, to FP, FPP, Columbia. On attitude of border patrol, interview by GM with Arthur M. Dailey, photographer of the West. On frequent consultations between FP and MacCormack, interview by GM with Isador Lubin.

5. FPOHC, Bk. 4, pp. 471–79; FP, *TRIK*, 183–85; FP letter to Hopkins, August 26, 1940, FPP, Columbia; letter from Robert T. Lansdale, Commissioner of N.Y. State Dept. of Welfare, to Bradley Buell, editor of *Survey Midmonthly*, March 14, 1946, PUK Papers, correcting FP on why Hopkins was chosen over Hodson.

6. Moley, *After Seven Years,* pp. 173–74.

7. FPOHC, Bk. 4, p. 487; Salmond, *The Civilian Conservation Corps,* pp. 16–18.

8. FPOHC, Bk. 4, pp. 298–301, 487–89.

9. Salmond, *The Civilian Conservation Corps,* pp. 21–25.

10. FPOHC, Bk. 4, pp. 482–83, 490; on Persons, 493–98. Salmond, *The Civilian Conservation Corps,* p. 27: Persons "a happy choice."

11. FPOHC, Bk. 4, pp. 302–21; Department of Labor *Annual Report, 1933,* p. 5; memorandum of a discussion of the conference by FP and Clara Beyer, April 18, 1946, FPP, Columbia (in file *TRIK,* II). Shown by GM to CB and confirmed by her. CMB Papers, folder 180.

Chapter 21

(*pages 257–276*)

1. Moley, *After Seven Years,* pp. 172–75.

2. FPOHC, Bk. 4, pp. 478–79. On reasons for the choice of Hopkins, see Chap. 20, above, note 5.

3. Fight over public works, FPOHC, Bk. 5, pp. 1–90; FP, *TRIK,* pp. 268–77. FP as champion of program within cabinet, interview by GM with Lewis Douglas. FDR's "conflict," FP, *TRIK,* p. 270, and growth national product, p. 273.

4. Douglas, quoted by Schlesinger, *Coming of the New Deal,* p. 9; interview by GM with Douglas.

5. FP, *TRIK,* pp. 270, 269.

6. On Black Bill, FPOHC, Bk. 4, pp. 439–52; FP, *TRIK,* pp. 192–96; FP, *PAW,* pp. 134–37. Also, J. R. Anderson, thesis, pp. 209–13, pointing out, "The ideas for the National Industrial Recovery Act came from too many sources to give authorship of it to any one person, but Miss Perkins made the first official public proposal along its lines." Some discussion of it: Bernstein, *Collective Bargaining,* pp. 29–31; Huthmacher, *Wagner,* pp. 142–45; Freidel, *FDR, Launching the New Deal,* pp. 418–21; quoting an interesting comment by C. E. Wyzanski, Jr., on FP: she was "outside the

whole circle of developments." *New York Times*, April 20, 1933, 5:4; and April 26, 1933, 5:4.

7. FP, *TRIK*, pp. 197–98; FPOHC, Bk. 5, pp. 1–90, "Background of the NRA."

8. FP, *PAW*, p. 143.

9. Ickes, *Diary*, Vol. 1, p. 28. For the bill as it developed see account in *New York Times*, April 29, 1933, 1:5. FP, *TRIK*, p. 271, says Wagner's bill originally did not include public works. Huthmacher, *Wagner*, p. 147, disagrees. In any event the joint bill by April 29 had a full public works program.

10. *New York Times*, April 15, 1933, 2:2; see Furman, *Washington By-line*, pp. 163–64.

11. Quoted in Freidel, *FDR, Launching the New Deal*, p. 431.

12. FP, *TRIK*, p. 273.

13. FPOHC, Bk. 5, pp. 75–84.

14. Interview by GM with Lewis Douglas.

15. FPOHC, Bk. 5, pp. 21–22. Her description of Johnson at these meetings was confirmed by Robert K. Straus, who was present at most as Johnson's aide. Interview by GM with Straus.

16. FPOHC, Bk. 5, pp. 32, 54, 92–3.

17. FPOHC, Bk. 5, pp. 94–101, FP, *TRIK*, pp. 200–1.

18. FPOHC, Bk. 5, pp. 144–45.

19. FPOHC, Br. 5, p. 143; cf. Bk. 7, pp. 32, 42–43; speech before American Law Institute confirmed by C. E. Wyzanski, Jr., in letter to GM.

20. FPOHC, pp. 146 71; FP, *TRIK*, pp. 202–203; Johnson, *The Blue Eagle*, pp. 210–11. Though FP says she drove Johnson to his hotel, Robert K. Straus, who was in the front seat beside the chauffeur, remembers that they were taken to the airport, which, considering the shortness of time, seems more likely. Interview by GM with Straus.

Chapter 22

(*pages 277–291*)

1. Schlesinger, *Coming of the New Deal*, p. 21, citing Rexford G. Tugwell's *Diary*, May 6, 1933.

2. Charles E. Wyzanski, Jr., OH, Columbia, pp. 153, 174–79.

3. Interviews by GM with Ilo B. Wallace, and on "sharing expenses," with Agnes Leach. On the dinner guests, letters of C. E. Wyzanski, Jr., to GM and of Edward Arpee citing memories of Mary Ward, SWC and Charles C. Rumsey, Jr.

4. Interviews by GM with Father Lloyd Goodrich, Plank's successor at St. Thomas, and with Ilo B. Wallace. FP letter to Alfred Q. Plank, June 24, 1944, FPP, Columbia.

5. Interviews by GM with Rev. Mother Virginia, Sister Fidelia and Father Earle Hewitt Maddux, all at All Saints Convent.

6. FP letter to Carl Hovey, January 2, 1945, FPP, Columbia.

7. See note 8, below, on St. Bede Lectures. Graham, *Encore for Reform*, pp. 106–107, 111, 149, 169, 145, 161. One of his examples was Ernest Poole, a

close friend of FP (FPOHC, Bk. 1, p. 362 and married to Margaret Poole), who felt out of touch with the New Deal, p. 179.

8. St. Bede Lectures — 1948, at the Guild Hall of St. Thomas Church, 1 West Fifty-third St., New York City. FP was the second of three speakers, each of whom gave three lectures. Hers, "The Christian in the World," divided: (1) A Christian Order of Society (2) The Vocation of the Laity (3) The Good Life, Community and Individual, FPP, Columbia. Humanitarianism is not enough, 1:7, 2:48, 3:46; part of the Christian, 3:36; immigration example, 1:26–29. (She had used the "man must administer laws" sentence in an article for *Fortune*, September 1941.)

9. FP's "standards" (Robert Moses), "religion" (Isador Lubin), "principles" (Charles E. Wyzanski, Jr., and Agnes Leach), interviews with GM. The same or similar words, however, were used by almost everyone interviewed.

10. St. Bede Lectures: man's destiny, 1:24; pattern of cooperation, 3:26; Unitarian question and response, 3:46. She identfiied the labor leader as Sidney Hillman in the transcript of "Tape 13," p. 14, of "Lectures during 1957," FPP, Cornell. On conscience, "Tape 13," above.

11. FPOHC, Bk. 4, p. 492; FP, *TRIK*, p. 204; Ickes, *Diary*, Vol. 1, p. 99, cf. FPOHC, Bk. 7, p. 88.

12. *New York Times*, April 30, 1933, 16:5; Furman, *Washington By-line*, p. 165.

13. FPOHC, Bk. 4, pp. 67–70; Furman, *Washington By-line*, pp. 62–63. For a problem in protocol, Ickes, *Diary*, Vol. 2, p. 88.

14. FPOHC, Bk. 4, p. 71; cf. Bk. 3, pp. 420–24.

15. *New York Times*, March 18, 1933, 15:4.

16. FP letter to Genevieve Parkhurst, January 9, 1932, and cf. to Grace Hegger Lewis, November 20, 1933, both in FPP, Columbia.

17. FPOHC, Bk. 2, pp. 186–90; Bk. 4, p. 115.

18. *New York Times*, April 19, 1933, 2:2; interviews by GM with Isador Lubin and Aryness Joy Wickens.

19. FPOHC, Bk. 4, p. 368. Agnes Leach told GM that both FDR and ER thought FP should make a complete disclosure of her husband's illness to Washington reporters before her first press conference. They urged Leach to suggest it to FP. Leach refused, "it was not my concern," and suggested that the Roosevelts do it.

20. Furman, *Washington By-line*, pp. 162–63.

21. Sidney Skolsky, "Tintypes," March 24, 1933, clipping in FPP, Columbia. Furman, above, pp. 62–63. FP, "Eight Years as Madame Secretary," *Fortune*, September 1941. (FP preferred Madam, see Chap. 2, note 3.)

22. The press, FPOHC, Bk. 4, pp. 334–74; "a great mistake," pp. 338, 355. Schlesinger, *The Coming of the New Deal*, p. 562: "By according the press the *privilege* (italics added) of regular interrogation, Roosevelt established the presidential press conference is a quasi-constitutional status as the American equivalent of the parliamentary question period — a status which future presidents could downgrade to their peril." FP hoped Eisenhower would have the stature to be able to do it. FPOHC, Bk. 4, pp. 347, 370.

23. "Shoes" speech, New York *Herald Tribune*, May 23, 1933, 18:2; FPOHC,

Bk. 5, pp. 475–76. Editorial, Montgomery *Advertiser,* May 25, 1933 and
angry letters, FDR Library, OF, 15, Labor Dept. Misc. 1933–38. Letter
to FP from Eleanor Dangerfield, May 25, 1933, FPP, Columbia. *New York
Times* editorial, June 2, 1933, 18:4.

24. The incident took place on March 12, 1935, while she was testifying
before the Senate Labor Committee. The chairman ordered the photographer to hand over his plate. The press "retaliated" by making it a front
page story the next day, e.g. San Francisco *Chronicle,* March 13, 1935, 1:2.

25. FP, "Eight Years," etc. *Fortune,* above.

26. For an analysis of her press relations, J. R. Anderson's thesis, pp. 86–93,
and Biddle, *In Brief Authority,* pp. 10, 11, 15. On James V. Fitzgerald,
FPOHC, Bk. 6, pp. 495–97; "a real flat tire," interview by GM with
Lubin, also with Gladys Burch and Aryness Joy Wickens.

27. *Time,* April 28, 1941, p. 18.

Chapter 23

(pages 292–305)

For this chapter I found the Ph.D. thesis of Hilda Kessler Gilbert, "The
United States Department of Labor in the New Deal Period," a useful source
for figures, citations and bibliography.

1. "Jurisdiction-minded" — letter to FP from James F. Byrnes, June 11, 1945,
and cf. FP letter to K. Augusta Sutton, June 8, 1945, both in FPP, Columbia. Cf. FPOHC, Bk. 7, p. 824; Bk. 8, p. 113; Bk. 5, p. 357. Also interview by J. P. Grossman with Clara Beyer, November 5, 1965, p. 10.
Against these should be set Harold D. Smith, Director of the Budget
Bureau, in his Diary, May 6, 1939, quoted in Richard Polenberg, *Reorganizing Roosevelt's Government, 1936–1939* (Cambridge, Harvard
University Press, 1966), pp. 90–91. But on the whole, and particularly
in the war years, her record seems good.

2. MacMahon and Millett, *Federal Administrators,* p. 3.

3. The aliens were decreasing because of the decline in immigration and
death or naturalization of those already here. Numerous speeches by
MacCormack, FPP, Connecticut. Also, speeches by Edward J. Shaughnessy, April 2, 1937, and James L. Houghteling, October 31, 1939, both in
FPP, Columbia. Merger of bureaus, Executive Order 6166, June 10,
1933. The saving, interdepartmental memo, January 8, 1934, FPP,
Columbia.

4. Brown trial, *New York Times,* December 1933; naturalization trials,
Dept. of Labor *Appropriation Bill for 1935,* Hearings (1934), p. 81.
Dept. of Labor, *Annual Report, 1940,* pp. 8–9.

5. Professed humanity, MacCormack speeches, May 9, 1933 and January 7,
1936, also memorandum to branch and division heads, November 11,
1933; figures on aliens, speech, January 7, 1936; Mexican example, speech
May 9, 1933, and Russian, January 7, 1936. All in FPP, Connecticut.

6. Policy, increased discretion. Dept. of Labor *Appropriation Bill for 1936,*
Hearings (1935), pp. 88–91. FDR weak on due process, e.g. his failure
to support an antilynching bill for Negroes and his incarceration of

citizens of Japanese ancestry during World War II; C. E. Wyzanski, Jr., OH, Columbia, p. 268, "He was not so concerned with due process as he might have been." The reforms a bright chapter, "Recent Developments in the Deportation Process" by Reuben Oppenheimer, *Michigan Law Review*, January 1938, p. 384; also letters to FP from Judge Charles F. Amidon, July 20, 1933, and Josephine Pisani, February 10, 1939, both in FPP, Columbia. Figures on deportations, Dept. of Labor *Appropriations Bill for 1936*, Hearings (1935), p. 90.

7. Vaguely in mind: FP's note on Abbott memorandum to FP, April 13, 1934. Abbott wrote, "The assumption that from an industrial standpoint women and children should be classed together is unjust to both . . . Women are adults, are in industry to stay, and such handicaps as they have and that should be taken account of are not those of children." Cf. FP's letter to Lewis Douglas, May 25, 1933, on ideas for reorganization: to continue the Children's Bureau separate and to merge the Women's Bureau, Conciliation Bureau and Bureau of Labor Statistics into a single Bureau of Labor Information and Service. It was dropped. All in FPP, Columbia.

8. Anderson, *Women at Work*, pp. 184–85. Cf. Anderson memorandum to FP, May 27, 1933, on the possibility of the merger discussed by FP in letter to Douglas, above, FPP, Columbia.

9. Lenroot OH, Columbia, pp. 63–64C, 141, 173.

10. Interview by GM and letters from Newman; also interview by GM with Isador Lubin, and MacMahon and Millett, *Federal Administrators*, p. 405. Anderson, *Women at Work*, pp. 140–41, 148–49, 182–85, 238–43. See Witte, *Development of Social Security Act*, pp. 165–70.

11. Jay. Testimony as to her competence and brusqueness came from all sources. FP's developing relationship, letter to Jay, July 13, 1932, and Jay to FP, August 1 and 3, 1936, June 7, 1938, all in FPP, Columbia. Sense of guilt, FPOHC, Bk. 4, pp. 202–3, confirmed by SWC and Gladys Burch, interviews with GM. FP letter of apology for Jay's brusqueness, to Comtesse de Pierrefou, July 31, 1942, FPP, Columbia. On Harrison, FPOHC, Bk. 4, pp. 377, 383, 388–92; see Reilly interview with Jonathan Grossman, pp. 6, 23 and confirmed in all interviews by GM.

12. Discredited. "Instead of a System! Appraisal of the Doak Reorganization of the Federal Employment Offices" by Ruth M. Kellogg, *Survey Graphic*, No. 22, pp. 165–67, March 1933; Ewan Clague, OH (Soc. Sec.), Columbia, pp. 20, 86; and cf. Huthmacher, *Wagner*, p. 78.

13. Persons. Interview by GM with his son, Edward B. Persons. For FP's relations with him, e.g. letter to him, February 9, 1934, Employment 1934 file, p. 149; letter to him, December 13, 1935, and his reply, December 18, 1935, Emp. 1935, p. 149; and letter to him, January 31, 1936, Emp. 1936, p. 148; all folders in FPP, NA.

Persons and the CCC, Salmond, *The Civilian Conservation Corps*, pp. 88–102. In FPP, NA, files as indicated: letter FP to FDR (drafted by Persons), June 1, 1933, White House 1933, Box 81; memorandum Jay to Persons, April 24, 1935, Empl.-Labor Policy, Box 150, asking for draft of letter below; letter FP to ER, May 7, 1935, White House 1935, Box 80; "be not sent," FP memorandum to Persons, July 29, 1935, with typed note, "This file is not to be returned to Mr. Persons if he requests it. Request must be submitted to the Secretary if anyone in his office makes it," Empl.-Labor Policy, Box 150 (includes several letters and drafts); memorandums Persons to FP, August 14, 1935, Empl. Texas, Box 46, September 7, 1935 and same (including several letters) CCC 1935, Box 23; letter from FERA administrator in Ohio to Persons, April 27, 1936, Box 23.

14. Gilbert, thesis, pp. 191–93: "The outstanding contribution of the U.S.E.S. was insistence on a merit system of selecting personnel in state agencies." When FP received a letter from one of Farley's assistants asking for a list of all non-civil service positions, she wrote on it "Forget," Ambrose O'Connell to FP, May 16, 1933, FPP Columbia. FP letter to John B. Andrews, secretary of the American Association of Labor Legislation, sets out the history of Civil Service requirements and exemptions in the USES. JBA papers.

15. Battle. FPOHC, Bk. 7, pp. 242–43; interviews by GM with Clara Beyer, Isador Lubin and Thomas H. Eliot; quotation from Beyer.

16. Conciliation and Kerwin. FPOHC, Bk. 4, pp. 287–97; C. E. Wyzanski, Jr., OH, Columbia, p. 222; Ewan Clague, OH, Columbia, Bk. 2, p. 183. Letter to FP from Howard T. Colvin, June 16, 1945, on improvement in service since 1932, FPP, Columbia. "Work of the world," FPOHC, Bk. 4, p. 271; Bk. 8, p. 195.

17. Memorandum McGrady to FP, January 16, 1934, FPP, Columbia. For an example of Congressional pressure, see "Memo for Col. McIntyre," June 16, 1934, prepared in answer to Senator Guffey's inquiries about patronage positions in Pennsylvania, FDR Library, OF 15, 1933–34, Box 1.

18. McGrady. Letter FP to FDR, February 1, 1933, quoted at length in Chap. 19, this book. Her initial suspicion turning to trust, interviews by GM with Thomas H. Eliot, Isador Lubin and Gerard Reilly. For a harsh view of McGrady (and of FP) by two angry, left-wing labor writers, see Bruce Minton and John Stuart, *Men Who Lead Labor* (New York, Modern Age Books, 1937), pp. 55–85.

19. Quoted in Anderson, thesis, p. 83. Cf. Ewan Clague on her accent and manner in testifying, OH, Columbia, Bk. 2, p. 173. For an effort to counteract her difficulties see FP conciliatory letter, August 17, 1933, to Senator Frederic C. Walcott of the Committee on Labor and Education, FPP, Columbia.

20. FP talks too much: Ickes, *Diary*, Vol. 1, pp. 152, 407, 491, 569, 694; Vol. 3, pp. 67, 120, 190; FP has "ideas," Vol. 1, p. 482. Cf. Farley, *Story*, p. 54, ". . . she did considerable talking at official family sessions." On "Feminine" as pejorative, e.g. Ickes, *Diary*, Vol. 3, pp. 25 and 540: "Lilienthal had been both feminine and unfair" and "The President was just a little feminine in his attack upon me." Ilo Wallace thought some of Ickes's ambivalence toward FP was caused by the fact that FP knew as much or "more" than he about public works. Interview by GM with Ilo Wallace.

21. Gilbert, thesis, p. 41.

22. Stewart. MacMahon and Millet, *Federal Administrators*, pp. 421–2; Herring, *Public Administration*, p. 286; *New York Times*, July 3, 1932, I,

3:2; New York *Herald Tribune,* July 3, 1932, 7:5; FP telegram and Stewart's reply, n.d., FPP, Columbia; interviews by GM with Ewan Clague and Aryness Joy Wickens; Clague, OH (Soc. Sec.), Columbia, pp. 20–22, 87; Clague, OH, Columbia, Bk. 1, pp. 44–48, 55–58, 67–68, 91–92; FPOHC, Bk. 3, p. 452; Bk. 4, pp. 132, 236, 243 (some details not correct).

23. Stewart to FDR, November 28, 1932, FPP, Columbia. On BLS, Ewan Clague, OH citations above.

24. Clague, *The Bureau of Labor Statistics,* viii, pp. 19–21.

25. Lubin, OH, Columbia, pp. 1–54 and interview with GM.

26. Lubin's reforms, Wickens, OH, Columbia, pp. 13, 20–25, interview with GM and Jonathan Grossman: Clague, *The BLS,* p. 21; see also *Journal of Electrical Workers and Operators,* July 1935, pp. 281–83, 309–10, FPP, Columbia. Figures on Employment and Payroll Index, Gilbert, thesis, p. 43.

27. Interview by GM with Lubin; Wickens, OH, above.

28. Layers of assistants. Interviews by Jonathan Grossman with Gerard Reilly and Clara Beyer; interview by GM with Lucille Buchanan.

29. FP herself doubted Wyzanski's allegiance to the party, though never his loyalty to the administration so long as he worked for it; FPOHC, Bk. 7, p. 23. McGrady's report, FPP, NA, Appropriations 1933–35, Box 3. On the "striking results" of appointments on merit, letter of Ewan Clague to FP, March 29, 1940, FPP, NA, Employment Service, Box 107. The Dept. of Labor as a dumping ground for incompetents, FPOHC, Bk. 4, p. 245.

Chapter 24

(*pages 306–324*)

1. Ickes, *Back to Work,* p. 27.

2. Ickes, above, pp. 31–32.

3. FP's attitude on function of Dept. of Labor, FPOHC, Bk. 3, pp. 549–54; Bk. 5, p. 347. On men forced into unions, cf. letter to FP from Roger Lapham, April 13, 1935, reviewing labor problems on the Pacific Coast, FPP, Columbia.

4. Tour of steel mills, FP, *TRIK,* pp. 217–21; the long quotation, pp. 219–20; FPOHC, permission, Bk. 5, pp. 322–30; Mckeesport, pp. 330–36; Homestead, pp. 336–43; Sparrows Point, pp. 343–46. Letter to FP, August 3, 1933, from L. F. Coles, a Negro worker, commending her actions at Homestead, FPP, Columbia. *New York Times* stories, July 28–31, 1933. Also, Brody, *Steelworkers in America, The Nonunion Era.*

5. *New York Times,* August 1, 1933, 12:3, and 13:1; and August 6, 1933, IV, 4:7.

6. FP, *TRIK,* pp. 221–23, long quotation; FPOHC, Bk. 5, pp. 311–20; *New York Times,* August 16, 1933, 1:1.

7. For the longshoremen's strike of 1934 I have relied particularly on the San Francisco *Chronicle;* Bernstein, *Turbulent Years;* Larrowe, *Harry Bridges;* Galenson, *The CIO Challenge to the AFL* and Joseph P. Goldberg, *The Maritime Story* (Cambridge, Harvard University Press, 1957).

8. Telegram Johnson to Ickes, FPP, Columbia.

9. FP with Hull and Cummings, including quotations, FPOHC, Bk. 6, pp. 293–308; FP, *TRIK*, pp. 312–15. Her sources: one of her best, beside McGrady, was Paul Smith, financial editor of the *Chronicle*. She also talked at length with Roger Lapham, president of the American-Hawaiian Steamship Line. Lapham in his OH, University of California, Berkeley, p. 95, says of McGrady: "He was pretty well following orders from the Secretary of Labor. He daily phoned her, and she was his boss, and he didn't deviate too much from his orders." Quoted by permission of the director of the Bancroft Library. Hull in his Memoirs, p. 198, states that he had a meeting with Cummings and Perkins and that "Cummings and I agreed that the Federal Government should not take direct action." FP believed that Hull, when he came to write his *Memoirs,* simply had forgotten how strongly he had advocated direct action, FPOHC, Bk. 6, p. 313.

10. FP's cable, at 12:15 A.M., July 15, 1934, is a clear summary of the situation, ending, "the situation is serious but not yet hopeless"; FDR Library, OF 407-B. There is no cable from Hull on that date on the strike. There is an undated cable from Cummings, which might be their joint cable. It sets out the President's powers to intervene, but ends "situation apparently improving. Recent encouraging developments may make an affirmative action undesirable"; FDR Library, OF 407-B. It is tempting to think that FP persuaded them to that view. Howe's view, FPOHC, Bk. 6, p. 311. Ickes's view, FPOHC, Bk. 6, p. 308, was that calling out the military was "the craziest thing I ever heard of."

11. FDR on *Houston* cablegram to FP, July 16, 1934, FDR Library, PSF Labor Dept. In FPP, Columbia, see letter from Bridges to FDR, June 29, 1934, on aims of the strike (cf. FPOHC, Bk. 6, p. 381) and a report on the strike, August 3, 1934, from Thomas H. Eliot of Labor Dept's Solicitor's office to FP.

12. San Francisco *Chronicle,* July 18, 1934, 5.

13. San Francisco *Chronicle,* July 21, 1934.

14. On FP and legion, San Francisco *Chronicle,* August 12 through 16, 1934.

15. Incidents at University of California, interview by GM with Clara Beyer; at St. George's Church, New York City, *New York Times,* April 9, 1935, 9:1.

16. There are many letters to FDR on this point, in FDR Library, OF 15, Labor Dept. Misc., 1933–1938. Apparently as many women as men, perhaps more, thought her incompetent *because* she was a woman, e.g., letter of Isabelle C. Rikerson to FDR: "Women are not constituted emotionally for such a job."

Chapter 25

(*pages 325–340*)

1. FP to PCW, n.d., but in another's hand "11/1/1934." FPP, Coggeshall.

2. Interview by GM with Vira Peters Towle, who heard it from the Roundses.

3. Interview by GM with SWC; interview by Edward Arpee with Mary Ward.

4. FPOHC, Bk. 9, p. 2; letter M. B. Bruère to FP, August 8, 1933, FPP, Columbia; same, June 27, 1934, and other correspondence on the book, FPP, FDR Library, Box 2. Among those who worked on it were Rev. Harry Emerson Fosdick, Father Francis Haas, Miss Powell of the Nyack Public Library and the Industrial Department of the YWCA; see two letters to R. Critchell Rimington, June 8 and June 14, 1934, FPP, Columbia. In the Department of Labor Isador Lubin, in particular, worked on it. A vestige of the book's original plan can be seen in its footnote on p. 223.

5. Royalty statement from John Day Co., FPP, Columbia. Quoted review by Stuart Chase, New York *Herald Tribune* (Sunday), May 27, 1934, Section VII, p. 1; other reviews, New York *Herald Tribune,* May 24, 1934, by Lewis Gannett; *New York Times,* May 24, 1934, by John Chamberlain; *New York Times* (Sunday) May 27, 1934, by William McDonald; *Saturday Review of Literature,* June 23, 1934, by Suzanne La Follette.

6. FP, *PAW,* pp. 37–38.

7. FP, *PAW,* p. 140.

8. FP, *PAW,* p. 122.

9. FP, *PAW,* p. 224.

10. *Saturday Review of Literature,* June 23, 1934, by Suzanne La Follette.

11. Roger Lapham, OH, University of California, Berkeley, p. 85. Quoted by permission of the director of the Bancroft Library.

12. Quoted in Leon H. Keyserling, "Why the Wagner Act?" *The Wagner Act: After Ten Years,* ed. by Louis G. Silverberg (Washington, Bureau of National Affairs, 1945), pp. 12–13, from a speech by Wagner to the National Democratic Club Forum, May 8, 1937. See also "The Ideal Industrial State — As Wagner Sees It," *New York Times Magazine,* May 9, 1937, p. 23.

13. FP constantly stated her concept of the labor department as the department for all workers, organized or unorganized. E.g., the department's *Annual Report, 1933* and *1937* both p. 1. Also her address to the employees of the department, October 4, 1939, on the duties of the Secretary of Labor, FPP, NA, Box 5, Employees Meetings. And FPOHC, Bk. 4, p. 277.

14. FPOHC, Bk. 5, pp. 360–76; Robert K. Straus, Johnson's assistant, in letters and an interview with GM, confirmed all of FP's remarks except her account of Straus's persuading Robinson to come to Washington. That incident involved another secretary.

15. FPOHC, Bk. 5, pp. 376–381.

16. FP, *TRIK,* p. 212.

17. FDR quotation, FPOHC, Bk. 5, p. 479; FP, *TRIK,* p. 211.

18. FPOHC, Bk. 5, p. 354, FP, *TRIK,* p. 227; cf. Johnson's opinion expressed in his last interview as NRA administrator (he was in the hospital) on the day his resignation became effective, *New York Times,* October 16, 1934, 14:2. Interview by GM with R. K. Straus.

19. Interview by GM with R. K. Straus.

20. FP, *TRIK,* p. 237; Johnson, *Blue Eagle,* p. 311.

21. Huthmacher, *Wagner,* pp. 163–68; see memorandum of Johnson to FDR, June 26, 1934, FPP, Columbia.

22. FP, *TRIK*, pp. 241, 243 and FPOHC, Bk. 5, pp. 512–27.
23. Interview with R. K. Straus. Johnson's note to Straus, ". . . Also I don't want anybody suggesting vacations for me. This has reached the proportions of a conspiracy and finally was suggested by the President today." The date is unclear but is either March or June 26, 1934. Cf. FPOHC, Bk. 5, pp. 108, 528–29, in which Blackwell Smith also speaks to her about easing Johnson out.
24. FPOHC, Bk. 5, pp. 356, 108–13 (poisonous cup, p. 111), pp. 545–53; cf. Bk. 7, p. 622.
25. Johnson's quotation, Schlesinger, *Coming of the New Deal*, p. 153. The book was *The Corporate State* by Raffaello Vigilone, see FP, *TRIK*, p. 206. On Johnson's views, FP, *TRIK*, p. 241 and FPOHC, Bk. 5, pp. 368–69.
26. FPOHC, Bk. 5, pp. 557–75; Johnson, *Blue Eagle*, pp. 387–91.
27. FDR's illusion, FPOHC, Bk. 5, p. 99. Humiliation, FPOHC, Bk. 5, pp. 574–75.
28. FPOHC, Bk. 7, pp. 47–69, a section entitled "Schechter Case," and also 104–9; NRA "washed up," p. 64. FP, *TRIK*, pp. 251–52.

Chapter 26
(pages 341–356)
For the account of the origins and passage of the Social Security Act, I have relied particularly on:

Witte, *The Development of the Social Security Act,* and three of his speeches, all in FPP, Columbia: "Old Age Security, The National Picture," October 2, 1954, "A Balanced Program in Employment Security," October 8, 1954, and "Twenty Years of Social Security," August 15, 1955. The last is an excellent short account of the act and its passage, and was published in the *Social Security Bulletin,* Vol. 18, No. 10, October 1955. Also, his essay, "Organized Labor and Social Security" in *Labor and the New Deal,* ed. by Milton Derber and Edwin Young (Madison, University of Wisconsin Press, 1957).

Altmeyer, *The Formative Years of Social Security*.

FP, *TRIK*, pp. 278–301; her lecture on the subject at Cornell, November 5, 1957, FPP, Cornell (typescript at FPP, Columbia); her copy of the Committee on Economic Security's Reports, FPP, Connecticut; much material, particularly exchanges with Witte, at FPP, Radcliffe; her correspondence with Paul U. Kellogg, PUK Papers.

1. Anderson, thesis, p. 107, citing FP to FDR, April 17, 1934, FDR Library, OF 121A, Unemployment Insurance file. Cf. FP, lecture at Cornell, November 5, 1957, FPP, Cornell, and Ickes, *Diary*, Vol. 1, p. 163. Witte, "Organized Labor and Social Security," p. 248 fn. 5, believes the idea for the bill originated with Brandeis, passed to Elizabeth Brandeis and Paul Raushenbush, then to FP, who relayed it to Wagner.
2. FP, *TRIK*, pp. 279, 281. Cf. Altmeyer, OH, Columbia, pp. 94–96.
3. The executive order, No. 6757, is printed in full in Witte, *Development,* p. 201.
4. On Altmeyer. Interview by GM with Isador Lubin; Thomas H. Eliot,

OH, Columbia, p. 16; Lavinia Engle, OH, Columbia, pp. 8, 57, 59; and Altmeyer, OH, Columbia, pp. 98, 189, 192; on reason chosen, Altmeyer, *Formative Years*, p. ix.

5. On Witte. "A government man," introduction by Wilbur J. Cohen to Witte, *Development*, p. xv. Interview by GM with Isador Lubin. Eliot, OH, Columbia, p. 15; Engle, OH, Columbia, p. 77.

6. On functions. Witte, *Development*, pp. 18–20, 68. Cf. Altmeyer, *Formative Years*, pp. 8, 15.

7. Witte, *Development*, p. 28.

8. On Advisory Council. Witte, *Development*, pp. 42, 53–54, 63. The representatives of labor had the poorest record of attendance, p. 54.

9. FP, *TRIK*, pp. 284–85. Cf. discussion on this point among Kellogg, Witte, and FP in letters January 31, 1935 to February 19, 1935, PUK Papers. For a statement by Witte, November 1, 1934, on "Limitations and Value of Unemployment Insurance," FPP, Radcliffe, Box 72, folder 938. For FDR's financial reason, statement made in presence of T. H. Eliot, interview by GM with Eliot. For his political reason, Schlesinger's *Coming of the New Deal*, p. 308, citing R. G. Tugwell, "Roosevelt and Hoover," *Antioch Review*, Winter 1953–54.

10. Altmeyer, *Formative Years*, p. 13; FP, *TRIK*, p. 189.

11. The ten programs: unemployment insurance, old age insurance, old age assistance, aid to dependent children, maternal and child health aid, child welfare services, crippled children services, public health work, vocational rehabilitation and pensions for the blind.

12. Attendance. Minutes of the meetings, FPP, Connecticut. Sandwiches, Eliot, OH, Columbia, p. 18 and interview by GM.

13. FP's radio address was on August 13, the editorial appeared August 25. For correspondence with doctors, FPP, Radcliffe, Box 72, folders 944 and 945. Altmeyer, *Formative Years*, p. 57, on fate of health insurance recommendations. For the list of thirteen studies under way by September, see "Information Primer," a news release on the Committee's activities. FPP, Radcliffe, Box 72, folder 938.

14. "States-righter." FPOHC, Bk. 2, p. 631 and interview by GM with Isador Lubin. Also see "The Secretary of Labor Cooperates" by John B. Andrews, December 1942, particularly the penultimate paragraph and FP's speech reported in Newark *Evening News*, November 17, 1936, 4:1; both in FPP, Columbia.

15. Altmeyer, *Formative Years*, p. 55. It bothered FP, Eliot, OH, Columbia, and interview by GM.

16. "Mistake," Witte, *Development*, p. 35.

17. Brown, *An American Philosophy of Social Security*, p. 16. Brown's defense of their action is a half-truth. He offers as evidence that the Committee was not considering old age insurance, "the printed program of the conference lists unemployment insurance, but makes no mention of old age insurance." True. But it lists "Old Age Security," which included the insurance plan, and two of the four discussion leaders for the topic were I. M. Rubinow and Abraham Epstein, the outstanding old age insurance advocates. And old age insurance was discussed. Among the stories, *New York Times*, November 15, 1934, 1:1.

18. FP's statement, *New York Times,* November 16, 1934, 1:6. A reporter at her press conference claimed that a committee member had described FDR's speech as the "kiss of death" for old age security, but when challenged he refused to identify his source. Krock's column, "In Washington," November 20, 1934, 20:5. FP wrote to him, November 26, 1934, complaining that he had not checked with her or Witte, FPP, Columbia. Witte *Development,* pp. 46–47. Brown, above, 16–17.

19. Witte, *Development,* p. 40.

20. Kellogg's importance, e.g. Altmeyer, OH, Columbia, p. 11. For his views, see correspondence, January 31 to May 4, 1935, to Witte and FP, PUK Papers.

21. Kellogg to FP, May 9, 1934, PUK Papers. Cf. FP, *TRIK,* p. 283.

22. Abbott's anger. Kellogg to Witte, February 19, 1935, PUK Papers.

23. FP to Kellogg, February 19, 1935, PUK Papers.

24. See Witte letter to Kellogg, January 31, 1935, PUK Papers. Also, Witte, "Organized Labor and Social Security," p. 254.

25. FP to Kellogg, February 19, 1935; his reply, February 22, 1935; PUK Papers.

26. Witte, *Development,* p. 42. FPOHC, Bk. 8, p. 146.

27. Witte, *Development,* p. 70. Also, Witte, "Organized Labor and Social Security," p. 250.

28. Meeting at the Perkins-Rumsey house. Witte, *Development,* p. 64, describes it as "probably the most important of all meetings of the Committee." No minutes were kept, and he does not say what was decided. Altmeyer in a letter to GM wrote, "I think what Mr. Witte meant . . . was not that it disposed of basic issues but that it agreed with the language used so that he could complete his report." The locking the door, etc., interview by GM with Alice Cook, who was told by FP.

29. Witte, *Development,* pp. 68–69.

30. Witte, *Development,* p. 74. He was present at the latter part of the meeting. Also, Altmeyer, *Formative Years,* pp. 29, 26. In 1944, following an increase in the scope and amount of benefits payable under the old age insurance program, Congress amended the Social Security Act to authorize appropriations from the general tax revenues to pay for them. According to FP, "the President didn't like it, but he was interested in extending social security . . . I don't think he ever realized that that was the exact system which he had rejected in at least a modified form when the Committee on Economic Security had reported it to him in 1934." FP, *TRIK,* p. 301.

31. Altmeyer, *Formative Years,* pp. 34, 36, 41, 47–49; Witte, *Development,* pp. 78, 144, 102, 139, 145.

32. Witte, *Development,* p. 76. For a staff analysis of interest in the country for and against social insurance, as of late November 1934, Memorandum: Trend of Interest in Security Program, FPP, Radcliffe, Box 72, folder 938. *New York Times,* January 20, 1935, IV, 8:2.

33. Witte, *Development,* p. 96. Among her speeches, at St. George's Church, New York City, see Chap. 24, this book.

34. Letter Charles E. Wyzanski, Jr., to Augustus N. Hand, August 13, 1935, CEW Papers. Among the guests were Morgenthau, Cummings, Josephine

Roche, Robert Wagner, Congressmen Robert L. Doughton (chairman of the House Ways and Means Committee) and David J. Lewis.

35. Interview by GM with Leonard Adams; see Chap. 35, this book.

Chapter 27
(*pages 357–368*)

1. December 18, 1934.
2. FP letter to editor, The *Times* of London, July 22, 1935, FPP, Columbia.
3. Interview by GM with Clara Beyer.
4. FP, *TRIK*, p. 75; FPOHC, Bk. 4, pp. 512–26; interview by GM with SWC. Richard D. McKinzie, *The New Deal for Artists* (Princeton, Princeton University Press, 1973), pp. 6, 32, 63. In a mural Biddle painted for the Dept. of Justice he put himself at a sewing machine in a sweatshop with FP close by. FP letter to Thomas G. Corcoran, February 28, 1939, FPP, Columbia.
5. *New York Times*, November 8, 1936, 6:2.
6. Interview by GM with Walter Evers.
7. FPOHC, Bk. 4, pp. 357–59, *New York Times*, January 26, 1935, 16:7.
8. Quilts. E.g., letters to FP from Stella Waterbury Tenney, September 25, 1933, from Mrs. B. Boyd Mason, November 10, 1934, and from Mrs. William McElhoe, January 25, 1938; also material in Box 2 "Biographical"; all in FPP, Columbia. FPOHC, Bk. 3, p. 284.
9. Letter from Stephen T. Early to J. V. Fitzgerald, October 14, 1934, FDR Library, OF 15, Labor Dept.
10. Witte, "Organized Labor and Social Security," in Derber and Young, *Labor and the New Deal*, pp. 241, 244, 271.
11. Potofsky, OH, Columbia, pp. 289–92. Cf. Brophy, OH, Columbia, pp. 1021–25.
12. FDR wanted Gov. Herbert H. Lehman to appoint Flynn, who had supported FDR against AES at the 1932 convention, in place of Senator Royal S. Copeland, whom FDR would appoint ambassador to Germany. In the event Copeland continued in the Senate.
13. FPOHC, Bk. 3, p. 85.
14. Huthmacher, *Wagner*, p. 124; e.g., FP letter to "Dear Governor Al," September 28, 1944, FPP, Columbia.
15. *New York Times*, May 15, 1935, 5:1; August 2, 1934, 19:6; May 26, 1936, II, 8:5. Letter Jay to FP, August 1, 1936, FPP, Columbia. FP was the chief speaker at the International Confederation of Business and Professional Women's Conference, *New York Times*, July 31, 1936, 5:1. Most of her trip, however, was concerned with the International Labor Organization.
16. A full account is in Furman, *Washington By-line*, p. 241; *New York Times*, June 25, 1936, 12:8; on her part in the convention and campaign, FPOHC, Bk. 7, pp. 1–15.
17. FPOHC, Bk. 7, pp. 6–9.
18. FPOHC, above; FP, *TRIK*, pp. 122–24.
19. Thomas Stokes, *Chip Off My Shoulder* (Princeton, Princeton University Press, 1940), pp. 458–60, reprinted in Leuchtenburg, *The New Deal*.

20. The feelings of the Progressives analyzed, Graham, *Encore for Reform,* pp. 31–39, 69–73, 174.
21. FP letter to Aileen Osborn, April 16, 1936, FPP, Columbia.
22. FP, *TRIK,* too rich, p. 124; shortcomings, p. 4. Cf. pp. 156, 368, 385. Her clear view of the good and bad in FDR was much admired in her biography.

Chapter 28

(*pages 369–377*)

1. Letter to FP from R. K. Keyes. Though dated January 18, 1936, it clearly should be 1935. The letter has several other typing mistakes. FPP, Columbia.
2. Letter FP to R. K. Keyes, January 23, 1935, FPP, Columbia.
3. Letter FP to R. K. Keyes, November 2, 1935, FFP, Columbia.
4. Letter FP to R. K. Keyes, May 29, 1936, FPP, Columbia. The three women were Meta Glass of Sweetbriar, Millicent Carey McIntosh of the Brearley School and Marjorie Hope Nicolson of Smith. Glass was president of Sweetbriar College from 1925 to 1946. McIntosh later became president of Barnard College, and Nicolson became the first woman chairman of the department of English and Comparative Literature at Columbia University.
5. Letter FP to R. K. Keyes, May 29, 1936, FPP, Columbia.
6. Letter to FP from Mary Woolley, Marks, *Life and Letters of Mary Emma Woolley,* p. 165.
7. Letter FP to R. K. Keyes, May 29, 1936, FPP, Columbia. The most detailed account of the episode in FPP is Alva Morrison's reply to Mrs. Maurice D. Cooper, February 19, 1937. It is a long document with several exhibits. Less interesting, more soothing accounts were published in the *Mount Holyoke Alumnae Quarterly.*
8. Description of the meeting from Marks, above, pp. 173–78. She was a fervent supporter of Woolley, writing at a time, 1952–55, when most participants were still alive to be consulted. It is doubtful that the as yet undisclosed minutes of this meeting will recount details.
9. On the consternation and gradual division among the alumnae, interview by GM with Vira Peters Towle: "The general feeling was that the committee had not tried to find a woman and had railroaded the selection through." Letter to the trustees from Josephine Bolding 1902, Perkins's classmate; e.g., other letters, Mary E. Bolton, Miriam Brailey, Sophonisba P. Breckinridge, Phyllis R. Fenner, Sarah Truair Hollands, Elizabeth Mitchell, Julia E. Moody, Esther L. Richards, Amy Rowland, Helen F. Schrack, Vira Peters Towle, Sarah A. Whitehurst, all in FPP, Columbia.
10. Telegram FP to editor, Florence Clement, July 19, 1936, FPP, Columbia. Woolley and the editor, Marks, above, p. 181.
11. Interview by GM with Elizabeth Mason.
12. Nicolson's letter is an exhibit in Morrison's answer to Mrs. Cooper, above, note 7.
13. Letter to FP from Marion Park, July 21, 1936; letter Jay to Park, July 25,

1936; both in FPP, Columbia. Millicent Carey McIntosh, in a letter to GM, August 6, 1974, wrote: "I was interviewed for the Mount Holyoke job by Mr. Morrison. It was a very pleasant talk, but I said at the beginning that I could not allow my name to be considered because my children were too young, and my husband would not be able to leave New York. Actually the job was never formally offered to me, at least I didn't feel that it was. This presented a problem later, because the opposition to Dr. Ham wrote and asked me if I *had* had a definite offer. I replied that I had not. They made much of this in their sheet called "Tell it to the Marines," saying that the committee said falsely that I had been offered the job and had turned it down . . . I got no feeling when I talked with Mr. Morrison that the committee would prefer to have a man."

14. Interview by GM with Elizabeth Mason.
15. "Comment on Trustee meetings and Alumnae Council meetings, March 5, 6 and 7, 1937. Mount Holyoke College, South Hadley." FPP, Columbia.
16. Letter FP to Mrs. L. R. Rounds, May 1, 1937, FPP, Columbia.
17. Letter FP to Felix Frankfurter, June 7, 1945, FPP, Columbia.
18. Letter FP to R. G. Ham, Januray 21, 1941, FPP, Columbia.
19. Adapted from minutes of meeting, May 13, 1944. She received several congratulatory letters on the statement, e.g. Olive Copeland and Frank C. Myers; all in FPP, Columbia.
20. Letter to the trustees from Josephine Bolding, October 13, 1936, FPP, Columbia.

Chapter 29

(*pages 378–395*)

In this first section, on the Public Contracts or Walsh-Healey Act, I have relied particularly upon an address by the administrator, L. Metcalfe Walling, at the Department of Labor, November 30, 1939, FPP, Columbia; a speech by Walling before the Seventh Annual Labor Conference at the department, December 11, 1940, FDR Library, PSF Labor Dept.; Chap. 12 of the Ph.D. thesis of Hilda Kessler Gilbert, "The United States Department of Labor in the New Deal Period"; and *Public Contracts and Private Wages, Experience Under the Walsh-Healey Act* by Herbert C. Morton. Also FPOHC, Bk. 7, pp. 16–46, a section entitled "Walsh-Healey Public Contracts Act."

1. FP speech at National Conference of Social Work, Montreal, *New York Times,* June 11, 1935, 19:1; cf. FP speech to Good Neighbor League, New York City, *New York Times,* October 8, 1936, 15:2, "If the way in which it was attempted in the first place was not the right way, then the ingenuity of the people of the United States will find another way."
2. Anderson, thesis, p. 54, citing FDR to Marvin McIntyre, June 13, 1935, FDR Library, OF, Box 526; Morton, *Public Contracts,* p. 7.
3. Described in FP, *TRIK,* p. 254.
4. FP, *TRIK,* pp. 248–49, 255.
5. Gilbert, thesis, p. 219, citing First Deficiency Appropriation Bill for 1937, Hearings before the Subcommittee of the House Committee on Appro-

priations, Seventy-fifth Congress, first session (1937), p. 358; and Department of Labor Appropriation Bill for 1937, Hearings, Seventy-fifth Congress, first session (1936). Morton, *Public Contracts,* p. 12, cites an opinion that the $10,000 limitation excluded 99 percent of the contracts by number and 75 percent by value.

6. Gilbert, thesis, p. 218, citing Dept. of Labor Appropriation Bill for 1938, Hearings before Subcommittee of House Committee on Appropriations, Seventy-fifth Congress, first session (1937), pp. 66–68.

7. Gilbert, thesis, p. 226, citing *Annual Report of the Secretary of Labor,* fiscal year *1940,* p. 32, and same, fiscal *1941,* p. 45.

8. Walling, address at Dept. of Labor, November 30, 1939, FPP, Columbia.

9. Morton, *Public Contracts,* p. 29, "During the first year . . . the Secretary issued eight determinations covering industries employing more than 150,000 workers." *Perkins* v. *Lukens Steel Company,* 310 U.S. 113 (1940); FPOHC, Bk. 7, pp. 29, 41–42; Walling; address, above, p. 16.

10. Walling, address, above, p. 22.

Of the particular value for the National Labor Relations Act: Bernstein, *The New Deal Collective Bargaining Policy,* Chaps. ix and x (an appendix prints the complete act); Huthmacher, *Wagner,* Chap. 11; Brody, "The Emergence of Mass Production Unionism" in Braemon et al. *Change and Continuity in Twentieth-Century America,* and R. W. Fleming, "The Significance of the Wagner Act," in Derber and Young, *Labor and the New Deal.* Also FPOHC, Bk. 7, pp. 135–219, a section entitled "National Labor Relations Board," and her lecture at Cornell, February 27, 1957, "Labor Union History and Administration," FPP, Cornell.

11. FP, *TRIK,* p. 239; FPOHC, Bk. 7, p. 141. Wagner represented a congressional initiative, which in the next quarter-century would almost disappear under the impact of successive "strong" executives.

12. Huthmacher, *Wagner,* pp. 50, 107, 175.

13. Interview by GM with Lubin.

14. Huthmacher, *Wagner,* p. 193, citing speech of March 18, 1934.

15. FPOHC, Bk. 7, pp. 138, 147; Shor, thesis, pp. 76–97, citing his interview with FP, May 23, 1952; Anderson, thesis, pp. 271–79, a summary built on interesting sources. On one-sidedness and majority rule, Fleming, "The Significance of the Wagner Act," in Derber and Young, *Labor and the New Deal,* pp. 138, 144: "Majority rule means certain inequities for minorities but more strength and stability for the unit . . . The sponsors of the Wagner Act wanted to develop a strong independent labor movement . . . With such an objective m.r. was an essential ingredient . . . In this light disagreement with the m.r. principle as applied to collective bargaining more nearly reflects basic disagreeemnt with the avowed objective of a strong independent labor movement than a concern for inequities which may be perpetrated upon minority groups." For Wagner's views on these questions, see Leon H. Keyserling, "Why the Wagner Act" in *The Wagner Act: Ten Years After,* ed. by Louis G. Silverberg (Washington, Bureau of National Affairs, 1945), pp. 18–20, 23–25.

16. FP, *TRIK,* p. 243; FPOHC, Bk. 7, p. 138; Shor, thesis, pp. 80–81, 87; Galenson, *The CIO Challenge to the AFL,* pp. 612, 641.

17. FP, *TRIK*, pp. 240–44; FPOHC, Bk. 7, pp. 146–49.
18. Shor, thesis, p. 80, "only reluctantly" FP to Shor in interview; FP, *TRIK*, p. 239; FPOHC, Bk. 7, p. 147.
19. Brody, "The Emergence of Mass-Production Unionism" in Braemon et al. *Change and Continuity;* and Fleming, "The Significance of the Wagner Act" in Derber and Young, *Labor and the New Deal.* Figures from Dulles, *Labor in America,* p. 280.
20. FP, *TRIK*, p. 245; FPOHC, Bk. 7, pp. 151–66. In FPOHC she claims she called more than two hundred persons to fill the three positions, p. 154; in her Cornell lecture she says twenty-nine, still a large number considering the background work to be done before the position is offered.
21. FPOHC, Bk. 7, pp. 173–75. The problem was often resolved by allowing the AFL contract to finish its term. "The G— D— Labor Board," by Walter Gellhorn and S. L. Linfield, *Fortune,* October 1938, pp. 52–57, 115–23.
22. FP, *TRIK*, pp. 242–43; FPOHC, Bk. 7, p. 149.
23. For the account following, including her interviews with Madden, Smith and Wagner, FPOHC, Bk. 7, pp. 170, 176–83. Millis and Brown, *From the Wagner Act,* pp. 174–89, particularly p. 185; "In the early years, when violations were very widespread, the employer who wished to live within the law generally was careful to avoid discussing any issue as to unionization with his employees." But then on p. 189: "In sum, there was in the experience little evidence of unreasonable restraint of employers by Board decisions."
24. FPOHC, Bk. 7, pp. 181, 742. She felt the ideas came from Nathan Witt, originally assistant counsel to the board and later its executive secretary. In 1953 Witt refused to disclose to the Senate Internal Security Committee whether he was or ever had been a communist. Edwin Smith similarly refused. *New York Times,* May 22, 1953, 12:3. At the time of testifying Smith was registered at the Department of Justice as a foreign agent for the Soviet Union, the People's Republic of China and satellite countries. He imported news photographs, literature and music. FP has a long discussion on Smith and Witt's influence on him. FPOHC, Bk. 7, pp. 160–66, 179–88, 202–208, 218.

    Interview with Reilly by Jonathan Grossman, p. 33: "With the exception of Ed Smith who was one of her great mistakes . . . she was pretty knowledgeable about who Communist people were either outside of the government but trying to have a finger in it or who had gotten into the government. But on Smith apparently because he may not have been a Communist until he was subjected to Pressman's influence on the Labor Board, she trusted him a great deal."

25. Millis and Brown, *From the Wagner Act,* p. 80, citing also the Attorney General's Committee, Final Report, pp. 58–59: "numerically and otherwise, the life-blood of the administrative process — negotiations and informal settlements."
26. FPOHC, Bk. 7, pp. 198–201; independent and unpredictable, FP, *TRIK*, p. 245. Also, FP Cornell lecture, February 27, 1957, "Labor Union History and Administration," p. 27, FPP, Cornell.

27. AFL, *Proceedings of the Sixtieth Annual Convention, 1940,* pp. 501–2;
    Proceedings of the Sixty-First Convention, 1941, pp. 330–31. Cf. FP letter
    to Harry Bridges, Janauary 17, 1936, FPP, Columbia.
28. Shor, thesis, p. 87.

Of particular value for the Fair Labor Standards Act: FP, *TRIK,* "Wages
and Hours," pp. 246–67; Burns, *Congress on Trial,* pp. 67–82.

29. FPOHC, Bk. 7, "Supreme Court Fight," pp. 70–134. FP, *TRIK,* p. 256.
30. Ickes, *Diary,* Vol. 1, p. 531. FPOHC, Bk. 7, p. 112: "Ickes was always, for
    as long as I can remember, for going after the Supreme Court."
31. FPOHC, Bk. 7, pp. 75–77.
32. FPOHC, Bk. 7, pp. 107–108.
33. FPOHC, Bk. 2, p. 230.
34. *West Coast Hotel* v. *Parrish,* 300 U.S. 379; *NLRB* v. *Jones and Laughlin
    Steel Corp.,* 301 U.S. 1; *Steward Machine Co.* v. *Davis,* 301 U.S. 548;
    Helvering v. *Davis,* 301 U.S. 619; interview by GM with T. H. Eliot.
35. FP, *TRIK,* p. 257, ascribes the idea to Grace Abbott.
36. Shor, thesis, p. 175, citing United States Congress, Senate, Fair Labor
    Standards Act of 1937, joint hearings before the Committee on Education
    and Labor, United States Senate, and the Committee on Labor, United
    States House of Representatives, Seventy-fifth Congress, first session
    (Washington, Government Printing Office, 1937), pp. 178 ff. Harrison
    on FP, *Congressional Record,* July 30, 1937, p. 7872.
37. FP, *TRIK,* p. 261.
38. Interview by GM with Reilly.
39. FP, *TRIK,* pp. 265–66.
40. "Not sound," interview with Reilly by J. P. Grossman; "boiler," inter-
    view with Reilly by GM.
41. *Annual Report of the Secretary of Labor, 1939,* p. 198.
42. Reilly recalled that Andrews was FP's third choice, preceded by Leon
    Henderson and Isador Lubin, interview by GM.
43. "Memorandum of a Conversation with the President on Thursday, Oc-
    tober 13, 1938." FPP, Columbia. Interview by GM with Reilly; FPOHC,
    Bk. 3, p. 637. For Andrews's continued fight for independent power, *New
    York Times,* March 3, 1939, 1:4.
44. Interview by GM with Gladys Burch. *New York Times,* October 18,
    1939, 1:3: headline, "Andrews Resigns, Col. Fleming Gets His Post, with
    No Explanation of Wage-Hours Shift."
45. Memorandum FP to FDR, August 18, 1939, FDR Library, PSF, Labor
    Dept.
46. E.g., letter from A. S. Barger to FDR, November 3, 1939; and correspon-
    dence between FP and Consumers' League of New York (Helene P. Gans,
    secretary), November–December 1939, FPP, NA, Box 138, Wage-Hours,
    Fleming. The appointment required special legislation, enabling him to
    retain his army commission in addition to holding a civilian post.
47. Lubin, OH, Columbia, p. 67. Also interview with Reilly by J. P. Gross-
    man, p. 17.
48. *United States* v. *Darby,* 312 U.S. 100.
49. On "the purge," FPOHC, Bk. 7, pp. 311–25: "I was shocked by it," p. 312;

she thought it "politically foolish" and "part of the court fight," p. 314. "I never talked to Roosevelt about this," p. 312.
50. Leuchtenburg, *FDR and the New Deal*, p. 256.

Chapter 30

(*pages 396–406*)

1. FP letters, all in FPP, Columbia, to Gertrude Ely, January 4, 1937; to Daisy Harriman, January 4, 1937; Beatrice Hale, February 9, 1937; Sarah McDonald, July 17, 1937; Louise Rounds, July 19, 1937; Jo Davidson, January 11, 1938; "takes one back," Anna Olney, September 22, 1939; to SWC, January 18, 1941; interview by GM with SWC.
2. FPOHC, Bk. 3, p. 85; Tully, *F.D.R., My Boss*, pp. 58–59.
3. FPOHC, Bk. 6, p. 415.
4. A copy of Edmondson's Star-of-David "Roosevelt's Supreme Council," FPP, Columbia. Eventually a criminal suit was started against Edmondson for libeling Virginia Gildersleeve, Dean of Barnard College, FP and the Jewish religion. In the spring of 1938 on the request of the prosecutor the court dismissed the indictment for fear of giving Edmondson's ideas the publicity he sought for them by appearing to persecute him. See *New York Times* for February 8, 1938, 14:5; April 19, 1938, 44:3; May 11, 1938, 15:2. FPOHC, Bk. 6, p. 414.
5. Clerk at Newton. Letter to FP from Frank M. Grant, October 29, 1938, FPP, Columbia. FPOHC, Bk. 6, p. 413.
6. FPP, Mount Holyoke. Partly because of Perkins's negligence in filling out forms the Alumnae Office constantly misinformed those who inquired about her. But surely FP never said her daughter's name was Penelope, as the office informed C. N. Stone, May 16, 1933. See also the Registrar's letter to Malcolm S. Hallman, May 6, 1940, FPP, Columbia.
7. All in FPP, Columbia: letter to FP from Pauline (Mrs. Wagner) MacMillan, January 18, 1936; letter FP in reply published *New York Times*, April 5, 1936, 43:3; letter to FP from Mrs. Milton Brown, February 3, 1938, reporting a lecturer on circuit saying that FP was a Russian who had changed her name; FP letter to Rev. Wayne White, denying Russian Jewish ancestry, July 11, 1939; FP correspondence with William Lee Bishop, January–February 1942, on alleged Russian origin.
8. On start of recession, FP letter to Gertrude Ely, January 4, 1937 [*sic*, almost certainly should be 1938], FPP, Columbia. FDR quotation, Leuchtenburg, *Franklin D. Roosevelt and the New Deal*, p. 250 with important fn. explaining variance from *FDR Public Papers*, IV, p. 425.
9. Of particular value for the strike, Fine, *Sit-Down*. Murphy to FP, FPOHC, Bk. 6, p. 128. FPOHC has a long section on the strike and its background, Bk. 6, pp. 67–247.
10. FPOHC, Bk. 6, pp. 130–34. Her memory of the press conference is correct in substance and wrong in detail; too many of the reporters who must have been present agree on the details. The original story in a mild form appeared on the front page of e.g. the Washington *Evening Star*, January 26, 1937, *New York Times*, New York *Herald Tribune* and San Francisco *Chronicle*, all January 27, 1937. In each case the story was followed the next day by an editorial or column against her position.

Mark Sullivan in the Washington *Evening Star,* January 28, 1937, 11:4, puts the issue most clearly. There are good accounts of the press conference by Paul W. Ward in the Baltimore *Sun,* January 27, 1937, 1:1 and the New York *Herald Tribune,* January 27, 1937, 10:1.

11. FPOHC, Bk. 6, p. 136. See Garner's letter to Farley in Farley, *Story,* pp. 84–86: "I think he has been over-reached in some things or else he has arrived at conclusions which to my mind can't be sustained from a standpoint of statesmanship or patriotism. I refer particularly to the sit-down strikes and mass lawlessness, which, to me, is intolerable and will lead to great difficulty, if not destruction."

12. FPOHC, Bk. 6, p. 141.

13. FPOHC, Bk. 6, pp. 112–16; Sulzberger's story, *New York Times,* January 31, 1937, 1:1. Interview with Reilly by J. P. Grossman, p. 10, says she had a cold at the time and may have sounded hoarse on the phone, but "she was never emotional about labor disputes. She took those rather philosophically." The story is repeated in one form or another in, e.g. Fine, *Sit-Down,* p. 259, *Commentator,* February 1938, pp. 106–10, *Time,* February 8, 1937, p. 15, began and ended its account of the Sloan episode, "A woman scorned . . . almost in tears."

14. Anderson, thesis, citing Washington *Star,* March 20, 1937.

15. Sloan phone call and on his character, FPOHC, Bk. 6, pp. 203–19; short memorandum of call, dated January 29, 1937, FPP, Coggeshall. Letter FP to Joseph T. Robinson, January 27, 1937, FPP, Columbia. Letter published, *New York Times,* January 28, 1937, 1:1; congressional comment, January 29, 1937, 4:4; Krock column, January 30, 1937, 16:5. See Shor thesis, p. 94.

16. Farley, *Story,* p. 160.

17. Figures from Galenson, *The CIO Challenge to the AFL,* pp. 587–88.

18. Interview by GM with Clara Beyer, who was in the room when FP talked to Lewis. FP previously had warned Lewis about Pressman, FPOHC, Bk. 8, pp. 474–76. Also interview with Beyer by J. P. Grossman. For Reilly on FP and communists, see his interview by J. P. Grossman, p. 33, quoted in Chap. 29, note 24, above. Also, after the collapse of one effort to get the AFL and CIO together, in which Lewis at the last minute tore up the document and walked out, Philip Murray came to FP's office the next day to apologize. In Reilly's presence he told FP that until Lewis had shown the agreement to Pressman he (Lewis) had been in favor of it. Pressman, however, in Murray's presence, had argued against it, offering reasons, not one of which Lewis had used the next day at the public meeting. FPOHC, Bk. 7, p. 742, on communist techniques FP saw in New York. FP weak on communists, e.g., John Philip Frey, president of the Metal Trades Dept. of the AFL, OH, Columbia, pp. 508–9, 556, and 698.

Chapter 31

(*pages 407–419*)

Of particular use in this chapter: FP, *TRIK,* pp. 315–19; FPOHC, "San Francisco: Harry Bridges," Bk. 6, pp. 371–472, and "Impeachment," Bk. 6, pp. 473–542; the material in a folder "Bridges Case" in FPP, Columbia;

Larrowe's *Harry Bridges,* which seldom cites sources but so far as I could check it was always accurate; and an interview by GM with Gerard Reilly.

1. Letter of Edward J. Shaughnessy, Acting Commissioner of Immigration and Naturalization, to Mrs. Frank H. Stanberg, of the DAR, Los Angeles, January 13, 1937, quotes the report and gives a history of the bureau's investigation of Bridges, FPP, Columbia.
2. Evidence unusual: FP statement to House Judiciary Committee, February 8, 1939, FPP, Radcliffe, Box 77, folder 1021 and FPP, NA, Immigration, General, January–May, 1939, Box 51. See FPOHC, Bk. 6, p. 454.
3. 95 F2nd 976.
4. FP statement, note 2 above, and FPOHC, Bk. 6, p. 469. Memorandum on Bridges and Strecker cases by Reilly for FP, July 29, 1938, FPP, Columbia.
5. FPOHC, Bk. 6, pp. 469–72. She does not identify the man but describes him as "one rather sober critic who didn't lose his head." Her quotation, p. 472.
6. Figures from Leuchtenburg, *Franklin D. Roosevelt and the New Deal,* p. 280.
7. *New York Times,* August 31, 1938; September 7, 1938; September 9, 1938.
8. *New York Times,* October 25, 1938, 1:3; New York *Herald Tribune,* October 26, 1938, 13:2; FP letters to Mrs. William Brown Meloney, November 3 and 17, 1938; and letter to FP from Lutie E. Sterns, October 29, 1938; all FPP, Columbia.
9. Fine, *Sit-Down,* p. 337; FDR press conference, October 25, 1937.
10. Dies letter to Solicitor General Robert Jackson, *New York Times,* October 30, 1938, 1:4; urging Ickes, Hopkins, FP to resign, *New York Times,* November 25, 1938, 3:6.
11. Letter to FP from Kevin Emmett Perkins, n.d., FDR Library, OF 15, Labor Dept. Misc. 1933–38.
12. On the alleged tie-in between the witness, Harpers Knowles and the Industrial Association, undated Associated Press story in unidentified news clipping, "Legion Spurns Dies Witness," and memorandum from Reilly to FP, December 20, 1938, discussing evidence of it collected by a Senate committee; both FPP, Columbia. Relations with Bridges, e.g. letter to FP, July 27, 1942 from Westbrook Pegler asking if her niece was married to Bridges, FPP, Columbia.
13. FPOHC, Bk. 6, p. 484.
14. FP knew Parsons before going to Washington, FPOHC, Bk. 2, p. 501. Letter to FP from Parsons, January 16, 1939, and their subsequent correspondence, FPP, Columbia (filed under Dorothy McAllister).
15. FP letter to Mary T. Norton, January 21, 1939; the letter as read with subsequent questions in the House, FPP, Columbia, (filed under Dorothy McAllister). FP paying, memorandum Reilly to FP, March 17, 1939, FPP, Columbia. Impeachment resolution, *New York Times,* January 25, 1939, 1:2.
16. FPOHC, Bk. 6, p. 479.
17. Memorandum MacCormack to FP, July 26, 1935, analyzing Dies's figures and suggesting the mistakes by which he may have reached them, FPP, Connecticut.

18. FPOHC, Bk. 6, p. 479.

19. *New York Times* editorials, January 25, 1939, 20:2, "not on a par"; February 10, 1939, 22:2, questioning her actions (she drafted a letter to the editor but followed Wyzanski's advice not to send it) ; April 18, 1939, 22:2, "the wisdom of this postponement has always been open to question. It does not become clearer now that the Strecker decision is known." On early Christians and grandmother, FPOHC, Bk. 6, p. 488.

20. FPOHC, Bk. 6, pp. 489–90. Letter to FP from Myrtle Dies, February 26, 1939, thanking FP for *Listen the Wind,* which "cheered" Dies very much.

21. Sumners. Interview by GM with Reilly. The two federal judges were Harold Louderback, acquitted by the Senate in 1933, and Halsted L. Ritter, convicted in 1936. See "Impeachment of Federal judges: An Historical Overview" by Frank Thompson, Jr., and Daniel H. Pollitt, *North Carolina Law Review,* Vol. 49, 1970–71, pp. 87–121. FPOHC, Bk. 6, p. 505.

22. FPOHC, Bk. 6, p. 512. Two others who thought the attack was entirely political and certain to fail were Congressmen John W. MacCormack and Andrew J. May; letters in FPP, Columbia.

23. ER to Anne Choate, February 2, 1939, quoted by Lash, *Eleanor and Franklin,* pp. 463–64. The propensity of women to believe the charge of communism was also made about those in Portland, Oregon, by William Lee Bishop, letter to FP, January 25, 1942, FPP, Columbia.

24. FPOHC, Bk. 6, pp. 508–25; Joan of Arc, p. 518; Michener, p. 514; long morning, p. 525. Interview by GM with Reilly: He is certain that FP is mistaken in stating that Parnell Thomas, who was not a member of the committee, was present. Reilly remembered Michener shouting, p. 514, and Samuel Hobbs of Alabama asking the question about aliens, p. 522. In Reilly's interview by Grossman, p. 9, he described FP's performance as "extremely impressive." Because the hearing was held in executive session there is no public record of it. For her statement, see note 2, above.

25. The Judiciary Committee's Report is Report No. 311, March 24, 1939, *Congressional Record,* March 25, 1939, p. 3285. Resolution tabled, *Congressional Record,* March 24, 1939, p. 3273. A discussion of the Republican maneuver by which the Additional Views were added, *Congressional Record,* March 30, 1939, p. 3552.

26. Copies of the speeches of Thomas and Meed, FPP, Columbia.

27. Martin's speech, *Congressional Record,* April 3, 1939, p. 3741. Others complaining about the lack of publicity, Kate F. O'Connor, to FP, n.d., and Nora B. Felt to FP, April 16, 1939, FPP, Columbia.

28. *Kessler* v. *Strecker,* 307 U.S. 22.

29. Larrowe, *Bridges,* pp. 147–49, 214, offers evidence of the favorable attitude of San Francisco newspapers to Landis. Landis report, pp. 245, 246, in FPP, Columbia. A summary of it appeared in the *New York Times,* December 31, 1939, 12:2. Landis, OH, Columbia, p. 58. He noticed that though the letters came from all over, most came from Detroit and Brooklyn, even more than from California. Remarks of Leland M. Ford, *Congressional Record,* January 12, 1942, p. 259. Cf. Ford's letter to FP, June 19, 1941, in which he rehearses all her shortcomings, FPP, Columbia.

30. *New York Times,* April 3, 1941, 19:1: "The Committee, in its report to the House, said it was not advised as to 'who is responsible for such a grossly inexcusable oversight' but that whoever was should be made to answer for it." Reilly memorandum to FP, April 5, 1941, analyzing Hoover's testimony on the Bridges case, FPP, Columbia. On the Episcopal convention, May 13 and 14, *New York Times,* May 15, 1941, 18:2; New York *Herald Tribune,* May 15, 1941, 13:1; letter from C. C. Burlingham to Bishop William T. Manning, May 19, 1941, and letter of Canon B. I. Bell to FP, June 3, 1941, both in FPP, Columbia.

31. FP to Dewey McKinley Taft, October 1, 1941, and FP to Philip A. Bennett, November 26, 1941, both in FPP, Columbia. Bennett's speech, *Congressional Record,* November 10, 1941, p. 8743 ff.; his limited correction, *Congressional Record,* November 28, 1941, p. 9248.

32. Letters to FP from Mrs. Arthur Solberg, January 31, 1939, from Harry Lundeberg, June 18, 1945, and from P. J. McMullan, May 31, 1941, all in FPP, Columbia. In FPOHC, Bk. 7, p. 26, citing John A. Ryan's *A Living Wage,* she defines it as: "More than just enough to feed and house a person against the storm; it is enough to make it possible for him to participate in a modest way in the elementary culture of his community, such as being able to send his children to school rather than putting them to work." On her optimism, FP letter to Ruth Cowan, December 13, 1940, FPP, Columbia.

Chapter 32

(pages 420–438)

1. The seven states passing minimum wage laws early in 1933: Connecticut, Illinois, New Hampshire, New Jersey, New York, Ohio and Utah. The nine with existing laws: California, Colorado, Massachusetts, Minnesota, North Dakota, Oregon, South Dakota, Washington and Wisconsin. *New York Times,* July 12, 1933, 8:6.

2. The first National Conference was planned chiefly by FP, Boris Stern of the BLS and Jean Flexner of the Children's Bureau. FP's correspondence in this period with John B. Andrews, secretary of the American Association for Labor Legislation, displays what she was attempting to do, JBA Papers. Proceedings of the First National Conference for Labor Legislation, FPP, Radcliffe, Vols. 78–84. Reports of the conferences, 1934–42, are at Radcliffe. See also CMB Papers, folders 181–84.

3. Clara Beyer memo to FP, "Suggestions for Miss Perkins' Address, IAGLO Convention," accompanying her letter to FP, August 11, 1959, FPP, Columbia. Interview GM with Beyer. FPOHC, Bk. 1, pp. 313–15; Bk. 2, p. 480. Zimmer, Address on Division of Labor Standards, June 21, 1939, 5, FPP, Columbia.

4. Failure of experts. John B. Andrews, "The Secretary of Labor Cooperates," *American Labor Legislation Review,* Vol. 31, No. 4, p. 160, December 1942, FPP, Columbia. Interview by GM with Beyer. Proceedings of first conference, above, note 2.

5. Quoted in MacMahon and Millett, *Federal Administrator,* p. 372.

6. Interview by GM with Beyer. The division of work and prestige within the

division tends to confirm her statement and also letter of A. L. Fletcher, Commissioner of Labor of North Carolina, to FP, October 10, 1935, FPP, NA, Box 40, Second Annual Conference on Labor Legislation.

7. Interview by GM with Beyer.

8. Durkin's letter quoted in Beyer memorandum to FP, January 19, 1935, FPP, NA, Box 59, Labor Standards 1935. A. L. Fletcher to FP, October 10, 1935, FPP, NA, Box 40, Second National Conference on Labor Legislation. On drawing state and union officials together, interview by GM with Beyer; on J. Tone, Zimmer, address, above, note 3, p. 4, identified by Beyer to GM.

9. Beyer memorandum to FP, "Suggestions for Address," p. 4, see above, note 3.

10. Silicosis conferences, FP letter to John B. Andrews, March 24, 1936, letters March 30, 1929 and March 4, 1936, all JBA Papers. The conferences were held on February 26, March 11 and April 14. Cf. *New York Times,* May 3, 1936, 17:1. On cadavers, interview by GM with Beyer. On all aspects of division's work, CMB Papers, folders 187–204.

11. Zimmer, address, p. 5, see above, note 3. See Elizabeth Brandeis, "Organized Labor and Protective Labor Legislation" in Derber and Young, *Labor and the New Deal,* pp. 213–17: "The attitudes of state federation representatives at these . . . conferences suggests that forces other than organized labor probably took the lead in securing state hour and wage laws."

12. Description by Andrews, "The Secretary . . . Cooperates," p. 159, see above, note 4.

13. The ribbons, interview by GM with Beyer; doodles, interview by GM with Beyer and Lucille Buchanan; Gamble, interview by GM with Buchanan; other incidents from the proceedings, above, note 2. Letter William L. Connolly to FDR, January 8, 1945, FPP, Columbia. FP's estimate FPOHC, Bk. 4, p. 282; also Bk. 2, p. 473.

14. FP, *TRIK,* Chap. 26, "Approaches to World Order," is entirely on the ILO, pp. 337–46. It is sometimes said that Wyzanski rather than Perkins was the prime mover in the project to join the ILO. In an interview with GM he denied it. Also Wyzanski, OH, Columbia, pp. 228 ff.

15. *Congressional Record,* April 3, 1936, p. 4933. Committee of the Whole House on the State of the Union for consideration of the bill, H.R. 12098 making appropriations for fiscal year ending June 30, 1937.

16. Dept. of Labor *Annual Report, 1937,* p. 1. On her approach and attitude toward the ILO, interviews by GM with Clara M. Beyer, Carol Riegelman Lubin, Isador Lubin and Charles E. Wyzanski, Jr.

17. FPOHC, Bk. 7, p. 384. She also never questioned Farley directly, Bk. 7, p. 500.

18. FPOHC, Bk. 7, pp. 383, 389, 826.

19. FPOHC, Bk. 7, pp. 827, 389.

20. FP letter to Ernest G. Draper, July 11, 1945, FPP, Columbia. FPOHC, Bk. 7, "we've won," p. 15, cf. pp. 823–24. Derber, *The American Idea of Industrial Democracy, 1865–1965,* p. 298, thinks this change in attitude was "perhaps the single most significant" of the period.

21. FPOHC, Bk. 7, p. 411. In stating that FDR had his mind made up as

early as April or May she puts the decision a few weeks or even months earlier than most historians have believed. This perhaps supports Farley's claim, *Story*, p. 306, that FDR consistently lied about his intentions to his friends and colleagues while wrapping his deceit in a cloak of patriotism. See Donahoe, *Private Plans and Public Dangers*, p. 161; Leuchtenburg, *Franklin D. Roosevelt and the New Deal*, p. 315; Burns, *Roosevelt, Lion and Fox*, pp. 408–28, 532–33, who doesn't set a date but thinks FDR would have run again regardless of the war.

22. Kelly in control, Ickes, *Diary* Vol. 3, p. 122 and Farley, *Story*, p. 224. FP's opinion, FPOHC, Bk. 2, p. 306. Farley, *Story*, p. 309, thought the hidden, amplified chants "beyond all decency."

23. FPOHC, Bk. 7, pp. 460–61.

24. FPOHC, Bk. 7, p. 464. Cf. Bk. 7, p. 537: "The President used to talk to me about things that were none of my darn business." Krock, OH, Columbia, p. 47.

25. FPOHC, Bk. 7, p. 476. Interview by GM with Ilo B. Wallace, who confirmed that ER took her hand. Time has not healed the wounds of that night for Mrs. Wallace. My question about the hand was to have been the first of several about the convention. But as I asked it, she stiffened and said, "Oh, let's not talk about that," while a look of pain so fresh, so actual suffused her face, that I stopped.

26. Farley, *Story*, p. 302. Harshly advised, Sherwood, *Roosevelt and Hopkins*, p. 179. FP has an interesting account of Sherwood's difficulties in writing the book, FPOHC, Bk. 7, pp. 532–39.

27. Farley, *Story*, pp. 301, 238.

28. Protecting others: e.g. Farley, *Story*, p. 219, credits Perkins with persuading FDR to call him. By the time of her OH (c. 1953), she was uncertain whether she had done it, FPOHC, Bk. 7, p. 470. She went to a testimonial dinner for Farley in New York on July 10, 1944. In FPOHC, Bk. 7, p. 502, she has an account of warmhearted FDR urging her to go: "He's been a good fellow to us." But a White House file memo, July 1, 1944, records her request for permission to go and FDR's response: "I think the whole thing depends on her own desires. No reason she should not go — that is perfectly all right. On the other hand, I think she should make the decision." FDR Library, PSF Labor Perkins. She instinctively did the decent thing and frequently helped others to it.

29. On FDR: FPOHC, Bk. 7, pp. 561–64; cf. her summary of FDR as a war President, FP, *TRIK*, pp. 384–87. Cf. *TRIK*, pp. 163–65.

30. On Farley, FPOHC, Bk. 7, pp. 485–509. The three men: Farley, Jesse Jones and Thomas Lamont, a partner in J. P. Morgan & Co.

31. On Hopkins, FPOHC, Bk. 7, pp. 563–64.

32. Her attempt to resign, FPOHC, Bk. 7, pp. 823–30; Bk. 9, pp. 123–31. The *New York Times* on its front page announced that her resignation had been accepted, November 25, 1940, 1:2: "It was learned authoritatively last night . . . Miss Perkins confided the news to old friends on a visit here last week." Both she and the White House denied the resignation, but the *Times*, November 26, 1940, 26:1, reported that "highly placed persons insisted tonight" that the rumor was true. Fiorello La Guardia or Paul McNutt was considered her most likely successor.

Chapter 33

(*pages 439–455*)

1. Interview by GM with Alice Cook, who said that FP "would *never* talk about the Civil Service Commission." FP, *TRIK,* p. 384.
2. Interview by GM with C. E. Wyzanski, Jr.
3. FP letter to FDR, September 15, 1939, FPP, Columbia. On declaring the national emergency, Rosenman, *Working with Roosevelt,* pp. 283–84.
4. FPOHC, Bk. 7, p. 845. Cf. Ickes, *Diary,* Vol. 3, p. 302, where he laments that because of FP atrocities could not be recounted at cabinet meetings.
5. *New York Times,* March 16, 1939, 3:2. On FDR, FP and Ickes on finger-printing Ickes, *Diary,* Vol. 3, p. 609, recording FP as saying, "The whole thing is a racket stimulated by the people who supply the materials."
6. Interview by GM with Reilly, who was present, and repeated his re-marks in his interview by J. P. Grossman. Also FPOHC, Bk. 9, pp. 72–76; and stressed in Klutz, "The Woman Nobody Knows," *Collier's,* August 5, 1944, quoting some of her remarks to a National Conference for Labor Legislation.
7. FPOHC, Bk. 8, pp. 158–62; Bk. 6, pp. 443–44; FP, *TRIK,* pp. 360–61. For an account of what followed the transfer, see Biddle, *In Brief Authority,* pp. 106–22.
8. *Congressional Record,* May 27, 1940, p. 6916. For FP's letter in reply to Taber, May 27, 1940, copies of which were sent to 58 congressmen and senators, FPP, Columbia. Name-calling, FPOHC, Bk. 3, p. 264; women's vote, etc., FP, *TRIK,* p. 136.
9. There has been considerable debate as to whether FDR intended a re-buke to FP by the transfer. A memorandum, January 9, 1941, to FDR from James Rowe, Jr., asking the reasons for it, stated, "I have always assumed it resulted quite logically from the developments in the world situation, i.e. immigration and naturalization had changed from a prob-lem particularly pertinent to American labor and has become a useful defense weapon in terms of national defense and should be related to the other defensive activities of the Department of Justice." FDR marked this "O.K., F.D.R.," FDR Library, OF 15, Labor Dept. Lubin, interview by GM, thought no rebuke had been intended or taken. Reilly, interview by J. P. Grossman, p. 24, thought that privately "she resented it."
10. Conrat, Maisie and Richard. *Executive Order 9066* (Los Angeles, Cali-fornia Historical Society, 1972). Interviews by GM with Deane and Eleanor Malott.
11. FPOHC, Bk. 8, p. 96.
12. FPOHC, Bk. 8, pp. 154–57; also her speech to Pen and Brush Club, April 19, 1945, FPP, Columbia. FP letter, August 15, 1942, to Samuel Rosenman, with accompanying memorandum to Harold Smith, FPP, Columbia. Memorandum from Mary La Dame to FP, December 4, 1941, with FP's marginal notes, FPP, NA, Adm. General 1939, p. 1.
13. Lubin, OH, Columbia, pp. 76–77. Letter to FP, c. March 24, 1942, from Mrs. A. Williamson Walton, FPP, Columbia.
14. FP, *TRIK,* pp. 373–74; FPOHC, Bk. 7, p. 616.

15. FPOHC, Bk. 8, p. 240. Memorandum from A. Ford Hinrichs to FP, March 16, 1943, on women in war work, FPP, Columbia.
16. FPOHC, Bk. 8, p. 123; Hershey, pp. 126–27, also p. 227.
17. FPOHC, Bk. 8, lampshades pp. 127–28, mechanic, p. 129.
18. *New York Times*, November 1, 1942, 52:2. FP letter to FDR, November 2, 1942, FPP, Columbia. For other examples of holding the line: FP letter, April 24, 1942, to the chairman of the Senate Judiciary Committee opposing a bill, S2425, to suspend all holidays, because experience shows need of them, FPP, NA, Bills Misc. 1942, p. 89. Also correspondence in March, April and May 1942 on proposed use of child labor in anticipated farm labor shortage, FPP, NA, Children's Bureau 1942, p. 93.
19. FP, *TRIK*, pp. 374–75. Memorandum from Clara Beyer to FP, December 22, 1941, FPP, NA, Box 114, Labor Standards.
20. FP letter, May 15, 1943, to Lawrence M. C. Smith, with attached summary of conference statements, FPP, Columbia.
21. *New York Times* editorial, March 13, 1942, and Frank Kent column in Washington *Star*, March 20, 1942. FP letter, March 23, 1942, to Kent with attached memorandum, FPP, NA, Wage and Hour General (40-hour week), 138. Also in same NA ref., FP letter to Lauchlin Currie, February 19, 1942, and to Senator Elbert D. Thomas, March 18, 1942, as well as I. L. Sharfman to FP, February 26, 1942. Also FP letter, December 17, 1940, to FDR, with speech by L. M. Walling on provisions of Public Contracts Act in defense work, FDR Library, PSF, Labor Dept.
22. Letter to FP and FDR, March 25, 1942, from Alice B. Long, FPP, Columbia. Proved clearly, FP, *TRIK*, p. 375. Grossman, *The Dept. of Labor*, p. 57, the cites the preservation of labor standards as "perhaps the Labor Department's most effective war activity."
23. FPOHC, Bk. 8, p. 206.
24. FPOHC, Bk. 8, p. 212.
25. ER, *Women of Courage*, p. 193. Memorandum to FP, July 27, 1942, from Warner W. Gardner on History of the War Labor Board Executive Order, FPP, Columbia. Memorandum Report of War-Labor Conference convened December 17, 1941, FPP, Radcliffe, Box 76, folder 990.
26. FP, *TRIK*, pp. 367–69; FPOHC, Bk. p. 201. FP letter to Mrs. John Bradshaw, June 16, 1943, FPP, Columbia.
27. Figures from Dulles, *Labor in America*, p. 335.
28. The Controversy over the Cost of Living Index is recounted from various points of view in: Arnow, *Attack on the Cost of Living Index;* Clague, *The Bureau of Labor Statistics*, pp. 217–27; Goulden, *Meany*, pp. 111–16; Wickens, OH, Columbia, pp. 31–56. Also interviews GM with Hinrichs, Wickens, Lubin and Clague.

Chapter 34
(pages 456–465)

1. FP letter to Harriet Laidlaw, October 27, 1944, FPP, Columbia.
2. FP, *TRIK*, pp. 388–90; FPOHC, Bk. 8, p. 286. Bishop, *FDR's Last Year*, opening chapters, of which typically p. 14: "If Mrs. Roosevelt and Anna were told anything it was that Admiral McIntire advised the President

that 'he could quite easily go on with the activities of the presidency.'"
In fact the doctors as early as May 1944 put him on a schedule of no
more than four hours work a day; see p. 38. Bishop's book is the most
detailed account of FDR's medical history. Another source, Lord Moran,
Churchill (Boston, Houghton Mifflin, 1966), pp. 242–43, dates a heart
attack for FDR as early as June 1944, before the convention. James
MacGregor Burns, "FDR: The Untold Story of His Last Year," *Saturday
Review*, April 11, 1970, thinks FDR's heart trouble of little significance.

3. Goldmark, *Impatient Crusader*, pp. 180–88; handful FPOHC, Bk. 8, p.
   532; also Bk. 7, p. 443.

4. Chafe, *The American Woman*, pp. 164–65.

5. Her opposition: see interview with James Dodson by J. P. Grossman,
   p. 18. Grant, "Confessions of a Feminist," *American Mercury*, December
   1943, Vol. 57, No. 240, pp. 684–91.

6. FP letter, July 8, 1944, to Dorothy McAllister; letter, July 8, 1944, to
   Jane Grant; reply Grant to FP, July 14, 1944; all in FPP, NA, Equal
   Rights, p. 89. Grant to FP, June 12, 1953, FPP, Columbia.

7. Seemly: FP letter, July 8, 1944, to Dorothy McAllister; FP letter, July 10,
   1944, to Florence A. Armstrong; both FPP, NA, Equal Rights, p. 89.
   Argument for and against protective legislation summarized in Baker,
   Technology and Women's Work, pp. 393–442, and Chafe, *The American
   Woman*, pp. 112–132. FP at the convention, *New York Times*, July 19,
   1944, 13:6 and July 21, 1944, 12:3, 6.

8. FP, *TRIK*, pp. 392–94.

9. "You must"; interview by GM with T. H. Eliot, to whom FP repeated
   the exchange. Wyzanski, who heard of it from Eliot, was inclined to believe it because "that was the kind of courage she had, and demanded."
   Mrs. Woodrow Wilson, FPOHC, Bk. 8, p. 286.

10. Letter to FP, April 16, 1945, from C. C. Burlingham, who wrote "FD was
    never disappointed" etc. FP because of that phrase showed the letter to
    ER and repeated it in a number of her own letters. FP reply to Bur-
    lingham, May 7, 1945; to Ethel Van Benthuysen, May 4, 1945; to Mary
    Simkhovitch, June 11, 1945; to Basil O'Connor, June 11, 1945, about a
    Roosevelt memorial: "The last personal letter that the President ever
    wrote to me had these words in it: 'There is still a great deal to be done'";
    to Sir Arthur and Lady Salter, May 4, 1945, speaking of FDR and the
    emotion in the country on his death: "For a brief time somebody obeyed
    the Christian injunction to 'love thy neighbor as thyself,' and the neigh-
    bors loved him back"; and to Harry Hopkins, May 16, 1945. All in FPP,
    Columbia.

11. FPOHC, Bk. 8, pp. 843–51; Albertson, *Roosevelt's Farmer*, p. 397; Biddle,
    In Brief Authority, pp. 364–66.

12. Recognition Dinner: menu, list of sponsors and Green's speech, FPP,
    Columbia. Also Washington *Evening Star*, June 27, 1945, June 28, 1945.
    Interview with A. J. Wickens by J. P. Grossman.

13. Schwellenbach's succession: FPOHC, Bk. 8, pp. 848–72; "laugh and
    laugh," p. 869. In these 25 pages she hits again and again at "the great
    strong man successor" who did no better with strikes than she but was
    given a much easier time by the press. Interviews by GM with Beyer,

Buchanan, Burch, Dempsey and Dodson. Interviews by GM with Clague and Hinrichs on the BLS. Cf. Clague, *The Bureau of Labor Statistics,* p. 227; also Clague, OH, Columbia, Bk. 2, pp. 218–22, 244–45.

The Washington *Evening Star,* June 30, 1945, A1:2; July 1, 1945, A1:2 and A4:5; July 3, 1945, A1:5 (the General Order story); July 14, 1945, A4:3 (his first radio address). *New York Times,* July 1, 1945, 16:5, Schwellenbach being sworn with FP present (a picture) and announcement of his proposed reorganization; July 12, 1945, 9:3, his remarks on the BLS.

Schwellenbach's tenure as Secretary had many elements of tragedy. He entered with high hopes, not all of which were mistaken or unreasonable. Soon after, his close adviser, John R. Steelman was appointed to the White House staff and used the position to undermine Schwellenbach's influence with Truman. His wife, apparently overexcited by his new place in the world, became, in the opinion of one of his colleagues, "enough to drive any man into the asylum." As a senator and a judge he had managed staffs of fewer than ten and had little idea of how to administer a department employing thousands. His authority was threatened by the great wave of postwar strikes, and a Republican Congress elected in 1946 began the following year to cut the heart out of the department on the excuse that it was too friendly to labor. By June 1948 the appropriation which for fiscal year 1947 had been $113 million had been reduced to $15 million and the staff to 3,340, the smallest number in almost twenty-five years. Under these blows Schwellenbach gradually lost any will to work, became ill and in June 1948 died in office. Interviews and sources, above. The quotation is taken from a longer one in Grossman, *The Dept. of Labor,* p. 65–66.

Chapter 35

(*pages 469–481*)

1. FPOHC, Bk. 2, pp. 588–99.
2. Copies of her tax returns and work sheets, FPP, Columbia. She did her own returns and almost invariably made arithmetical or other small errors, which kept her constantly in correspondence with the IRS. In 1949 she sent the estimated tax return by mistake to the Collector of Customs in Portland instead of the IRS.
3. Truman: Lubin, OH, Columbia, p. 96; interview by GM with Deane Malott. FP letter to PCW, June 27, 1945, FPP, Columbia.
4. Interview by GM with Agnes Leach, SWC and Gladys Burch. FP letter to SWC, January 8, 1941; see also letter to SWC, May 9, 1941; letter to Robert Whitman, July 1, 1941; and letter to FP from Margaret Poole; all FPP, Columbia.
5. Hare as a "handicap," FP letter to her first cousin, Mrs. J. C. Johnston, March 3, 1945, FPP, Columbia.
6. Interview by GM with Nannie Burgess Glidden.
7. Correspondence of GM and Miranda Masocco Levy, and interview with SWC.

8. On *TRIK:* FPOHC, Bk. 9, pp. 1–32; correspondence George Bye, Howard Taubman, Viking Press (B. W. Huebsch, Marshall Best) and Charles Burton; memorandum of her meeting with IRS Commissioner George Schoenman, March 12, 1948; all FPP, Columbia. Interviews GM with Gerard Reilly and Taubman. Bruère letter quoted in FPOHC, Bk. 9, p. 27.

9. On whether Hopkins made the remark, which he later denied, Farley, *Story,* p. 156, and Krock, OH, Columbia, pp. 60–66, both of whom were convinced he had.

10. Interviews by GM with SWC, Aryness Joy Wickens; Lubin, OH, Columbia, p. 73; Wickens, OH, Columbia, p. 67; interview with Wickens by J. P. Grossman.

11. Memorandum on Private Charity, FPP, Coggeshall. Cf. her statements in her master's essay for Columbia, such as that relief is only an expedient until "society adjusts itself and provides adequate incomes and adequate education to all its workers."

12. FP letter to Albert Jay Nock, March 1, 1944, after reading his book *Memoirs of a Superfluous Man,* FPP, Columbia.

13. On these ideas, Coughlin, *Church and State in Social Welfare,* pp. viii, 20–21, 27, 137 and 140.

14. FPOHC, Bk. 8, p. 848; nearest to heart, FP letter, May 22, 1941, to authors (Drew Pearson and Robert Allen) of "Washington Merry-Go-Round" column, FPP, Columbia. She was the fourth woman to serve as commissioner; annual salary was $15,000.

15. FPOHC, Bk. 9, pp. 33, 154; interview by GM with SWC.

16. FP decision in Wonnacott case, U.S. Civil Service Commission, FPP, Columbia. Letter to FP from W. Arthur McCoy, head of Examination Division, June 28, 1951, FPP, Columbia. Letter to Maurice F. Neufeld from Vera T. Garland with the CSC's tribute (one of the best) to FP on her death, FPP, Neufeld. McCoy is described in FPOHC, Bk. 9, pp. 138–39; Mrs. Garland, pp. 148–49.

17. FP speech reported in the *Christian Science Monitor,* October 31, 1946, 8. Sections of it quoted with approval in letter to FP, November 2, 1946, from Gertrude E. T. MacDonald; see also letter to FP, October 30, 1946, from anonymous worker; both FPP, Columbia. Cf. Klutz, "The Woman Nobody Knows," *Collier's,* August 5, 1944.

18. Neufeld letter to Mrs. J. W. Garland, January 10, 1966, FPP, Neufeld.

19. FP notes in Yasulaitus case, U.S. CSC, FPP, Columbia.

20. FP notes in Tilley case, U.S. CSC, FPP, Columbia.

21. FP letter to Gertrude Ely, August 19, 1944, FPP, Columbia.

22. FP letter to Sam Rayburn, March 5, 1952, FPP, Columbia.

23. FP letters to SWC, September 4, 1951, and August 18, 1952, FPP, Coggeshall.

24. Interview by GM and correspondence with Leonard Adams. Exchange between FP and Mary Dreier, January 5 and 22, 1953; also exchange between FP and Evangeline Jordan, January 14 and February 10, 1953; all FPP Columbia.

25. Letter to FP with information from Aryness Joy Wickens, April 7, 1953; from University of Illinois: Tom Page, June 23, 1953, R. W. Fleming,

March 10 and 24, 1953; all FPP, Columbia. Interview by GM with Gerard Reilly.

Chapter 36
(pages 482–490)

1. Interview by GM with Margaret Janeway.
2. Clipping describing her speech and visit to Cornell, Ithaca *Journal*, May 20, 1955, FPP, Columbia. Among the faculty were Martin P. Catherwood, Maurice F. Neufeld, Leonard P. Adams and Alice H. Cook.
3. Interview by GM with Martin P. Catherwood. Cf. letter of Mark Daly to FP, January 16, 1929, FPP, Columbia.
4. Interview by GM with Deane Malott.
5. Letter to FP from M. Slade Kendrick, December 12, 1957, FPP, Columbia.
6. Interviews by GM with Agnes Leach and Margaret Janeway.
7. FP's duties at Cornell and finances: two memoranda, May 26, 1958 and April 23, 1959, letter to FP from Alice Cook, August 13, 1959, letters to FP from John W. McConnell, May 18, 1960, March 30, 1962; all FPP, Columbia. Also examination of her income tax worksheets and New York and federal estate tax returns. In the last fifteen years of her life lecturing had a large part. Among other institutions besides Cornell at which she conducted seminars: Salzburg, Princeton and the University of Illinois (twice). Others at which she delivered anywhere from one to four lectures: Amherst, Bologna, California (L.A.), Carleton, Colgate, Hamilton, Notre Dame, Williams and Wisconsin. At the time of her death she had lectures scheduled at Syracuse, Kalamazoo and Illinois.
8. Her frugality and sense of not being rich: unanimous testimony of friends. The handbag: interview by GM with Alice Cook.
9. The Telluride Association was founded in 1911 and endowed by Lucien L. Nunn, an electrical engineer and pioneer in the high-voltage transmission of alternating current, who developed electrical systems in the Rocky Mountain states. The association consists of about eighty members, most of them students in their middle twenties, who own and administer the association's assets. Its chief program is maintaining the Telluride House at Cornell and filling it each year with about thirty college and graduate students, all on Telluride grants. There is a smaller house, similarly operated, at the University of California at Berkeley. The association also runs summer programs for students about to enter their last year of secondary schooling and assists Deep Springs Junior College, also endowed by Nunn, where all students are on full scholarship. In 1963 the association voted to grant FP permanent residence at Telluride House at Cornell, and after her death it created a Frances Perkins Memorial Fellowship in Industrial and Labor Relations. In 1974 the fellowship was held by a woman. Interview by GM with Beatrice MacLeod, executive secretary of the association.
10. Neufeld letter to Mrs. J. W. Garland, January 10, 1966, FPP, Neufeld, and interview by GM with Neufeld.
11. Interviews by GM with SWC, Deane and Eleanor Malcott and others at Cornell.

12. Letter to FP from Mrs. Archer (Helen) Sinclair, June 19, 1962, quoting Charlotte Drake on cornerstone, FPP, Columbia.

13. Understanding FDR, FPOHC, Bk. 3, pp. 341–59, particularly 351–52; "Roosevelt had great reserves — terrific reserves — within himself that I doubt he ever revealed to anybody, even his wife. I think he revealed part of himself to one person, part of himself to another . . . Al Smith, on the other hand, had many fewer reserves. I lay part of that to . . . the habits engendered by his youth in an Irish-American community where everybody was poor . . . there were no pretenses . . . Roosevelt grew up in an entirely different way and he had many reserves because there were many things to protect, many things to conceal. There were many pretenses."

14. Her "purest admiration." The phrase is from Neufeld's tribute to FP at a memorial service.

15. FP, *TRIK*, pp. 161–63. FPOHC, Bk. 2, pp. 230–31.

16. Moses, *Tribute to Governor Smith,* p. 39; Neufeld letter to GM and interview by GM with Moses. At the 1960 annual meeting of the American Historical Association FP was chairman of a session entitled "Personality and Biography in American History." At the 1962 annual meeting she served as commentator at a session entitled "Changing Views of the Relation Between Social Welfare and Politics."

17. Interviews by GM with Alice Cook and others at Cornell.

18. Interview by GM with Howard Taubman. Letter from Daniel P. Moynihan to FP, September 17, 1963, FPP, Neufeld; interview by GM with Anne Barrett.

19. Interviews by GM with SWC and Margaret Janeway.

20. Interviews by GM with SWC, Maurice Neufeld and Agnes Leach. The letter of instruction, FP to Rev. Gordon Wadhams, June 18, 1945, FPP, Columbia; see also letter of instructions in case of death in Europe, FP to Frances Jurkowitz, January 14, 1956, FPP, Neufeld. Two good short summaries of her character are Neufeld's tribute and the Civil Service Commission's tribute sent out to all employees, May 18, 1965, as Letter No. A-150; both in FPP, Neufeld. A third and longer is C. E. Wyzanski, Jr.'s letter published in a cut version by *New York Times,* May 19, 1965, 46:4. A copy of the uncut original is in FPP, Mt. Holyoke.

Bibliography

UNPUBLISHED MATERIAL

1. Manuscript collections primarily by or about Frances Perkins.
2. Other manuscript collections in which Frances Perkins figures.
3. Unpublished studies.
4. Interviews
  (a) by George Martin
  (b) by Dr. Jonathan P. Grossman
  (c) by Edward Arpee
5. Personal correspondence, with George Martin.
6. Reminiscences, oral histories, etc.
  (a) Columbia University
  (b) University of California, Berkeley

PUBLISHED MATERIAL

7. By Frances Perkins
  (a) Books
  (b) Articles
8. Primarily about Frances Perkins
  (a) Books
  (b) Articles
9. Other books (those used only for one or two specific points are described in the appropriate note).

The abbreviations used in the Notes are given first. FP stands for Frances Perkins and FPP for Frances Perkins Papers.

Unpublished Material

1. Manuscript collections primarily by or about Frances Perkins.

She distributed her papers among several libraries, apparently without plan. A librarian would suggest that she give her papers to his library, and she would agree, sending along whatever files were at hand. Then she would do nothing more until another librarian stirred her sense of responsibility, and off would go some more files — to a different library. The final gift, by far the largest, was to Columbia in 1955, the year she completed her oral history for that university. Since Perkins's death in 1965 her daughter has added to the Columbia collection.

FPOHC: Her Oral History at Columbia's Oral History Research Office. The double-spaced typescript runs 5056 pages, transcribing 102 tape-recorded interviews with Dean Albertson in the years 1951 through June 1955. She discusses her childhood and family life as well as her career.

FPP, Columbia: Her papers in Columbia's Rare Book and Manuscript Library (Special Collections). The largest collection of her papers outside the National Archives; the primary collection for her years before and after her service in the federal government, and even for the federal years the equal, perhaps, of the collection in the National Archives.

FPP, Radcliffe: Her papers in the Schlesinger Library, Radcliffe College. Almost exclusively a collection from her years as Secretary of Labor, 1933–45. Particularly strong on the International Labor Organization and on the origins and development of the Social Security Act (but see FPP, Connecticut).

FPP, Connecticut: Her papers in the American Women's Collection of Connecticut College Library. A small collection, but with a complete set of the Reports of the Committee on Economic Security (the Social Security Act) and many papers pertaining to immigration under Commissioner Daniel W. MacCormack, 1933–37. Also a few papers of her years as New York's Industrial Commissioner, 1929–33.

FPP, FDR Library: Her papers at the Franklin D. Roosevelt Library under her own name (not to be confused with Perkins material in the Roosevelt papers; see below). A very small collection. Some material on the Unemployment Conference at Albany, April 1932, on *People At Work,* drafts of articles and speeches and letters on National Defense.

FPP, Mount Holyoke: Her papers at Mount Holyoke consist chiefly of her correspondence with the Alumnae Office, her replies to its questionnaires and such miscellany as the only discovered announcement of her wedding. The library has copies of the 1902 Class Book and the subsequent Class Letters (published in 1903, 1906, 1909, 1915 and 1924) in which each member described in a letter what she was doing and thinking.

FPP, Cornell: Her papers at the New York State School of Industrial and Labor Relations, Martin P. Catherwood Library, Cornell, consist chiefly of drafts and transcripts of her lectures delivered at the university, 1957–65. In them she ranged over all periods of her life.

FPP, Neufeld: In the final eight years of her life, while teaching at Cornell, she relied greatly for friendship and assistance of all kinds on Professor Maurice F. Neufeld of the School of Industrial and Labor Relations. He has a small collection of letters and documents pertaining to those years, her death and subsequent projects involving her name.

FPP, Civil Service Commission: A collection of clippings, articles, speeches and press releases, many of which are not found elsewhere. They are described in *Fifty United States Civil Service Commissioners,* published by the commission's library, 1971.

FPP, Coggeshall: Perkins's daughter, Susanna Coggeshall, has many papers, which she is sorting before giving to Columbia. They pertain chiefly to early years and family matters.

FPP, Coggeshall, AES: The drafts of the opening chapters of her biography of Alfred E. Smith, which she did not live to finish. Several chapters are fairly polished; others, no more than notes. But the draft is a valuable source for the early years of her life and career.

2. Other manuscript collections in which Frances Perkins figures:

FPP, NA: Records of the Department of Labor, 1933–45 at the National Archives. The material has an excellent annotated card index made by Oswald L. Harvey, historian of the department, 1938–62, and kept at the department.

FDR Library: Roosevelt's papers contain much Perkins material. His presidential papers are divided: the President's Secretary's File (PSF), the Official File (OF) and the President's Personal File (PPF). There is also Perkins material in his pre-presidential papers. Among other collections in the library with Perkins material are those of Mary Dewson, Eleanor Roosevelt and Henry Wallace as Vice-President.

CMB Papers: The papers of Clara M. Beyer in the Schlesinger Library, Radcliffe College. Beyer worked at the U.S. Department of Labor from 1928 to 1958. Besides working with FP, she was a friend, and there is much Perkins material in the collection, particularly on the Division of Labor Standards and the conferences sponsored. Often in the Notes this is included as part of the author's interview with CMB.

PUK Papers: The papers of Paul Underwood Kellogg, the editor of *Survey* and *Survey Graphic,* at the Social Welfare History Archives Center, University of Minnesota, have considerable Perkins material, particularly for the years 1930–45 and for the Social Security Act.

CEW Papers: The papers of Charles E. Wyzanski, Jr., at the Harvard Law School Library. He was Solicitor of Labor, 1933–35, and a constant friend of Perkins thereafter. In his letters to others there are many references to her; also some correspondence between them.

JBA Papers: The papers of John B. Andrews, secretary of the American Association for Labor Legislation, at the New York State School of Industrial and Labor Relations, Cornell, have correspondence from 1918 to 1941.

3. Unpublished studies.

Anderson, James Russell. "The New Deal Career of Frances Perkins, Secretary of Labor, 1933–1939." PhD. thesis, Western Reserve University, January, 1968. (In connction with this thesis, in 1965 Dr. Grossman conducted some of the interviews recorded below.)

Curlee, Joan Ethelyn. "Some Aspects of the New Deal Rationale: The Pre-1936 Writings of Six of Roosevelt's Advisers." Ph.D. thesis, Vanderbilt University, June 1957. (The six are Berle, Perkins, Moley, Ickes, Tugwell and Wallace.)

Gilbert, Hilda Kessler. "The United States Department of Labor in the New Deal Period." PhD. thesis, University of Wisconsin, October 1942. (On the examining board were Edwin E. Witte, as Major Professor, Selig Perlman and Howard Becker. Gilbert's notes are extensive, and she is particularly good on excerpting the *Congressional Record* and analyzing appropriations.)

Gillette, J. William. "Welfare State Trail Blazer: New York State Factory Investigating Commission, 1911–1915." Master's essay, Columbia University, 1956.

MacEachron, David Wells. "The Role of the United States Department of Labor," Ph.D. thesis, Harvard University, April 1953 (using interviews with Perkins, Wyzanski and others).

Perkins, Frances. "The United States Department of Labor." Address to Department employees, Oct. 4, 1939. FPP, NA, Box 5, Employees Meetings.

———— "The Christian in the World." The St. Bede Lectures, delivered at the Guild Hall of St. Thomas Church (Episcopal), New York City, 1948. Three lectures: "A Christian Order of Society," "The Vocation of the Laity" and "The Good Life, Community and Individual." FPP, Columbia.

———— "A Study of Malnutrition in 107 Children from Public School." Her master's thesis. On file in Rare Book and Manuscript Library (Special Collections), Columbia, in Columbia University Theses, 1910, Vol. 18, Political Science, P–R.

Schramm, Sarah Slavin. "Section 213: Woman Overboard." Paper delivered at the Second Berkshire Conference on The History of Women, Radcliffe College, 1974. On file at Schlesinger Library, Radcliffe, and FDR Library. (During the Depression, under Section 213, many women in government service married to men in government service were fired for that reason alone.)

Shor, Edgar L. "The Role of the Secretary of Labor." Ph.D. thesis, University of Chicago, December 1954 (using interviews with Perkins, Lubin, Reilly and others).

4. Interviews.

(a) Conducted by George Martin, 1970–74, and in almost every case followed by correspondence.

Leonard P. Adams
Edward Arpee
Anne Barrett
Clara M. Beyer
Alison Bishop
Jane Bruère
Lucille Buchanan
Gladys H. Burch
Alison Bruère Carnahan
Martin P. Catherwood
Ewan Clague
Calvert Coggeshall

Susanna Wilson Coggeshall
Arthur M. Dailey
James E. Dempsey
James E. Dodson
Lewis W. Douglas
Thomas H. Eliot
Walter Evers
Sister Fidelia
Helene P. Gans
Anna Glidden
Nannie Glidden
Lloyd Goodrich

Jonathan P. Grossman	Maurice F. Neufeld
Anthony Gualtieri	Pauline M. Newman
Oswald L. Harvey	Edward B. Persons
A. Ford Hinrichs	Gerard D. Reilly
Margaret Janeway	Charles C. Rumsey, Jr.
Olga Knopf	Alfred Santoro
Robert M. Lake	Katherine Santoro
Agnes B. Leach	James A. Spargo, Jr.
Carol Riegelman Lubin	Robert K. Straus
Isador Lubin	Howard Taubman
Beatrice MacLeod	Lea Demarest Taylor
Earle Hewitt Maddux	Vira Peters Towle
Deane Malott	George Trowbridge
Eleanor Malott	Reverend Mother Virginia
Mary V. Marvin	Ilo B. Wallace
Elizabeth Mason	Aileen O. Webb
Robert Moses	Aryness Joy Wickens
Hinda Neufeld	Charles E. Wyzanski, Jr.

(b) Conducted by the historian of the Department of Labor, Dr. Jonathan P. Grossman, 1965, and on file at the department.

Clara M. Beyer	Gerard D. Reilly
James E. Dodson	Aryness Joy Wickens

(c) Conducted by Edward Arpee for GM, 1971. Mary Ward

5. *Personal correspondence with George Martin.*

Arthur Altmeyer	Miranda Masocco Levy
Ethel O'Dell Black	Nancy Mansbach
Emmanuel Celler	Marion E. Martin
George Cheever	Millicent Carey McIntosh
Leroy Ford	Thomas J. Mittler
Sue Gentry	Mary Piper
Florence Polk Holding	

6. *Reminiscences, Oral History Research Office.*
    (a) Columbia University

Arthur Altmeyer	Isador Lubin
Robert S. Binkerd	Langdon P. Marvin
John Brophy	Frances Perkins
Henry Bruère	Jacob S. Potofsky
Ewan Clague (2)	Lee Pressman
Thomas H. Eliot	Samuel I. Rosenman
Lavinia Engle	Laurence A. Tanzer
John Philip Frey	Aryness Joy Wickens
Arthur Krock	Leo Wolman
James M. Landis	Charles E. Wyzanski, Jr.
Katharine Lenroot	

(b) Bancroft Library, University of California, Berkeley.
Roger Lapham

Published Material

7. *By Frances Perkins.*

(a) Books

FP, *PAW — People at Work* (New York, John Day Company, 1934) .
FP, *TRIK — The Roosevelt I Knew* (New York, Viking, 1946) .
   Two Views of American Labor (the second view by J. Paul St. Sure)
   (Los Angeles, Institute of Industrial Relations, University of California,
   1965) . (The "essence" of a series of lectures by Perkins delivered in
   1963 and entitled "Labor Under the New Deal" and the "New Frontier.")

(b) Articles — listed by date of publication.

A selection of articles found useful. In the twenty years from 1926 to 1946
many were written for her signature by editors or reporters and others were
sometimes reprinted with a new title and slight changes. While she was
Secretary of Labor someone prepared a bibliography of her writings from
1910 to August 1937. It listed 148 articles and 31 by others about her: FPP,
Radcliffe and New York Public Library. A Supplement prepared in May
1945 listed 113 articles and 10 by others about her: FPP, Columbia. Several
other less complete bibliographies are also in FPP, Columbia. *Fifty United
States Civil Service Commissioners,* published by the commission, lists what is
available in its library, including a number of later speeches and articles not
found elsewhere.

"Some Facts Concerning Certain Undernourished Children," *Survey,* Oct.
   1, 1910, Vol. 25, pp. 68–72. (Her first published work and appropriately
   in a magazine with which she continued a close connection. The article
   is her essay for a master's degree at Columbia, shorn of all tables and cut
   to the bone. The essay is on file in the Rare Book and Manuscript Library (Special Collections) at Columbia University Theses, 1910, Vol. 18,
   Political Science, P–R.)
Testimony on Cellar Bakeries in New York. New York (State) Factory Investigating Commission. *Preliminary Report, 1912,* Vol. 1, pp. 310–33.
"The Fire Bills." *Survey,* Feb. 22, 1913, Vol. 29, pp. 732–33. (An analysis
   of five fire safety bills proposed by the Factory Investigating Commission.)
"The Factory Inspector." In *Careers for Women,* ed. Catherine Filene (Boston, Houghton Mifflin, 1920) , pp. 255–60 (Also completely revised in an
   enlarged edition, 1934. Both are interesting accounts of the job with
   some figures on the number of inspectors.)
"After-Care for Industrial Compensation Cases." In National Conference of
   Social Work. *Proceedings, 1921,* pp. 58–63.
"Do Women in Industry Need Special Protection? Yes — Frances Perkins;
   We Don't Know — Elizabeth Faulkner Baker." *Survey,* February 15,
   1926, Vol. 55, pp. 529–32, 582–83.

"Industrial Relations." In *An Outline of Careers for Women, A Practical Guide to Achievement* (New York, Doubleday, 1928), pp. 221–29. (Interesting facts about positions open to women, and salaries.)

"My Job," *Survey,* March 15, 1929, Vol. 61, No. 12, pp. 773–75. (Address at the luncheon in her honor on her appointment as Industrial Commissioner of New York.)

Reprinted with slightly different wording in *American Labor Legislation Review,* June 1929, Vol. 19. pp. 164–70.

"Helping Industry To Help Itself." *Harper's Magazine,* October 1930. Vol. 161, pp. 624–30.

"Frances Perkins on Unemployment." *Women's Journal,* November 1930. Vol. 15, No. 11, pp. 8–10, 41–42.

"A Cooperative Program Needed for Industrial Stabilization." American Academy of Political and Social Science. *Annals,* March 1931. Vol. 154, pp. 124–130.

"Unemployment Insurance, An American Plan to Protect Workers and Avoid the Dole." *Survey,* Nov. 1, 1931, Vol. 67, pp. 117–19, 173. (Her recommendations for an interstate insurance authority, based on her study of the British system.)

Excerpts also appeared in the (American) *Review of Reviews,* December 1931. Vol. 84, pp. 72–73.

"Cost of Five-Dollar Dress." *Survey Graphic,* February 1933, Vol. 22, pp. 75–78.

"Toward Security; the Bill before Congress for Unemployment Insurance." *Survey Graphic,* March 1934, Vol. 23, pp. 116–17, 144.

"Frances Perkins, Secretary of Labor, Explains the New Deal," *Pictorial Review,* March 1934, Vol. 35, pp. 7, 58–65 (Taken almost entirely from her book *People at Work*).

"The Way of Security." *Survey Graphic,* December 1934, Vol. 23, pp. 620–22, 629.

"The Social Security Act." *Vital Speeches,* September 9, 1935, Vol. 1, pp. 792–94. (Her Labor Day Address on the radio, September 2, 1935.) Reprinted in full in *The New Deal,* ed. by William E. Leuchtenburg (New York, Harper & Row, 1968), pp. 81–86.

"Fair Labor Standards Bill." *American Federationist,* July 1937, Vol. 44, pp. 709–16.

"Grace Abbott: Public Servant." *The Child* (U.S. Children's Bureau), August 1939, Vol. 4, pp. 27–29. (What she chose to admire in Abbott reveals much about herself.)

"Eight Years as Madame Secretary." *Fortune,* September 1941, Vol. 24, pp. 76–79, 94. (The most self-revealing of her articles.)

"My Recollections of Florence Kelley." *Social Service Review,* March 1954, Vol. 28, No. 1.

"The Man Behind Roosevelt." *The New Republic,* June 21, 1954, Vol. 130, pp. 18. (A review of Lela Stile's boigraphy of Louis Howe.)

"Franklin Roosevelt's Apprenticeship." *The New Republic,* April 25, 1955, Vol. 132, pp. 19–21. (A review of Bernard Bellush's *Franklin D. Roosevelt as Governor of New York*.)

8. Primarily about Frances Perkins.

(a) Books

Lawson, Don. *Frances Perkins, First Lady of the Cabinet.* New York: Abelard-Schuman, 1967.

Myers, Elisabeth P. *Madam Secretary: Frances Perkins.* New York: Julian Messner, 1972.

(Both are juveniles and written before much of the Perkins material became available.)

(b) Articles (listed by date of publication)

"Behind the Rail: Being the Story of a Woman Lobbyist." by Leroy Scott, *The Metropolitan Magazine,* July 1912. (Passage of the 54-Hour Bill in the New York State legislature.)

"Commissioner Perkins." *Survey,* March 1, 1919, Vol. 41, p. 803. (Editorial comment on her appointment to the New York State Industrial Commission.)

"Story of Frances Perkins." by Augusta W. Hinshaw, *Century,* September 1927, Vol. 114, pp. 596–605. (A rare instance in which Perkins actively cooperated with the writer. See letter to Hinshaw, July 27, 1925, FPP, Columbia.)

"Miss Commissioner Perkins." *Survey,* January 15, 1929, Vol. 61, p. 478. (Editorial on her appointment as Industrial Commissioner of New York.)

"Frances Perkins, Industrial Crusader." by Inis W. Jones, *World's Week,* April 1930. Vol. 59, 64–67, 114. (An editorial based on this article appeared in *Review of Reviews,* May 1930, p. 109.)

"For Secretary of Labor, Frances Perkins." by Jane Addams, *Forum,* February 1933, Vol. 89, Suppl. p. 9. (A letter to the editor.)

"The Department of Labor: A Challenge." *Nation,* Feb. 22, 1933. Vol. 136, p. 192.

"Madam Secretary Perkins." *Survey,* March 1933, Vol. 69, p. 110.

"Issues and Men and A Woman — Frances Perkins." by Oswald G. Villard, *Nation,* March 8, 1933.

"Miss Perkins Talks of the Tasks Ahead." by Alice R. Hager, *New York Times Magazine,* May 7, 1933, pp. 3, 17.

"Madam Secretary: The Illustrious Frances Perkins." by Corinne, M. Low, *Pictorial Review,* June 1933. Vol. 34, pp. 4, 41–42.

"Triumvirate. Three Great Women of the Labor Department: Frances Perkins, Mary Anderson, Grace Abbott." by Frances Parkinson Keyes, *Delineator,* September 1933, Vol. 123, pp. 7, 40–42.

"Madame Secretary: A Profile. " by Russell Lord, *The New Yorker,* September 2 and 9, 1933.

"Fearless Frances." by Ray Tucker, *Collier's,* July 28, 1934, Vol. 94, pp. 16, 35. (In the same issue an editorial, "Sheep and Goats in the Cabinet," ranked Perkins very high.)

"Miss Perkins Sees New Hope for Labor." by S. J. Woolf, *New York Times Magazine,* August 5, 1934, pp. 3, 10.

"Frances Perkins, Liberal Politician." by Marguerite Young, *American Mercury,* August 1934, Vol. 32, pp. 398–407. (A hostile article; describes a meeting that FP describes quite differently in FPOHC, Bk. 7, pp. 240–51.)

"The Woman and the Hour: Frances Perkins." *Barron's, the National Financial Weekly,* October 1, 1934, Vol. 14, pp. 12, 15.

"New Roads to Security." by H. F. Pringle, *American Magazine,* February 1935, Vol. 119, pp. 48–50.

"Please Excuse Miss Perkins." by Paul W. Ward, *Nation,* March 27, 1935, Vol. 140, p. 353. (A harsh attack on her person as much as her policies.)

"Miss Perkins wins Geneva's Acclaim: Officials of I.L.O. impressed by her views as she seeks world textile pact." by Clarence K. Streit, *New York Times* Section IV, August 16, 1936, 4:8.

"Secretary Perkins Has the Hardest Government Job." by Owen L. Scott, Washington *Star,* February 7, 1937, Section D, 2:1.

"A Person Named Perkins." by Carlisle Bargeron, *The Commentator,* February 1938, pp. 106–110.

"Miss Perkins Forsees New Gains for Labor." by S. J. Woolf, *New York Times Magazine,* March 6, 1938, pp. 8, 21.

"Shoot the Works: Miss Perkins Reconsidered." by Heywood Broun, *The New Republic,* April 13, 1938, Vol. 144, p. 302 (Favorable) .

"Madame Secretary; A Study in Bewilderment." by Benjamin Stolberg, *Saturday Evening Post,* July 27, 1940, Vol. 213, pp. 9–11. (Rose Schneiderman wrote the magazine a letter of protest, FPP, Columbia.)

"Madame Secretary." by Aryness Joy, *Mount Holyoke Alumnae Quarterly,* November 1941, Vol. 25, no. 3, pp. 99–101.

"The Secretary of Labor Cooperates." by John B. Andrews, *American Labor Legislation Review,* December 1942, Vol. 32, pp. 159–162. (About the National Conferences on Labor Legislation.)

"The Woman Nobody Knows." by Jerry Klutz and Herbert Asbury, *Colliers,* August 5, 1944, Vol. 114, pp. 21, 30–32. (Perkins thought the article "wrong about almost everything that is significant." FP Letter to Gertrude Ely, August 19, 1944, FPP, Columbia. The judgment is too harsh. The articles is one of the few to stress her dislike of regimentation, fingerprinting, medical questionnaires etc.)

9. Other books (those used only for one or two specific points are described in the appropriate note) :

Adams, Graham, Jr. *Age of Industrial Violence, 1910–15: The Activities and Findings of the United States Commission on Industrial Relations.* New York: Columbia University Press, 1966.

Addams, Jane. *20 Years at Hull House.* New York :Macmillan, 1911.

Albertson, Dean. *Roosevelt's Farmer, Claude R. Wickard in the New Deal.* New York: Columbia University Press, 1961.

Alcock, Antony. *History of the International Labour Organization.* London: Macmillan, 1971.

Alinsky, Saul. *John L. Lewis, An Unauthorized Biography.* New York: Putnam's, 1949.

Altmeyer, Arthur J. *The Formative Years of Social Security.* Madison: University of Wisconsin Press, 1968.

Anderson, Mary. *Woman at Work: The Autobiography of Mary Anderson as told to Mary N. Winslow.* Minneapolis: University of Minnesota Press, 1951.

Arnow, Kathryn Smul. *The Attack on the Cost of Living Index.* (In the Inter-University Case Program) . Indianapolis: Bobbs-Merrill, 1952.

Bain, Richard C. *Convention Decisions and Voting Records.* Washington: Brookings Institution, 1960.

Baker, Elizabeth Faulkner. *Technology and Woman's Work.* New York: Columbia University Press, 1964.

Bellush, Bernard. *Franklin D. Roosevelt as Governor of New York.* New York: Columbia University Press, 1955. Republished, New York: AMS Press, 1968.

Bernstein, Irving. *The New Deal Collective Bargaining Policy.* Los Angeles: University of California Press, 1950.

––––––– *The Lean Years, A History of the American Worker, 1920–1933.* Boston: Houghton Mifflin, 1966.

––––––– *Turbulent Years, A History of the American Worker, 1933–1941.* Boston: Houghton Mifflin, 1970.

Biddle, Francis. *In Brief Authority.* New York: Doubleday, 1962.

Bishop, Jim. *FDR's Last Year, April 1944–April 1945.* New York: Morrow, 1974.

Blum, John Morton. *From the Morgenthau Diaries, Years of Crisis, 1928–1938.* 3 vols. Boston: Houghton Mifflin, 1959.

Braeman, John et al. (eds.) . *Change and Continuity in Twentieth-Century America.* Columbus: Ohio State University Press, 1964. (Includes "The Emergence of Mass-Production Unionism" by David Brody.)

Brody, David (ed.) . *The American Labor Movement.* New York: Harper & Row, 1971.

––––––– *Steelworkers in America, The Nonunion Era.* Cambridge: Harvard University Press, 1960.

––––––– (See Braeman, above)

Brown, J. Douglas. *An American Philosophy of Social Security, Evolution and Issues.* Princeton: Princeton University Press, 1972.

Burns, James MacGregor. *Roosevelt: The Lion and the Fox.* New York: Harcourt Brace, 1956.

––––––– *Congress on Trial: The Legislative Process and the Administrative State.* New York: Harper, 1949. Republished, New York: Gordian, 1966. (For account of the passage of the Fair Labor Standards Act.)

Caro, Robert A. *The Power Broker, Robert Moses and the Fall of New York.* New York: Knopf, 1974.

Chafe, William Henry. *The American Woman, Her Changing Social, Economic and Political Roles, 1920–1970.* New York: Oxford University Press, 1972.

Chambers, Clarke A. *Seedtime of Reform, American Social Service and Social Action, 1918–1933.* Minneapolis: University of Minnesota Press, 1963. In paperback, Ann Arbor: University of Michigan Press, 1967.

––––––– *Paul U. Kellogg and the Survey: Voices for Social Welfare and Social Justice.* Minneapolis: University of Minnesota Press, 1971.

Clague, Ewan. *The Bureau of Labor Statistics.* New York: Praeger, 1968.

Cole, Arthur C. *A Hundred Years of Mount Holyoke College: The Evolution of an Educational Ideal.* New Haven: Yale University Press, 1940.

Coughlin, Bernard J. *Church and State in Social Welfare.* New York: Columbia University Press, 1965.

Cushman, David Quimby, *The History of Ancient Sheepscot and Newcastle (including the genealogies of more than four hundred families)*, Bath, Maine: 1882.

Dahlberg, Jane S. *The New York Bureau of Municipal Research, Pioneer in Government Administration.* New York: New York University Press, 1966.

Davis, Allen F. *Spearheads for Reform, The Social Settlements and the Progressive Movement, 1890–1914.* New York: Oxford University Press, 1967.

Davis, Kenneth S. *FDR: The Beckoning of Destiny, 1882–1928.* New York: Putnam's, 1972.

Derber, Milton. *The American Idea of Industrial Democracy, 1865–1965.* Urbana: University of Illinois Press, 1970.

Derber, Milton and Edwin Young (eds.) . *Labor and the New Deal.* Madison: University of Wisconsin Press, 1957.

Devine, Edward T. *When Social Work Was Young.* New York: Macmillan, 1939.

Donahoe, Bernard F. *Private Plans and Public Dangers, The Story of FDR's Third Nomination.* South Bend: University of Notre Dame Press, 1965.

Douglas, Lewis W. *The Liberal Tradition.* New York: Van Nostrand, 1935.

Douglas, Paul H. *In the Fullness of Time, The Memoirs of Paul H. Douglas.* New York: Harcourt Brace, 1972.

Dubofsky, Melvyn. *When Workers Organize, New York City in the Progressive Era.* Amherst: University of Massachusetts Press, 1968.

Dulles, Foster Rhea. *Labor in America.* New York: Crowell, 1949.

Farley, James A. *Jim Farley's Story, The Roosevelt Years.* New York, McGraw-Hill, 1948.

Fine, Sidney. *Sit-Down, The General Motors Strike of 1936–37.* Ann Arbor: University of Michigan Press, 1969.

Finley, Joseph E. *The Corrupt Kingdom, The Rise and Fall of the United Mine Workers.* New York: Simon and Schuster, 1972.

Flynn, Edward J. *You're the Boss.* New York: Viking, 1947.

Freidel, Frank. *Franklin D. Roosevelt.* 4 vols. thus far. Boston: Little, Brown, 1952–1973. 1. *The Apprenticeship.* 2. *The Ordeal.* 3. *The Triumph.* 4. *Launching the New Deal.*

Furman, Bess. *Washington By-line, The Personal History of a Newspaperwoman.* New York: Knopf, 1949.

Galenson, Walter. *The CIO Challenge to the AFL, A History of the American Labor Movement, 1935–1941.* Cambridge: Harvard University Press, 1960.

Gilchrist, Beth Bradford. *The Life of Mary Lyon.* Boston: Houghton Mifflin, 1910.

Goldmark, Josephine. *Impatient Crusader: Florence Kelley's Life Story.* Urbana: University of Illinois Press, 1953.

Goulden, Joseph C. *Meany.* New York: Atheneum, 1972. (A biography of George Meany of the AFL.)

Graham, Otis L., Jr. *An Encore for Reform: The Old Progressives and the New Deal.* New York: Oxford University Press, 1967.

Grossman, Jonathan P. *The Department of Labor.* New York: Praeger, 1973.

Handlin, Oscar. *Al Smith and His America.* Boston: Little, Brown, 1958.

Harbaugh, William H. *Lawyer's Lawyer: The Life of John W. Davis.* New York: Oxford University Press, 1973.

Herring, Pendleton. *Public Administration and the Public Interest.* New York: McGraw-Hill, 1936. Reissued, New York: Russell & Russell, 1967.

Hofstadter, Richard. *The Age of Reform: From Bryan to F.D.R.* New York: Knopf, 1955.

Hull, Cordell, with Andrew Berding. *The Memoirs of Cordell Hull.* New York: Macmillan, 1948.

Huthmacher, J. Joseph. *Senator Robert F. Wagner and the Rise of Urban Liberalism.* New York: Atheneum, 1968.

Ickes, Harold L. *The Secret Diary of Harold L. Ickes.* 3 vols. New York: Simon and Schuster, 1953–1954.

—————— *Back to Work.* New York: Macmillan, 1935.

Johnson, Hugh S. *The Blue Eagle from Egg to Earth.* New York: Doubleday, 1935.

Josephson, Matthew. *Sidney Hillman: Statesman of Labor.* New York: Doubleday, 1952.

—————— with Hannah Josephson. *Al Smith: Hero of the Cities (A Political Portrait Drawing upon the Papers of Frances Perkins).* Boston: Houghton Mifflin, 1969.

Kraditor, Aileen S. *The Ideas of the Woman Suffrage Movement, 1890–1920.* New York: Columbia University Press, 1965.

Krock, Arthur. *Memoirs, Sixty Years on the Firing Line.* New York: Funk & Wagnalls, 1968.

Larrowe, Charles P. *Harry Bridges: The Rise and Fall of Radical Labor in the United States.* New York: Lawrence Hill, 1972.

Lash, Joseph P. *Eleanor and Franklin, The Story of Their Relationship Based on Eleanor Roosevelt's Private Papers.* New York: Norton, 1972.

—————— *Eleanor: The Years Alone.* New York: Norton, 1972.

Leuchtenburg, William E. *Franklin D. Roosevelt and the New Deal, 1932–1940.* New York: Harper, 1963.

—————— (ed.) *The New Deal: A Documentary History.* New York: Harper, 1968.

Lewinson, Edwin R. *John Purroy Mitchel: The Boy Mayor of New York.* New York: Astra Books, 1965.

Lombardi, John. *Labor's Voice in the Cabinet: A History of the Department of Labor from its Origin to 1921.* New York, Columbia University Press, 1942. Republished, New York: AMS Press, 1968.

Lubell, Samuel. *The Future of American Politics.* New York: Harper, 1952.

Lubove, Roy. *The Struggle for Social Security, 1900–1935.* Cambridge: Harvard University Press, 1968.

MacMahon, Arthur W. and John D. Millett. *Federal Administrators, A Biographical Approach to the Problem of Departmental Management.* New York: Columbia University Press, 1939. Reprinted, New York: AMS Press, 1967.

Marks, Jeannette. *Life and Letters of Mary Emma Woolley*. Washington, D.C.: Public Affairs, 1955.

Marshall, F. Ray. *The Negro and Organized Labor*. New York: John Wiley, 1965.

Millis, Harry A. and Emily Clark Brown. *From the Wagner Act to Taft-Hartley, A Study of National Labor Policy and Labor Relations*. Chicago: Chicago University Press, 1950.

Moley, Raymond. *After Seven Years, A Political Analysis of the New Deal*. New York: Harper, 1939. As a Bison paperback, Lincoln: University of Nebraska Press, 1971.

———— *27 Masters of Politics, In a Personal Perspective*. New York: Funk & Wagnalls, 1949.

Morton, Herbert C. *Public Contracts and Private Wages, Experience Under the Walsh-Healey Act*. Washington: Brookings Institution, 1965.

Moses, Robert. *A Tribute to Governor Smith*. New York: Simon & Schuster, 1962.

Nathan, Maud. *The Story of an Epoch-Making Movement*. New York: Doubleday, 1926. (A history of the Consumers' Leagues.)

Neufeld, Maurice F. *A Representative Bibliography of American Labor History*. Ithaca: Cornell University Press, 1964.

Nevins, Allan, and John A. Krout (eds.). *The Greater City: New York, 1898–1948*. New York: Columbia University Press, 1948.

O'Connor, Richard. *The First Hurrah, A Biography of Alfred E. Smith*. New York: Putnam's, 1970.

Patten, Simon N. *The New Basis of Civilization*. New York: Macmillan, 1907. A new edition, edited and with an introduction by Daniel M. Fox, was published by Harvard University Press in 1968.

Patterson, James T. *The New Deal and the States: Federalism in Transition*. Princeton: Princeton University Press, 1969.

Polenberg, Richard. *Reorganizing Roosevelt's Government, 1936–1939*. Cambridge: Harvard University Press, 1966.

Riis, Jacob A. *How the Other Half Lives: Studies among the Tenements of New York*. New York: Scribner's, 1890. A new edition, edited by Sam Bass Warner, Jr., was published by Harvard University Press in 1970, with an introduction, explanatory notes and additional line drawings and photographs.

Rodgers, Cleveland. *Robert Moses: Builder of Democracy*. New York: Holt, 1952.

Roosevelt, Eleanor. *This I Remember*. New York: Harper, 1949.

———— with Lorena A. Hickok. *Ladies of Courage*. New York: Putnam's, 1954. (Chapter 7 is chiefly on Perkins.)

Roosevelt, Elliott and James Brough. *An Untold Story: The Roosevelts of Hyde Park*. New York: Putnam's, 1973.

Rosenman, Samuel I. *Working with Roosevelt*. New York: Harper, 1952.

Rollins, Alfred B., Jr. *Roosevelt and Howe*. New York: Knopf, 1962.

Salmond, John A. *The Civilian Conservation Corps, 1933–1942: A New Deal Case Study*. Durham: Duke University Press, 1967.

Schlesinger, Arthur M., Jr. *The Age of Roosevelt*. 3 vols. Boston: Houghton

Mifflin, 1957–1960. 1. *The Crisis of the Old Order, 1919–1933.* 2. *The Coming of the New Deal.* 3. *The Politics of Upheaval.*

Schneider, David M. and Albert Deutsch. *The History of Public Welfare in New York State, 1867–1940.* Chicago: University of Chicago Press, 1938–41.

Schneiderman, Rose and Lucy Goldthwaite. *All for One.* New York: Paul S. Eriksson, Inc., 1967.

Schwarz, Jordan A. *The Interregnum of Despair: Hoover, Congress and the Depression.* Urbana: University of Illinois Press, 1970.

Sherwood, Robert E. *Roosevelt and Hopkins: An Intimate History.* Revised edition. New York: Harper, 1950.

Smith, Alfred E. *Up to Now: An Autobiography.* New York Viking, 1929.

Smith, Russell E. and Dorothy Zietz. *American Social Welfare Institutions.* New York: John Wiley, 1970.

Stein, Leon. *The Triangle Fire.* Philadelphia: Lippincott, 1962.

Taft, Philip. *The AF of L: From the Death of Gompers to the Merger.* New York: Harper, 1959. Republished, New York: Octagon, 1970.

Taylor, Graham. *Chicago Commons Through Forty Years.* Chicago: Chicago Commons Association, 1936.

Trattner, Walter I. *Homer Folks, Pioneer in Social Welfare.* New York: Columbia University Press, 1968.

Trolander, Judith Ann. *Settlement Houses and the Great Depression.* Detroit: Wayne State University Press, 1975.

Tully, Grace. *F.D.R., My Boss.* New York: Scribner's, 1949.

United States Government. *The Anvil and the Plow: A History of the United States Department of Labor.* Washington, D.C.: U.S. Government Printing Office, 1963.

Warner, Emily Smith with Daniel Hawthorne. *The Happy Warrior: A Biography of My Father.* New York: Doubleday, 1956.

Witte, Edwin E. *The Development of the Social Security Act.* Madison: University of Wisconsin Press, 1963.

Yellowitz, Irwin. *Labor and the Progressive Movement in New York State, 1897–1916.* Ithaca: Cornell University Press, 1965.

Index

Entries concerning Frances Perkins are listed in sub-indexes under her name as follows: Career (with alphabetical entries further subdivided by parts, as in the table of contents) and Private Life.